Essential Latin Dictionary

Latin–English
English–Latin

Alastair Wilson BA

Revised by Valentina Asciutti

T0271748

For UK order enquiries: please contact Bookpoint Ltd, 130 Milton Park, Abingdon, Oxon OX14 4SB. *Telephone:* +44 (0) 1235 827720. *Fax:* +44 (0) 1235 400454. Lines are open 09.00–17.00, Monday to Saturday, with a 24-hour message answering service. Details about our titles and how to order are available at www.teachyourself.com

For USA order enquiries: please contact McGraw-Hill Customer Services, PO Box 545, Blacklick, OH 43004-0545, USA. *Telephone:* 1-800-722-4726. *Fax:* 1-614-755-5645.

For Canada order enquiries: please contact McGraw-Hill Ryerson Ltd, 300 Water St, Whitby, Ontario L1N 9B6, Canada. *Telephone:* 905 430 5000. *Fax:* 905 430 5020.

Long renowned as the authoritative source for self-guided learning – with more than 50 million copies sold worldwide – the *Teach Yourself* series includes over 500 titles in the fields of languages, crafts, hobbies, business, computing and education.

British Library Cataloguing in Publication Data: a catalogue record for this title is available from the British Library.

Library of Congress Catalog Card Number: on file.

First published in UK 1965 as TeachYourself Latin Dictionary by Hodder Education, part of Hachette UK, 338 Euston Road, London NW1 3BH.

First published in US 1992 by The McGraw-Hill Companies, Inc.

This edition published 2010.

Previously published as Teach Yourself Latin Dictionary

The *Teach Yourself* name is a registered trade mark of Hodder Headline.

Typeset by Transet Ltd, Coventry, England.
Printed and bound in Great Britain by Clays Ltd, Elcograf S.p.A.

The publisher has used its best endeavours to ensure that the URLs for external websites referred to in this book are correct and active at the time of going to press. However, the publisher and the author have no responsibility for the websites and can make no guarantee that a site will remain live or that the content will remain relevant, decent or appropriate.

Hachette UK's policy is to use papers that are natural, renewable and recyclable products and made from wood grown in sustainable forests. The logging and manufacturing processes are expected to conform to the environmental regulations of the country of origin.

Impression number 10 9 8 7 6 5
Year 2018

Contents

Credits

Front cover: Oxford Illustrators Ltd

Foreword

This dictionary is intended for anyone with an interest in the Latin language.

This new edition of our classic Latin dictionary has been revised and now includes

- *One-, five- and ten-minute summaries of the Latin language. These short articles are intended to allow readers to come away with useful information about Latin if they have only one, five, or ten minutes available.*
- *Fifty 'author insight boxes' containing short information about elements of Latin that are difficult to grasp or that are essential for everyone to know. These can be tips to help the learner remember a particular grammar rule or key vocabulary and phrases.*

The study of a foreign language should always begin with a good understanding of the basic grammar rules of such a language; therefore, the learner should always have to hand a good Latin grammar book such as **Essential Latin Grammar***, by Gregory Klyve, in the same series.*

Only got a minute?

Latin is an Italic language originally spoken in the region of central Italy called *Latium* (today Lazio) and the ancient city of Rome, the *aeterna urbs*. With the Roman conquest, Latin spread throughout Italy, the Mediterranean and Europe. The so called Romance languages such as Catalan, French, Italian, Portuguese, Romanian, and Spanish are descended directly from Latin; many other languages, English included, although not directly derived from Latin, have inherited and acquired much of their vocabulary from it.

Latin is a perfect language with a very precise set of grammatical rules; it is a synthetic language where affixes are attached to fixed stems of words to express gender, number, and case in nouns, pronouns and adjectives; this process is called declension. Latin nouns, pronouns and adjectives therefore decline; there are five declensions in Latin and every declension has six cases (*nominative*, *accusative*, *vocative*, *genitive*, *dative* and *ablative*); each case has a specific meaning and function. In Modern English, nouns have distinct singular and plural forms; so in a way, they *decline* to reflect their grammatical number. On the other hand, verbs are conjugated in Latin; there are four main conjugations where affixes are attached to fixed stems of verbs to denote person, number, tense, voice, mood, and aspect.

Latin is not a spoken language today but there are traces of Latin in many modern languages and in every sentence we speak. Some examples of Latin words or expressions commonly used in everyday speech are:

- *a.m./p.m.* stand for *ante/post meridiem* (before/after midday)
- *etc.* stands for *et cetera* (and other things)
- *forum* is a marketplace, the real social and political centre of a town, today commonly used to denote an online space used for discussion.

5 Only got five minutes?

Latin is an Italic language originally spoken in the region of central Italy called *Latium* (today Lazio) and the ancient city of Rome, the *aeterna urbs*. With the Roman conquest, Latin spread throughout Italy, the Mediterranean and Europe. Britain was occupied by the Romans from AD 43 to AD 410 and during this time Latin was the main language used in the island, apart from Scotland. *'Veni, Vidi, Vici'* (= I came, I saw, I conquered) is the famous sentence reportedly written by Julius Caesar in 47 BC after his expedition to Britain. However, the conquest of Britain didn't start until AD 43 with the invasion led by Claudius. Roman rule ended in AD 410 and Britain was then overrun by Anglo-Saxons in the following years, so that there was no major Latin influence on the language at this stage; Anglo-Saxon was indeed the predominant tongue. However, when Norman and Angevin kings ruled England for some 300 years, the Latin-based French was incorporated into Middle English, adding enormous richness to it. So, Latin influence was back into the English language, this time through French. The so called Romance languages such as Catalan, French, Italian, Portuguese, Romanian, and Spanish are instead descended directly from Latin but many other languages, English included, although not directly derived from Latin, have inherited and acquired much of their vocabulary from it.

Latin is a perfect language with a very precise set of grammatical rules; it is a synthetic language where affixes are attached to fixed stems of words to express gender, number, and case in nouns, pronouns and adjectives; this process is called declension. Latin nouns, pronouns and adjectives therefore decline; there are five declensions in Latin and every declension has six cases (*nominative, accusative, vocative, genitive, dative* and *ablative*). Each case has a specific meaning and function: *nominative* is the case of the subject, *accusative* is the case of the direct object, *vocative* is the case used when addressing someone, *genitive* is the case that shows possession, *dative* is the case of the indirect object and *ablative* is a case with several functions, its main meanings being 'by', 'with', 'from', 'at', 'in' and 'on'. There is also an old seventh case, called the *locative* case, used to indicate a location, corresponding to the English 'in' or 'at'. This is far less common than the other six cases of Latin nouns and usually applies to cities, small towns, and small islands, along with a few common nouns (e.g. *domi* = at home). In the first and second declension singular, its form coincides with the genitive (e.g. *Romae* = in Rome). In the first and second declension plural, and in the other declensions, it coincides with the dative and ablative (e.g. *Athenis* = at Athens). The meaning of the cases can also change when these are used with prepositions. Prepositions are short words that stand in front of a noun or pronoun to introduce an adverbial phrase; in Latin prepositions can take either the accusative or the ablative, only the preposition in can take both cases: 'in + a noun in the ablative case' means 'in', 'at', 'on', (e.g. *in schola* = at school) 'in + a noun in the accusative case' means 'into', 'onto', 'towards' (e.g. *in scholam* – into the school). The main prepositions in Latin are: a) prepositions with accusative: *in* (into), *ad* (to), *per* (through, by means of, on account of), *ante* (before), *contra* (against), *ob/propter* (because of, on account of), *post* (after), *praeter* (along, except), *prope* (near), *trans* (across); b) prepositions with ablative: *cum* (with), *a/ab/e/ex/de* (by, from, out of – de + ablative can also mean about), *in* (in, at, on). Even in Modern English, nouns have distinct singular and plural forms; so in a way, they *decline* to reflect their grammatical number. On the other hand, verbs are conjugated in Latin; there are four main conjugations (first, second, third and fourth) and a mixed conjugation (third and fourth) where affixes are attached to fixed stems of verbs to denote person, number, tense, voice, mood, and aspect. There are six tenses in Latin (i.e. present, imperfect, future, perfect, pluperfect, and future perfect), three grammatical moods (i.e. indicative, imperative and subjunctive, in addition to the infinitive, participle, gerund, gerundive and supine), three persons (first, second, and third), two numbers (singular and plural) and three voices (active, passive and deponent).

Verbs are described by their principal parts (e.g. *amo, amare, amavi, amatum*):

- The first principal part is the first person (or third person for impersonal verbs) singular, present tense, indicative, active (or passive for verbs lacking an active voice).
- The second principal part is the present infinitive active (or passive for verbs lacking an active voice).
- The third principal part is the first person (or third person for impersonal verbs) singular, perfect, indicative, active (or passive when there is no active forms).
- The fourth principal part is the supine form. It usually shows the neuter (*-um*) of the participle. It can also be the future participle when the verb cannot be made passive.

Latin lacks indefinite and definite articles.

Latin is not a spoken language today but there are traces of Latin in many modern languages and in every sentence we speak. Some examples of Latin words or expressions commonly used in everyday speech are:

- *a.m./p.m.* stand for *ante/post meridiem* (before/after midday)
- *etc.* stands for *et cetera* (and other things)
- *forum* is a marketplace, the real social and political centre of a town, today commonly used to denote an online space used for discussion
- *e.g.* stands for *exempli gratia* (for example)
- *i.e.* stands for *id est* (that is, namely)

10 Only got ten minutes?

Latin is an Italic language originally spoken in the region of central Italy called *Latium* (today Lazio) and the ancient city of Rome, the *aeterna urbs*. With the Roman conquest, Latin spread throughout Italy, the Mediterranean and Europe. Britain was occupied by the Romans from AD 43 to AD 410 and during this time Latin was the main language used in the island, apart from Scotland. 'Veni, Vidi, Vici' (= I came, I saw, I conquered) is the famous sentence reportedly written by Julius Caesar in 47 BC after his expedition to Britain. However, the conquest of Britain didn't start until AD 43 with the invasion led by Claudius. Britain was then overrun by Anglo-Saxons in the years following the end of the Roman rule, so that there was no major Latin influence on the language at this stage; Anglo-Saxon was indeed the predominant tongue. However, when Norman and Angevin kings ruled England for some 300 years, the Latin-based French was incorporated into Middle English, adding enormous richness to it. So, Latin influence was back into the English language, this time through French. The so called Romance languages such as Catalan, French, Italian, Portuguese, Romanian, and Spanish are descended directly from Latin but many other languages, English included, although not directly derived from Latin, have inherited and acquired much of their vocabulary from it. English has taken some of its Latin-based words direct from Latin, others through an intermediary language such as French (e.g. wine comes from vinum). Moreover, some English words look similar to Latin because both English and Latin are Indo-European languages. The Indo-European family extends from the Atlantic coasts of Europe to India. In Europe four big-groups can be detected: Hellenic, represented by the various dialects of Greek; Italic, mostly consisting of Latin; Germanic, including English, German, and the Scandinavian languages;

and Celtic, including Welsh and Irish. Latin is also the ancestor of the Romance languages, as mentioned above. So, in a way, Latin is not a dead language but it persists in all the modern Romance languages, which represent the evolution of its spoken forms.

Latin is a perfect language with a very precise set of grammatical rules; it is a synthetic language where affixes are attached to fixed stems of words to express gender, number, and case in nouns, pronouns and adjectives; this process is called declension. Latin nouns, pronouns and adjectives therefore decline; there are five declensions in Latin and every declension has six cases (*nominative, accusative, vocative, genitive, dative* and *ablative*). Each case has a specific meaning and function: nominative is the case of the subject, accusative is the case of the direct object, *vocative* is the case used when addressing someone, genitive is the case that shows possession, *dative* is the case of the indirect object and *ablative* is a case with several functions, its main meanings being 'by', 'with', 'from', 'at', 'in' and 'on'. There is also an old seventh case, called the *locative* case, used to indicate a location, corresponding to the English 'in' or 'at'. This is far less common than the other six cases of Latin nouns and usually applies to cities, small towns, and small islands, along with a few common nouns (e.g. *domi* = at home). In the first and second declension singular, its form coincides with the genitive (e.g. *Romae* = in Rome). In the first and second declension plural, and in the other declensions, it coincides with the dative and ablative (e.g. *Athenis* = at Athens). The meaning of the cases can also change when these are used with prepositions. Prepositions are short words that stand in front of a noun or pronoun to introduce an adverbial phrase; in Latin prepositions can take either the accusative or the ablative, only the preposition in can take both cases: 'in + a noun in the ablative case' means 'in', 'at', 'on', (e.g. *in schola* = at school) 'in + a noun in the accusative case' means 'into', 'onto', 'towards' (e.g. *in scholam* – into the school). The main prepositions in Latin are: a) prepositions with accusative: *in* (into), *ad* (to), *per* (through, by means of, on account of), *ante* (before), *contra* (against), *ob/propter* (because of, on account of), *post* (after),

praeter (along, except), *prope* (near), *trans* (across); b) prepositions with ablative: *cum* (with), *a/ab/e/ex/de* (by, from, out of – de + ablative can also mean about), *in* (in, at, on). Even in Modern English, nouns have distinct singular and plural forms; so in a way, they *decline* to reflect their grammatical number. On the other hand, verbs are conjugated in Latin; there are four main conjugations (first, second, third and fourth) and a mixed conjugation (third and fourth; e.g. *capio*) where affixes are attached to fixed stems of verbs to denote person, number, tense, voice, mood, and aspect. There are six tenses in Latin (i.e. present, imperfect, future, perfect, pluperfect, and future perfect), three grammatical moods (i.e. indicative, imperative and subjunctive, in addition to the infinitive, participle, gerund, gerundive and supine), three persons (first, second, and third), two numbers (singular and plural) and three voices (active, passive and deponent). The indicative mood is used to state something as a fact or to ask a question. The imperative expresses a command, an order. The subjunctive is used, among other functions, to express doubt or unlikelihood. The infinitive can be described as a verbal noun. It acts as a verb when it is active or passive, has a present, future and past tense and can govern cases; it can also act as a noun, when it is neuter and it stands in the nominative or accusative case. The participle can be defined as an adjective formed from a verb; there are three tenses of participle in Latin: present, future and perfect. As adjectives, participles agree in case, number and gender with the noun or pronoun to which they refer. The gerundive is a verbal adjective; it is a passive adjective, based on a verb, ending in *-ndus, -a, -um* like a fist-and-second-declension-adjective, meaning 'to be -ed' and frequently expressing the idea of obligation (e.g. *hoc faciendum est* = this must be done).The gerundive usually has the agent expressed in the dative case or *a/ab* + a noun in the ablative case. The gerund, as much as the infinitive can be described best as a verbal noun; it is a neuter noun, formed from a verb; this form is never nominative and is mostly used with a preposition. Finally, the supine is that part of a verb from which other parts of the verb can be predicated, especially the passive forms. Verbs can have active, passive or deponent forms. Deponent verbs are those verbs that have a passive form but they are translated with an active meaning (e.g. *utor* = I use); also, there are the so-called semi-deponent verbs; they adopt active forms in some tenses and deponent forms in others (e.g. *audeo* = I dare).

Verbs are described by its principal parts (e.g. *amo, amare, amavi, amatum*):

- The first principal part is the first person (or third person for impersonal verbs) singular, present tense, indicative, active (or passive for verbs lacking an active voice).
- The second principal part is the present infinitive active (or passive for verbs lacking an active voice).
- The third principal part is the first person (or third person for impersonal verbs) singular, perfect, indicative, active (or passive when there is no active form).
- The fourth principal part is the supine form. It usually shows the neuter (*-um*) of the participle. It can also be the future participle when the verb cannot be made passive.

Only the principal parts of irregular verbs or verbs with their own individual forms are given in the dictionary. Regular verbs have the following endings:
am-o, am-are, am-avi, am-atum
mo-eo, mon-ere, mon-ui, mon-itum
leg-o, leg-is, leg-i, lec-tum
aud-io, aud-is, aud-ivi / aud-ii, aud-itum

Some of the most important verbs with irregular principal parts to remember are:

- *ago, agere, egi, actum* = I do
- *augeo, augere, auxi, auctum* = I increase
- *cado, cadere, cecidi, casum* = I fall, I die
- *capio, capere, cepi, captum* = I take
- *coepi, coepisse, coeptus* = I have begun
- *credo, credere, credidi, creditum* = I believe
- *curro, currere, cucurri, cursum* = I run
- *dico, dicere, dixi, dictum* = I say
- *do, dare, dedi, datum* = I give

- *edo, edere, edi, esum* = I eat
- *emo, emere, emi, emptum* = I buy
- *eo, ire, ii/ivi, itum* = I go
- *facio, facere, feci, factum* = I make
- *fero, ferre, tuli, latum* = I bring
- *fio, fieri, factus* = I become
- *gero, gerere, gessi, gestum* = I do, conduct
- *iubeo, iubere, iussi, iussum* = I order
- *malo, malle, malui* = I prefer
- *maneo, manere, mansi, mansum* = I wait
- *mitto, mittere, misi, missum* = I send
- *nolo, nolle, nolui* = I do not want
- *odi, odisse, osus* = I hate
- *possum, posse, potui* = I can
- *sto, stare, steti, statum* = I stand
- *sum, esse, fui, futurus* = I am
- *tollo, tollere, sustuli, sublatum* = I lift
- *traho, trahere, traxi, tractum* = I drag
- *volo, velle, volui* = I want

Latin lacks indefinite and definite articles.

Latin is not a spoken language today but there are traces of Latin in many modern languages and in every sentence we speak. Some examples of Latin words or expressions commonly used in everyday speech are:

- *a.m./p.m.* stand for *ante/post meridiem* (before/after midday)
- *etc.* stands for *et cetera* (and other things)
- *forum* is a marketplace, the real social and political centre of a town, today commonly used to denote an online space used for discussion
- *e.g.* stands for *exempli gratia* (for example)
- *i.e.* stands for *id est* (namely)

Introduction

The chief benefit that a knowledge of Latin confers is the ability to read the works of the Roman authors, particularly those of the Golden and Silver Ages of Latin Literature, i.e. 60 BC–AD 100. This dictionary has been compiled with this in mind, and also with an eye to the 'non-specialist'. To this end, the equivalents in the Latin–English section of the dictionary have been presented in as simple and 'modern' a form as possible, while at the same time the most important distinctions in meaning which each Latin word bears have been indicated. The vocabulary has been based on that commonly used by the authors of the period mentioned above, and a person who is acquainted with Latin grammar and the common forms of the Latin language should be able, with a little help from this dictionary, to read them without much difficulty. *Teach Yourself Latin Grammar*, by Gregory Klyve, may be of assistance to those who are not so acquainted, or whose memory has been dimmed by the passage of time.

In the English–Latin section, the Latin equivalent given is that which represents the best general meaning of the English, and which is used in that sense by a Classical author. Occasionally, however, where no exact Latin equivalent for an English word exists, it has been necessary to give a short circumlocution: in this case the phrase given is always translated into English, e.g. **disinterested** neutri favens (**favouring neither side**). Where several different meanings are borne by the same word, or where ambiguity may occur, care has been taken to differentiate between the various meanings, e.g. **order**, *nn*, (**arrangement**), ordo, *m*; (**in —**), *adj*, dispŏsĭtus; (**command, direction**), iussum, *n*; (**class, rank**), ordo, *m*; (**in — to**), ut.

Where fuller information is required about any of the words given in the dictionary, reference should be made to Lewis and Short's *Latin Dictionary* (Oxford University Press, 1963), available on line via the Perseus Digital Library, at **http://www.perseus.tufts.edu/**, which comprises a magnificent collection of primary and secondary Classical sources.

Advice on learning vocabulary

If you are gifted with a good memory, you will find it particularly easy to learn Latin vocabulary, especially if you try to link in your mind new Latin words and any English derivatives of them which you can think of, e.g. **mare**—sea—marine; **nauta**—ship—nautical. A high proportion of Latin words have quite common English derivatives. If you do this, not only will your interest in both languages grow, but you will begin to form an impression of the debt which our language owes to that of the Romans.

If on the other hand, you are one of those who find it difficult to make words stick, then here is a piece of simple advice – not to be despised because of its simplicity – which might help you to retain words in your memory. To learn a new word it is not only essential to find out and to understand its meaning, but also to see it working in relationship to other words, and to 'meet' it as many times as possible immediately after first acquaintance. It is therefore advisable to re-read the piece in which you originally met the word two or three times after you have learned it, and to make an effort to find the same word again within a day or two of first meeting it, otherwise you may find, on ultimately seeing it again, that it has 'gone'. Above all, try to maintain your interest in learning new vocabulary, for without such an interest no learning of real or lasting nature can take place.

Abbreviations used

( ) Brackets are used to indicate alternative forms.

See *Teach Yourself Latin Grammar*, by Gregory Klyve, for an explanation of the grammar terms used.

a, um   see adj.

abl.   ablative case.

acc.   accusative case.

acis⎫ genitive singular ending of nouns indicating that they
atis⎭ belong to the third declension.

adj.   adjective, **a, um, era, erum** after an adjective indicates that it declines like a noun of the first or second declensions, **e** that it declines like a noun of the third declension.

adv.   adverb. The adverb ending is often given, e.g. **e, iter, nter, um, o**, and should be attached to the *stem* of the adjective, e.g. **abditus** (*adj*); **abdite** (*adv*).

ae genitive singular ending of a noun, indicating that it belongs to the first declension.

arum genitive plural ending, indicating that the noun belongs to the first declension.

auxil. auxiliary verb.

c. common gender.

comp. comparative adjective or adverb.

conj. conjunction.

cris, cre nominative feminine and neuter endings, indicating that an adjective declines like a noun of the third declension.

cl. clause.

dat. dative case; also some verbs take a dative case after them.

defect. a defective verb; i.e. it has not all its parts.

demonst. demonstrative pronoun.

dep. see v. dep.

e see adj.

ei genitive singular ending of noun, indicating that it belongs to the fifth declension.

enis⎱ genitive singular endings of nouns indicating that they
etis⎰ belong to the third declension.

exclam. exclamation.

f. feminine gender.

f.pl. feminine plural.

fut. future.

genit. genitive case.

i, ii genitive singular ending of noun, indicating that it belongs to the second declension.

icis⎱ genitive singular endings of nouns indicating that they
inis⎰ belong to the third declension.

impers. impersonal verb.

indecl. indeclinable.

inf. infinitive.

interj. interjective.

interr. interrogative.

irreg. irregular verb.

is genitive singular of noun, indicating that it belongs to the third declension.

iter see adv.

itis genitive singular ending of noun, indicating that it belongs to the third declension.

ium genitive plural ending of noun, indicating that it belongs to the third declension.

loc locative case

m. masculine gender.

m.pl. masculine plural.

n. neuter gender.

nn. noun.

nter see adv.

ntis genitive singular ending of some nouns and adjectives of the third declension.

num numeral.

n.pl. neuter plural.

obj. objective.

onis } genitive singular noun ending, indicating that the noun
oris } belongs to the second declension.

orum genitive plural ending, indicating that a noun belongs to the second declension.

partic. participle.

pass. a passive verb, conjugated in the passive voice only.

perf. perfect.

pers. personal.

phr. phrase.

pl. plural.

poss. possessive.

prep. preposition: the case taken by the preposition is usually indicated.

pres. present.

pron. pronoun.

pron. adj. pronominal adjective; a pronoun which declines and agrees like an adjective.

reflex. reflexive.

rel. relative.

semi-dep. semi-deponent; verbs which are deponent in some of their tenses.

sup(erl). superlative adjective or adverb.

tis } genitive singular ending of some nouns and adjs. of
tris } the third declension.

um genitive plural ending of noun, indicating that it belongs to the third declension.

ūs genitive singular ending of noun, indicating that it belongs to the fourth declension.

v. vb. verb. The conjugation to which a verb belongs is indicated by the figure 1, 2, 3, or 4. In the case of third conjugation verbs, and other verbs whose perfect stem and supine are not regular, these are given with the verb, e.g. **aboleo, evi, itum.** If none of these parts are given, it may be assumed that the verb is regularly conjugated; if some, but not all parts are given, it may be assumed that the ones not given are not in regular use.

v. dep.   verb deponent.

v.i.   verb intransitive, i.e. a verb which does not have a direct object.

v. impers.   verb impersonal.

v.i.t.   a verb which can be used intransitively or transitively. The separate uses are indicated by the use of the semi-colon, e.g. **abhorreo**, *v.i.t.*, 2, to shrink back (intransitive); to disagree with (transitive).

voc.   vocative case.

v.t.   verb transitive, i.e. a verb which has a direct object.

Alphabet

The Latin alphabet contained 23 letters:

A B C D E F G H I K L M N O P Q R S T V X Y Z

Pronunciation

Although there is not complete agreement about the way in which the Romans spoke Latin, this is one method of pronunciation which many people believe to have been used by the Romans.

Vowels

ă (short a) as in 'fat'; ā (long a) as in 'father'.
ĕ (short e) as in 'net'; ē (long e) as in 'they'.
ĭ (short i) as in 'pin'; ī (long i) as in 'police'.
ŏ (short o) as in 'not'; ō (long o) as in 'note'.
ŭ (short u) as 'oo' in 'wood'; ū (long u) as 'oo' in 'mood'.

In the dictionary ᾱ̆, ĕ̄, ĭ̄, ŏ̄, ŭ̄ represent the respective vowels with the combined long (macron ‾) and short (breve ˇ) marks (e.g. 'ăprīcor'). This mark is used to indicate that the syllable is anceps. In Latin, vowels could be long or short; anceps syllables could be both.

Diphthongs

Two vowels pronounced together to form one sound are called diphthongs, e.g. ae, au, oe, and are pronounced as follows.

ae, as in 'ai' in 'aisle'.
au, as 'ow' in 'cow'.
oe, as in 'oi' in 'oil'.

Consonants

These are mostly pronounced as in English, but note:

c is always hard, as in 'cat'.

g is always hard, as in 'get'.

i, when it is used as a consonant, is always pronounced as 'y' in 'yellow' e.g. *iam*, 'yam'.

s is always pronounced as in 'son'.

t is always pronounced as in 'top'.

v is pronounced as 'w' in 'wall', e.g. *servi*, pronounced 'serwee'.

th is pronounced as 't' and *ch* as 'k'.

Latin–English dictionary

A

> **Insight**
>
> There is no **definite article** in Latin. Therefore there are no Latin words to express the English 'the'. Likewise, there is no **indefinite article** in Latin. Thus, there are no Latin words to express the English 'a' and 'an'.

ā, ăb *prep. with abl*, by (agent); from (place, time); in, at (position); since

ăbăcus, i *m*, sideboard, counting or gaming board, slab

ăbălĭēno *v.t.* 1, to estrange, make a legal transfer

ăbăvus, i *m*, great-great-grandfather, ancestor

abdĭcātĭo, ōnis *f*, renunciation of office

abdĭco *v.t.* 1, to resign

abdīco, xi, ctum *v.t.* 3 to refuse assent

abdĭtus, a, um *adj, adv, ē*, hidden, secret

abdo, didi, dĭtum *v.t.* 3, to conceal

abdōmĕn, ĭnis *n*, belly

ăberro *v.i.* 1, to go astray

ăbhinc *adv*, ago

ăbhorrĕo *v.i.t.* 2, to shrink back; disagree with

ăbi see ăbĕo

ăbĭcĭo, iēci, iectum *v.t.* 3, to throw away

abiectus, a, um *adj, adv, ē*, downcast

ăbiēgnus, a um *adj*, made of fir

ăbĭēs, ĕtis *f*, fir

ăbīgo, ĕre, ēgi, actum *v.t.* 3, to drive away

ăbĭtĭo, ōnis *f*, departure

abiūdico *v.t.* 1, to deprive by legal sentence

abiungo, nxi, nctum *v.t.* 3, to unyoke

> **Insight**
>
> **Third declension nouns** have a great variety of endings in the nominative singular. What unites them all is that the genitive singular always has the same ending (*-is*). Therefore, when learning third-declension nouns, it is essential to memorize both the nominative and the genitive singular.

abdūco, xi, ctum *v.t.* 3, to lead away

ăbĕo *v.i.* 4, to go away

abiūro *v.t.* 1, to deny on oath

ablātus, a, um *adj.* from **aufĕro**, taken away

> **Insight**
>
> The **ablative** is a case with many usages and meanings. The basic meanings are 'by', 'with', 'from', 'at', 'in' or 'on'. Many prepositions take the ablative determining the meaning of the noun. Many verbs are followed by the ablative case (e.g. *utor*).

ablēgātĭo, ōnis *f,* banishment

ablēgo *v.t.* 1, to send away

ablŭo, ŭi, ūtum *v.t.* 3, to wash away

ablūtĭo, ōnis *f,* ablution, washing

abnĕgo *v.t.* 1, to refuse

abnormis, e *adj,* irregular

abnŭo, ŭi, ūtum *v.i.t.* 3, to refuse

ăbŏlĕo, ēvi, ĭtum *v.t.* 2, to destroy

ăbŏlesco, ēvi *v.i.* 3, to decay

ăbŏlĭtĭo, ōnis *f,* abolition

ăbolla, ae *f,* cloak

ăbōmĭnor *v.t.* 1, *dep,* to wish away (being ominous)

ăbŏrīgĭnes, um *m.pl,* natives

ăbortĭo, ōnis *f,* miscarriage

ăbortus, ūs *m,* abortion

abrādo, si, sum *v.t.* 3, to scrape off

abrĭpĭo, ŭi, reptum *v.t.* 3, to drag away

abrōdo, si, sum *v.t.* 3, to gnaw away

abrŏgātĭo, ōnis *f,* repeal

abrŏgo *v.t.* 1, to repeal

abrumpo, rūpi, ruptum *v.t.* 3, to break off

abruptus, a, um *adj,* steep

abscēdo, cessi, cessum *v.i.* 3, to go away

abscīdo, cīdi, scīsum *v.t.* 3, to cut off

abscindo, scĭdi, scissum *v.t.* 3, to tear away

abscīsus, a, um *adj, adv,* ē, steep

abscondĭtus, a, um *adj, adv,* ē, hidden

abscondo, di, dĭtum *v.t.* 3, to conceal

absens, entis *adj,* absent

absentĭa, ae *f,* absence

absĭlĭo *v.i.* 4, to jump away

absĭmĭlis, e *adj,* unlike

absinthium, ii *n,* absinth

absisto, stĭti *v.i.* 3, to stand aloof

absŏlūtĭo, ōnis *f,* acquittal

absŏlūtus, a, um *adj, adv,* ē, discordant

absolvo, vi. sŏlūtum *v.t.* 3, to unfasten, acquit

absŏnus, a, um *adj, adv,* ē, discordant

absorbĕo, bŭi, ptum *v.t.* 2, to swallow up

absquĕ *prep. with abl,* without

abstēmĭus, a, um *adj,* sober

abstergĕo, rsi, rsum *v.t.* 2, to wipe off

absterrĕo *v.t.* 2, to frighten away

abstinens, ntis *adj, adv,* nter, temperate

abstĭnentĭa, ae *f,* self-restraint

abstĭnĕo, ŭi, tentum *v.i.t.* 2, to abstain from; restrain

abstrăho, xi, ctum *v.t.* 3, to drag away

abstrūdo, si, sum *v.t.* 3, to push away

abstrūsus, a, um *adj, adv,* ē, hidden

absum, esse, abfui (afui) *v.i. irreg,* to be absent

absūmo, mpsi, mptum *v.t.* 3, to take away, use up

absurdus, a, um *adj, adv,* ē, stupid, tuneless

ăbundans, ntis *adj, adv,* nter, plentiful

ăbundantĭa, ae *f,* plenty

ăbundo *v.i.* 1, to overflow

ăbūtor, i, usus sum *v.* 3, *dep, with abl,* to use up, abuse

āc *conj,* and

ăcācĭa, ae *f,* acacia

ăcădēmĭa, ae *f,* academy

accēdo, cessi, cesssum *v.i.* 3, to approach

accēlĕro *v.i.t.* 1, to hurry; quicken

accendo, ndi, nsum *v.t.* 3, to set on fire

accensĕo, ŭi, nsum *v.t.* 2, to add to

accensus, i *m,* attendant

accentus, ūs *m,* accentuation

acceptĭo, ōnis *f,* acceptance

acceptum, i *n,* receipt

acceptus, a, um *adj,* agreeable

accessĭo, ōnis *f,* approach, increase

accessus, ūs *m,* approach

accīdo, cīdi, cīsum *v.t.* 3, to cut

accĭdo, cĭdi *v.i.* 3, to fall upon, happen

accingo, nxi, nctum *v.t.* 3, to equip, put on

accĭo *v.t.* 4, to summon

accĭpĭo, cēpi, ceptum *v.t.* 3, to receive

accĭpĭter, tris *m,* hawk

accītus, ūs *m*, summons
acclāmātĭo, ōnis *f*, shout
acclāmo *v.t.* 1, to shout at
acclīnis, e *adj*, leaning on
acclīno *v.t.* 1, to lean
acclīvis, e *adj*, uphill
acclīvĭtas, ātis *f*, ascent
accŏla, ae *c*, neighbour
accŏlo, cŏlui, cultum *v.t.* 3, to live near
accommŏdātus, a, um *adj*, *adv*, ē, suitable
accommŏdātĭo, ōnis *f*, compliance
accommŏdo *v.t.* 1, to adapt
accommŏdus, a, um *adj*, suitable
accresco, crēvi, crētum *v.i.* 3, to grow
accrētĭo, ōnis *f*, increase
accŭbĭtĭo, ōnis *f*, reclining
accŭbo *v.i.* 1, to lie near, recline at table
accumbo, cŭbŭi, cŭbĭtum *v.i.* 3, to lie near, recline at table
accŭmŭlo *v.t.* 1, to heap up
accūro *v.t.* 1, to take care of
accūrātus, a, um *adj*, *adv*, ē, prepared carefully, precise
accurro, curri, cursum *v.i.* 3, to run to
accūsātio, ōnis *f*, accusation
accūsātor, ōris *m*, accuser
accūso *v.t.* 1, to accuse
ācer, cris, e *adj*, *adv*, ĭter, keen
ăcer, ĕris *n*, maple tree
ăcerbĭtas, ātis *f*, bitterness

ăcētārĭa, ōrum *n.pl*, salad
ăcētum, i *n*, vinegar
ăcĭdus, a, um *adj*, *adv*, ē, sour
ăcĭes, ēi *f*, edge, pupil of eye, battle line, keeness
ăcĭnăces, is *m*, scimitar
ăcĭnus, i *m* (um, i *n*), berry
ăcĭpenser, ĕris *m*, sturgeon
aclys, ўdis *f*, small javelin
ăcŏnĭtum, i *n*, aconite
acquĭesco, ēvi, ĕtum *v.i.* 3, to rest, aquiesce
acquīro, sīvi, sītum *v.t.* 3, to procure
ācrĭmōnĭa, ae *f*, sharpness
ācrĭter *adv*, keenly
acta, ōrum *n.pl* acts, records
actĭo, ōnis *f*, act, legal action
actor, ōris *m*, driver, plaintiff, performer
actŭarĭus, a, um *adj*, swift
actŭārĭus, i *m*, notary
actum, i *n*, deed
actus, a, um see ăgo
actus, ūs *m*, impulse, act (of drama)
ăcūlĕātus, a, um *adj*, prickly
ăcūlĕus, i *m*, sting
ăcūmĕn, ĭnis *n*, point, sting
ăcŭo, ŭi, ūtum *v.t.* 3, to sharpen
ăcus, ūs *f*, needle, pin
ăcūtus, a, um *adj*, *adv*, ē, sharp
ad *prep. with acc*, to, towards, near (place), about (time), for (purpose)

Insight

In Latin the 'place to which' is expressed by **in/ad** with a noun in the accusative case (*ad oppidum* = to the town). The 'place from which' by **a/ab/e/ex/de** with the ablative (*ex oppido* = from the town). The 'place where' by **in** with the ablative (*in oppido* = in the town).

ăcerbo *v.t.* 1, to embitter
ăcerbus, a, um *adj*, bitter, keen
ăcernus, a, um *adj*, made of maple
ăcerra, ae *f*, incense-box
ăcervo *v.t.* 1, to heap up
ăcervus, i *m*, heap

ădaequo *v.i.t.* 1, to be equal; to make equal
ădaequo *v.i.t.* 1, to be equal; to make equal
ădāmas, ntis *m*, steel, diamond
ădāmo *v.t.* 1, to love deeply

ădăpĕrĭo, ŭi, rtum *v.t.* 4, to open fully

ădaugĕo, xi, ctum *v.t.* 2, to increase

addīco, xi, ctum *v.t.* 3, to assent, award

addictĭo, ōnis *f,* adjudication

addictus, a, um *adj,* dedicated

addo, dĭdi, dĭtum *v.t.* 3, to add to

addŭbĭto *v.i.t.* 1, to doubt

addūco, xi, ctum *v.t.* 3, to lead to, influence

ădemptĭo, ōnis *f,* seizure

ădĕo *v.i.* 4, to approach, attack

ădĕo *adv,* so much, so long

ădeps, ĭpis *c,* fat

ădeptĭo, ōnis *f,* attainment

ădĕquĭto *v.i.* 1, to gallop up

ădhaerĕo, si, sum *v.i.* 2, to cling to

ădhaeresco, si, sum *v.i.* 3, to cling to

ădhĭbĕo *v.t.* 2, to apply, invite

ădhortātĭo, ōnis *f,* encouragement

ădhortor *v.t.* 1, *dep,* to encourage

ădhuc *adv,* still

adiăcĕo *v.i.* 2, to adjoin

adĭcĭo, iēci, iectum *v.t.* 3, to throw to, add to

ădĭgo, ēgi, actum *v.t.* 3, to drive to, compel

ădĭmo, ēmi, emptum *v.t.* 3, to take away

ădĭpiscor, eptus *v.t.* 3, *dep,* to obtain

ădĭtus, ūs *m,* approach

adiūdĭco *v.t.* 1, to assign

adiŭmentum, i *n,* assistance

adiunctĭo, ōnis *f,* union

adiungo, xi, ctum *v.t.* 3, to join to

adiūro *v.t.* 1, to swear, confirm

adiūtor, ōris *m,* helper

adiŭvo, iūvi, iūtum *v.t.* 1, to precipitate

admētĭor, mensus *v.t.* 4, *dep,* to measure out

admĭnĭcŭlum, i *n,* prop

admĭnister, tri *m,* servant

admĭnistrātĭo, ōnis *f,* aid, management, arrangement

admĭnistro *v.t.* 1, to assist, manage

admīrābilis, e *adj, adv,* ĭter, wonderful

admīrātĭo, ōnis *f,* admiration

admīror *v.t.* 1, *dep,* to wonder at

admiscĕo, scŭi, xtum *v.t.* 2, to mix with

admissārĭus, ii *m,* stallion

admissĭo, ōnis *f,* reception

admissum, i *n,* fault

admitto, mīsi, ssum *v.t.* 3, to let in, let go, incur, commit

admixtĭo, ōnis *f,* mixture

admŏdum *adv,* up to the limit, very much, nearly

admŏnĕo *v.t.* 2, to remind

admŏnĭtĭo, ōnis *f,* warning

admŏnĭtus, ūs *m,* suggestion

admordĕo, di, sum *v.t.* 2, to bite at

admōtĭo, ōnis *f,* application

admŏvĕo, mōvi, mōtum *v.t.* 2, to conduct, assault

admurmŭrātĭo, ōnis *f,* murmur

admurmŭro *v.i.* 1, to murmur at

adn- see ann...

ădŏlĕo, ŭi, ultum *v.i.* 3, to grow up

ădŏlescens, ntis *adj,* young

ădŏlescens, ntis *c,* young person

ădŏlescentĭa, ae *f,* youth

ădŏlescentŭlus, i *m,* very young man

ădŏlesco, ēvi, ultum *v.i.* 3, to grow up

ădŏpĕrĭo, ŭi, rtum *v.t.* 4, to cover up

ădoptātĭo, ōnis *f,* adoption

ădoptĭo, ōnis *f,* adoption

ădoptīvus, a, um *adj,* adoptive

ădopto *v.t.* 1, to choose, adopt

ădor, ōris *n,* grain

ădōrātĭo, ōnis *f,* adoption

ădōrĕa, ae *f,* reward for bravery

ădŏrĭor, ortus *v.t.* 4, *dep,* to attack, undertake

ădorno *v.t.* 1, to equip, decorate

ădōro *v.t.* 1, to worship, entreat

adrādo, si, sum *v.t.* 3, to shave

adsum, esse, adfui *v.i, irreg,* to be near

ads... see ass...

ădūlātĭo, ōnis *f,* flattery

ădūlātor, ōris *m,* flatterer

ădūlor *v.t.* 1, *dep,* to flatter

ădulter, ĕri *m,* adulterer

ădultĕra, ae *f,* adulteress

ădultĕrātĭo, ōnis *f,* adulteration

ădultĕrīnus, a, um *adj,* false

ădultĕrĭum, ii *n,* adultery

ădultĕro *v.i.t.* 1, to commit adultery; to falsify, pollute

ădultus, a, um   *adj,* grown up
ădumbrātĭo, ōnis   *f,* sketch
ădumbro   *v.t.* 1, to sketch
ăduncus, a, um   *adj,* hooked
ădurgĕo   *v.t.* 2, to press
ădūro, ssi, stum   *v.t.* 3, to scorch
ădusque   *prep. with acc,* right up to
ădusta, ōrum   *n.pl,* burns
ădustus, a, um   *adj,* burnt
advĕho, xi, ctum   *v.t.* 3, to carry to
advĕna, ae   *c,* stranger
advĕnĭo, vēni, ventum   *v.t.* 4, to reach
advento   *v.t.* 1, to approach
adventus, ūs   *m,* arrival
adversārĭus, ii   *m,* opponent
adversārĭus, a, um   *adj,* opposite, opposing
adversor   *v.* 1, *dep, with dat,* to oppose
adversus, a, um   *adj,* opposite; (of winds) contrary
adversus   *prep. with acc,* opposite
adversum   *adv,* opposite
adverto, ti, sum   *v.t.* 3, to direct towards
advespĕrascit, avit   *v. impers,* evening approaches
advĭgĭlo   *v.i.* 1, to keep watch
advŏcātĭo, ōnis   *f,* summons, legal assistance
advŏcātus, i   *m,* legal adviser
advŏco   *v.t.* 1, to call, summon help
advŏlo   *v.i.* 1, to fly towards
advolvo, vi, ūtum   *v.t.* 3, to roll, grovel before
ădȳtum, i   *n,* sanctuary
aedēs, is   *f,* temple; pl. house

aedīcŭla, ae   *f,* shrine, niche
aedĭfĭcātor, ōris   *m,* builder
aedĭfĭcĭum, ii   *n,* building
aedĭfĭcātĭo, ōnis   *f,* constructing
aedĭfĭco   *v.t.* 1, to build
aedīlīcĭus, a, um   *adj,* of an aedile
aedīlis, is   *m,* aedile – Roman magistrate
aedīlĭtas, ātis   *f,* aedileship
aedĭtŭus, i   *m,* verger
aeger, ra, rum   *adj,* ill, sad
aegis, ĭdis   *f,* shield
aegrē   *adv,* with difficulty, scarcely, amiss, with displeasure
aegresco   *v.i.* 3, to fall ill
aegrĭtūdo, ĭnis   *f,* illness, grief
aegrōtātĭo, ōnis   *f,* sickness
aegrōto   *v.i.* 1, to be ill
aegrōtus, a, um   *adj,* ill
aemŭlātĭo, ōnis   *f,* rivalry
aemŭlor   *v.t.* 1, *dep,* to rival, envy
aemŭlus, a, um   *adj,* rivalling
aēnĕus, a, um   *adj,* of bronze
aenigma, ătis   *n,* riddle
aequābĭlis, e   *adj, adv, ĭter,* similar, uniform
aequābĭlĭtas, ātis   *f,* equality
aequaevus, a, um   *adj,* of equal age
aequālis, e   *adj, adv, ĭter,* level, contemporary
aequālĭtas, ātis   *f,* uniformity
aequē   *adv,* equally, justly
aequĭlībrĭum, ii   *n,* horizontal position
aequĭnoctĭum, i   *n,* equinox
aequĭpăro   *v.i.t.* 1, to equal; compare
aequĭtas, ātis   *f,* equality, fariness, calmness

Insight

Latin has two words that are commonly translated by 'house': *domus* and *aedes*. The fourth declension noun *domus* means 'house' as well as 'home'; the third declension noun aedes means 'house' if used in its plural form, otherwise it is translated as 'temple'. The noun *casa* which means 'house/home' in Italian, Spanish, Portuguese and Catalan means 'cottage' in Latin.

aequo *v.i.t.* 1, to equalize; match, raze
aequor, ŏris *n*, even surface, sea
aequum, i *n*, plain, justice
aequus, a, um *adj*, flat, friendly, equal, reasonable

aether, ĕris *m*, upper air, heaven
aethĕrĭus, a, um *adj*, celestial
Aethĭops, ŏpis *m*, Aethiopian, negro
aethra, ae *f*, upper air
aevum, i *n*, lifetime, generation

Insight

aequus and *equus* are pronounced the same but they are two distinct words. *Aequus* means 'even', hence the English words 'equations', 'equal', 'equality' and so on. Equus means 'horse', hence 'equine', 'equestrian' etc.

āēr, ris *m*, air
aerārĭa, ae *f*, mine
aerārĭum, i *n*, treasury
aerārĭus, a, um *adj*, of bronze, of the treasury
aerātus, a, um *adj*, bronze covered
aerĕus, a, um *adj*, of bronze
aerĭpes, ĕdis *adj*, bronze-footed
āĕrĭus, a, um *adj*, lofty
aerūgo, ĭnis *f*, rust, envy
aerumna, ae *f*, suffering
aerumnōsus, a, um *adj*, wretched
aes, aeris *n*, copper, money
aescŭlētum, i *n*, oak-forest
aescŭlĕus, a, um *adj*, oaken
aescŭlus, i *f*, oak
aestas, ātis *f*, summer
aestĭfer, ĕra, ĕrum *adj*, hot, sultry
aestĭmābĭlis, e *adj*, valuable
aestĭmātĭo, ōnis *f*, valuation
aestĭmātor, ōris *m*, valuer
aestĭmo *v.t.* 1, to value, assess
aestīva, ōrum *n.pl*, summer camp
aestīvus, a, um *adj, adv*, ē, summer-like
aestŭārĭum, ii *n*, creek, air-hole
aestŭo *v.i.* 1, to seethe, glow
aestŭōsus, a, um *adj, adv*, ē, sweltering
aestus, ŭs *m*, heat, tide, rage, excitement
aetas, ātis *f*, age, lifetime
aetātŭla, ae *f*, tender age
aeternĭtas, ātis *f*, eternity
aeternus, a, um *adj, adv*, um, everlasting

affābĭlis, e *adj, adv*, ĭter, courteous
affătim *adv*, enough
affātus *partic. from* **affor**
affectātĭo, ōnis *f*, pretension, whim
affectātus, a, um *adj* far-fetched
affectĭo, ōnis *f*, disposition, whim
affecto *v.t.* 1, to strive after
affectus, ūs *m*, mood, sympathy
affĕro, afferre, attŭli, allātum *v.t, irreg*, to bring to, announce, help, produce, confer
affĭcĭo, affēci, ctum *v.t.* 3, to influence, seize
affigo, xi, xum *v.t.* 3, to fasten to
affingo, nxi, ictum *v.t.* 3, to add to, fabricate
affinis, e *adj*, neighbouring, related
affīnĭtas, ātis *f*, kinship
affirmātē *adv*, explicitly
affirmātĭo, ōnis *f*, assertion
affirmo *v.t.* 1, to assert
affixus, a, um *adj*, fastened to
afflātus, ūs *m*, breath, blast
afflicto *v.t.* 1, to trouble, shatter
afflictus, a, um *adj*, damaged, prostrate
afflīgo, xi, ctum *v.t.* 3, to dash to the ground, damage
afflo *v.t.* 1, to breathe on, inspire
afflŭens, ntis *adj, adv*, nter, rich in
afflŭo, xi, xum *v.i.* 3, to flow towards, flock in
affor *v.t.* 1, to speak to, accost
affulgĕo, ulsi *v.i.* 2, to shine on

affundo, ūdi, ūsum *v.t.* 3, to pour on, in

Āfrĭcus (ventus) S.W. wind

āfui see **absum**

ăgāso, ōnis *m*, groom

ăgĕ! come on!

ăgellus, i *m*, small field

ăgens, ntis *adj*, powerful

ăger, gri *m*, field, territory

agger, ĕris *m*, mound, rampart

aggĕro, ssi stum *v.t.* 3, to convey

aggĕro *v.t.* 1, to heap up

agglŏmĕro *v.t.* 1, to add to

aggrăvo *v.t.* 1, to make heavier or worse

aggrĕdior, grĕssus *v.t.* 3, *dep*, to approach, attack, undertake

aggrĕgo *v.t.* 1, to adhere, join

aggressus see **aggrĕdior**

ăgĭlis, e *adj, adv*, ĭter, active

ăgĭlĭtas, ātis *f*, activity

ăgĭtātĭo, ōnis *f*, quick movement, contemplation

ăgĭtātor, ōris *m*, charioteer

ăgĭtātus, a, um *adj*, driven, dogged

ăgĭto *v.t.* 1, to drive, shake, swing, torment, mock, consider

agmen, ĭnis *n*, marching column

agna, ae *f*, ewe lamb

agnātus, a, um *adj*, related (male line)

agnĭtĭo, ōnis *f*, recognition

agnōmen, ĭnis *n*, surname, additional name

agnosco, nŏvi, ĭtum *v.t.* 3, to recognize, acknowledge

agnus, i *m*, lamb

ăgo, ēgi, actum *v.t.* 3, to drive, steal, bring, do, negotiate, pass (time), act, lead (life)

ăgrārĭus, a, um *adj*, agrarian

ăgrārĭi, ōrum *m.pl*, land reformers

ăgrestis is *m*, peasant

ăgrestis, e *adj*, rural, coarse

agrĭcŏla, ae *m*, farmer, countryman

agrĭcultūra, ae *f*, agriculture

āio *v, defect*, to assert

āla, ae *f*, wing, armpit, porch

ălăcer, cris, e *adj, adv*, ĭter, brisk, vigorous

ălăcrĭtas, ātis *f*, briskness

ălăpa, ae *f*, slap

ălauda, ae *f*, lark

albārĭum, ii *n*, whitewash

albātus, a, um *adj*, clothed in white

albĕo *v.i.* 2, to be white

albesco *v.i.* 3, to become white

album, i *n*, whiteness, register

albus, a, um *adj*, white

alces, is *f*, elk

alcēdo, ĭnis *f*, kingfisher

alcўon, ŏnis *f*, kingfisher

alcўŏnēus, a, um *adj*, halcyon

ālĕa, ae *f*, gambling, a game with dice, chance, hazard

ālĕātor, ōris *m*, gambler

ālĕs, ĭtis *adj*, winged

ālĕs, ĭtis *c*, bird

alga, ae *f*, seaweed

algĕo, si *v.i.* 2, to feel cold

algĭdus, a, um *adj*, cold

algor, ōris *m*, coldness

ălīā *adv*, in a different way

ălīās ... ălīās *adv*, at one time ... at another time, otherwise

ălĭbi *adv*, elsewhere

ălĭcŭbi *adv*, somewhere

ălĭcunde *adv*, from somewhere

ălĭēnātĭo, ōnis *f*, transfer, aversion, delirium

ălĭēnātus, a, um *adj*, alienated

ălĭēnĭgĕna, ae *m*, foreigner

ălĭēno *v.t.* 1, to transfer, estrange

ălĭēnus, a, um *adj*, someone else's, strange, hostile, unsuitable

ălĭēnus, i *m*, stranger

ălĭēnum, i *n*, stranger's property

ālĭger, ĕra, ĕrum *adj*, winged

ālĭi see **ālĭus**

ălĭmentum, i *n*, nourishment

ălĭmōnĭum, ii *n*, nourishment

ălĭō *adv*, to another place

ălĭōqui(n) *adv*, in other respects

ālĭpēs, ēdis *adj*, wing-footed

ălĭquā *adv*, somehow

ălĭquamdĭu *adv*, for some time

ălĭquando *adv*, at some time

ălĭquantus, a, um *adj, adv*, ō, um, somewhat, some

ălĭqui, qua, quod *pron, adj*, some, any

ălĭquis, quid *pron*, someone, something

ălĭquō *adv*, to some place
ălĭquot *adj*, several
ălĭquŏtĭes *adv*, at different times
ălīter *adv*, otherwise
ălĭunde *adv*, from elsewhere
ălĭus, a, ud *pron, adj*, other,
  different
allābor, psus *v*. 3, *dep*, to glide,
  flow towards
allapsus, ūs *m*, stealthy approach
allātro *v.t*. 1, to bark at
allecto *v.t*. 1, to entice
allēgo *v.t*. 1, to commission
allĕgo, ēgi, ectum *v.t*. 3, to elect
allēgŏrĭa, ae *f*, allegory
allĕvātĭo, ōnis *f*, raising up
allĕvo *v.t*. 1, to lift up, relieve
allĭcĭo, exi, ectum *v.t*. 3, to attract
allīdo, si, sum *v.t*. 3, to strike
allĭgo *v.t*. 1, to bind, fasten
allĭno, ēvi, ĭtum *v.t*. 3, to bedaub
allĭum, i *n*, garlic
allŏcūtĭo, ōnis *f*, speech, address
allŏquĭum, ii *n*, exhortation
allŏquor, lŏcūtus *v.t*. 3, *dep*, to
  speak to, exhort, console
allūdo, si, sum *v.i.t*. 3, to play,
  joke; sport with
allŭo, ŭi *v.t*. 3, to wash against,
  bathe
allŭvĭes, ēi *f*, pool
allŭvĭo, ōnis *f*, inundation
almus, a, um *adj*, nourishing,
  kind
alnus, i *f*, alder
ălo, ŭi, altum *v.t*. 3, to nourish,
  cherish, encourage
ălŏē, ēs *f*, aloe
alpīnus, a, um *adj*, Alpine
alsĭus, a, um *adj*, cold, chilly
alsus, a, um *adj*, cold, chilly
altāre, altāris *n*, high altar
altārĭa, ĭum *n.pl*, high altar
alter, ĕra, ĕrum *adj*, one or the
  other of two, second
altercātĭo, ōnis *f*, dispute
altercor *v.i*. 1, *dep*, to quarrel
alterno *v.i.t*. 1, to hesitate;
  alternate
alternus, a, um *adj*, alternate
altĕrŭter, ra, rum *adj*, one or the
  other, either
altĭlis, e *adj*, fattened, rich

altĭsŏnus, a, um *adj*, high sounding
altĭtūdo, ĭnis *f*, height, depth
altor, ōris *m*, foster-father
altrix, īcis *f*, foster-mother
altum, i *n*, the deep (sea)
altus, a, um *adj*, high, deep, great
ālūcĭnor *v.i*. 1, *dep*, to wander in
  the mind
ălumna, ae *f*, foster-child
ălumnus, i *m*, foster-child
ălūta, ae *f*, soft leather
alvĕārĭum, ii *n*, beehive
alvĕus, i *m*, salver, channel,
  canoe
alvus, i *f*, belly, stomach
ămābĭlis, e *adj, adv*, ĭter, lovable,
  amiable
āmando *v.t*. 1, to remove
āmans, ntis *adj*, fond
āmans, ntis *m*, lover
ămārĭtĭes, ēi *f*, bitterness
ămārus, a, um *adj*, bitter
ămātor, ōris *m*, lover
ămātōrĭum, ii *n*, love-philtre
ămātōrĭus, a, um *adj*, amatory
ambactus, i *m*, vassal
ambāges, is *f*, roundabout way
ambĭgo *v.i*. 3, to waver, go about
ambĭgŭĭtas, ātis *f*, double sense
ambĭgŭum, i *n*, uncertainty
ambĭgŭus, a, um *adj, adv*, ē,
  doubtful, changeable
ambĭo *v.i.t*. 4, to go round; solicit
ambĭtĭo, ōnis *f*, canvassing
ambĭtĭōsus, a, um *adj, adv*, ē,
  embracing, fawning
ambĭtus, ūs *m*, going round,
  circuit, bribery
ambō, ae, ō *adj*, both
ambrŏsĭa, ae *f*, food of the gods
ambrŏsĭus, a, um *adj*, immortal
ambŭlātĭo, ōnis *f*, walk
ambŭlātor, ōris *m*, walker
ambŭlo *v.i*. 1, to walk, lounge
ambūro, ssi, stum *v.t*. 3, to singe
ambustum, i *n*, burn
amellus, i *m*, star-wort
āmens, ntis *adj*, out of one's mind
āmentĭa, ae *f*, madness
āmentum, i *n*, strap
ămĕs, ĭtis *m*, pole, shaft
ămĕthystus, i *f*, amethyst
ămīca, ae *f*, friend, mistress

ămĭcĭo

ămĭcĭo, ŭi, ctum *v.t.* 4, to wrap
ămĭcĭtĭa, ae *f*, friendship
ămictus, ūs *m*, cloak
ămĭcŭlum, i *n*, cloak
ămĭcus, i *m*, friend
ămĭcus, a, um *adj, adv*, ē, friendly
āmissĭo, ōnis *f*, loss
ămĭta, ae *f*, paternal aunt
āmitto, mĭsi, missum *v.t.* 3, to let
    go, dismiss, lose
amnis, is *m*, river
ămo *v.t.* 1, to love, like

anceps, cĭpĭtĭs *adj*, two-headed,
    doubtful
ancĭle, is *n*, oval shield
ancilla, ae *f*, maidservant
ancŏrāle, is *n*, cable
ānellus, i *m*, small ring
anfractus, ūs *m*, circuitous route,
    digression
angĭna, ae *f*, quinsy
angĭportus, ūs *m*, alley
ango, xi, ctum *v.t.* 3, to strangle,
    torment

Insight

The perfect tense (e.g. *amavi*) has three basic meanings: a) a
completed action in past time; b) an action in the past seen
from the point of view of the present; c) a present state
arising from past action.

ămoenĭtas, ātis *f*, pleasantness
ămoenus, a, um *adj, adv*, ē,
    charming
āmōlĭor *v.t.* 4, *dep*, to remove,
    refute
ămor, ōris *m*, love, desire
āmŏvĕo, mōvi, tum *v.t.* 2, to
    remove
amphĭthĕātrum, i *n*, amphitheatre
amphŏra, ae *f*, two-handled jar
amplector, xus *v.t.* 3, *dep*, to
    embrace
amplexus, ūs *m*, embrace
amplĭfĭcātĭo, ōnis *f*, enlargement
amplĭfĭco *v.t.* 1, to enlarge
amplĭo *v.t.* 1, to enlarge
amplĭtūdo, ĭnis *f*, width, size
amplĭus *comp. adv*, more
amplus, a, um *adj, adv*, ē, ĭter,
    spacious, great, glorious
ampulla, ae *f*, bottle
ampŭtātĭo, ōnis *f*, pruning
ampŭto *v.t.* 1, to cut away
ămurca, ae *f*, dregs of oil
ămӯlum, i *n*, starch
ăn *conj*, or: also used to introduce
    a question
ănăphŏră, ae *f*, recurrence
ănăs, ătis *f*, duck
ănătĭcŭla, ăe *f*, duckling

angor, ōris *m*, strangling, distress
anguilla, ae *f*, eel
anguīnĕus, a, um *adj*, snaky
anguĭpēs, ĕdis *adj*, snake-footed
anguĭs, is *c*, snake
angŭlātus, a, um *adj*, angular
angŭlāris, e *adj*, angular
angŭlus, i *m*, corner
angustĭae, ārum *f.pl.*, defile,
    straits, difficulties
angustus, a, um *adj, adv*, ē,
    narrow, difficult
ănhēlĭtus, ūs *m*, panting, vapour
ănhēlo *v.i.t.* 1, to pant; exhale
ănhēlus, a, um *adj*, panting
ănĭcŭla, ae *f*, little old woman
ănīlis, e *adj, adv*, ĭter, old
    womanish
ănĭma, ae *f*, breeze, breath, life,
    soul
ănĭmadversĭo, ōnis *f*, attention,
    reproof
ănĭmadverto, ti, sum *v.t.* 3, to pay
    attention to, notice, punish
ănĭmăl, ālis *n*, animal
ănĭmālis, e *adj, adv*, ĭter, of air,
    living
ănĭmans, ntis *adj*, living
ănĭmātus, a, um *adj*, disposed,
    courageous
ănĭmo *v.i.t.* 1, to have life; revive,
    give life to

ănĭmōsus, a, um *adj, adv,* ē, bold
ănĭmōsus, a, um *adj,* gusty, living, spirited
ănĭmus, i *m,* soul, mind, memory, opinion, anger, purpose, courage, attitude
annāles, ĭum *m.pl,* chronicles
annālis, e *adj,* annual
annĕ introduces a question
annecto, xŭi, xum *v.t.* 3, to fasten to, add
annĭtor, nīsus nixus *v.i.* 3, *dep,* to lean against, exert oneself
ănnivversārĭus, a, um *adj,* anniversary
anno *v.i.* 1, to swim to
annon *conj,* or not
annōna, ae *f,* annual produce, grain price
annōsus, a, um *adj,* old
annŏtātĭo, ōnis *f,* annotation, note
annŏto *v.t.* 1, to note down
annŭa, ōrum *n.pl,* annuity
annŭmĕro *v.t.* 1, to pay, include
annŭo, ŭi, ŭtum *v.i.* 3, to nod, assent
annus, i *m,* year
annŭus, a, um *adj,* annual, yearly
ănōmălĭa, ae *f,* anomaly
anquīro, sīvi, sītum *v.t.* 3, to search for
ansa, ae *f,* handle, opportunity
anser, ĕris *m,* goose
antĕ *prep. with acc,* before, in front of
antĕ (antĕā) *adv,* before
antĕcēdo, ssi, ssum *v.i.t.* 3, to distinguish oneself; precede
antĕcello *v.i.t.* 3, to be outstanding; surpass
antĕcessĭo, ōnis *f,* antecedent
antĕcursor, ōris *m,* advanced guard
antĕ-ĕo *v.i.* 4, to go before, excel
antĕfĕro, ferre, tŭli, lātum *v.t, irreg,* to carry in front, prefer
antĕgrĕdĭor, gressus *v.t.* 3, *dep,* to go in front
antĕhāc *adv,* previously
antĕlūcānus, a, um *adj,* before day-break
antĕmĕrīdĭānus, a, um *adj,* before midday

antĕmitto, mīsi, missum *v.t.* 3, to send on
antenna, ae *f,* sail-yard
antĕpōno, pŏsŭi, ĭtum *v.t.* 3, to place in front
antĕquam *conj,* before
antēris, ĭdis *f,* buttress (pl.)
antes, ĭum *m.pl.* ranks
antĕsignānus, i *m,* in front of the standard, selected soldier
antesto, ĕti *v.i.* 1, to stand before, excel
antestor *v.* 1, *dep,* to call a witness
antĕverto, ti, sum *v.t.* 3, to precede, anticipate
anthrōpŏphăgus, i *m,* cannibal
antīcus, a, um *adj,* foremost
antīcĭpo *v.t.* 1, to anticipate
antīdŏtum, i *n,* remedy
antīpŏdes, um *m.pl,* antipodes
antīquĭtas, ātis *f,* age, olden times
antīqui, ōrum *m.pl,* old writers
antīquus, a, um *adj, adv,* ē, old
antistĕs, ĭtis *m,* *f,* high priest
antistĭta, ae *f,* high priestess
antlĭa, ae *f,* pump
antrum, i *n,* cave
ānŭlus, i *m,* ring
ănus, ūs *f,* old woman
anxĭētas, ātis *f,* anxiety
anxĭus, a, um *adj, adv,* ē, troubled
ăpăgĕ! *interj,* begone
ăper, pri *m,* wild boar
ăpĕrĭo, rŭi, rtum *v.t.* 4, to open, explain
ăpertus, a, um *adj, adv,* ē, open, frank
ăpex, ĭcis *m,* summit, crown
ăpis, is *f,* bee
ăpiscor, aptus *v.t.* 3, *dep,* to reach for, acquire
ăpĭum, ii *n,* parsley
ăplustre, is *n,* stern
ăpo, (*no perf.*) aptum *v.t.* 3, to fasten
ăpŏcha, ae *f,* receipt
ăpŏthēca, ae *f,* store-place
appărātĭo, ōnis *f,* preparation
appărātus, a, um *adj, adv,* ē, ready, elaborate
appărātus, ūs *m,* preparation, apparatus, pomp

appārĕo

appārĕo *v.i.* 2, to appear
appārītĭo, ōnis *f*, service
appārītor, ōris *m*, public servant
appăro *v.t.* 1, to prepare
appellātĭo, ōnis *f*, calling appeal, title
appellātor, ōris *m*, appellant
appellātus, a, um *adj*, called
appello, ŭli, ulsum *v.t.* 3, to drive towards, land
appello *v.t.*1, to speak to, appeal to, name
appendix, ĭcis *f*, supplement
appendo, ndi, nsum *v.t.* 3, to weigh
appĕtens, ntis *adj, adv*, nter, eager for
appĕtentĭa, ae *f*, desire
appĕtītĭo, ōnis *f*, desire
appĕtītus, ūs *m*, attack, passion
appĕto, ii, ītum *v.i.t.* 3, to approach; strive after
applĭcātĭo, ōnis *f*, inclination
applĭco *v.t.* 1, to affix, attach, steer
appōno, pŏsŭi, sĭtum *v.t.* 3, to put near, apply, add

àprīcor *v.i.* 1, *dep*, to sun oneself
àprīcus, a, um *adj*, sunny
Ÿprīlis (mensis) April
aptātus, a, um *adj*, suitable
apto *v.t.* 1, to adjust
aptus, a, um *adj, adv*, ē, suitable
ăpŭd *with acc*, at the house of, in the works of, amongst, near
ăqua, ae *f*, water, rain; *pl*, spa
ăquaeductus, ūs *m*, aqueduct
ăquālis, is *c*, wash-basin
ăquārĭus, ii *m*, water-bearer, a sign of the zodiac
ăquātĭcus, a, um *adj*, watery
ăquātĭlis, e *adj*, aquatic
ăquātĭo, ōnis *f*, water-fetching
ăquātor, ōris *m*, water-carrier
ăquīla, ae *f*, eagle, standard
ăquīlĭfer, ĕri *m*, standard-bearer
ăquīlīnus, a, um *adj*, aquiline
ăquīlo, ōnis *m*, north wind, north
ăquīlōnāris, e *adj*, northern
ăquor *v.i.* 1, *dep*, to fetch water
ăquōsus, a, um *adj*, moist, rainy
āra, ae *f*, altar
ărānĕa, ae *f*, spider, web
ărānĕus i *m*, spider, web

Insight

Appositions are nouns or nouns-plus-adjectives phrases that add further information about a noun already mentioned in the sentence (e.g. a 'red-brick building' house). Nouns are said to be 'in apposition' to another noun.

---

apporto *v.t.* 1, to conduct
appŏsĭtus *adj, adv*, ē, bordering, suitable
apprĕhendo, di, sum *v.t.*3, to seize, understand
apprīmus, a, um *adj, adv*, ē, very first
approbātĭo, ōnis *f*, sanction
approbo *v.t.* 1, to approve, make satisfactory
appropĕro *v.i.t.* 1, to hurry; speed up
appropinquātĭo, ōnis *f*, approach
appropinquo *v.i.* 1, to approach
appulsus, ūs *m*, landing, approach
àprīcātĭo, ōnis *f*, sunning

ărātĭo, ōnis *f*, cultivation
ărātor, ōris *m*, ploughman
ărātrum, i *n*, plough
arbĭter, tri *m*, witness, umpire
arbĭtrātus, ūs *m*, free-will
arbĭtrĭum, ii *n*, verdict, power, inclination
arbĭtror *v.i.* 1, *dep*, to think, decide
arbor, ŏris *f*, tree
arbŏrĕus, a, um *adj*, tree-like
arbustum, i *n*, plantation
arbŭtum, i *n*, wild strawberry
arbŭtus, i *f*, wild strawberry tree
arca, ae *f*, box, dungeon
arcānus, a, um *adj, adv*, ō, secret
arcĕo *v.t.* 2, to confine, keep off

arcessītus, a, um *adj,* sent for, far-fetched

arcesso, sīvi, sītum *v.t.* 3, to send for

archĭtector *v.t.* 1, *dep,* to design

archĭtectūra, ae *f,* architecture

archĭtectus, i *m,* architect

arcĭtĕnens, ntis *adj,* armed with bow

arctŏs, i *f,* Bear, North Pole

arctūrus, i *m,* chief star in constellation Boötes

arcŭla, ae *f,* small box

arcŭo *v.t.* 1, to bend

arcus, ūs *m,* rainbow, arch

ardĕa, ae *f,* heron

ardens, ntis *adj, adv,* **nter,** burning, eager

ardĕo, arsi, sum *v.i.* 2, to burn, be eager

ardesco, arsi *v.i* 3, to catch fire

ardor, ōris *m,* blaze, desire

ardŭus, a, um *adj,* high, difficult

ārĕa, ae *f,* open space, threshing-floor

ărēna, ae *f,* sand, arena

ărēnātum, i *n,* mortar, plaster

ărēnōsus, a, um *adj,* sandy

ārens, ntis *adj,* parched

ārĕo *v.i.* 2, to be dry

āresco, ŭi *v.i.* 3, to dry up

argentārĭa, ae *f,* bank, silver-mine

argentārĭus, ii *m,* banker, broker

argentātus, a, um *adj,* silver-plated

argentĕus, a, um *adj,* silver

argentum, i *n,* silver, money

argilla, ae *f,* white clay

argūmentātĭo, ōnis *f,* proof

argūmentor *v.i.* 1, *dep,* to prove

argūmentum, i *n,* proof, content, artistic aim

argŭo, ŭi, ūtum *v.t.* 3, to prove, accuse, convict

argūtĭae, ārum *f.pl,* liveliness

argūtus, a, um *adj, adv,* **ē,** clear, witty, rattling

ārĭdĭtas, ātis *f,* dryness

ārĭdum, i *n,* dry land

ārĭdus, a, um *adj,* dry

ărĭes, tis *m,* ram, battering-ram

ărista, ae *f,* ear of corn

ărithmētĭca, ōrum *n.pl,* arithmetic

arma, ōrum *n.pl,* armour, shield, weapons, army, equipment

armāmenta, ōrum *n.pl,* gear, tackle

armāmentārĭum, ii *n,* arsenal

armāmentum, i *n,* ship's tackle

armārĭum ii *n,* cupboard

armātura, ae *f,* equipment, (light-)armed troops

armātus, a, um *adj,* equipped

armentārĭus, ii *m,* herdsman

armentum, i *n,* plough-animal, herd

armĭfer, ĕra, ĕrum *adj,* warlike, armoured

armĭger, ĕra, ĕrum *adj,* warlike, armoured

armilla, ae *f,* bracelet

armĭpŏtens, ntis *adj,* valiant

armĭsŏnus, a, um *adj,* with clashing armour

armo *v.t.* 1, to arm, equip

armus, i *m,* shoulder, side

ăro, *v.t.* 1, to plough

arquātus, a, um *adj,* bent

arrectus, a, um *adj,* steep

arrēpo, psi, ptum *v.i.* 3, to creep towards

arrha, ae *f,* money given as a pledge

arrīdĕo, si, sum *v.i.* 2, to laugh at, favour

arrĭgo, rexi, rectum *v.t.*3, to erect, excite

arrĭpĭo, ŭi, reptum *v.t.* 3, to seize, indict

arrŏgans, ntis *pres. partic, adj, adv,* **nter,** haughty

arrŏgantĭa, ae *f,* haughtiness

arrŏgo, *v.t.* 1, to claim, confer

ars, tis *f,* art, skill, theory, habit, stratagem

artē *adv,* closely

arthrītĭcus, a, um *adj,* arthritic

artĭcŭlātim *adv,* piece by piece

artĭcŭlo, *v.t.* 1, to articulate

artĭcŭlus, i *m,* joint, movement

artĭfex, fĭcis *m,* artist, author

artĭfĭcĭōsus, a, um *adj, adv,* **ē,** skilful

artĭfĭcĭum, ii *n,* trade, skill; *pl,* intrigue

arto *v.t.* 1, to compress

artus, ūs *m,* limb

artus, a, um *adj, adv,* **ē,** confined

ărun, ărus... see **hărun, hărus...**

arvīna, ae *f,* grease

arvum, i *n,* cultivated land

arvus, a, um *adj,* ploughed

arx, cis *f,* citadel

as, assis *m,* pound weight, coin

ascendo, ndi, nsum *v.i.t.* 3, to climb

ascensus, ūs *m,* ascent

ascĭa, ae *f,* adze

ascĭo *v.t.* 4, to receive

ascisco, īvi, ītum *v.t.* 3, to admit

ascītus, ūs *m,* reception

ascrībo, psi, ptum *v.t.* 3, to insert, enrol, attribute

ascriptivus, a, um *adj,* supernumerary

ascriptus, a, um *adj,* appointed

ăsella, ae *f,* small ass

ăsellus, i *m,* small ass

ăsīnus, i *m,* ass, simpleton

aspectābĭlis, e *adj,* visible

aspecto *v.t.* 1, to look at eagerly

aspectus, ūs *m,* look, sight

asper, ĕra, ĕrum *adj, adv,* **ē,** rough, bitter, austere, adverse

aspĕrĭtas, ātis *f,* roughness

aspĕrum, i *n,* rough ground

aspergo, si, sum *v.t.* 3, to scatter, sprinkle, defile

aspergo, ĭnis *f,* sprinkling, spray

aspĕrĭtas, ātis *f,* roughness

aspernātĭo, ōnis *f,* disdain

aspernor *v.t.* 1, *dep,* to despise

aspĕro *v.t.* 1, to roughen, rouse

aspersĭo, ōnis *f,* sprinkling

aspĭcĭo, exi, ectum *v.t.* 3, to look at

aspīrātĭo, ōnis *f,* exhalation

aspīro *v.i.t.* 1, to aspire to; breathe on

aspis, ĭdis *f,* adder

asporto, *v.t.* 1, to carry away

assĕcla, ae *c,* attendant

assectātĭo, ōnis *f,* attendance

assectātor ōris *m,* follower

assector *v.t.* 1, *dep,* to wait upon

assensĭo, ōnis *f,* approval

assensus, ūs *m,* approval

assentātĭo, ōnis *f,* flattery

assentātor, ōris *m,* flatterer

assentĭor, sus *v.* 4, *dep, with dat,* to agree with

assentor *v.* 1, *dep, with dat,* to flatter

assĕquor, sĕcūtus *v.t.* 3, *dep,* to pursue, overtake, comprehend

asser, ĕris *m,* stake

assĕro, rŭi, sertum *v.t.* 3, to claim, set free

assertor, ōris *m,* protector

asservo *v.t.* 1, to keep, guard

assessor, ōris *m,* assessor

assĕvērātĭo, ōnis *f,* assertion

assĕvēro *v.t.* 1, to assert

assīdĕo, sēdi, sessum *v.i.* 2, to sit by, wait upon, blockade, resemble

assīdŭĭtas, ātis *f,* constant presence

assīdŭus, a, um *adj, adv,* **ē,** constantly present

assignātĭo, ōnis *f,* allotment

assigno *v.t.* 1, to distribute

assīlĭo, ŭi, sultum *v.i.* 4, to spring upon

assĭmĭlis, e *adj, adv,* **ĭter,** like

assĭmŭlo *v.i.t.* 1, to resemble, imitate

assĭmŭlātus, a, um *adj,* similar

assisto, astĭti *v.i.* 3, to stand near, aid

assŏlĕo *v.i.* 2, to be in the habit of doing

assŭefăcĭo, fēci, factum *v.t.* 3, to make someone used to

assŭesco, ēvi, ētum *v.i.t.* 3, to become used to; familiarize

assŭētūdo, ĭnis *f,* habit

assŭētus, a, um *adj,* customary

assulto *v.t.* 1, to jump on, attack

assultus, ūs *m,* attack

assūmo, mpse, mptum *v.t.* 3, to take up, adopt

assŭo *v.t.* 3, to sew on

assurgo, surrexi, rectum *v.i.* 3, to rise, stand up

assŭla, ae *f,* splinter, chip

assus, a, um *adj,* roasted; **assa, ōrum,** *n.pl,* turkish bath

ast see **at**

astĭpŭlātor, ōris *m,* assistant

astĭpŭlor *v.* 1, *dep, with dat,* to bargain with

asto, stĭti *v.i.* 1, to stand near

astrĕpo *v.i.t.* 3, to make a noise; applaud

astringo, nxi, ctum *v.t.* 3, to bind, fasten, cool, limit
astrictus, a, um *adj, adv,* ē, tight, concise
astrŏlŏgĭa, ae *f,* astronomy
astrŏlŏgus, i *m,* astronomer
astrum, i *n,* star, constellation
astrŭo, xi, ctum *v.t.* 3, to build near, add
astŭpĕo *v.i.* 2, to be astonished
astus, ūs *m,* dexterity, craft
astūtĭa, ae *f,* dexterity, slyness
astūtus, a, um *adj, adv,* ē, shrewd, sly
ăsўlum, i *n,* place of refuge
at *conj,* but, on the other hand
ătăvĭa, ae *f,* ancestor
ătăvus, i *m,* ancestor
āter, tra, trum *adj,* black, deadly
ăthĕŏs, i *m,* atheiest
athlēta, ae *c,* wrestler, athlete
ătŏmus, i *f,* atom
atque *conj,* and, and also
atqui *conj,* but, nevertheless
ātrāmentum, i *n,* ink, varnish
ātrātus, a, um *adj,* in mourning
ātrĭensis, is *m,* house-steward
ātrĭŏlum, i *n,* ante-room
ātrĭum, ii *n,* hall, forecourt
àtrōcĭtas, ātis harshness, cruelty
àtrox, ōcis *adj, adv,* ĭter, horrible, fierce, stern
attactus, ūs *m,* touch
attămen *adv,* but nevertheless
attendo, di, tum *v.t.* 3, to stretch out, give attention to
attentĭo, ōnis *f,* attention
attento *v.t.* 1, to try, attack
attentus, a, um *adj, adv,* ē, engrossed, frugal
attĕnŭo *v.t.* 1, to impair, reduce
attĕro, trīvi, trītum *v.t.* 3, to rub away, exhaust

attĭnĕo, ŭi, tentum *v.i.t.* 2, to strech, concern; retain
attingo, tĭgi, tactum *v.t.* 3, to touch, reach, attack
attollo *v.t.* 3, to raise
attondĕo, di, sum *v.t.* 2, to shear
attŏnĭtus, a, um *adj, adv,* ē, astonished
attŏno, ŭi, ĭtum *v.t.* 1, to stun
attorquĕo *v.t.* 2, to hurl
attrăho, xi, ctum *v.t.* 3, to drag towards, attract
attrecto *v.t.* 1, to handle
attrĭbŭo, ŭi, ŭtum *v.t.* 3, to assign
attrĭbūtum, i *n,* predicate
attrītus, ūs *m,* rubbing against
auceps, ŭpis *c,* bird-catcher, eavesdropper
auctĭo, ōnis *f,* auction, increase
auctĭōnor *v.i.* 1, *dep,* to hold an auction
auctor, ōris *c,* creator, master, witness, supporter, author
auctōrĭtas, ātis *f,* influence, power
auctumnālis, e *adj,* autumnal
auctumnus, a, um *adj,* autumnal
auctumnus, i *m,* autumn
auctus, a, um *adj,* enlarged
auctus, ūs *m,* increase
aucŭpĭum, ii *n,* bird-catching
aucŭpor, v.i.t. 1, *dep,* to go bird-catching; pursue, watch for
audācĭa, ae *f,* boldness, insolence
audax, ācis *adj, adv,* cter, bold, rash
audens, ntis *adj, adv,* nter, bold
audentĭa, ae *f,* boldness
audĕo, ausus *v.i.t.* 2 *semi-dep,* to dare
audĭentĭa, ae *f,* hearing, audience
audĭo, v.t. 4, to hear, understand, obey

Insight

There is no way of distinguishing between the first person singular, future tense, indicative of third and fourth conjugation verbs and the first person singular, present tense, subjunctive (e.g. *dicam, audiam*) except by context.

audītĭo, ōnis *f*, a hearing, report
audītor, ōris *m*, hearer, pupil
audītus, ūs *m*, sense of hearing
aufĕro, ferre, abstŭli, ablātum *v.t, irreg*, to take away, rob, obtain
aufŭgĭo, fūgi, ĭtum *v.i.* 3, to run away
augĕo, xi, ctum *v.i.t.* 2, to grow; enlarge
augesco *v.i.* 3, to grow
augur, ŭris *c*, diviner, prophet
augŭrālis, e *adj*, prophetic
augŭrātus, ūs *m*, office of augur
augŭrĭum, ii *n*, omen, augury
augŭrĭus, a, um *adj*, augural
augŭror *v.t.* 1, *dep*, to prophesy, suppose
augustus, a, um *adj, adv*, ē, venerable
aula, ae *f*, palace, court
aulaeum, i *n*, curtain
aulicus, i *m*, courtier

auspĭcātō *adv*, after taking the auspices
auspĭcĭum, ii *n*, divination
auspĭcor *v.i.t.* 1, *dep*, to take the auspices, begin
auster, tri *m*, south wind
austērus, a, um *adj, adv*, ē, harsh, severe
austrālis, e *adj*, southern
austrīnus, a, um *adj*, southern
ausum, i *n*, bold attempt
aut *conj*, or, **aut ... aut**, either ... or
autem *conj*, but
autumnālis *adj*, autumnal
autŭmo *v.i.* 1, to assert
auxĭlĭa, ōrum *n.pl*, auxiliary troops
auxĭlĭāris, e *adj*, helping
auxĭlĭāres, ĭum *m.pl*, auxiliary troops
auxĭlĭor *v.* 1, *dep, with dat.* to help
auxĭlĭum ii *n*, help

Insight

Auxiliary verbs, such as 'will', 'do', 'have', are used to help the main verb, defining its mood, tense and aspect. The word 'auxiliary' comes from the Latin *auxilium* (= help). Latin only uses auxiliary verbs in the perfect, pluperfect and future perfect deponent and passive.

aura, ae *f*, air, soft breeze, sky, publicity, gleam
aurārĭa, ae *f*, gold mine
aurātus, a, um *adj*, gilded
aurĕus, i *m*, gold piece
aurĭcŏmus, a, um *adj*, golden-haired
aurĭcŭla, ae *f*, ear
aurĭfer, ĕra, ĕrum *adj*, gold-producing
aurĭfex, fĭcis *m*, goldsmith
aurīga, ae *c*, charioteer
aurĭger, ĕra, ĕrum *adj*, bearing gold
auris, is *f*, ear
aurītus, a, um *adj*, long-eared
aurōra, ae *f*, dawn
aurum, i *n*, gold
ausculto *v.i.t.* 1, to listen
auspex, ĭcis *c*, diviner

ăvārĭtĭa, ae *f*, greediness
ăvārus, a, um *adj, adv*, ē, greedy
ăve! (*pl*, **ăvete**)   hail! farewell!
āvĕho, vexi, ctum *v.t.* 3, to carry away
āvello, velli, vulsum *v.t.* 3, to tear away
ăvēna, ae *f*, oats, shepherd's pipe
ăvĕnācĕus, a, um *adj*, oaten
āvĕo *v.t.* 2, to long for
ăvĕo *v.i.* 2, to be well
āversor *v.t.* 1, *dep*, to turn away from, avoid
āversor, ōris *m*, embezzler
āversus, a, um *adj*, backwards, hostile
āverto, ti, sum *v.t.* 3, to push aside, steal, estrange
ăvĭa, ae *f*, grandmother
ăvĭārĭum, ii *n*, bird-haunts

ăvĭdĭtas, ātis *f*, eagerness, desire
ăvĭdus, a, um *adj, adv,* ē, greedy
ăvis, is *f*, bird
ăvītus, a, um *adj*, ancestral
āvĭum, ii *n*, pathless place
āvĭus, a, um *adj*, pathless
āvŏcātĭo, ōnis *f*, calling away, distraction
āvŏco *v.t.* 1, to call away
āvŏlo *v.i.* 1, to fly away
ăvuncŭlus, i *m*, uncle
ăvus, i *m*, grandfather
axis, is *m*, axle, chariot, region

B

bāca, ae *f*, berry
bācātus, a, um *adj*, pearl-set
baccar, ăris *n*, fox-glove
baccha, ae *f*, bacchanal
bacchānālĭa, ĭum *n.pl*, orgies of Bacchus
bacchātĭo, ōnis *f*, orgy
bacchor, *v.i.* 1, *dep*, to rave
bācĭfer, ĕra, ĕrum *adj*, berry-bearing
băcillum, i *n*, stick
băcŭlum, i *n*, stick, sceptre
bāiŭlo, *v.t.* 1, to carry a load
bāiŭlus, i *m*, porter
bālaena, ae *f*, whale
bălănus, i *f*, acorn
bălàtro, ōnis *m*, comedian
bālātus, ūs *m*, bleating
balbus, a, um *adj, adv,* ē, stammering
balbūtĭo *v.i.t.* 4, to stammer
ballista, ae *f*, artillery engine
balnĕae, ārum *f.pl*, baths

balsămum, i *n*, balm
baltĕus, i *m*, belt, sword-belt
bărāthrum, i *n*, abyss
barba, ae *f*, beard
barbărĭa, ae *f*, foreign country, rudeness
barbărus, i *m*, foreigner, stranger
barbărus, a, um *adj, adv,* ē, foreign, rude, savage
barbātus, a, um *adj*, bearded
barbĭtos *m, f,* (*pl,* a), lute, lyre
bardus, a, um *adj*, stupid
bāro, ōnis *m*, blockhead
barrus, i *m*, elephant
băsĭlĭca, ae *f*, town-hall
băsĭlĭcus, a, um *adj*, royal
bāsĭo, *v.t.* 1, to kiss
băsis, is *f*, pedestal, base
bāsĭum, ii *n*, kiss
battŭo, ŭi *v.t.* 3, to fence; beat
bĕātĭtas, ātis *f*, happiness
bĕātĭtūdo, ĭnis *f*, happiness
bĕātus, a, um *adj, adv,* ē, happy, fortunate
bellans   see bello
bellārĭa, ōrum *n.pl*, dessert
bellātor, ōris *m*, warrior
bellātrix, īcis *f*, female-warrior
bellē *adv*, prettily
bellĭcōsus, a, um *adj*, warlike
bellĭcum, i *n*, signal for march or attack
bellĭcus, a, um *adj*, military
bellĭger, ĕra, ĕrum *adj*, warlike
bellĭgĕro *v.t.* 1, to wage war
bellis, ĭdis *f*, daisy
bello, *v.i.* 1 (bellor, *v.i.* 1, *dep*), to make war

··

Insight

The stem of a noun or a verb is that part of the word to which endings are added and which does not change or decline. For example, *bell-* is the stem of *bellum* (= war); am- is the stem of *amo* (= I love).

··

balnĕātor, ōris *m*, bath-keeper
balnĕum, i *n*, bath
bālo, *v.i.* 1, to bleat

bellum, i *n*, war
bellus, a, um *adj*, pretty
bēlŭa, ae *f*, beast

běně *adv*, well, very

běnědīco, xi, ctum *v.i.t.* 3, to praise

běnědictĭo, ōnis *f*, blessing

běněfăcĭo, fēci, factum *v.t.* 3, to do well, oblige

běněfactum, i *n*, good deed

běněfícentĭa, ae *f*, kind treatment

běněfícĭārĭi, ōrum *m.pl*, privileged soldiers (excused fatigues)

běněfícĭum, ii *n*, a kindness

běněfícus, a, um *adj*, obliging

běněvŏlentĭa, ae *f*, good will

běněvŏlus, a, um *adj, adv,* **ē**, well disposed

běnignē *adv*, thank you; no thank you; courteously

běnignus, a, um *adj*, kind, fruitful

běnignĭtas, ātis *f*, kindness

běo, *v.t.* 1, to bless, enrich

bes, bessis *m*, eight ounces

bestĭa, ae *f*, wild beast

bestĭārĭus, ii *m*, wild-beast fighter

bestĭŏla, ae *f*, small animal

bēta, ae *f*, beet

betŭla, ae *f*, birch

biblĭa, ōrum *n.pl*, the Bible

biblĭŏpōla, ae *m*, bookseller

biblĭŏthēca, ae *f*, library

biblĭŏthēcārĭus, ii *m*, librarian

bĭvo, bĭbi, ĭtum *v.t.* 3, to drink

bĭbŭlus, a, um *adj*, given to drink, porous

bĭceps, cĭpĭtis *adj*, two-headed

bĭcŏlōr, ōris *adj*, two-coloured

bĭcornis, e *adj*, two-pronged

bĭdens, ntis *m*, hoe

bĭdŭum, ii *n*, space of two days

bĭennĭum, ii *n*, space of two years

bĭfārĭam *adv*, in two ways

bĭfer, ěra, ěrum *adj*, blooming or fruiting twice a year

bĭfĭdus, a, um *adj*, cut in two

bĭfŏris, e *adj*, with double opening

bĭformis, e *adj*, two-shaped

bĭfrons, ntis *adj*, two-headed

bĭfurcus, a, um *adj*, two-pronged

bīgae, ārum *f.pl*, pair of horses, two-horsed chariot

bīgātus, a, um *adj*, stamped with a two-horsed chariot (of coins)

bĭiŭgus, a, um *adj*, yoked two together

bīlībris, e *adj*, weighing two pounds

bĭlinguis, e *adj*, bilingual

bīlĭōsus, a, um *adj*, bilious

bīlis, is *f*, bile

bīmăris, e *adj*, lying between two seas

bīmărītus, i *m*, bigamist

bīmembris, e *adj*, half-man, half-beast

bīmestris, e, *adj*, two months old

bīmus, a, um *adj*, two years old

bīni, ae, a *adj*, two each, a pair

bĭpartĭo *v.t.* 4, to bisect

bĭpartīto *adv*, in two ways

bĭpědālis, e *adj*, measuring two feet

bĭpennĭfer, ěra, ěrum *adj*, carrying a double-edged axe

bĭpennis, e *adj*, double-edged

bĭpēs, ědis *adj*, two-legged

bĭrēmis, e *adj*, two-oared

bĭrēmis, is *f*, a galley with two banks of oars

bis *adv*, twice

bĭsextĭlis, e *adj* (of years) leap

bĭsulcus, a, um *adj*, cloven

bĭtūmen, ĭnis *n*, bitumen

bĭvĭum, ii *n*, crossroad

bĭvĭus, a, um *adj*, going in two directions

blaesus, a, um *adj*, stammering

blandīmentum, i *n*, flattery

blandĭor, *v.* 4, *dep, with dat,* to flatter

blandĭtĭa, ae *f*, flattery

blandus, a, um *adj, adv,* **ē**, smooth-tongued, enticing

blasphēmo, *v.t.* 1, to revile

blătěro *v.t.* 1, to babble

blătěro, ōnis *m*, gabbler

blatta, ae *f*, cockroach, moth

bŏārĭus, a, um *adj*, of cattle

bōlētus, i *m*, mushroom

bombyx, ȳcis *m*, silk, silk-worm

bŏnĭtas, ātis *f*, excellence

bŏna, ōrum *n.pl*, goods, property

bŏnum, i *n*, goodness, profit

bŏnus, a, um *adj*, good

Insight

Most adjectives add -ior to the stem to form the comparative and -issimus to form the superlative (*longus-longior-longissimus*). However, there are several irregularities, the most common of which are: *bonus-melior-optimus, malus-peior-pessimus, magnus-maior-maximus.*

....

bŏrĕas, ae *m*, north wind
bŏrēus, a, um *adj*, northern
bōs, bŏvis *c*, ox; *pl*, cattle
bŏvārĭus see boārius
brācae, ārum *f.pl*, trousers
brācātus, a, um *adj*, wearing trousers, foreign
bracchĭum, ii *n*, forearm, branch, dike
bractĕa, ae, *f*, thin metal plate
branchĭae, ārum *f.pl*, fish gills
brassĭca, ae *f*, cabbage
brĕvī *adv*, in a short time, in a few words
brĕvĭārĭum, ii *n*, summary
brĕvis, e *adj, adv*, ĭter, short, brief
brĕvĭtas, ātis *f*, conciseness, shortness
brūma, ae *f*, shortest day, winter
brūmālis, e *adj*, wintry
brūtus, a, um *adj*, unwieldy, dull
būbo, ōnis *m*, owl
būbulcus, i *m*, ploughman
būbŭlus, a, um *adj*, of cattle
bucca, ae *f*, the cheek
buccŭla, ae *f*, small mouth, helmet
būcĭna, ae *f*, trumpet
būcŭla, ae *f*, heifer
būfo, ōnis *m*, toad
bulbus, i *m*, bulb
bulla, ae *f*, bubble, knob, amulet
bullo, *v.i.* 1, to bubble
būmastus, i *f*, grape which grows in large bunches
būris, is *m*, plough-beam
bustum, i *n*, funeral pyre, grave
būtyrum, i *n*, butter
buxifer, ĕra, ĕrum *adj*, growing box trees
buxum, i *n*, boxwood

buxus, i *f*, box tree
byssus, i *f*, cotton

C

căballus, i *m*, packhorse
cācăbus, i *m*, saucepan
căchinnātĭo, ōnis *f*, guffaw
căchinno, *v.i.* 1, to laugh aloud
căchinnus, i *m*, laughter, jeering
căcūmen, ĭnis *n*, extremity, peak
căcūmĭno *v.t.* 1, to make into a point
cădāver, ĕris *n*, corpse
cădo, cĕcĭdi, cāsum *v.i.* 3, to fall, wane, occur, decay
cādūcĕātor, ōris *m*, herald
cādūcĕum, i *n* (us, i *m*), herald's staff, Mercury's wand
cādūcĭfer, ĕra, ĕrum *adj*, carrying a herald's staff (Mercury)
cădūcus, a, um *adj*, falling, doomed
cădus, i *m*, large jar (for liquids)
caecĭtas, ātis *f*, blindness
caeco *v.t.* 1, to blind
caecus, a, um *adj*, blind, hidden
caedēs, is *f*, slaughter
caedo, cĕcīdi, caesum *v.t.* 3, to cut, strike, slaughter
caelātor, ōris *m*, engraver
caelātūra, ae *f*, carving
caelebs, lībis *adj*, unmarried
caelĕs, ĭtis *adj*, heavenly
caelĭtes, um *pl*, gods
caelestĭa, ĭum *n.pl*, the heavenly bodies
caelestis, e *adj*, heavenly
caelestis, is *m*, god
caelībātus, ūs *m*, celibacy

caelĭcŏla, ae *m.* *f*, inhabitant of heaven

caelĭfer, ĕra, ĕrum *adj*, supporting the heavens (Atlas)

caelo *v.t.* 1, to engrave

caelum, i *n*, heaven, climate

caelum, i *n*, chisel

caementum, i *n*, quarry stone

caenum, i *n*, dirt

caepa, ae *f* (e, is *n*), onion

caerĭmōnĭa, ae *f*, religious ceremony, awe

caerŭlĕus(lus), a, um *adj*, dark blue

caesărĭēs, ēi *f*, the hair

caesim *adv*, by cutting

caesĭus, a, um *adj*, green- or grey-eyed

caespĕs, ĭtis *m*, a turf

caestus, ūs *m*, boxing glove

caetra, ae *f*, native shield

cǎlǎmister, tri *m*, curling-iron; *pl*, flourishes

cǎlǎmĭtas, ātis *f*, disaster

cǎlǎmĭtōsus, a, um *adj, adv*, ē, destructive, unhappy

cǎlǎmus, i *m*, cane, reed-pen

cǎlǎthus, i *m*, basket

calcǎr, āris *n*, spur, stimulus

calcĕāmentum, i *n*, shoe

calcĕo *v.t.* 1, to shoe

calcĕus, i *m*, shoe

calcĭtrātus, ūs *m*, kicking

calcĭtro *v.i.* 1, to kick, resist

calco *v.t.* 1, to tread on, oppress

calcŭlātor, ōris *m*, accountant

calcŭlus, i *m*, pebble, calculation, vote, piece (chess, draughts)

cǎlěfǎcĭo, fēci, factum *v.t.* 3, to heat, excite

cǎlěo *v.i.* 2, to be warm, roused

cǎlesco *v.i.* 3, to become warm

cǎlĭdus, a, um *adj*, warm, hot, hot-headed

cǎlĭga, ae *f*, leather boot

cǎlĭgātus, a, um *adj*, weraing soldier's boots

cǎlĭgĭnōsus, a, um *adj*, obscure

cālĭgo, ĭnis *f*, mist, gloom

cālĭgo *v.i.* 1, to steam, be dark

cǎlix, ĭcis *m*, cup

calyx see calix

callĕo *v.i.t.* 2, to be callous, insensible; to know by experience

callĭdĭtas, ātis *f*, skill, cunning

callĭdus, a, um *adj, adv*, ē, skilful, sly

callis, is *m*, footpath

callum, i *n*, hard or thick skin

cālo, ōnis *m*, soldier's servant, menial

cǎlor, ōris *m*, heat, ardour

caltha, ae *f*, marigold

cǎlumnĭa, ae *f*, trickery, libel

cǎlumnĭātor, ōris *m*, slanderer

cǎlumnĭor *v.t.* 1, *dep*, to blame or accuse unjustly

calva, ae *f*, scalp

calvārĭa, ae *f*, skull

calvĭtĭum, i *n*, baldness

calvus, a, um *adj*, bald

calx, cis *f*, heel

calx, cis *f*, limestone, chalk

cǎmēlŏpardǎlis, is *f*, giraffe

cǎmēlus, i *m*, camel

cǎmēna, ae *f*, muse

cǎmĕra, ae *f*, vault

cǎmīnus, i *m*, forge, furnace

campester, tris, e *adj*, on level ground

campestre, is *n*, wrestling trunks

campus, i *m*, plain, open country, opportunity, scope

cǎmŭr, ŭra, ŭrum *adj*, curved inwards

cǎnālis, is *m*, pipe, groove

cancelli, ōrum *m.pl*, railings

cancer, cri *m*, crab

candēla, ae *f*, candle

candēlābrum, i *n*, candlestick

candens, ntis *adj*, shining white, glowing hot

candĕo *v.i.* 2, to shine, glow

candesco, ŭi *v.i.* 3, to glisten

candĭdātus, i *m*, candidate

candĭdus, a, um *adj, adv*, ē, dazzling white, beautiful, honest

candor, ōris *m*, whiteness, beauty, honesty

cānens, ntis *adj*, grey, white

cānĕo *v.i.* 2, to be white, grey

cānesco *v.i.* 3, to grow white

cānīcŭla, ae *f*, small dog, Dog-star

cānīnus, a, um *adj*, dog-like

cānis, is *c*, dog, Dog-star

cānistrum, i *n*, open basket

cānĭtĭes (*no genitive*) *f*, grey hair, old age

canna, ae *f*, reed, flute
cannăbis, is *f*, hemp
căno, cěcĭni, cantum *v.i.t.* 3, to sing, play; prophesy
cănor, ōris *m*, tune
cănōrus, a, um *adj*, melodious
cantērĭus see **canthērĭus**
cantātor, ōris *m*, singer
canthăris, ĭdis *f*, beetle
canthărus, i *m*, tankard
canthērĭus, ii *m*, mule, rafter
cantĭcum, i *n*, song
cantĭlēna, ae *f*, hackneyed song
canto *v.i.t.* 1, to sing, act; predict
cantor, ōris *m*, singer, actor
cantus, ūs *m*, music, prophecy, singing
cānus, a, um *adj*, white, old
căpācĭtas, ātis *f*, capacity
căpax, ācis *adj*, roomy, capable
căpella, ae *f*, she-goat
căper, pri *m*, goat
căpesso, īvi, ītum *v.t.* 3, to seize, undertake, reach for
căpillāmentum, i *n*, wig
căpillāre, is *n*, hair oil
căpillātus, a, um *adj*, hairy
căpillus, i *m*, the hair
căpĭo, cēpi, captum *v.t.* 3, to take, capture, tempt, choose, obtain, undertake, hold, grasp

capsa, ae *f*, box, satchel
captātor, ōris *m*, fortune hunter
captĭo, ōnis *f*, fraud, quibble
captīvĭtas, ātis *f*, captivity
captīvus, a, um *adj* (i *m*), prisoner
capto *v.t.* 1, to chase, entice
captus, ūs *m*, grasp, capacity
captus, a, um *adj*, taken, disabled
căpŭlus, i *m*, tomb, handle
căpŭt, ĭtis *n*, head, person, chief, origin, summit, status, paragraph, chapter
carbăsěus, a, um *adj*, made of flax, linen
carbăsus, i *f*, flax, linen
carbo, ōnis *m*, charcoal, coal
carbuncŭlus, i *m*, ruby, carbuncle
carcer, ěris *m*, prison, jailbird
carchēsĭum, ii *n*, goblet, masthead
cardĭăcus, a, um *adj*, dyspeptic
cardo, ĭnis *m*, hinge, crisis
cardŭus, i *m*, thistle
cărěo *v.i.* 2, (*with abl.*) to lack
cărex, ĭcis *f*, reed-grass
cărĭes (*no genitive*) *f*, decay
cărĭca, ae *f*, dried fig
cărīna, ae *f*, hull, keel, boat
cărĭōsus, a, um *adj*, decayed
cārĭtas, ātis *f*, costliness, affection
carmen, ĭnis *n*, song, poem
carnārĭum, ii *n*, larder

Insight

In Latin verbs are conjugated. There are four conjugations and a mixed one, the third-and-fourth conjugation which takes its endings mainly from the third but also partly from the fourth conjugation. An example of a mixed conjugation verb is *capio* (= I take).

căpistrum, i *n*, halter
căpĭtālis, e *adj*, of life and death, criminal, dangerous
capra, ae *f*, she-goat
căprěa, ae *f*, wild she-goat, roe
căprěŏlus, i *m*, roebuck, prop
căprĭcornus, i *m*, capricorn
căprĭficus, i *f*, wild fig tree
căprĭgěnus, a, um *adj*, goat-born
căprīnus, a, um *adj*, of a goat

carnĭfex, ĭcis *m*, executioner
carnĭfĭcīna, ae *f*, execution, torment
carnĭfĭco *v.t.* 1, to execute
carnĭvŏrus, a, um *adj*, carnivorous
carnōsus, a, um *adj*, fleshy
căro, carnis *f*, flesh, meat
carpentum, i *n*, chariot
carpo, psi, ptum *v.t.* 3, to pluck, graze, slander, weaken, pass over

carptim *adv,* separately
carrus, i *m,* two-wheeled cart
cartĭlāgo, ĭnis *f,* cartilage
cārus, a, um *adj, adv,* **ē,** dear
căsa, ae *f,* cottage, hut
căsĕus, i *m,* cheese
căsĭa, ae *f,* cinnamon (tree)
casses, ĭum *m.pl,* hunting-net, spider's web
cassis, ĭdis *f,* helmet
cassĭda, ae *f,* helmet
cassus, a, um *adj,* empty, vain
castănĕa, ae *f,* chestnut
castē *adv,* purely
castellum, i *n,* stronghold
castīgātĭo, ōnis *f,* punishment
castīgātor, ōris *m,* critic
castīgo *v.t.* 1, to correct, punish
castĭmōnĭa, ae *f,* purity
castītas, ātis *f,* chastity
castor, ŏris *m,* beaver
castra, ōrum *n.pl.,* camp

sly
cauda, ae *f,* tail
caudex, ĭcis *m,* tree trunk, ledger
caulae, ārum *f.pl,* hole, enclosure
caulis, is *m,* stem, cabbage
caupo, ōnis *m,* retailer, innkeeper
caupōna, ae *f,* shop, inn
caupōnor *v.t.* 1, *dep,* to trade
causa, ae *f,* reason, cause, motive; *abl.* **causā** for the sake of
causĭdīcus, i *m,* counsel
causor *v.i.t.* 1, *dep,* to make excuses; plead
cautē *adv,* cautiously
cautēs, is *f,* crag, rock
cautĭo, ōnis *f,* precaution
cautus, a, um *adj,* safe, cautious
căvĕa, ae *f,* den, coop
căvĕo, căvi, cautum *v.i.t.* 2, to be on one's guard; stipulate
căverna, ae *f,* cave, ship's hold
căvillātĭo, ōnis *f,* jeering

Insight

Pluralia tantum are nouns that either have only the plural form or change their meaning when plural. Some examples are: *copia, -ae* = abundance/copiae, *-arum* = forces and *castrum, -i* = fort/*castra, -orum* = camp.

castrensis, e *adj,* of the camp, military
castro *v.t.* 1, to castrate
castrum, i *n,* fort
castus, a, um *adj,* pure, virtuous
cāsū *adv,* accidentally
cāsus, ūs *m,* fall, chance, mishap
cătăpulta, ae *f,* catapult
cătaracta, ae *f,* waterfall, portcullis
cătellus i *m,* (**a, ae** *f*), puppy
cătēna, ae *f,* chain, fetter
cătēnātus, a, um *adj,* chained
căterva, ae *f,* crowd, company
cătervātim *adv,* by companies
căthēdra, ae *f,* chair
cătillus, i *m,* dish
cătīnus, i *m,* bowl, dish
cătŭlus, i *m,* puppy, young animal
cătus, a, um *adj, adv,* **ē,** intelligent,

căvillor *v.i.t.* 1, *dep,* to jeer; taunt, quibble
căvo *v.t.* 1, to hollow out
căvum, i, *n* (**us, i** *m*), hole
căvus, a, um *adj,* hollow
cēdo, cessi, cessum *v.i.t.* 3, to move, yield, happen; befall
cēdo *imperative,* here! say! give!
cĕdrus, i *f,* cedar (wood, tree, oil)
cĕlĕbĕr, ĕbris, ĕbre *adj,* much frequented, crowded, famous
cĕlĕbrātĭo, ōnis *f,* crowd, festival
cĕlĕbrātus, a, um *adj,* popular, usual, well-known
cĕlĕbrĭtas, ātis *f,* crowd, fame
cĕlĕbro *v.t.* 1, to frequent, use, celebrate, praise, proclaim, solemnize
cĕlĕr, ĕris, ĕre *adj, adv,* **ĭter,** swift, lively, rash

cĕlĕrĭtas, ātis *f*, speed
cĕlĕro *v.i.t.* 1, to hurry; quicken
cella, ae *f*, store room
cellārĭus, i *m*, butler
cēlo *v.t.* 1, to conceal
cĕlox, ōcis *f*, yacht
celsus, a, um *adj*, high, eminent
cēna, ae *f*, dinner
cēnācŭlum, i *n*, attic, refectory
cēnātĭo, ōnis *f*, dining room
cēnātus, a, um *adj*, having dined
cēno *v.i.t.* 1, to dine; eat
cēnsĕo, ŭi, censum *v.t.* 2, to
   assess, give an opinion
censor, ōris *m*, censor
censōrĭus, a, um *adj*, censorial
censūra, ae *f*, censorship
census, ūs *m*, census, wealth
centaurēum, i *n*, herb (centaury)
centaurus, i *m*, a Centaur
centēni, ae, a *adj* a hundred each
centēsĭmus, a, um *adj*, hundredth
centĭens (centĭes) *adv*, a hundred
   times
centĭmănus, a, um *adj*, hundred-
   handed
cento, ōnis *m*, patchwork
centum, a hundred
centumgĕmĭnus, a, um *adj*, a
   hundredfold
centumpondĭum, ii *n*, weight of a
   hundred pounds
centŭplex, plĭcis *adj* hundredfold
centŭrĭa, ae *f*, division, century
centŭrĭātim *adv*, by hundreds
centŭrĭo, ōnis *m*, centurion
centŭrĭo *v.t.* 1, to divide into
   centuries
cēnŭla, ae *f*, small dinner
cēra, ae *f*, wax, writing tablet
cĕrăsus, i *f*, cherry (tree)
cerdo, ōnis *m*, handicraftsman
cĕrĕbrōsus, a, um *adj*, hot-headed
cĕrĕbrum, i *n*, brain,
   understanding
cērĕus, a, um *adj*, of wax
cērĕus, i *m*, wax taper
cervisia, ae *f*, beer
cērintha, ae *f*, wax flower
cerno, crēvi, crētum *v.t.* 3, to
   perceive, decide
cernŭus, a, um *adj*, headfirst
cēro *v.t.* 1, to smear with wax

cerrītus, a, um *adj*, frantic, crazy
certāmen, ĭnis *n*, struggle
certātim *adv*, eagerly
certātĭo, ōnis *f*, contest
certē *adv*, undoubtedly
certĭōrem făcĭo to inform
certō *adv*, certainly
certo *v.i.t.* 1, to struggle; contest
certus, a, um *adj*, certain, fixed
cērussa, ae *f*, white lead
cerva, ae *f*, doe
cervīcal, ālis *n*, pillow
cervīnus, a, um *adj*, of a deer
cervisia   see cerevisia
cervix, īcis *f*, neck
cervus, i *m*, deer
cessātĭo, ōnis *f*, loitering
cessātor, ōris *m*, idler
cessātrix, īcis *f*, idler
cesso *v.i.t.* 1, to loiter, cease; fail
cĕtārĭum, ii *n*, fishpond
cĕtārĭus, ii *m*, fishmonger
cētĕrōqui *adv*, in other respects
cētĕrum *adv*, otherwise, but yet
cētĕrus, a, um *adj*, *adv*, um, the
   rest, remainder
cētus, i *m*, sea monster, whale
ceu *adv*, as, just as
chălybs, ўbis *m*, steel
charta, ae *f*, writing paper
chĕlўdrus, i *m*, water snake
chĕrăgra, ae *f*, gout in the hand
chīrŏgrăphum, i *n*, handwriting
chīrurgĭa, ae *f*, surgery
chīrurgus, i *m*, surgeon
chlămys, ўdis *f*, military cloak
chorda, ae *f*, string of a musical
   instrument
chŏrēa, ae *f*, dance
chŏrus, i *m*, dance, chorus, group
Christus, i *m*, Christ
Christĭānus, a, um *adj*, Christian
cĭbārĭa, ōrum *n.pl*, food
cĭbārĭus, a, um *adj*, of food
cĭbōrĭum, ii *n*, drinking-cup
cĭbus, i *m*, food
cĭcāda, ae *f*, grasshopper
cĭcātrix, īcis *f*, scar
cĭcer, ĕris *n*, chick pea
cĭcīnus, a, um *adj*, of the cici tree
cĭcōnĭa, ae *f*, stork
cĭcur, ūris *adj*, tame
cĭcūta, ae *f*, hemlock

cĭĕo, cīvi, cĭtum *v.t.* 2, to rouse, move, summon

cĭlĭcĭum, ii *n*, coarse cloth

cīmex, ĭcis *m*, but

cincinnātus, a, um *adj*, with ringlets

cincinnus, i *m*, lock of hair

cinctus, ūs *m*, girdle

cĭnĕrĕus, a, um *adj*, ash-coloured

cingo, nxi, nctum *v.t.* 3, to enclose, encircle, fasten on, crown, besiege

cingŭla, ae *f*, (um, i *n*), girdle

cĭnis, ĕris *m*, ashes, death

cippus, i *m*, stake

circā *adv, and prep. with acc*, round about

circenses, ĭum *m.pl.*, The Games

circīnus, i *m*, pair of compasses

circĭter *adv. and prep. with acc*, round about, near

circĭtor, ōris *m*, patrol

circŭĭtĭo, ōnis *f*, patrolling

circŭĭtus, ūs *m*, circuit

circŭlor *v.i.* 1, *dep*, to form a group

circŭlus, i *m*, circle, orbit

circum *adv, and prep. with acc*, around, near

circŭmăgo, ēgi, actum *v.t.* 3, to wheel, drive round, pass (time)

circumcīdo, cīdi, cīsum *v.t.* 3, to cut around, reduce

circumcīsus, a, um *adj*, cut off

circumclūdo, si, sum *v.t.* 3, to shut in, surround

circumdătus, a, um *adj*, surrounded

circumdo, dĕdi, dătum *v.t.* 1, to put around, shut in, surround

circumdūco, xi, ctum *v.t.* 3, to lead around

circŭmĕo, circŭĭtum *v.i.t.* 4, to go around; surround, canvass

circumfĕro, ferre, tŭli, lātum *v.t, irreg*, to carry or pass around

circumflecto, xi, xum *v.i.t.* 3, to bend, turn around

circumflŭo, xi, ctum *v.i.t.* 3, to flow round; overflow with

circumfŏrānĕus, a, um *adj*, movable

circumfundo, fūdi, fūsum *v.t.* 3, to pour around, envelop, hem in

circumgrĕdĭor, gressus *v.i.t.* 3, *dep*, to go around

circumĭcĭo, iēci, ctum *v.t.* 3, to throw or set round

circumiectus, a, um *adj*, surrounding

circumlīgo *v.t.* 1, to tie round

circumlĭno, (*no perf.*) ĭtum *v.t.* 3, to besmear

circummitto, mīsi, missum *v.t.* 3, to send around

circummūnĭo *v.t.* 4, to fortify round

circumplector, xus *v.t.* 3, *dep*, to embrace, surround

circumplĭco *v.t.* 1, to wind round

circumrōdo, di *v.t.* 3, to nibble round

circumscrībo, psi, ptum *v.t.* 3, to draw a line round, restrict, deceive

circumscriptĭo, ōnis *f*, circle, outline

circumsĕdĕo, sēdi, sessum *v.t.* 2, to surround, blockade

circumsisto, stĕti *v.t.* 3, to stand around; surround

circumsŏno *v.t.* 1, to resound; fill with sound

circumspecto *v.t.* 1, to look round; survey carefully

circumspectus, a, um *adj*, guarded, considered

circumspectus, ūs *m*, contemplation, spying

circumspĭcĭo, spexi, ctum *v.i.t.* 3, to look around, take care; survey, search for

circumsto stĕti *v.i.t.* 1, to stand around; surround, besiege

circumtextus, a, um *adj*, woven round

circumtŏno, ŭi, *v.t.* 1, to thunder around

circumvādo, si *v.t.* 3, to envelop

circumvallo *v.t.* 1, to surround with a wall, blockade

circumvector, *v.* 1, *dep*, to ride around

circumvĕhor, vectus *v.t.* 3, *dep*, to ride around

circumvĕnĭo, vēni, ventum *v.t.* 4, to surround

circumvŏlĭto, *v.i.t.* 1, to flit; fly around

circumvŏlo, *v.t.* 1, to fly around

circumvolvo, volvi, vŏlūtum *v.t.* 3, to roll around

circus, i   *m*, circle, ring

cīris, is *f*, sea bird

cirrus, i   *m*, curl

cis   *prep. with acc*, on this side of, within

cīsĭum, ii   *n*, two-wheeled vehicle

cista, ae *f*, box, chest

cisterna, ae *f*, cistern

cĭtātus, a, um *adj*, urged on, quick

cĭtĕrĭor *comp. adj*, on this side

cĭthăra, ae *f*, guitar, lute

cĭthărista, ae *m*, guitar-player

cĭthăroedus, i *m*, a singing guitar player

cĭto *adv*, soon, quickly

cĭto, *v.t.* 1, to incite, call

cĭtrā *adv, and prep. with acc*, on this side (of)

cĭtrĕus, a, um *adj*, of citrus wood, of the citrus tree

cĭtrō *adv, (with ultro)* to and fro, backwards and forwards

citrus, i *f*, citrus tree

cĭtus, a, um *adj*, swift, quick

cīvĭcus, a, um *adj*, of a citizen, civic, civil

cīvīlis, e *adj, adv*, ĭter, of a citizen, civic, civil

cīvis, is *c*, citizen

cīvĭtas, ātis *f*, citizenship, the state, the citizens

clādes, is *f*, disaster, massacre

clam *adv, and prep. with acc*, secretly; unknown to

clāmĭto *v.i.t.* 1, to call out

clāmo, *v.i.t.* 1, to shout; declare

clāmor, ōris *m*, shout, applause

clāmōsus, a, um *adj*, noisy, bawling

clandestīnus, a, um *adj, adv,* ō, secret, hidden, furtive

clangor, ōris *m*, noise, clash

clārĕo *v.i.* 2, to shine, be famous

clāresco, clārŭi *v.i.* 3, to become clear or famous

clārĭtas, ātis *f*, brightness, renown

clārĭtūdo, ĭnis *f*, renown

clārus, a, um *adj, adv,* e, clear, bright, plain, famous

classĭārĭi, ōrum *m.pl*, marines

classĭcum, i *n*, battle signal

classis, is *f*, fleet, class or muster of citizens

claudĕo *v.i.* 2, (*no perf*), to limp, be lame

claudĭco *v.i.* 1, to limp, be lame

claudĭcātĭo, ōnis *f*, limping

claudo, si, sum *v.t.* 3, to shut, cut off, enclose, blockade

claudus, a, um *adj*, lame

claustra, ōrum *n.pl*, lock, bolt, barricade

clausŭla, ae *f*, conclusion, end

clausum, i *n*, enclosed space

clāva, ae *f*, club, cudgel

clāvĭger, ĕra, ĕrum *adj*, club-armed

clāvĭger, ĕri *m*, key-bearer

clāvis, is *f*, key

clāvŭlus, i *m*, small nail

clāvus, i *m*, nail, tiller, stripe

clēmens, ntis *adj, adv,* nter, gentle, mild, merciful

clēmentĭa, ae *f*, mildness, mercy

clĕpo, psi, ptum *v.t.* 3, to steal

clepsўdra, ae *f*, water-clock

clĭens, ntis *c*, retainer, follower

clĭentēla, ae *f*, patronage, train of dependants

clĭpĕus, i *m*, Roman round shield

clītellae, ārum *f.pl*, saddle bags

clīvōsus, a, um *adj*, hilly

clīvus, i, *m*, slope, hill

clŏāca, ae *f*, sewer, drain

clūnis, is *m,   f*, buttock, haunch

cŏăcervo *v.t.* 1, to pile together

cŏactor, ōris *m*, money collector

cŏacum, i *n*, a thick covering

cŏactus, a, um *adj, adv,* ē, forced

cŏaequo *v.t.* 1, to level, equalize

cŏagmento *v.t.* 1, to join together

cŏagŭlo *v.t.* 1, to coagulate

cŏalesco, ălŭi, ălĭtum *v.i.* 3, to grow together, combine

cŏargŭo, ŭi *v.t.* 3, to convict, refute, demonstrate

cŏarto *v.t.* 1, to compress

coccĭnĕus, a, um *adj*, scarlet

coccum, i *n*, scarlet colour

cochlĕa, ae *f*, snail, spiral

cŏclĕa, ae *f*, snail, spiral

cŏclĕar, āris *n*, spoon

coctĭlis, e *adj*, baked, burned

cŏcus, i *m*, cook

cōdex, ĭcis *m*, tree trunk, ledger

cōdĭcilli, ōrum *m.pl*, notebook

cŏēmo, ēmi, emptum *v.t.* 3, to buy up

coenum, i *n*, dirt

cŏĕo *v.i.* 4, to assemble, unite, encounter, conspire

(coepĭo) coepi, coeptum *v.i.t.* 3, *defect*, to begin

coeptum, i *n*, attempt

coeptus, ūs, *m*, undertaking

cŏercĕo, *v.t.* 2, to confine, curb

cŏercĭtĭo, ōnis *f*, coercion, restraint

coetus, ūs *m*, meeting, crowd

cōgĭtātĭo, ōnis *f*, thought, reflection, purpose

cōgĭtātum, i *n*, idea, thought

cōgĭtātus, a, um *adj*, thought out

cōgĭto *v.t.* 1, to consider, think, be disposed towards, plan

cognātĭo, ōnis *f*, blood relationship, family

cognātus, a, um *adj*, related by birth; (*as a noun*) blood-relative

cognĭtĭo, ōnis *f*, study, knowledge, recognition, idea, trial

cognĭtor, ōris *m*, legal representative

cognĭtus, a, um *adj*, known, approved

cognōmen, ĭnis *n*, surname

cognōmĭnis, e *adj*, of the same name

cognosco, gnōvi, gnĭtum *v.t.* 3, to learn, understand, inquire

cōgo, cŏēgi, cŏactum *v.t.* 3, to collect, compel, restrict

cŏhaerens see cohaerĕo

cŏhaerĕo, si, sum *v.i.* 2, to cling together, agree with

cŏhēres, ēdis *c*, fellow heir

cŏhĭbĕo *v.t.* 2, to hold together, confine, restrain

cŏhŏnesto *v.t.* 1, to honour

cŏhorresco, horrŭi *v.i.* 3, to shudder

cŏhors, tis *f*, company of soldiers (¹/₁₀ of a legion); enclosure

cŏhortālis, e *adj*, of the poultry farm

cŏhortātĭo, ōnis *f*, encouragement

cŏhortor *v.t.* 1, *dep*, to encourage

cŏĭtĭo, ōnis *f*, meeting, conspiracy

cŏĭtus, ūs *m*, meeting, crowd, sexual intercourse

cŏlăphus, i *m*, blow, cuff

collăbĕfacto *v.t.* 1, to dislodge

collăbĕfĭo, fieri, factus *irreg*, to be overthrown, disabled

collābor, psus *v.i.* 3, to fall, faint, decay

collăcrĭmo *v.i.t.* 1, to weep; deplore

collactĕus, i *m*, (a, ae *f*) foster brother (sister)

collātĭo, ōnis *f*, collection, encounter, comparison

collaudo *v.t.* 1, to praise highly

collēga, ae *m*, partner, colleague

collēgĭum, ii *n*, organization, body of officials

collĭbet *v. impers*, 2, it is agreeable

collīdo, si, sum *v.t.* 3, to beat or strike together

collĭgo, lēgi, ctum *v.t.* 3, to collect, compress, consider

collĭgo *v.t.* 1, to tie together

collīno, lēvi, lĭtum *v.t.* 3, to besmear, defile

collīnus, a, um *adj*, hilly

collis, is *m*, hill, high ground

collŏcātĭo, ōnis *f*, setting up, giving in marriage

collŏco *v.t.* 1, to arrange, give in marriage, invest, employ

collŏquĭum, ii *n*, conversation

collŏquor, cūtus *v.i.* 3, *dep*, to hold a conversation, discuss

collūcĕo *v.i*, 2, to shine

collūdo, si, sum *v.i.* 3, to play with, be in collusion with

collum, i *n*, neck, throat

collumna see columna

collŭo, lŭi, lūtum *v.t.* 3, to rinse

collūsĭo, ōnis *f*, collusion

collūsor, ōris *m*, playmate

collustro *v.t.* 1, to illumine

collŭvĭo, ōnis *f*, heap of rubbish

collŭvĭes (*no genit.*) *f*, heap of rubbish

cŏlo, ŭi, cultum *v.t.* 3, to cultivate, improve, worship, study

cōlo *v.t.* 1, to filter

cŏlŏcāsĭa, ae *f*, marsh-lily

cōlon, i *n*, colon

cŏlōna, ae *f*, farmer's wife

cŏlōnĭa, ae *f,* Roman outpost, colonial settlement, farm

cŏlōnus, i *m,* farmer, colonist

cŏlor, ōris *m,* colour, dye, beauty

cŏlōrātus, a, um *adj,* coloured

cŏlōro *v.t.* 1, to colour, dye

cŏlossus, i *m,* gigantic statue

cŏlŭber, bri *m,* (bra, ae, *f*) snake

cōlum, i *n,* strainer, colander

cŏlumba, ae *f,* (us, i *m*) dove

cŏlumbārĭum, ii *n,* dovecot

cŏlumbīnus, a, um *adj,* of a dove, dove-coloured

cŏlŭmella, ae *f,* small pillar

cŏlŭmen, ĭnis *n,* summit, prop

cŏlumna, ae *f,* pillar, post

cŏlurnus, a, um *adj,* of hazel

cŏlus, ūs *f,* distaff

cŏma, ae *f,* hair, crest, foliage

cŏmans, ntis *adj,* hairy

cŏmātus, a, um *adj,* long-haired

combĭbo, bĭbi *v.t.* 3, to drink up

combūro, ussi, ustum *v.t.* 3, to burn, consume completely

cŏmĕdo, ēdi, ĕsum *v.t.* 3, to eat up, waste

cŏmes, ĭtis *c,* companion, attendant

cŏmētes, ae *m,* comet

cōmĭcus, a, um *adj, adv,* ē, comic

cōmĭcus, i *m,* comedian

cōmis, e *adj, adv,* ĭter, courteous, obliging

cōmissātĭo, ōnis *f,* drinking party

cōmissātŏr, ōris *m,* reveller

cōmissor *v.i.* 1, *dep,* to have a party

cōmĭtas, ātis *f,* affability

cŏmĭtātus, a, um *adj,* accompanied

cŏmĭtātus, ūs *m,* escort, retinue

cŏmĭtĭa, ōrum *n.pl,* Roman assembly for electing magistrates

cŏmĭtĭālis, e *adj,* of the elections; (*with* morbus) epilepsy

cŏmĭtĭum, ii *n,* assembly place for voting

cŏmĭtor *v.t.* 1, *dep,* to accompany

commăcŭlo *v.t.* 1, to stain

commĕātus, ūs *m,* expedition, leave of absence, convoy, supplies

commĕmŏrātĭo, ōnis *f,* mention

commĕmŏro *v.t.* 1, to remember, relate

commendātīcĭus, a, um *adj,* commendatory

commendātĭo, ōnis *f,* recommendation

commendo *v.t.* 1, to entrust, recommend

commentārĭus, ii *m,* (ium, ii *n*) notebook, record

commentātĭo, ōnis *f,* careful study

commentīcĭus, a, um *adj,* thought-out, imaginary, false

commentor *v.i.t.* 1, *dep,* to study

commentor, ōris *m,* inventor

commentum, i *n,* fabrication

commĕo, *v.i.* 1, to come and go, frequent

commercĭum, ii *n,* fabrication

commĕrĕo *v.t.* 2, to deserve fully, be guilty of

commĭgro *v.t.* 1, to migrate

commīlĭtĭum, ii *n,* comradeship

commīlĭto, ōnis *m,* comrade

commĭnātĭo, ōnis *f,* threats

commĭniscor, mentus *v.t.* 3, *dep,* to devise, invent

commĭnor *v.t.* 1, *dep,* to threaten

commĭnŭo, ŭi, ūtum *v.t.* 3, to crush, lessen, weaken

commĭnus *adv,* at close quarters

commiscĕo, scŭi, xtum *v.t.* 2, to mix together

commĭsĕror *v.t.* 1, *dep,* to pity

commissĭo, ōnis *f,* opening of the games, prepared speech

commissum, i *n,* offence, secret

commissūra, ae *f,* knot, joint

committo, mīsi, ssum *v.t.* 3, to connect, engage in, begin, entrust, do something wrong, bring together in combat

commŏdātum, i *n,* loan

commŏdē *adv,* appropriately, just in time

commŏdĭtas, ātis *f,* benefit

commŏdo *v.t.* 1, to adjust, lend, be kind to, oblige

commŏdum, i *n,* convenient time or opportunity, advantage

commŏdus, a, um *adj,* suitable, obliging, advantageous

commŏnĕfăcĭo, fēci, factum *v.t.* 3, to remind, impress upon

commŏnĕo *v.t.* 2, to impress upon

commonstro *v.t.* 1, to point out
commŏrātĭo, ōnis *f,* delay
commŏror *v.t.* 1, *dep,* to wait, stay
commōtĭo, ōnis *f,* commotion, excitement
commōtus, a, um *adj,* aroused
commŏvĕo, mōvi, mōtum *v.t.* 2, to shake, move, arouse, disturb
commūnĭcātĭo, ōnis *f,* communication
commūnĭco *v.t.* 1, to share with another, consult, unite, partake
commūnĭo *v.t.* 4, to fortify strongly
commūnĭo, ōnis *f,* partnership
commūnē, is *n,* community, state
commūnis, e *adj, adv, ĭter,* common, general
commūnĭtas, ātis *f,* fellowship
commūtābĭlis, e *adj,* changeable
commūtātĭo, ōnis *f,* change
commūto, *v.t.* 1, to change, exchange
cōmo, mpsi, mptum *v.t.* 3, to arrange, comb, braid, adorn
cōmoedĭa, ae *f,* comedy
cōmoedus, a, um *adj,* comic
cōmoedus, i *m,* comic actor
compactum, i *n,* agreement
compactus, a, um *adj,* thick set
compāges, is *f,* joint, structure
compār, ăris *adj,* equal, like
compār, ăris *m,* companion
compărātĭo, ōnis *f,* comparison, preparation
compărātīvus, a, um *adj,* comparative
compārĕo *v.t.* 2, to be evident
compăro *v.t.* 1, to pair off, compare, make ready, provide
compello, pŭli, pulsum *v.t.* 3, to collect, compel
compello *v.t.* 1, to address, rebuke
compendĭārĭus, a, um *adj,* short
compendĭum, ii *n,* gain, saving, abbreviation
compensātĭo, ōnis *f,* compensation
compenso *v.t.* 1, to make things balance, compensate
compĕrendĭno *v.t.* 1, to remand
compĕrĭo, pĕri, pertum *v.t.* 4, to ascertain
compertus, a, um *adj,* proved

compēs, ĕdis *f,* chain, shackle for the feet
compesco, scŭi *v.t.* 3, to restrain
compĕtītor, ōris *m,* rival
compĕto, īvi, ītum *v.t.* 3, to correspond, coincide
compīlo *v.t.* 1, to plunder
compingo, pēgi, pactum *v.t.* 3, to construct, fasten together
compĭtum, i *n,* crossroad
complāno *v.t.* 1, to level
complector, xus *v.t.* 3, *dep,* to embrace, value, enclose, understand
complēmentum, i *n,* complement
complĕo, ēvi, ētum *v.t.* 2, to fill up, supply
complexĭo, ōnis *f,* combination
complexus ūs *m,* embrace, love
complīco *v.t.* 1, to fold up
complōrātĭo, ōnis *f,* lamentation
complōrātus ūs *m,* lamentation
complōro *v.t.* 1, to lament
complūres, a *pl, adj,* several
compōno, pŏsŭi, pŏsĭtum *v.t.* 3, to put together, unite, build, arrange, compare, put to sleep, adjust, pretend, agree upon
comporto *v.t.* 1, to bring together
compŏs, ŏtis *adj, with genit. or abl,* having control of
compŏsĭtĭo, ōnis *f,* arranging
compŏsĭtus, a, um *adj, adv, ē,* well-arranged, suitable **ex compŏsĭto,** by previous agreement
comprĕhendo, di, sum *v.t.* 3, to seize, perceive, recount, understand
comprĕhensĭo, ōnis *f,* arrest
comprĭma, pressi, pressum *v.t.* 3, to press together, restrain
comprŏbo *v.t.* 1, to approve, prove
comptus, a, um *adj,* dressed-up
compulsus, a, um *adj,* collected, driven
compungo, nxi, nctum *v.t.* 3, to prick, sting
compŭto *v.t.* 1, to calculate
cōnāmen, ĭnis *n,* effort
cōnāta, ōrum *n.pl,* undertaking

cōnātum, i *n*, attempt

cōnātus, ūs *m*, effort, enterprise

concăvus, a, um *adj*, hollow, arched

concēdo, cessi, ssum *v.t.* 3, to go away, yield; permit

concĕlĕbro *v.t.* 1, to frequent, celebrate, notify

concentus, ūs *m*, harmony

conceptĭo, ōnis *f*, comprehension, conception

conceptus, ūs *m*, gathering

concertātĭo, ōnis *f*, dispute

concerto *v.t.* 1, to dispute

concessĭo ōnis *f*, permission

concessu (*abl*), by permission

concessus, a, um *adj*, yielded, confirmed

concha, ae *f*, shellfish, oyster-shell, Triton's trumpet

conchȳlĭum, ii *n*, shellfish

concĭdo, cĭdī *v.i.* 3, to collapse

concīdo, cīdi, cīsum *v.t.* 3, to cut up, kill, annihilate

concĭĕo, īvi, ĭtum *v.t.* 2, to bring together

concĭlĭābŭlum, i *n*, assembly-place

concĭlĭātĭo, ōnis *f*, union

concĭlĭātor, ōris *m*, promoter

concĭlĭo *v.t.* 1, to unite, win over, bring about

concĭlĭum, ii *n*, meeting, assembly

concinnĭtas, ātis *f*, elegance

concinnus, a, um *adj, adv*, ē, well-adjusted, graceful

concĭno, nŭi *v.t.* 3, to harmonize; celebrate

concĭpĭo, cēpi, ceptum *v.t.* 3, to take hold of, become pregnant, understand, formulate, designate

concīsus, a, um *adj, adv*, ē, cut short

concĭtātĭo, ōnis *f*, quick motion

concĭtātus, a, um *adj, adv*, ē, swift, roused

concĭto *v.t.* 1, to stir up, rouse

conclāmo *v.t.* 1, to shout out; call upon

conclāve, is *n*, room

conclūdo, si, sum *v.t.* 3, to enclose, include, conclude

concoctĭo, ōnis *f*, digestion

concŏlor, ōris *adj*, similar in colour

concŏquo, xi, ctum *v.t.* 3, to boil together, digest, put up with

concordĭa, ae *f*, agreement

concordo *v.i.* 1, to agree

concors, cordis *adj, adv*, ĭter, of the same mind

concrēdo, dĭdi, dĭtum *v.t.* 3, to entrust

concrĕmo *v.t.* 1, to burn up

concrĕpo, ŭi, ĭtum *v.i.t.* 3, to creak, crack; rattle, clash

concresco, crēvi, tum *v.i.* 3, to grow together, harden

concrētus, a, um *adj*, hardened

concŭbīna, ae *f*, concubine

concŭbĭus, a, um, *adj*, (*with* nox) at dead of night

conculco *v.t.* 1, to trample on

concŭpisco, cŭpīvi, ĭtum *v.t.* 3, to long for, strive after

concurro, curri, cursum *v.i.* 3, to rush together, assemble, join battle

concursātĭo, ōnis *f*, running together

concursĭo, ōnis *f*, running together

concurso *v.i.t.* 1, to run, travel about, skirmish; frequent

concursus, ūs *m*, rush, collision

concŭtĭo, cussi, ssum *v.t.* 3, to shake, disturb, terrify, examine

condemno *v.t.* 1, to convict

condenso *v.t.* 1, to condense

condensus, a, um *adj*, thick

condĭcĭo, ōnis *f*, agreement, proposition, terms, alliance, rank, situation

condīmentum, i *n*, seasoning

condĭo *v.t.* 4, to pickle

condiscĭpŭlus, i *m*, school friend

condisco, dĭdĭci *v.t.* 3, to learn carefully

condĭtor, ōris *m*, builder, author, founder

condĭtus, a, um *adj*, fashioned, composed

condītus, a, um *adj*, savoury

condo, dĭdi, dĭtum *v.t.* 3, to construct, found, store up, hide, thrust in

condŏlesco, lŭi *v.i.* 3, to suffer pain

condōno *v.t.* 1, to present, give up, surrender, pardon

condūco, xi, ctum *v.i.t.* 3, to be useful; collect, connect, hire

conductĭo, ōnis *f,* hiring

conductor, ōris *m,* tenant, contractor

conductum, i *n,* tenement

conductus, a, um *adj,* hired

cōnecto, xŭi, xum *v.t.* 3, to tie together, involve

confarrĕātĭo, ōnis *f,* marriage

confectĭo, ōnis *f,* arrangement, completion

confectus, a, um *adj,* completed, exhausted

confercĭo, (*no perf.*) **fertum** *v.t.* 4, to cram, stuff together

confĕro, ferre, tŭli, collātum *v.t, irreg,* to bring together, contribute, confer, talk about, engage, fight, compare, condense, convey, postpone; (*reflex.*) to betake oneself, go

confertus, a, um *adj, adv,* **ē,** crowded

confessĭo, ōnis *f,* confession

confessus, a, um *adj,* admitted

confestim *adv,* immediately

confĭcĭo, fēci, fectum *v.t.* 3, to complete, produce, exhaust, kill

confĭdens, ntis *adj, adv,* **nter,** bold, impudent

confĭdentĭa, ae *f,* boldness

confido, fīsus sum *v.i.* 3, *semi-dep,* to feel confident; *with dat,* to trust

configo, xi, xum *v.t.* 3, to nail, fasten together, transfix

confingo, nxi, ctum *v.t.* 3, to fashion, invent

confīnis, e, *adj,* adjoining

confīnĭum, ii *n,* border

confirmātĭo, ōnis *f,* encouragement, confirming

confirmātus, a, um *adj,* resolute

confirmo, *v.t.* 1, to strengthen, encourage, prove

confīsus, a, um *adj,* trusting

confĭtĕor, fessus *v.t.* 2, *dep,* to acknowledge, own

conflàgro *v.i.* 1, to burn

conflicto *v.t.* 1, to strike or dash together, ruin, harass

conflīgo, xi, ctum *v.i.t.* 3, to fight, struggle; strike or dash together

conflo *v.t.* 1, to kindle, cause

conflŭens, ntis *m,* confluence of rivers

conflŭo, xi *v.i.* 3, to flow together, unite, come in crowds

confŏdĭo, fōdi, fossum *v.t.* 3, to dig thoroughly, stab, pierce

conformātĭo, ōnis *f,* shaping

conformo *v.t.* 1, to form, fashion

confrăgōsus, a, um *adj,* broken

confringo, frēgi, fractum *v.t.* 3, to smash up

confŭgĭo, fūgi *v.i.* 3, to run away for help, take refuge

confundo, fūdi, sum *v.t.* 3, to pour together, confuse

confūsĭo, ōnis *f,* blending, disorder

confūsus, a, um *adj, adv,* **ē,** disorderly

confūto *v.t.* 1, to repress, silence

congĕlo *v.i.t.* 1, to freeze; thicken

congĕmĭno *v.t.* 1, to redouble

congĕmo, ŭi *v.i.t.* 3, to sigh; mourn

congĕrĭes, ēi *f,* heap

congĕro, ssi, stum *v.t.* 3, to bring together, accumulate

congestus, ūs *m,* heap

congĭārĭum, ii *n,* gratuity

congĭus, ii *m,* six-pint measure

conglŏbo *v.t.* 1, to gather, press into a ball

conglūtĭno *v.t.* 1, to glue or cement together, unite

congrĕdĭor, gressus *v.i.* 3, *dep,* to meet, encounter

congrĕgātĭo, ōnis *f,* assembly

congrĕgo *v.t.* 1, to collect into a flock, unite

congressus, ūs *m,* meeting, combat

congrŭens, ntis *adj, adv,* **nter,** appropriate, proper, consistent

congrŭentĭa, ae *f,* agreement

congrŭo, ŭi *v.t.* 3, to meet, coincide

cōnĭcĭo, iēci, iectum *v.t.* 3, to hurl, infer, drive

coniecto v.t. 1, to hurl, foretell
coniectūra, ae f, inference
coniectus, ūs m, throwing, heap
coniectus, a, um adj, thrown together
cōnĭfer, ĕra, ĕrum adj, cone-bearing
cōnĭtor, nīsus (nixus) v.i. 3, dep, to strive, struggle towards
cōnīvĕo, nīvi v.i. 2, to wink, blink
coniŭgĭum, ii n, union, marriage
coniunctĭo, ōnis f, uniting, junction
coniunctus, a, um adj, adv, ē, near, connected, allied
coniungo, nxi, nctum v.t. 3, to join together, marry
coniunx, iŭgis m, f, husband, wife
coniūrātĭo, ōnis f, conspiracy
coniūrātus, i m, conspirator
coniūro v.i. 1, to conspire, band together
conl... see coll...
connecto see cōnecto
conīvĕo see cōnīvĕo
connūbĭum, ii n, marriage
cōnōpèum, i n, gauze net
cōnor v.t. 1, dep, to try, undertake
conquĕror, questus v.i.t. 3, dep, to complain (of)
conquĭesco, quĭēvi, quĭētum v.i. 3, to rest, pause
conquīro, quīsīvi, sītum v.t. 3, to search for
conquīsītĭo, ōnis f, search
conquīsītus, a, um adj, sought after
consălūto v.t. 1, to greet
consānesco, ŭi v.i. 3, to heal
consanguĭnĕus, a, um adj, related by blood
consanguĭnĭtas, ātis f, blood relationship
conscendo, di, sum v.i.t. 3, to embark; mount
conscĭentĭa, ae f, joint knowledge, moral sense
conscindo, ĭdi, issum v.t. 3, to tear in pieces
conscisco, scīvi, ītum v.t. 3, to make a joint resolution, decree, inflict

conscĭus, a, um adj, sharing knowledge of, (with sibi) conscious of
conscĭus, i m, accomplice
conscrībo, psi, ptum v.t. 3, to enroll, enlist, compose
conscriptus, i m, senator
consĕco, cŭi, ctum v.t. 1, to cut up
consecrātĭo, ōnis f, consecration
consecro v.t. 1, to dedicate, doom
consector v.t. 1, dep, to pursue eagerly, imitate
consĕnesco, nŭi v.i. 3, to grow old or weak
consensĭo, ōnis f, agreement, plot
consensus, ūs m, agreement, plot
consentānĕus, a, um adj, suited
consentĭo, sensi, sum v.i.t. 4, to agree, conspire, resolve; plot
consĕquens, ntis adj, according to reason, fit
consĕquor, sĕcūtus v.t. 3, dep, to follow, pursue, overtake, attain, obtain
consĕro, sēvi, sĭtum (sătum) v.t. 3, to plant, sow
consĕro, rŭi, rtum v.t. 3, to fasten together
consertus, a, um adj, adv, ē, joined, close, serried
conservātĭo, ōnis f, maintenance
conservo v.t. 1, to maintain, keep safe
conservus, i m, fellow slave
consessus, ūs m, assembly
consīdĕrātus, a, um adj, adv, ē, well-considered, cautious, discreet
consīdĕrātĭo, ōnis f, consideration
consīdĕro v.t. 1, to examine, contemplate
consīdo, sēdi, sessum v.i. 3, to sit down, take up position, subside
consigno v.t. 1, to seal, certify
consĭlĭārĭus, ii m, adviser
consĭlĭor v.i. 1, dep, to consult
consĭlĭum, ii n, plan, deliberation, policy, advise, assembly, wisdom
consĭmĭlis, e adj, quite like
consisto, stĭti, stĭtum v.i. 3, to stand, halt, take up position, endure, settle
consōbrīnus, i m (a, ae, f), cousin
consŏcĭātus, a, um adj, united
consŏcĭo v.t. 1, to share, unite

consōlātĭo, ōnis *f,* comfort

consōlātor, ōris *m,* comforter

consōlor *v.t.* 1, *dep,* to comfort

consŏnans, ntis (*with* **littera**), consonant

consŏno, ŭi *v.i.* 1, to resound, harmonize, agree

consŏnus, a, um *adj, adv,* **ē,** fit, harmonious

consōpĭo *v.t.* 4, to put to sleep

consors, rtis *adj,* partner

conspectus, ūs *m,* look, sight, view, presence

conspectus, a, um *adj,* distinguished, visible

conspergo, si, sum *v.t.* 3, to sprinkle

conspĭcĭo, spexi, ctum *v.t.* 3, to look at, understand

conspĭcor *v.t.* 1, *dep,* to catch sight of

conspĭcŭus, a, um *adj,* visible, striking

conspīrātĭo, ōnis *f,* agreement, plot

conspīro *v.i.* 1, to agree, plot

consponsor, ōris *m,* joint surety

conspŭo, (no perf.), ūtum *v.t.* 3, to spit on, cover

constans, ntis *adj, adv* **nter,** firm, resolute, consistent

constantĭa, ae *f,* firmness, consistency

constat *v. impers,* it is agreed

consternātĭo, ōnis *f,* dismay

consterno, strāvi, strātum *v.t.* 3, to cover over

consterno *v.t.* 1, to alarm, provoke

constĭtŭo, ŭi, ūtum *v.t.* 3, to put, place, draw up, halt, establish, arrange, determine, decide

constĭtūtĭo, ōnis *f,* arrangement, establishment

constĭtūtum i *n,* agreement

constĭtūtus, a, um *adj,* arranged

consto, stĭti, stātum *v.i.* 1, to agree with, endure, be established, exist, consist of, cost

constrātus, a, um *adj,* covered

constringo, nxi, ctum *v.t.* 3, to tie up, restrain

construo, xi, ctum *v.t.* 3, to heap up, build

constūpro *v.t.* 1, to ravish

consŭēfăcĭo, fēci, factum *v.t.* 3, to accustom

consŭesco, sŭēvi, sŭētum *v.i.t.* 3, to be accustomed; train

consŭētūdo, ĭnis *f,* habit, custom, intimacy

consŭētus, a, um *adj,* customary

consŭl, ŭlis *m,* consul (highest Roman magistrate)

consŭlāris, e *adj,* of a consul

consŭlātus, ūs *m,* consulship

consŭlo, ŭi, sultum *v.i.t.* 3, to consider, consult; *with dat,* promote the interests of

consulto *v.i.t.* 1, to deliberate; consult

consultor, ōris *m,* adviser, client

consultum, i *n,* decision, decree

consultus, a, um *adj, adv,* **ē, ō,** well considered

consummātĭo, ōnis *f,* summing-up, completion

consūmo, mpsi, mptum *v.t.* 3, to use, eat up, consume, waste, destroy

consumptĭo, ōnis *f,* wasting, use

consurgo, surrexi, surrectum *v.i.t.* 3, to stand up, rise

contăbŭlātĭo, ōnis *f,* flooring

contăbŭlo *v.t.* 1, to board over

contactus, ūs *m,* touch, contact, contagion

contāgĭo, ōnis *f,* touch, contact, contagion

contāmĭnātus, a, um *adj,* impure

contāmĭno *v.t.* 1, to blend, stain

contĕgo, xi, ctum *v.t.* 3, to cover up, hide

contemnendus, a, um *adj,* contemptible

contemno, mpsi, mptum *v.t.* 3, to despise

contemplātĭo, ōnis *f,* observation

contemplor *v.t.* 1, *dep,* to observe

contemptor, ōris *m,* despiser

contemptus, ūs *m,* contempt

contemptus, a, um *adj,* despicable

contendo, di, tum *v.i.t.* 3, to strive, march, fight, stretch; compare, make a bid for

contentĭo, ōnis *f,* struggle, effort, contrast, dispute

contentus, a, um *adj*, strained
contentus, a, um *adj*, satisfied
conterminus, a, um *adj*, bordering on
contero, trīvi, trītum *v.t.* 3, to grind, wear away, waste
conterrĕo *v.t.* 2, to frighten
contestor *v.t.* 1, *dep*, to call to witness
contexo, ūi, xtum *v.i.t.* 3, to weave together; build, compose
contextus, ūs *m*, connection
contĭcesco, tĭcŭi *v.i.* 3, to be silent, cease
contignātĭo, ōnis *f*, wooden floor
contĭgŭus, a, um *adj*, adjoining
contĭnens, ntis *f*, continent
contĭnens, ntis *adj, adv,* **nter,** moderate, adjacent, unbroken
contĭnentĭa, ae *f*, self-restraint
contĭnĕo, ŭi, tentum *v.t.* 2, to keep together, contain, enclose, restrain
contingo, tĭgi, tactum *v.i.t.* 3, to happen; touch, border on, reach
contĭnŭātĭo, ōnis *f*, succession
contĭnŭō *adv*, immediately
contĭnŭo *v.t.* 1, to connect, to do one thing after another
contĭnŭus, a, um *adj*, unbroken
contĭo, ōnis *f*, meeting, speech
contĭonātor, ōris *m*, demagogue
contĭonor *v.* 1, *dep*, to expound
contorquĕo, torsi, tortum *v.t.* 2, to twist, brandish, hurl
contortĭo, ōnis *f*, twisting, intricacy
contortus, a, um *adj, adv,* **ē,** energetic, complicated
contrā *adv, prep. with acc,* opposite, facing, contrary to
contractĭo, ōnis *f*, contraction
contractus, a, um *adj*, compressed
contrādīco, xi, cutm *v.t.* 3, to reply
contrādictĭo, ōnis *f*, reply
contrăho, xi, ctum *v.t.* 3, to bring together, shorten, produce, check
contrārĭum, ii *n*, the contrary
contrārĭus, a, um *adj, adv,* **ē,** opposite, injurious
contrecto *v.t.* 1, to handle, feel
contrĕmisco, mŭi *v.i.t.* 3, to quake; tremble at
contrĭbŭo, ŭi, ūtum *v.t.* 3, to quake; tremble at

contrĭbŭo, ŭi, ūtum *v.t.* 3, to incorporate, unite
contristo *v.t.* 1, to sadden, cloud
contrītus, a, um *adj*, worn out
contrōversĭa, ae *f*, dispute
contrōvērsus, a, um *adj*, questionable
contrŭcīdo *v.t.* 1, to slash
contŭbernālis, is *c*, messmate
contŭbernĭum, ii *n*, companionship
contŭĕor *v.t.* 2, *dep*, to survey
contŭmācĭa, ae *f*, obstinacy
contŭmax, ācis *adj, adv,* **ĭter,** stubborn, insolent
contŭmēlĭa, ae *f*, insult
contŭmēlĭōsus, a, um *adj*, abusive
contŭmŭlo *v.t.* 1, to bury
contundo, tŭdi, tūsum *v.t.* 3, to grind, crush, subdue
conturbo *v.t.* 1, to confuse
contus, i *m*, pole
contūsum, i *n*, bruise
cōnūbĭum, ĭi, *n*, marriage
cōnus, i *m*, cone, helmet-tip
convălesco, lŭi *v.i.* 3, to regain strength or health
convallis, is *f*, valley
convecto *v.t.* 1, to collect
convĕho, xi, ctum *v.t.* 3, to bring together
convello, velli, vulsum *v.t.* 3, to tear up
convĕnĭens, ntis *adj, adv,* **nter,** consistent, appropriate
convĕnĭenta, ae *f*, consistency, symmetry
convĕnĭo, vēni, ventum *v.i.t.* 4, to assemble, agree with; meet
convĕnit *impers*, it is agreed, it is right, it suits
conventum, i *n*, agreement
conventus, ūs *m*, meeting, assizes
conversĭo, ōnis *f*, revolution
conversus, a, um *adj*, reversed, turned, transposed
converto, ti, sum *v.i.t.* 3, to turn; change, alter
convexus, a, um *adj*, arched
convīcĭum, ii *n*, outcry, squabbling, abuse
convictor, ōris *m*, close friend
convictus, ūs *m*, intimacy
convinco, vīci, victum *v.t.* 3, to conquer, prove

convīva, ae *c*, guest
convīvĭum, ii *n*, dinner party
convīvor *v.i.* 1, *dep*, to banquet
convŏco *v.t.* 1, to call together
convŏlo, *v.i.* 1, to flock together
convolvo, volvi, vŏlūtum *v.t.* 3, to roll up, interweave
convulsĭo, ōnis *f*, convulsion
convulsus, a, um *adj*, torn-up
cŏŏpĕrĭo, rŭi, rtum *v.t.* 4, to cover up, overwhelm
cŏoptātĭo, ōnis *f*, election
cŏopto *v.t.* 1, to nominate, elect
cŏŏrĭor, ortus *v.i.* 4, *dep*, to arise, break out
cŏphĭnus, i *m*, wicker basket
cōpĭa, ae *f*, abundance, power, supply, opportunity; *pl*, forces
cōpĭōsus, a, um *adj, adv, ē*, well-supplied, eloquent
cōpŭla, ae *f*, thong, grappling iron
cōpŭlo *v.t.* 1, to link, join
cŏquo, xi, ctum *v.t.* 3, to cook, burn, ripen, devise, harass
cŏquus, i *m*, cook
cŏr, cordis *n*, heart, mind
cŏrălĭum, ii *n*, coral
cōram *adv and prep. with abl*, in the presence of, openly
corbis, is *c*, basket
corbīta, ae *f*, merchant ship
cordātus, a, um *adj*, shrewd
cŏrĭārĭus ii, *m*, tanner
cŏrĭum, ii *n*, skin, hide, leather, layer, stratum
cornĕus, a, um *adj*, horny
cornĕus, a, um *adj*, of cornel wood
cornĭcen, ĭnis *m*, horn-player
cornĭcŭla, ae *f*, jackdaw
cornĭcŭlum, i *n*, little horn, feeler
cornĭger, ĕra, ĕrum *adj*, horned
cornĭpēs, ĕdis *adj*, hoofed
cornix, īcis *f*, crow
cornū, ūs *n*, horn, hoof, beak, tributary, promontory, knob, wing of army, bow, trumpet, drinking horn
cornum, i *n*, cornel-cherry
cornus, i *f*, cornel-cherry tree, cornel-wood javelin
cŏrōna, ae *f*, garland, wreath, crown, ring, circle, crowd

cŏrōno *v.t.* 1, to crown, encircle
corpŏrĕus, a, um *adj*, physical
corpŭlentus, a, um *adj*, corpulent
corpus, ŏris *n*, body
correctĭo, ōnis *f*, improvement
corrector, ōris *m*, reformer
corrēpo, psi *v.i.* 3, to creep
corrĭgĭa, ae *f*, shoe lace
corrĭgo, rexi, ctum *v.t.* 3, to put right, improve
corrĭpĭo, pŭi, pertum *v.t.* 3, to snatch, plunder, attack, shorten
corrōbŏro *v.t.* 1, to strengthen
corrūgo *v.t.* 1, to wrinkle
corrumpo, rūpi, ptum *v.t.* 3, to destroy, corrupt, spoil
corrŭo, ŭi *v.i.t.* 3, to collapse; overthrow
corruptēla, ae *f*, corruption
corruptor, ōris *m*, corruptor, seducer
corruptus, a, um *adj, adv, ē*, spoiled, damaged, tainted
cortex, īcis *m*, bark, rind
cortīna, ae *f*, kettle, cauldron
cŏrusco *v.i.t.* 1, to glitter; shake
cŏruscus, a, um *adj*, glittering, vibrating
corvus, i *m*, raven
cŏrўlus, i *f*, hazel shrub
cŏrymbus, i *m*, cluster of fruit or flowers
cōrўtŏs, i *m*, quiver
cōs, cōtis *f*, flintstone
costa, ae *f*, rib, wall
cŏthurnus, i *m*, hunting-boot, buskin (worn by tragic actors)
cottīdĭānus, a, um *adj, adv, ō*, daily, usual
cottīdĭē/cotidie *adv*, daily
cŏturnix, īcis *f*, quail
coxendix, īcis *f*, hip
crabro, ōnis *m*, hornet
crambē, es *f*, cabbage, kale
crāpŭla, ae *f*, intoxication
crās *adv*, tomorrow
crassĭtūdo, ĭnis *f*, thickness
crassus, a, um *adj, adv, ē*, thick, fat, solid
crastĭnus, a, um *adj*, of tomorrow
crātēr, ĕris *m*, mixing-bowl, basin
crātēra, ae *f*, mixing-bowl, basin
crātĭcŭla, ae *f*, gridiron

crātis, is *f*, wicker-work, hurdle
crĕātĭo, ōnis *f*, appointing
crĕātor, ōris *m*, founder, creator
crĕātrix, īcis *f*, mother
crēber, bra, brum *adj, adv*, **ō**, think, numerous, repeated
crēbresco, brŭi *v.i.* 3, to become frequent, gain strength
crēdens, ntis *c*, believer
crēdĭbĭlis, e *adj, adv* **īter**, credible, probable
crēdĭtor, ōris *m*, creditor
crēdo, dĭdi, dĭtum *v.t.* 3, to lend, entrust, trust, believe in (*with dat*); suppose
crēdŭlĭtas, ātis *f*, credulity
crēdŭlus, a, um *adj*, ready to believe
crĕmo *v.t.* 1, to burn
crĕo *v.t.* 1, to produce, appoint
crĕpĭda, ae *f*, sandal
crĕpīdo, ĭnis *f*, pedestal, dike
crĕpĭtācŭlum, i *n*, rattle
crĕpĭto *v.i.* 1, to rattle, rustle
crĕpĭtus, ūs *m*, rattling, clashing, cracking
crĕpo, ŭi, ĭtum *v.i.t.* 1, to rattle, creak, jingle; prattle about
crĕpundĭa, ōrum *n.pl*, child's rattle
crĕpuscŭlum, i *n*, twilight, dusk
cresco, crēvi, crētum *v.i.* 3, to arise, grow, appear, thrive
crēta, ae *f*, chalk
crētus, a, um *adj*, arisen, born of
crībro *v.t.* 1, to sift
crībrum, i *n*, sieve
crīmen, ĭnis *n*, accusation, offence
crīmĭnātĭo, ōnis *f*, accusation, calumny
crīmĭnor *v.t.* 1, *dep*, to accuse
crīmĭnōsus, a, um *adj, adv*, **ē**, slanderous, culpable
crīnālis, e *adj*, of the hair
crīnis, is *m*, the hair
crīnītus, a, um *adj*, long-haired
crispo *v.i.t.* 1, to curl; brandish
crispus, a, um *adj*, curled, quivering
crista, ae *f*, crest, plume
cristātus, a, um *adj*, crested
crītĭcus, i *m*, critic
crŏcĕus, a, um *adj*, of saffron or yellow

crōcĭo *v.i.* 4, to croak
crōcŏdīlus, i *m*, crocodile
crŏcus, i *m* (**um, i**, *n*), crocus
crŭcĭātus, ūs *m*, torture, pain
crŭcĭo *v.t.* 1, to torture
crūdēlis, e *adj, adv*, **īter**, cruel
crūdēlĭtas, ātis *f*, crulelty
crūdesco, dŭi *v.i.* 3, to get worse
crūdĭtas, ātis *f*, indigestion
crūdus, a, um *adj*, raw, fresh, unripe, cruel
crŭento *v.t.* 1, to stain with blood
crŭentus, a, um *adj*, bloodstained, bloodthirsty
crŭmēna, ae *f*, small purse
crŭor, ōris *m*, blood (from a wound), murder
crūs, ūris *n*, leg, shin
crusta, ae *f*, crust, bark, mosaic
crustŭlārĭus, ii *m*, confectioner
crustŭlum, i *n*, confectionery
crustum, i *n*, confectionery
crux, ŭcis *f*, cross
crypta, ae *f*, cloister, vault
crystallum, i *n*, crystal
cŭbĭculārĭus, ii *m*, chamber-servant
cŭbĭcŭlum, i *n*, bedroom
cŭbĭcus, a, um *adj*, cubic
cŭbīle, is *n*. bed, lair
cŭbĭtăl, ālis *n*, cushion
cŭbĭtum, i *n*, elbow
cŭbĭtus, i *m*, elbow
cŭbĭtum see **cŭbo**
cŭbo, ŭi, ĭtum *v.i.* 1, to lie down, sleep, lie ill, slant
cŭcullus, i *m*, hood
cŭcŭlus, i *m*, cuckoo
cŭcŭmis, ĕris *m*, cucumber
cŭcurbĭta, ae *f*, cup
cūdo *v.t.* 3, to beat, strike, stamp
cūius, a, um *interr. adj*, whose?
cūius *genit. of* **qui, quis**
culcĭta, ae *f*, mattress, cushion
cŭlex, īcis *m*, gnat, mosquito
cŭlīna, ae *f*, kitchen, food
cullĕus, i *m*, leather bag
culmen, ĭnis *n*, summit, roof
culmus, i *m*, stem, stalk
culpa, ae *f*, blame, fault, weakness
culpābĭlis, e *adj*, culpable
culpandus, a, um *adj*, culpable
culpo *v.t.* 1, to blame
culter, tri *m*, knife, ploughshare

cultor, ōris *m*, cultivator, supporter, inhabitant
cultrix, īcis *f*, female inhabitant
cultūra, ae *f*, cultivation, care
cultus, a, um *adj*, cultivated, elegant
cultus, ūs, *m*, farming, education, culture-pattern, reverence, dress
cŭlullus, i, *m*, drinking-cup
cum *conj*, when, whenever, since, although **cum ... tum**, both ... and, not only ... but also
cum *prep. with abl*, together with; *it is attached to the abl. case of personal prons*, e.g. **mecum**, with me

cūpa, ae *f*, barrel, cask
cūpēdĭa, ōrum *n.pl*, delicacies
cŭpĭdē *adv*, eagerly
cŭpĭdĭtas, ātis *f*, desire, longing
cŭpīdo, ĭnis *f*, lust, greed
cŭpĭdus, a, um *adj*, eager, longing for, greedy, passionate
cŭpĭens, ntis *adj, adv*, **nter**, eager or longing for
cŭpĭo, īvi, ītum *v.t.* 3, to desire
cùpressus, i *f*, cypress tree
cūr *adv*, why
cūra, ae *f*, care, attention, management, anxiety
cūrātĭo, ōnis *f*, administration, cure

Insight

Cum used as a preposition and when followed by the ablative case means 'with'; *cum* used as a conjunction means 'when', 'whenever', 'since' and 'although'. It can be followed by both the indicative and the subjunctive.

---

cumba, ae *f*, small boat
cŭmĕra, ae *f*, box, chest
cŭmīnum, i *n*, cumin (plant)
cumquĕ *adv*, however, whenever
cŭmŭlātus, a, um *adj, adv*, **ē**, full, increased
cŭmŭlo *v.t.* 1, to heap up, complete
cŭmŭlus, i *m*, heap, 'last straw'
cūnābŭla, ōrum *n.pl*, cradle
cūnae, ārum *f.pl*, cradle
cunctans, ntis *adj, adv*, **nter**, loitering, sluggish
cunctātĭo, ōnis *f*, delay, doubt
cunctātor, ōris *m*, loiterer, cautious person
cunctor *v.i.* 1, *dep*, to hesitate, delay
cunctus, a, um *adj*, all together
cŭnĕātim *adv*, wedge-shaped
cŭnĕo *v.t.* 1, to fasten with wedges
cŭnĕus, i *m*, wedge, wedge-shaped block of theatre seats or troop formation
cŭnīcŭlum, i *n*, tunnel, mine
cŭnīcŭlus, i *m*, rabbit

cūrātor, ōris *m*, manager
cūrātus, a, um *adj*, urgent
curcŭlĭo, ōnis *m*, weevil
cūrĭa, ae *f*, senate house, city ward
cūrĭālis, e *adj*, of the same ward
cūrĭōsus, a, um *adj, adv*, **ē**, careful, inquisitive
cūro *v.t.* 1, to take care of; *with acc. and gerundive*, to see to it that ..., to arrange, command
currĭcŭlum, i *n*, racecourse, chariot, racing, career
curro, cŭcurri, cursum *v.i.* 3, to run
currus, ūs *m*, chariot
cursim *adv*, swiftly
curso *v.i.* 1, to run to and fro
cursor, ōris *m*, runner, courier
cursus, ūs *m*, running, journey, speed, direction
curtus, a, um *adj*, shortened, humble
cŭrūlis, e *adj*, of a chariot; **sella cŭrūlis**, ivory chair of office used by high magistrates
curvāmen, ĭnis *n*, curve
curvo *v.t.* 1, to bend

curvus, a, um *adj*, bent, stooping
cuspis, ĭdis *f*, point, lance, spit, sting
custōdĭa, ae *f*, watch, guard, imprisonment, guard-room
custōdĭo *v.t.* 4, to guard, watch, keep, preserve
custos, ōdis *c*, guardian, gaoler
cŭtis, is *f*, skin, surface
cўăthus, i *m*, small ladle
cўcnēus, a, um *adj*, of a swan
cўcnus, i *m*, swan
cўlindrus, i *m*, roller, cylinder
cymba, ae *f*, small boat
cymbălum, i *n*, cymbal, bell
cymbĭum, ii *n*, bowl, basin
Cўnĭcus, i *m*, a Cynic philosopher
cўpărissus, i *f*, cypress tree

D

dactўlus, i , *m*, dactyl (metrical foot consisting of one long and two short syllables)
daedălus, a, um *adj*, skilful
daemŏnĭum, ii *n*, demon
damma (dāma), ae *f*, deer
damnātĭo, ōnis *f*, condemnation
damnātōrĭus, a, um *adj*, condemnatory
damnātus, a, um *adj*, guilty
damno *v.t.* 1, to condemn
damnōsus, a, um *adj*, *adv* ē, destructive
damnum, i *n*, damage, loss, fine
daps, dăpis *f*, formal banquet
dătĭo, ōnis *f*, distribution
dător, ōris *m*, giver
dē *prep. with abl*, from, down from, about, concerning, on account of
dĕa, ae *f*, goddess
dĕalbo *v.t.* 1, to whitewash
dĕambŭlo *v.i.* 1, to take a walk
dĕarmo *v.t.* 1, to disarm
dēbacchor *v.i.* 1, *dep*, to rage
dēbellātor, ōris *m*, conqueror
dēbello *v.i.t.* 1, to finish a war; subdue
dēbĕo *v.i.t.* 2, to be indebted; owe, (one) ought
dēbĭlis, e *adj*, disabled, weak

dēbĭlĭtas, ātis *f*, weakness
dēbĭlĭtātĭo, ōnis *f*, maiming, enervating
dēbĭlĭto *v.t.* 1, to cripple, weaken
dēbĭtor, ōris *m*, debtor
dēbĭtum, i *n*, debt
dēbĭtus, a, um *adj*, owed
dēcanto *v.i.* 1, to sing repeatedly
dēcēdo, ssi, ssum *v.i.* 3, to go away, cease, yield, resign
dĕcem *indecl. adj*, ten
Dĕcember (mensis) December
dĕcempĕda, ae *f*, measuring rod (ten feet long)
dĕcempĕdātor, ōris *m*, surveyor
dĕcemvĭrālis, e *adj*, of the decemviri
dĕcemvĭrātus, ūs *m*, the rank of decemvir
dĕcemvĭri, ōrum *m.pl*, commission of ten (early rulers of Rome)
dĕcens, ntis *adj*, *adv*, nter, proper, graceful
dĕcentĭa, ae *f*, comeliness
dēceptus, a, um *adj*, deceived
dēcerno, crēvi, crētum *v.i.t.* 3, to decide, resolve; fight
dēcerpo, psi, ptum *v.t.* 3, to pluck, gather
dēcertātĭo, ōnis *f*, struggle
dēcerto *v.i.t.* 1, to fight it out; struggle for
dēcessĭo, ōnis *f*, departure
dēcessus, ūs *m*, departure
dĕcet, cŭit *v.* 2, *impers*, it is becoming or proper
dēcĭdo, cĭdi *v.i.* 3, to fall down, die, perish
dēcĭdo, cīdi, cīsum *v.t.* 3, to cut off, settle
dĕcĭēs, (dĕcĭens) *adv*, ten times
dĕcĭma, ae *f*, tenth part, tithe
dĕcĭmānus, a, um *adj*, of tithes, of the tenth legion; **porta dĕcĭmāna**, main camp gate
dĕcĭmo *v.t.* 1, to punish every tenth man, decimate
dĕcĭmus, a, um *adj*, tenth
dēcĭpĭo, cēpi, ptum *v.t.* 3, to deceive
dēcīsĭo, ōnis *f*, decision
dēclāmātĭo ōnis *f*, practice in public speaking

dēclāmātor, ōris *m*, speech
expert
dēclāmātōrĭus, a, um *adj*,
rhetorical
dēclāmo *v.i.* 1, to practise
speaking
dēclāro *v.t.* 1, to make clear
dēclīnātĭo, ōnis *f*, avoidance,
bending
dēclīno *v.i.t.* 1, to turn aside
dēclīve, is *n*, slope
dēclīvis, e *adj*, sloping downwards
dēclīvĭtas, ātis *f*, slope
dēcoctor, ōris *m*, bankrupt
dēcoctus, a, um   *adj*, boiled,
refined
dēcŏlor, ōris *adj*, discoloured
dēcŏlōro *v.t.* 1, to discolour
dēcŏquo, xi, ctum *v.t.* 3, to boil
down, go bankrupt
dēcor, ōris *m*, elegance
dēcŏro *v.t.* 1, to adorn
dēcōrum, I *n*, decency
dēcōrus, a, um *adj, adv*, ē,
becoming, proper, elegant
dēcrĕpĭtus, a, um *adj*, decrepit
dēcresco, crēvi, tum *v.i.* 3, to
diminish, wane
dēcrētum, i *n*, decree, decision
dēcŭma, dēcŭmānus see decim...
dēcumbo, cŭbŭi *v.i.* 3, to lie down,
lie ill
dēcŭrĭa, ae *f*, section of ten
dēcŭrĭo *v.t.* 1, to divide into
sections
decŭrĭo, ōnis *m*, the head of ten,
superintendent
dēcurro, cŭcurri, cursum   *v.i.* 3, to
run down, complete a course,
manoeuvre, have recourse to
dēcursus, ūs *m*, descent, course,
manoeuvre, attack
dĕcus, ŏris *n*, ornament,
splendour
dĕcussātĭo, ōnis *f*, intersection
dēcŭtĭo, cussi, ssum *v.t.* 3, to
shake off, beat off
dēdĕcet, cŭit *v.* 2, *impers*, it is
unbecoming
dēdĕcŏro *v.t.* 1, to disgrace
dēdĕcus, ŏris *n*, disgrace, shame
dēdĭcātĭo, ōnis *f*, dedication
dēdĭco *v.t.* 1, to dedicate

dēdignor *v.t.* 1, *dep*, to disdain
dēdisco, dīdĭci *v.t.* 3, to forget
dēdītīcĭus, ii *m*, prisoner-of-war
dēdītĭo, ōnis   *f*, surrender
dēdĭtus, a, um *adj*, addicted to
dēdo, dēdĭdi, dĭtum *v.t.* 3, to give
up, surrender, devote
dēdŏcĕo *v.t.* 2, to teach one not to
...
dēdŏlĕo *v.i.* 2, to stop grieving
dēdūco, xi, ctum *v.t.* 3, to bring,
lead down, withdraw, conduct,
escort, mislead, subtract, launch
dēductĭo, ōnis *f*, diversion,
transplanting, inference
dēductus, a, um *adj*, fine-spun
dĕerro *v.i.* 1, to go astray
dēfătīgātĭo, ōnis *f*, exhaustion
dēfătīgo *v.t.* 1, to exhaust
dēfectĭo, ōnis *f*, rebellion, failure,
eclipse
dēfectus, ūs *m*, rebellion, failure,
eclipse
dēfectus, a, um *adj*, worn out
dēfendo, di, sum   *v.t.* 3, to repel,
defend, support
dēfensĭo, ōnis *f*, defence
dēfensor, ōris   *m*, protector
dēfĕro, ferre, tŭli, lātum *v.t, irreg*,
to bring down or away, convey,
refer, announce, indict, offer
dēfervesco, fervi *v.i.* 3, to cool
down
dēfessus, a, um *adj*, weary
dēfĕtiscor, fessus *v.i.* 3, *dep*, to
grow tired
dēfĭcĭo, fēci, fectum *v.i.t.* 3, to fail,
disappear, revolt; desert
dēfīgo, xi, xum *v.t.* 3, to fasten
down, astound
dēfingo, nxi *v.t.* 3, to shape
dēfīnĭo *v.t.* 4, to mark off, restrict,
define
dēfīnītĭo, ōnis   *f*, definition
dēfīnītus, a, um *adj, adv*, ē, precise
dēfixus, a, um *adj*, fixed
dēflàgrātĭo, ōnis *f*, destruction by
fire
dēflàgro *v.i.* 1, to burn out
dēflecto, xi, xum *v.i.t.* 3, to swerve;
divert
dēflĕo, ēvi, ētum *v.t.* 2, to deplore
dēflōresco, rŭi *v.i.* 3, to wither

dēflŭo, xi, xum *v.i.* 3, to flow down, vanish

dēfŏdĭo, fōdi, ssum *v.t.* 3, to dig deep, bury

dēfŏre *fut. infinitive* (**dēsum**)

dēformis, e *adj*, deformed, ugly

dēformĭtas, ātis *f*, ugliness

dēformo *v.t.* 1, to shape

dēformo, *v.t.* 1, to disfigure

dēfossus, a, um *adj*, buried

dēfraudo *v.t.* 1, to cheat

dēfrĭco, cŭi, ctum *v.t.* 1, to rub hard

dēfringo, frēgi, fractum *v.t.* 3, to break up, break off

dēfrŭtum, i *n*, syrup

dēfŭgĭo, fūgi *v.i.t.* 3, to escape; avoid

dēfunctus, a, um *adj*, having finished, deceased

dēfundo, fūdi, fūsum *v.t.* 3, to pour out

dēfungor, functus *v.* 3, *dep, with abl*, to bring to an end

dēgĕner, ĕris *adj*, unworthy of one's birth, ignoble

dēgenĕro *v.i.t.* 1, to deteriorate; impair

dēgo, dēgi *v.i.t.* 3, to live; spend

dēgrandĭnat *v. impers*, it is hailing, ceasing to hail

dēgrăvo, *v.t.* 1, to weigh down

dēgrĕdĭor, gressus *v.i.* 3, *dep*, to step down, dismount

dēgusto *v.t.* 1, to taste, graze

dēhinc *adv*, from here, hence, next, afterwards

dēhisco, hīvi *v.i.* 3, to split open, gape

dēhŏnesto *v.t.* 1, to disgrace

dēhortor *v.t.* 1, *dep*, to dissuade

dēĭcĭo, iēci, iectum *v.t.* 3, to throw down, drive out, lower

dēiectus, a, um *adj*, downcast

dēiectus, ūs *m*, descent, felling

dēin *adv*, from there, after that, afterwards

dēindĕ *adv*, from there, after that, afterwards

dēinceps *adv*, in succession

dēlābor, lapsus *v.i.* 3, *dep*, to fall, sink, glide down

dēlasso *v.t.* 1, to tire out

dēlātĭo, ōnis *f*, accusation

dēlātor, ōris *m*, informer

dēlectābĭlis, e *adj*, delightful

dēlectātĭo, ōnis *f*, delight, pleasure

dēlecto *v.t.* 1, to allure, charm

dēlectus, a, um *adj*, chosen

dēlectus, ūs *m*, choice, selection, levy

dēlectum hăbēre to hold a levy

dēlēgo *v.t.* 1, to dispach, assign, attribute

dēlēnīmentum, i *n*, allurement

dēlēnĭo *v.t.* 4, to soothe, charm

dēlĕo, lēvi, lētum *v.t.* 2, to destroy, finish

dēlībĕrātĭo, ōnis *f*, careful thought

dēlībĕrātus, a, um *adj*, settled

dēlībĕro *v.t.* 1, to consider, consult, resolve

dēlībo *v.t.* 1, to taste, pluck, detract from

dēlībūtus, a, um *adj*, smeared

dēlĭcātus, a, um *adj, adv*, e, charming, luxurious

dēlĭcĭae, ārum *f.pl*, pleasure, luxury, sweetheart, pet

dēlictum, i *n*, crime, offence

dēlĭgo, lēgi, lectum *v.t.* 3, to pick, choose, gather

dēlĭgo *v.t.* 1, to tie down

dēlinquo, līqui, lictum *v.i.* 3, to fail, offend

dēlīrātĭo, ōnis *f*, silliness

dēlĭrĭum, ii *n*, delirium

dēlīro *v.i.* 1, to be out of one's mind

dēlīrus, a, um *adj*, crazy

dēlĭtesco, tŭi *v.i.* 3, to lurk

delphīnus, i *m*, dolphin

dēlūbrum, i *n*, sanctuary

dēlūdo, si, sum *v.t.* 3, to mock

dēmando *v.t.* 1, to entrust

dēmens, ntis *adj, adv*, **nter**, out of one's mind

dēmensum, i *n*, ration

dēmentĭa, ae *f*, insanity

dēmĕrĕo *v.t.* 2, to deserve, oblige

dēmergo, si, sum *v.t.* 3, to immerse, sink

dēmētĭor, mensus *v.t.* 4, *dep*, to measure off

dēmēto, messŭi, ssum *v.t.* 3, to mow, reap, gather

dēmigro *v.i.* 1, to emigrate
dēmĭnŭo, ŭi, ūtum *v.t.* 3, to lessen, infringe
dēmĭnūtĭo, ōnis *f,* decrease
dēmīror *v.i.* 1, *dep,* to wonder
dēmissĭo, ōnis *f,* abasement
dēmissus, a, um *adj, adv,* ē, lowlying, drooping, downcast, shy
dēmitto, mīsi, ssum *v.t.* 3, to send down, lower, descend, enter upon, lose heart
dēmo, mpsi, mptum *v.t.* 3, to take away, remove
dēmōlĭor *v.t.* 4, *dep,* to pull down, destroy
dēmonstrātĭo, ōnis *f,* indication
dēmonstro *v.t.* 1, to point out
dēmŏrĭor, mortŭus *v.i.* 3, *dep,* to die
dēmŏror *v.i.t.* 1, *dep,* to loiter; restrain
dēmŏvĕo, mōvi, mōtum *v.t.* 2, to remove, put aside
dēmum *adv,* at last, not until then, only
dēmūto *v.i.t.* 1, to change
dēnārĭus, ii *m,* small Roman silver coin
dēnăto *v.i.* 1, to swim down
dēnĕgo *v.t.* 1, to deny completely
dēni, ae, a, *adj,* ten each, ten
dēnĭque *adv,* and then, at last, in short
dēnōmĭno *v.t.* 1, to name
dēnormo *v.t.* 1, to disfigure
dēnŏto *v.t.* 1, to mark, point out
dens, ntis *m,* tooth, prong
denso *v.t.* 1, to thicken, close up
densus, a, um *adj,* thick, frequent
dentālĭa, ĭum *n.pl,* plough-beam
dentātus, a, um *adj,* with teeth
dentĭfrĭcĭum, ii *n,* tooth-powder
dentĭo *v.i.* 4, to teethe
dentītĭo, ōnis *f,* teething
dentiscalpĭum, ii *n,* toothpick
dēnūbo, psi, ptum *v.i.* 3, to marry
dēnūdo *v.t.* 1, to lay bare
dēnuntĭātĭo, ōnis *f,* declaration
dēnuntĭo *v.t.* 1, to announce, command, warn
dēnŭō *adv,* anew, again
dĕorsum *adv,* downwards
dēpăciscor see **dēpĕciscor**

dēpasco, pāvi, pastum *v.t.* 3, to feed on, consume
dēpĕciscor, pectus (pactus) *v.t.* 3, *dep,* to bargin for
dēpĕcūlor *v.t.* 1, *dep,* to plunder
dēpello, pŭli, pulsum *v.t.* 3, to drive away, dissuade
dēpendĕo *v.i.* 2, to hang down, depend on
dēpendo, di, sum *v.t.* 3, to spend, pay
dēperdo, dĭdi, dĭtum *v.t.* 3, to destroy, lose
dēpĕrĕo *v.i.* 4, to perish completely, die with love for
dēpingo, pinxi, pictum *v.t.* 3, to paint, portray, sketch
dēplōro *v.i.t.* 1, to lament; deplore
dēpōno, pŏsŭi, pŏsĭtum *v.t.* 3, to put aside, entrust, bet, get rid of
dēpŏpŭlātĭo, ōnis *f,* pillaging
dēpŏpŭlor *v.t.* 1, *dep,* to plunder
dēporto *v.t.* 1, to carry down, carry away, banish, earn
dēposco, pŏposci *v.t.* 3, to demand, challenge
dēpŏsĭtum, i *n,* deposit, trust
dēprāvātĭo, ōnis *f,* corruption
dēprāvo *v.t.* 1, to pervert, corrupt
dēprĕcātĭo, ōnis *f,* pleading, intercession
dēprĕcātor, ōris *m,* pleader
dēprĕcor *v.t.* 1, *dep,* to avert by prayer, beseech, plead for
dēprĕhendo, di, sum *v.t.* 3, to catch, overtake, discover
dēpressus, a, um *adj,* low-lying
dēprĭmo, pressi, pressum *v.t.* 3, press down, sink, suppress
dēproelĭor *v.i.* 1, *dep,* to battle fiercely
dēprōmo, mpsi, mptum *v.t.* 3, to fetch out
dēprŏpĕro *v.i.t.* 1, to hasten; prepare hastily
dēpugno *v.i.* 1, to fight it out
dēpulsĭo, ōnis *f,* warding off
dēpūto *v.t.* 1, to prune
dērĕlinquo, līqui, lictum *v.t.* 3, to abandon completely
dērīdĕo, si, sum *v.t.* 2, to mock
dērĭgesco, gŭi *v.i.* 3, to stiffen
dērĭpĭo, rĭpŭi, reptum *v.t.* 3, to tear off, pull down

dērīsor, ōris *m*, scoffer
dērīvātĭo, ōnis *f*, turning off
dērīvo *v.t.* 1, to divert water
dērŏgo *v.t.* 1, to remove, restrict
dērōsus, a, um *adj*, nibbled
dēruptus, a, um *adj*, broken, steep
dēsaevĭo *v.i.* 4, to rage
dēscendo, di, sum *v.i.* 3, to go down, come down, go into battle, penetrate, resort to
dēscensus, ūs *m*, descent
dēscisco, īvi, ītum *v.i.* 3, to revolt, desert, degenerate
dēscrībo, psi, ptum *v.t.* 3, to transcribe, describe, define, arrange
dēscripta, ōrum *n.pl*, records
dēscriptĭo, ōnis *f*, sketch, description, arrangement
dēsĕco, cŭi, ctum *v.t.* 1, to cut off
dēsĕro, rŭi, rtum *v.t.* 3, to abandon
dēserta, ōrum *n.pl*, desert
dēsertor, ōris *m*, deserter
dēsertus, a, um *adj*, abandoned
dēservĭo *v.i.* 4, to serve wholeheartedly
dēses, ĭdis *adj*, indolent
dēsĭdĕo, sēdi *v.i.* 2, to sit idle
dēsīdĕrĭum, ii *n*, longing, grief, request
dēsīdĕro *v.t.* 1, to miss, crave for
dēsīdĭa, ae *f*, idleness
dēsĭdĭōsus, a, um *adj*, lazy
dēsīdo, sēdi *v.i.* 3, to sink down
dēsignātĭo, ōnis *f*, description, arrangement
dēsignātor, ōris *m*, master of ceremonies, undertaker
dēsignātus, a, um *adj*, elect
dēsigno *v.t.* 1, to mark out, indicate, appoint
dēsĭlĭo, sĭlŭi, sultum *v.i.* 4, to jump down
dēsĭno, sĭi, ĭtum *v.i.t.* 3, to cease; put an end to
dēsĭpĭo *v.i.* 3, to be foolish
dēsisto, stĭti, stĭtum *v.i.* 3, to leave off, halt
dēsōlātus, a, um *adj*, forsaken
dēsōlo *v.t.* 1, to abandon
dēspecto *v.t.* 1, to look down on
dēspectus, ūs *m*, view down on

dēspectus, a, um *adj*, despicable
dēspērātĭo, ōnis *f*, hopelessness
dēspērātus, a, um *adj*, past hope
dēspēro *v.i.t.* 3, to despair; give up as lost
dēspĭcĭo, exi, ctum *v.i.t.* 3, to look down; despise
dēspŏlĭo *v.t.* 1, to plunder
dēspondĕo, di, nsum *v.t.* 2, to promise (in marriage)
dēspūmo *v.t.* 1, to skim off
dēspŭo *v.i.t* 3, to spit; reject
dēstillo *v.i.* 1, to trickle, drip
dēstĭnātĭo, ōnis *f*, purpose
dēstĭnātum, i *n*, aim, intention
dēstĭnātus, a, um *adj*, fixed
dēstĭno *v.t.* 1, to secure, intend
dēstĭtŭo, ŭi, ūtum *v.t.* 3, to place, desert
dēstĭtūtus, a, um *adj*, abandoned
dēstringo, nxi, ctum *v.t.* 3, to strip off, unsheath, graze
dēstrŭo, xi, ctum *v.t.* 3, to demolish
dēsŭesco, sŭēvi, sŭētum *v.i.t.* 3, to become unused; cease to use
dēsŭētus, a, um *adj*, disused
dēsultor, ōris *m*, acrobat on horseback
dēsum, dĕesse, dēfŭi *v.i*, to be lacking, fail, desert
dēsūmo, mpsi, mptum *v.t.* 3, to select
dēsŭpĕr *adv*, from above
dēsurgo *v.i.* 3, to rise from
dētĕgo, xi, ctum *v.t.* 3, to expose
dētentus, a, um *adj*, kept back
dētergĕo, si, sum *v.t.* 2, to wipe clean
dētĕrĭor, ĭus *adj*, lower, worse
dētĕrĭus *adv*, worse, less
dētermĭno *v.t.* 1, to fix limits
dētĕro, trīvi, trītum *v.t.* 3, to rub or wear away, impair
dēterrĕo *v.t.* 2, to discourage
dētestābĭlis, e *adj*, detestable
dētestātĭo, ōnis *f*, cursing
dētestor *v.t.* 1, *dep*, to curse, loathe, ward off
dētexo, xŭi, xtum *v.t.* 3, to weave, finish
dētĭnĕo, tĭnŭi, tentum *v.t.* 2, to keep back, delay, lengthen

dētŏno, ŭi *v.i.* 1, to thunder, cease thundering

dētorquĕo, si, tum *v.t.* 2, to turn aside, distort

dētrăho, xi, ctum *v.t.* 3, to pull down, remove, deprecate

dētrecto *v.t.* 1, to reject, detract from

dētrīmentum, i *n*, loss, damage, defeat

dētrūdo, si, sum *v.t.* 3, to push down, dislodge

dētrunco *v.t.* 1, to lop off

dēturbo *v.t.* 1, to throw down

dĕūro, ussi, ustum *v.t.* 3, to burn

dĕus, i *m*, god

dēvinco, vīci, ctum *v.t.* 3, to conquer completely

dēvinctus see **dēvincĭo**

dēvīto *v.t.* 1, to avoid

dēvĭus, a, um *adj*, out-of-the-way

dēvŏco *v.t.* 1, to call away

dēvŏlo, *v.i.* 1, to fly down

dēvolvo, volvi, vŏlūtum *v.t.* 3, to roll down

dēvŏro *v.t.* 1, to gulp down

dēvōtĭo, ōnis *f*, consecration

dēvōtus, a, um *adj*, devoted

dēvŏvĕo, vōvi, vōtum *v.t.* 2, to dedicate, doom, devote

dexter, tĕra, tĕrum (tra, trum) *adj*, on the right, skilful, suitable

Insight

The following second declension nouns have minor irregularities in their declension: **deus** (= god) has nominative plural *dei* or *di*, genitive plural *deorum* or *deum*, ablative plural *deis* or *dis*; **vir** (= man) has genitive plural *virorum* or *virum*.

dēvasto *v.t.* 1, to devestate

dēvĕho, xi, ctum *v.t.* 3, to carry down, carry away

dēvĕnĭo, vēni, ventum *v.i.* 4, to come down, arrive at

dēversor *v.i.* 1, *dep*, to lodge

dēversor, ōris *m*, lodger

dēversōrĭum, ii *n*, inn

dēverto, ti, sum *v.i.t.* 3, to lodge, stay; turn aside

dēvexus, a, um *adj*, sloping down

dēvĭa, ōrum *n.pl*, lonely places

dēvincĭo, nxi, nctum *v.t.* 4, to tie up, endear

dextĕra (dextra), ae *f*, right hand

dextĕrĭtas, ātis *f*, dexterity

dextrorsum *adv*, on the right

di *pl.* of **dĕus**

dĭădēma, ătis *n*, crown, diadem

dĭăgōnālis, e *adj*, diagonal

dĭălectĭcus, a, um *adj*, of debate

dĭălŏgus, i *m*, conversation

dĭārĭa, ōrum *n.pl*, rations

dīca, ae *f*, lawsuit

dīcācĭtas, ātis *f*, wit

dīcax, ācis *adj*, witty

dīcĭo, ōnis *f*, dominion, power

dīco *v.t.* 1, to dedicate, devote

Insight

The **ablative absolute** is a Latin construction where both noun and verb are in the ablative case. In addition to this, the verb is always a participle. It is independent of the structure of the rest of the sentence (*Caesar, his dictis, ...* = Caesar, after saying these things...).

dīco, xi, ctum *v.t.* 3, to say, tell, appoint

dicta see **dictum**

dictāta, ōrum *n.pl*, written exercises

dictātĭo, ōnis *f*, dictation

dictātor, ōris *m*, dictator (Roman magistrate appointed in emergencies)

dictātūra, ae *f*, dictatorship

dictĭo, ōnis *f*, speaking, style

dictĭto *v.t.* 1, to repeat, dictate, compose

dicto *v.t.* 1, to declare, dictate

dictum, i *n*, saying, proverb, order

dictus, a, um *adj*, said, told

dīdo, dīdĭdi, dīdĭtum *v.t.* 3, to distribute

dīdūco, xi, ctum *v.t.* 3, to divide, scatter

dĭēs, dĭēī *m,f*, day

diffĕro, differre, distŭli, dīlātum *v.i.t*, *irreg*, to differ; scatter, publish, defer

differtus, a, um *adj*, crowded

diffibŭlo *v.t.* 1, to unbuckle

difficĭlis, e *adj*, *adv*, **ē**, **ĭter**, difficult, surly

difficultas, ātis *f*, difficulty, obstinacy

diffīdens, ntis *adj*, distrustful

diffīdentĭa, ae *f*, mistrust, despair

diffīdo, fīsus sum *v.i.* 3, *semi-dep*, *with dative*, to mistrust, despair

diffindo, fīdi, fīsum *v.t.* 3, to split, divide

diffingo *v.t.* 3, to re-shape

diffĭtĕor *v.t.* 2, *dep*, to deny

difflŭo *v.i.* 3, to flow away

diffŭgĭo, fūgi *v.i.* 3, to disperse

diffundo, fūdi, dūsum *v.t.* 3, to pour out, scatter

diffūsus, a, um *adj*, *adv*, **ē**, spread out, wide

dīgĕro, gessi, gestum *v.t.* 3, to separate, arrange, interpret

dīgesta, ōrum *n.pl*, digest of writings

dĭgĭtus, i *m*, finger, toe, inch

dīglădĭor *v.i.* 1, *dep*, to fight fiercely

dignātĭo, ōnis *f*, reputation

dignĭtas, ātis *f*, worthiness, rank, authority

dignor *v.t.* 1, *dep*, to consider someone worthy

dignus, a, um *adj*, *adv* **ē**, *with abl*, worthy, suitable

dīgrĕdĭor, gressus *v.i.* 3, *dep*, to go away

dīgressĭo, ōnis *f*, digression

dīgressus, ūs *m*, departure

dīiūdĭco *v.t.* 1, to decide

diiun... see **disiun...**

dīlābor, lapsus *v.i.* 3, *dep*, to dissolve, scatter, perish

dīlăcĕro *v.t.* 1, to tear apart, or to pieces

dīlănĭo *v.t.* 1, to tear apart, or to pieces

dīlātĭo, ōnis *f*, delay

dīlāto *v.t.* 1, to enlarge

dīlātor, ōris *m*, delayer

dīlātus, a, um *adj*, scattered

dīlectus, a, um *adj*, beloved

dīlĭgens, ntis *adj*, *adv*, **nter**, scrupulous, thrifty

dīlĭgentĭa, ae *f*, care, economy

dīlĭgo, lexi, lectum *v.t.* 3, to value highly

dīlūcesco, luxi *v.i.* 3, to grow light, dawn

dīlūcĭdus, a, um *adj*, clear

dīlūcŭlum, i *n*, dawn

dīlŭo, ŭi, ūtum *v.t.* 3, to wash away, dilute, drench, weaken

dīlūtum, i *n*, solution

dīlŭvĭes, ēi *f* (...ĭum, ii, *n*), flood, destruction

dīmētĭor, mensus *v.t.* 4, *dep*, to measure out

dīmĭcātĭo, ōnis *f*, struggle

**dīmĭco, ** *v.i.* 1, to struggle

dīmĭdĭātus, a, um *adj*, halved

dīmĭdĭum, ii *n*, a half

dīmĭdĭus, a, um *adj*, half

dīmissĭo, ōnis *f*, sending out

dīmitto, mīsi, missum *v.t.* 3, to send away, break up, disband, throw away, give up

dīmŏvĕo, mōvi, mōtum *v.t.* 2, to divide, part, remove

dīnŭmĕro *v.t.* 1, to count up

dĭplōma, ātis *n*, official letter of recommendation

dīra, ōrum *n.pl,* curses

dīrectus, a, um *adj, adv,* **ē,** straight, level

dīreptĭo, ōnis *f,* plundering

dīreptor, ōris *m,* plunderer

dīrĭgo, rexi, ctum *v.t.* 3, to put in a straight line, arrange

dīrĭmo, ēmi, emptum *v.t.* 3, to part, divide, interrupt

dīrĭpĭo, ŭi, reptum *v.t.* 3, to tear apart, plunder

dīrumpo, rūpi, ptum *v.t.* 3, to break in pieces, sever

dīrŭo, ŭi, ŭtum *v.t.* 3, to destroy

dīrus, a, um *adj,* fearful, ill-omened

discēdo, cessi, cessum *v.i.* 3, to depart, abandon, gape, deviate

disceptātĭo, ōnis *f,* discussion

discepto *v.t.* 1, to debate

discerno, crēvi, tum *v.t.* 3, to separate, distinguish between

discerpo, psi, ptum *v.t.* 3, to tear in pieces

discessus, ūs *m,* departure

discĭdĭum, ii *n,* separation

discinctus, a, um *adj,* casually dressed, slovenly

dīscindo, cĭdi, cissum *v.t.* 3, to cut to pieces, divide

discingo, nxi, nctum *v.t.* 3, to take off or undo (clothing)

disciplīna, ae *f,* teaching, knowledge, system, tactics

discĭpŭlus, i *m,* pupil

disclūdo, si, sum *v.t.* 3, to keep apart, separate

disco, dĭdĭci *v.t.* 3, to learn

discŏlor, ōris *adj,* of different colours

discordĭa, ae *f,* disagreement

discordo *v.i.* 1, to differ

discors, dis *adj,* disagreeing

discrĕpantĭa, ae *f,* discrepancy

discrĕpo, ŭi *v.i.* 1, to differ

dīscrībo, scripsi, ptum *v.t.* 3, to distribute

discrīmen, ĭnis *n,* division, distinction, crisis, danger

discrīmĭno *v.t.* 1, to divide

discrŭcĭo *v.t.* 1, to torture

discumbo, cŭbŭi, cŭbĭtum *v.i.* 3, to recline at table

discurro, curri, cursum *v.i.* 3, to run about

discursus, ūs *m,* bustle, activity

discus, i *m,* discus, quoit

discŭtĭo, cussi, ssum *v.t.* 3, to shatter, disperse

dīsertus, a, um *adj, adv,* **ē,** fluent, clear

disĭcĭlo, ĭēci, ctum *v.t.* 3, to scatter, destroy

disiunctus, a, um *adj, adv,* **ē,** distant, abrupt

disiungo, nxi, nctum *v.t.* 3, to separate, unyoke

dispar, ăris *adj,* unlike, unequal

dispăro *v.t.* 1, to divide

dispello, pŭli, pulsum *v.t.* 3, to drive away, scatter

dispendĭum, ii *n,* expense, cost

dispenso *v.t.* 1, to pay out, distribute, manage

disperdo, dĭdi, dĭtum *v.t.* 3, to spoil, ruin

dispĕrĕo *v.i.* 4, to perish

dispergo, si, sum *v.t.* 3, to scatter about

dispertĭo *v.t.* 4, to distribute

dispĭcĭo, spexi, ctum *v.i.t.* 3, to look around; discern, reflect on

displīcĕo *v.i.* 2, to displease

dispōno, pŏsŭi, pŏsĭtum *v.t.* 3, to arrange, dispose

dispŏsĭtus, a, um *adj,* arranged

dispungo, xi, ctum *v.t.* 3, to check

dispūtātĭo, ōnis *f,* debate, dispute

dispūtātor, ōris *m,* debater

dispūto *v.i.t* 1, theorize; examine, discuss

dissēmĭno *v.t.* 1, to spread about

dissensĭo, ōnis *f,* disagreement

dissentĭo, si, sum *v.i.* 4, to disagree, differ

dissĕrēnat *v.impers.* 1, to be clear

dissĕro, rŭi, rtum *v.t.* 3, to discuss, argue

dissĭdĕo, ēdi, essum *v.i.* 2, to differ, disagree

dissĭlĭo, ŭi *v.i.* 4 to leap apart, split

dissĭmĭlis, e *adj, adv,* **ĭter,** unlike, different

dissĭmĭlĭtūdo, ĭnis *f,* unlikeness

dissĭmŭlātus, a, um *adj,* disguised

dissĭmŭlo *v.t.* 1, to disguise, hide

dissĭpātĭo, ōnis *f,* scattering, destruction

dissĭpo *v.t.* 1, to scatter, rout
dissŏcĭābĭlis, e *adj,* dividing
dissŏcĭo *v.t.* 1, to estrange
dissŏlūtĭo, ōnis *f,* break-up,
destruction
dissŏlūtus, a, um *adj,* loose
dissolvo, solvi, sŏlūtum *v.t.* 3, to
unloose, separate, pay, annul,
destroy
dissŏnus, a, um *adj,* discordant
dissuādĕo, si, sum *v.t.* 2, to advise
against
dissulto *v.i.* 1, to burst apart
distans, ntis *adj,* distant
distendo, di, tum *v.t.* 3, to stretch
out, distend, torture
distentus, a, um *adj,* full
distentus, a, um *adj,* busy
distinctĭo, ōnis *f,* difference
distinctus, a, um *adj, adv,* ē,
separate, clear, adorned
distĭnĕo, tĭnŭi, tentum *v.t.* 2, to
keep apart, perplex, hinder
distinguo, nxi, nctum *v.t.* 3, to
separate, discriminate, adorn
disto *v.i.*1, to be distant, differ
distorquĕo, rsi, rtum *v.t.* 2, to
twist, distort, torture
distortĭo, ōnis *f,* distortion
distortus, a, um *adj,* deformed
distractĭo, ōnis *f,* division
distractus, a, um *adj,* bewildered
distrăho, xi, ctum *v.t.* 3, to pull
apart, divide, distract, perplex
distrĭbŭo, ŭi, ūtum *v.t.* 3, to
distribute
distrĭbūtē *adv,* methodically
distrĭbūtĭo, ōnis *f,* distribution
districtus, a, um *adj,* busy, strict
distringo, nxi, ctum *v.t.* 3, to
stretch tight, distract the
attention
disturbo *v.t.* 1, to disturb,
demolish, frustrate
dīto *v.t.* 1, to enrich
dĭū *adj,* a long time
dĭurnus, a, um *adj,* daily
dĭurna ōrum *n.pl,* records
dĭūtĭnus, a, um *adj,* long-lasting
dĭūtĭus *comp. adv,* longer
dĭūturnĭtas, ātis *f,* long duration
dĭūturnus, a, um *adj, adv,* ē, long-
lasting

dīva, ae *f,* goddess
dīvello, velli, vulsum *v.t.* 3, to tear
to pieces, destroy
dīvendo, (*no perfect*)*, itum* *v.t.* 3,
to retail
dīverbĕro *v.t.* 1, to cut
dīversĭtas, ātis *f,* disagreement
dīversus, a, um *adj, adv,* ē,
opposite, contrary, hostile,
separate, different
dīverto, ti, sum *v.i.* 3, to diverge
dīves, ĭtis *adj,* rich
dīvĭdo, vīsi, sum *v.t.* 3, to separate,
distribute, destroy
dīvĭdŭus, a, um *adj,* divisible
dīvīnĭtas, ātis *f,* divinity
dīvīnĭtus *adv,* providentially
dīvīno *v.t.* 1, to prophesy
dīvīnus, a, um *adj, adv,* ē, divine,
prophetic, superhuman
dīvinus, i *m,* prophet
dīvīsĭo, ōnis *f,* division
dīvīsor, ōris *m,* distributor of
bribes to electors
dīvĭtĭae, ārum *f.pl,* wealth
dīvortĭum, ii *n,* separation
dīvulgo *v.t.* 1, to make known
dīvum, i *n,* sky
dīvus, a, um *adj,* divine
dīvus, i *m* (a, ae *f*), god, (goddess)
do, dĕdi, dătum *v.t.* 1, to give
dŏcĕo, ŭi, doctum *v.t.* 2, to teach,
inform
dŏcĭlis, e *adj,* easily taught
doctor, ōris *m,* teacher
doctrīna, ae *f,* teaching, education,
learning
doctus, a, um *adj, adv,* ē, learned,
skilled
dŏcŭmentum, i *n,* lesson, example
dōdrans, ntis *m,* three quarters
dogma, ătis *n,* doctrine, dogma
dŏlābra, ae *f,* pickaxe
dŏlĕo *v.i.t.* 2, to suffer pain;
grieve, deplore
dōlĭum, ii *n,* large jar
dŏlo *v.t.* 1, to chop, beat
dŏlor, ōris *m,* pain, sorrow
dŏlōsus, a, um *adj,* deceitful
dŏlus, i *m,* fraud, trick
dŏmābĭlis, e *adj,* tamable
dŏmestĭcus, a, um *adj,* of the
home

dŏmestĭci, ōrum *m.pl*, family,
  servants, escort
dŏmi *loc*, at home

dōtātus, a, um *adj*, endowed
dōto *v.t.* 1, to endow

Insight

In Latin, nouns are declined. There are five declensions.
Each declension has six cases: nominative, accusative,
genitive, vocative, dative, ablative. Moreover, there is an old
seventh case, the locative, which still survives in some
expressions and which tells us where something is happening
(e.g. domi = at home).

---

dŏmĭcĭlĭum, ii *n*, dwelling place
dŏmĭna, ae *f*, mistress, lady
dŏmĭnans, ntis *adj*, ruling
dŏmĭnātĭo, ōnis *f*, absolute rule
dŏmĭnātus, ūs *m*, absolute rule
dŏmĭnĭum, ii *n*, banquet, property-
  ownership
dŏmĭnor *v.i.* 1, *dep*, to reign
dŏmĭnus, i *m*, master, owner

drachma, ae *f*, small Greek silver
  coin
drăco, ōnis *m*, water snake
drŏmas, ădis *m*, dromedary
drўas, ădis *f*, wood nymph
dŭbĭē *adv*, doubtfully
dŭbĭtātĭo, ōnis *f*, doubt,
  uncertainity
dŭbĭto *v.i.t.* 1, to hesitate; doubt

Insight

The ending for the **vocative** is the same as the nominative for
all nouns of all declensions except for second declension
masculine nouns ending in -**us** where the vocative singular
ends in -**e** (*dominus* nom. – *domine* voc.).

---

dŏmĭto *v.t.* 1, to tame
dŏmĭtor, ōris *m*, tamer
dŏmĭtus, a, um *adj*, tamed
dŏmo, ŭi, ĭtum *v.t.* 1, to tame,
  conquer
dŏmus, ūs *f*, house, home
dōnārĭum, ii *n*, altar, sanctuary
dōnātĭo, ōnis *f*, donation
dōnātus, a, um *adj*, presented
dōněc *conj*, while, until
dōno *v.t.* 1, to present, remit
dōnum, i *n*, gift, present
dorcas, ădis *m*, gazelle
dormĭo *v.i.* 4, to sleep
dormĭto *v.i.* 1, to fall asleep
dorsum, i *n*, the back, ridge, ledge
dōs, dōtis *f*, dowry
dōtālis, e *adj*, of a dowry

dŭbīum, ii *n*, doubt
dŭbĭus, a, um *adj*, doubtful,
  dangerous
dŭcēni, ae, a *adj*, two hundred
  each
dŭcenti, ae, a *adj*, two hundred
dūco, xi, ctum *v.t.* 3, to lead,
  marry, construct, receive,
  prolong, consider
ductĭlis, e *adj*, moveable, malleable
ductor, ōris *m*, leader
ductus, ūs *m*, bringing, leadership
dūdum *adv*, some time ago,
  formerly
dulcē *adv*, sweetly
dulcēdo, ĭnis *f*, sweetness, charm
dulcĭtūdo, ĭnis *f*, sweetness, charm

dulcis, e *adj, adv,* **ĭter,** sweet, pleasant, dear

dum *conj,* while, until, provided that

dūmētum, i *n,* thicket

dummŏdo *adv,* as long as

dūmōsus, a, um *adj,* bushy

dūmus, i *m,* bramble

dumtaxat *adv,* in so far as, merely, at least

dŭŏ, ae, ŏ *adj,* two

dŭŏdĕcīes *adv,* twelve times

dŭŏdĕcim *adj,* twelve

dŭŏdĕcīmus, a, um *adj,* twelfth

dŭŏdēni, ae, a *adj,* twelve each

dŭŏdēvīcensīmus, a, um *adj,* eighteenth

dŭŏdēvīginti *adj,* eighteen

dŭŏvĭri, ōrum *m.pl,* board or commission of two men

dùplex, ĭcis *adj, adv,* **ĭter,** double, deceitful

dùplĭco *v.t.* 1, to double

dùplus, a, um *adj,* double

dūra, ōrum *n.pl,* hardship

dūrābĭlis, e *adj,* durable

dūrātus, a, um *adj,* hardened

dūrē *adv,* roughly

dūresco, rŭi *v.i.* 3, to harden

dūrītĭa, ae *f,* hardness, strictness, austerity

dūro *v.i.t.* 1, to be hard, endure; harden

dūrus, a, um *adj, adv,* **ē, ĭter,** hard, rough, harsh, stern

dux, dŭcis *m,* leader, commander

dўnastes, ae *m,* chieftain

dўsentĕrĭa, ae *f,* dysentery

dyspnoea, ae *f,* asthma

E

ē *prep. with abl,* out of, from, since

ĕa see **is**

ĕādem see **idem**

ĕātĕnus *adv,* so far

ĕvĕnus, i *f,* ebony (tree)

ēbĭbo, bi, bĭtum *v.t.* 3, to drink up, absorb, squander

ēblandĭor *v.t.* 4, *dep,* to obtain by flattery

ēbrĭĕtas, ātis *f,* drunkenness

ēbrĭōsus, a, um *adj,* addicted to drink

ēbrĭus, a, um *adj,* drunk

ēbullĭo *v.t.* 4, to boast about

ēbŭlum, i *n,* dwarf elder

ēbŭr, ŏris *n,* ivory

ēburnĕus, a, ūm *adj,* of ivory

ecce *demonstrative adv,* see!

ĕchīnus, i *m,* hedgehog, sea urchin, rinsing bowl

ēchō, ūs *f,* echo

ecquando *interr. adv,* at any time?

ecqui, ae, od *interr. pron, adj,* any? anyone?

ecquis, id *interr. pron,* anyone? anything?

ēdācītas, ātis *f,* gluttony

ĕdax, ācis *adj,* greedy

ēdentŭlus, a, um *adj,* toothless

ēdīco, xi, ctum *v.t.* 3, to publish, declare

ēdictum, i *n,* proclamation

ēdisco, dĭdĭci *v.t.* 3, to learn by heart, study

ēdissĕro, rŭi, rtum *v.t.* 3, to explain in full

ēdĭtĭo, ōnis *f,* bringing out, publishing

ēdĭtus, a, um *adj,* high, raised, brought out

ēdo, ēdi, ēsum *v.t.* 3, to eat

ēdo, dĭdi, dĭtum *v.t.* 3, to produce, bring out, declare, cause, erect

ēdŏcĕo, cŭi, ctum *v.t.* 2, to teach thoroughly

ēdŏmo, ŭi, ĭtum *v.t.* 1, to subdue

ēdŭcātĭo, ōnis *f,* bringing up, education

ēdūco, xi, ctum *v.t.* 3, to lead or bring out, summon, educate, erect

ēdūco *v.t.* 1, to bring up (child)

ĕdūlis, e *adj,* eatable

effātus, a, um *adj,* established

effectĭo, ōnis *f,* doing, performing

effectus, a, um *adj,* completed

effectus, ūs *m,* accomplishment

effēmĭnātus, a, um *adj,* effeminate

effĕrātus, a, um *adj,* wild

effĕro, efferre, extŭli, ēlātum *v.t, irreg,* to bring out, bury, declare, raise; *in passive or with* **se,** to be haughty

effĕro *v.t.* 1, to brutalize

effĕrus, a, um *adj,* savage

effervesco, ferbŭi *v.i.* 3, to boil up, rage

effervo *v.i.* 3, to boil over
effētus, a, um *adj,* exhausted
efficax, ācis *adj,* efficient
efficiens, ntis *adj, adv,* nter, efficient
efficio, fēci, fectum *v.t.* 3, to bring about, complete, produce
effictus, a, um *adj,* fashioned
effiges, ēi *f,* portrait, copy
effingo, nxi, ctum *v.t.* 3, to shape, fashion, portray
efflāgito *v.t.* 1, to request urgently
efflo *v.t.* 1, to breathe out
efflōresco, rŭi *v.i.* 3, to bloom
efflŭo, xi *v.i.* 3, to flow out, vanish
effŏdĭo, fōdi, fossum *v.t.* 3, to dig out, dig up
effor *v.t.* 1, *dep,* to speak out
effrēnātus, a, um *adj,* unruly
effrēnus, a, um *adj,* unrestrained
effringo, frēgi, fractum *v.t.* 3, to break open, smash
effŭgĭo, fŭgi *v.i.t.* 3, to escape; flee from, avoid
effŭgĭum, ii *n,* escape
ĕffulgĕo, si *v.i.* 2, to gleam
effundo, fūdi, fūsum *v.t.* 3, to pour out, let loose, squander; *in passive or with reflexive,* to rush out
effūsĭo, ōnis *f,* outpouring, profusion
effūsus, a, um *adj, adv,* ē, poured out, spread out, wide, loosened
effūtĭo *v.t.* 4, to blurt out
ĕgĕlĭdus, a, um *adj,* cool
ĕgens, ntis *adj,* in want of
ĕgēnus, a, um *adj,* in want of
ĕgĕo *v.i.* 2, *with abl,* to be in need of
ēgĕro, ssi, stum *v.t.* 3, to bring out
ĕgestas, ātis *f,* poverty
ĕgŏ *pers. pron,* I

ĕgŏmet *pron,* I myself
ēgrĕdĭor, gressus *v.i.t.* 3, *dep,* to go or come out; leave, exceed
ēgrĕgĭus, a, um *adj, adv,* ē, distinguished
ēgressus, ūs *m,* departure, passage
ēheu! alas!
ēiă! hey! I say!
ēiăcŭlor *v.t.* 1, *dep,* to shoot out
ēīcĭo, iēci, iectum *v.t.* 3, to drive out, expel, wreck; *with reflexive,* to rush out
ēiecto *v.t.* 1, to vomit
ēiūro *v.t.* 1, to reject on oath, abandon
ēius *genit. of* is, ea, id
ēiusmŏdi in such a manner
ēlābor, lapsus *v.i.* 3, *dep,* to slip away, escape
ēlăbōrātus, a, um *adj,* elaborate
ēlăbōro *v.i.t.* 1, to make an effort; take pains with
ēlanguesco, gŭi *v.i.* 3, to grow feeble
ēlātĭo, ōnis *f,* lifting up, passion
ēlātro *v.t.* 1, to bark loudly
ēlātus, a, um *adj,* raised, lofty
ēlectĭo, ōnis *f,* selection
ēlectrum, i *n,* amber
ēlectus, a, um *adj,* selected
ēlĕgans, ntis, *adj, adv,* nter, refined, tasteful
ēlĕgantĭa, ae *f,* refinement
ēlĕgi, ōrum *m.pl,* elegy
ēlĕgĭa, ae *f,* elegy
ēlĕmentum, i *n,* element, first principle; *pl,* rudiments
ēlĕphantus, I *m,* elephant, ivory
ēlĕvo *v.t.* 1, to lift up, weaken, disparage
ēlĭcĭo, cŭi, cĭtum *v.t.* 3, to lure out, call out

Insight

The **dative** is the case of an indirect object. It also indicates the person to whose advantage/disadvantage something is done, the agent showing by whom something is done and possession with the verb 'to be' (*est mihi pecunia*). The main meanings are 'to', 'for', 'by' and 'from'. Several verbs are followed by the dative.

ēlīdo, si, sum *v.t.* 3, to knock or force out, shatter

ēlīgo, lēgi, ctum *v.t.* 3, to choose

ēlinguis, e *adj,* speechless

ēlixus, a, um *adj,* boiled

ellychnĭum, ii *n,* lampwick

ēlŏco *v.t.* 1, to let (a farm)

ēlŏcūtĭo, ōnis *f,* expression, elocution

ēlŏgĭum, ii *n,* saying, inscription

ēlŏquens, ntis *adj,* eloquent

ēlŏquentĭa, ae *f,* eloquence

ēlŏquor, ēlŏcūtus *v.t.* 3, *dep,* to speak out, declare

ēlūcĕo, xi *v.i.* 2, to shine out

ēluctor *v.i.t.* 1, *dep,* to struggle out; struggle out of

ēlūdo, si, sum *v.t.* 3, to evade, cheat, frustrate

ēlūgĕo, xi *v.t.* 2, to mourn for

ēlŭo, ŭi, ūtum *v.t.* 3, to wash off, clean

ēlūtus, a, um *adj,* insipid

ēlŭvĭes *(no genit)* *f,* inundation

ēlŭvĭo, ōnis *f,* inundation

ēmancĭpo *v.t.* 1, to set free, transfer, sell

ēmāno *v.i.* 1, to flow out, arise from

embŏlĭum ii *n,* interlude

ēmendātĭo, ōnis *f,* correction

ēmendātor, ōris *m,* corrector

ēmendātus, a, um *adj,* faultless

ēmendo *v.t.* 1, to correct

ēmentĭor *v.t.* 4, *dep,* to assert falsely

ēmercor *v.t.* 1, *dep,* to purchase

ēmĕrĕo *v.t.* 2, (ēmĕrĕor *v.t.* 2, *dep*), to deserve, earn, complete one's military service

ēmergo, si, sum *v.i.* 3, to come out, escape

ēmĕrĭtus, a, um *adj,* worn out

ēmētĭor, mensus *v.t.* 4, *dep,* to measure out, travel over

ēmīco, ŭi, ātum *v.i.* 1, to spring out, appear

ēmĭgro *v.i.* 1, to depart

ēmĭnens, ntis *adj,* projecting, distinguished

ēmĭnentĭa, ae *f,* prominence

ēmĭnĕo *v.i.* 2, to stand out, excel

ēmĭnus *adv,* from or at a distance

ēmissārĭum, ii *n,* drain, vent

ēmissārĭus, ii *m,* spy

ēmissĭo, ōnis *f,* sending out, hurling (of missiles)

ēmitto, mīsi, ssum *v.t.* 3, to send out, produce, publish; with manū, to set free

ēmo, ēmi, emptum *v.t.* 3, to buy

ēmŏdŭlor *v.t.* 1, *dep,* to sing

ēmollĭo *v.t.* 4, to soften

ēmŏlŭmentum, i *n,* effort, profit

ēmŏrĭor, mortuus *v.i.* 3, *dep,* to die

ēmŏvĕo, mōvi, tum *v.t.* 2, to remove, shake

empīrĭcus, a, um *adj,* empirical

emplastrum, i *n,* plaster

empŏrĭum, ii *n,* market

emptĭo, ōnis *f,* purchase

emptor, ōris *m,* buyer

ēmunctus, a, um *adj,* clean, shrewd

ēmungo, nxi, nctum *v.t.* 3, to wipe the nose

ēmūnĭo *v.t.* 4, to fortify

ēn! see! come!

ēnarro *v.t.* 1, to expound

ēnascor, nātus *v.i.* 3, *dep,* to spring up, be born

ēnāto *v.i.* 1, to swim away

ēnectus, a, um *adj,* killed

ēnĕco, ŭi, ctum *v.t.* 1, to kill, exhaust

ēnervo *v.t.* 1, to weaken

ĕnim *conj,* for, indeed

ĕnimvēro *conj,* certainly

ēnīsus, a, um *adj,* strenuous

ēnĭtĕo *v.i.* 2, to shine out

ēnĭtesco, tŭi *v.i.* 3, to shine out

ēnītor, nīsus (nixus) *v.i.t.* 3, *dep,* to struggle upwards, climb, strive; give birth to, ascend

ēnixus, a, um *adj, adv,* ē, strenuous, earnest

ēno *v.i.* 1, to swim out or away

ēnōdātĭo, ōnis *f,* explanantion

ēnōdis, e *adj,* smooth, clear

ēnōdo *v.t.* to elucidate

ēnormis, e *adj,* enormous, shapeless

ēnormĭtas, ātis *f,* shapelessness

ēnōto *v.t.* 1, to note down

ensĭger, ĕra, ĕrum *adj,* carrying a sword

ensis, is *m,* sword

ēnūclěātus, a, um *adj, adv,* **ē,**
pure, clear, simple
ēnūměrātǐo, ōnis *f,* counting,
recapitulation
ēnǔměro *v.t.* 1, to count, relate
ēnuntǐo *v.t.* 1, to disclose, declare
ěo, īre, īvi (ii), ǐtum *v.i, irreg,* to go;
with **pedibus,** to vote for

ěquǔlěus, i, *m,* colt, the rack
ěquus, i *m,* horse
ěra, ae *f,* lady of the house
ērādīco *v.t.* 1, to root out
ērādo, si, sum *v.t.* 3, to scrape out,
abolish
ērectus, a, um *adj,* upright, noble,
haughty, resolute

Insight

As well as English, Latin has some **irregular** verbs. Irregular
verbs are those verbs that do not follow any of the set
patterns. They are not in any of the four conjugations, and
have their own individual forms. An example of irregular
verb is *eo* (= I go).

ěō *adv,* to that place, to such an
extent, so long, besides
eo ... quo, (*with comparatives*) the
more ... the more
ěōdem *adv,* to the same place, to
the same point or purpose
èōus, i *m,* (**a, um** *adj*), east
ěphēbus, i *m,* a youth
ěphippǐum, ii *n,* saddle
ěphǒrus, i *m,* Spartan magistrate
ěpǐcus, a, um *adj,* epic
ěpiscǒpus, i *m,* bishop
ěpǐgramma, ǎtis *n,* inscription
ěpistǒla, ae *f,* letter
ěpistǒmǐum, ii *n,* valve
ěpǐtǒmē (ěpǐtǒma), ēs *f,*
abridgement
ěpǒs *n,* epic poem
ēpōto, pōtum *v.t.* 1, to drink up
ěpǔlae, ārum *f.pl,* food, banquet
ěpǔlor *v.i.t.* 1, *dep,* to banquet; eat
ěqua, ae *f,* mare
ěquārǐa, ae *f,* stud of horses
ěques, ǐtis *m,* horseman, knight
ěquester, tris, tre *adj,* of a
horseman, of cavalry
ěquǐdem *adv,* indeed, of course,
for my part
ēquīnus, a, um *adj,* of horses
ěquǐtātǐo, ōnis *f,* riding on
horseback
ěquǐtātus, ūs *m,* cavalry
ěquǐto *v.i.* 1, to ride

ērēpo, psi *v.i.t.* 3, to creep out;
creep over
ergā *prep. with acc,* towards
ergastǔlum, i *n,* detention centre
ergō *adv,* therefore; *prep.*
following genit, on account of
ērǐgo, rexi, rectum *v.t.* 3, to raise
up, encourage
ěrīlis, e *adj,* of the master, or
mistress
ērǐǐo, rǐpǔi, reptum *v.t.* 3, to snatch,
take away; *with reflexive,* to
escape
ērǒgātǐo, ōnis *f,* paying out
ērǒgo *v.t.* 1, to pay out, squander
errābundus, a, um *adj,* wandering
errātǐcus, a, um *adj,* wandering
errātǐcus, a, um *adj,* rambling
errātum, i *n,* mistake
erro *v.i.* 1, to stray, err
erro, ōnis *m,* wanderer
error, ōris *m,* straying, mistake
ěrǔbesco, bǔi *v.i.* 1, to blush, feel
ashamed
ērūca, ae *f,* caterpillar
ēructo *v.t.* 1, to belch, emit
ērǔdǐo *v.t.* 4, to polish, instruct
ērǔdītǐo, ōnis *f,* learning
ērǔdītus, a, um *adj, adv,* **ē,**
learned, skilled
ērumpo, rūpi, ptum *v.i.t.* 1, to
break out; burst
ērǔo, ǔi, ǔtum *v.t.* 3, to throw out,
dig out, destroy, rescue

ēruptĭo, ōnis *f*, break out
ĕrus, i *m*, master of the house
ervum, i *n*, wild pea
esca, ae *f*, food, bait
ēscendo, di, sum *v.i.* 3, to climb
ēscensĭo, ōnis *f*, aascent
escŭlentus, a, um *adj*, eatable
esse see sum
essĕdārĭus, i *m*, chariot fighter
essĕdum, i *n,* war chariot
ēsŭrĭens, ntis *adj*, hungry
ēsŭrĭo *v.i.t.* 4, to be hungry; long
  for
ĕt *conj*, and, as

ēventus, ūs *m*, occurrence, result,
  fortune
ēverbĕro *v.t.* 1, to strike hard
ēverro, verri, versum *v.t.* 3, to
  sweep out
ēversĭo, ōnis *f*, destruction
ēversor, ōris *m*, destroyer
ēversus, a, um *adj*, overthrown
ēverto, ti, sum *v.t.* 3, to overthrow,
  ruin
ēvĭdens, ntis *adj*, apparent
ēvĭgĭlo *v.i.t.* 1, to wake up; keep
  awake, keep watch through
ēvincĭo, nxi, nctum *v.t.* 4, to bind
  round

Insight

There are several words in Latin that mean 'and': et, atque,
ac, and -que joined to the second of two words; *et...et*
means 'both...and'; *aut...aut* or *vel...vel* mean 'either...or';
neque means 'and not'; *neque...neque* or *nec...nec* mean
'neither...nor'.

ĕtĕnim *conj*, and indeed
ĕtĭam *conj*, also, even, still
ĕtĭamnum, ĕtĭamnunc *adv*, even
  then, till now
etsi *conj*, although, even if
eu! well done!
eurīpus, i *m*, canal
eurōus, a, um *adj*, eastern
eurus, i *m*, east wind
ēvādo, si, sum *v.i.* 3, to go out,
  escape; leave behind
ēvăgor *v.i.t.* 1, *dep*, to stray;
  overstep
ēvălesco, lŭi *v.i.* 3, to grow strong,
  to be able
ēvānesco, nŭi *v.i.* 3, to vanish
ēvānĭdus, a, um *adj*, vanishing
ēvasto *v.t.* 1, to devastate
ēvĕho, xi, ctum *v.t.* 3, to carry out;
  in passive, to ride or move out
ēvello, velli, vulsum *v.t.* 3, to tear
  out, eradicate
ēvĕnĭo, vēni, ventum *v.i.* 4, to
  come out, turn out, result
ēventum, i *n*, occurrence, result,
  fortune
ēventus, ūs *m*, occurrence, result,
  fortune

ēvinco, vīci, ctum *v.t.* 3, to
  conquer completely, succeed
ēviscĕro *v.t.* 1, to tear apart
ēvīto *v.t.* 1, to avoid
ēvŏcāti, ōrum *m.pl*, reservists
ēvŏco *v.t.* 1, to call out
ēvŏlo *v.i.* 1, to fly away
ēvolvo, vi, vŏlūtum *v.t.* 3, to unroll
  (and read a book), disclose
ēvŏmo, ŭi, ĭtum *v.t.* 3, to spit out,
  vomit
ēvulsĭo, ōnis *f*, pulling out
ex (ē) *prep. with abl*, out of, from,
  after, since, on account of,
  according to, made of
exăcerbo *v.t.* 1, to irritate
exactĭo, ōnis *f*, debt or tax
  collecting, expelling
exactor, ōris *m*, expeller,
  superintendent, tax collector
exactus, a, um *adj*, accurate
exăcŭo, ŭi, ūtum *v.t.* 3, to sharpen,
  stimulate
exadversum (...us) *adv and prep.
  with acc*, opposite
exaedĭfĭco *v.t.* 1, to construct
exaequo *v.t.* 1, to place equal
exaestŭo *v.i.* 1, to seethe
exaggĕro *v.i.* 1, to heap up

exăgĭto *v.t.* 1, to disturb
exalbesco, bŭi *v.i.* 3, to turn pale
exāmen, ĭnis *n*, crowd, swarm
exāmĭno *v.t.* 1, to weigh, test
exănĭmātĭo, ōnis *f*, terror
exănĭmātus, a, um *adj*, out of breath
exănĭmis, e *adj*, lifeless
exănĭmus, a, um *adj*, lifeless
exănĭmo *v.t.* 1, to deprive of breath, kill, terrify
exardesco, arsi, sum *v.i.* 3, to be inflamed
exāresco, rŭi *v.i.* 3, to dry up
exăro *v.t.* 1, to plough, write
exaspĕro *v.t.* 1, to roughen, provoke
exauctōro *v.t.* 1, to discharge honourably or dishonourably from army
exaudĭo *v.t.* 4, to hear, grant
excandesco, dŭi *v.i.* 3, to glow
excēdo, ssi, ssum *v.i.t.* 3, to depart, die; leave, exceed
excellens, ntis *adj, adv,* **nter**, distinguished, excellent
excello, cellŭi, lsum *v.i.* 3, to be eminent, excel
excelsus, a, um *adj*, distinguished
exceptĭo, ōnis *f*, restriction
excepto *v.t.* 1, to catch
excerno, crēvi, crētum *v.t.* 3, to separate
excerpo, psi, ptum *v.t.* 3, to select
excessus, ūs *m*, departure
excĭdĭum, ii *n*, destruction
excĭdo, cĭdi *v.i.* 3, to fall from, escape, disappear, slip the memory, fail in
excĭdo, cĭdi, cīsum *v.t.* 3, to cut down, destroy
excĭo *v.t.* 4, to call or bring out
excĭpĭo, cēpi, ceptum *v.t.* 3, to take out, make an exception, receive, capture, follow after, overhear, intercept

excĭtātus, a, um *adj*, roused, vigorous
excĭto *v.t.* 1, to rouse up, excite
exclāmātĭo, ōnis *f*, exclamation
exclāmo *v.i.t.* 1, to call out
exclūdo, si, sum *v.t.* 3, to shut out, drive out, remove, hinder, hatch
exclūsĭo, ōnis *f*, exclusion
excōgĭto *v.t.* 1, to think out
excŏlo, cŏlŭi, cultum *v.t.* 3, to cultivate, improve, refine
excŏquo, xi, ctum *v.t.* 3, to boil away, purify
excors, dis *adj*, stupid
excresco, crēvi, crētum *v.i.* 1, to grow up
excrētus, a, um *adj*, full-grown
excrētus, a, um *adj*, separated
excrŭcĭo *v.t.* 1, to torture
excŭbĭae, ārum *f.pl*, watch, guard
excŭbĭtor, ōris *m*, watchman
excŭbo, ŭi, ĭtum *v.i.* 1, to sleep out of doors, keep watch
excūdo, di, sum *v.t.* 3, to hammer out
exculco *v.t.* 1, to trample down
excurro, cŭcurri, cursum *v.i.* 3, to run out, make a sortie, extend
excursĭo, ōnis *f*, attack, invasion, sally
excursus, ūs *m*, attack, invation, sally
excūsābĭlis, e *adj*, excusable
excūsātĭo, ōnis *f*, excuse
excūso *v.t.* 1, to excuse, plead in excuse
excŭtĭo, cussi, cussum *v.t.* 3, to shake off, get rid of, hurl, examine
exēdo, ēdi, ēsum *v.t.* 3, to eat up
exemplar, āris *n*, copy, model
exemplum, i *n*, copy, model, precedent, warning, example

Insight

Some abbreviated expressions that are commonly used in English come from Latin: For example **e.g.** stands for *exempli gratia*; **i.e.** stands for *id est*; **etc.** stands for *et cetera*; **p.s.** stands for *post scriptum*; **a.m./p.m.** stand for *ante/post meridiem*.

exemptus, a, um *adj*, removed

exĕo *v.i.t.* 4, to depart, run out (time); die; cross, avoid

exercĕo *v.t.* 2, to keep busy, train, exercise, pester

exercĭtātĭo, ōnis *f*, practice

exercĭtātus, a, um *adj*, trained

exercĭtor, ōris *m*, trainer

exercĭtus, ūs *m*, army

exercĭtus, a, um *adj*, trained, harrassed

exhālātĭo, ōnis *f*, exhalation

exhālo *v.t.* 1, to breathe out

exhaurĭo, si, stum *v.t.* 4, to draw out, exhaust, empty

exhaustus, a, um *adj*, drained, worn out

exhērēdo *v.t.* 1, to disinherit

exhĭbĕo *v.t.* 2, to present, display, procure, cause

exhĭbĭtus, a, um *adj*, produced

exhĭlăro *v.t.* 1, to delight

exhorresco, rŭi *v.i.t.* 3, to tremble; shrink from, dread

exhortor *v.t.* 1, *dep*, to encourage

exiens see **exeo**

exĭgo, ēgi, actum *v.t.* 3, to drive out, enforce, demand, complete, examine, estimate, spend (time)

exĭgŭĭtas, ātis *f*, small size

exĭgŭus, a, um *adj, adv*, **ē**, small, short

exīlis, e *adj, adv*, **ĭter** small, thin, feeble, insignificant

exĭlĭum, ii *n*, exile

exīmĭus, a, um *adj, adv*, **ē**, unusual, distinguished

exĭmo, ēmis, emptum *v.t.* 3, to take away, free, waste

exĭnānĭo *v.t.* 4, to empty

exindē (exin) *adv*, from there, then, next, accordingly

existĭmātĭo, ōnis *f*, opinion, reputation, character

existĭmātor, ōris *m*, critic

existĭmo *v.t.* 1, to estimate, think

exĭtĭābĭlis, e *adj*, fatal, deadly

exĭtĭālis, e *adj*, fatal, deadly

exĭtĭōsus, a, um *adj*, destructive

exĭtĭum, ii *n*, destruction

exĭtus, ūs *m*, departure, outlet, conclusion, result, death

exōlesco, ŏlēvi, lētum *v.i.* 3, to grow up, disappear

exŏnĕro *v.t.* 1, to unload

exoptātus, a, um *adj*, longed for

exopto *v.t.* 1, to long for

exōrābĭlis, e *adj*, easily persuaded

exordĭor, orsus *v.t.* 4, *dep*, to begin, weave

exordĭum, ii *n*, beginning, introduction

exŏrĭor, ortus *v.i.* 4, *dep*, to spring up, arise, appear

exornātĭo, ōnis *f*, decoration

exorno *v.t.* 1, to equip, adorn

exōro *v.t.* 1, to prevail upon

exorsus, a, um *adj*, begun

exortus, ūs *m*, rising

exōsus, a, um *adj*, hating, detested

expăvesco, pāvi *v.i.t.* 3, to be afraid; dread

expect... see **exspect...**

expēdĭo *v.t.* 4, to set free, prepare, arrange, explain; *impers*, it is expedient

expēdĭo *v.t.* 4, to set free, prepare, arrange, explain; *impers*, it is expedient

expēdītĭo, ōnis *f*, campaign

expēdītē *adv*, promptly

expēdītus, a, um *adj*, ready

expēdītus, i *m*, soldier in light-marching order

expello, pŭli, pulsum *v.t.* 3, to drive away

expendo, di, sum *v.t.* 3, to pay out, consider, pay the penalty

expergēfăcĭo, fēci, factum *v.t.* 3, to arouse

expergiscor, perrectus *v.i.* 3, *dep*. to awake

expĕrĭens, ntis *adj*, enterprising

expĕrĭentĭa, ae *f*, experiment, practice

expĕrīmentum, i *n*, proof, experience

expĕrĭor, pertus *v.t.* 4, *dep*, to prove, test, try; *perf*, know from experience

expers, rtis *adj*, devoid of

expertus, a, um *adj*, proved

expĕto, īvi (ii), ītum *v.t.* 3, to long for, aim at, reach

expĭātĭo, ōnis *f*, atonement

expĭlo *v.t.* 1, to plunder

expīlātĭo, ōnis *f*, plundering

expingo, nxi, ctum *v.t.* 3, to paint
expĭo *v.t.* 1, to atone for
expiscor *v.t.* 1, *dep,* to search out
explānātĭo, ōnis *f,* explanation
explāno *v.t.* 1, to explain
explĕo, ēvi, ētum *v.t.* 2, to fill up, fulfil, finish
explētĭo, ōnis *f,* satisfying
explētus, a, um *adj,* full, complete
explĭcātĭo, ōnis *f,* unfolding, explanation
explĭcātus, a, um *adj,* spread-out, plain
explĭco *v.t.* 1, (or ... ŭi ... ĭtum) to unfold, spread out, deploy, arrange, explain
explōdo, si, sum *v.t.* 3, to hiss off the stage, disapprove
explōrātor, ōris *m,* spy, scout
explōrātus, a, um *adj, adv,* ē, established, certain
explōro *v.t.* 1, to search out, spy, test
expŏlĭo *v.t.* 4, to polish
expōno, pŏsŭi, pŏsĭtum *v.t.* 3, to expose, put on shore, explain
exporto *v.t.* 1, to carry away
exposco, pŏposci *v.t.* 3, to implore, require
expŏsĭtĭo, ōnis *f,* elucidation
expŏsĭtus, a, um *adj,* accessible
expostūlātĭo, ōnis *f,* complaint
expostūlo *v.t.* 1, to demand, upbraid, complain
expressus, a, um *adj,* clear
exprĭmo, pressi, pressum *v.t.* 3, to press out, model, extort
exprŏbrātĭo, ōnis *f,* reproach
exprŏbo *v.t.* 1, to reproach
exprōmo, mpsi, mptum *v.t.* 3, to fetch out, display, explain
expugnātĭo, ōnis *f,* capture by assault
expugno *v.t.* 1, to storm, capture
expurgo *v.t.* 1, to purify, justify
exquīro, sīvi, sītum *v.t.* 3, to search out
exquīsītus, a, um *adj, adv,* ē, choice, excellent
exsanguis, e *adj,* bloodless, weak
exsătĭo *v.t.* 1, to satisfy
exsătŭro *v.t.* 1, to satiate
exscensĭo, ōnis *f,* landing

exscindo, ĭdi, issum *v.t.* 3, to destroy completely
exscrībo, psi, ptum *v.t.* 3, to write out, copy
exsēco, cŭi, ctum *v.t.* 1, to cut out, cut off
exsècrābĭlis, e *adj,* accursed
exsècrātĭo, ōnis *f,* curse
exsècrātus, a, um *adj,* accursed
exsècror *v.i.t.* 1, *dep,* to take an oath; curse
exsĕcūtĭo, ōnis *f,* execution
exsĕquĭae, ārum *f.pl,* funeral
exsĕquor, sĕcūtus *v.t.* 3, *dep,* to pursue, follow, carry out, describe, avenge
exsĕro, rŭi, rtum *v.t.* 3, to put out, uncover, protrude
exserto *v.t.* 1, to stretch out
exsicco *v.t.* 1, to dry up
exsĭlĭo, īlŭi *v.i.* 4, to leap out, jump up
exsĭlĭum, ii *n,* exile
exsisto, stĭti, stĭtum *v.i.* 3, to come out, appear, arise, exist
exsolvo, solvi, sŏlūtum *v.t.* 3, to unloose, free, discharge
exsomnis, e *adj,* sleepless
exsorbĕo *v.t.* 2, to suck up
exsors, rtis *adj,* specially chosen, deprived of
exspătĭor *v.i.* 1, *dep,* to digress, launch out
exspectātĭo, ōnis *f,* expectation
exspectātus, a, um *adj,* desired
exspecto *v.t.* 1, to look out for, wait for, hope for
exspergo (spargo) (*no perf.*), **spersus** *v.t.* 3, to scatter
exspīrātĭo, ōnis *f,* breathing out
exspīro *v.i.t.* 1, to rush out, expire, cease; breathe out
exspŏlĭo *v.t.* 1, to plunder
exstĭmŭlo *v.t.* 1, to goad on
exstinctor, ōris *m,* destroyer
exstinctus, a, um *adj,* destroyed, extinct
exstinguo, nxi, nctum *v.t.* 3, to quench, kill, destroy
exstirpo *v.t.* 1, to uproot
exsto *v.i.* 1, to project, be conspicuous, exist
exstructĭo, ōnis *f,* structure

exstrŭo, xi, ctum *v.t.* 3, to heap up, build up

exsūdo *v.t.* 1, to toil or sweat at

exsul (exul), ŭlis *c,* an exile

exsŭlo (exulo) *v.i.* 1, to live in exile

exsultans, ntis *adj,* boastful

exsultātǐo, ōnis *f,* rapture

exsultim *adv,* friskingly

exsulto *v.i.* 1, to jump about, run riot, boast

exsŭpěrābǐlis, e *adj,* surmountable

exsŭpěro *v.i.t.* 1, to get the upper hand; pass over, exceed

exsurdo *v.t.* 1, to deafen, dull

exsurgo, surrexi *v.i.* 3, to rise, stand up

exsuscǐto *v.t.* 1, to awaken

exta, ōrum *n.pl,* the inwards

extemplō *adv,* immediately

extendo, di, tum *v.t.* 3, to stretch out, enlarge, prolong

extentus, a, um *adj,* extensive

extěnŭātǐo, ōnis *f,* attenuation

extěnŭo *v.t.* 1, to diminish, weaken

exter (extěrus), ěra, ěrum *adj,* external, strange, foreign

extergěo, si, sum *v.t.* 2, to plunder

extěrǐor, us *comp. adj,* outer

extermǐno *v.t.* 1, to expel

externus, a, um *adj,* external, foreign

extěro, trīvi, trītum *v.t.* 3, to rub off, wear away

exterrěo *v.t.* 2, to frighten

extǐmesco, mǔi *v.i.t.* 2, to be afraid; to dread

extollo, sustŭli *v.t.* 3, to raise

extorquěo, si, sum *v.t.* 2, to wrench away from, extort

extorris, e *adj,* exiled

extrā *adv and prep. with acc.* outside, beyond, except

extrǎho, xi, ctum *v.t.* 3, to drag out, release, prolong

extrānĕus, i *m,* stranger

extrǎordǐnārǐus, a, um *adj,* extraordinary

extrēma, ōrum *n.pl,* last resort

extrēmǐtas, ātis *f,* extremity

extrēmum, i *n,* the end

extrēmum *adv,* for the last time, finally

extrēmus, a, um *adj,* furthest, the end of, or extremity of

extrīco *v.t.* 1, to disentangle

extrinsěcus *adv,* from, or on, the outside

extrūdo, si, sum *v.t.* 3, to push out

extundo, tŭdi, tūsum *v.t.* 3, to force out, hammer out

exturbo *v.t.* 1, to drive away

exūběro *v.i.* 1, to be abundant

exul see **exsul**

exulcěro *v.t.* 1, to aggravate

exūlŭlo *v.i.* 1, to howl

exundo *v.i.* 1, to overflow

exŭo, ŭi, ūtum *v.t.* 3, to strip, deprive of, discard

exūro, ussi, ustum *v.t.* 3, to burn up, consume

exustǐo, ōnis *f,* conflagration

exŭvǐae, ārum *f.pl,* stripped-off clothing or equipment

F

fǎba, ae *f,* bean

fābella, ae *f,* short story

fǎber, bri *m,* smith, carpenter

fǎbrǐca, ae *f,* workshop, a trade, a skilled work

fǎbrǐcātǐo, ōnis *f,* structure

fǎbrǐcātor, ōris *m,* maker

fǎbrǐcor *v.t.* 1, *dep,* (**fabrǐco** *v.t.* 1), to construct, form

fǎbrīlis, e *adj,* of a craftsman

fābŭla, ae *f,* story, play

fābŭlor *v.t.* 1, *dep,* to talk, chat

fābŭlōsus, a, um *adj,* legendary

fǎcesso, cessi, ītum *v.i.t.* 3, to depart; perform, cause

fǎcētǐae, ārum *f.pl,* witticisms

fǎcētus, a, um *adj, adv,* **ē,** courteous, elegant, witty

fǎcǐes, ēi *f,* face, shape, appearance

fǎcǐlǐě *adv,* easily

fǎcǐlis, e *adj,* easy, quick, good-natured

fǎcǐlǐtas, ātis *f,* ease, affability

fǎcǐnus, ŏris *n,* deed, crime

fǎcǐo, fēci, factum *v.i.t.* 3, to do, act, to side with (**cum, ab**), or against (**contra**), to be useful; to make, do, produce, assert, pretend, practise (trade)

factĭo, ōnis *f*, faction, party
factĭōsus, a, um *adj*, mutinous
factĭto *v.t.* 1, to keep doing
factum, i *n*, deed
făcultas, ātis *f*, power, opportunity, supply
fācundĭa, ae *f*, eloquence
fācundus, a, um *adj, adv*, ē, eloquent
faecŭla, ae *f*, wine dregs
faenĕrātĭo, ōnis *f*, moneylending
faenĕrātor, ōris *m*, moneylender
faenĕrātōrĭus, a, um *adj*, usurious
faenĕror *v.t.* 1, *dep* (**faenĕro,** *v.t.* 1), to lend on interest
faenīlĭa, ĭum *n.pl*, hayloft
faenum, i *n*, hay
faenus, ŏris *n*, interest, profit
faex, cis *f*, dregs, sediment
fāgĭnĕus (nus), a, um *adj*, of beech
fāgus, i *f*, beech tree
fălārĭca, ae *f*, burning missile
falcātus, a, um *adj*, armed with scythes, curved
falcĭfer, ĕra, ĕrum *adj*, holding a sickle
falco, ōnis *m*, falcon
fallācĭa, ae *f*, trick, deceit
fallax, ācis *adj, adv*, ĭter, deceitful, fallacious
fallo, fĕfelli, falsum *v.t.* 3, to deceive, betray, escape to notice of, appear
falsum, i *n*, falsehood
falsus, a, um *adj, adv*, ē, or ō, false, counterfeit, deceptive
falx, cis *f*, scythe, hook
fāma, ae *f*, rumour, public opinion, reputation, fame
fāmes, is *f*, hunger, famine
fămĭlĭa, ae *f*, domestic servants, family property, crowd or set
fămĭlĭāris, e *adj, adv*, ĭter, domestic, intimate
fămĭlĭāris, is *m*, friend
fămĭlĭārĭtas, ātis *f*, friendship
fāmōsus, a, um *adj*, notorious
fămŭla, ae *f*, maid-servant
fămŭlātus, ūs *m*, servitude
fămŭlor *v.i.* 1, *dep*, to serve, wait on
fămŭlus, i *m*, servant
fānātĭcus, a, um *adj*, inspired, frantic

fandus, a, um *adj*, lawful
fānum, i *n*, temple, shrine
fār, farris *n*, grain, corn
farcīmen, ĭnis *n*, sausage
farcĭo, rsi, rtum *v.t.* 4, to cram
fărīna, ae *f*, flour
farrāgo, ĭnis *f*, hotchpotch
fartor, ōris *m*, poultry farmer
fartum, i *n*, stuffing
fartūra, ae *f*, cramming, padding
fās *n*, *(indeclinable)*, divine law, right
fascēs, ĭum *m.pl*, bundle of rods and axes; symbol of magistrates' power of scourging and beheading
fascĭa, ae *f*, band, headband
fascĭcŭlus, i *m*, small bundle
fascĭnātĭo, ōnis *f*, bewiching
fascĭno *v.t.* 1, to charm, enchant
fascĭnum, i *n*, lucky charm
fascĭŏla, ae *f*, small bandage
fascis, is *m*, bundle, pack
fassus, a, um *participle*, having acknowledged
fasti, ōrum *m.pl*, working days, calendar
fastīdĭo *v.i.t.* 4, to be disgusted; to loathe
fastīdĭōsus, a, um *adj, adv*, ē, scornful, squeamish, disagreeable
fastīdĭum, ii *n*, loathing, scorn
fastīgātus, a, um *adj, adv*, ē, sloping
fastīgĭum, ii *n*, gable, top, bottom, slope
fastīgo *v.t.* 1, to make jointed
fastus, a, um (**dĭes**), court-day
fastus, ūs *m*, arrogance
fātālis, e *adj, adv*, ĭter, destined, deadly
fătĕor, fassus *v.t.* 2, *dep*, to admit, confess
fātĭdĭcus, a, um *adj*, prophetic
fātĭfer, ĕra, ĕrum *adj*, deadly
fătīgātĭo, ōnis *f*, exhaustion
fătīgātus, a, um *adj*, exhausted
fătīgo *v.t.* 1, to weary, harass, torment
fătisco *v.i.* 3, to fall apart
fătŭĭtas, ātis *f*, foolishness
fātum, i *n*, destiny, calamity, prophetic saying

fătŭus, a, um *adj,* foolish

faucēs, ĭum *f.pl,* throat, narrow passage

faustus, a, um *adj, adv,* **ē,** fortunate

fautor, ōris *m,* supporter

fautrix, īcis *f,* patroness

făvĕo, fāvi, fautum *v.i.* 2, *with dat;* to favour, befriend

făvilla, ae *f,* embers

făvor, ōris *m,* goodwill, applause

făvōrābĭlis, e *adj,* popular

făvus, i *m,* honeycomb

fax, făcis *f,* torch, stimulus

febrĭcŭlōsus, a, um *adj* feverish

fĕbris, is *f,* fever

Fĕbrŭārĭus (mensis) February

fĕbrŭum, i *n,* atonement

fēcundĭtas, ātis *f,* fertility

fēcundo *v.t.* 1, to fertilize

fēcundus, a, um *adj,* fertile, abundant

fel, fellis *n,* gall-bladder, poison, bitterness

fēles, is *f,* cat

fēlīcĭtas, ātis *f,* happiness

fēlix, īcis *adj, adv,* **īter,** happy, fortunate, abundant

fēmĭna, ae *f,* woman

fēmĭnĕus, a, um *adj,* feminine

fĕmur, ŏris (ĭnis) *n,* thigh

fēn... see **faen...**

fĕnestra, ae *f,* window

fĕra, ae *f,* wild animal

fērālis, e *adj,* of the dead

fĕrax, ācis *adj,* fertile

fercŭlum, i *n,* barrow, dish

fĕrē *adv,* almost, nearly, usually

fĕrentārĭus, ii *m,* light-armed soldier

fĕrètrum, i *n,* bier

fērĭae, ārum *f.pl,* holidays

fērĭātus, a, um *adj,* on holidays

fērīnus, a, um *adj,* of wild animals

fĕrĭo *v.t.* 4, to strike, kill; (*with* **foedus**), to make treaty

fĕrĭtas, ātis *f,* wildness

fermē *adv,* almost, usually

fermentum, i *n,* yeast, beer

fĕro, ferre, tŭli, lātum *v.t, irreg,* to bear, bring, move, produce, plunder, offer, tolerate, show, assert; **fertur, ferunt,** it is said

fĕrōcĭa, ae *f,* high spirits, ferocity

fĕrōcĭtas, ātis *f,* high spirits, ferocity

fĕrōcĭter *adv,* bravely, fiercely

fĕrox, ōcis *adj,* brave, fierce

ferrāmentum, i *n,* iron tool

ferrātus, a, um *adj,* iron-clad

ferrĕus, a, um *adj,* made of iron

ferrūgĭnĕus, a, um *adj,* rusty, dark red

ferrūgo, ĭnis *f,* rust, dark red

ferrum, i *n,* iron, sword

ferrūmen, ĭnis *n,* cement, glue, solder

ferrūmĭno *v.t.* 1, to cement, solder

fertĭlis, e *adj,* fertile

fertĭlĭtas, ātis *f,* fertility

fĕrŭla, ae *f,* stalk, rod

fĕrus, a, um *adj,* wild, cruel

fĕrus, i *m,* wild animal

fervĕfăcĭo, fēci, factum *v.t.* 3, to heat, melt

fervens, ntis *adj, adv,* **nter,** burning, boiling hot

fervĕo, bŭi *v.i.* 2, to boil, burn, rage, swarm

fervĭdus, a, um *adj,* burning, impetuous

fervor, ōris *m,* heat, passion

fessus, a, um *adj,* tired

festīnans, ntis *adj, adv,* **nter,** in haste

festīnātĭo, ōnis *f,* haste

festīno *v.i.t.* 1, to hurry

festīnus, a, um *adj,* quick

festīvĭtas, ātis *f,* humour

festīvus, a, um *adj, adv,* **ē,** witty, lively, cheerful

festum, i *n,* holiday, banquet

festus, a, um *adj,* festive, gay

fētĕo *v.i.* 2, to stink

fētĭāles, ĭum *m.pl,* college of priests concerned with war ceremonies

fētĭdus, a, um *adj,* stinking

fētor, ōris *m,* stench

fētūra, ae *f,* bearing of young, young brood

fētus, a, um *adj,* pregnant, fruitful, newly delivered

fibra, ae *f,* fibre, nerve

fībŭla, ae *f,* brooch, pin

fībŭlo *v.t.* 1, to fasten

fictīlis, e *adj*, made of clay
fictīle, is (ia, ĭum) *n*, earthern pottery
fictor, ōris *m*, designer
fictus, a, um *adj*, imagined
ficus, i or **ūs** *f*, fig tree
fidēlis, e *adj*, *adv*, **ĭter**, faithful, true, sure
fidēlĭtas, ātis *f*, faithfulness
fidens, ntis *adj*, *adv*, **nter** self-confident
fidentĭa, ae *f*, confidence
fĭdes, ĕi *f*, trust, faith, confidence, honesty, promise
fĭdes, ĭum *f.pl*, lute, guitar
fĭdĭcen, ĭnis *m*, lute-player
fĭdo, fīsus sum *v*. 3, *semi-dep. with dat*; to trust
fidūcĭa, ae *f*, confidence
fidus, a, um *adj*, trustworthy
fĭĕri see **fio**
figo, xi, xum *v.t*. 3, to fix, fasten, transfix
figŭlāris, e *adj*, of a potter
figŭlus, i *m*, potter
figūra, ae *f*, shape, phantom, atom, nature
figūrātus, a, um *adj*, shaped
figūro *v.t*. 1, to shape
fīlĭa, ae *f*, daughter
fīlĭŏla, ae *f*, little daughter
fīlĭŏlus, i *m*, little son
fīlĭus, i *m*, son
fīlix, ĭcis *f*, hair, fern
fīlum, i *n*, thread, texture
fimbrĭae, ārum *f.pl*, threads, fringe
fĭmus, i *m*, manure
findo, fĭdi, ssum *v.t*. 3, to split
fīnes, ĭum *m.pl*, territory
fingo, nxi, ctum *v.t*. 3, to shape, adorn, imagine, devise
fĭnĭo *v.t*. 4, to enclose, limit, prescribe, end, die
fĭnis, is *m*, boundary, limit, end
fĭnĭtĭmus, a, um *adj*, adjoining
fĭnĭtĭmi, ōrum *m.pl*, neighbours
fĭnītor, ōris *m*, surveyor
fio, fĭĕri, factus sum *v*, *irreg*, to become, happen
firmāmen, ĭnis *n*, prop, support

firmāmentum, i *n*, prop, support
firmĭtas, ātis *f*, strength, firmness
firmĭtūdo, ĭnis *f*, strength, firmness
firmo *v.t*. 1, to strengthen, encourage, promise
firmus, a, um *adj*, *adv*, **ē, ĭter**, strong, stable, constant, true
fiscella, ae *f*, small basket, muzzle
fiscīna, ae *f*, small basket
fiscus, i *m*, purse, imperial treasury
fissīlis, e *adj*, breakable
fissum, i *n*, cleft, chink
fissūra, ae *f*, split, chink
fistūca, ae *f*, rammer
fistŭla, ae *f*, pipe, tube
fistŭlātor, ōris *m*, piper
fisus, a, um *adj*, trusting, relying on
flābellum, i *n*, small fan
flābra, ōrum *n.pl*, gusts
flaccĭdus, a, um *adj*, flabby
flăgello *v.t*. 1, to whip
flăgellum, i *n*, whip, thong
flāgĭtātĭo, ōnis *f*, demand
flāgĭtĭōsus, a, um *adj*, *adv*, **ē**, disgraceful
flāgĭtĭum, ii *n*, disgraceful conduct, shame
flāgĭto *v.t*. 1, to demand
flăgrans, ntis *adj*, burning
flăgro *v.i*. 1, to blaze, glow
flăgrum, i *n*, whip
flāmen, ĭnis *m*, priest
flāmen, ĭnis *n*, blast
flāmĭnĭum, ii *n*, priesthood
flamma, ae *f*, flame, blaze
flammĕum, i *n*, bridal veil
flammĕus, a, um *adj*, flaming
flammĭfer, ĕra, ĕrum *adj*, flame-carrying
flammo *v.i.t*. 1, to burn
flātus, ūs *m*, blowing, bluster
flāvens, ntis *adj*, yellow
flāvĕo *v.i*. 2, to be golden, yellow
flāvesco *v.i*. 3, to turn golden
flāvus, a, um *adj*, golden, yellow
flēbĭlis, e *adj*, *adv*, **ĭter**, lamentable, tearful

flecto, xi, xum *v.i.t.* 3, to turn; bend, curve, wheel, persuade

flĕo, ēvi, tum *v.i.t.* 2, to weep; mourn

flētus, ūs *m*, weeping

flexĭbĭlis, e *adj*, flexible

flexĭo, ōnis *f*, curve

flexŭōsus, a, um *adj*, crooked

flexus, ūs *m*, bend, turning

flictus, ūs *m*, collision

flō *v.i.t.* 1, to blow

floccus, i *m*, lock of wool

flōrens, ntis *adj*, shining, flourishing

flōrĕo *v.i.* 2, to bloom, flourish

flōresco *v.i.* 3, to come into flower, flourish

flōrĕus, a, um *adj*, made of flowers

flōrĭdus, a, um *adj*, blooming

flōs, ōris *m*, flower, ornament

floscŭlus, i *m*, small flower

fluctŭo *v.i.* 1, to ripple, undulate, hesitate

fluctŭōsus, a, um *adj*, billowy

fluctus, ūs *m*, wave

flŭens, ntis *adj*, lax, fluent

flŭentum, i *n*, stream, flood

flŭĭdus, a, um *adj*, flowing, slack

flŭĭto *v.i.* 1, to flow, float

flūmen, ĭnis *n*, river, flood

flūmĭnĕus, a, um *adj*, of a river

flŭo, xi, xum *v.i.* 3, to flow, wave, vanish

flŭvĭālis, e *adj*, of a river

flŭvĭus, ii *m*, river

fluxĭo, ōnis *f*, flowing

fluxus, a, um *adj*, fluid, slack

fōcāle, is *n*, necktie

fŏcŭlus, i *m*, brazier

fŏcus, i *m*, fireplace, home

fŏdĭco *v.t.* 1, to dig, nudge, stab

fŏdĭo, fōdi, fossum *v.i.t.* 3, to dig; dig up, prick, stab

foedĕrātus, a, um *adj*, allied

foedĭtas, ātis *f*, filthiness

foedo *v.t.* 1, to disfigure, disgrace, stain

foedus, a, um *adj, adv*, ē, filthy, shameful

foedus, ĕris *n*, treaty, contract

foet... see **fet...**

fŏlĭum, ii *n*, leaf

follĭcŭlus, i *m*, small bag

follis, is *m*, pair of bellows

fōmentum, *n*, poultice, comfort

fōmes, ĭtis *m*, firewood

fons, ntis *m*, fountain, origin

fontĭcŭlus, i *m*, small fountain

for *v.i.t.* 1, *dep*, to speak; say, predict

fŏrāmen, ĭnis *n*, hole

fŏrās *adv*, out-of-doors

forceps, ĭpis *m, f*, tongs, pincers

fŏrĕ = futurum esse see **esse**

fŏrem = essem see **esse**

fŏrensis, e *adj*, concerning the courts of law

fŏres, um *f.pl*, door, entrance

forfex, ĭcis *f*, scissors (*usually in pl.*)

fŏrĭca, ae *f*, public convenience

fŏrĭcŭlae, ārum *f. pl*, shutters

fŏris, is *f*, door, entrance

fŏris *adv*, outside, from outside

forma, ae *f*, form, shape, beauty

formīca, ae *f*, ant

formīdābĭlis, e *adj*, fearful

formīdo *v.i.t.* 1, to be afraid; fear

formīdo, ĭnis *f*, fear, terror

formīdŭlōsus, a, um *adj, adv*, ē, dreadful, fearful

formo *v.t.* 1, to shape

formōsus, a, um *adj*, beautiful

formŭla, ae *f*, rule, principle, agreement, lawsuit

fornax, ācis *f*, oven

fornix, ĭcis *m*, arch, vault

fors, rtis *f*, chance, luck

fors *adv*, perhaps

forsan *adv*, perhaps

forsĭtan *adv*, perhaps

fortassē *adv*, perhaps

fortē *adv*, by chance

fortis, e *adj, adv,* ĭter, strong, brave

fortĭtūdo, ĭnis *f*, bravery

fortŭĭtō(ū) *adv*, by chance

fortŭĭtus, a, um *adj*, accidental

fortūna, ae *f*, luck, fate, fortune (good or bad), circumstances, property

fortūnātus, a, um *adj, adv*, ē, lucky, happy

fortūno *v.t.* 1, to enrich, bless

fŏrum, i *n*, marketplace, business

Insight

The Latin term *forum* means 'marketplace' but it also relates to the legal and business centre of a town. Nowadays the term *forum* is commonly used to indicate an online space for discussion.

fŏrus, i *m*, gangway, passage, row of seats

fossa, ae *f*, ditch

fossĭo, ōnis *f*, excavation

fossor, ōris *m*, digger, miner

fŏvĕa, ae *f*, pit, pitfall

fŏvĕo, fōvi, fōtum *v.t.* 2, to warm, caress, love

fractūra, ae *f*, fracture

fractus, a, um *adj*, weak, feeble

frāga, ōrum *n.pl*, strawberries

frăgĭlis, e *adj*, brittle, frail

frăgĭlĭtas, ātis *f*, frailty

fragmen, ĭnis *n*, fracture, splinter

fragmentum, i *n*, fragment

frăgor, ōris *m*, crash

frăgōsus, a, um *adj*, rugged, crashing

fragro *v.i.* 1, to smell

frăgum, i *n*, strawberry plant

frango, frēgi, fractum *v.t.* 3, to break, crush, weaken

frāter, tris *m*, brother

frāternĭtas, ātis *f*, brotherhood

frāternus, a, um *adj*, *adv*, **ē**, brotherly

frātrĭcīda, ae *m*, a fratricide

fraudātĭo, ōnis *f*, deceit

fraudātor, ōris *m*, deceiver

fraudo *v.t.* 1, to cheat, defraud

fraudŭlentus, a, um *adj*, deceitful

fraus, dis *f*, deceit, crime, mistake, injury

fraxĭnĕus, a, um *adj*, of ash

fraxĭnus, i *f*, ash tree

frĕmĭtus, ūs *m*, murmur, roar

frĕmo, ŭi, ĭtum *v.i.t.* 3, to roar, murmur, howl; grumble at

frĕmor, ōris *m*, murmuring

frendĕo, ŭi, frēsum *v.i.* 2, to gnash the teeth, crush

frēno *v.t.* 1, to bridle, curb

frēnum, i *n*, bridle, restraint

frĕquens, ntis *adj*, *adv*, **nter**, usual, repeated, crowded

frĕquentātĭo, ōnis *f*, frequency

frĕquentĭa, ae *f*, crowd

frĕquento *v.t.* 1, to frequent, repeat, crowd, celebrate

frĕtum, i *n*, channel, strait

frĕtus, a, um *adj. with abl*, relying on

frĭco, cŭi, ctum *v.t.* 1, to rub

frictus, a, um *adj*, rubbed, **(frico)**; roasted **(frigo)**

frīgĕo *v.i.* 2, to be cold or languid, to be slighted

frīgesco, frixi *v.i.* 3, to grow cold, become languid

frīgĭdus, a, um *adj*, cold, stiff, feeble, spiritless

frīgĭda, ae *f*, cold water

frīgo, xi, ctum *v.t.* 3, to roast

frīgus, ŏris *n*, cold, winter

fringilla, ae *f*, small bird, robin, chaffinch

frondātor, ōris *m*, pruner

frondĕo *v.i.* 2, to be in leaf

frondesco, dŭi *v.i.* 3, to come into leaf

frondĕus, a, um *adj*, leafy

frondōsus, a, um *adj*, leafy

frons, dis *f*, foliage, leaf

frons, ntis *f*, forehead, front, appearance

fructŭōsus, a, um *adj*, fruitful, ádvantageous

fructus, ūs *m*, enjoyment, fruit, profit

frūgālis, e *adj*, *adv*, **ĭter**, thrifty, careful

frūgālĭtas, ātis *f*, thrift, worth

frūges, um *f.pl*, see **frux**

frūgi *indecl. adj*, worthy, useful

frūgĭfer, ĕra, ĕrum *adj*, fertile

frūmentārĭus, a, um *adj*, of corn

frūmentor *v.i.* 1, *dep*, to fetch corn

frūmentum, i *n*, corn

frŭor, fructus *v.* 3, *dep. with abl*, to enjoy

frustrā *adv*, in vain

frustrātĭo, ōnis *f*, deception, frustration

frustror *v.t.* 1, *dep*, to deceive

frustum, i *n*, piece

frŭtex, ĭcis *m*, bush

frŭtĭcētum, i *n*, thicket

frŭtĭcōsus, a, um *adj*, bushy

frux, frūgis *f*, fruit, crops, value, result

fūcātus, a, um *adj*, painted, counterfeit

fūco *v.t.* 1, to paint, dye

fūcōsus, a, um *adj*, coloured, spurious

fūcus, i *m*, rouge, disguise

fūcus, i *m*, drone

fŭga, ae *f*, flight, exile

fŭgax, ācis *adj*, runaway, swift

fŭgĭens, ntis *adj*, runaway, swift

fŭgĭens, ntis *adj*, fleeing

fŭgĭo, fūgi, fŭgĭtum *v.i.t.* 3, to run away; flee from, avoid

fŭgĭtīvus, a, um *adj*, fugitive

fŭgĭtīvus, i *m*, runaway slave, deserter

fŭgĭto *v.t.* 1, to flee, avoid

fŭgo *v.t.* 1, to rout, chase

fulcĭo, fulsi, fultum *v.t.* 4, to prop up, strenghen

fulcrum, i *n*, foot (of couch)

fulgens, ntis *adj*, shining

fulgĕo, lsi *v.i.* 2, to flash, shine

fulgĭdus, a, um *adj*, flashing, shining

fulgor, ōris *m*, lightning, gleam, splendour

fulgur, ŭris *n*, lightning

fulgŭrat *v. impers*, it lightens

fūlĭca, ae *f*, moorhen

fūlīgo, ĭnis *f*, soot

fūlīgĭnōsus, a, um *adj*, sooty

fulmen, ĭnis *n*, thunderbolt, lightning

fulmĭnĕus, a, um *adj*, of lightning, destructive, brilliant

fulmĭno *v.i.* 1, to thunder

fultūra, ae *f*, prop, tonic

fulvus, a, um *adj*, deep yellow

fūmĕus, a, um *adj*, smoky

fūmĭdus, a, um *adj*, smoky

fūmĭfer, ĕra, ĕrum *adj*, smoking, steaming

fūmĭfĭcus, a, um *adj*, smoking, steaming

fūmĭgo *v.t.* 1, to smoke out, fumigate

fūmo *v.i.* 1, to smoke

fūmōsus, a, um *adj*, smoky, smoke-dried

fūmus, i *m*, smoke

fūnāle, is *n*, cord, torch

functĭo, ōnis *f*, performing

functus, a, um *partic. adj*, *with abl*, having completed

funda, ae *f*, sling, missile

fundāmen, ĭnis *n*, foundation

fundāmentum, i *n*, foundation

fundĭtor, ōris *m*, slinger

fundĭtus *adv*, from the bottom, completely

fundo, fūdi, fūsum *v.t.* 3, to pour out, spread out, scatter, overthrow, produce

fundo *v.t.* 1, to found, fix

fundus, i *m*, the bottom, a farm

fundus, i *m*, guarantor

fūnèbris, e *adj*, of a funeral

fūnĕrĕus, a, um *adj*, of a funeral

fūnĕro *v.t.* 1, to bury, kill

fūnesto *v.t.* 1, to pollute

fūnestus, a, um *adj*, fatal, sad

fungor, functus *v.* 3, *dep, with abl*, to perform, complete

fungus, i *m*, mushroom, fungus

fūnis, is *m*, rope

fūnus, ĕris *n*, funeral, death, ruin

fūr, fūris *c*, thief, rogue

fūrax, ācis *adj*, light-fingered

furca, ae *f*, two-pronged fork or pole for punishment

furcĭfer, ĕri *m*, gallows-bird

furcilla, ae *f*, small fork

furcŭla, a *f*, fork-shaped prop, ravine

fŭrens, ntis *adj*, raging

furfur, ŭris *m*, bran

fŭrĭae, ārum *f.pl*, rage, frenzy, avenging Furies

fŭrĭālis, e *adj*, *adv*, ĭter, raging, wild

fūrĭbundus, a, um *adj*, raging
fūrĭo *v.t.* 1, to enrage
fūrĭōsus, a, um *adj*, raging
furnus, i *m*, oven
fūro, ŭi *v.i.* 3, to rage, be mad
fūror *v.t.* 1, *dep*, to steal
fūror, ōris *m*, rage, fury
furtim *adv*, stealthily
furtīvus, a, um *adj*, stolen, secret
furtum, i *n*, theft, trick
furtō *adv*, secretly
fūruncŭlus, i *m*, pilferer, sore, boil
furvus, a, um *adj*, gloomy, swarthy
fuscīna, ae *f*, trident
fusco *v.t.* 1, to blacken, darken
fuscus, a, um *adj*, dark, swarthy
fūsĭlis, e *adj*, fluid, soft
fustis, is *m*, cudgel, club
fūsus, a, um *adj*, spread out, wide
fūsus, i *m*, spindle
futtĭlis (fūtĭlis), e, *adj*, worthless
futtĭlĭtas (fūtĭlĭtas), ātis *f*,
   worthlessness
fŭtūra, ōrum *n.pl*, the future
fŭtūrum, i *n*, the future
fŭtūrus, a, um *adj*, future

G

gaesum, i *n*, heavy Gallic javelin
galbĭnus, a, um *adj*, greenish-
   yellow
gălĕa, ae *f*, helmet
gălĕo *v.t.* 1, to issue with helmets
gălērum, i *n*, **(us, i** *m*)**, hat
galla, ae *f*, oak-apple
gallīna, ae *f*, hen
gallīnārĭum, ii *n*, hen-house

garrĭo *v.t.* 4, to chatter
garrŭlĭtas, ātis *f*, chattering
garrŭlus, a, um *adj*, talkative
gărum (garon), i *n*, fish sauce
gaudĕo, gāvīsus *v.i.t.* 2, *semi-dep*,
   to rejoice
gaudĭum, ii *n*, joy, delight
gausăpa, ae *f*, rough clothing
gāvĭa, ae *f*, seabird
gāza, ae *f*, treasure (of Persia)
gĕlĭdus, a, um *adj*, *adv*, **ē**, ice-cold,
   frosty
gĕlo *v.i.t.* 1, to freeze
gĕlum, i (gĕlu, ūs) *n*, frost, cold
gĕmellus, a, um *adj*, **(us, i** *m*)**,
   twin
gĕmĭno *v.t.* 1, to double, pair
gĕmĭnus, a, um *adj*, twin
gĕmĭni, ōrum *m.pl*, twins
gĕmĭtus, ūs *m*, lamentation
gemma, ae *f*, bud, jewel, goblet,
   signet-ring
gemmārĭus, ii *m*, jeweller
gemmātus, a, um *adj*, set with
   jewels
gemmĕus, a, um *adj*, set with
   jewels
gemmo *v.i.* 1, to come into bud
gĕmo, ŭi, ĭtum *v.i.t.* 3, to groan,
   creak; deplore
gĕna, ae *f*, the cheek
gĕner, ĕri *m*, son-in-law
gĕnĕrālis, e *adj*, of a certain kind,
   general
gĕnĕrātim *adv*, in classes, in
   general
gĕnĕrātor, ōris *m*, breeder
gĕnĕro *v.t.* 1, to create, produce;
   (*passive*) be born

Insight

The **genitive** is the case that shows possession, author or
source; it completes the meaning of a noun by describing the
content or material of it. The dominant meaning is therefore
'of'.

---

gallus, i *m*, cock
gānĕa, ae *f*, eating-house
gānĕo, ōnis *m*, glutton
gannĭo *v.i.* 4, to bark, snarl
gannītus, ūs *m*, chattering

gĕnĕrōsus, a, um *adj*, *adv*, **ē**, of
   noble birth, generous
gĕnesta, ae *f*, small shrub with
   yellow flowers, broom

gĕnĕtīvus, a, um *adj*, inborn
gĕnĕtrix, īcis *f*, mother
gĕnĭālis, e *adj, adv*, ĭter, bridal, cheerful
gĕnĭtālis, e *adj*, of birth, fruitful
gĕnĭtor, ōris *m*, father
gĕnĭus, ii *m*, guardian angel
gens, ntis *f*, clan, race, descendant, nation
gentīlĭcĭus, a, um *adj*, of the same clan
gentīlis, e *adj*, of the same clan
gentīlis, is *c*, relative
gĕnu, ūs *n*, knee
gĕnŭīnus, a, um *adj*, innate
gĕnŭīnus, a, um *adj*, of the cheek or jaw
gĕnus, ĕris *n*, birth, race, kind, type, descendant
gĕōgrăphĭa, ae *f*, geography
gĕōmĕtres, ae *m*, mathematician
gĕōmĕtrĭa, ae *f*, geometry
germānĭtas, ātis *f*, brotherhood
germānus, a, um *adj*, own
germānus, i *m*, (a, ae *f*), brother, (sister)
germen, ĭnis *n*, bud, sprig
germĭno *v.i.* 1, to bud
gĕro, gessi, stum *v.t.* 3, to bear, wear, bring, produce, behave, display, carry on, honour

gestus, a, um *adj*, achieved, carried
gibber, ĕris *m*, hump; *as adj*, hunchbacked
gibbus, i *m*, hump; *as adj*, hunchbacked
gĭgantēus, a, um *adj*, of giants
gīgās, ntis *m*, giant
gigno, gĕnŭi, gĕnĭtum *v.t.* 3, to give birth to; (*passive*) be born
gilvus, a, um *adj*, pale yellow
gingīva, ae *f*, gum
glăber, bra, brum *adj*, bald
glăcĭālis, e *adj*, frozen
glăcĭes, ēi *f*, ice
glăcĭo *v.t.* 1, to freeze
glădĭātor, ōris *m*, gladiator
glădĭātōrĭus, a, um *adj*, gladiatorial
glădĭus, ii *n*, sword
glaeba (glēba), ae *f*, clod
glans, ndis *f*, acorn, bullet
glārĕa, ae *f*, gravel
glaucus, a, um *adj*, blue-grey
glēba *see* glaeba
glis, glīris *m*, dormouse
glisco, m *v.i.* 3, to swell, grow
glŏbōsus, a, um *adj*, spherical
glŏbus, i *m*, ball, crowd
glŏmĕro *v.t.* 1, to gather into a heap, crowd together
glŏmus, ĕris *n*, ball of thread

Insight

The **gerund** and **gerundive** are two different things. The gerund is a 'verbal noun' and it therefore declines like a second declension noun (*ars regendi* = the art of ruling); the gerundive is a verbal adjective and it therefore declines like a first-and-second declension adjective (*hoc faciendum est* = this must be done).

gerrae, ārum *f.pl*, nonsense
gĕrŭlus, i *m*, porter
gestāmen, ĭnis *n*, load
gestātĭo, ōnis *f*, riding, driving
gestĭo *v.i.* 4, to be joyful, desire passionately
gesto *v.t.* 1, to carry, wear, have
gestus, ūs *m*, posture, gesture

glōrĭa, ae *f*, glory, boasting
glōrĭātĭo, ōnis *f*, boasting
glōrĭor *v.i.t.* 1, *dep*, to boast
glōrĭōsus, a, um *adj, adv*, ē, famous, conceited
glossārĭum, ii *n*, glossary
glūten, ĭnis *n*, glue
glūtĭnātor, ōris *m*, bookbinder

glūtĭno *v.t.* 1, to glue
gluttĭo *v.t.* 4, to gulp
gnārus, a, um *adj. with genit,*
acquainted with, expert in
gnātus, a, um *adj,* born
gnāv... see nāv...
gossypĭum, ii *n,* cotton
grăcĭlis, e *adj,* slender
grăcĭlĭtas, ātis *f,* slenderness
grăcŭlus, i *m,* jackdaw
grădātim, *adv,* gradually
grădātĭo, ōnis *f,* gradation, climax
grădĭor, gressus *v.i.* 3, *dep,* to
walk, go, move
grădus, ūs *m,* pace, step, rank,
position, station, stair, plait
graecor *v.i.* 1, *dep,* to live like the
Greeks
grallae, ārum *f.pl,* stilts
grāmen, ĭnis *n,* grass
grāmĭnĕus, a, um *adj,* grassy
grammătĭca, ae *f,* grammar
grammătĭcus, i *m,* grammarian
grānārĭa, ōrum *n.pl,* granary
grānātus, a, um *adj,* with many
seeds
grandaevus, a, um *adj,* old
grandĭlŏquus, a, um *adj,* boastful
grandĭnat *v.* 1, *impers,* it is hailing
grandis, e *adj,* full-grown, large,
old, strong, noble
grando, ĭnis *f,* hail, hailstorm
grānum, i *n,* grain, seed
grānōsus, a, um *adj,* seedy
grassātor, ōris *m,* idler, footpad
grassor *v.i.* 1, *dep,* to hang about,
attack, rage
grātē *adv,* gratefully, willingly
grātes *f.pl,* thanks
grātĭa, ae *f,* esteem, friendship,
charm, beauty, kindness, favour,
gratitude; *in abl,* for the sake of;
grātĭīs (grātīs), as a favour; *pl,*
thanks
grātĭfĭcātĭo, ōnis *f,* doing favours
grātĭfĭcor *v.* 1, *dep,* to do as a
favour, oblige
grātĭōsus, a, um *adj,* popular
grātor *v.i.t.* 1, *dep,* to congratulate
grātŭītus, a, um *adj,* voluntary
grātŭlātĭo, ōnis *f,* rejoicing
grātŭlor *v.i.t.* 1, *dep,* to
congratulate

grātus, a, um *adj,* pleasing, grateful
grăvāte *adv,* unwillingly
grăvēdo, ĭnis *f,* cold, catarrh
grăvĕŏlens, ntis *adj,* stinking
grăvesco *v.i.* 3, to grow heavy
grăvĭdus, a, um *adj,* pregnant
grăvis, e *adj, adv,* **ĭter,** heavy,
loaded, low, pregnant, severe,
unpleasant, serious, urgent,
important
grăvĭtas, ātis *f,* weight, heaviness,
severity, dignity, urgency
grăvo *v.t.* 1, to load, oppress
grăvor *v.i.t.* 1, *dep,* to be irritated
or reluctant; not to tolerate
grĕgālis, e *adj,* of the herd,
gregarious
grĕgārĭus, a, um *adj,* common
grĕgātim *adv,* in herds
grĕmĭum, ii, *n,* bosom, lap
gressus, ūs *m,* step, way
grex, grĕgis *m,* flock, herd
grūmus, i *m,* hillock
grunnĭo *v.i.* 4, to grunt
grunnītus, ūs *m,* grunt
grus, grŭis *m, f,* crane
grўllus, i *m,* grasshopper
gryps, gryphis *m,* griffin
gŭbernācŭlum, i *n,* rudder
gŭbernātĭo, ōnis *f,* management
gŭbernātor, ōris *m,* steersman
gŭberno *v.t.* 1, to steer, manage
gŭla, ae *f,* throat, appetite
gŭlōsus, a, um *adj,* gluttonous
gummi *n, (indecl.),* gum
gurges, ĭtis *m,* whirlpool, abyss
gustātĭo, ōnis *f,* taste
gustātus, ūs *m,* sense of taste
gusto *v.t.* 1, to taste
gustus, ūs *m,* tasting, snack
gutta, ae *f,* drop, spot
guttur, ŭris *n,* throat
gutus (guttus), i *m,* flask
gymnāsĭum, ii *m,* gymnasium
gymnĭcus, a, um *adj,* gymnastic
gypsātus, a, um *adj,* covered with
lime
gypso *v.t.* 1, to plaster
gypsum, i *n,* white line
gўrus, i *m,* circuit, ring

H

hăbēna, ae *f,* thong, rein
hăbĕo *v.t.* 2, to have, keep, be able, render, esteem, use, deal with , know; *with* in animo to intend
hăbĭlis, e *adj,* convenient, expert
hăbĭtābĭlis, e *adj,* habitable
hăbĭtātĭo, ōnis *f,* residence
hăbĭto *v.i.t.* 1, to live; inhabit
hăbĭtus, ūs *m,* condition, bearing, state, dress, shape
hāc *adv,* by this way, here
hactĕnus *adv,* up to this point
haec see **hic**
haedus, i *m,* young goat
haemorrhăgĭa, ae *f,* haemorrhage
haerĕo, si, sum *v.i.* 2, to hang, cling, hesitate
haesĭtans, ntis *adj,* hesitant
haesĭtantĭa, ae *f,* stammering
haesĭtātĭo, ōnis *f,* embarrassment
haesĭto *v.i.* 1, to hesitate
hālītus, ūs *m,* breath, steam
hālo *v.i.t.* 1, to breathe; exhale
hăma, ae *f,* bucket
hāmātus, a, um *adj,* hooked
hāmus, i *m,* hook, fish hook
hăra, ae *f,* coop, pen, sty
hărēna, ae *f,* sand, arena
hărēnārĭus, a, um *adj,* of sand
hărēnōsus, a, um *adj,* sandy
hărĭŏlor *v.i.* 1, *dep,* to foretell
hărĭŏlus, i *m,* prophet
harmŏnĭa, ae *f,* harmony
harpăgo, ōnis *m,* grappling-hook
hărundo, ĭnis *f,* reed, fishing rod, shaft, shepherd's pipe
hăruspex, ĭcis *m,* clairvoyant
hasta, ae *f,* spear, lance
hastāti, ōrum *m.pl,* pike-men; front line of a Roman army
hastīle, is *n,* spear shaft
haud (haut) *adv,* not at all
haudquāquam *adv,* by no means
haurĭo, si, stum *v.t.* 4, to draw up, drink in, drain, exhaust
haustus, ūs *m,* a drink, draught
hav... see **av...**
hĕbĕnus, i *f,* ebony
hĕbĕo *v.i.* 2, to be dull
hĕbes, ĕtis *adj,* blunt, dull
hĕbesco *v.i.* 3, to grow dull
hĕbĕto *v.t.* 1, to blunt
hĕdĕra, ae *f,* ivy
hei *interj,* ah! alas!
hellŭo, ōnis *m,* glutton
hellŭor *v.i.* 1, *dep, with abl,* to squander
hem! (em!) *interj,* ah! indeed!
hēmĭcyclĭum, ii *n,* semicircle
hēmisphaerĭum, ii *n,* hemisphere
hĕra, ae *f,* lady of the house
herba, ae *f,* grass, plant
herbārĭus, a, um *adj,* of plants
herbĭdus, a, um *adj,* grassy
herbōsus, a, um *adj,* grassy
hercŭle (hercle)! by Hercules!
hĕrĕ *adv,* yesterday
hērēdĭtārĭus, a, um *adj,* ïinherited
hērēdĭtas, ātis *f,* inheritance
hēres, ēdis *c,* heir, heiress
hĕri *adv,* yesterday
hĕrīlis, e *adj,* of the master or mistress
hernĭa, ae *f,* rupture
hērōĭcus, a, um *adj,* heroic
hēros, ōis *m,* demigod
hĕrus, i *m,* master of the house
hespĕris, ĭdis *adj,* western
hespĕrĭus, a, um *adj,* western
hesternus, a, um *adj,* yesterday's
heu! *interj,* oh! alas!
heus! *interj,* hallo there!
hexămĕter, tri *m,* a verse metre consisting of six feet
hĭans see **hĭo**
hĭātus, ūs *m,* aperture
hīberna, ōrum *n.pl,* winter quarters
hībernācŭla, ōrum *n.pl,* tents to spend winter in
hīberno *v.i.* 1, to spend the winter
hībernus, a, um *adj,* of winter
hibrĭda, ae *c,* cross breed
hīc, haec, hōc *pron,* this
hīc *adv,* here
hĭĕmālis, e *adj,* of winter
hĭĕmo *v.i.t.* 1, to spend the winter; freeze
hĭems (hiemps), hĭĕmis *f,* winter, stormy weather
hĭlăris, e *adj, adv,* **ē,** cheerful
hĭlărĭtas, ātis *f,* gaiety
hĭlăro *v.t.* 1, to cheer up
hillae, ārum *f.pl,* sausage

hinc *adv*, from here, hence
hinnĭo *v.i.* 4, to neigh
hinnītus, ūs *m*, neighing
hinnŭlĕus, i *m*, young stag
hĭo *v.i.* 1, to gape open
hippŏpŏtămus, i *m*, hippopotamus
hircīnus, a, um *adj*, of a goat
hircus, i *m*, goat
hirsūtus, a, um *adj*, shaggy
hirtus, a, um *adj*, rough, shaggy
hīrūdo, ĭnis *f*, leech
hĭrundĭnīnus, a, um *adj*, of swallows
hĭrundo, ĭnis *f*, a swallow
hisco, — *v.i.t.* 3, to gape; whisper
hispĭdus, a, um *adj*, rough, shaggy
histŏrĭa, ae *f*, story, account
histŏrĭcus, a, um *adj*, historical
histŏrĭcus, i *m*, historian
histrĭo, ōnis *m*, actor
hĭulcus, a, um *adj*, gaping; (of speech) badly connected
hoc see **hic**
hŏdĭē *adv*, today
hŏdĭernus, a, um *adj*, of today
hŏlus, ĕris *n*, vegetables
hŏluscŭlum, i *n*, small vegetable
hŏmĭcīda, ae *c*, murderer
hŏmĭcīdĭum, ii *n*, homicide
hŏmo, ĭnis *c*, human being

hŏnor (hŏnos), ōris *m*, esteem, public office, reward, charm
hŏnōrārĭus, a, um *adj*, honorary
hŏnōrātus, a, um *adj*, respected
hŏnōrĭfĭcus, a, um *adj, adv*, **ē**, complimentary
hŏnōro *v.t.* 1, to honour, respect, adorn
hŏnos see **hŏnor**
hŏnus... see **ŏnus...**
hōra, ae *f*, hour, time, season
hōrārĭum, ii *n*, hourglass
hordĕŏlus, i *m*, sty (eye)
hordĕum, i *n*, barley
hŏrĭŏla, ae *f*, fishing boat
hornŏtīnus, a, um *adj*, this year's
hornus, a, um *adj*, this year's
hōrŏlŏgĭum, ii *n*, clock
horrendus, a, um *adj*, terrible
horrĕo *v.i.t.* 2, to bristle, tremble; dread
horresco, horrŭi *v.i.* 3, to become ruffled or frightened
horrĕum, i *n*, barn, warehouse
horrĭbĭlis, e *adj*, terrible
horrĭdŭlus, a, um *adj*, rough
horrĭdus, a, um *adj, adv*, **ē**, rough, bristly, wild, uncouth
horrĭfer, ĕra, ĕrum *adj*, dreadful
horrĭfĭco *v.t.* 1, to ruffle, terrify
horrĭfĭcus, a, um *adj*, terrible

Insight

Latin has two words *homo* and *vir* that are commonly translated as 'man' but there is an important distinction between them. **Vir** is an adult male in contrast with **femina** 'woman'. The word **homo** means 'human being', the creature made of humus 'earth' and consequently subject to death, by contrast with a god, who lives forever and so is **immortalis** (lit. 'not dying', not subject to mors 'death').

hŏmullus, i *m*, puny man
hŏmuncŭlus, i *m*, puny man
hŏnestas, ātis *f*, honour, good name, integrity
hŏnesto *v.t.* 1, to honour, adorn
hŏnestum, i *n*, integrity
hŏnestus, a, um *adj, adv*, **ē**, respectable, esteemed, eminent

horrĭsŏnus, a, um *adj*, with fearful sounds
horror, ōris *m*, bristling, trembling, chill, terror
hortāmen, ĭnis *n*, encouragement
hortātĭo, ōnis *f*, encouragement
hortātor, ōris *m*, encourager
hortātus, ūs *m*, encouragement

hortor *v.t.* 1, *dep*, to encourage, urge, cheer on

hortŭlus, i *m*, little garden

hortus, i *m*, garden

hospĕs, ĭtis, *m*, (**hospĭta, ae** *f*), host(ess), guest, stranger

hospĭtālis, e *adj*, hospitable

hospĭtĭum, ii *n*, hospitality, friendship, lodgings

hostĭa, ae *f*, sacrificial victim

hostĭcus, a, um *adj*, of the enemy

hostīlis, e *adj, adv,* **ĭter**, hostile

hostis, is *c*, enemy, stranger

hūc *adv*, to this place or point

hui! *interj*, oh!

huius *genitive of* **hic**

hūiuscĕmŏdi, hūiusmŏdi *pron. adj*, (indecl.) of this sort

hūmāna, ōrum *n.pl*, human affairs

hūmānĕ *adv*, like a reasonable human being, courteously

hūmānĭtas, ātis *f*, humanity, gentleness, refinement

hūmānĭter *adv*, see **hūmānē**

hūmānus, a, um *adj*, human, mortal, humane, gentle, kind

hūmecto *v.t.* 1, to moisten

hūmĕo *v.i.* 2, to be wet

hūmĕrus, i *m*, shoulder, arm

hūmi *adv*, on or to the ground

hūmĭdus, a, um *adj*, damp, wet

hūmĭlis, e *adj, adv,* **ĭter**, low, humble, abject

hūmĭlĭtas, ātis *f*, lowness, insignificance, meanness

hūmo *v.t.* 1, to bury

hūmor, ōris *m*, liquid

hūmus, i *f*, the ground, region

hўăcinthus(os), i *m*, blue iris

hўaena, ae *f*, hyena

hўălus, i *m*, glass

hybrĭda, ae *c*, crossbreed

hўdra, ae *f*, seven-headed water snake

hydrĭa, ae *f*, jug

hydrops, ōpis *m*, dropsy

hydrus, i *m*, water snake

hўmen, mĕnis *m*, marriage

hўperbŏlē, es *f*, exaggeration, hyperbole

hystrĭx, ĭcis *f*, porcupine

I

ĭambēus, a, um *adj*, iambic

ĭambus, i *m*, iambic foot (two syllables, short followed by long)

ĭanthĭnus, a, um *adj*, violet in colour

ĭāpyx, iapўgis *m*, West-North-West wind

ĭaspis, ĭdis *f*, jasper

ĭbi *adv*, there, then

ĭbĭdem *adv*, in that same place, at that very moment

ĭbis, ĭdis *f*, scared bird, ibis

ĭcĭo (ĭco), īci, ictum *v.t.* 3, to hit, strike (a bargain)

ictus, ūs *m*, blow, stroke, shot

id see **is**

idcirco *adv*, for that reason

īdem, ĕădem, ĭdem *pron*, the same

īdentĭdem *adv*, repeatedly

īdĕo *adv*, for that reason

ĭdĭōta, ae *m*, layman

ĭdōnĕus, a, um *adj*, suitable, capable, sufficient

īdus, ŭum *f.pl*, the ides, 13th or 15th day of the month

īdyllĭum, ii *n*, idyll

īgĭtur *adv*, therefore, then

ignārus, a, um *adj*, unaware

ignāvĭa, ae *f*, laziness, cowardice

ignāvus, a, um *adj, adv,* **ē**, lazy, cowardly

ignesco *v.i.* 3, to catch fire

ignĕus, a, um *adj*, burning

ignĭcŭlus, i *m*, spark

ignĭfer, ĕra, ĕrum *adj*, fiery

ignis, is *m*, fire, glow

ignōbĭlis, e *adj*, unknown, obscure

ignōbĭlĭtas, ātis *f*, obscurity

ignōmĭnĭa, ae *f*, disgrace

ignōmĭnĭōsus, a, um *adj*, shameful

ignōrans, ntis *adj*, unaware

ignōrantĭa, ae *f*, ignorance

ignōrātĭo, ōnis *f*, ignorance

ignōro *v.i.t.* 1, to be unaware (of)

ignosco, nōvi, nōtum *v.t.* 3 *(with dat. of person)*, to forgive

ignōtus, a, um *adj*, unknown, of low birth

ii see **is**

īlex, ĭcis *f*, evergreen, oak

īlĭa, ĭum *n.pl*, groin, flank
īlĭcet *adv*, immediately
īlĭco *adv*, immediately
īlignus, a, um *adj*, of oak
illa see **ille**
illăbĕfactus, a, um *adj*, unbroken
illābor, psus *v.i.* 3, *dep*, to slip, glide, fall
illac *adv*, on that side
illăcessītus, a, um *adj*, unprovoked
illăcrĭmābĭlis, e *adj*, unlamented
illăcrĭmo *v.i.* 1, to weep over
illaesus, a, um *adj*, unhurt
illaetābĭlis, e *adj*, gloomy
illăquĕo *v.t.* 1, to ensnare
illātus see **infero**
ille, a, ud *pron*, *adj*, that, he, she, it

illud see **ille**
illūdo, si, sum *v.i.t.* 3, to play; mock, ridicule
illūmĭno *v.t.* 1, to light up
illustris, e *adj*, lighted up, distinct, distinguished
illustro *v.t.* 1, to elucidate, make famous
illŭvĭes, ēi *f*, dirt
īmāgo, ĭnis *f*, statue, picture, copy, echo, conception
imbēcillĭtas, ātis *f*, weakness
imbēcillus, a, um *adj*, weak
imbellis, e *adj*, unwarlike
imber, bris *m*, rain, shower
imberbis, e *adj*, beardless
imbĭbo, bĭbi *v.t.* 3, to drink in
imbrex, ĭcis *f*, gutter, tile

Insight

On its own the pronoun *ille, illa, illud* means 'that man', 'that woman', 'that thing' depending on gender and context. Often, however, it is used as if it was a personal pronoun and is best translated as 'he', 'she', 'it'.

---

illĕcĕbra, ae *f*, charm, allurement, bait
illĕcĕbrōsus, a, um *adj*, alluring
illĕpĭdus, a, um *adj*, ill-mannered, rude
illex, ĭcis *c*, decoy
illībātus, a, um *adj*, unimpaired
illībĕrālis, e *adj*, mean
illic *adv*, there, over there
illĭcĭo, lexi, ctum *v.t.* 3, to allure, entice
illĭcĭtus, a, um *adj*, forbidden
illīco *adv*, there, immediately
illīdo, si, sum *v.t.* 3, to strike, dash, beat
illīgo *v.t.* 1, to tie, fasten
illinc *adv*, from there
illĭno, lēvi, lĭtum *v.t.* 3, to smear, spread
illittĕrātus, a, um *adj*, illiterate
illīus *genitive of* **ille**
illō *adv*, to that place
illōtus, a, um *adj*, dirty
illūc *adv*, to that place
illūcesco, luxi *v.i.* 3, to grow light, dawn, shine

imbrĭfer, ĕra, ĕrum *adj*, rainy
imbŭo, ŭi, ūtum *v.t.* 3, to soak, infect, instil, train
īmĭtābĭlis, e *adj*, easily intimidated
īmĭtātĭo, ōnis *f*, imitation
īmĭtātor, ōris *m*, imitator
īmĭtātrix, ĭcis *f*, imitator
īmĭtor *v.t.* 1, *dep*, to imitate
immădesco, dŭi *v.i.* 3, to become wet
immānĭa, ĭum *n.pl*, horrors
immanis, e *adj*, *adv*, **ē, ĭter**, enormous, frightful, savage
immānītas, ātis *f*, enormity, barbarism, vastness
immansuētus, a, um *adj*, untamed
immātūrus, a, um *adj*, untimely, immature
immĕdĭcābĭlis, e *adj*, incurable
immĕmor, ōris *adj*, heedless
immĕmōrātus, a, um *adj*, unmentioned
immensĭtas, ātis *f*, immensity
immensum, i *n*, immensity
immensus, a, um *adj*, measureless, endless

immĕrens, ntis *adj*, undeserving, innocent

immergo, si, sum *v.t.* 3, to dip, plunge, immerse

immĕrĭtus, a, um *adj*, undeserved

immētātus, a, um *adj*, unmeasured

immìgro, *v.i.* 1, to go into

immìnĕo *v.i.* 2, to overhang, overlook, threaten, strive for

immĭnŭo, ŭi, ūtum *v.t.* 3, to reduce, weaken, destroy

immĭnūtĭo, ōnis *f*, weakening

immĭnūtus, a, um *adj*, unabated

immiscĕo, scŭi, xtum *v.t.* 2, to mix in, blend, unite

immĭsĕrābĭlis, e *adj*, unpitied

immĭsĕrĭcors, cordis *adj*, merciless

immissĭo, ōnis *f*, admission

immītis, e *adj*, harsh, rough

immitto, mīsi, ssum *v.t.* 3, to send in, let fly, incite, allow to grow wild

immo *adv*, on the contrary

immōbĭlis, e *adj*, immovable

immōbĭlĭtas, ātis *f*, immobility

immŏdĕrātus, a, um *adj, adv*, **ē**, excessive

immŏdĭcus, a, um *adj*, excessive

immŏlātĭo, ōnis *f*, sacrifice

immŏlo *v.t.* 1, to sacrifice, kill

immŏrĭor, mortŭus *v.i.* 3, *dep*, to die, die away

immortāles, ĭum *m.pl*, the gods

immortālis, e *adj*, immortal

immortālĭtas, ātis *f*, immortality

immōtus, a, um *adj*, unmoved

immūgĭo *v.i.* 4, to roar, resound

immundus, a, um *adj*, dirty

immūnis, e *adj*, exempt, idle, devoid of

immūnĭtas, ātis *f*, exemption

immūnītus, a, um *adj*, unfortified

immurmŭro *v.i.* 1, to murmur at

immūtābĭlis, e *adj*, unchangeable

immūtātĭo, ōnis *f*, interchange

immūto *v.t.* 1, to change, alter

impācātus, a, um *adj*, unsubdued

impar, ăris *adj, adv*, **ĭter**, unequal, uneven

impărātus, a, um *adj*, unprepared

impastus, a, um *adj*, hungry

impătĭens, ntis *adj*, impatient

impăvĭdus, a, um *adj*, fearless

impeccābĭlis, e *adj*, faultless

impēdīmenta, ōrum *n.pl*, luggage

impĕdīmentum, i *n*, obstacle

impĕdĭo *v.t.* 4, to hinder, entangle, hamper

impĕdītus, a, um *adj*, difficult; (soldiers) in full marching-kit

impĕdītĭo, ōnis *f*, obstruction

impello, pŭli, pulsum *v.t.* 3, to strike upon, drive on, urge, overthrow

impendens, ntis *adj*, overhanging

impendĕo *v.i.t.* 2, to overhang; threaten

impendĭum, ii *n*, cost, expense

impendo, di, sum *v.t.* 3, to expend, devote

impĕnĕtrābĭlis, e *adj*, impenetrable

impensa, ae *f*, cost, expense

impensus, a, um *adj, adv*, **ē**, large, strong, expensive

impĕrātor, ōris *m*, general

impĕrātōrĭus, a, um *adj*, of a general

impĕrātum, i *n*, order

imperfectus, a, um *adj*, incomplete

impĕrĭōsus, a, um *adj*, powerful, mighty, tyrannical

impĕrītĭa, ae *f*, inexperience

impĕrĭto *v.i.t.* 1, to command

impĕrītus, a, um *adj, with genit*, unskilled, or inexperienced in

impĕrĭum, ii *n*, power, command, control, dominion

impermissus, a, um *adj*, forbidden

impĕro *v.t.* 1, *with dat. of person*, to command, impose on, demand, requisition, rule

impertĭo *v.t.* 4, to share

impervĭus, a, um *adj*, impervious

impĕtĭbĭlis, e *adj*, intolerable

impĕtrābĭlis, e *adj*, attainable

impĕtro *v.t.* 1, to obtain, get

impĕtus, ūs *m*, attack, impetuosity, impulse

impexus, a, um *adj*, uncombed

impĭĕtas, ātis *f*, lack of respect for duty, disloyalty

impĭger, gra, grum *adj*, energetic

impingo, pēgi, pactum *v.t.* 3, to thrust, drive, strike (something) against

impĭus, a, um *adj*, undutiful, unpatriotic, disloyal, wicked
implācābĭlis, e *adj*, implacable
implācātus, a, um *adj*, unsatisfied
implăcĭdus, a, um *adj*, rough
implecto, xi, xum *v.t.* 3, to plait, interweave
implĕo, ēvi, ētum *v.t.* 2, to fill, complete, fulfil
implĭcātĭo, ōnis *f*, entwining, complication
implĭcātus, a, um *adj*, entangled, confused
implĭco *v.t.* 1, to entangle, involve, grasp, unite
implōrātĭo, ōnis *f*, entreaty
implōro *v.t.* 1, to implore, beg for
implūmis, e *adj*, unfledged, callow
implŭvĭum, ii *n*, rain-tank in floor of atrium of Roman house
impŏlītus, a, um *adj*, unpolished
impōno, pŏsŭi, pŏsĭtum *v.t.* 3, to place in or on, impose, assign
importo *v.t.* 1, to carry in, import, cause
importūnĭtas, ātis *f*, insolence
importūnus, a, um *adj*, *adv*, ē, inconvenient, unsuitable, troublesome, rude
impŏtens, ntis *adj*, powerless, weak, violent, headstrong
impŏtentĭa, ae *f*, violence
impransus, a, um *adj*, fasting
imprĕcātĭo, ōnis *f*, imprecation, curse

imprŏbĭtas, ātis *f*, wickedness
imprŏbo *v.t.* 1, to disapprove
imprŏbus, a, um *adj*, *adv*, ē, bad, wicked, violent, enormous, shameless
imprōvĭdus, a, um *adj*, not anticipating
imprōvīsus, a, um *adj*, *adv*, o, unexpected
imprūdens, ntis *adj*, *adv*, nter, unsuspecting, unaware
imprūdentĭa, ae *f*, lack of foresight
impūbes, is *adj*, youthful
impŭdens, ntis *adj*, shameless
impŭdentĭa, ae *f*, impudence
impŭdīcĭtĭa, ae *f*, shameful behaviour
impŭdīcus, a, um *adj*, shameless, lewd, disgusting
impugno *v.t.* 1, to attack
impulsor, ōris *m*, instigator
impulsus, ūs *m*, pressure, impulse, suggestion
impūnĕ *adv*, without punishment
impūnĭtas, ātis *f*, impunity
impūnītus, a, um *adj*, unpunished
impūrus, a, um *adj*, filthy
impŭto *v.t.* 1, to reckon, ascribe, impute
īmus, a, um *adj*, lowest, last
in *prep. with abl*, in, on, within, among; *with acc*, into, towards, till, against
ĭnaccessus, a, um *adj*, inaccessible

Insight

A **preposition** is a short word that stands in front of a noun or pronoun to produce an adverbial phrase. In Latin prepositions can be followed either by the accusative or the ablative. Only the preposition *in* can be followed by both cases, having in each instance a different meaning.

imprĕcor *v.t.* 1, *dep*, to pray for something for someone
impressĭo, ōnis *f*, imprint, onset
impressus, a, um *adj*, stamped, printed
imprīmīs *adv*, especially
imprĭmo, pressi, ssum *v.t.* 3, to stamp, imprint, engrave

ĭnaedĭfĭco *v.t.* 1, to build on
ĭnaequābĭlis, e *adj*, uneven, unlike
ĭnaequālis, e *adj*, uneven, unlike
ĭnaequālĭtas, ātis *f*, inequality
ĭnaestĭmābĭlis, e *adj*, inestimable
ĭnămābĭlis, e *adj*, hateful
ĭnămāresco *v.i.* 3, to become bitter

ĭnambŭlo *v.i.* 1, to walk up and down

ĭnāne, is *n*, emptiness

ĭnănĭmus, a, um *adj*, lifeless

ĭnānis, e *adj, adv*, ĭter, empty, useless, vain

ĭnānĭtas, ātis *f*, emptiness

ĭnărātus, a, um *adj*, unploughed

ĭnardesco, arsi *v.i.* 3, to catch fire, glow

ĭnassŭētus, a, um *adj*, unaccustomed

ĭnaudax, ācis *adj*, timid

ĭnaudĭo *v.t.* 4, to hear

ĭnaudītus, a, um *adj*, unheard of

ĭnaugŭro *v.i.t* 1, to divine omens; to consecrate, inaugurate

ĭnaurātus, a, um *adj*, golden

ĭnauro *v.t.* 1, to cover with gold

ĭnauspĭcātus, a, um *adj*, without good omens

ĭnausus, a, um *adj*, unattempted

incaedŭus, a, um *adj*, uncut

incălesco, călŭi *v.i.* 3, to grow hot, glow

incallĭdus, a, um *adj*, stupid

incandesco, dŭi *v.i.* 3, to grow hot, glow

incānesco, nŭi *v.i.* 3, to grow grey or white

incanto *v.t.* 1, to chant, bewitch

incānus, a, um *adj*, grey, white

incassum *adv*, in vain

incastīgātus, a, um *adj*, unpunished

incautus, a, um *adj, adv*, ē, rash, careless, unexpected

incēdo, cessi, ssum *v.i.* 3, to advance, appear, enter

incendĭārĭus, ii *m*, and incendiary

incendĭum, ii *n*, fire, heat

incendo, cendi, censum *v.t.* 3, to burn, excite, irritate

incensus, a, um *adj*, unregistered

incensus, a, um *adj*, burning, excited

inceptĭo, ōnis *f*, an attempt, undertaking

inceptum, i *n*, an attempt, undertaking

incertum, i *n*, uncertainity

incertus, a, um *adj*, uncertain, hesitating, doubtful

incesso, cessīvi *v.t.* 3, to attack, accuse

incessus, ūs   *m*, walk, pace, approach

incesto *v.t.* 1, to pollute

incestum , i *n*, adultery, incest

incestus, a, um   *adj*, impure

incĭdo, cĭdi, cāsum *v.i.* 3, to fall into or upon, meet, happen, occur

incīdo, cīdi, sum *v.t.* 3, to cut into, carve, interrupt

incingo, nxi, nctum *v.t.* 3, to encircle

incĭpĭo, cēpi, ceptum *v.i.t.* 3, to begin; undertake

incīsĭo, ōnis *f*, an incision

incĭtāmentum, i *n*, incentive

incĭtātĭo, ōnis *f*, instigation, energy

incīsūra, ae *f*, cutting, incision

incĭtātus, a, um *adj*, swift

incĭto *v.t.* 1, to urge on, rouse, excite, inspire

incĭtus, a, um *adj*, swift

incĭto *v.t.* 1, to urge on, rouse, excite, inspire

incĭtus, a, um *adj*, swift

inclāmo *v.i.t.* 1, to cry out; call out, to rebuke, abuse

inclēmens, ntis *adj, adv*, nter, harsh, severe

inclēmentĭa, ae *f*, harshness

inclīnātĭo, ōnis *f*, leaning, tendency

inclīno *v.i.t.* 1, to sink, yield; bend, turn, change

inclīnātus, a, um *adj*, bent, disposed

inclĭtus, a, um *adj*, famous

inclūdo, si, sum *v.t.* 3, to shut in, include, finish

inclūsĭo, ōnis *f*, confinement

inclŭtus, a, um *adj*, famous

incoctus, a, um *adj*, uncooked

incognĭtus, a, um *adj*, unknown

incŏhātus, a, um *adj*, incomplete

incŏho *v.i.t.* 1, to begin; undertake

incŏla, ae *c*, inhabitant

incŏlo, lŭi *v.i.t.* 3, to settle; inhabit

incŏlŭmis, e *adj*, safe, sound

incŏlŭmĭtas, ātis *f*, safety

incŏmĭtātus, a, um *adj*, unaccompanied

incommŏdĭtas, ātis *f*, unsuitability

incommŏdo *v.i.* 1, to be annoying
incommŏdum, i *n*, disadvantage
incommŏdus, a, um *adj, adv,* ē,
troublesome, unsuitable
incompertus, a, um *adj*, unknown
incompŏsĭtus, a, um *adj*, badly
arranged
incomptus, a, um *adj*, unadorned
inconcessus, a, um *adj*, illict
inconcinnus, a, um *adj*, awkward
incondĭtus, a, um *adj*, irregular,
confused, rude
inconsĭdĕrātus, a, um *adj, adv,* ē,
thoughtless, inconsiderate
inconsōlābĭlis, e *adj*, inconsolable
inconstans, ntis *adj, adv,* nter,
inconsistent, fickle
inconstantĭa, ae *f*, inconstancy
inconsultus, a, um *adj, adv,* ē,
without advice, indiscreet
inconsumptus, a, um *adj*,
unconsumed
incontāmĭnātus, a, um *adj*,
uncontaminated
incontĭnens, ntis *adj, adv,* nter,
immoderate
incŏquo, xi, ctum *v.t.* 3, to boil,
dye
incorruptus, a, um *adj*, unspoiled
incrēbresco, brŭi *v.i.* 3, to
increase, become prevalent
incrēdĭbĭlis, e *adj, adv,* ĭter,
incredible, unbelievable
incrēdŭlus, a, um *adj*, unbelieving
incrēmentum, i *n*, increase
increpo, ŭi, ĭtum *v.i.t.* 1, to rattle,
clatter; blare out, rebuke,
reprimand
incresco, ēvi *v.i.* 3, to grow
incrŭentus, a, um *adj*, bloodless
incrusto *v.t.* 1, to coat over
incŭbo, ŭi, ĭtum *v.i.* 1, to lie in or
on, rest on, fall upon
inculco *v.t.* 1, to trample on, cram
in, force on, obtude
incultus, a, um *adj, adv,* ē,
uncultivated, unpolished
incumbo, cŭbŭi, ĭtum *v.i.* 3, to lean
or lie on, overhang, fall upon,
take pains over, influence
incūnābŭla, ōrum *n.pl*, cradle,
birthplace, origin, swaddling
clothes

incūrĭa, ae *f*, neglect
incūrĭōsus, a, um *adj, adv,* ē,
indifferent
incurro, curri, cursum *v.i.t.* 3, to
run at, happen; attack
incursĭo, ōnis *f*, raid, attack
incurso *v.i.t* 1, to run to; attack,
strike
incursus, ūs *m*, attack
incurvo *v.t.* 1, to bend
invurvus, a, um *adj*, bent
incūs, ūdis *f*, anvil
incūso *v.t.* 1, to accuse, blame
incustōdītus, a, um *adj*, unguarded
incŭtĭo, cussi, cussum *v.t.* 3, to
strike upon, hurl, inflict
indāgātĭo, ōnis *f*, investigation
indāgo *v.t.* 1, to track down
indāgo, ĭnis *f*, enclosing
indĕ *adv*, from there, then
indēbĭtus, a, um *adj*, not due
indĕcor, ŏris *adj*, disgraceful
indĕcŏro *v.t.* 1, to disgrace
indĕcōrus, a, um *adj, adv,* ē,
unbecoming, unsightly,
disgraceful
indēfensus, a, um *adj*, undefended
indēfessus, a, um *adj*, unwearied
indēlēbĭlis, e *adj*, indestructible
indēlībātus, a, um *adj*, untouched
indemnātus, a, um *adj*,
unsentenced
indēprensus, a, um *adj*, unnoticed
index, ĭcis *m, f*, forefinger,
informer, sign, list
indĭcĭum, ii *n*, information,
evidence, proof, indication
indĭco *v.t.* 1, to show, indicate,
give evidence
indīco, xi, ctum *v.t.* 3, to
announce, appoint, impose
indictus, a, um *adj*, unsaid
indĭdem *adv*, from the same place
indĭes *adv*, from day to day
indiffĕrens, ntis *adj*, indifferent
indĭgĕna, ae *adj*, native
indĭgĕo *v.i.* 2, to need, want
indĭgestus, a, um *adj*, confused
indignans, ntis *adj*, enraged
indignātĭo, ōnis *f*, indignation
indignĭtas, ātis *f*, shameful
behaviour, unworthiness
indignor *v.t.* 1, *dep*, to be
indignant at, scorn

indignus, a, um *adj, adv,* **ē,**
unworthy, shameful, cruel
indĭgus, a, um *adj,* needing
indīlĭgens, ntis *adj, adv,* **nter,**
careless
indīlĭgentĭa, ae *f,* carelessness
indiscrētus, a, um *adj,* unseparated
indīsertus, a, um *adj,* at a loss for
words
indīvĭdŭus, a, um *adj,* indivisible
indo, dĭdi, dĭtum *v.t.* 3, to put or
place upon or into, attach
indŏcĭlis, e *adj,* unteachable,
untaught
indoctus, a, um *adj,* untaught
indŏles, is *f,* inborn abilities
indŏleso, lŭi *v.i.* 3, to be in pain, to
be troubled
indŏmĭtus, a, um *adj,* untamed
indormĭo *v.i.* 4, to fall asleep over
indōtātus, a, um *adj,* without a
dowry, poor
indŭbĭto *v.i.* 1, to distrust
indŭbĭus, a, um *adj,* not doubtful
indūco, xi, ctum *v.t.* 3, to lead in,
conduct, exhibit, spread over, put
on (clothes), induce, resolve,
cancel
inductĭo, ōnis *f,* introduction,
exhibition, intention
indulgens, ntis *adj, adv,* **nter,** kind,
indulgent, fond
indulgentĭa, ae *f,* indulgence
indulgĕo, si, tum *v.i.t.* 2, *with dat,*
to be kind to; permit, grant
indŭo, ŭi, ūtum *v.t.* 3, to put on
(garment), assume
indūro *v.t.* 1, to harden
indūsĭum, ii *n,* woman's petticoat
industrĭa, ae *f,* diligence; *with* **de**
or **ex** on purpose
industrĭus, a, um *adj,* diligent
indūtĭae, ārum *f.pl,* truce
indūtus, a, um *adj,* clothed
ĭnēdĭa, ae *f,* fasting
ĭnēlĕgans, ntis *adj, adv,* **nter,**
unrefined
ĭnēluctābĭlis, e *adj,* unavoidable
ĭnemptus, a, um *adj,* unbought
ĭnēnarrābĭlis, e *adj,* indescribable
ĭnĕo *v.i.t.* 4, to begin; enter,
calculate, estimate, contrive
ĭneptĭae, ārum *f.pl,* absurdities

ĭneptus, a, um *adj, adv,* **ē,**
improper, inept, foolish
ĭnermis, e *adj,* unarmed
ĭners, rtis *adj,* unskilful, idle,
sluggish
ĭnertĭa, ae *f,* ignorance, idleness
ĭnērŭdītus, a, um *adj,* illiterate
ĭnēvītābĭlis, e *adj,* unavoidable
ĭnexcūsābĭlis, e *adj,* inexcusable
ĭnexercĭtātus, a, um *adj,* untrained
ĭnexhaustus, a, um *adj,*
inexhaustible
ĭnexōrābĭlis, e *adj,* inexorable
ĭnexpectātus, a, um *adj,*
unexpected
ĭnexpertus, a, um *adj,*
inexperienced, untried
ĭnexplābĭlis, e *adj,* irreconcilable
ĭnexplēbĭlis, e *adj,* insatiable
ĭnexplētus, a, um *adj,* unsatisfied
ĭnexplĭcābĭlis, e *adj,* inexplicable
ĭnexplōrātus, a, um *adj,*
unexplored
ĭnexpugnābĭlis, e *adj,* impregnable
ĭnexstinctus, a, um *adj,*
imperishable
ĭnextrīcābĭlis, e *adj,* inextricable
infàbrē *adv,* unskilfully
infăcētus, a, um *adj,* coarse
infāmĭa, ae *f,* disgrace
infāmis, e *adj,* disreputable
infāmo *v.t.* 1, to disgrace
infandus, a, um *adj,* unutterable
infans, ntis *adj,* speechless
infans, ntis *c,* child, baby
infantĭa, ae *f,* speechlessness,
infancy
infātŭo *v.t.* 1, to make a fool of
infaustus, a, um *adj,* unfortunate
infector, ōris *m,* dyer
infectus, a, um *adj,* unfinished
infēcundus, a, um *adj,* unfruitful
infēlix, īcis *adj,* unhappy,
unfortunate, barren
infensus, a, um *adj,* enraged
infĕri, ōrum *m.pl,* the dead
infĕrĭae, ārum *f.pl,* sacrifices in
honour of the dead
infĕrĭor, ĭus *adv,* lower, later,
younger, inferior
infĕrĭus *adv,* lower
infernus, a, um *adj,* lower,
underground

inferi, ōrum *m.pl*, inhabitants of
the underworld, the dead
infero, inferre, intŭli, illātum *v.t*,
irreg, to bring to or against,
attack, produce, inflict
inferus, a, um *adj*, below, lower
infervesco, ferbŭi *v.i*. 3, to boil
infesto *v.t*. 1, to attack, molest
infestus, a, um *adj, adv*, ē,
dangerous, hostile, unsafe
inficĭo, fēci, fectum *v.t*. 3, to stain,
dye, taint, corrupt
infidēlis, e *adj*, untrustworthy
infidēlĭtas, ātis *f*, treachery
infidus, a, um *adj*, treacherous
infigo, xi, xum *v.t*. 3, to fix into,
drive in, imprint
infimus, a, um *adj*, lowest
infindo, fĭdi, fissum *v.t*. 3, to cut
into
infinĭtas, ātis *f*, endlessness
infinĭtus, a, um *adj, adv*, ē,
unlimited, endless
infirmātĭo, ōnis *f*, weakening
infirmĭtas, ātis *f*, weakness
infirmo *v.t*. 1, to weaken, annul
infirmus, a, um *adj, adv*, ē, weak
infit *v, defect*, he (she, it) begins
infitĭas ĕo (ire, ii) to deny
infitĭātĭo, ōnis *f*, denial
infitĭātor, ōris *m*, bad debtor
infitĭor *v.t*. 1, *dep*, to deny
inflammātĭo, ōnis *f*, inflammation,
setting on fire
inflammo *v.t*. 1, to set on fire
inflātus, ūs *m*, blast
inflātus, a, um *adj*, puffed up,
haughty, inflated
inflecto, xi, xum *v.t*. 3, to bend
inflētus, a, um *adj*, unmourned
inflexĭbĭlis, e *adj*, inflexible
inflexĭo, ōnis *f*, bending
infligo, xi, ctum *v.t*. 3, to strike
(something) against
inflo *v.t*. 1, to blow into
inflŭo, xi, xum *v.i*. 3, to flow into,
crowd in
infŏdĭo, fōdi, fossum *v.t*. 3, to dig
in, bury
informātĭo, ōnis *f*, outline
informis, e *adj*, shapeless
informo *v.t*. 1, to shape, sketch,
educate

infortūnātus, a, um *adj*,
unfortunate
infrā *adv, and prep. with acc*,
below, under
infractĭo, ōnis *f*, breaking
infractus, a, um *adj*, broken,
exhausted
infrĕmo, ŭi *v.i*. 3, to growl
infrendĕo *v.i*. 2, to gnash the teeth,
threaten
infrēnis, e (us, a, um) *adj*,
unbridled
infrēno *v.t*. 1, to bridle, curb
infrĕquens, ntis *adj*, rare, not well
filled
infrĕquentĭa, ae *f*, scantiness
infringo, frēgi, fractum *v.t*. 3, to
break off, crush, weaken
infŭla, ae *f*, headband, ribbon
infundĭbŭlum, i *n*, funnel
infundo, fūdi, fūsum *v.t*. 3, to pour
out, lay before, impart
infusco *v.t*. 1, to darken,
stain
infūsus, a, um *adj*, streaming or
falling over
ingĕmĭno *v.i.t*. 1, to increase;
repeat, redouble
ingĕmisco, mŭi *v.i*. 3, to sigh
ingĕmo, ŭi *v.i.t*. 3, to groan;
lament, mourn
ingĕnĕro *v.t*. 1, to produce
ingĕnĭōsus, a, um *adj, adv*, ē,
talented, adapted to
ingĕnĭum, ii *n*, natural disposition,
abilities, intelligence
ingens, ntis *adj*, huge, famous
ingĕnŭĭtas, ātis *f*, good birth,
gentlemanly character
ingĕnŭus, a, um *adj, adv*, ē,
natural, inborn, freeborn, frank,
honourable
ingĕnŭus, i *m*, (a, ae *f*), freeborn
man or woman
ingĕro, gessi, gestum *v.t*. 3, to
carry, throw or thrust into
ingigno, gĕnŭi, gĕnĭtum *v.t*. 3, to
implant, produce
inglōrĭus, a, um *adj*, inglorious
inglŭvĭes, ēi *f*, gizzard, maw
ingrātĭis *adv*, unwillingly
ingrātus, a, um *adj, adv*, ē,
unpleasant, ungrateful

ingrăvesco *v.i.* 3, to become heavy or worse

ingrăvo *v.t.* 1, to aggravate

ingrĕdĭor, gressus *v.i.t.* 3, *dep*, to advance; enter, upon

ingressĭo, ōnis *f*, entering, pace

ingressus, ūs *m*, entrance, inroad, commencement

ingrŭo, ŭi *v.i.* 3, to attack

inguen, ĭnis *n*, groin, abdomen

ingurgĭto *v.t.* 1 (*with* **se**) to gorge, addict one's self to

ĭnhăbĭlis, e *adj*, unwieldy, incapable

ĭnhăbĭtābĭlis, e *adj*, uninhabitable

ĭnhaerĕo, si, sum *v.i.* 2, to cling to, adhere to

ĭnhaeresco, haesi, haesum *v.i.* 3, to cling to, adhere to

ĭnhĭbĕo *v.t.* 2, to restrain

ĭnhĭo *v.i* 1, to gape, gaze

ĭnhŏnestus, a, um *adj*, shameful

ĭnhŏnōrātus, a, um *adj*, unhonoured

ĭnhorrĕo *v.i.* 2, to bristle, shiver

ĭnhorresco *v.i.* 3, to bristle, shiver

ĭnhospĭtālis, e *adj*, inhospitable

ĭnhospĭtus, a, um *adj*, inhospitable

ĭnhūmānĭtas, ātis *f*, barbarity, niggardliness

ĭnhūmānus, a, um *adj, adv*, ē, ĭter, savage, uncivilized, rude

ĭnhūmātus, a, um *adj*, unburied

ĭnĭbi *adv*, there

ĭnĭcĭo, iēci, iectum *v.t.* 3, to throw into, seize, inspire

ĭnĭmīcĭtĭa, ae *f*, enmity

ĭnĭmīco *v.t.* 1, to make into enemies

ĭnĭmīcus, a, um *adj, adv*, ē, unfriendly, hostile

ĭnĭmīcus, i *m*, (**a, ae** *f*), enemy

ĭnīquĭtas, ātis *f*, unevenness, difficulty, injustice

ĭnīquus, a, um *adj, adv*, ē, uneven, unfair, unfortunate, hostile, disadvantageous

ĭnĭtĭo *v.t.* 1, to initiate

ĭnĭtĭo *adv*, in the beginning

ĭnĭtĭum, ii *n*, beginning, origin; *pl*, first principles, sacred rites

ĭnĭūcundus, a, um *adj, adv*, ē, unpleasant

iniungo, nxi, nctum *v.t.* 3, to join on to, inflict, impose

iniūrātus, a, um *adj*, without taking an oath

iniūrĭa, ae *f*, injury, wrong

iniūrĭōsus, a, um *adj*, wrongful

iniussu *adv*, without orders

iniussus, a, um *adj*, of one's accord

iniustĭtĭa, ae *f*, injustice

iniustus, a, um *adj, adv*, ē, unjust, wrongful, harsh

innascor, nātus *v.i.* 3, *dep*, to be born in, grow up in

innăto *v.t.* 1, to swim, float in

innātus, a, um *adj*, innate

innāvĭgābĭlis, e *adj*, unnavigable

innecto, xŭi, xum *v.t.* 3, to tie, fasten, attach, contrive

innītor, nixus (nīsus) *v.* 3, *dep*, *with dat. or abl*, to lean on

inno *v.i.* 1, to swim, float in

innŏcens, ntis *adj*, harmless, blameless

innŏcentĭa, ae *f*, integrity

innŏcŭus, a, um *adj*, harmless

innoxĭus, a, um *adj*, harmless, innocent, unhurt

innūbus, a, um *adj*, unmarried

innŭmĕrābĭlis, e *adj*, countless

innŭmĕrus, a, um *adj*, countless

innŭo, ŭi, ūtum *v.i* 3, to nod, hint

innuptus, a, um *adj*, unmarried

ĭnobservātus, a, um *adj*, unperceived

ĭnoffensus, a, um *adj*, untouched, uninterrupted

ĭnōlesco, lēvi, lĭtum *v.i* 3, to grow in, take root

ĭnŏpĭa, ae *f*, lack, need

ĭnŏpīnans, ntis *adj*, unaware

ĭnŏpīnātus, a, um *adj, adv*, ē, ō, unexpected

ĭnŏpīnus, a, um *adj*, unexpected

ĭnopportūnus, a, um *adj*, unfitting, inopportune

ĭnops, ŏpis *adj*, helpless, needy

ĭnordĭnātus, a, um *adj*, in disorder

ĭnornātus, a, um *adj*, unadorned

inquam *v, irreg*, I say

inquĭes, ētis *f*, restlessness

inquĭētus, a, um *adj*, restless

inquĭlīnus, i *m*, lodger

inquĭnātus, a, um *adj,* filthy

inquĭno *v.t.* 1, to stain, corrupt

inquīro, sīvi, sītum *v.t.* 3, to search for, examine

inquīsītĭo, ōnis *f,* legal investigation

insălūbris, e *adj,* unhealthy

insălūtātus, a, um *adj,* without saying goodbye

insānābĭlis, e *adj,* incurable

insānĭa, ae *f,* madness, folly

insānĭo *v.i.* 4, to be insane, to rage

insānĭtas, ātis *f,* disease

insānus, a, um *adj, adv,* ē, insane, frantic, excessive

insătĭābĭlis, e *adj,* insatiable

inscĭens, ntis *adj,* unaware

inscĭentĭa, ae *f,* ignorance, inexperience

inscĭtĭa, ae *f,* ignorance, inexperience

inscītus, a, um *adj, adv,* ē, ignorant, stupid

inscĭus, a, um *adj,* unaware

inscrībo, psi, ptum *v.t.* 3, to write on, attribute

inscriptĭo, ōnis *f,* title

insculpo, psi, ptum *v.t.* 3, to engrave

insēco, cŭi, ctum *v.t.* 1, to cut up

insectātĭo, ōnis *f,* pursuit

insectātor, ōris *m,* pursuer

insector *v.t.* 1, *dep,* to pursue, reproach

insectum, i *n,* insect

insĕnesco, nŭi *v.i.* 3, to grow old at

insĕpultus, a, um *adj,* unburied

insĕquor, sĕcūtus *v.i.t.* 3, *dep,* to follow; pursue, reproach

insĕro, sēvi, sĭtum *v.t.* 3, to implant, ingraft

insĕro, rŭi, rtum *v.t.* 3, to put in, introduce

inserto *v.t.* 1, to insert

inservĭo *v.i.* 4, to serve, be submissive to, attend to

insīdĕo, sēdi, sessum *v.i.t.* 2, to sit upon, be fixed; occupy, inhabit

insīdĭae, ārum *f.pl,* ambush, plot; *with* ex *or* per, craftily

insīdĭor *v.* 1, *dep, with dat,* to lie in ambush

insīdĭōsus, a, um *adj, adv,* ē, cunning, dangerous

insīdo, sēdi, sessum *v.i.t.* 3, to settle on or in; occupy

insigne, is *n,* mark, sign, costume, signal, ornament

insignĭo *v.t.* 4, to make distinguished

insignis, e *adj,* conspicuous, famous, distinguished

insĭlĭo, ŭi *v.i.* 4, to spring upon

insĭmŭlo *v.t.* 1, to accuse

insincērus, a, um *adj,* tainted

insĭnŭo *v.i.t.* 1, to penetrate; insinuate

insĭpĭens, ntis *adj,* foolish

insĭpĭentĭa, ae *f,* folly

insisto, stĭtĭ *v.i.t.* 3, to step, stand, begin, halt; devote oneself to

insĭtus, a, um *adj,* inborn

insŏlens, ntis *adj, adv,* nter, unusual, unaccustomed, haughty

insŏlentĭa, ae *f,* strangeness, novelty, affectation, arrogance

insŏlĭtus, a, um *adj,* unaccustomed, unusual

insomnĭa, ae *f,* sleeplessness

insomnis, e *adj,* sleepless

insomnĭum, ii *n,* dream

insŏno, ŭi *v.i.* 1, to resound

insons, ntis *adj,* innocent, harmless

inspecto *v.t.* 1, to look at

inspērans, ntis *adj,* not hoping

inspērātus, a, um *adj,* unhoped for, unexpected

inspergo, si, sum *v.t.* 3, to sprinkle

inspĭcĭo, spexi, spectum *v.t.* 3, to examine, consider

inspīro *v.t.* 1, to breathe on, inspire

instăbĭlis, e *adj,* unsteady, changeable

instans, ntis *adj,* present

instar *n, indecl,* resemblance, appearance, value; *with genit,* as big as, like

instauro *v.t.* 1, to renew

insterno, strāvi, strātum *v.t.* 3, to spread or cover over

instīgo *v.t.* 1, to incite

instillo *v.t.* 1, to instil

instĭmŭlo *v.t.* 1, to spur on

instinctus, ūs *m*, impulse

instinctus, a, um *adj*, incited

instītor, ōris *m*, commercial traveller

instĭtŭo, ŭi, ūtum *v.t.* 3, to set up, appoint, undertake, resolve, arrange, train

instĭtūtĭo, ōnis *f*, arrangement, custom, education

instĭtūtum, i *n*, purpose, plan, custom

insto, stĭti, stātum *v.i.* 1, to stand over, harass, impend, urge on, pursue

instructus, a, um *adj*, arranged, provided with

instrūmentum, i *n*, tool, stores

instrŭo, xi, ctum *v.t.* 3, to erect, arrange, provide, teach

insŭāvis, e *adj*, unpleasant

insuesco, ēvi, ētum *v.i.t.* 3, to become accustomed; to accustom

insuētus, a, um *adj*, unaccustomed to, unusual

insŭla, ae *f*, island, block of flats

insŭlānus, i *m*, islander

insulsĭtas, ātis *f*, silliness

insulsus, a, um *adj, adv, ē*, tasteless, silly

insulto *v.i.t.* 1, to jump, leap; to spring at, abuse

insum, inesse, infŭi *v.i, irreg*, to be in, be contained in

insūmo, mpsi, mptum *v.t.* 3, to employ, expend

insŭo, ŭi, ūtum *v.t.* 3, to sew on

insŭper *adv, and prep. with acc*, moreover, besides; above

insŭpĕrābĭlis, e *adj*, insurmountable

insurgo, surrexi, rectum *v.i.* 3, to arise, rise to

insŭsurro *v.i.t.* 1, to whisper

intābesco, bŭi *v.i.* 3, to waste away

intactus, a, um *adj*, untouched, unattempted, chaste

intāmĭnātus, a, um *adj*, pure

intectus, a, um *adj*, uncovered

intĕger, gra, grum *adj, adv, ē*, untouched, perfect, blameless, unspoiled, undecided

intĕgo, xi, ctum *v.t.* 3, to cover

intĕgrĭtas, ātis *f*, completeness, uprightness

intĕgro *v.t.* 1, to renew, refresh

intĕgŭmentum, i *n*, covering, disguise

intellĕgens, ntis *adj*, understanding

intellĕgentĭa, ae *f*, understanding

intellĕgo, xi, ctum *v.t.* 3, to understand, perceive

intĕmĕrātus, a, um *adj*, pure

intempĕrans, ntis *adj*, extravagant

intempĕrantĭa, ae *f*, extravagance

intempĕrĭes, ēi *f*, inclement weather, violence

intempestīvus, a, um *adj, adv, ē*, untimely, inconvenient

intempestus, a, um *adj*, unseasonable, unhealthy; (*with* **nox**) the dead of night

intendo, di, tum (sum) *v.t.* 3, to stretch or spread out, aim, direct, threaten, concentrate, intend

intentātus, a, um *adj*, untried

intentĭo, ōnis *f*, tension, effort, application

intentus, a, um *adj, adv, ē*, stretched, bent, intent

intĕpesco, pŭi *v.i.* 3, to grow warm

inter *adv, and prep. with acc*, among, between, during

intercēdo, cessi, ssum *v.i.* 3, to go between, intervene, occur

intercessĭo, ōnis *f*, veto, intervention

intercessor, ōris *m*, mediator, surety, user of the veto

intercīdo, di, sum *v.t.* 3, to cut up

intercīdo, di *v.i.* 3, to happen, fall down, perish

intercĭpĭo, cēpi, ceptum *v.t.* 3, to intercept, seize, steal

interclūdo, si, sum *v.t.* 3, to block, cut off, hinder, separate, blockade

intercurro, curri, cursum *v.i.* 3, to run between, intercede

interdīco, dixi, dictum *v.t.* 3, to prohibit, banish

interdictum, i *n*, prohibition

interdĭu *adv*, in the daytime

interdum *adv*, sometimes

intĕrĕā *adv*, meanwhile

intĕrĕo, ĭi, ĭtum *v.i.* 4, to perish, die, become lost

intĕrest see intersum

interfector, ōris *m*, murderer

interfĭcĭo, fēci, fectum *v.t.* 3, to kill, destroy

interflŭo, xi *v.i.* 3, to flow between

interfūsus, a, um *adj*, poured between, interposed, stained

intĕrim *adv*, meanwhile

intĕrĭmo, ēmi, emptum *v.t.* 3, to take away, destroy, kill

intĕrĭor, ĭus *comp. adj*, inner

intĕrĭus *adv*, inside

intĕrĭtus, ūs *m*, annihilation

interĭăcĕo *v.i.* 2, to lie between

interĭcĭo, iēci, iectum *v.t.* 3, to put or throw between

interiectus, a, um *adj*, interposed

interlābor, lapsus *v.i.* 3, *dep*, to glide or flow between

interlĕgo, lēgi, lectum *v.t.* 3, to pluck, pick

interlūcĕo, luxi *v.i.* 2, to shine out, appear

interlŭo *v.t.* 3, to flow between

intermĭnātus, a, um *adj*, endless

intermiscĕo, scŭi, xtum *v.t.* 2, to intermix

intermissĭo, ōnis *f*, interruption, cessation

intermitto, mīsi, missum *v.i.t.* 3, to cease; neglect, omit, stop, pause, interrupt

intermortŭus, a, um *adj*, lifeless

internĕcīnus, a, um *adj*, deadly, internecine

internĕcĭo, ōnis *f*, massacre

internecto *v.t.* 3, to bind up

internosco, nōvi nōtum *v.t.* 3, to distinguish between

internuntĭus, ii *m*, negotiator

internus, a, um *adj*, internal

interpellātĭo, ōnis *f*, interruption

interpello *v.t.* 1, to interrupt

interpŏlo *v.t.* 1, to furbish

interpōno, pŏsŭi, ĭtum *v.t.* 3, to put between, introduce; *with* se, to interfere; *with* fidem, to pledge

interpŏsĭtĭo, ōnis *f*, insertion

interprĕs, ĕtis *c*, negotiatior

interprĕtātĭo, ōnis *f*, explanation

interprĕtor *v.t.* 1, *dep*, to explain

interpunctĭo, ōnis *f*, punctuation

interpungo, nxi, ctum *v.t.* 3, to punctuate

interquĭesco, quĭēvi, quĭētum *v.i.* 3, to rest for a while

interregnum, i *n*, vacancy in the kingship or high office

interrex, rēgis *m*, regent

interrĭtus, a, um *adj*, fearless

interrŏgātor, ōris *m*, questioner

interrŏgātum, i *n*, question

interrŏgo *v.t.* 1, to inquire

interrumpo, rūpi, ruptum *v.t.* 3, to break up, interrupt

intersaepĭo, psi, ptum *v.t.* 4, to hedge in, cut off

interscĭndo, scĭdi, scissum *v.t.* 3, to tear down, divide

intersĕro, rŭi, rtum *v.t.* 3, to interpose

intersum, esse, fŭi *v.i*, *irreg*, to lie between, differ, take part in; interest, *v*, *impers*, it concerns, it is of importance

intertexo, xŭi, xtum *v.t.* 3, to intertwine

intervallum, i *n*, space, pause

intervĕnĭo, vēni, ventum *v.i.* 4, to interrupt, happen, prevent

interventus, ūs *m*, intervention

intervīso, si, sum *v.t.* 3, to inspect, visit occasionally

intestābĭlis, e *adj*, abominable

intestīna, ōrum *n.pl*, intestines

intestīnus, a, um *adj*, internal

intexo, xŭi, xtum *v.t.* 3, to interlace

intĭmus, a, um *adj*, inmost

intŏlĕrābĭlis, e *adj*, intolerable

intŏlĕrandus, a, um *adj*, intolerable

intŏlĕrans, ntis *adj*, *adv*, nter, impatient, intolerable

intŏno, ŭi *v.i.* 1, to thunder

intonsus, a, um *adj*, unshaven

intorquĕo, si, sum *v.t.* 2, to twist, sprain, hurl

intrā *adv*, and *prep. with acc*, on the inside, within

intractābĭlis, e *adj*, unmanageable

intractātus, a, um *adj*, untried

intrĕmo, ŭi *v.i.* 3, to tremble

intrĕpĭdus, a, um *adj*, fearless

intrō *adv*, within, inside

intro *v.i.t.* 1, to enter

intrōdūco, xi, ctum *v.t.* 3, to lead in, introduce
intrōductĭo, ōnis *f*, introduction
intrōeo *v.i.* 4, to enter
intrōfĕro, ferre, tŭli, lātum *v.t, irreg*, to bring in
intrōgrĕdĭor, gressus *v.i.* 3, *dep*, to enter
intrŏĭtus, ūs *m*, entrance
intrōmitto, mīsi, ssum *v.t.* 3, to send in
introrsum (us) *adv*, within
intrōspĭcĭo, spexi, spectum *v.t.* 3, to look into, examine
intŭĕor *v.t.* 2, *dep*, to look at
intŭmesco, mŭi *v.i.* 3, to swell
intus *adv*, within, inside
intūtus, a, um *adj*, unguarded
ĭnultus, a, um *adj*, unavenged
ĭnumbro *v.t.* 1, to shade
ĭnundātĭo, ōnis *f*, flooding
ĭnundo *v.i.t.* 1, to overflow; flood
ĭnungo, nxi, unctum *v.t.* 3, to anoint
ĭnurbānus, a, um *adj*, rude
ĭnūro, ssi, stum *v.t.* 3, to brand
ĭnūsĭtātus, a, um *adj, adv, ē*, unusual, strange
ĭnūtĭlis, e *adj*, useless
ĭnūtĭlĭtas, ātis *f*, uselessness
invādo, si, sum *v.i.t.* 3, to enter; attack, invade, seize
invălĭdus, a, um *adj*, weak
invĕho, xi, ctum *v.t.* 3, to carry, bring to; *passive or reflex*, to ride, drive, attack (with words)
invĕnĭo, vēni, ventum *v.t.* 4, to find, meet with, devise
inventĭo, ōnis *f*, invention
inventor, ōris *m*, inventor
inventum, i *n*, invention
invĕnustus, a, um *adj*, unattractive
invĕrēcundus, a, um *adj*, immodest
invergo *v.t.* 3, to pour on
inversus, a, um *adj*, inverted, perverted
inverto, ti, sum *v.t.* 3, to turn upside down, exchange
invespĕrascit *v, impers*, evening is approaching
investīgātĭo, ōnis *f*, investigation
investīgo *v.t.* 1, to search for
invĕtĕrasco, rāvi *v.i.* 3, to grow old, become permanent

invĕtĕrātus, a, um *adj*, old-established
invĕtĕro *v.t.* 1, to endure
invĭcem *adv*, alternately
invictus, a, um *adj*, unconquered, invincible
invĭdĕo, vīdi, vīsum *v.t.* 2, *with dat*; to envy, grudge
invĭdĭa, ae *f*, envy, ill will
invĭdĭōsus, a, um *adj, adv, ē*, jealous, enviable
invĭdus, a, um *adj*, envious
invĭgĭlo *v.i.* 1, to be watchful
invĭŏlātus, a, um *adj*, unharmed
invīso, si, sum *v.t.* 3, to visit
invīsus, a, um *adj*, hated
invīsus, a, um *adj*, unseen
invītātĭo, ōnis *f*, challenge, invitation
invīto *v.t.* 1, to invite, challenge, tempt
invītus, a, um *adj*, unwilling
invĭus, a, um *adj*, pathless
invŏcātus, a, um   *adj*, uninvited
invŏco *v.t.* 1, to appeal to
invŏlĭto *v.i.* 1, to hover
invŏlo *v.i.t.* 1, to fly at; attack
invŏlūcrum, i *n*, wrapper
invŏlūtus, a, um *adj*, intricate
involvo, volvi, vŏlūtum *v.t.* 3, to roll on, wrap up, envelop
invulnĕrābĭlis, e *adj*, invulnerable
ĭō *interj*, oh! ah! ho!
ipse, a, um (*genit*, **ipsius**, dat, **ipsi**), *emphatic pron*, himself, herself, itself, precisely, just
īra, ae *f*, anger
īrācundĭa, ae *f*, rage, temper
īrācundus, a, um *adj*, irritable
īrascor, īrātus *v.* 3, *dep, with dat*, to be angry with
īrātus, a, um *adj*, angry
ire see **ĕo**
īris, ĭdĭs *f*, iris
īrōnĭa, ae *f*, irony
irpes, ĭcis *m*, harrow
irrĕmĕābĭlis, e *adj*, irretraceable
irrĕpĕrābĭlis, e *adj*, irrecoverable
irrĕpertus, a, um *adj*, undiscovered
irrēpo, psi, ptum *v.i.* 3, to creep in, insinuate oneself
irrĕquĭētus, a, um *adj*, restless
irrētĭo *v.t.* 4, to entangle

irrĕtortus, a, um *adj*, not turned
back

irrĕvŏcābĭlis, e *adj*, irrevocable

irrīdĕo, si, sum *v.i.t.* 2, to joke,
jeer; mock, ridicule

irrĭgātĭo, ōnis *f*, irrigation

irrĭgo *v.t.* 1, to water, refresh

irrĭgŭus, a, um *adj*, well-watered,
moistening

irrīsĭo, ōnis *f*, mockery

irrīsus, ūs *m*, mockery

irrīsor, ōris *m*, scoffer

irrītābĭlis, e *adj*, irritable

irrītāmen, ĭnis *n*, incentive

irrītāmentum, i *n*, incentive

irrīto *v.t.* 1, to provoke

irrĭtus, a, um *adj*, invalid,
unsuccessful

irrŏgo *v.t.* 1, to propose (against
someone), inflict

irrōro *v.t.* 1, to bedew

irrumpo, rūpi, ptum *v.i.t.* 3, to
break in; attack, interrupt

irrŭo, ŭi *v.i.* 3, to rush in, seize

irruptus, a, um *adj*, unbroken

īs, ĕa, id *demonst. pron*, he, she, it,
that

ischĭas, ădis *f*, sciatica

iste, a, ud *demonst. pron*, that

isthmus, i *m*, isthmus

istīc *adv*, there

istinc *adv*, from there

istūc *adv*, to that place

ĭtă *adv*, in such a way, so

ĭtăque *conj*, and so, therefore

ĭtem *adv*, likewise, also

ĭter, ĭtĭnĕris *n*, route, journey,
march

ĭtĕrātĭo, ōnis *f*, repetition

ĭtĕro *v.t.* 1, to repeat

ĭtĕrum *adv*, again

ĭtĭdem *adv*, in the same way

ĭtĭo, ōnis *f*, travelling

J (consonantal i)

ĭăcĕo *v.i.* 2, to lie (recumbent), lie
sick

ĭăcĭo, iēci, iactum *v.t.* 3, to throw,
lay down

iactans, ntis *pres. part, adj*,
boastful

iactantĭa, ae *f*, ostentation

iactātĭo, ōnis *f*, tossing, bragging

iactātor, ōris *m*, braggart

iacto *v.t.* 1, to throw about, boast

iactūra, ae *f*, throwing overboard,
sacrifice

iactus, ūs *m*, throw, shot

ĭăcŭlātor, ōris *m*, thrower

ĭăcŭlātrix, īcis *f*, huntress

ĭăcŭlor *v.t.* 1, *dep*, to hurl

ĭăcŭlum, i *n*, javelin

iam *adv*, already, now

iamdūdum *adv*, a long time ago

iamprīdem *adv*, for a long time
now

ĭānĭtor, ōris *m*, doorkeeper

ĭānŭa, ae *f*, door, entrance

Iānŭārĭus (mensis) January

iēcur, ōris *n*, liver

iēiūnĭtas, ātis *f*, meagreness

iēiūnĭum, ii *n*, fast, hunger

iēiūnus, a, um *adj*, hungry, barren

ientācŭlum, i *n*, breakfast

iento *v.i.* 1, to breakfast

iŏcātĭo, ōnis *f*, joke

iŏcor *v.i.t.* 1, *dep*, to joke

iŏcōsus, a, um *adj*, humorous

iŏcŭlārĭs, e *adj*, amusing

iŏcŭlātor, ōris *m*, joker

iŏcus, i *m*, joke

iŭba, ae *f*, mane, crest

iŭbar, ăris *n*, radiance

iŭbĕo, iussi, iussum *v.t.* 2, to
order, tell

iūcundĭtas, ātis *f*, pleasantness

iūcundus, a, um *adj*, pleasant

iūdex, ĭcis *m*, judge

iudicialis, e *adj*, judicial

iudicatio, ōnis *f*, judgement

iūdĭcĭum, ii *n*, trial, verdict, court,
discretion, judgement

iūdĭco *v.t.* 1, to judge, decide

iŭgālis, e *adj*, yoked together

iŭgāles *m.pl*, chariot horses

iūgĕrum, i *n*, acre (approx.)

iūgis, e *adj*, perpetual

iūglans, dis *f*, walnut

iŭgo *v.t.* 1, to marry, connect

iŭgōsus, a, um *adj*, mountainous

iŭgŭlo *v.t.* 1, to cut the throat

iŭgum, i *n*, yoke, bench, mountain-
ridge

Iūlĭus (mensis), July

iūmentum, i *n*, pack animal
iuncĕus, a, um *adj*, made of rushes
iuncōsus, a, um *adj*, full of rushes
iunctĭo, ōnis *f*, junction
iunctūra, ae *f*, joint
iuncus, i *m*, bullrush
iungo, nxi, nctum *v.t.* 3, to join
iūnĭor *comp. adj*, from iŭvĕnis, younger
iūnĭpĕrus, i *f*, juniper tree
Iūnĭus (mensis) June
iūrātor, ōris *m*, commissioner of oaths
iūrātus, a, um *adj*, bound by oath
iurgĭum, ii *n*, quarrel
iurgo *v.i.t.* 1, to quarrel; upbraid
iūris consultus, i *m*, lawyer
iūris dictĭo, ōnis *f*, jurisdiction
iūro *v.i.t.* 1, to take an oath; to swear by
iūs, iūris *n*, law, legal status, right, authority
iūs, iūris *n*, soup
iusiūrandum, i *n*, oath
iussum, i *n*, order
iusta, ōrum *n.pl*, due ceremonies
iustē *adv*, rightly
iustĭtĭa, ae *f*, justice
iustĭtĭum *n*, holiday for lawcourts, public mourning
iusum, i *n*, fairness
iustus, a, um *adj*, fair, lawful
iŭvĕnālis, e *adj*, youthful
iŭvenca, ae *f*, heifer
iŭvencus, i *m*, bullock
iŭvĕnesco, nŭi *v.i.* 3, to reach youth
iŭvĕnīlis, e *adj*, youthful
iŭvĕnis, is *m, f*, young person; (*adj*) young
iŭvĕnor *v.i.* 1, *dep*, to act youthfully
iŭventa, ae *f*, the age of youth
iŭventas, ātis *f*, the age of youth
iŭventus, ūtis *f*, the age of youth
iŭvo, iūvi, iūtum *v.t.* 1, to help, gratify; iŭvat (*impers, with acc*), it pleases, it is of use
iuxtā *adv, and prep. with acc*, near
iuxtim *adv, and prep. with acc*, next to

K

Kalendae, ārum *f.pl*, the Kalends, the first day of the month

L

lăbĕfăcĭo, fēci, factum *v.t.* 3, to shake, loosen, overthrow
lăbĕfacto *v.t.* 1, to shake, destroy
lăbellum, i *n*, a lip
lăbellum, i *n*, tub, basin
lābes, is *f*, sinking, downfall
lābes, is *f*, spot, blemish
lăbo *v.i.* 1, to totter, waver
lābor, lapsus *v.i.* 3, *dep*, to slip, slide, glide, pass away, be mistaken
lăbor, ōris *m*, work, toil, workmanship, distress
lăbŏrĭōsus, a, um *adj, adv,* ē, laborious, industrious
lăbōro *v.i.t.* 1, to strive, be in trouble or difficulty; to make, prepare
lăbrum, i *n*, lip
lābrum, i *n*, tub, basin
lăbўrinthus, i *m*, labyrinth
lac, lactis *n*, milk
lăcer, ĕra, ĕrum *adj*, mangled
lăcerna, ae *f*, cloak
lăcĕrātĭo, ōnis *f*, laceration
lăcĕro *v.t.* 1, to tear, rend, censure, destroy
lăcerta, ae *f* (us, i *m*), lizard
lăcertōsus, a, um *adj*, brawny
lăcertus, i *m*, arm, strength
lăcertus, i *m*, lizard, newt
lăcesso, īvi, ītum *v.t.* 3, to provoke, attack, irritate, urge
lăcĭnĭa, ae *f*, edge of garment
lăcrĭma, ae *f*, tear
lăcrĭmābilis, e *adj*, mournful
lăcrĭmo *v.i.* 1, to weep
lăcrĭmōsus, a, um *adj*, tearful
lactens, ntis *f*, very young (unweaned) animal
lactĕus, a, um *adj*, milky
lacto *v.i.t.* 1, to have milk; suck
lactūca, ae *f*, lettuce
lăcūna, ae *f*, ditch, pond, gap

lăcūnar

lăcūnar, āris *n*, ceiling
lăcus, ūs *m*, lake, tank, tub
laedo, si, sum *v.t.* 3, to injure, offend
laena, ae *f*, cloak
laetābĭlis, e *adj*, joyful
laetĭfĭco *v.t.* 1, to delight
laetĭtĭa, ae *f*, joyfulness
laetor *v.i.*, *dep*, to rejoice
laetus, a, um *adj, adv,* **ē**, glad, cheerful, willing, pleased, prosperous, beautiful
laeva, ae *f*, the left hand
laevus, a, um *adj*, on the left side, unfortunate, foolish
lăgănum, i *n*, a cake
lăgēna, ae *f*, wine jar
lăgōis, ĭdis *f*, grous
lăgōpūs, ŏdis *f*, grouse
lăguncŭla, ae *f*, small bottle
lambo, bi, bĭtum *v.t.* 3, to lick
lāmentābĭlis, e *adj*, mournful
lāmentātĭo, ōnis *f*, mourning
lāmentor *v.i.t.* 1, *dep*, to weep; mourn
lāments, ōrum *n.pl*, moaning
lămĭa, ae *f*, witch, vampire
lāmĭna, ae *f*, thin metal plate
lampas, ădis *f*, torch
lāna, ae *f*, wool
lancĕa, ae *f*, lance, spear
lānĕus, a, um *adj*, woollen
languens, ntis *adj*, faint, weak
languĕo *v.i.* 2, to be faint or listless
languesco, gŭi *v.i.* 3, to become faint or listless
languĭdus, a, um *adj*, faint, weary, sluggish
languor, ōris *m*, weakness, weariness, sluggishness
lănĭātus, ūs *m*, laceration
lānĭcĭum, ii *n*, wool
lănĭēna, ae *f*, butcher's stall
lānĭfĭcus, a, um *adj*, weaving
lānĭger, ĕra, ĕrum *adj*, fleecy
lănĭo *v.t.* 1, to mutilate
lănista, ae *m*, fencing master
lănĭus, ii *m*, butcher
lanterna, ae *f*, lamp, torch
lānūgo, ĭnis *f*, down, hair
lanx, ncis *f*, dish, plate
lăpăthus, i *f*, sorrel

lăpĭcīda, ae *m*, quarryman
lăpĭcīdīnae, ārum *f.pl*, stone quarries
lăpĭdātĭo, ōnis *f*, stoning
lăpĭdĕus, a, um *adj*, of stone
lăpĭdōsus, a, um *adj*, stony
lăpillus, i *m*, pebble, grain
lăpis, ĭdis *m*, stone, milestone, jewel
lappa, ae *f*, burr
lapso *v.i.* 1, to slip, stumble
lapsus, a, um *adj*, fallen, sinking, ruined
lapsus, ūs *m*, fall, slip, gliding
lăquĕar, āris *n*, ceiling
lăquĕātus, a, um *adj*, panelled
lăquĕus, i *m*, noose, snare
lar, ăris *m*, guardian deity of a house, home
largĭor *v.t.* 4, *dep*, to lavish, give
largĭtas, ātis *f*, abundance
largĭtĭo, ōnis *f*, generous distribution, bribery
largĭtor, ōris *m*, briber, generous giver
largus, a, um *adj, adv,* **ē, ĭter**, abundant, lavish, large
lārĭdum (lardum), i *n*, lard
lārix, ĭcis *f*, larch
larva, ae *f*, ghost, mask
lascīvĭa, ae *f*, playfulness
lascīvĭo *v.i.* 4, to frolic
lascīvus, a, um *adj*, playful, licentious
lassĭtūdo, ĭnis *f*, weariness
lasso *v.t.* 1, to tire, fatigue
lassus, a, um *adj*, exhausted
lātē *adv*, far and wide
lătèbra, ae *f*, hiding-place, subterfuge
lătèbrōsus, a, um *adj*, full of hiding places, secret
lătens, ntis *adj, adv,* **nter**, hidden, secret
lătĕo *v.i.* 2, to lie hidden, keep out of sight
lăter, ĕris *m*, brick, tile, ingot
lătĕrīcĭus, a, um *adj*, made of bricks
lătex, ĭcis *m*, liquid
lătĭbŭlum, *n*, hiding-place
Lătīnē *adv*, in Latin
lătĭto *v.i.* 1, to lie hidden

lātĭtūdo, ĭnis *f*, breadth
lātor, ōris *m*, proposer of a law
lātrātor, ōris *m*, a barker
lātrātus, ūs *m*, barking
lātrīna, ae *f*, water-closet
lātro *v.i.t.* 1, to bark; bark at
lătro, ōnis *m*, robber
lătrōcĭnĭum, ii *n*, robbery, fraud, robber-band
lătrōcĭnor *v.i.* 1, *dep*, to practise highway robbery
lătruncŭlus, i *m*, robber
lātus, a, um *adj, adv*, ē, wide
lătus, ĕris *n*, the side, flank, lungs
laudābĭlis, e *adj*, praiseworthy
laudātĭo, ōnis *f*, praises, eulogy
laudātor, ōris *m*, praiser
laudātus, a, um *adj*, praiseworthy
laudo *v.t.* 1, to praise, name

lectĭo, ōnis *f*, selection, reading aloud
lector, ōris *m*, reader
lectŭlus, i *m*, sofa, couch
lectus, a, um *adj*, chosen, excellent
lectus, i *m*, bed, couch
lectus, ūs *m*, reading
lēgātĭo, ōnis *f*, delegation
lēgātum, i *n*, legacy
lēgātus, i *m*, ambassador, delegate, lieutenant-general
lēges see lex
lēgĭfer, ĕra, ĕrum *adj*, law-giving
lēgĭo, ōnis *f*, Roman legion (4,000–6,000 soldiers)
lēgĭōnārĭus, a, um *adj*, of a legion
lēgĭtĭmus, a, um *adj*, legal, legitimate, proper, right

Insight

Active verbs usually have four **principal parts**. Deponent verbs have three. The principal parts give the first person singular present tense, the infinitive, the first person singular perfect tense, and the supine (e.g. *laudo, laudare, laudavi, laudatum*).

---

laurĕa, ae *f*, laurel (tree)
laurĕātus, a, um *adj*, crowned with laurel (of victory)
laurĕus, a, um *adj*, of laurel
laurus, i *f*, laurel
laus, dis *f*, praise, merit
lautē *adv*, elegantly
lautĭtĭa, ae *f*, elegance
lautŭmĭae, ārum *f.pl*, stone quarry
lautus, a, um *adj*, elegant, splendid, noble
lăvātĭo, ōnis *f*, ablution, washing
lăvo, lāvi, lautum *v.i.t.* 1 or 3, to wash or wet
laxĭtas, ātis *f*, spaciousness
laxo *v.t.* 1, to enlarge, loosen, relax, relieve, weaken
laxus, a, um *adj*, wide, loose
lĕa, ae *f*, lioness
lĕaena, ae *f*, lioness
lĕbes, ētis *m*, copper basin
lectīca, ae *f*, sedan, litter

lēgo *v.t.* 1, to send with a commission, appoint as a deputy, leave as a legacy
lĕgo, lēgi, lectum *v.t.* 3, to read, gather, select, steal, pass through, sail by, survey
lĕgūmen, ĭnis *n*, pulse, beans
lembus, i *m*, yacht, cutter
lĕmŭres, um *m.pl*, ghosts, spirits
lēna, ae *f*, bawd
lēnīmen, ĭnis *n*, alleviation, palliative
lēnīmentum, i *n*, alleviation, palliative
lēnĭo *v.t.* 4, to soften, soothe
lēnis, e *adj, adv*, ĭter, soft, smooth, gentle, calm
lēnĭtas, ātis *f*, gentleness
lēno, ōnis *m*, pimp, seducer
lēnōcĭnĭum, ii *n*, pandering, ornamentation
lēnōcĭnor *v.* 1, *dep, with dat*, to flatter, promote

lens

lens, ntis *f*, lentil
lentesco *v.i.* 3, to become soft or sticky
lentīgo, ĭnis *f*, freckle
lentĭtūdo, ĭnis *f*, apathy, sluggishness
lento *v.t.* 1, to bend
lentus, a, um *adj, adv*, **ē**, slow, flexible, sticky, tedious, calm (of character)
lēnuncŭlus, i *m*, boat

lībāmentum, i *n*, drink offering
lībella, ae *f*, small coin
lībellus, i *m*, small book, pamphlet, diary
lībens, ntis *adj, adv*, **nter**, with pleasure, willing
līber, ĕra, ĕrum *adj, adv*, **nter**, free, frank
līber, ĕri *m*, Baccus, wine
līber, ĕri *m*, child
līber, bri *m*, book, tree bark

Insight

The word *liber* in Latin is a bit confusing: *liber, liberi* means child while *liber, libri* means book. *Liber, Liberi* (capital letter) stands for Baccus, therefore wine. Also, the first-and-second-declension adjective *liber, -a, -um* means free.

---

lĕo, ōnis *m*, lion
lĕpĭdus, a, um *adj, adv*, **ē**, charming, elegant, pleasant
lĕpor (lĕpos), ōris *m*, charm, pleasantness, wit
lĕŏrārĭum, ĭī *n*, warren
leprae, ārum *f.pl*, leprosy
lĕprōsus, a, um *adj*, leprous
lĕpus, ŏris *m*, a hare
lĕpuscŭlus, i *m*, leveret
lētālis, e *adj*, fatal
lēthargĭcus, a, um *adj*, lethargic
lēthargus, i *m*, stupor
lētĭfer, ĕra, ĕrum *adj*, deadly
lētum, i *n*, death
lĕvāmen, ĭnis *n*, consolation, comfort
lĕvāmentum, i *n*, consolation, comfort
lĕvātĭo, ōnis *f*, raising
lĕvis, e *adj, adv*, **ĭter**, light, mild, light-armed, agile, trivial, unreliable
lēvis, e *adj*, smooth, soft
lĕvĭtas, ātis *f*, inconstancy
lēvĭtas, ātis *f*, smoothness
lĕvo *v.t.* 1, to raise, relieve, take away, support, soothe, release
lēvo *v.t.* 1, to smooth
lex, lēgis *f*, law, condition
lībāmen, ĭnis *n*, drink offering

lībĕrālis, e *adj, adv*, **ĭter**, honourable, generous
lībĕrālĭtas, ātis *f*, generosity
lībĕrātĭo, ōnis *f*, release
lībĕrātor, ōris *m*, liberator
lībĕri, ōrum *m.pl*, children
lībĕro *v.t.* 1, to release, free from slavery, acquit
lībertas, ātis *f*, freedom
lībertīnus, i *m*, freedman
lībertīnus, a, um *adj*, of a freedman
lībertus, i *m*, a freedman
lībet, lībŭit, lībĭtum est *v.* 2, *impers*, it is agreeable
lībīdĭnōsus, a, um *adj*, lecherous
lībīdo, ĭnis *f*, desire, passion, whim
lībo *v.t.* 1, to taste, touch, pour out an offering of wine
lībra, ae *f*, Roman pound (12 oz.), pair of scales
lībrāmentum, i *n*, a weight
lībrārĭus, i *m*, secretary
lībrārĭus, a, um *adj*, of books
lībrātus, a, um *adj*, balanced
lībrīlis, e *adj*, weighing a pound
lībro *v.t.* 1, to balance, hurl
lībum, i *n*, pancake
līburna, ae *f*, fast sailing ship
līcenter *adv*, without restraint
līcentĭa, ae *f*, freedom, licence
līcĕo *v.i.* 2, to be for sale, be valued at

līcĕor *v.t.* 2, to be for sale, be valued at

līcĕor *v.t.* 2, *dep*, to bid (for)

līcet, cŭit, cĭtum est *v.* 2, *impers*, it is allowed, one may

līcet *conj*, although

līcĭtus, a, um *adj*, permitted

līcĭtātĭo, ōnis *f*, bidding

līcĭum, ii *n*, a thread

lictor, ōris *m*, official attendant of high magistrates

līēn, ēnis *m*, spleen

līgāmen, ĭnis *n*, bandage

līgāmentum, i *n*, ligament

lignārĭus, ii *m*, carpenter, joiner

lignātĭo, ōnis *f*, wood gathering

lignātor, ōris *m*, wood cutter

lignĕus, a, um *adj*, wooden

lignor *v.i.* 1, *dep*, to collect wood

lignum, i *n*, wood

līgo *v.t.* 1, to tie, bind

līgo, ōnis *m*, hoe

līgŭla, ae *f*, small tongue (of land); tongue of a shoe

līgūrĭo *v.t.* 4, to lick, desire

līgustrum, i *n*, a plant, privet

līlĭum, ii *n*, lily

līma, ae *f*, file

līmax, ācis *f*, slug

limbus, i *m*, border, edge

līmen, ĭnis *n*, doorstep, door, lintel

līmĕs, ĭtis *m*, boundary, track

līmo *v.t.* 1, to file, polish, finish

līmōsus, a, um *adj*, slimy, muddy

limpĭdus, a, um *adj*, clear, bright

līmus, a, um *adj*, aslant

līmus, i *m*, slime, mud

līmus, i *m*, apron

līnāmentum, i *n*, linen, lint

līnĕa, ae *f*, thread, string, line, end, goal

līnĕāmentum, i *n*, line, feature

līnĕus, a, um *adj*, linen

lingo, nxi *v.t.* 3, to lick

lingua, ae *f*, tongue, speech, language

līnĭger, ĕra, ĕrum *adj*, clothed in linen

līno, lēvi, lītum *v.t.* 3, to daub, smear over

linquo, līqui *v.t.* 3, to leave

lintĕo, ōnis *m*, linen weaver

linter, tris *f*, boat, tray

lintĕum, i *n*, linen

lintĕus, a, um *adj*, of linen

līnum, i *n*, flax, linen, thread, rope, net

lippĭtūdo, ĭnis *f*, inflammation of the eyes

lippus, a, um *adj*, blear-eyed

līquĕfăcĭo, fēci, factum *v.t.* 3, to melt, dissolve

līquĕfactus, a, um *adj*, molten

līquens, ntis *adj*, liquid

līquĕo, līqui *v.i.* 2, to be clear

līquesco, līcŭi *v.i.* 3, to melt

līquĭdus, a, um *adj*, liquid, flowing, clear

līquo *v.t.* 1, to melt, filter

līquor *v.i.* 3, *dep*, to melt, flow

līquor, ōris *m*, a liquid

līs, tis *f*, dispute, lawsuit

lītĭgĭōsus, a, um *adj*, quarrelsome

lītĭgo *v.i.* 1, to quarrel

līto *v.i.t.* 1, to make a sacrifice with favourable omens; appease

lītŏrĕus, a, um *adj*, of the seashore

littĕra, ae *f*, a letter of the alphabet

littĕrae, ārum *f.pl*, a letter, document, literature, learning

littĕrātus, a, um *adj*, educated

littĕrŭla, ae *f*, small letter, moderate literary knowledge

lītūra, ae *f*, smear, erasure

lītus, ōris *n*, seashore

lītŭus, i *m*, augur's staff, trumpet

līvens, ntis *adj*, bluish

līvĕo *v.i.* 2, to be black and blue

līvĭdus, a, um *adj*, bluish, black and blue, envious

līvor, ōris *m*, leaden colour, envy, malice

lixa, ae *m*, camp-follower

lŏca, ōrum *n.pl*, a region

lŏcātĭo, ōnis *f*, placing, arrangement, lease

lŏco *v.t.* 1, to place, arrange, give in marriage, lease, contract for

lŏcŭlāmentum, i *n*, box

lŏcŭlus, i *m*, satchel, purse

lŏcŭplēs, ētis *adj*, wealthy

lŏcŭplēto *v.t.* 1, to enrich

lŏcus, i *m*, place, position, topic, subject, cause, reason

lŏcusta, ae *f*, locust

lŏcūtĭo, ōnis *f*, speaking, pronunciation, phrase

lōdix, īcis *f*, blanket

lŏgĭca, ōrum *n.pl*, logic

lŏgĭcus, a, um *adj*, logical

lōlīgo, ĭnis *f*, cuttlefish

lŏlīum, ii *n*, darnel

longaevus, a, um *adj*, ancient

longē *adv*, far off, greatly

longinquĭtas, ātis *f*, duration, distance

longinquus, a, um *adj*, distant, strange, prolonged

longĭtūdo, ĭnis *f*, length

longŭrĭus, ii *m*, long pole

longus, a, um *adj*, long, tall, vast, distant, tedious

lŏquācĭtas, ātis *f*, talkativeness

lŏquax, ācis *adj*, *adv*, **ĭter**, talkative, babbling

lŏquēla, ae *f*, speech, discourse

lŏquor, lŏcūtus *v.i.t.* 3, *dep*, to speak; tell, mention, declare

lōrīca, ae *f*, breastplate

lōrĭpēs, pĕdis *adj*, bandy-legged

lōrum, i *n*, strap, whip

lōtos (lōtus), i *f*, lotus tree

lūbens, lŭbet see **libens, libet**

lūbrĭcus, a, um *adj*, slippery, dangerous, deceitful

lŭcellum, i *n*, slight profit

lūcĕo, xi *v.i.* 2, to shine

lūcet *v. impers*, day breaks

lūcerna, ae *f*, lamp

lūcesco *v.i.* 3, to dawn

lūcĭdus, a, um *adj*, bright, clear

lūcĭfer, ĕra, ĕrum *adj*, light-bringing

lūcĭfer, ĕri *m*, morning star

lūcĭfŭgus, a, um *adj*, retiring

lùcrātīvus, a, um *adj*, profitable

lùcror *v.t.* 1, *dep*, to gain, win

lùcrum, i *n*, profit, advantage

luctāmen, inis *n*, wrestling, struggle

luctātĭo, ōnis *f*, wrestling, struggle

luctātor, ōris *m*, wrestler

luctĭfĭcus, a, um *adj*, woeful

luctor *v.i.* 1, *dep*, to struggle

luctŭōsus, a, um *adj*, sorrowful

luctus, ūs *m*, grief, mourning (clothes)

lūcùbrātĭo, ōnis *f*, night-work

lūcŭlentus, a, um *adj*, bright

lūcus, i *m*, wood, grove

lūdĭbrĭum, ii *n*, mockery, jest, laughing-stock

lūdĭbundus, a, um *adj*, playful

lūdĭcer, ĭcra, ĭcrum *adj*, sportive, theatrical

ludĭcrum, i *n*, public show or games, a play

lūdĭdĭcātĭo, ōnis *f*, mocking

lūdĭfĭcor *v.i.t.* 1, *dep* **(lūdĭffĭco** *v.t.* 1), to mock, deceive

lūdīmăgister, tri *m*, schoolmaster

lūdīus, ii *m*, pantomime-actor

lūdo, si, sum *v.i.t.* 3, to play, frolic; mock, deceive

lūdus, i *m*, a play, game, public games, school, joke

lŭes, is *f*, an epidemic

lūgĕo, xi, ctum *v.i.t.* 2, to mourn

lūgŭbris, e *adj*, lamentable, disastrous

lumbus, i *m*, loin

lūmen, ĭnis *n*, light, lamp, gleam, life, eye, glory

lūna, ae *f*, moon

lūnāris, e *adj*, lunar

lūnātus, a, um *adj*, crescent-shaped

lūno *v.t.* 1, to bend into a crescent-shape

lŭo, lŭi *v.t.* 3, to pay a debt or penalty, undergo, atone for

lŭpāta, ōrum *n.pl*, horse-bit

lŭpātus, a, um *adj*, jagged

lŭpīnus, a, um *adj*, of the wolf

lŭpīnus, i *m*, lupin (plant)

lŭpus, i *m*, wolf, pike (fish), a jagged bit, hook

lūrĭdus, a, um *adj*, lurid, sallow

luscīnĭa, ae *f*, nightingale

lūsor, ōris *m*, player, mocker

lustrālis, e *adj*, expiatory

lustrātĭo, ōnis *f*, purification by sacrifice

lustro *v.t.* 1, to to purify by sacrifice, wander over, review

lustrum, i *n*, den, wood

lustrum, i *n*, purificatory sacrifice, period of five years

lūsus, ūs *m*, play, sport, game

lūtĕŏlus, a, um *adj*, yellow

lūtĕus, a, um *adj*, golden-yellow

lŭtĕus, a, um *adj*, muddy, worthless

lūtra, ae *f*, otter

lūtŭlentus, a, um *adj,* filthy
lūtum, i *n,* yellow
lūtum, i *n,* mud, clay
lux, lūcis *f,* light, dawn, day, life, brightness, glory
luxŭrĭa, ae *f,* luxuriance, extravagance
luxŭrĭo *v.i.* 1, **(luxŭrĭor,** *v.* 1, *dep),* to be overgrown, to have in excess, run riot
luxŭrĭōsus, a, um *adj,* luxuriant, excessive
luxus, ūs *m,* extravagance, pomp
lychnūcus, i *m,* lamp-stand
lychnus, i *m,* light, lamp
lympha, ae *f,* water
lymphātus, a, um *adj,* frenzied
lyncēus, a, um *adj,* sharp-eyed
lynx, cis *c,* lynx
lўra, ae *f,* lute, poetry, song
lўrĭcus, a, um *adj,* of the lute, lyric

M

măcellum, i *n,* food market
măcer, cra, crum *adj,* lean, thin
mācĕrĭa, ae *f,* wall
mācĕro *v.t.* 1, to soften, weaken, torment
māchĭna, ae *f,* engine, machine, battering-ram, trick, plan
māchĭnālis, e *adj,* mechanical
māchĭnātĭo, ōnis *f,* contrivance, machine, trick
māchĭnātor, ōris *m,* engineer, inventor
māchĭnor *v.t.* 1, *dep,* to design, plot
măcĭes, ēi *f,* thinness, poverty
macte or **macti** *(voc. of* **mactus),** good luck! well done!
macto *v.t.* 1, to sacrifice a victim, reward, honour, destroy
mactus, a, um *adj,* worshipped
măcŭla, ae *f,* spot, stain, fault, mesh
măcŭlo *v.t.* 1, to stain, disgrace
măcŭlōsus, a, um *adj,* spotted, dishonoured
mădĕfăcĭo, fēci, factum *v.t.* 3, to soak, drench
mădens, ntis *adj,* moist, drunk
mădĕo *v.i.* 2, to be moist, to drip, to be boiled, softened

mădesco, dŭi *v.i.* 3, to become wet
mădīdus, a, um *adj,* soaked
maena, ae *f,* small salted fish
maenĭānum, i *n,* balcony
maerens, ntis *adj,* mourning
maerĕo *v.i.t.* 2, to mourn; bewail
maeror, ōris *m,* grief, mourning
maestĭtĭa, ae *f,* sadness
maestus, a, um *adj,* sad
măga, ae *f,* witch
māgālĭa, ĭum *n.pl,* huts
măgĭcus, a, um *adj,* magic
măgis *comp. adv* **(magnus),** more, rather
măgister, tri *m,* master, leader, director, teacher
măgistĕrĭum, ii *n,* president's position
măgistra, ae *f,* mistress
măgistrātus, ūs *m,* magistracy, magistrate
magnănĭmĭtas, ātis *f,* magnanimity
magnănĭmus, a, um *adj,* great-hearted
magnes, ētis *m,* magnet
magnētĭcus, a, um *adj,* magnet
magni see **magnus**
magnĭfĭcentĭa, ae *f,* nobleness, splendour, boasting
magnĭfĭcus, a, um *adj, adv,* **ē,** noble, distinguished, sumptuous, bragging
magnĭlŏquentĭa, ae *f,* high-sounding language
magnĭtūdo, ĭnis *f,* size
magnŏpĕrē *adv,* very much
magnus, a, um *adj,* large, great; **magni** or **magno** at a high price
măgus, i *m,* magician
Māius (mensis) May
māiestas, ātis *f,* greatness, grandeur, sovereignty, treason
māior *comp. adj,* larger, greater;
māiōres, um *m.pl,* ancestors, the Senate; **maior nātu** older
māla, ae *f,* cheekbone, jaw
mălăcĭa, ae *f,* calm at sea
malagma, ātis *n,* poultice
mălē *adv,* badly, exceedingly; often reverses the meaning of an adj: **male sānus** deranged
mălĕdīcens, ntis *adj,* abusive

mălĕdīco, xi, ctum *v.i.* 3, to abuse, slander

mălĕdictĭo, ōnis *f,* abuse

mălĕdictum, i *n,* abusive word

mălĕdīcus, a, um *adj,* abusive

mălĕfĭcĭum, ii *n,* wrongdoing

mălĕfĭcus, a, um *adj,* evil-doing

mălĕsuādus, a, um *adj,* persuading towards wrong

mălĕvŏlens, ntis *adj,* spiteful

mălĕvŏlentĭa, ae *f,* malice

mălĕvŏlus, a, um *adj,* spiteful

mălignus, a, um *adj,* malicious

mălĭtĭa, ae *f,* malice

mălĭtĭōsus, a, um *adj,* wicked

mallĕus, i *m,* hammer

mālo, malle, mālŭi *v.t, irreg,* to prefer

mālŏbăthrum, i *n,* a costly ointment

mālum, i *n,* apple, fruit

mălum, i *n,* evil, misfortune

mălus, a, um *adj,* bad, harmful

mālus, i *m,* mast

malva, ae *f,* the mallow

mamma, ae *f,* breast, teat

manceps, cĭpis *m,* contractor

mancĭpĭum, ii *n,* legal purchase, right of ownership, slave

mancĭpo *v.t.* 1, to sell, transfer

mancus, a, um *adj,* maimed

mandātum, i *n,* order, commission

mandātus, ūs *m,* order, commission

mando *v.t.* 1, to order, commission, commit

mandūco *v.t.* 1, to chew

māne *n, indecl,* morning; *adv,* in the morning

mănĕo, nsi, nsum *v.i.t.* 2, to stay, remain, continue; await

mānes, ĭum *m.pl,* deified ghosts of the dead

mănĭcae, ārum *f.pl,* glove, gauntlet, handcuff

mănĭfestus, a, um *adj, adv,* ō, clear, apparent

mănĭpŭlāris, e *adj,* belonging to a company (a soldier)

mănĭpŭlus, i *m,* handful, bundle, company of soldiers

mannus, i *m,* coach-horse, pony

māno *v.i.t.* 1, to flow, trickle; pour out

mansĭo, ōnis *f,* a stay, inn

mansŭĕfăcĭo, fēci, factum *v.t.* 3, to tame, civilize

mansŭesco, sŭēvi, sŭētum *v.i.* 3, to grow tame or gentle

mansŭētus, a, um *adj,* gentle

mansŭētūdo, ĭnis *f,* gentleness

mansūrus, a, um *adj,* lasting

mantēle, is *n,* towel, cloth

mantĭca, ae *f,* suitcase

mănūbĭae, ārum *f.pl,* money from the sale of booty

mănūbrĭum, ii *n,* handle

mănūmissĭo, ōnis *f,* the freeing of a slave

mănūmitto, mīsi, missum *v.t.* 3, to set free a slave

mănus, ūs *f,* hand, bravery, combat, violence, grappling-iron, armed band

māpālĭa, ĭum *n.pl,* African huts

mappa, ae *f,* towel, napkin

marcĕo *v.i.* 2, to be weak

marcesco *v.i.* 3, to wither

marcĭdus, a, um *adj,* decayed

māre, is *n,* the sea

marga, ae *f,* marl

margărīta, ae *f,* pearl

margo, ĭnis *m, f,* edge, border

mărīnus, a, um *adj,* of the sea

mărīta, ae *f,* wife

mărītālis, e *adj,* matrimonial

mărĭtĭmus, a, um *adj,* of the sea

mărītus, a, um *adj,* matrimonial

mărītus, i *m,* husband

marmor, ŏris *n,* marble, statue; *in pl,* surface of the sea

marmŏrĕus, a, um *adj,* of marble

martĭālis, e *adj,* sacred to Mars

Martĭus (mensis) March

martyr, ўris *c,* martyr

martyrĭum, ii *n,* martyrdom

mās, măris *adj,* male

mascŭlus, a, um *adj,* male, bold

massa, ae *f,* lump, mass

mătellĭo, ōnis *m,* pot

māter, tris *f,* mother

māterfămĭlĭas, mātrisfămĭlĭas *f,* mistress of the house

mătĕrĭa, ae *f,* timber, materials, topic, opportunity

matĕris, is *f*, Celtic javelin

māternus, a, um *adj*, maternal

mātertĕra, ae *f*, maternal aunt

māthēmătĭca, ae *f*, mathematics

māthēmătĭcus, a, um *adj*, mathematical

mātrĭcīda, ae *c*, murderer of his (her) mother

mātrĭmōnĭum, ii *n*, marriage

mātrōna, ae *f*, married woman

mātrōnālis, e *adj*, of a married woman

mātūrē *adv*, at the proper time, soon, quickly

mātūresco, rŭi *v.i.* 3, to ripen

mātūrĭtas, ātis *f*, ripeness

mātūro *v.i.t.* 1, to ripen, hurry; bring to maturity

mātūrus, a, um *adj*, mature, ripe, early

mātūtĭnus, a, um *adj*, of the morning

maxilla, ae *f*, jawbone, jaw

maxĭmē *adv*, expecially, very

maxĭmus, a, um *sup. adj*, very large or great

māxŏnŏmus, i *m*, dish

me *acc. or abl.* of ĕgŏ

mĕātus, ūs *m*, motion, course

mĕdĕor *v.* 2, *dep*, *with dat*, to heal, remedy, amend

mĕdĭastīnus, i *m*, drudge

mēdĭca, ae *f*, a kind of clover

mēdĭcābĭlis, e *adj*, curable

mēdĭcāmen, ĭnis *n*, remedy, drug

mēdĭcāmentum, i *n*, remedy, drug

mēdĭcāmentārĭus, a, um *adj*, of drugs

mēdĭcīna, ae *f*, the art of medicine, remedy

mēdĭco *v.t.* 1, to heal, sprinkle, dye

mĕdĭcor *v.t.* 1, *dep*, to heal

mĕdĭcus, a, um *adj*, healing

mĕdĭcus, i *m*, doctor, surgeon

mēdimnum, i *n*, bushel

mĕdĭōcris, e *adj*, *adv*, ĭter, ordinary, insignificant

mĕdĭōcrĭtas, ātis *f*, a middle state, insignificance

mĕdĭtātĭo, ōnis *f*, contemplation, preparation

medĭtātus, a, um *adj*, considered

mĕdĭterrānĕus, a, um *adj*, inland

mĕdĭtor *v.i.t.* 1, *dep*, to consider, muse; study, intend, practise

mĕdĭum, ii *n*, middle, the public

mĕdĭus, a, um *adj*, middle, neutral

mĕdĭus, i *m*, mediator

mĕdulla, ae *f*, kernel, marrow

mēio *v.i.* 3, to urinate

mĕl, mellis *n*, honey

mĕlanchŏlĭcus, a, um *adj*, melancholic

mēles, is *f*, badger

mĕlīmēla, ōrum *n.pl*, honey apples

mĕlĭor, us *comp. adj*, better

mĕlissphyllum, i *n*, balm

mĕlĭus *comp. adv*, better

mellĭfer, ĕra, ĕrum *adj*, honey producing

mellĭfĭco *v.t.* 1, to make honey

mellītus, a, um *adj*, of honey

mēlo, ōnis *m*, melon

mĕlos, i *n*, tune, song

membrāna, ae *f*, skin, parchment

membrātim *adv*, piece by piece

membrum, i *n*, limb, division

mĕmmĭni, isse *v.i*, *defective*, to remember

mĕmor, ŏris *adj*, remembering, mindful

mĕmŏrābĭlis, e *adj*, memorable

mĕmŏrandus, a, um *adj*, memorable

mĕmŏrātus, a, um *adj*, renowned

mĕmŏrĭa, ae *f*, memory, posterity, historical account, tradition

mĕmŏro *v.t.* 1, to mention

menda, ae *f*, defect

mendācĭum, ii *n*, a lie

mendax, ācis *adj*, lying, false

mendīcĭtas, ātis *f*, poverty

mendīco *v.i.* 1, to beg

mendīcus, a, um *adj*, needy

mendīcus, i *m*, beggar

mendōsus, a, um *adj*, *adv*, ē, faulty, false

mendum, i *n*, blunder, defect, mistake

mens, ntis *f*, mind, intellect, understanding, intention, courage

mensa, ae *f*, table, course; **sĕcunda mensa** dessert

mensārĭus, ii *m*, banker

mensis, is *m*, month

mensor, ōris *m*, valuer, surveyor

menstrŭus, a, um *adj*, monthly

mensūra, ae *f*, measurement, quantity

mensus, a, um *adj*, measured off

menta, ae *f*, mint

mentĭo, ōnis *f*, recollection, mention

mentĭor *v.i.t.* 4, *dep*, to lie, cheat; counterfeit, imitate

mentītus, a, um *adj*, counterfeit

mentum, i *n*, chin

mĕo *v.i.* 1, to go

mĕrācus, a, um *adj*, unmixed

mercātor, ōris *m*, wholesaler

mercātūra, ae *f*, trade

mercātus, ūs *m*, trade, market

mercēdŭla, ae *f*, small wages

mercēnārĭus, a, um *adj*, hired

merces, ēdis *f*, pay, wages, rent, interest, reward

merces (*pl*) see **merx**

mercor *v.t.* 1, *dep*, to buy

mĕrens, ntis *adj*, deserving

mĕrĕo *v.t.* (**mĕrĕor** *v. dep*) 2, to deserve, earn; *with* **stīpendĭa**, to serve as a soldier

mĕrètrīcĭus, a, um *adj*, of prostitutes

mĕrètrix, trīcis *f*, prostitute

merges, ĭtis *f*, sheaf

mergo, si, sum *v.t.* 3, to immerse

mergus, i *m*, seabird (diver)

mĕrīdĭānus, a, um *adj*, of midday

mĕrīdĭes, ēi *m*, midday, south

mĕrĭtōrĭus, a, um *adj*, bringing in money

mĕrĭtum, i *n*, reward, benefit, fault, blame

mĕrĭtus, a, um *adj*, *adv*, **ē**, deserved, deserving

mĕrops, ŏpis *m*, bee-eating bird

merso *v.t.* 1, to immerse, drown

mĕrŭla, ae *f*, blackbird

mĕrum, i *n*, pure wine

mĕrus, a, um *adj*, pure, only, genuine

merx, cis *f*, goods, commodities

messis, is *f*, harvest, crops

messor, ōris *m*, harvester

mēta, ae *f*, winning-post, end, cone

mĕtallĭcus, a, um *adj*, metallic

mĕtallĭcus, i *m*, miner

mĕtallum, i *n*, mine, metal

mētātor, ōris *m*, surveyor

mētĭor, mensus *v.t.* 4, *dep*, to measure, distribute, traverse, estimate, value

mĕto, ssŭi, ssum *v.t.* 3, to mow, gather, cut down

mētor *v.t.* 1, *dep*, to measure, mark out, traverse

mètrĭcus, a, um *adj*, metrical

mĕtŭendus, a, um *adj*, formidable

mĕtŭo, ŭi, ūtum *v.i.t.* 3, to be afraid; to fear

mĕtus, ūs *m*, fear, awe

mĕus, a, um *adj*, my, mine: **mĕi, ōrum** *m.pl*, my relatives

mīca, ae *f*, crumb

mīco, ŭi *v.i.* 1, to tremble, sparkle

mìgrātĭo, ōnis *f*, migration

mìgro *v.i.* 1, to depart, change

mīlĕs, ĭtis *c*, soldier, army

mīlia see **mille**

mīlĭārĭum, ii *n*, milestone

mīlĭtāris, e *adj*, military

mīlĭtāris, is *m*, soldier

mīlĭtĭa, ae *f*, military service, warfare

mīlĭto *v.i.* 1, to serve as a soldier

mīlĭum, ii *n*, millet

mille (*pl*, **mīlia**, *with genit.*) a thousand; **mille passus**, or **passuum**, a mile

millēsĭmus, a, um *adj*, the thousandth

millĭes (millĭens) *adv*, a thousand times

milŭīnus, a, um *adj*, kite-like

milŭus, i *m*, kite, gurnard

mīmĭcus, a, um *adj*, farcical

mīmus, i *m*, mime, mimic actor

mīna, ae *f*, Greek silver coinage

mīnae, ārum *f.pl*, threats

mīnax, ācis *adj*, *adv*, **ĭter**, threatening, projecting

mīnĭmē *sup. adv*, very little

mīnĭmus, a, um *sup. adj*, very small

mĭnister, tri *m*, **mĭnistra, ae** *f*, servant, assistant

mĭnistĕrĭum, ii *n*, service, occupation

mĭnistrātor, ōris *m*, servant

mĭnistro *v.t.* 1, to wait upon, serve, manage

mĭnĭtor *v.i.t.* 1, *dep*, to threaten

mĭnĭum, ii red-lead

mĭnor *v.i.t.* 1, *dep*, to threaten

mĭnor, us *comp. adj*, smaller

mĭnŭo, ŭi, ūtum *v.i.t.* 3, to ebb; to reduce, weaken, chop up

mĭnus *comp. adv*, less

mĭnuscŭlus, a, um *adj*, rather small

mĭnūtal, ālis *n*, mincemeat

mĭnūtātim *adv*, little by little

mĭnūtus, a, um *adj, adv*, ē, small

mīrābĭlis, e *adj, adv*, ĭter, wonderful, strange

mīrācŭlum, i *n*, a wonder, marvel

mīrandus, a, um *adj*, wonderful

mīrātĭo, ōnis *f*, surprise

mīrātor, ōris *m*, admirer

mīrĭfĭcus, a, um *adj, adv*, ē, marvellous, extraordinary

mīror *v.i.t.* 1, *dep*, to be amazed; to marvel at, admire

mīrus, a, um *adj, adv*, ē, marbellous, extraordinary

miscĕo, scŭi, xtum *v.t.* 2, to mix, unite, disturb

mĭsellus, a, um *adj*, wretched

mĭser, ĕra, ĕrum *adj, adv*, ē, wretched, pitiable, worthless

mĭsĕrābĭlis, e *adj, adv*, ĭter, pitiable, sad

mĭsĕrandus, a, um *adj*, pitiable

mĭsĕrātĭo, ōnis *f*, pity

mĭsĕrĕor *v.* 2, *dep, with genit*, to pity

mĭsĕret (me, te, etc.) *v.* 2, *impers*, it distresses (me), I pity, am sorry for

mĭsĕresco *v.i.* 3, to feel pity

mĭsĕrĭa, ae *f*, misfortune, wretchedness

mĭsĕrĭcordĭa, ae *f*, pity

mĭsĕrĭcors, dis *adj*, merciful

mĭsĕror *v.t.* 1, *dep*, to lament, pity

missĭle, is *n*, missile, javelin

missĭlis, e *adj*, that is thrown

missĭo, ōnis *f*, throwing, discharge, release

missus, ūs *m*, dispatching, throwing, shot

mītella, ae *f*, turban, bandage

mītesco *v.i.* 3, to grow mild or soft or ripe

mītĭgātĭo, ōnis *f*, mitigation

mītĭgo *v.t.* 1, to make soft or ripe, to tame, soothe

mītis, e *adj*, mild, ripe, calm

mĭtra, ae *f*, headband

mitto, mīsi, missum *v.t.* 3, to send, announce, cease, release, throw, escort

mītŭlus, i *m*, sea mussel

mixtūta, ae *f*, mixture

mixtus, a, um *adj*, mixed

mōbĭlis, e *adj, adv*, ĭter, movable, agile, flexible, fickle

mōbĭlĭtas, ātis *f*, speed, inconstancy

mŏdĕrāmen, ĭnis *n*, rudder, management

mŏdĕrātĭo, ōnis *f*, moderation, restraint

mŏdĕrātor, ōris *m*, manager

mŏdĕrātus, a, um *adj, adv*, ē, moderate

mŏdĕror *v.t.* 1, *dep*, to restrain, govern

mŏdestĭa, ae *f*, moderation, discretion, modesty

mŏdestus, a, um *adj, adv*, ē, modest, gentle

mŏdĭcus, a, um *adj, adv*, ē, modest, ordinary

mŏdĭfĭcātus, a, um *adj*, measured

mŏdĭus, ii *m*, peck, measure

mŏdŏ *adv*, only, but, just, lately; non mŏdŏ not only; mŏdŏ … mŏdŏ at one time … at another time

mŏdŭlātor, ōris *m*, musician

mŏdŭlor *v.t.* 1, *dep*, to sing, play

mŏdŭlātus, a, um *adj*, sung, played

mŏdŭlus, i *m*, a small measure

mŏdus, i *m*, measure, quantity, rhythm, limit, restriction, end, method, way

moechus, i *m*, adulterer

moenĭa, ĭum *n.pl*, ramparts

mŏla, ae *f*, millstone, grain mixed with salt to be sprinkeld on sacrificial animals

mŏlāris, is *m*, millstone

mōles, is *f*, mass, bulk, dam, pier, power, difficulty

mŏlestĭa, ae *f*, trouble, affectation

mŏlestus, a, um *adj, adv,* ē,
  troublesome, affected
mōlīmen, ĭnis *n,* undertaking,
  attempt
mōlīmentum, i *n,* undertaking,
  attempt
mōlĭor *v.i.t.* 4, to strive, depart; to
  rouse, construct, attempt
mŏlĭtor, ōris *m,* miller
mōlītor, ōris *m,* contriver
mollesco *v.i.* 3, to grow soft
mollĭo *v.t.* 4, to soften, restrain
mollis, e *adj, adv,* ĭter soft, supple,
  tender, effeminate
mollĭtĭa, ae *f,* softness, weakness
mollĭtĭes, ēi *f,* softness, weakness
mollĭtūdo, ĭnis *f,* softness,
  weakness
mŏlo, ŭi, ĭtum *v.t.* 3, to grind
mōmentum, i *n,* movement,
  motion, moment, instant, cause,
  influence, importance
mŏnăcha, ae *f,* nun
mŏnastērĭum, ii *n,* monastery
mŏnēdŭla, ae *f,* jackdaw
mŏnĕo *v.t.* 2, to warn, advise,
  remind, instruct, tell

monstrum, i *n,* omen, monster
monstrŭōsus, a, um *adj,* strange,
  monstrous
montānus, a, um *adj,* of a
  mountain, mountainous
montĭcŏla, ae *c,* mountain-dweller
montĭvăgus, a, um *adj,* wandering
  in the mountains
montŭōsus, a, um *adj,*
  mountainous
mŏnŭmentum, i *n,* monument,
  memorial, written record
mŏra, ae *f,* delay, hindrance
mōrālis, e *adj,* moral
mōrātus, a, um *adj,* mannered;
mŏrātus *partic. from* mŏror,
  having delayed
morbĭdus, a, um *adj,* diseased
morbus, i *m,* illness, disease
mordax, ācis *adj,* biting, stinging
mordĕo, mŏmordi, morsum *v.t.* 2,
  to bite, clasp, sting
mordĭcus, a, um *adj,* by biting
mōres see mos
mŏrētum, i *n,* salad
mŏrĭbundus, a, um *adj,* dying
mŏrĭens, ntis *adj,* dying

Insight

The imperfect tense (e.g. *monebam*) refers to an action that
is uncompleted; the action is depicted as continuing, or being
repeated, or beginning or being attempted. The most
common translations for the imperfect are: 'I was -ing', 'I
used to –', 'I began to –', 'I tried to –'.

mŏnēta, ae *f,* the mint, coin
mŏnētālis, e *adj,* of the mint
mŏnīle, is *n,* necklace, collar
mŏnĭtĭo, ōnis *f,* warning
mŏnĭtor, ōris *m,* adviser, instructor
mŏnĭtum, i *n,* advice
mŏnĭtus, ūs *m,* warning, omen
mŏnŏcĕros, ōtis *m,* unicorn
mŏnŏpōlĭum, ii *n,* monopoly
mons, ntis *m,* mountain
monstrātĭo, ōnis *f,* showing,
  pointing out
monstrātor, ōris *m,* teacher
monstro *v.t.* 1, to show, tell

mŏrĭor, mortŭus *v.i.* 3, *dep,* to die
mŏror *v.i.t.* 1, *dep,* to delay
mōrōsĭtas, ātis *f,* fretfulness
mōrōsus, a, um *adj,* fretful,
  fastidious
mors, mortis *f,* death
morsus, ūs *m,* bite, pungency
mortālis, e *adj,* mortal, human,
  temporary
mortālis, is *c,* human being
mortālĭtas, ātis *f,* mortality
mortārĭum, ii *n,* a mortar
mortĭfer, ĕra, ĕrum *adj,* fatal
mortŭus, a, um *adj,* dead

mortŭus, i *m*, dead person
mōrum, i *n*, blackberry
mōrus, i *f*, blackberry-bush
mos, mōris *m*, custom, manner, habit, fashion; *in pl*, character
mōtăcilla, ae *f*, wagtail
mōtĭo, ōnis *f*, motion
mōto *v.t.* 1, to move about
mōtus, ūs *m*, motion, movement, impulse, emotion, rebellion
mŏvĕo, mōvi, mōtum *v.t.* 2, to move, stir, excite, cause
mox *adv*, soon, immediately
mūcĭdus, a, um *adj*, musty
mūcor, ōris *m*, mouldiness
mūcōsus, a, um *adj*, mucous
mūcro, ōnis *m*, sword's point
mūgil, is *m*, mullet
mūgĭnor *v.i.* 1, *dep*, to hesitate
mūgĭo *v.i.* 4, to low, bellow, groan, crash
mūgītus, ūs *m*, bellowing, roaring
mūla, ae *f*, she-mule
mulcĕo, si, sum *v.t.* 2, to stroke, soothe
mulco *v.t.* 1, to maltreat
mulctra, ae *f*, milk-bucket
mulctrārĭum, ii *n*, milk-bucket
mulgĕo, si, sum *v.t.* 2, to milk
mūlĭēbris, e *adj, adv*, ĭter, female, effeminate
mūlĭer, ĕris *f*, woman, wife
mūlĭercŭla, ae *f*, girl
mūlĭo, ōnis *m*, mule-driver
mullus, i *m*, mullet
mulsum, i *n*, honey-wine
multa, ae *f*, penalty, fine
multātĭo, ōnis *f*, penalty, fine
multi see multus
multĭfārĭam *adv*, on many sides
multĭplex, ĭcis *adj*, with many windings, numerous, many
multĭplĭcātĭo, ōnis *f*, multiplication
multĭplĭco *v.t.* 1, to multiply
multĭtūdo, ĭnis *f*, crowd, great number
multō *adv*, a great deal
multo *v.t.* 1, to punish
multum *adv*, very much, greatly
multus, a, um *adj*, much; *pl*, many
mūlus, i *m*, mule
mundĭtĭa, ae *f*, cleanliness, neatness
mundĭtĭes, ēi *f*, cleanliness, neatness

mundo *v.t.* 1, to cleanse
mundus, a, um *adj*, clean, elegant
mundus, i *m*, world, universe, ornaments
mūnĕro *v.t.* 1 (mūnĕror, *v.t.* 1, *dep.*), to reward, honour
mūnĭa, ōrum *n.pl*, duties
mūnĭceps, cĭpis *c*, citizen
mūnĭcĭpālis, e, *adj*, municipal
mūnĭcĭpĭum, ii *n*, self-governing town
mūnĭfĭcentĭa, ae *f*, generosity
mūnĭfĭcus, a, um *adj, adv*, ē, generous
mūnīmen, ĭnis *n*, rampart, protection
mūnīmentum, i *n*, rampart, protection
mūnĭo *v.t.* 4, to fortify, secure, make a way
mūnītĭo, ōnis *f*, fortification
mūnītor, ōris *m*, engineer
mūnītus, a, um *adj*, fortified
mūnus, ĕris *n*, service, duty, employment, post, tax, gift, public show
mūnuscŭlum, i *n*, small present
mūrālis, e *adj*, of a wall
mūrex, ĭcis *m*, purple fish, purple dye, pointed rock
mūrĭa, ae *f*, brine, pickle
murmur, ŭris *n*, murmur, crash
murmŭro *v.i.* 1, to murmur, roar
murra, ae *f*, myrrh (tree)
murrĕus, a, um *adj*, perfumed with myrrh
mūrus, i *m*, wall, defence
mūs, mūris *c*, mouse
mūsa, ae *f*, goddess of the arts
musca, ae *f*, a fly
muscĭpŭlum, i *n*, mousetrap
muscōsus, a, um *adj*, mossy
muscŭlus, i *m*, little mouse, mussel, muscle, military shed
muscus, i *m*, moss
mūsēum, i *n*, museum
mūsĭca, ae *f*, music
mūsĭcus, a, um *adj*, musical
mūsĭcus, i *m*, musician
musso *v.i.* 1, to mutter, be silent, be in doubt
mustēla, ae *f*, weasel
mustum, i *n*, new wine

mūtābĭlis, e *adj*, changeable
mūtābĭlĭtas, ātis *f*, changeableness
mūtātĭo, ōnis *f*, alteration
mŭtĭlo *v.t.* 1, to cut off, maim
mŭtĭlus, a, um *adj*, maimed
mūto *v.i.t.* 1, to alter, change
mūtŭlus, i *m*, bracket
mūtŭō *adv*, in turns
mūtŭor *v.t.* 1, *dep*, to borrow
mūtus, a, um *adj*, dumb, mute
mūtŭum, i *n*, loan
mūtŭus, a, um *adj*, borrowed,
   mutual
mȳrīca, ae *f*; mȳrīce, es *f*, a shrub,
   tamarisk
myrr... see murr...
myrtētum, i *n*, myrtle grove
myrtĕus, a, um *adj*, of myrtle
myrtum, i *n*, myrtle berry
myrtus, i *f*, myrtle tree
mysta (es), ae *f*, priest of Ceres'
   mysteries
mystērĭum, ii *n*, secret rites
mystĭcus, a, um *adj*, mystical

N

naevus, i *m*, wart, mole
Nāĭās, ădis *f*, water-nymph
nam *conj*, for

nasturtĭum, ii *n*, cress
nāsus, i *m*, nose
nāsūtus, a, um *adj*, large-nosed
nāta, ae *f*, daughter
nātālīcĭus, a, um *adj*, birthday
nātālis, e *adj*, of birth
nātālis, is *m*, birthday
nătantes, um *f.pl*, fish
nătātĭo, ōnis *f*, swimming
nătātor, ōris *m*, swimmer
nātĭo, ōnis *f*, race, nation
nătis, is, *f*, buttock
nātīvus, a, um *adj*, created, inborn,
   natural
năto *v.i.* 1, to swim, float, waver
nătrix, īcis *f*, water snake
nātūra, ae *f*, nature
nātūrālis, e *adj*, *adv*, ĭter, by birth,
   natural
nātus, ūs *m*, birth
nātus, i *m*, son
nātus, a, um *adj*, born, aged
nauarchus, i *m*, ship's master
naufrăgĭum, ii *n*, shipwreck
naufrăgus, a, um *adj*, shipwrecked
naumāchĭa, ae *f*, mock sea fight
nausĕa, ae *f*, seasickness
nausĕābundus, a, um *adj*, seasick
nausĕo *v.i.* 1, to be seasick
nauta, ae *m*, sailor

Insight

All nouns of the **first declension** are feminine except for a
few nouns that are masculine by meaning, such as *nauta*
(= sailor), *agricola* (= farmer), and *scriba* (= clerk, secretary).

---

namque *conj*, for indeed
nanciscor, nactus *v.t.* 3, *dep*, to
   obtain, meet with, find
nānus, i *m*, dwarf
nāpus, i *m*, turnip
narcissus, i *m*, narcissus
nardus, i *f*, perfumed balm
nāris, is *f*, nostril; *pl*, nose
narrātĭo, ōnis *f*, narrative
narrātor, ōris *m*, narrator
narro *v.t.* 1, to tell, relate
narthēcĭum, ii *n*, medicine chest
nascor, nātus *v.i.* 3, *dep*, to be
   born, rise, proceed

nautĭcus, a, um *adj*, nautical
nāvālĭa, ĭum *n.pl*, dockyard
nāvāle, is *n*, dockyard
nāvālis, e *adj*, naval
nāvĭcŭla, ae *f*, boat
nāvĭcŭlārĭus, ii *m*, shipowner
nāvĭfrăgus, a, um *adj*, ship
   wrecking
nāvĭgābĭlis, e *adj*, navigable
nāvĭgātĭo, ōnis *f*, sailing
nāvĭger, ĕra, ĕrum *adj*, navigable
nāvĭgĭa, ōrum *n.pl*, ships, shipping
nāvĭgĭum, ii *n*, ship, boat
nāvĭgo *v.i.t.* 1, to sail; navigate

nāvis, is *f*, ship; **nāvis longa,** warship

nāvīta, ae *m*, **(nauta)**, sailor

nāvĭter *adv*, completely

nāvo *v.t.* 1, to do vigorously

nāvus, a, um *adj*, hard-working

nē *conj*, lest; **nē ... quidem,** not even ...

-nĕ attached to the first word of a sentence to form a question

nē *interj*, indeed, truly

nēbŭla, ae *f*, mist, fog, smoke

nēbŭlo, ōnis *m*, rascal, wretch

nēbŭlōsus, a, um *adj*, misty

nĕc *adv*, not; *conj*, and not; **nĕc ... nĕc,** neither ... nor

necdum *conj*, not yet

nĕcessārĭus, a, um *adj, adv*, **ō,** unavoidable, necessary, related

nĕcessārĭus, ii *m*, relative

nĕcesse *indecl. adj*, unavoidable

nĕcessĭtas, ātis *f*, necessity, compulsion, destiny

nĕcessĭtūdo, ĭnis *f*, necessity, relationship

necnĕ *adv*, or not

nec-non and also

nĕco *v.t.* 1, to kill

nĕcŏpīnans, ntis *adj*, unaware

nĕcŏpīnātus, a, um *adj, adv*, **ō,** unexpected

nĕcŏpīnus, a, um *adj*, unexpected

nectar, ăris *n*, the drink of the gods

nectărĕus, a, um *adj*, of nectar

necto, xŭi, xum *v.t.* 3, to tie, fasten together

nĕcŭbi *adv*, so that nowhere

nēdum *conj*, still less

nĕfandus, a, um *adj*, abominable, heinous, wrong

nĕfārĭus, a, um *adj*, heinous, wrong

nĕfas *n, indecl*, wrong, sin

nefastus, a, um *adj, with* **dies,** a day on which neither trials nor public meetings could be held, wicked, unlucky

nĕgātĭo, ōnis *f*, denial

nĕgĭto *v.t.* 1, to persist in denying

neglectus, a, um *adj*, despised

neglĕgens (neglĭgens), ntis *adj*, careless, indifferent

neglĕgentĭa, ae *f*, carelessness

neglĕgo, xi, ctum *v.t.* 3, to neglect, slight, despise

nĕgo *v.i.t.* 1, to say no (not); refuse

nĕgōtĭātĭo, ōnis *f*, wholesale business, banking

nĕgōtĭātor, ōris *m*, wholesaler, banker

nĕgōtĭor *v.i.* 1, *dep*, to carry on business, trade or banking

nĕgōtĭōsus, a, um *adj*, busy

nĕgōtĭum, ii *n*, business, occupation, difficulty

nēmo, ĭnis *m, f*, nobody

nĕmŏrālis, e *adj*, woody

nĕmŏrōsus, a, um *adj*, woody

nempĕ *conj*, certainly

nĕmus, ŏris *n*, wood, grove

nēnĭa, ae *f*, funeral hymn, sad song, popular song

nĕo, nēvi, nētum *v.t.* 2, to spin

nĕpa, ae *f*, scorpion

nĕpos, ōtis *m, f*, grandson (...daughter), descendant, spendthrift

neptis, is *f*, granddaughter

nēquam *indecl. adj, adv* **nēquĭter,** worthless, bad

nēquăquam *adv*, not at all

nĕque *adv*, not; *conj*, and not; **nĕque ... nĕque,** neither ... nor

nĕquĕo, īvi (ĭi), ĭtum *v.i.* 4, to be unable

nēquīquam *adv*, in vain

nēquĭtĭa, ae *f*, worthlessness, idleness, extravagance

nervōsus, a, um *adj, adv*, **ē,** sinewy, energetic

nervus, i *m*, sinew, string of musical instrument or bow

nescĭo *v.t.* 4, not to know, to be unable

nescĭus, a, um *adj*, unaware

neu *adv*, and so that ... not

neuter, tra, trum *adj*, neither the one nor the other

neutĭquam *adv*, not at all

neutrō *adv*, neither way

nēve *adv*, and so that ... not

nex, nĕcis *f*, death, slaughter

nexĭlis, e *adj*, tied together

nexum, i *n*, slavery for debt, obligation

nexus, ūs *m*, tying together
nī *conj*, unless
nictātĭo, ōnis *f*, winking
nicto *v.i.* 1, to wink, blink
nīdor, ōris *m*, steam, smell
nīdŭlus, i *m*, little nest
nīdus, i *m*, nest, home; *in pl*, nestlings
nĭger, gra, grum *adj*, black, dark, ill-omened, funereal
nigrans, ntis *adj*, black
nigresco, grŭi *v.i.* 3, to grow dark
nĭhil (nīl) *n, indecl*, nothing
nĭhĭli of no value
nĭhĭlōmĭnus *adj*, nevertheless
nĭhĭlum, i *n*, nothing
nīl *n, indecl*, nothing
nimbĭfer, ĕra, ĕrum *adj*, stormy, rainy
nimbōsus, a, um *adj*, stormy, rainy
nimbus, i *m*, heavy rain, rain-cloud, cloud
nīmīrum *adv*, without doubt
nĭmis *adv*, too much
nĭmĭum *adv*, too much
nĭmĭum, ii *n*, excess
nĭmĭus, a, um *adj*, excessive
ningit *v.i.* 3, *impers*, it is snowing
nĭsĭ *conj*, if not, unless
nĭsus, ūs *m*, pressure, effort, labour of childbirth

nĭtrum, i *n*, soda
nĭvālis, e *adj*, snowy, cold
nĭvĕus, a, um *adj*, snowy, white
nĭvōsus, a, um *adj*, snowy
nix, nĭvis *f*, snow
nixor *v.i.* 1, *dep*, to strive
nixus, ūs *m*, pressure, effort, labour of childbirth
no *v.i.* 1, to swim
nōbīlis, e *adj*, famous, noble
nōbīlĭtas, ātis *f*, fame, noble birth
nōbīlĭto *v.t.* 1, to make famous
nōbis *dat. or abl. of* **nos**
nŏcens, ntis *adj*, wicked, bad, harmful, injurious
nŏcĕo *v.i.* 2, *with dat*, to harm
nocte *adv*, at night
noctĭlūca, ae *f*, moon
noctĭvăgus, a, um *adj*, wandering at night
noctu *adv*, at night
noctŭa, ae *f*, night owl
nocturnus, a, um *adj*, nocturnal
nōdo *v.t.* 1, to tie in a knot
mōdōsus, a, um *adj*, knotty, difficult
nōdus, i *m*, knot, knob, band, obligation, difficulty
nōli, nōlīte *imper*, do not ...
nōlo, nolle, nōlŭi *v, irreg*, to be unwilling

Insight

The imperative forms of *nolo*, **noli/nolite** are used for a negative command; they mean 'don't!' and are followed by the infinitive of the verb (e.g. *noli clamare* = don't shout!).

nītēdŭla, ae *f*, dormouse
nĭtens, ntis *adj*, bright, shining, sleek, beautiful
nĭtĕo *v.i.* 2, to shine, to look handsome, thrive
nĭtěsco, tŭi *v.i.* 3, to shine
nĭtĭdus, a, um *adj*, shining, sleek, handsome, refined
nītor, nīsus (nixus) *v.i.* 3, *dep*, to lean, press forward, fly, make an effort, argue
nĭtor, ōris *m*, brightness, splendour, beauty, elegance

nōmen, ĭnis *n*, name, debt, fame, repute, excuse, reason
nōmenclātor, ōris *m*, slave who reminded his master of the names of the people he met
nōmĭnātim *adj*, by name
nōmĭnātĭo, ōnis *f*, nomination
nōmĭnātus, a, um *adj*, renowned
nōmĭno *v.t.* 1, to name, make famous
nŏmisma, ătis *n*, a coin
nōn *adv*, not

nōnae, ārum *f.pl*, the Nones; 5th or 7th day of the month
nōnāgēni, ae *adj*, ninety each
nōnāgēsĭmus, a, um *adj*, ninetieth
nōnāgĭes *adv*, ninety times
nōnāgintā *indecl. adj*, ninety
nondum *adj*, not yet
nongenti, ae, a *adj*, nine hundred
nonnĕ *adv*, used to introduce a question expecting the answer 'yes'
nonnēmo, ĭnis *m*, someone
nonnĭhil *n*, something
nonnĭsi *adv*, only
nonnullus, a, um *adj*, several
nonnumquam *adv*, sometimes
nōnus, a, um *adj*, ninth
norma, ae *f*, rule, pattern, standard
nōs *pron, pl*. of **ĕgŏ**, we, us

nŏvēnus, a, um *adj*, nine each
nŏverca, ae *f*, stepmother
nŏvīcĭus, a, um *adj*, new
nŏvĭens *adv*, nine times
nŏvĭes *adv*, nine times
nŏvissĭmus, a, um *adj*, last; in *m.pl*, or **nŏvissĭmum agmen** rear ranks
nŏvĭtas, ātis *f*, novelty, unusualness
nŏvo *v.t.* 1, to renew, refresh, change
nŏvus, a, um *adj*, new, recent, fresh; **nŏvus hŏmo** an upstart; **nŏvae res** revolution
nox, noctis *f*, night
noxa, ae *f*, injury, harm fault, crime

Insight

Personal pronouns **nos** (= we) and **vos** (= you plural) have two forms for the genitive plural: *nostri* and *vestri* are objective (*cupidus nostri* = desirous of us), *nostrum* and *vestrum* are partitive (*unus vestrum* = one of you).

---

noscĭto *v.t.* 1, to know, observe
nosco, nōvi, nōtum *v.t.* 3, to get to know, know, recognize, acknowledge
noster, tra, trum *adj*, our, ours
nostras, ātis *adj*, of our country
nŏta, ae *f*, mark, sign, brand
nŏtābĭlis, e *adj*, noteworthy
nŏtātĭo, ōnis *f*, branding, observation
nŏthus, a, um *adj*, illegitimate, counterfeit
nōtĭo, ōnis *f*, investigation
nōtĭtĭa, ae *f*, fame, knowledge
nŏto *v.t.* 1, to mark, write, indicate, brand, reprimand
nōtus, a, um *adj*, well-known
nŏtus, i *m*, the south wind
nŏvācŭla, ae *f*, razor
nŏvālis, is *f*, fallow land
nŏvellus, a, um *adj*, young, new
nŏvem *indecl. adj*, nine
Nŏvember (mensis) November
nŏvendĭālis, e *adj*, lasting nine days

noxĭa, ae *f*, injury, harm, fault, crime
noxĭus, a, um *adj*, harmful, guilty
nūbes, is *f*, cloud
nūbĭfer, ĕra, ĕrum *adj*, cloud-capped, cloud-bringing
nūbĭla, ōrum *n.pl*, the clouds
nūbĭlis, e *adj*, marriageable
nūbĭlus, a, um *adj*, overcast
nūbo, psi, ptum *v.i.t.* 3, *with dat*, to marry
nŭclĕus, i *m*, nut, kernel
nūdĭus *with a number* **(tertĭus)** (three) days ago
nūdo *v.t.* 1, to strip, expose
nūdus, a, um *adj*, naked, destitute of, poor, simple
nūgae, ārum *f.pl*, jokes, nonsense, trifles
nūgātor, ōris *m*, silly person
nūgātŏrĭus, a, um *adj*, trifling
nūgor *v.i.* 1, *dep*, to play the fool
nullus, a, um *adj*, none, no
nullus, ĭus *m*, no-one

num *adv*, used to introduce a question expecting answer 'no'; whether

nūmen, ĭnis *n*, divine will, divine power, divinity

nŭmĕrābĭlis, e *adj*, able to be counted

nŭmĕrātor, ōris *m*, counter

nŭmĕrātum, i *n*, ready money

nŭmĕro *v.t.* 1, to count, pay out, number

nŭmĕrō *adv*, in number, just

nŭmĕrōsus, a, um *adj, adv*, **ē**, numerous, rhythmic

nŭmĕrus, i *m*, number, band (of soldiers), class, category, sequence, rhythm, poetic metre

nummārĭus, a, um *adj*, of money

nummātus, a, um *adj*, rich

nummus, i *m*, money, a Roman silver coin, farthing

numquam *adv*, never

numquid *interr. adv*, is there anything…?

nunc *adv*, now, at present

nuncia, nuncius … see **nunt**…

nuncŭpo *v.t.* 1, to call, name

nundĭnae, ārum *f.pl*, ninth day, market-day

nundĭnātĭo, ōnis *f*, trading

nundĭnor *v.i.t.* 1, *dep*, to trade; buy, sell

nunquam *adv*, never

nuntĭātĭo, ōnis *f*, announcement

nuntĭo *v.t.* 1, to announce, tell

nuntĭus, i *m*, messenger, message

nūper *adv*, lately, recently

nupta, ae *f*, wife, bride

nuptĭae, ārum *f.pl*, marriage

nuptĭālis, e *adj*, of marriage

nuptus, a, um *adj*, married

nŭrus, ūs *f*, daughter-in-law, young wife

nusquam *adv*, nowhere

nūto *v.i.* 1, to nod, waver

nūtrīcĭus, a, um *adj*, foster-father

nūtrīco *v.t.* 1, to nurse, rear

nūtrīcula, ae *f*, nurse

nūtrīmen, ĭnis *n*, nourishment

nūtrīmentum, i *n*, nourishment

nūtrĭo *v.t.* 4, to feed, bring up, support

nūtrix, īcis *f*, nurse

nūtus, ūs *m*, nod, command

nux, nŭcis *f*, nut

nympha, ae *f*, bride, nymph (demi-goddess inhabiting woods, trees, fountains, etc.)

O

ŏb *prep. with acc*, on account of, in front of

ŏbaerātus, a, um *adj*, involved in debt

ŏbambŭlo *v.i.* 1, to walk about

obdo, dĭdi, dĭtum *v.t.* 3, to shut, place, expose

obdormĭo *v.i.* 4, to fall asleep

obdormisco *v.i.* 3, to fall asleep

obdūco, xi, ctum *v.t.* 3, to lead forward, bring forward, cover over, swallow

obdūresco, rŭi *v.i.* 3, to become hardened

obdūro *v.i.* 1, to persist

ŏbēdĭens, ntis *adj*, obedient

ŏbēdĭentĭa, ae *f*, obedience

ŏbēdĭo *v.i.* 4, to obey, be subject to

ŏbĕliscus, i *m*, obelisk

ŏbĕo *v.i.t.* 4, to go to meet, die, set (constellations); to go to, reach, travel over, visit, undertake, perform

ŏbĕquĭto *v.i.* 1, to ride towards

ŏbēsĭtas, ātis *f*, fatness

ŏbēsus, a, um *adj*, fat, dull

ōbex, ĭcis *m, f*, bolt, barrier

obĭăcĕo *v.i.* 2, to lie opposite

ōbĭcĭo, iēci, iectum *v.t.* 3, to throw forward, expose, oppose, taunt, reproach

obiectātĭo, ōnis *f*, reproach

obiecto *v.t.* 1, to place against, expose, reproach, accuse

obiectus, ūs *m*, opposing, putting in the way

obiectus, a, um *adj*, lying opposite

ŏbĭtus, ūs *m*, setting, downfall

obiurgātĭo, ōnis *f*, rebuke

obiurgātor, ōris *m*, blamer

obirgātōrĭus, a, um *adj*, reproachful

obiurgo *v.t.* 1, to blame, rebuke

oblectāmen, ĭnis *n*, pleasure, delight

oblectāmentum, i *n*, pleasure, delight

oblecto *v.t.* 1, to amuse, please

oblīgātĭo, ōnis *f*, obligation

oblīgo *v.t.* 1, to bind, put under obligation, render liable

oblīmo *v.t.* 1, to cover with mud, squander

oblīno, lēvi, lĭtum *v.t.* 3, to besmear, defile

oblīquo *v.t.* 1, to bend aside

oblīquus, a, um *adj, adv*, ē, slanting, sideways

oblīvĭo, ōnis *f*, oblivion

oblīvĭōsus, a, um *adj*, forgetful, producing forgetfulness

oblīviscor, oblītus *v.* 3, *dep, with genit*, to forget

oblīvĭum, ii *n*, oblivion

oblŏquor, lŏcūtus *v.i.* 3, *dep*, to contradict, accompany a song

obluctor *v.i.* 1, *dep*, to struggle against

obmūtesco, tŭi *v.i.* 3, to become speechless

obnītor, xus *v.i.* 3, to become speechless

obnītor, xus *v.i.* 3, *dep*, to push or struggle against

obnixus, a, um *adj*, resolute

obnoxĭus, a, um *adj*, resolute

obnoxĭus, a, um *adj*, liable to, submissive, indebted

obnūbo, psi, ptum *v.t.* 3, to veil

obnuntĭātĭo, ōnis *f*, announcement of bad omens

obnuntĭo *v.t.* 1, to announce bad omens

ŏboedĭens, oboedĭo see obēd...

ŏbŏrĭor, ortus *v.i.* 4, *dep*, to arise, appear

obrēpo, psi, ptum *v.t.* 3, to creep up to, surprise

obrĭgesco, gŭi *v.i.* 3, to stiffen

obrŏgo *v.t.* 1, to invalidate

obrŭo, ŭi, ŭtum *v.t.* 3, to overwhelm, bury, hide

obsaepĭo, psi, ptum *v.t.* 4, to fence in

obscēnĭtas, ātis *f*, obscenity, foulness

obscēnus, a, um *adj*, ominous, filthy, obscene

obscūrĭtas, ātis *f*, uncertainty, lowness

obscūro *v.t.* 1, to darken, hide

obscūrus, a, um *adj, adv*, ē, dark, shady, indistinct, ignoble, humble, reserved

obsĕcrātĭo, ōnis *f*, appeal

obsĕcro *v.t.* 1, to implore

obsĕcundo *v.t.* 1, to humour, obey

obsēp... see obsaep...

obsĕquens, ntis *adj*, amenable

obsĕquĭum, ii *n*, compliance, obedience

obsĕquor, sĕcūtus *v.* 3, *dep, with dat*, to comply with, submit to, humour

obsĕro *v.t.* 1, to fasten

obsĕro, sēvi, sĭtum *v.t.* 3, to sow, plant

observans, ntis *adj*, attentive

observantĭa, ae *f*, attention, respect

observātĭo, ōnis *f*, care, observation

observo *v.t.* 1, to watch, take note of, respect, comply with

obses, ĭdis *m, f*, hostage

obsessĭo, ōnis *f*, blockade

obsessor, ōris *m*, besieger

obsĭdĕo, sēdi, sessum *v.t.* 2, to besiege, hem in, frequent

obsĭdĭo, ōnis *f*, siege

obsīdo *v.t.* 3, to besiege

obsignātor, ōris *m*, witness

obsigno *v.t.* 1, to seal up

obsisto, stĭti, stĭtum *v.i.* 3, to resist, oppose

obsĭtus, a, um *adj*, covered over

obsŏlesco, lēvi, lētum *v.i.* 3, to wear out, decay

obsŏlētus, a, um *adj*, worn out, low, mean

obsōnĭum, ii *n*, eatables

obsōnātor, ōris *m*, caterer

obsōno *v.t.* 1, (obsōnor *v.i.* 1, *dep*), to cater

obsorbĕo *v.t.* 2, to swallow

obstĕtrix, īcis *f*, midwife

obstĭnātĭo, ōnis *f*, firmness, obstinacy

obstĭnātus, a, um *adj, adv*, ē, determined, resolute, stubborn obstĭpesco, pŭi *v.i.* 3, to be amazed

obstīpus, a, um *adj*, bent

obsto, stĭti, ātum *v.i.* 1, *with dat,* to obstruct, withstand

obstrĕpo, ŭi, ĭtum *v.i.* 3, to roar at, resound

obstringo, nxi, ctum *v.t.* 3, to tie up, put under obligation

obstrŭo, xi, ctum *v.t.* 3, to build up, barricade, impede

obstŭpĕfăcĭo, fēci, factum *v.t.* 3, to astonish

obstŭpesco, pŭi *v.i.* 3, to be stupified, amazed

obsum, obesse, obfŭi *v.i, irreg,* to hinder, injure

obsŭo, ŭi, ūtum *v.t.* 3, to sew up

obsurdesco, dŭi *v.i.* 3, to grow deaf

obtĕgo, xi, ctum *v.t.* 3, to cover up

obtempĕro *v.t.* 1, *with dat,* to comply with

obtendo, di, tum *v.t.* 3, to spread before, hide

obtentus, ūs *m*, outspreading

obtĕro, trīvi, trītum *v.t.* 3, to crush to pieces

obtestātĭo, ōnis *f*, appeal

obtestor *v.t.* 1, *dep,* to call as a witness, implore

obtexo, xŭi *v.t.* 3, to cover up

obtĭcesco, tĭcŭi *v.i.* 3, to be struck dumb

obtĭnĕo, nŭi, tentum *v.i.t.* 2, to prevail, continue; keep, hold, gain, obtain

obtingo, tĭgi *v.i.* 3, to befall

obtorpesco, pŭi *v.i.* 3, to become stiff

obtorquĕo, si, tum *v.t.* 2, to twist, wrench

obtrectātĭo, ōnis *f*, disparagement

obtrectātor, ōris *m*, slander

obtrecto *v.i.t.* 1, to disparge

obtrunco *v.t.* 1, to trim, kill

obtundo, tŭdi, tūsum *v.t.* 3, to blunt, weaken, deafen, annoy

obtūrācŭlum, i *n*, stopper

obtūrāmentum, i *n*, stopper

obturbo *v.t.* 1, to disturb

obtūro *v.t.* 1, to close

obtūsus, a, um *adj*, blunt, dull

obtūtus, ūs *m*, gaze, stare

ŏbumbro *v.t.* 1, to overshadow

ŏbuncus, a, um *adj*, hooked

ŏbustus, a, um *adj*, hardened in fire

obvĕnĭo, vēni, ventum *v.i.* 4, to meet, befall one, happen

obversor *v.i.* 1, *dep,* to move to and fro, hover

obversus, a, um *adj*, directed towards

obverto, ti, sum *v.t.* 3, to turn downwards

obvĭam *adv, with verbs of motion,* towards, against

obvĭus, a, um *adj*, in the way, so as to meet, courteous, exposed

obvolvo, volvi, vŏlūtum *v.t.* 3, to wrap round, cover

occaeco *v.t.* 1, to blind, hide

occāsĭo, ōnis *f*, opportunity

occāsus, ūs *m*, setting (of sun, etc.) downfall, ruin

occĭdens, ntis *m*, the west

occĭdentālis, e *adj*, west

occīdĭo, ōnis *f*, massacre

occīdo, cīdi, cīsum *v.t.* 3, to strike down, crush, kill

occĭdo, cĭdi, cāsum *v.i.* 3, to fall, perish, set (of sun, etc.)

occĭdŭus, a, um *adj*, setting, western

occīsĭo, ōnis *f*, slaughter

occlūdo, si, sum *v.t.* 3, to close

occo *v.t.* 1, to harrow

occŭbo *v.i.* 1, to lie down, rest

occŭlo, lŭi, ltum *v.t.* 3, to hide

occultātĭo, ōnis *f*, concealment

occulto *v.t.* 1, to hide

occultus, a, um *adj, adv,* ē, hidden, secret

occumbo, cŭbŭi, cŭbĭtum *v.i.* 3, to die

occŭpātĭo, ōnis *f*, employment

occŭpātus, a, um *adj*, busy

occŭpo *v.t.* 1, to seize, occupy, attack, anticipate, fill

occurro, curri, cursum *v.i.* 3, to meet

occursātĭo, ōnis *f*, greeting

occurso *v.i.* 1, to meet, attack

occursus, ūs *m*, meeting

ōcĕănus, i *m*, ocean

ŏcellus, i *m*, small eye, darling
ōchra, ae *f*, ochre
ōcĭor, ĭus *comp. adj*, swifter
ōcĭus *adv*, more quickly
òcrĕa, ae *f*, leg-shield, greave
octāvus, a, um *adj*, eighth
octĭens (octĭes) *adv*, eight times
octingenti, ae, a *pl. adj*, eight
   hundred
octŏ *indecl. adj*, eight
Octōber (mensis) October
octōgēsĭmus, a, um *adj*, eightieth
octōginta *indecl. adj*, eighty
octōgōnum, i *n*, octagon
octōni, ae, a *pl. adj*, eight each
octōphŏron, i *m*, sedan carried by
   eight men
ŏcŭlārĭus, a, um *adj*, of the eyes
ŏcŭlus, i *m*, eye, bud
ōdi, ōdisse *v.t*, *defect*, to hate
ŏdĭōsus, a, um *adj, adv, ē*, hateful,
   troublesome
ŏdĭum, ii *n*, odour, smell
ŏdor, ōris *m*, odour, smell
ŏdōrātĭo, ōnis *f*, smell
ŏdōrātus, ūs *m*, smelling
ŏdōrātus, a, um *adj*, scented
ŏdōrĭfer, ĕra, ĕrum *adj*, fragrant
ŏdōro *v.t*. 1, to perfume
ŏdōror *v.t*. 1, *dep*, to smell out,
   investigate
ŏdōrus, a, um *adj*, fragrant
oestrus, i *m*, gad fly
offa, ae *f*, morsel
offendo, di, sum *v.i.t*. 3, to make a
   mistake; strike against, meet
   with, find, offend
offensa, ae *f*, hatred, crime
offensĭo, ōnis *f*, stumbling, dislike,
   displeasure
offensus, a, um *adj*, offensive,
   offended
offĕro, offerre, obtŭli, oblātum *v.t*,
   irreg, to offer, show, cause, bring
officīna, ae *f*, workshop
officĭo, fēci, fectum *v.i*. 3, to
   obstruct, hinder
officĭōsus, a, um *adj, adv, ē*,
   obliging, courteous
officĭum, ii *n*, kindness, duty,
   employment, office
offirmātus, a, um *adj*, firm
offulgĕo, si *v.i*. 2, to shine on,
   appear

offundo, fūdi, fūsum *v.t*. 3, to pour
   out, spread over
ŏhē *interj*, ho there!
ŏlĕa, ae *f*, olive
ŏlĕācĕus, a, um *adj*, oily
ŏlĕārĭus, a, um *adj*, of oil; (...i
   m), oil-seller
ŏlĕaster, stri *m*, wild olive tree
ŏlens, ntis *adj*, fragrant, rank
ŏlĕo, ŭi *v.i.t*. 2, to smell of
ŏlĕum, i *n*, olive oil
olfăcĭo, fēci, factum *v.t*. 3, to smell
ŏlĭdus, a, um *adj*, stinking
ōlim *adv*, once upon a time, once,
   sometime in the future
ŏlĭtor, ōris *m*, market gardener
ŏlīva, ae *f*, olive tree, olive branch
ŏlīvētum, i *n*, olive grove
ŏlīvĭfer, ĕra, ĕrum *adj*, olive
   growing
ŏlīvum, i *n*, oil
olla, ae *f*, pot, jar
ŏlor, ōris *m*, swan
ŏlōrīnus, a, um *adj*, of swans
ŏlus, ĕris *n*, vegetables
ŏmāsum, i *n*, tripe
ōmen, ĭnis *n*, omen, sign
ōmĭnor *v.t*. 1, *dep*, to forbode
ōmitto, mīsi, missum *v.t*. 3, to put
   aside, give up, leave out
omnĭgĕnus, a, um *adj*, of all kinds
omnīno *adv*, altogether, entirely
omnĭpārens, ntis *adj*, all-producing
omnĭpŏtens, ntis *adj*, almighty
omnes, ĭum *c, pl*, all men
omnĭa, ĭum *n.pl*, all things
omnis, e *adj*, all, every
omnĭvăgus, a, um *adj*, wandering
   everywhere
ŏnăger (grus), i *m*, wild as
ŏnĕrārĭa, ae *f*, merchant ship
ŏnĕrārĭus, a, um *adj*, of, or for,
   freight
ŏnĕro *v.t*. 1, to load, oppress
ŏnĕrōsus, a, um *adj*, burdensome
ŏnŭs, ĕris *n*, load, burden
ŏnustus, a, um *adj*, loaded, full
ŏnyx, ychis *m, f*, yellow marble
ŏpāco *v.t*. 1, to cover, shade
ŏpācus, a, um *adj*, shady
ŏpālus, i *m*, opal
ŏpem (*no nomin.*) *f*, power,
   wealth, help

ŏpĕra

ŏpĕra, ae *f*, exertion, effort; *in pl*, workmen
ŏpĕram do to give careful attention to
ŏpĕrārĭus, a, um *adj*, of labour
ŏpĕrārĭus, ii *m*, labourer
ŏpercŭlum, i *n*, lid, cover
ŏpĕrĭo, ŭi, ŏpertum *v.t.* 4, to cover, hide
ŏpĕror *v.i.* 1, *dep*, to work, labour, perform a sacrifice
ŏpĕrōsus, a, um *adj, adv*, ē, painstaking, busy, troublesome
ŏpertus, a, um *adj*, hidden
ŏpes, um *f.pl*, wealth, resource
ŏpĭfer, ĕra, ĕrum *adj*, helping
ŏpĭfex, ĭcis *c*, craftsman
ŏpīmus, a, um *adj*, fat, rich, fertile; spŏlĭa ŏpima arms won by a general in single combat with opposing general
ŏpīnābĭlis, e *adj*, imaginary
ŏpīnātĭo, ōnis *f*, supposition
ŏpīnātus, a, um *adj*, imagined
ŏpīnĭo, ōnis *f*, supposition, belief, reputation, rumour
ŏpīnor *v.i.t.* 1, *dep*, to suppose
ŏpĭpărē *adv*, sumptuously
ŏpĭtŭlor *v.i.* 1, *dep*, to help
ŏpĭum, ii *n*, opium
ŏportet *v.* 2, *impers, with acc. of person* it is necessary
oppĕrĭor, pertus *v.i.t.* 4, *dep*, to wait; wait for
oppĕto, īvi, ītum *v.t.* 3, to encounter (especially death)
oppĭdāni, ōrum *m.pl*, townspeople
oppĭdānus, a, um *adj*, provincial
oppĭdŭlum, i *n*, small town
oppĭdum, i *n*, town
oppignĕro *v.t.* 1, to pledge
oppĭlo *v.t.* 1, to shut, stop
opplĕo, ēvi, ētum *v.t.* 2, to fill up
oppōno, pŏsŭi, sĭtum *v.t.* 3, to place opposite, oppose, offer, expose, object
opportūnĭtas, ātis *f*, convenience, advantage
opportūnus, a, um *adj, adv*, ē, suitable, convenient
oppŏsĭtĭo, ōnis *f*, opposition
oppŏsĭtus, a, um *adj*, opposite
opprĭmo, pressi, ssum *v.t.* 3, to supress, close, surprise, hide

opprŏbrĭum, i *n*, scandal, taunt
oppugnātĭo, ōnis *f*, attack, siege
oppugnātor, ōris *m*, attacker
oppugno *v.t.* 1, to attack
ops, ŏpis *f*, power, aid
optābĭlis, e *adj*, desirable
optātĭo, ōnis *f*, wish
optātum, i *n*, wish
optātus, a, um *adj, adv*, ō, desired, pleasant
optĭmas, ātis *adj*, aristocratic
optĭmātes, um *c, pl*, the aristocratic party
optĭmus, a, um *adj, adv*, ē, best
optĭo, ōnis *f*, choice
optĭo, ōnis *m*, assistant
opto *v.t.* 1, to choose, desire
ŏpŭlens, ntis *adj*, rich
ŏpŭlentĭa, ae *f*, wealth
ŏpŭlentus, a, um *adj*, rich
ŏpus, ĕris *n*, work, task; ŏpus est there is need (a necessity)
ŏpuscŭlum, i *n*, a small work
ōra, ae *f*, border, sea coast, region
ōrācŭlum, i *n*, oracle
ōrātĭo, ōnis *f*, speech, language, eloquence
ōrātĭuncŭla, ae *f*, brief speech
ōrātor, ōris *m*, speaker, orator, ambassador
ōrātōrĭus, a, um *adj*, oratorical
orbĭcŭlātus, a, um *adj*, circular
orbis, is *m*, circle; orbis terrarum the world
orbĭta, ae *f*, track, rut
orbĭtas, ātis *f*, bereavement
orbo *v.t.* 1, to bereave, deprive
orbus, a, um *adj*, bereaved, destitute
orca, ae *f*, large tub
orchas, ādis *f*, olive
orchēstra, ae *f*, a place at the front of the theatre
orchis, is *f*, orchid
Orcus, i *m*, death, the Lower World
ordĭnārĭus, a, um *adj*, regular, usual, orderly
ordĭnātim *adv*, in proper order
ordĭnātus, a, um *adj*, orderly, regulated
ordĭne *adv*, in order
ordĭno *v.t.* 1, to arrange

ordĭor, orsus *v.i.t* 4, *dep*, to begin, undertake
ordo, ĭnis *m*, row, rank, band or company of soldiers, series, class of society
Òrēăs, ādis *f*, mountain-nymph
orgĭa, ōrum *n.pl*, revels in honour of Bacchus
ŏrĭchalcum, i *n*, copper ore
ŏrĭens, ntis *m*, the east
ŏrīgo, ĭnis *f*, beginning, origin, family, ancestor
ŏrĭor, ortus *v.i.* 4, *dep*, to arise, appear, originate
ŏrĭundus, a, um *adj*, descended or sprung from
ornāmentum, i *n*, equipment, decoration
ornātus, a, um *adj, adv*, ē, equipped, decorated
ornātus, ūs *m*, equipment, dress, ornament
orno *v.t.* 1, to equip, adorn, praise
ornus, i *f*, mountain ash
ōro *v.t.* 1, to plead, beg, pray
orsa, ōrum *n.pl*, undertaking, speech
orsus, ūs *m*, undertaking
ortus, ūs *m*, rising (of sun, etc.), beginning, source
ŏrȳsa, ae *f*, rice
ōs, ōris *n*, mouth, face, opening
ŏs, ossis *n*, bone
oscen, ĭnis *m*, singing bird from whose notes omens were taken
oscillātĭo, ōnis *f*, swinging
oscillum, i *n*, small mask
oscĭtātĭo, ōnis *f*, yawning
oscĭto *v.i.* 1, to gape, yawn
oscŭlor *v.i.t.* 1, *dep*, to kiss
oscŭlum, i *n*, mouth, kiss
ossĕus, a, um *adj*, made of bone
ossĭfrăgus, i *m*, sea eagle
ostendo, di, sum *v.t.* 3, to show, make known
ostentātĭo, ōnis *f*, display
ostento *v.t.* 1, to show, display
ostentum, i *n*, prodigy
ostĭārĭum, ii *n*, door tax
ostĭātim *adv*, from door to door
ostĭum, ii *n*, door, entrance
ostrĕa, ae *f*, oyster
ostrĕārĭum, ii *n*, oyster-bed

ostrum, i *n*, purple, purple coverings or dress
ōtĭor *v.i.* 1, *dep*, to be on holiday
ōtĭōsus, a, um *adj, adv*, ē, at leisure, unemployed, quiet
ōtĭum, ii *n*, leisure, peace
ŏvans, ntis *adj*, triumphant
ōvātus, a, um *adj*, oval
ŏvillus, a, um *adj*, of sheep
ŏvīlis, e *adj*, of sheep
ŏvīle, is *n*, sheepfold
ŏvis, is *f*, sheep
ŏvo *v.i.* 1, to exult
ōvum, i *n*, egg

P

păbo, ōnis *m*, wheelbarrow
pābŭlātĭo, ōnis *f*, collection of fodder
pābŭlātor, ōris *m*, forager
pābŭlor *v.i.* 1, *dep*, to look for fodder
pābŭlum, i *n*, food, fodder
pācālis, e *adj*, peaceful
pācātus, a, um *adj*, peaceful
pācĭfer, ĕra, ĕrum *adj*, peace-bringing
pācĭfĭcātĭo, ōnis *f*, pacification
pācĭfĭco *v.t.* 1, to make peace
pācĭfĭcus, a, um *adj*, peaceable
pāciscor, pactus *v.i.t.* 3, *dep*, to make a bargain; barter
pāco *v.t.* 1, to subdue, pacify
pactĭo, ōnis *f*, an agreement
pactum, i *n*, an agreement
pactus, a, um *adj*, agreed
paean, ănis *m*, hymn to Apollo
paedăgōgus, i *m*, slave who took chidren to school, and looked after them at home
paedor, ōris *m*, filth
paelex, ĭcis *f*, concubine
paenĕ *adv*, almost, nearly
paeninsŭla, ae *f*, peninsula
paenĭtens, ntis *adj*, repentant
paenĭtentĭa, ae *f*, penitence
paenĭtet *v.* 2, *impers, with acc. o f person*, it grieves
paenŭla, ae *f*, cloak
paenultĭmus, a, um *adj*, penultimate
paetus, a, um *adj*, with a slight cast in the eye

pāgānus, a, um *adj*, rural
pāgānus, i *m*, country-dweller
pāgĭna, ae *f*, page, leaf, book
pāgus, i *m*, village, district
pāla, ae *f*, spade
pălaestra, ae *f*, wrestling ground
or school, wrestling, rhetorical
exercise
pălam *adv*, openly; *prep. with abl*,
*i*n the presence of
pălētĭum, ii *n*, palace
pălātum, i *n*, palate
pălĕa, ae *f*, chaff
pălĭūrus, i *m*, Christ's thorn (plant)
palla, ae *f*, stole, robe
pallens, ntis *adj*, pale
pallĕo *v.i.* 2, to be pale
pallesco, pallŭi *v.i.* 3, to turn pale
pallĭātus, a, um *adj*, cloaked like
Greeks
pallĭdus, a, um *adj*, pale
pallĭŏlum, i *n*, hood
pallĭum, ii *n*, coverlet, cloak
pallor, ōris *m*, paleness
palma, ae *f*, palm, hand, oar-
blade, palm tree, broom, palm
wreath, prize, glory
palmāris, e *adj*, excellent, worthy
of the palm
palmātus, a, um *adj*, marked with
the hand, decorated with palm
palmĕs, ĭtis *m*, wine shoot
palmētum, i *n*, palm grove
palmĭfer, ĕra, ĕrum *adj*, palm-
bearing
palmōsus, a, um *adj*, with many
palm trees
palmŭla, ae *f*, oar-blade
palmus, i *m*, palm of hand, span
pālor *v.i.* 1, *dep*, to wander
palpèbra, ae *f*, eyelid
palpĭtātĭo, ōnis *f*, palpitation
palpĭto *v.i.* 1, to throb, pant
palpo *v.t.* 1, to stroke, carress
pălūdāmentum, i *n*, military cloak,
general's cloak
pălūdātus, a, um *adj*, dressed in
general's cloak
pălūdōsus, a, um *adj*, marshy
pălumbes, is *m, f*, wood-pigeon
pālus, i *m*, stake
pălus, ūdis *f*, marsh
păluster, tris, tre *adj*, marshy

pampĭnĕus, a, um *adj*, full of vine
leaves
pampĭnus, i *m, f*, vine shoot, vine
leaf
pănăcēa, ae *f*, a herb which
healed all diseases
panchrestus, a, um *adj*, good for
anything
pando, di, nsum *v.t.* 3, to unfold,
open out, spread out, publish
pandus, a, um *adj*, curved
pango, pĕpĭgi, pactum *v.t.* 3, to
fasten, settle, agree upon
pānis, is *m*, bread
pannōsus, a, um *adj*, tattered
pannus, i *m*, garment, rags
panthēra, ae *f*, panther
pantŏmīmus, i *m*, ballet dancer
păpāver, ĕris *n*, poppy
pāpīlĭo, ōnis *m*, butterfly
păpilla, ae *f*, breast, nipple
păpŭla, ae *f*, pimple
păpȳrĭfer, ĕra, ĕrum *adj*, papyrus
producing
păpȳrus, i *m, f*, paper
pār, păris *adj*, equal, suitable
pār, păris *m*, companion
părăbĭlis, e *adj*, easily procured
părăbŏla *f*, parable, comparison
părallēlus, a, um *adj*, parallel
părălўsis, is *f*, paralysis, palsy
părăsītus, i *m*, parasite
părātus, a, um *adj*, prepared
părātus, ūs *m*, preparation
parco, pĕperci, parsum *v.i.* 3, *with
dat*, to spare, desist
parcus, a, um *adj, adv*, ē, thrifty,
sparing, scanty
pārens, ntis *adj*, obedient
părens, ntis *m, f*, parent, ancestor,
founder
părentālĭa, ĭum *n.pl*, festival in
honour of dead relations
părentālis, e *adj*, parental
părento *v.t.* 1, to honour dead
relatives, avenge a relative's death
by killing
pārĕo *v.i.* 2, *with dat*, to obey, to
appear
părĭēs, ĕtis *m*, wall
părĭĕtĭnae, ārum *f.pl*, ruins
părĭlis, e *adj*, equal
părĭo, pĕpĕri, partum *v.t.* 3, to
bring forth, produce, acquire

părĭter, *adv*, equally, at the same time

parma, ae *f*, small round shield

parmŭla, ae *f*, small round shield

păro *v.t.* 1, to prepare, intend, obtain

părŏchus, i *m*, caterer

păroecĭa, ae *f*, parish

parra, ae *f*, owl

parrĭcīda, ae *c*, murderer of a parent of relative, assassin

parrĭcīdĭum, ii *n*, murder of a parent, or relative, treason

pars, partis *f*, part, party, faction, part in a play; *in pl*, duty, office; **in utramque partem** on both sides; **pro parte** to the best of one's ability

parsĭmōnĭa, ae *f*, thrift

partĭceps, cĭpis *adj*, *with genit*, sharing; (*as noun*) sharer

partĭcĭpo *v.t.* 1, to give a share of

partĭcŭla, ae *f*, small part

partim *adv*, partly

partĭo *v.t.* 4, to share, divide

partĭor *v.t.* 4, *dep*, to share, divide

partītĭo, ōnis *f*, division

partītus, a, um *adj*, divided

partŭrĭo *v.i.t.* 4, to be pregnant of in labour; produce

pārtus, ūs *m*, birth, confinement, offspring

părum *adv*, too little

părumper *adv*, for a short time

parvĭtas, ātis *f*, smallness

parvŭlus, a, um *adj*, slight

parvus, a, um *adj*, small, petty, short; **parvi**, of little value

pasco, pāvi, pastum *v.i.t.* 3, to feed; pasture, nourish

pascor, pastus *v.i.* 3, *dep*, to graze, feast

pascŭum, i *n*, pasture

pascŭus, a, um *adj*, for grazing

passer, ĕris *m*, sparrow, turbot

passim *adv*, in all directions

passum, i *n*, raisin wine

passus, a, um *adj*, spread out, dried

passus, a, um *partic. adj*, having suffered

passus, ūs *m*, step, pace

pastillus, i *m*, lozenge to dispel bad breath

pastor, ōris *m*, shepherd

pastōrālis, e *adj*, of shepherds, pastoral

pastōrĭcĭus, a, um *adj*, of shepherds, pastoral

pastōrĭus, a, um *adj*, of shepherds, pastoral

pastus, ūs *m*, pasture, food

pătĕfăcĭo, fēci, factum *v.t.* 3, to throw open, disclose

pătĕfactĭo, ōnis *f*, opening up

pătella, ae *f*, plate

pătens, ntis *adj*, open

pătĕo *v.i.* 2, to be open, to extend, to be evident

păter, tris *m*, father; *in pl*, forefathers, senators

pătĕra, ae *f*, saucer, bowl

păterfămĭlĭas, patrisfămĭlĭas *m*, master of the house

păternus, a, um *adj*, of a father

pătesco, pătŭi *v.i.* 3, to be opened, to extend, be evident

pătībĭlis, e *adj*, endurable

pătībŭlum, i *n*, fork-shaped yoke or gibbet

pătĭens, ntis *adj*, *adv*, **nter**, suffering, patient, hard

pătĭentĭa, ae *f*, endurance

pătĭna, ae *f*, pan, dish

pătĭor, passus *v.t.* 3, *dep*, to suffer, bear, allow

pătrĭa, ae *f*, fatherland

pătrĭarcha, ae *m*, patriarch

pătrĭcĭus, a, um *adj*, noble

pătrĭcĭus, i *m*, member of the Roman nobility

pătrĭmōnĭum, ii *n*, inherited estate

pătrītus, a, um *adj*, of one's father or ancestor

pătrĭus, a, um *adj*, of a father, hereditary, established, native

pătro *v.t.* 1, to perform, finish

pătrōcĭnĭum, ii *n*, defence

pătrōna, ae *f*, patroness

pătrōnus, i *m*, protector, patron, counsel

pătrŭēlis, is *c*, cousin

pătrŭus, i *m*, uncle

pătrŭus, a, um *adj*, of an uncle

pătŭlus, a, um *adj*, open wide

pauci, ae, a *pl. adj*, few

paucĭtas, ātis *f*, small number

paucŭlus, a, um *adj*, very few
paucus, a, um *adj*, few, little
paulātim *adv*, gradually
paulisper *adv*, for a short time
paulō *adv*, a little, somewhat
paulŭlum *adv*, a little, somewhat
paulum *adv*, a little, somewhat
pauper, ĕris *adj*, poor, meagre
pauper, ĕris *c*, a poor man
paupĕrĭes, ēi *f*, poverty
paupertas, ātis *f*, poverty
paupĕro *v.t.* 1, to impoverish
pausa, ae *f*, stop, end
păvĕfăcĭo, fēci, factum *v.t.* 3, to alarm
păvĕo, păvi *v.i.t.* 2, to be afraid; dread
păvesco *v.i.* 3, to become alarmed
păvĭdus, a, um *adj*, terrified
păvīmentum, i *n*, pavement
păvĭo *v.t.* 4, to beat, strike
păvĭto *v.i.t.* 1, to tremble (at)
pāvo, ōnis *m*, peacock
păvor, ōris *m*, anxiety, dread
pax, pācis *f*, peace, grace, favour, tranquillity; *in abl,* by permission
peccans, ntis *c*, offender
peccātor, ōris *m*, sinner
peccātum, i *n*, fault, mistake
pecco *v.i.t.* 1, to make a mistake; to miss
pecten, ĭnis *m*, comb, reed, rake, a plectrum to strike the strings of the lyre
pecto, pexi, xum *v.t.* 3, to comb
pectŏrālis, e *adj*, pectoral
pectus, ŏris *n*, breast, heart, soul, mind
pĕcŭārĭus, a, um *adj*, of cattle
pĕcŭārĭus, ii *m*, cattle-breeder
pĕcūlātor, ōris *m*, embezzler
pĕcūlātus, ūs *m*, embezzlement
pĕcūlĭāris, e *adj*, one's own, special
pĕcūlĭum, ii *n*, property, savings
pĕcūnĭa, ae *f*, money
pĕcūnĭārĭus, a, um *adj*, pecuniary
pĕcūnĭōsus, a, um *adj*, rich
pĕcus, ŏris *n*, cattle, herd
pĕcus, ŭdis *f*, an animal, beast
pĕdālis, e *adj*, a foot in length or thickness
pĕdes, ĭtis *m*, infantryman

pĕdes see **pes**
pĕdester, tris, tre *adj*, on foot, prosaic, plain
pĕdĕtemptim *adv*, gradually
pĕdīca, ae *f*, shackle, snare
pĕdīcŭlōsus, a, um *adj*, lousy
pĕdīcŭlus, i *m*, louse
pĕdīsĕquus, i *m*, footman
pĕdītātus, ūs *m*, infantry
pĕdum, i *n*, shepherd's crook
pēĭĕro *v.i.* 1, to swear falsely
pēior *comp. adj*, worse
pēius *comp. adv*, worse
pĕlăgus, i *n*, open sea
pellax, ācis *adj*, seductive
pellex, ĭcis *f*, concubine
pellĭcĭo, lexi, lectum *v.t.* 3, to allure, coax
pellĭcŭla, ae *f*, small skin
pellis, is *f*, skin, leather, tent
pellītus, a, um *adj*, clothed in skins
pello, pĕpŭli, pulsum *v.t.* 3, to strike, push, drive out, rout, affect, impress
pellūcĕo, xi *v.i.* 2, to shine through, be transparent
pellūcĭdus, a, um *adj*, transparent
pĕlōris, ĭdis *f*, mussel
pelta, ae *f*, small shield
pelvis, is *f*, basin
pĕnārĭus, a, um *adj*, for provisions
pĕnātes, ĭum *m.pl*, guardian deities of the home, home
pendĕo, pĕpendi *v.i.* 2, to hang, float, loiter, depend upon, be interrupted, be in suspense
pendo, pĕpendi, pensum *v.t.* 3, to weigh or pay out, ponder
pendŭlus, a, um *adj*, hanging, uncertain
pĕnĕs *prep. with acc,* in the power of
pĕnĕtrābĭlis, e *adj*, penetrable, penetrating
pĕnĕtrālĭa, ĭum *n.pl*, inner places or rooms
pĕnĕtrālis, e *adj*, inner
pĕnĕtro *v.i.t.* 1, to enter; penetrate
pēnĭcillum, i *n*, painter's brush, pencil
pēnĭcŭlāmentum, i *n*, train of a dress
pēnĭcŭlus, i *m*, brush
pēnis, is *m*, tail, penis

pĕnĭtus *adv*, inwardly, deep within, entirely

penna, ae *f*, feather, wing

pennātus, a, um *adj*, winged

pennĭger, ĕra, ĕrum *adj*, winged

pensĭlis, e *adj*, hanging

pensĭo, ōnis *f*, payment

pensĭto *v.t.* 1, to pay, weigh, ponder

penso *v.t.* 1, to weigh out, repay, consider

pensum, i *n*, a task

pēnūrĭa, ae *f*, need, want

pĕnus, ūs (*or* ĭ), *m, f*, store of food

pĕpo, ŏnis *m*, pumpkin

per *prep. with acc*, through, during, by means of, on account of

per... in compound words usually adds intensity: very ...

pĕractĭo, ōnis *f*, completion

pĕrăgo, ēgi, actum *v.t.* 3, to complete, relate, transfix

pĕràgro *v.t.* 1, to travel over

pĕrambŭlo *v.t.* 1, to go through

pĕrăro *v.t.* 1, to plough through

perbrĕvis, e *adj*, very short

perca, ae *f*, perch (fish)

percĕlĕbro *v.t.* 1, to say frequently

percello, cŭli, culsum *v.t.* 3, to upset, destroy, dishearten

percensĕo *v.t.* 2, to reckon up

perceptĭo, ōnis *f*, perception

percĭpĭo, cēpi, ceptum *v.t.* 3, to gather, perceive, understand

percontātĭo, ōnis *f*, *i*nquiry

percontor *v.i.t.* 1, *dep*, to investigate

percŏquo, xi, ctum *v.t.* 3, to boil, cook, heat

percrēbesco, bŭi *v.i.* 3, to become prevalent

percrĕpo, ŭi, ĭtum *v.i.* 1, to resound, ring

perculsus, a, um *adj*, upset

percurro, curri, cursum *v.i.t.* 3, to run; pass over, mention

percussĭo, ōnis *f*, beating

percussor, ōris *m*, assassin

percŭtĭo, cussi, cussum *v.t.* 3, to thrust through, kill, strike, astound

perdisco, dĭdĭci *v.t.* 3, to learn thoroughly

perdĭtor, ōris *m*, destroyer

perdĭtus, a, um *adj, adv*, ē, ruined, desperate, corrupt

perdix, īcis *c*, partridge

perdo, dĭdi, dĭtum *v.t.* 3, to destroy, waste, lose

perdŏcĕo *v.t.* 2, to teach thoroughly

perdŏmo, ŭi, ĭtum *v.t.* 1, to subdue completely

perdūco, xi, ctum *v.t.* 3, to conduct, bedaub, prolong, induce

perductor, ōris *m*, pimp

perdŭellĭo, ōnis *f*, treason

perdŭellis, is *m*, public enemy

pĕrēdo, ēdi, sum *v.t.* 3, to eat up

pĕrēgrē *adv*, abroad

pĕrēgrīnātĭo, ōnis *f*, travel abroad

pĕrēgrīnātor, ōris *m*, traveller

pĕrēgrīnor *v.i.* 1, *dep*, to live or travel abroad

pĕrēgrīnus, a, um *adj*, foreign

pĕrēgrīnus, i *m*, foreigner

pĕrendĭē *adv*, on the day after tomorrow

pĕrennis, e *adj*, everlasting

pĕrenno *v.i.* 1, to last, endure

pĕrĕo, ĭi, ĭtum *v.i.* 4, *irreg*, to pass away, disappear, die, to be ruined or wasted

pĕrĕquĭto *v.i.* 1, to ride about

pĕrerro *v.t.* 1, to wander through

perfectĭo, ōnis *f*, completion

perfectus, a, um *adj, adv*, ē, complete, perfect

perfĕro, ferre, tŭli, lātum *v.t, irreg*, to bring or bear through, convey, announce, complete, suffer

perfĭcĭo, fēci, fectum *v.t.* 3, to complete, finish

perfĭdĭa, ae *f*, treachery

perfĭdĭōsus, a, um *adj* treacherous

perfĭdus, a, um *adj*, treacherous

perflo *v.t.* 1, to blow through

perflŭo, xi *v.i.* 3, to flow through

perfŏdĭo, fōdi, fossum *v.t.* 3, to dig through

perfŏro *v.t.* 1, to bore through

perfrĭco, cŭi, cātum *v.t.* 1, to rub all over, put on a bold front

perfringo, frēgi, fractum *v.t.* 3, to shatter, infringe

perfrŭor, fructus *v.* 3, *dep*, *with abl*, to enjoy thoroughly

perfŭga, ae *m*, deserter
perfŭgĭo, fūgi *v.i.* 3, to flee for refuge, desert
perfŭgĭum, ii *n*, shelter
perfundo, fūdi, fūsum *v.t.* 3, to pour over, besprinkle
perfungor, functus *v.* 3, *dep, with abl*, to fulfil, discharge
perfŭro, — *v.i.* 3, to rage
pergo, perrexi, perrectum *v.i.t.* 3, to proceed, go; continue
pĕrhĭbĕo, ŭi, ĭtum *v.t.* 2, to extend, assert, name
pĕrhorresco, rŭi *v.i.t.* 3, to tremble; shudder at
pĕrīclĭtor *v.i.t.* 1, *dep*, to try, be in danger; test, endanger
pĕrīcŭlōsus, a, um *adj, adv, ē*, dangerous
pĕrīcŭlum, i *n*, danger, proof, attempt
pĕrĭmo, ēmi, emptum *v.t.* 3, to anihilate, prevent
pĕrinde *adv*, just as, equally
pĕrĭŏdus, i *f*, complete sentence
pĕrītĭa, ae *f*, experience, skill
pĕrītus, a, um *adj, adv, ē, with genit*, skilled, expert
periūrĭum, ii *n*, perjury
periūro see **pēiĕro**
periūrus, a, um *adj*, perjured, lying
perlābor, lapsus *v.i.* 3, *dep*, to glide through
perlectĭo, ōnis *f*, reading through
perlĕgo, lēgi, lectum *v.t.* 3, to survey, examine, read through
perlūcĕo, xi *v.i.* 2, to shine through, be transparent
perlŭo, ŭi, ūtum *v.t.* 3, to wash
perlūcĭdus, a, um *adj*, transparent
perlustro *v.t.* 1, to wander through
permănĕo, nsi, nsum *v.i.* 2, to flow through, penetrate
permansĭo, ōnis *f*, persisting
permĕo *v.t.* 1, to cross, penetrate
permētĭor, mensus *v.t.* 4, *dep*, to measure out, travel over
permiscĕo, scŭi, xtum *v.t.* 2, to mix together
permissĭo, ōnis *f*, permission, surrender
permissū *abl*, by permission

permitto, mīsi, missum *v.t.* 3, to let loose, commit, entrust; allow (*with dat*)
permōtĭo, ōnis *f*, excitement
permŏvĕo, mōvi, mōtum *v.t.* 2, to stir up, rouse
permulcĕo, mulsi, mulsum *v.t.* 2, to stroke, charm, flatter
permultus, a, um *adj, adv, ō*, or **um**, very much
permūtātĭo, ōnis *f*, exchange
permūto *v.t.* 1, to change
perna, ae *f*, leg of pork
pernĕgo *v.t.* 1, to deny flatly
pernĭcĭes, ēi *f*, disaster
pernĭcĭōsus, a, um *adj, adv, ē*, destructive
pernĭcĭtas, ātis *f*, agility
pernix, īcis *adj*, agile
pernocto *v.i.* 1, to stay all night
pernox, ctis *adj*, night-long
pēro, ōnis *m*, rawhide boot
pĕrōsus, a, um *adj*, detesting, detested
pĕrōro *v.t.* 1, to wind up a speech
perpendĭcŭlum, i *n*, plumb line
perpendo, pendi, pensum *v.t.* 3, to ponder, consider
perpĕram *adv*, untruly
perpĕtĭor, pessus *v.i.t.* 3, *dep*, to suffer; endure
perpĕtŭĭtas, ātis *f*, continuity
perpĕtŭus, a, um *adj, adv, ō*, perpetual, entire, continuous
perplexus, a, um *adj*, intricate
perpŏlĭo *v.t.* 4, to perfect
perprĭmo, pressi, ssum *v.t.* 3, to press hard
perpurgo *v.t.* 1, to clean up
perquam *adv*, very much
perquīro, sīvi, sītum *v.t.* 3, to make a careful search for
perrārō *adv*, very rarely
perrumpo, rūpi, ruptum *v.i.t.* 3, to break through
perscrībo, psi, ptum *v.t.* 3, to write in full
perscriptĭo, ōnis *f*, written entry or note
perscrūtor *v.t.* 1, *dep*, to examine
persĕco, cui, ctum *v.t.* 1, to cut up
persentĭo, si, sum *v.t.* 4, to perceive plainly, feel deeply

persĕquor, sĕcūtus *v.t.* 3, *dep*, to pursue, overtake, revenge

persĕvērantĭa, ae *f*, constancy

persĕvēro *v.i.t.* 1, to persevere; persist in

persīdo, sēdi, sessum *v.i.* 3, to penetrate

persisto, stĭti *v.i.* 3, to persist

persolvo, solvi, sŏlūtum *v.t.* 3, to pay out, give

persōna, ae *f*, mask, character, part, person

parsōnātus, a, um *adj*, fictitious

persŏno, ŭi, ĭtum *v.i.t.* 1, to resound; fill with sound

perspectus, a, um *adj*, well known

perspĭcācĭtas, ātis *f*, perspicacity

perspĭcax, ācis *adj*, astute

perspĭvĭo, spexi, spectum *v.t.* 3, to look at, examine, perceive

perspĭcŭĭtas, ātis *f*, clearness, perspicuity

perspĭcŭus, a, um *adj, adv*, ē, clear, evident

persto, stĭti, stātum *v.i.* 1, to endure, continue, persist

perstringo, nxi, ctum *v.t.* 3, to graze, blunt, stun, blame, allude to, slight

persuādĕo, si, sum *v.t.* 2, *with dat*, to persuade

persuāsĭo, ōnis *f*, conviction

persuāsus, a, um *adj*, settled; **persuāsum hăbēre** to be convinced

pertento *v.t.* 1, to consider

pertĕrĕbro *v.t.* 1, to bore through

perterrĕo *v.t.* 2, to frighten thoroughly

pertĭca, ae *f*, pole, rod

pertĭmesco, mŭi *v.i.t.* 3, to be very afraid; to fear greatly

pertĭnācĭa, ae *f*, obstinancy

pertĭnax, ācis *adj*, firm, constant, stubborn

perttĭnĕo *v.i.* 2, to extend, pertain, concern, be applicable

pertracto *v.t.* 1, to touch

pertundo, tŭdi, tūsum *v.t.* 3, to make a hole through

perturbātĭo, ōnis *f*, confusion

perturbātus, a, um *adj*, disturbed

perturbo *v.t.* 1, to disturb

pĕrungo, nxi, nctum *v.t.* 3, to besmear

pĕrūro, ssi, stum *v.t.* 3, to burn up, rub sore, nip

pervādo, si, sum *v.i.* 3, to spread through, pervade

pervăgātus, a, um *adj*, well-known

pervăgor *v.i.t.* 1, *dep*, to wonder through; pervade

pervĕho, xi, ctum *v.t.* 3, to carry through

pervello, velli *v.t.* 3, to pull, disparage

pervĕnĭo, vēnis, ventum *v.i.* 4, to reach, arrive at

perversĭtas, ātis *f*, obstinacy

perversus, a, um *adj*, askew, perverse

perverto, ti, sum *v.t.* 3, to overturn, destroy, corrupt

pervestīgo *v.t.* 1, to investigate

pervĭcācĭa, ae *f*, obstinacy

pervĭcax, ācis *adj, adv*, ĭter, stubborn, wilful

pervĭdĕo, vīdi, vīsum *v.t.* 2, to view, survey

pervĭgĭl, is *adj*, ever-watchful

pervĭgĭlātĭo, ōnis *f*, vigil

pervĭgĭlo *v.i.* 1, to remain awake all night

pervinco, vīci, victum *v.t.* 3, to gain victory over

pervĭus, a, um *adj*, able to be crossed or passed

pervŏlĭto *v.i.* 1, to flit about

pervŏlo *v.i.* 1, to fly about or through or to

pervŏlo, velle, vŏlŭi *v.i, irreg*, to wish greatly

pervulgo *v.t.* 1, to spread about

pēs, pĕdis *m*, foot; rope attached to a sail, sheet

pessĭmē *adv*, very badly

pessĭmus, a, um *adj*, very bad

pessŭlus, i *m*, latch

pessum *adv*, to the ground; **pessum ire**, to go to ruin

pestĭfer, era, ĕrum *adj*, destructive, harmful

pestĭlens, ntis *adj*, unhealthy

persĭlentĭa, ae *f*, infectious disease

pestis, is *f*, disease, ruin

pĕtăsātus, a, um *adj*, dressed for a journey

pĕtăsus, i *m*, travelling-hat

pĕtītīo, ōnis *f*, blow, candidature for office

pĕtītor, ōris *m*, candidate, plaintiff

pĕto, īvi, ītum *v.t.* 3, to make for, seek, aim at, request

pĕtōrĭtum, i *n*, four-wheeled carriage

petŭlans, ntis *adj*, impudent

pĕtŭlantĭa, ae *f*, impudence

pexus, a, um *adj*, new

phălanx, ngis *f*, military formation

phălĕrae, ārum *f.pl*, military decoration

phărĕtra, ae *f*, quiver

phărĕtrātus, a, um *adj*, wearing a quiver

pharmăcŏpōla, ae *m*, quack

phărus, i *f*, lighthouse

phăsēlus, i *m*, *f*, kidney bean, light boat, yacht

phengītes, ae *m*, selenite, mica

phĭlŏlŏgĭa, ae *f*, love of learning

phĭlŏlŏgus, *m*, man of learning

phĭlŏmēla, ae *f*, nightingale

phĭlŏsŏphĭa, ae *f*, philosophy

phĭlŏsŏphor *v.i.* 1, *dep*, to study philosophy

phĭlŏsŏphus, i *m*, philosopher

phĭlȳra, ae *f*, bark of the linden tree

phīmus, i *m*, dice-box

phōca, ae *f*, seal, sea-dog

phoenix, īcis *m*, bird which was said to live 500 years

phthĭsis, is *f*, phthisis

phȳlarchus, i *m*, chief, prince

phȳsĭca, ōrum *n.pl*, physics

phȳsĭcus, i *m*, naturalist

phȳsĭŏlŏgĭa, ae *f*, physiology

pĭācŭlāris, e *adj*, expiatory

pĭācŭlum, i *n*, sacrificial offering of atonement, victim, sin, crime

pīca, ae *f*, magpie

pīcĕa, ae *f*, pitch-pine

pīcĕus, a, um *adj*, pitch-black

pictor, ōris *m*, painter

pictūra, ae *f*, painting, picture

pictūrātus, a, um *adj*, embroidered

pictus, a, um *adj*, painted, decorated

pīcus, i *m*, woodpecker

pĭĕtas, ātis *f*, sense of duty, loyalty, mercy

pĭger, gra, grum *adj*, lazy, sluggish

pĭget (me, te) *v.* 2, *impers*, *it* annoys or displeases (me, you)

pigmentum, i *n*, paint, pigment

pignĕro *v.t.* 1, to pledge, pawn

pignĕror *v.t.* 1, *dep*, to take possession of

pignus, ŏris (ĕris) *n*, security, mortgage, pledge, bet

pĭgrĭtĭa, ae *f*, laziness, indolence

pĭgrĭtĭes, ēi *f*, laziness, indolence

pīla, ae *f*, pillar, pier

pīla, ae *f*, ball

pīlātus, a, um *adj*, armed with javelins

pīlentum, i *n*, carriage

pillĕātus, a, um *adj*, wearing a felt cap, *see below*

pillĕus, i *m* (pillĕum, i, *n*), felt cap, worn by Romans at festivals, and by freed slaves

pīlōsus, a, um *adj*, hairy

pĭlŭla, ae *f*, pill

pīlum, i *n*, the heavy javelin of the Roman infantry

pĭlus, i *m*, a hair, the hair

pīlus, i *m*, (*with* prīmus), senior centurion, senior division of trĭārĭi- men who fought in the 3rd rank

pīnētum, i *n*, a wood of pines

pīnĕus, a, um *adj*, of pinewood

pingo, nxi, ctum *v.t.* 3, to paint, decorate

pinguesco *v.i.* 3, to grow fat or fertile

pingue, is *n*, fat

pinguis, e *adj*, rich, fertile, plump, dull, stupid

pinguĭtūdo, ĭnis *f*, plumpness, richness

pīnĭfer, ĕra, ĕrum *adj*, pine-bearing

pīnĭger, ĕra, ĕrum *adj*, pine-bearing

pinna, ae *f*, feather, wing

pinnātus, a, um *adj*, winged

pinnĭger, ĕra, ĕrum *adj*, winged

pīnus, ūs (or i) *f*, pine tree

pĭo *v.t.* 1, to appease, atone for

pīpātus, ūs *m*, chirping

pīper, ĕris *n*, pepper

pīpĭlo *v.i.* 1, to chirp
pīpĭo *v.i.* 4, to chirp
pīrāta, ae *m*, pirate
pīrātĭcus, a, um *adj*, of pirates
pĭrum, i *n*, pear
pĭrus, i *f*, pear tree
piscātor, ōris *m*, fisherman
piscātōrĭus, a, um *adj*, of fishing or
 fishermen
piscātus, ūs *m*, fishing
piscīna, ae *f*, fish pond
piscis, is *m*, a fish
piscor *v.i.* 1, *dep*, to fish
piscōsus, a, um *adj*, full of fish
pistor, ōris *m*, miller, baker
pistrīnum, i *n*, mill
pistris, is (pistrix, īcis) *f*, sea-
 monster
pĭsum, i *n*, pea
pītuīta, ae *f*, phlegm
pĭī, ōrum *m.pl*, the departed
pĭus, a, um *adj, adv*, ē, dutiful,
 loyal, kind, affectionate
pix, pĭcis *f*, pitch
plācābĭlis, e *adj*, easily pacified,
 mild
plācātus, a, um *adj, adv*, ē,
 calmed, still
plăcens, ntis *adj*, pleasing
plăcenta, ae *f*, cake
plăcĕo *v.i.* 2, *with dat*, to please,
 to be welcome
plăcĭdus, a, um *adj, adv*, ē, quiet,
 calm, peaceful
plăcĭtus, a, um *adj*, agreeable
plāco *v.t.* 1, to reconcile, soothe
plāga, ae *f*, wound, blow
plăga, ae *f*, region
plăga, ae *f*, hunting-net
plăgĭārĭus, ii *m*, oppressor
plāgōsus, a, um *adj*, fond of
 flogging
plăgŭla, ae *f*, curtain
planctus, ūs *m*, lamentation
plango, nxi, nctum *v.t.* 3, to beat,
 strike, lament
plangor, ōris *m*, lamentation
plānĭtĭes, ēi *f*, plain
planta, ae *f*, shoot, twig
plantārĭa, ĭum *n.pl*, young trees
plantārĭum, ii *n*, plantation
plānum, i *n*, plain

plānus, a, um *adj, adv*, ē, flat,
 level, clear
plănus, i *m*, imposter, cheat
plătănus, i *f*, plane tree
plătēa, ae *f*, street
plauso, si, sum *v.i.t.* 3, to applaud;
 strike, beat
plausĭbĭlis, e *adj*, acceptable
plaustrum, i *n*, cart, waggon
plausus, ūs *m*, applause
plēbēcŭla, ae *f*, the mob
plēbēĭus, a, um *adj*, vulgar
plēbĭcŏla, ae *c*, demagogue
plebs (plēbes), is *f*, the common
 people
plecto *v.t.* 3, to punish
plectrum, i *n*, quill with which to
 strike a stringed instrument
plēnĭtūdo, ĭnis *f*, fulness
plēnus, a, um *adj, adv*, ē, full,
 laden, complete, plentiful
plērīque, aeque, ăque *adj*, most,
 very many
plērumque *adv*, for the most part
plerētis, ĭdis *f*, pleurisy
plīco *v.t.* 1, to fold up
plinthus, i *m, f*, plinth
plōrātus, ūs *m*, weeping
plōro *v.i.t.* 1, to weep; bewail
plostellum, i *n*, small cart
plŭit *v. impers*, it rains
plūma, ae *f*, feather, down
plumbĕus, a, um *adj*, made of
 lead, heavy
plumbum, i *n*, lead, bullet
plūmeus, a, um *adj*, downy, soft
plūrālis, e *adj*, plural
plūres, es, a *comp. adj*, more
plūrĭmum *adv*, very much
plūrĭmus, a, um *adj*, very much
plūs, plūris *n*, more
plūs *adv*, more
pluscŭlum, i *n*, somewhat more
plŭtĕus, i *m*, shed, parapet, shelf
plŭvĭa, ae *f*, rain
plŭvĭālis, e *adj*, rainy
plŭvĭus, a, um *adj*, rainy
pōcŭlum, i *n*, cup, beaker
pŏdàgra, ae *f*, gout
pŏdĭa, ae *f*, sail-rope
pŏdĭum, ii *n*, height, balcony
pŏēma, ătis *n*, poem

poena, ae *f,* punishment, penalty
poenālis, e *adj,* penal
pŏēsis, is *f,* poetry
pŏēta, ae *m,* poet
pŏētĭcus, a, um *adj,* poetical
poi! *interj,* indeed!
pŏlĭo *v.t.* 4, to polish, improve
pŏlītĭcus, a, um *adj,* political
pŏlītus, a, um *adj, adv, ē,* polished, refined
pollens, ntis *adj,* powerful
pollĕo *v.i.* 2, to be powerful, to prevail
pollex, ĭcis *m,* thumb
pŏllĭcĕor *v.i.t.* 2, *dep,* to promise
pollĭcĭtātĭo, ōnis *f,* promise
pollĭcĭtum, i *n,* promise
pollinctor, ōris *m,* undertaker
pollŭo, ŭi, ūtum *v.t.* 3, to pollute, contaminate
pŏlus, i *m,* pole, north-pole
pŏlўpus, i *m,* polypus
pōmārĭum, ii *n,* orchard
pōmārĭus, ii *m,* fruiterer
pōmĕrīdĭnus, a, um *adj,* in the afternoon
pōmĭfer, ĕra, ĕrum *adj,* fruit-bearing
pōmoerĭum, ii *n,* open space inside and outside city walls
pompa, ae *f,* procession, retinue, pomp
pōmum, i *n,* fruit
pōmus, i *f,* fruit tree
pondĕro *v.t.* 1, to consider
pondĕrōsus, a, um *adj,* ponderous
pondo *adv,* by weight
pondus, ĕris *n,* weight, mass, influence, authority
pōne *adv. and prep. with acc,* behind, after
pōno, pŏsŭi, pŏsĭtum *v.t.* 3, to put, place, set, plant, wager, invest, spend, lay aside, appoint, calm, allege, propose
pons, ntis *m,* bridge
pontĭcŭlus, i *m,* drawbridge
pontĭfex, ĭcis *m,* high-priest
pontĭfĭcĭus, a, um *adj,* of a high-priest
pontus, i *m,* the sea
pŏpa, ae *m,* priest's assistant
pŏpīna, ae *f,* restaurant

poplĕs, ĭtis *m,* knee
pŏpŭlāris, e *adj, adv, ĭter,* of the people, popular, democratic
pŏpŭlāris *c,* fellow-countryman
pŏpŭlāres, ĭum *m.pl,* the people's party
pŏpŭlātĭo, ōnis *f,* devastation
pŏpŭlātor, ōris *m,* plunderer
pōpŭlĕus, a, um *adj,* of poplars
pŏpŭlo *v.t.* 1, to plunder, devastate
pŏpŭlor *v.t.* 1, *dep,* to plunder, devastate
pŏpŭlus, i *m,* the people
pōpŭlus, i *f,* poplar tree
porcīna, ae *f,* pork
porcŭlus, i *m,* young pig; (*with* mărīnus) porpoise
porcus, i *m,* pig
porrectĭo, ōnis *f,* extension
porrectus, a, um *adj,* extended
porrĭcĭo, ēci, ctum *v.t.* 3, to offer to the gods
porrĭgo, rexi, rectum *v.t.* 3, to stretch out, offer
porrīgo, ĭnis *f,* dandruff
porro *adv,* forwards, next, moreover
porrum, i *n,* leek
porta, ae *f,* gate, door
portendo, di, tum *v.t.* 3, to foretell
portentum, i *n,* omen, monster
portĭcus, ūs *f,* colonnade
portĭo *in phrase,* **pro portĭōne** in proportion
portĭtor, ōris *m,* customs officer
portĭtor, ōris *m,* boatman
porto *v.t.* 1, to carry, bring
portōrĭum, ii *n,* customs duty
portŭōsus, a, um *adj,* with many harbours
portus, ūs *m,* harbour, refuge
posco, pŏposci *v.t.* 3, to demand
pŏsĭtĭo, ōnis *f,* placing, situation
pŏsĭtus, a, um *adj,* situated
pŏsĭtus, ūs *m,* arrangement, disposition
possessĭo, ōnis *f,* seizure, occupation
possessor, ōris *m,* possessor
possĭdĕo, sēdi, sessum *v.t.* 2, to be master of, possess
possīdo, sēdi, sessum *v.t.* 3, to take possession of, occupy

possum, posse, pŏtŭi *v.i. irreg*, to be able, to have power

postŭmus, a, um *adj*, last-born, posthumous

Insight

possum is a combination of the stem **pot-** meaning 'power' (e.g. *potestas, potentia, potens*) and the verb *sum* (I am). So possum means 'I am able to', 'I can'. Hence the English words 'possibility', 'possible', 'impossible', etc.

post *adv, and prep. with acc*, behind, backwards, after

pōtātĭo, ōnis *f*, drinking
pōtātor, ōris *m*, drinker

Insight

Post is a preposition, followed by a noun or a pronoun in the accusative case (post meridiem = after midday); **postea** is an adverb (= afterwards); **postquam** is a conjunction (= after...). Likewise, **ante** is a preposition that takes the accusative (before), **antea** is an adverb and **antequam** is a conjunction.

postĕā *adv*, afterwards
postĕāquam *conj*, after
postĕri, ōrum *m.pl*, posterity
postĕrĭor, ĭus *comp. adj*, next, worse
postĕrĭtas, ātis *f*, posterity
postĕrĭus *adv*, later
postĕrus, a, um *adj*, next
postgĕnĭti, ōrum *m.pl*, posterity
posthăbĕo *v.t.* 2, to postpone, neglect
posthāc *adv*, in future
postīcum, i *n*, back door
postis, is *m*, door-post
postmŏdo *adv*, afterwards
postpōno, pŏsŭi, pŏsĭtum *v.t.* 3, to postpone, neglect
postquam *conj*, after, when
postrēmo *adv*, at last
postrēmus, a, um *adj*, the last
postrīdĭē *adv*, on the next day
postŭlāta, ōrum *n.pl*, demand, request
postŭlātĭo, ōnis *f*, demands, requests
postŭlo *v.t.* 1, to demand, prosecute, accuse

pŏtens, ntis *adj*, powerful, master of (*with genit*)
pŏtentātus, ūs *m*, power, rule
pŏtentĭa, ae *f*, power, authority
pŏtestas, ātis *f*, power, dominion, control, value, force, ability, permission, opportunity
pōtĭo, ōnis *f*, a drink
pŏtĭor *v.* 4, *dep, with abl*, to obtain, hold, possess
pŏtĭor, ĭus *comp. adj*, preferable
pŏtis, e *adj*, possible
pŏtĭus *adv*, preferably
pōto *v.i.t.* 1, to drink
pōtor, ōris *m*, drinker
pōtus, a, um *adj*, intoxicated, drained
pōtus, ūs *m*, a drink
prae *adv, and prep. with abl*, before, in comparison with
prae se ferre (gĕrere) to reveal
praeăcŭo, ŭi, ūtum *v.t.* 3, to sharpen
praeăcūtus, a, um *adj*, pointed
praebĕo *v.t.* 2, to offer, give, show
praevăvĕo, cāvi, cautum *v.i.t.* 2, to be on one's guard; prevent

praecēdo, cessi, cessum *v.i.t.* 3, to lead the way; precede

praecellens, ntis *adj,* excellent

praecelsus, a, um *adj,* very high

praeceps, cĭpĭtis *adj,* headlong

praeceps, cĭpĭtis *n,* precipice, danger

praeceptor, ōris *m,* teacher

praeceptum, i *n,* rule, maxim, order, command

praecerpo, psi, ptum *v.t.* 3, to gather before time

praecīdo, cīdi, cīsum *v.t.* 3, to cut off, cut short

praecingo, nxi, nctum *v.t.* 3, to encircle, gird

praecĭno, nŭi, centum *v.i.t.* 3, to sing before; predict

praecĭpĭo, cēpi, ceptum *v.t.* 3, to receive in advance, anticipate, advise, teach

praecĭpĭto *v.i.t* 1, to rush down; throw headlong

praecĭpŭus, a, um *adj, adv,* **ē,** particular, especial, excellent

praeclārus, a, um *adj, adv,* **ē,** splendid, excellent

praeclūdo, si, sum *v.t.* 3, to close

praeco, ōnis *m,* herald

praecōnĭum, ii *n,* office of herald, proclamation

praecōnĭus, a, um *adj,* of a herald

praecordĭa, ōrum *n.pl,* midriff, heart

praecox, ŏcis *adj,* premature

praecurro, cŭcurri, cursum *v.i.t.* 3, to run in front; excel

praecursor, ōris *m,* scout, spy

praecŭtĭo, cussi, cussum *v.t.* 3, to brandish in front

praeda, ae *f,* plunder, prey

praedātor, ōris *m,* plunderer

praedātōrĭus, a, um *adj,* predatory

praedĭātor, ōris *m,* estate agent

praedĭcātĭo, ōnis *f,* proclamation, commendation

praedĭco *v.t.* 1, to proclaim, declare, praise

praedīco, xi, ctum *v.t.* 3, to predict, advise, command

praedictĭo, ōnis *f,* prediction

praedictum, i *n,* prediction

praedisco *v.t.* 3, to learn beforehand

praedĭtus, a, um *adj,* provided with

praedĭum, ii *n,* farm, estate

praedīvĕs, ĭtis *adj,* very rich

praedo, ōnis *m,* robber

praedor *v.i.t.* 1, *dep,* to plunder

praedūco, xi, ctum *v.t.* 3, to make or put in front

praedulcis, e *adj,* very sweet

praedūrus, a, um *adj,* very hard

praeĕo, ĭi, ĭtum *v.i.t.* 4, to lead the way; recite, dictate

praefātĭo, ōnis *f,* preface

praefectūra, ae *f,* superintendence

praefectus, i *m,* director, commander, governor

praefĕro, ferre, tŭli, lātum *v.t, irreg,* to carry in front, offer, prefer, show

praefĭcĭo, fēci, fectum *v.t.* 3, to put in command

praefĭdens, ntis *adj,* overconfident

praefīgo, xi, xum *v.t.* 3, to fix in front

praefinĭo *v.t.* 3, to fix, appoint

praeflŭo *v.i.* 3, to flow past

praefŏdĭo, fōdi *v.t.* 3, to dig in front

praefor, fātus *v.i.t.* 1, *dep,* to say in advance

praefringo, frēgi, fractum *v.t.* 3, to break off

praefulgĕo, si *v.i.* 2, to glitter

praegestĭo *v.i.* 4, to desire greatly

praegnans, ntis *adj,* pregnant

praegrăvis, e *adj,* very heavy

praegrĕdĭor, gressus *v.i.t.* 3, *dep,* to go in advance

praeiūdĭcātus, a, um *adj,* preconceived

praeiūdĭcĭum, ii *n,* precedent (at law)

praeiūdĭco *v.t.* 1, to pre-judge

praelābor, lapsus *v.i.t.* 3, *dep,* to glide or flow along or past

praelambo *v.t.* 3, to taste in advance

praelūcĕo, xi *v.i.* 2, to carry a light in front

praemandāta, ōrum *n.pl,* warrant of arrest

praemĕdĭtātĭo, ōnis *f,* premeditation

praemĕdĭtor *v.t.* 1, *dep*, to premeditate

praemitto, mīsi, missum *v.t.* 3, to send in advance

praemĭum, ii *n*, booty, reward

praemŏnĕo *v.t.* 2, to forewarn

praemūnĭo *v.t.* 4, to fortify

praenăto *v.i.* 1, to flow past

praenĭtĕo *v.i.* 2, to outshine

praenōmen, ĭnis *n*, first (Christian) name

praenosco *v.t.* 3, to learn in advance

praenuntĭo *v.t.* 1, to predict

praenuntĭus, a, um *adj*, foreboding

praenuntĭus, i *m*, foreteller

praeoccŭpo *v.t.* 1, to seize in advance

praeopto *v.t.* 1, to prefer

praepărātĭo, ōnis *f*, preparation

praepăro *v.t.* 1, to prepare

praepĕdĭo *v.t.* 4, to bind, obstruct

praependĕo *v.i.* 2, to hang down in front

praepes, ĕtis *adj*, swift

praepes, ĕtis *c*, bird

praepinguis, e *adj*, very fat

praepōno, pŏsŭi, pŏsĭtum *v.t.* 3, to put first, put in command, prefer

praepŏsĭtĭo, ōnis *f*, preference

praepŏsĭtus, i *m*, chief, head

praepostĕrus, a, um *adj*, preposterous

praepŏtens, ntis *adj*, very powerful

praeprŏpĕrus, a, um *adj*, sudden, precipitate

praerĭpĭo, rĭpŭi, reptum *v.t.* 3, to snatch away

praerōdo, rōsum *v.t.* 3, to nibble

praerŏgātīva, ae *f*, the Roman tribe to which the first vote was allotted

praerumpo, rūpi, ruptum *v.t.* 3, to break off

praeruptus, a, um *adj*, steep

praes, dis *m*, security, bail

praesaepe, is *n*, stable, pen

praesaepĭo, psi, ptum *v.t.* 4, to barricade

praesāgĭo *v.t.* 4, to have a presentiment or premonition

praesāgĭum, ii *n*, a foreboding

praesāgus, a, um *adj*, foretelling

praescisco *v.t.* 3, to learn in advance

praescĭus, a, um *adj*, knowing in advance

praescrībo, psi, ptum *v.t.* 3, to order, appoint, prescribe

praescriptĭo, ōnis *f*, excuse, order, law

praescriptum, i *n*, order, law

praesens, ntis *adj*, present, prompt, powerful, resolute, helping

praesensĭo, ōnis *f*, foreboding

praesentĭa, ae *f*, presence

praesentĭa, ĭum *n.pl*, present circumstances

praesentĭo, si, sum *v.t.* 4, to have a premonition

praesēpe see **praesaepe**

praesertim *adv*, especially

pareses, ĭdis *adj*, guarding

praeses, ĭdis *c*, guardian, chief

praesĭdĕo, sēdi *v.i.t.* 2, to guard, direct, superintend

praesĭdĭum, ii *n*, garrison, fortification, camp

praesignis, e *adj*, excellent, distinguished

praestābĭlis, e *adj*, excellent, distinguished

praestans, ntis *adj*, excellent, distinguished

praestantĭa, ae *f*, excellence

praestat *v.* 1, *impers*, it is preferable

praestīgĭae, ārum *f.pl*, juggling tricks

praestĭtŭo, ŭi, ūtum *v.t.* 3, to appoint in advance

praesto *adv*, ready, present

praesto, stĭti, stĭtum *v.i.t.* 1, to be superior; surpass, vouch for, perform, fulfil, show, give, offer

praestringo, nxi, ctum *v.t.* 3, to tie up, graze, blunt

praestrŭo, xi, ctum *v.t.* 3, to build or block up

praesum praeesse, praefŭi *v.i, irreg, with dat*, to be in command of

praesūmo, mpsi, mptum *v.t.* 3, to anticipate, imagine in advance

praetento, di, tum *v.t.* 3, to hold out, pretend

praetento *v.t.* 1, to examine in advance

praeter *adv, and prep. with acc,* past, beyond, beside, except, unless

praetĕrĕā *adv,* besides, henceforth

praetĕrĕo, ĭi, ĭtum *v.i.t.* 4, to pass by; go past, omit, neglect

praeterflŭŏ, xi, ctum *v.i.* 3, to flow past

praetergrĕdĭor, gressus *v.i.t.* 3, *dep,* to pass beyond

praetĕrĭtus, a, um *adj,* past, gone

praeterlābor, lapsus *v.i.t.* 3, *dep,* to glide or flow past

praetermissĭo, ōnis *f,* omission

praetermitto, mīsi, missum *v.t.* 3, to let pass, omit, neglect

praeterquam *adv,* besides, except

praetervĕhor, vectus *v.i.t.* 3, *dep,* to sail, ride or drive past

praetervŏlo *v.i.t.* 1, to escape; fly past

praetexo, xŭi, xtum *v.t.* 3, to edge, border, pretend

praetexta, ae *f,* purple-edged toga worn by Roman magistrates and children

praetexta, ae *f,* a tragedy

praetextātus, a, um *adj,* wearing the toga praetexta

praetextus, a, um *adj,* wearing the toga praetexta

praetor, ōris *m,* chief, head, Roman magistrate concerned with administration of justice

praetōrĭum, ii *n,* general's tent, governor's residence

praetōrĭus, a, um *adj,* of the praetor or general

praetūra, ae *f,* praetorship

praeūro, ussi, ustum *v.t.* 3, to burn at the end

praeustus, a, um *adj,* burnt, frostbitten

praevălĕo *v.i.* 2, to be superior

praevălĭdus, a, um *adj,* very strong

praevĕhor, ctus *v.i.t.* 3, *dep,* to ride, fly or flow in front

praevĕnĭo, vēni, ventum *v.i.t.* 4, to come before; outstrip

praeverto, ti *v.t.* 3, to outstrip, anticipate, prevent

praevertor, sus *v.i.t.* 3, *dep,* to concentrate one's attention (on)

praevĭdĕo, vīdi, vīsum *v.t.* 2, to anticipate, see in advance

praevĭus, a, um *adj,* leading the way

prandĕo, di, sum *v.i.t.* 2, to breakfast, lunch (on)

prandĭum, ii *n,* breakfast, luncheon

pransus, a, um *adj,* having breakfasted

prātensis, e *adj,* growing in meadows

prātŭlum, i *n,* small meadow

prātum, i *n,* meadow

prāvĭtas, ātis *f,* deformity, depravity

prāvus, a, um *adj, adv,* **ē,** wrong, bad, deformed

prĕcārĭus, a, um *adj, adv,* **ō,** obtained by prayer

prĕcātĭo, ōnis *f,* prayer

prĕcĭae, ārum *f.pl,* grapevine

prĕcor *v.i.t.* 1, *dep,* to pray, beg

prĕhendo, di, sum *v.t.* 3, to seize, detain, take by surprise

prĕhenso *v.t.* 1, to grasp, detain

prēlum, i *n,* wine-press

prĕmo, ssi, ssum *v.t.* 3, to press, grasp, cover, close, pursue closely, load, overwhelm, plant, prune, check, repress

prendo see **prĕhendo**

prensus, a, um *adj,* grasped

presso *v.t.* 1, to press

pressus, ūs *m,* pressure

pressus, a, um *adj,* subdued, compact

prĕtĭōsus, a, um *adj, adv,* **ē,** valuable, costly

prĕtĭum, ii *n,* price, value, money, wages, reward

prex, prĕcis *f,* prayer, request

prīdem *adv,* long ago

prīdĭē *adv,* on the day before

prīmaevus, a, um *adj,* youthful

prīmārĭus, a, um *adj,* of the first rank, chief

prīmĭgĕnus, a, um *adj,* primitive

prīmĭpīlus see **pilus**

prīmĭtĭae, ārum *f.pl,* first fruits

prīmō *adv*, at first
prīmordĭa, ōrum *n.pl*, origin
prīmōris, e *adj*, first, front end
prīmōres, um *m.pl*, nobles
prīmum *adv*, at first; **cum prīmum** as soon as; **quam prīmum** as soon as possible
prīmus, a, um *adj*, first, chief
princeps, cĭpis *adj*, first, chief
princeps, cĭpis *m*, chief, originator
princĭpālis, e *adj*, original, primitive, principal
princĭpālis, is *m*, overseer
princĭpātus, ūs *m*, the first place, command, rule
princĭpĭo *adv*, in the beginning
princĭpĭum, ii *n*, origin; *in pl*, principles, elements
prĭor, ĭus *comp. adj*, previous, former
prĭōres, um *m.pl*, ancestors
priscus, a, um *adj*, ancient
prisma, ătis *n*, prism
pristĭnus, a, um *adj*, primitive
prĭus *comp. adv*, previously
prĭusquam *conj*, before
prīvātim *adv*, privately
prīvātĭo, ōnis *f*, taking-away
prīvātus, a, um *adj*, private
prīvātus, i *m*, private citizen
prīvigna, ae *f*, step-daughter
prīvignus, i *m*, step-son
prīvĭlēgĭum, ii *n*, bill or law concerned with an individual
prīvo *v.t*. 1, to deprive, release
prīvus, a, um *adj*, one's own
prō *prep. with abl*, before, in front of, on behalf of, instead of, just as, on account of, according to, in relation to
prō! (prōh!) *interj*, Ah! Alas!
prŏăvus, i *m*, great-grandfather
prŏbābĭlis, e *adj, adv*, **ĭter**, likely, pleasing
prŏbābĭlĭtas, ātis *f*, probability
prŏbātĭo, ōnis *f*, trial, proving
prŏbātus, a, um *adj*, tried, good
prŏbĭtae, ātis *f*, honesty
prŏbo *v.t*. 1, to try, test, approve of, recommend, prove
prŏboscis, ĭdis *f*, elephant's trunk
prŏbrōsus, a, um *adj*, shameful

prŏbrum, i *n*, disgraceful deed, lechery, disgrace, abuse
prŏbus, a, um *adj, adv*, **ē**, good, honest, virtuous
prŏcācĭtas, ātis *f*, impudence
prŏcax, ācis *adj*, impudent
prŏcēdo, cessi, cessum *v.i*. 3, to go forward, advance, turn out, prosper
prŏcella, ae *f*, storm, violence
prŏcellōsus, a, um *adj*, tempestuous
prŏcer, ĕris *m*, chief, prince
prŏcērĭtas, ātis *f*, height
prŏcērus, a, um *adj*, tall
prŏcessus, ūs *m*, advance
prŏcĭdo, di *v.i*. 3, to fall flat
prŏcinctus, ūs *m*, readiness for battle
prŏclāmo *v.t*. 1, to cry out
prŏclīno *v.t*. 1, to bend forwards
prŏclīve, is *n*, slope, descent
prŏclīvis, e *adj*, sloping downhill, liable, willing
prōconsul, is *m*, provincial govenor
prŏcrastĭno *v.t*. 1, to defer
prŏcrĕātĭo, ōnis *f*, procreation
prŏcrĕātor, ōris *m*, creator
prŏcrĕo *v.t*. 1, to produce
prŏcŭbo *v.i*. 1, to lie stretched-out
prŏcūdo, di, sum *v.t*. 3, to forge
prŏcul *adv*, in the distance
prŏculo *v.t*. 1, to trample on
prŏcumbo, cŭbŭi, cŭbĭtum *v.i*. 3, to lean or fall forwards, sink
prŏcūrātĭo, ōnis *f*, administration
prŏcūrātor, ōris *m*, manager, agent
prŏcūro *v.t*. 1, to look after
prŏcurro, curri, cursum *v.i*. 3, to run forward, project
prŏcus, i *m*, suitor
prōdĕo, ĭi, ĭtum *v.i*. 3, to come forward, appear
prōdesse see **prōsum**
prōdĭgĭōsus, a, um *adj*, strange, marvellous
prōdĭgĭum, ii *n*, omen, monster
prōdĭgus, a, um *adj*, wasteful
prōdĭtĭo, ōnis *f*, treachery
prōdĭtor, ōris *m*, traitor
prōdo, dĭdi, dĭtum *v.t*. 3, to bring out, relate, betray, bequeath

prōdūco, xi, ctum *v.t.* 3, to lead forward, prolong, produce, promote

prōductus, a, um *adj, adv,* ē, prolonged

proelīor *v.i.* 1, *dep,* to join battle

proelīum, ii *n,* battle

prŏfāno *v.t.* 1, to desecrate

prŏfānus, a, um *adj,* wicked, common

prŏfectĭo, ōnis *f,* departure

prŏfectō *adv,* certainly

prŏfectus, ūs *m,* advance

prŏfectus, a, um *adj,* having advanced

prŏfěro, ferre, tŭli, lātum *v.t, irreg,* to bring out, extend, defer, reveal, mention; *with* gradum, to proceed; *with* signa, to march forward

prŏfessor ōris *m,* teacher, professor

prŏfessĭo, ōnis *f,* declaration

prŏfessus, a, um *adj,* avowed

prŏfestus, a, um *adj,* working (days)

prŏfĭcĭo, fēci, fectum *v.i.t.* 3, to progress; perform, help

prŏfĭciscor, prŏfectus *v.i.* 3, *dep,* to set out, originate

prŏfĭtěor, fessus *v.i.* 2, *dep,* to declare, acknowledge, promise

prŏflīgātus, a, um *adj,* wretched, dissolute

prŏflīgo *v.t.* 1, to overthrow

prōflo *v.t.* 1, to blow out

prŏflŭo, xi, xum *v.i.* 3, to flow out, proceed

prŏflŭens, ntis *adj,* fluent

prŏflŭvĭum, ii *n,* flowing out

prŏfor *v.t.* 1, *dep,* to speak, say

prŏfŭgĭo, fūgi *v.i.t.* 3, to escape; flee from

prŏfŭgus, a, um *adj,* fugitive

prŏfŭgus, i *m,* fugitive, exile

prŏfundo, fūdi, fūsum *v.t.* 3, to pour out, utter, squander

prŏfundum, i *n,* the deep, the sea, an abyss

prŏfundus, a, um *adj,* deep

prŏfūsĭo, ōnis *f,* outpouring, prodigal use

prŏfūsus, a, um *adj,* extravagant

prōgěněro *v.t.* 1, to beget

prōgěnĭes, ēi *f,* family, offspring

prōgigno, gěnŭi, gěnĭtum *v.t.* 3, to produce

prōgnātus, a, um *adj,* born

prōgnātus, i *m,* descendant

prōgrědĭor, gressus *v.i.* 3, *dep,* to advance, proceed

prōgressĭo, ōnis *f,* growth

prōgressus, ūs *m,* advance

proh! see prō!

prŏhĭběo *v.t.* 2, to prevent, prohibit, defend

prōĭectus, a, um *adj,* projecting

prōĭcĭo, iēci, iectum *v.t.* 3, to throw forward, extend, expel, yield, disdain

prōin or prŏindē *adv,* in the same way, equally, accordingly, therefore

prōlābor, lapsus *v.i.* 3, *dep,* to slip or slide forward, fall

prōlātĭo, ōnis *f,* postponement, mentioning

prōlāto *v.t.* 1, to postpone

prōles, is *f,* offspring, child

prōlētārĭus, ii *m,* citizen of lowest class

prōlixus, a, um *adj, adv,* ē, stretched out, fortunate

prōlŏgus, i *m,* prologue

prōlūdo, si, sum *v.i.* 3, to practise in advance

prōlŭo, lŭi, lūtum *v.t.* 3, to wash away, moisten

prōlūsĭo, ōnis *f,* prelude

prōlŭvĭes, ēi *f,* overflow

prōměrěo *v.t.* 2, to deserve, merit

prōměrěor *v.t.* 2, *dep,* to deserve, merit

prōmĭnens, ntis *adj,* prominent

prōmĭněo *v.i.* 2, to project

prōmiscŭus, a, um *adj,* common, indiscriminate

prōmissĭo, ōnis *f,* promise

prōmissum, i *n,* promise

prōmissus, a, um *adj,* hanging

prōmitto, mīsi, missum *v.t.* 3, to promise, assure

prōmo, mpsi, mptum *v.t.* 3, to bring out, produce, tell

prōmontŭrĭum, ii *n,* headland

prōmŏvěo, mōvi, mōtum *v.t.* 2, to move forward, extend

promptus, a, um *adj*, ready, quick
promptus, ūs *m*, only in phrase; **in promptu**, in public; **in promptu esse,** to be at hand
prōmulgo *v.t.* 1, to publish
prōmus, i *m*, butler
prōmūtŭus, a, um *adj*, loaned
prŏnĕpos, ōtis *m*, great-grandson
prōnōmen, ĭnis *n*, pronoun
prōnŭba, ae *f*, bridesmaid
prōnuntĭātĭo, ōnis *f*, proclamation
prōnuntĭo *v.t.* 1, to announce
prōnus, a, um *adj*, leaning or bending forward, disposed; setting, sinking (of stars, etc.)
prŏoemĭum, ii *n*, preface
prŏpāgātĭo, ōnis *f*, extension
prŏpāgo *v.t.* 1, to generate, extend
prŏpāto, ĭnis *f*, shoot (of plant), offspring, child
prōpălam *adv*, openly
prōpătŭlus, a, um *adj*, uncovered
prŏpe *adv, and prep. with acc*, near, nearly
prŏpĕdĭem *adv*, soon
prōpello, pŭli, pulsum *v.t.* 3, to push or drive forward
prŏpĕmŏdum *adv*, almost
prōpendĕo, di, sum *v.i.* 2, to be inclined or disposed
prōpensus, a, um *adj*, inclined, disposed
prŏpĕro *v.i.t.* 1, to hurry
prŏpĕrus, a, um *adj, adv,* ē, quick, hurrying
prŏpexus, a, um *adj*, combed forward
prŏpīno *v.t.* 1, to drink a toast
prŏpinquĭtas, ātis *f*, nearness, relationship
prŏpinquo *v.i.t.* 1, to approach; hasten
prŏpinquus, a, um *adj*, near
prŏpinquus, i *m*, relative
prŏpĭor, ĭus *comp. adj*, nearer
prŏpĭtĭus, a, um *adj*, kind, favourable
prŏpĭus *comp. adv*, nearer
prōpōno, pŏsŭi, pŏsĭtum *v.t.* 3, to but forward, state, display, offer
prōpŏsĭtĭo, ōnis *f*, representation, theme
prōpŏsĭtum, i *n*, plan, purpose

prŏprĭĕtas, ātis *f*, peculiarity
prŏprĭus, a, um *adj, adv,* ē, special, particular, its (his, her) own
propter *prep. with acc*, on account of, near; *adv*, nearby
proptĕrĕā *adv*, for that reason
prōpugnācŭlum, i *n*, rampart
prōpugnātĭo, ōnis *f*, defence
prōpugnātor, ōris *m*, defender
prōpugno *v.i.t.* 1, to make sorties; defend
prōpulso *v.t.* 1, to ward off
prōra, ae *f*, prow, ship
prōrēpo, psi, ptum *v.i.* 3, to creep out, crawl forward
prōrĭpĭo, pŭi, reptum *v.t.* 3, to drag forward; *with* se, to rush
prōrŏgātĭo, ōnis *f*, prolonging
prōrŏgo *v.t.* 1, to prolong, defer
prorsus (prorsum) *adv*, certainly, utterly
prōrumpo, rūpi, ruptum *v.i.t.* 3, to rush forward; send forward
prōrŭo, rŭi, rŭtum *v.i.t.* 3, to rush forward; overthrow
proscaenĭum ii *n*, stage
prōscindo, scĭdi, scissum *v.t.* 3, to tear up, plough
prōscrībo, psi, ptum *v.t.* 3, to publish, confiscate, outlaw
prōscriptĭo, ōnis *f*, confiscation, outlawing
prōscriptus, i *m*, outlaw
prōsēmĭno *v.t.* 1, to sow
prōsĕquor, sĕcūtus *v.t.* 3, *dep*, to accompany, follow, pursue, bestow, proceed with
prōsĭlĭo, ŭi *v.i.* 4, to leap up
prospecto *v.t.* 1, to look at, expect, await
prospectus, ūs *m*, view, sight
prospĕrus, a, um *adj, adv,* ē, favourable, fortunate
prospĕrĭtas, ātis *f*, prosperity
prospĕro *v.t.* 1, to make (something) successful
prōspĭcĭo, spexi, spectum *v.i.t* 3, to look out; discern, overlook, forsee
prōsterno, strāvi, strātum *v.t.* 3, to overthrow, prostrate
prōsŭbĭgo *v.t.* 3, to dig up

prōsum, prōdesse, prōfŭi *v.i, irreg, with dat,* to be useful

prōvincĭa, ae *f,* province, duty, sphere of duty

....

Insight

In German beer halls a common way of toasting is to raise one's stein and say, 'Prost!' where in English we might say, 'Cheers!' The word is a contraction of the Latin prosit and a relic of student slang that has passed into general use. Prosit (from prosum *be of benefit, be useful*) is an example of an optative subjunctive with the literal meaning may it benefit (i.e. *may the drinking of this benefit us*).

....

prōtectum, i *n,* eaves

prōtĕgo, xi, ctum *v.t.* 3, to cover, protect

prōtēlum, i *n,* team of oxen

prōtendo, di, sum (tum) *v.t.* 3, to stretch out, extend

prōtĕro, trīvi, trītum *v.t.* 3, to trample down, crush, destroy

prōterrĕo *v.t.* 2, to terrify

prōtervĭtas, ātis *f,* impudence

prōtervus, a, um *adj, adv, ē,* forward, impudent, violent

prōtĭnus *adv,* straightforwards, continuously, immediately

prōtrăho, xi, ctum *v.t.* 3, to drag forward, reveal

prōtrūdo, si, sum *v.t.* 3, to push out

prōturbo *v.t.* 1, to repel

prout *adv,* just as

prōvectus, a, um *adj,* advanced (of time)

prōvĕho, xi, ctum *v.t.* 3, to carry forward, advance, promote

prōvĕnĭo, vēni, ventum *v.i.* 4, to be born, thrive, occur, turn out (well or badly)

prōventus, ūs *m,* produce, result

prōverbĭum, ii *n,* proverb

prōvĭdens, ntis *adj,* prudent

prōvĭdentĭa, ae *f,* foresight

prōvĭdĕo, vīdi, vīsum *v.i.t.* 2, to make preparations; forsee, provide for

prōvĭdus, a, um *adj,* prudent

prōvincĭālis, e *adj,* provincial

prōvŏcātĭo, ōnis *f,* appeal

prōvŏco *v.i.t.* 1, to appeal; call out, challenge, rouse

prōvŏlo *v.i.* 1, to fly out

prōvolvo, volvi, vŏlūtum *v.t.* 3, to roll forward

proxĭmē *adv,* nearest, next

proxĭmĭtas, ātis *f,* proximity

proxĭmus, a, um *adj,* nearest, next, previous

prūdens, ntis *adj, adv,* **nter,** experienced, wise, sensible

prūdentĭa, ae *f,* experience, skill, discretion

prūīna, ae *f,* frost, snow

prūīnōsus, a, um *adj,* frosty

prūna, ae *f,* burning coal

prūnum, i *n,* plum

prūnus, i *f,* plum tree

prūrĭo *v.i.* 4, to itch

prūrītus, ūs *m,* itching

psallo, i *v.i.* 3, to play on an instrument

psalmus, i *m,* a psalm

psittăcus, i *m,* parrot

ptīsăna, ae *f,* pearl barley

pūbens, ntis *adj,* flourishing

pūbertas, ātis *f,* puberty, manhood

pūbes (pūber), ĕris *adj,* adult

pūbes, is *f,* young men

pūbesco, bŭi *v.i.* 3, to grow up, ripen

pūblĭcānus, i *m,* tax collector

pūblĭcātĭo, ōnis *f,* confiscation

pūblĭco *v.t.* 1, to confiscate

pūblĭcum, i *n,* a public place
pūblĭcus, a, um *adj, adv,* **ē,** of the state, public, general
pŭdendus, a, um *adj,* disgraceful
pŭdens, ntis *adj, adv,* **nter,** modest
pŭdet *v.* 2, *impers,* it brings shame
pŭdībundus, a, um *adj,* modest
pŭdīcĭtĭa, ae *f,* modesty, virtue
pŭdīcus, a, um *adj,* modest, pure
pŭdor, ōris *m,* a sense of decency, shyness
pŭella, ae *f,* girl, sweetheart, young wife
pŭellāris, e *adj,* girlish
pŭer, ĕri *m,* boy

pullārĭus, ii *m,* chicken-keeper
pullŭlo *v.i.* 1, to sprout
pullus, i *m,* young animal, chicken
pullus, a, um *adj,* dark, black
pulmentārĭum, ii *n,* sauce
pulmentum, i *n,* sauce
pulmo, ōnis *m,* lung
pulpĭtum, i *n,* platform
puls, pultis *f,* porridge
pulsātĭo, ōnis *f,* beating
pulso *v.t.* 1, to beat, push, touch, disturb
pulsus, ūs *m,* push, blow, beating
pulvĕrĕus, a, um *adj,* dusty

Insight

Second declension masculine nouns usually have the nominative singular ending in *-us* except for some nouns that end in *-er*. These nouns either keep the -e- in the other cases (*puer, pueri* = boy) or drop it (*ager, agri* = field).

pŭĕrīlis, e *adj,* youthful
pŭĕrĭtĭa (pŭertĭa), ae *f,* childhood, youth
pŭgil, īlis *m,* boxer
pŭgillāres, ĭum *m.pl.* writing tablets
pŭgĭo, ōnis *m,* dagger
pugna, ae *f,* fight, battle
pugnātor, ōris *m,* fighter
pugnax, ācis *adj,* warlike, quarrelsome
pugno *v.i.* 1, to fight, disagree, struggle
pugnus, i *m,* fist
pulcher, chra, chrum *adj, adv,* **ē,** beautiful, handsome, glorious

pulvĕrŭlentus, a, um *adj,* dusty
pulvīnar, āris *n,* couch
pulvīnus, i *m,* cushion
pulvis, ĕris *m,* dust
pūmex, ĭcis *m,* pumice stone
pūmĭlĭo, ōnis *m,* dwarf
punctim *adv,* with the point
punctum, i *n,* point, vote, moment
pungo, pŭpŭgi, punctum *v.t.* 3, to prick, sting, vex, annoy
pūnĭcĕus, a, um *adj,* red
pūnĭo *v.t.* (**pūnĭor** *v.t, dep.*) 4, to punish
pūpa, ae *f,* doll
pūpilla, ae *f,* orphan, ward
pūpillus, i *m,* orphan, ward

Insight

Adjectives are words which define the quality of a noun. Adjectives must agree with the nouns they are attached to in gender (feminine/masculine/neuter), case and number (singular/plural) (e.g. *pulchra puella* = beautiful girl).

pulchrĭtūdo, ĭnis *f,* beauty
pūlex, ĭcis *m,* flea

puppis, is *f,* ship's stern
pūpŭla, ae *f,* pupil of the eye

purgāmen, ĭnis *n*, refuse, filth

purgāmentum, i *n*, refuse, filth

purgātĭo, ōnis *f*, cleansing

purgo *v.t.* 1, to clean, purify, excuse, justify, atone for

purpŭra, ae *f*, purple, purple clothes

puprŭrĕus, a, um *adj*, purple, clothed in purple, brilliant

pūrum, i *n*, clear sky

pūrus, a, um *adj, adv*, **ē**, pure, clean, plain

pūs, pūris *n*, pus

pūsillus, a, um *adj*, little, petty

pūsĭo, ōnis *m*, urchin

pustŭla, ae *f*, pimple

pŭtāmen, ĭnis *f*, peel, shell

pŭtĕal, ālis *n*, fence of a well

pūtĕo *v.i.* 2, to stink

pŭter (pŭtris), tris, tre *adj*, decaying, rotten

pūtesco, pūtŭi *v.i.* 3, to rot

pŭtĕus, i *m*, well, pit

pūtĭdus, a, um *adj*, rotten, disgusting

pŭto *v.t.* 1, to think, prune

pŭtresco *v.i.* 3, to decay

pŭtrĭdus, a, um *adj*, rotten

pўra, ae *f*, funeral pyre

pўrămis, ĭdis *f*, pyramid

pўrum, i *n*, pear

pўrus, i *f*, pear tree

pўthon, ōnis *m*, python

pyxis, ĭdis *f*, box

Q

quā *adv*, where, in which direction, how; **qua ... qua**, partly...partly

quācumque *adv*, wheresoever

quàdra, ae *f*, square, dining table

quàdrāgĕni, ae, a *adj*, forty each

quàdrāgēsĭmus, a, um *adj*, fortieth

quàdrāgĭes *adv*, forty times

quàdrāginta *adv*, forty

quàdrans, ntis *m*, a quarter

quàdrātum, i *n*, square

quàdrātus, a, um *adj*, square

quàdrĭdŭum, ii *n*, period of four days

quàdrĭfārĭam *adv*, into four parts

quàdrĭfĭdus, a, um *adj*, split into four

quàdrīgae, ārum *f.pl*, four-horse team or chariot

quàdrĭĭŭgis, e *adj*, yoked in a four-horse team

quàdrĭĭŭgus, a, um *adj*, yoked in a four-horse team

quàdrĭlătĕrus, a, um *adj*, quadrilateral

quàdrīmus, a, um *adj*, four years old

quàdringēnārĭus, a, um *adj*, of four hundred each

quàdringenti, ae, a *adj*, four hundred

quàdringentĭes *adv*, four hundred times

quàdro *v.i.t.* 1, to be square, agree; make square, complete

quàdrum, i *n*, square

quàdrŭpĕdans, ntis *adj*, galloping

quàdrŭpēs, ĕdis *adj*, galloping, going on four feet

quàdrŭplex, ĭcis *adj*, quadruple

quàdrŭplum, i *n*, fourfold amount

quaero, sīvi, sītum *v.t.* 3, to search for, acquire, inquire

quaesītĭo, ōnis *f*, investigation

quaesītor, ōris *m*, investigator

quaesītum, i *n*, question

quaesītus, a, um *adj*, far-fetched

quaeso, īvi *v.t.* 3, to beseech, seek

quaestĭo, ōnis *f*, investigation, trial, case, question, problem

quaestor, ōris *m*, Roman magistrate in charge of public revenues

quaestōrĭus, a, um *adj*, of a quaestor

quaestŭōsus, a, um *adj*, profitable

quaestūra, ae *f*, quaestorship

quaestus, ūs *m*, gain, profit, employment

quālis, e *adj*, of what kind

quāliscumque, quālĕcumque *adj*, of whatever kind

quālĭtas, ātis *f*, state, condition

quālum, i *n*, basket, hamper

quam *adv*, how; *with comparatives*, than

quamdĭu *adv*, as long as, until

quamlĭbet *adv*, as much as you wish

quămobrem *adv*, why, wherefore
quamprīmum *adv*, as soon as
  possible
quamquam *conj*, although
quamvīs *conj*, although; *adv*, very
quando *adv*, when?, some time;
  conj, since, because
quandōcumque *adv*, whenever
quandōque *adv*, whenever, at
  some time or other
quandōquĭdem *adv*, since
quanti? at what price?
quantō *adv*, by as much as
quantŏpĕrē *adv*, how much
quantŭlus, a, um *adj*, how small
quantŭluscumque *adj*, however
  small
quantum *adv*, as much as
quantus, a, um *adj*, how great
quantuscumque *adj*, however big
quantusvis, quantāvis,
  quantumvis *adj*, as big as you
  like
quāpropter *adv*, wherefore
quārē *adv*, wherefore, why
quartānus, a, um *adj*, occurring on
  the fourth day
quartum *adv*, for the fourth time
quartō *adv*, for the fourth time
quartus, a, um *adj*, fourth
quăsĭ *adv*, as if, just as
quăsillum, i *n*, small basket
quassātĭo, ōnis *f*, shaking
quasso *v.t.* 1, to shake, shatter
quātĕnus *adv*, to what extent,
  how long, since
quăter *adv*, four times
quăterni, ae, a *pl. adj*, four each
quătĭo (*no perf.*), **quassum** *v.t.* 3,
  to shake, shatter, excite
quattŭor *indecl. adj*, four
quattŭordĕcim *indecl. adj*, fourteen
quĕ *conj*, add
quĕmadmŏdum *adv*, how
quĕo, ĭi, ĭtum *v.i.* 4, to be able
quercētum, i *n*, oak forest
quercus, ūs *f*, oak tree
quĕrēla, ae *f*, complaint
quĕrĭbundus, a, um *adj*,
  complaining
quĕrĭmōnĭa, ae *f*, complaint
quernus, a, um *adj*, of oak
quĕror, questus *v.i.t.* 3, *dep*, to
  complain

quĕrŭlus, a, um *adj*, full of
  complaints, cooing, chirping
questus, ūs *m*, complaint
qui, quae, quod *rel. pron*, who,
  which, what
quī *adv*, how, wherewith
quĭă *conj*, because
quicquid *pron*, whatever
quĭcumque, quaecumque,
quodcumque *pron*, whoever,
  whatever
quid *interr. pron*, what? why?
quīdam, quaedam, quoddam *pron*,
  a certain somebody or something
quĭdem *adv*, indeed; **ne ... quidem**,
  not even ...
quidni why not?
quĭes, ētis *f*, rest, quiet
quĭescens, ntis *adj*, quiescent
quĭesco, ēvi, ētum *v.i.* 3, to rest,
  keep quiet, sleep
quĭētus, a, um *adj*, calm
quīlībet, quaelībet, quodlībet *pron*,
  anyone or anything you like
quīn *conj*, that not, but that,
  indeed, why not
quīnam, quaenam, quodnam *pron*,
  who, what, which
quincunx, ncis *m*, five-twelfths,
  trees planted in oblique lines
qindĕcĭes *adv*, fifteen times
quindĕcim *indecl. adj*, fifteen
quingēni, ae, a *pl. adj*, five
  hundred each
quingenti, ae, a *pl. adj*, five
  hundred
quingentĭes *adv*, five hundred
  times
quīni, ae, a *pl. adj*, five each
quinquāgēni, ae, a *pl. adj*, fifty
  each
quinquāgēsĭmus, a, um *adj*,
  fiftieth
quinquāginta *indecl. adj*, fifty
quinquātrĭa, ōrum *n.pl*, festival of
  Minerva (19th–23rd March)
quinquĕ *indec. adj*, five
quinquennālis, e *adj*, quinquennial
quinquennis, e *adj*, every fifth year
quiquennĭum, ii *n*, period of five
  years
quīnquĕrēmis *adj*, ship with five
  banks of oars

quinquĭens *adv*, five times
Quintīlis (menis) July
quintus, a, um *adj*, fifth
quippe *adv*, certainly; *conj*, in as
   much as
quis, quid *interr pron*, who?
   which? what? *indef. pron*,
   anyone, anything
quisnam, quaenam,
   quidnam *interr. pron*, who?
   which?
quispĭam, quaepĭam,
   quodpĭam *indef. pron*, anybody,
   anything
quisquam, quaequam,
   quicquam *indef. pron*, anyone,
   anything
quisque, quaeque, quodque *indef.
   pron*, each, every, everybody,
   everything
quisquĭlīae, ārum *f.pl*, rubbish
quisquis, quaeque, quodquod
   indef. pron, whoever,
   whatever
quīvis, quaevis, quodvis *indef.
   pron*, anyone or anything you
   please
quō *adv. and conj*, wherefore,
   where to, whither, so that
quŏad *adv*, as long as, until, as,
   far as
quōcircā *conj*, wherefore
quōcumque *adv*, to whatever
   place
quod *conj*, because
quod *neuter* of qui
quōdammŏdo in a certain manner
quōmĭnus *conj*, that ... not
quōmŏdŏ *adv*, how
quondam *adv*, once, at times
quŏnĭam *adv*, since, because
quōquam *adv*, to any place
quŏque *conj*, also, too
quŏquō *adv*, to whatever place
quorsum (quorsus) *adv*, to what
   place, to what purpose
quŏt *indecl. adj*, how many
quŏtannis *adv*, every year
quŏtĭdĭānus, a, um *adj*, daily
quŏtĭdĭe *adv*, daily
quŏtĭes (quŏtĭens) *adv*, how often
quŏtĭescumquĕ *adv*, however
   often

quotquŏt *adv*, however many
quŏtus, a, um *adj*, how many
quŏusquĕ *adv*, how long
quum see cum

R

răbĭdus, a, um *adj*, raving mad
răbĭes (em, e) *f*, madness, anger
răbĭōsus, a, um *adj*, raging
răbŭla, ae *f*, argumentative lawyer
răcēmĭfer, ĕra, ĕrum *adj*, clustering
răcēmux, i *m*, bunch, cluster
rădīcĭtus *adv*, by the roots
rădĭans, ntis *adj*, shining
rădĭātĭo, ōnis *f*, shining
rădĭo *v.i.* 1, to shine
rădĭus, ii *m*, rod, spoke, radius,
   shuttle, ray
rădix, īcis *f*, root, radish, source
rādo, si, sum *v.t.* 3, to scrape,
   shave
raeda, ae *f*, carriage
raedārĭus, i *m*, coachman
raia, ae *f*, ray (fish)
rāmālĭa, ĭum *n.pl*, brushwood
rāmōsus, a, um *adj*, branching
rāmus, i *m*, branch
rāna, ae *f*, frog
rancĭdus, a, um *adj*, rancid
rānunculus, i *m*, tadpole
răpācĭtas, ātis *f*, rapacity
răpax, ācis *adj*, grasping
răphănus, i *m*, radish
răpĭdus, a, um *adj*, *adv*, ē, swift,
   violent, tearing
răpīna, ae *f*, robbery, plunder
răpĭo, ŭi, raptum *v.t.* 3, to seize,
   snatch, drag away
raptim *adv*, hurriedly
raptĭo, ōnis *f*, abduction
rapto *v.t.* 1, to snatch, drag away,
   plunder
raptor, ōris *m*, robber
raptum, i *n*, plunder
raptus, ūs *m*, robbery, rape
rāpŭlum, i *n*, turnip
rāpum, i *n*, turnip
rāresco *v.i.* 3, to grow thin, open
   out
rārĭtas, ātis *f*, looseness, rarity,
   infrequency

rārus, a, um *adj, adv,* **ē, ō,** loose, loose in texture, thin, scattered, straggling, few, remarkable, rare

rāsĭlis, e *adj,* polished

rastellus, i *m,* hoe, rake

rastrum i *n,* rake, hoe

rătĭo, ōnis *f,* account, calculation, business affairs, relationship, concern for, consideration, conduct, plan, reason, motive, reckoning, order, law, theory, system, way, manner

rătĭōcĭnor *v.i.t.* 1, *dep,* to calculate

rătĭōnālis, e *adj,* rational, theoretical

rătis, is *f,* raft

rătus, a, um *adj,* established; *(partic.)* having thought; **pro rătā,** proportionally

raucus, a, um *adj,* hoarse

rāvus, a, um *adj,* grey, tawny

rē, rēvērā *adv,* really

rēapse *adv* **(re ipsa)** in fact

rĕbellĭo, ōnis *f,* revolt

rĕbellis, e *adj,* rebellious

rĕbello *v.i.* 1, to rebel, rebuff

rĕbŏo *v.i.* 1, to re-echo

rĕcalcĭtro *v.i.* 1, to kick back

rĕcalfăcĭo, fēci *v.t.* 3, to warm

rĕcandesco, dŭi *v.i.* 3, to grow white or hot

rĕcanto *(no perf.)* *v.t.* 1, to retract

rĕcēdo, cessi, cessum *v.i.* 3, to retreat, withdraw

rĕcens, ntis *adj,* fresh, new

rĕcens *adv,* newly, recently

rĕcensĕo, ŭi, ītum *v.t.* 2, to count, rekon, survey, review

rĕcensĭo, ōnis *f,* review

rĕceptācŭlum, i *n,* shelter

rĕcepto *v.t.* 1, to recover

rĕceptor, ōris *m,* receiver

rĕceptus, ūs *m,* retreat

rĕcessus, ūs *m,* retreat, recess

rĕcĭdīvus, a, um *adj,* recurring

rĕcĭdo, cĭdi, cāsum *v.i.* 3, to fall back, recoil, return

rĕcīdo, cīdi, cīsum *v.t.* 3, to cut down, cut off, cut short

rĕcingo *(no perf.)* **cinctum** *v.t.* 3, to loosen

rĕcĭno *v.i.* 3, to re-echo

rĕcĭpĕro (rĕcŭpĕro) *v.t.* 1, to regain

rĕcĭpĭo, cēpi, ceptum *v.t.* 3, to take back, regain, receive, give an assurance; *with* **sē** to retreat, recover oneself

rĕcĭprŏco *v.i.t.* 1, to move backwards

rĕcĭprŏcus, a, um *adj,* receding

recĭtātĭo, ōnis *f,* reading aloud

rĕcĭtātor, ōris *m,* reader

rĕcĭto *v.t.* 1, to read aloud

rèclāmătĭo, ōnis *f,* remonstrance

rèclāmo *v.i.t.* 1, to resound; contradict loudly, remonstrate

rèclīno *v.t.* 1, to lean back

rèclūdo, si, sum *v.t.* 3, to reveal

rĕcognĭgĭo, ōnis *f,* review

rĕcognosco, gnōvi, gnītum *v.t.* 3, to recollect, investigate

rĕcŏlo, cŏlŭi, cultum *v.t.* 3, to cultivate again, renew

rĕconcĭlĭātĭo, ōnis *f,* re-establishment, reconciliation

rĕconcĭlĭo *v.t.* 1, to restore, reconcile

rĕcondĭtus, a, um *adj,* hidden

rĕcondo, dĭdi, dĭtum *v.t.* 3, to put away, hide

rĕcŏquo, xi, ctum *v.t.* 3, to cook again, forge again

rĕcordātĭo, ōnis *f,* recollection

rĕcordor *v.i.t.* 1, *dep,* to think over, remember

rĕcrĕātĭo, ōnis *f,* recovery

rĕcrĕo *v.t.* 1, to revive, reproduce

rĕcresco, crēvi, crētum *v.i.* 3, to grow again

rectā *adv,* straightforwards

rector, ōris *m,* master, leader, helmsman

rectum, i *n,* virtue

rectus, a, um *adj, adv,* **ē,** straight, upright, correct

rĕcŭbans, ntis *adj,* recumbent

rĕcŭbo *v.i.* 1, to lie back

rĕcumbo, cŭbŭi *v.i.* 3, to lie down

rĕcŭpĕrātĭo, ōnis *f,* recovery

rĕcŭpĕro *v.t.* 1, to recover, regain

rĕcurro, curri *v.i.* 3, to run back, return

rĕcurso *v.i.* 1, to return

rĕcursus, ūs *m,* return, retreat

rĕcurvo *v.t.* 1, to bend back

rĕcurvus, a, um *adj,* bent

rĕcūsātĭo, ōnis *f,* refusal

rĕcūso *v.t.* 1, to refuse

rĕcussus, a, um *adj,* roused

rĕdargŭo, ŭi *v.t.* 3, to contradict

reddo, dĭdi, dĭtum *v.t.* 3, to give back, deliver, pay, produce, render, translate, recite, repeat, resemble

rĕdemptĭo, ōnis *f,* buying back

rĕdemptor, ōris *m,* contractor

rĕdĕo, ĭi, ĭtum *v.i.* 4, to go back, return, be reduced to

rĕdĭgo, ēgi, actum *v.t.* 3, to bring back, restore, collect, reduce to

rĕdĭmīcŭlum, i *n,* necklace

rĕdmĭo *v.t.* 4, to encircle

rĕdĭmo, ēmi, emptum *v.t.* 3, to repurchase, ransom, release, hire, obtain

rĕdintĕgro *v.t.* 1, to restore

rĕdĭtus, ūs *m,* return

rĕdŏlĕo *v.i.t.* 2, to smell; smell of

rĕdōno *v.t.* 1, to restore

rĕdūco, xi, ctum *v.t.* 3, to bring back, restore

rĕductus, a, um *adj,* remote

rĕdundantĭa, ae *f,* redundancy

rĕdundo *v.i.* 1, to overflow, abound in

rĕdus, dŭcis *adj,* brought back

rĕfello, felli *v.t.* 3, to refute

rĕfercĭo, si, tum *v.t.* 4, to cram

rĕfĕro, fĕrre, rettŭli, rĕlātum *v.t, irreg,* to bring back, restore, repay, report, reply, propose, record, reckon, refer, resemble; *with* pedem, to retreat

rēfert *v. impers,* it is of importance, it matters

rĕfertus, a, um *adj,* filled

rĕfĭcĭo, fēci, fectum *v.t.* 3, to re-make, repair, refresh

rĕfĭgo, xi, xum *v.t.* 3, to unfix

rĕfingo *v.t.* 3, to renew

rĕflecto, xi, xum *v.i.t.* 3, to turn back; bend back

rĕflo *v.i.* 1, to blow back

rĕflŭo *v.i.* 3, to flow back

rĕformīdo (*no perf.*) *v.t.* 1, to dread, avoid

rĕfrāgor *v.i.* 1, *dep,* to resist

rĕfrēno *v.t.* 1, to curb, check

rĕfrĭco, ŭi *v.t.* 1, to scratch open

rĕfrīgĕro *v.t.* 1, to cool

rĕfrīgesco, frixi *v.i.* 3, to grow cool, grow stale

rĕfringo, frēgi, fractum *v.t.* 3, to break open, break off

rĕfŭgĭo, fūgi *v.i.t.* 3, to run away, escape; flee from, avoid

rĕfulgĕo, si *v.i.* 2, to shine

rĕfundo, fūdi, fūsum *v.t.* 3, to pour out, cause to overflow

rĕfūtandus *gerundive,* see rĕfūto

rĕfūto *v.t.* 1, to repress, refute

rēgālis, e *adj,* royal, splendid

rēgĭa, ae *f,* palace, court

rēgĭfĭcus, a, um *adj,* royal

rēgigno *v.t.* 3, to reproduce

rēgĭmen, ĭnis *n,* guidance

rēgīna, ae *f,* queen

rēgĭo, ōnis *f,* district, region, direction, boundary; ē rēgĭōne — in a straight line

rēgĭus, a, um *adj, adv,* ē, royal, magnificent

regnātor, ōris *m,* ruler

regno *v.i.t.* 1, to reign; rule

regnum, i *n,* kingdom, sovereignty, dominion

rĕgo, xi, ctum *v.t.* 3, to rule, guide, direct

rĕgrĕdĭor, gressus *v.i.* 3, *dep,* to return, retreat

rĕgressus, ūs *m,* return, retreat

rēgŭla, ae *f,* wooden ruler, model, pattern

rēgŭlus, i *m,* prince

rēĭcĭo, iēci, iectum *v.t.* 3, to throw back, repel, reject, postpone

rēiectĭo, ōnis *f,* rejection

rĕlābor, lapsus *v.i.* 3, *dep,* to slide or sink back

rĕlanguesco, gŭi *v.i.* 3, to grow faint, relax

rĕlātĭo, ōnis *f,* proposition

rĕlaxo *v.t.* 1, to loosen, ease

rĕlēgātĭo, ōnis *f,* banishment

rĕlēgo *v.t.* 1, to send away, banish

rĕlēgo, lēgi, lectum *v.t.* 3, to gather together, travel over again, read over again

rĕlĕvo *v.t.* 1, to lift up, lighten, comfort, refresh

rĕlictĭo, ōnis *f*, abandonment

rĕlictus, a, um *adj*, left

rĕlĭgĭo, ōnis *f*, piety, religion, religious scruple, good faith, conscientiousness, sanctity

rĕlĭgĭōsus, a, um *adj*, devout, scrupulous, precise, sacred

rĕlĭgo *v.t.* 1, to bind, fasten

rĕlĭno, lēvi *v.t.* 3, to unseal

rĕlinquo, rĕlĭqui, lictum *v.t.* 3, to leave, leave behind, abandon, surrender

rĕlĭquĭae, ārum *f.pl*, remains

rĕlĭquum, i *n*, remainder

rĕlĭquus, a, um *adj*, remaining

rĕlūcĕo, xi *v.i.* 2, to shine

rĕluctor *v.i.* 1, *dep*, to resist

rĕmănĕo, nsi *v.i.* 2, to stay behind, endure

rĕmĕdĭum, ii *n*, cure, relief

rĕmĕo *v.i.* 1, to return

rĕmētĭor, mensus *v.t.* 4, *dep*, to remeasure

rēmex, ĭgis *m*, oarsman

rēmĭgĭum, ii *n*, rowing, oars, rowers

rēmĭgo *v.i.* 1, to row

rĕmĭgro *v.i.* 1, to return

rĕmĭniscor *v.3*, *dep*, *with genit*, to remember

rĕmiscĕo (*no perf*.) mixtum *v.t.* 2, to mix up

rĕmissĭo, ōnis *f*, relaxation

rĕmissus, a, um *adj*, *adv*, ē, loose, gentle, cheerful

rĕmitto, mīsi, missum *v.i.t.* 3, to decrease; send back, send out, yield, loosen, slacken, grant, surrender, give up; *with infin*, to cease

rĕmollesco *v.i.* 3, to grow soft

rĕmordĕo (*no perf*.), morsum *v.t.* 2, to torment

rĕmŏror *v.i.t.* 1, *dep*, to loiter; obstruct

rĕmōtus, a, um *adj*, distant

rĕmŏvĕo, mōvi, mōtum *v.t.* 2, to remove, withdraw, set aside

rĕmūgĭo *v.i.* 4, to resound

rĕmulcum, i *n*, tow rope

rĕmūnĕrātĭo, ōnis *f*, reward

rĕmūnĕror *v.t.* 1, *dep*, to reward

rĕmurmŭro *v.i.t.* 1, to murmur back

rēmus, i *m*, oar

rĕnascor, nātus *v.i.* 3, *dep*, to be born again, spring up again

rēnes, um *m.pl*, kidneys

rĕnīdĕo *v.i.* 2, to glisten

rĕnŏvātĭo, ōnis *f*, revewal

rĕnŏvo *v.t.* 1, to renew, restore, refresh, repeat

rĕnuntĭātĭo, ōnis *f*, announcement

rĕnuntĭo *v.t.* 1, to report, announce, refuse, renounce

rĕnŭo, ŭi *v.i.t.* 3, to refuse

rĕor, rātus *v.t.* 2, *dep*, to suppose, think, believe

rĕpāgŭla, ōrum *n.pl*, bolts, bars

rĕpărābĭlis, e *adj*, able to be repaired

rĕpăro *v.t.* 1, to recover, repair, restore, refresh

rĕpello, pŭli, pulsum *v.t.* 3, to drive back, reject

rĕpendo, di, sum *v.t.* 3, to weigh out in return, repay

rĕpens, ntis *adj*, *adv*, ē, sudden

rĕpentīnus, a, um *adj*, *adv*, ō, sudden, unexpected

rĕpercussus, ūs *m*, reflection

rĕpercŭtĭo, cussi, cussum *v.t.* 3, to drive back, reflect

rĕpĕrĭo, repperi, rĕpertum *v.t.* 4, to find, discover

rĕpertor, ōris *m*, discoverer

rĕpĕto, ĭi, ītum *v.t.* 3, to attack again, re-visit, fetch back, resume, recollect, demand back

rĕpĕtundae, ārum *f.pl*, (*with res*), extortion

rĕplĕo, ēvi, ētum *v.t.* 2, to fill up, complete

rĕplētus, a, um *adj*, full

rēpo, psi, ptum *v.i.* 3, to creep

rĕpōno, pŏsŭi, pŏsĭtum *v.t.* 3, to replace, preserve, put away

rĕporto *v.t.* 1, to bring back, carry back, obtain

rĕposco *v.t.* 3, to demand back

rĕpraesentātĭo, ōnis *f*, representation

rĕpraesento *v.t.* 1, to display, do immediately

rĕprĕhendo, di, sum *v.t.* 3, to blame, rebuke, convict

rĕprĕhensĭo, ōnis *f*, blame

rĕprĭmo

rĕprĭmo, pressi, ssum *v.t.* 3, to keep back, check, restrain

rĕpŭdĭātĭo, ōnis *f,* refusal, renunciation

rĕpŭdĭo *v.t.* 1, to divorce, reject, scorn

rĕpugnans, ntis *adj,* contradictory, irreconcilable

rĕpugnantĭa, ae *f,* opposition, inconsistency

rĕpungo *v.i.* 1, to resist, disagree with

rĕpulsa, ae *f,* refusal, rejection

rĕpurgo *v.t.* 1, to clean

rĕpŭto *v.t.* 1, to ponder, reckon

rĕquĭes, ētis *f,* rest, relaxation

rĕquĭesco, ēvi, etum *v.i.* 3, to rest

rĕquīro, sīvi, sītum *v.t.* 3, to search for, enquire, need, notice to be missing

rēs, rĕi *f,* thing, matter, affair, reality, fact, property, profit, advantage, business, affair, lawsuit; **rēs nŏvae, rērum nŏvārum** *f.pl,* revolution; **respublĭca, rēīpublĭcae** *f,* the State, statesmanship

rēscindo, scĭdi, ssum *v.t.* 3, to cut down, break down, abolish

rēscisco, īvi, ītum *v.t.* 3, to learn, ascertain

rēscrībo, psi, ptum *v.t.* 3, to write back, reply, repay

rĕsĕco, ŭi, ctum *v.t.* 1, to cut off, curtail

rĕsĕro *v.t.* 1, to unlock, open

rĕservo *v.t.* 1, to save up, keep

rĕsĕs, ĭdis *adj,* inactive

rĕsīdĕo, sēdi *v.i.* 2, to remain, linger, sit

rĕsīdo, sēdi *v.i.* 3, to settle

rĕsĭdŭus, a, um *adj,* remaining

rĕsigno *v.t.* 1, to unseal, open

rĕsĭlĭo, ŭi *v.i.* 4, to recoil

rēsīna, ae *f,* resin

rĕsĭpĭo *v.t.* 3, to taste of

rĕsĭpisco, īvi *v.i.* 3, to revive

rĕsisto, stĭti *v.i.* 3, to stop, remain; *with dat,* to resist

rĕsolvo, solvi, sŏlūtum *v.t.* 3, to untie, release, open, relax, annul, abolish

rĕsŏno *v.i.t.* 1, to resound; re-echo with

rĕsŏnus, a, um *adj,* resounding

rĕsorbĕo *v.t.* 2, to re-swallow

respecto *v.t.* 1, to look at, respect

respectus, ūs *m,* looking back, retreat, refuge, respect

rēspergo, si, sum *v.t.* 3, to besprinkle

rēspĭcĭo, spexi, spectum *v.i.t.* 3, to look back, give attention; look at, regard, respect

rēspīrātĭo, ōnis *f,* breathing

rēspīro *v.i.t.* 1, to revive; breathe out, breathe

rēsplendĕo *v.i.* 2, to shine

rēspondĕo, di, sum *v.t.* 2, to reply, give advice, agree, correspond, answer one's hopes

rēsponso *v.t.* 1, to reply, resist

rēsponsum, i *n,* answer

respublĭca see rēs

rēspŭo, ŭi *v.t.* 3, to spit out, expel, reject

rēstinguo, nxi, nctum *v.t.* 3, to quench, extinguish

restis, is *f,* rope

rēstĭtŭo, ŭi, ūtum *v.t.* 3, to replace, rebuild, renew, give back, restore

rēstĭtūtĭo, ōnis *f,* restoration

rēsto, stĭti *v.i.* 1, to remain

rēstrictus, a, um *adj,* bound

rēstringo, nxi, ctum *v.t.* 3, to bind, restrain

rĕsulto (*no perf.*) *v.i.* 1, to jump back, resound

rĕsūmo, mpsi, mptum *v.t.* 3, to resume, take back, recover

rĕsŭpīnus, a, um *adj,* lying on one's back

rĕsurgo, surrexi, surrectum *v.i.* 3, to rise, reappear

rĕsurrectĭo, ōnis *f,* resurrection

rĕsuscĭto *v.t.* 1, to revive

rĕtardo *v.i.t.* 1, to delay

rēte, is *n,* net, snare

rĕtĕgo, xi, ctum *v.t.* 3, to uncover, reveal

rĕtendo, di, tum *v.t.* 3, to slacken

rĕtento *v.t.* 1, to keep back

rĕtento *v.t.* 1, to try again

rĕtexo, ŭi, xtum *v.t.* 3, to unravel, cancel

rĕtĭcĕo *v.i.t.* 2, to be silent; conceal
rĕtĭcŭlātus, a, um *adj*, net-like
rētĭcŭlum, i *n*, small net
rĕtĭnācŭlum, i *n*, rope, cable
rĕtĭnens, ntis *adj*, tenacious
rĕtĭnĕo, ŭi, tentum *v.t.* 2, to hold
 back, restrain, maintain
rĕtorquĕo, si, tum *v.t.* 2, to twist
 back, drive back
rĕtracto *v.t.* 1, to handle or
 undertake again, reconsider,
 refuse
rĕtrăho, xi, ctum *v.t.* 3, to draw
 back, call back, remove
rĕtrĭbŭo, ŭi, ūtum *v.t.* 3, to repay
rĕtrō *adv*, backwards, formerly,
 back, behind, on the other hand
rĕtrorsum(s) *adv*, backwards
rĕtundo, tŭdi, tūsum *v.t.* 3, to
 blunt, dull, weaken
rĕtūsus, a, um *adj*, blunt, dull
rĕus, i *m* (rĕa, ae, *f*), defendant,
 criminal, culprit
rĕvălesco, lŭi *v.i.* 3, to grow well
 again
rĕvĕho, xi, ctum *v.t.* 3, to bring
 back; *in passive*, to return
rĕvello, velli, vulsum *v.t.* 3, to pull
 out, tear away
rĕvĕnĭo, vēni, ventum *v.i.* 4, to
 return
rĕvērā *adv*, really
rĕvĕrens, ntis *adj*, reverent
rĕvĕrentĭa, ae *f*, respect
rĕvĕrĕor *v.t.* 2, *dep*, to revere
rĕverto, ti *v.i.* 3, to return
rĕvertor, versus *v.i.* 3, *dep*, to
 return
rĕvincendus *gerundive*, see revinco
rĕvincĭo, nxi, nctum *v.t.* 4, to bind,
 fasten
rĕvinco, vīci, victum *v.t.* 3, to
 conquer, convict
rĕvĭresco, rŭi *v.i.* 3, to grow green
 again
rĕvīso *v.i.t.* 3, to revisit
rĕvīvisco, vixi *v.i.* 3, to revive
rĕvŏcābĭlis, e *adj*, able, to be
 recalled
rĕvŏcāmen, ĭnis *n*, recall
rĕvŏcātĭo, ōnis *f*, recalling
rĕvŏco *v.t.* 1, to recall, restrain,
 refer

rĕvŏlo *v.i.* 1, to fly back
rĕvolvo, volvi, vŏlūtum *v.t.* 3, to
 unroll, repeat
rĕvŏmo, ŭi *v.t.* 3, to vomit up
rex, rēgis *m*, king
rhēda, ae *f*, carriage
rhētor, ŏris *m*, teacher of oratory
rhētŏrĭca, ae *f*, rhetoric
rhētŏrĭcus, a, um *adj*, rhetorical
rhīnŏcĕros, ōtis *m*, rhinoceros
rhombus, i *m*, magic circle, turbot
rhonchus, i *m*, snore, sneer
rīca, ae *f*, veil
rīcīnĭum, ii *n*, small veil
rictus, ūs *m*, gaping mouth
rīdĕo, si, sum *v.i.t.* 2, to laugh,
 smile; laugh at, ridicule
rīdīcŭlum, i *n*, joke
rīdīcŭlus, a, um *adj*, *adv*, ē,
 amusing, absurd
rīgĕo *v.i.* 2, to be stiff
rīgesco, gŭi *v.i.* 3, to stiffen
rīgĭdus, a, um *adj*, stiff, stern
rīgo *v.t.* 1, to wet, water
rīgor, ōris *m*, stiffness, hardness,
 chilliness, severity
rīgŭus, a, um *adj*, irrigating
rīma, ae *f*, crack, chink
rīmor *v.t.* 1, *dep*, to tear up,
 explore, examine
rīmōsus, a, um *adj*, leaky
rīpa, ae *f*, river back
rīsus, ūs *m*, laughter
rītĕ *adv*, rightly, properly
rītus, ūs *m*, religious ceremony,
 custom, way; **rītu** *with genit*, in
 the manner of
rīvālis, is *m*, rival
rīvŭlus, i *m*, brook
rīvus, i *m*, brook, stream
rixa, ae *f*, quarrel
rixor *v.i.* 1, *dep*, to quarrel
rōbīgĭnōsus, a, um *adj*, rusty
rōbīgo, ĭnis *f*, rust, mould
rōbŏro *v.t.* 1, to strengthen
rōbur, ŏris *n*, oak, strength, power,
 vigour, force
rōbustus, a, um *adj*, oaken, firm,
 strong, robust
rōdo, si, sum *v.t.* 3, to gnaw,
 corrode, slander
rŏgātĭo, ōnis *f*, proposed law or
 bill, request

rŏgātor, ōris *m*, polling-clerk

rŏgo *v.t.* 1, to ask; *with* legem, to propose (law), beg

rŏgus, i *m*, funeral pile

rōro *v.i.t.* 1, to drop, drip, trickle; wet, besprinkle

rōs, rōris *m*, dew, moisture

rŏsa, ae *f*, rose

rŏsārĭum, ii *n*, rose garden

roscĭdus, a, um *adj*, dewy

rŏsētum, i *n*, rosebed

rŏsĕus, a, um *adj*, of roses, rose-coloured

rostra, ōrum *n.pl*, speaker's platform

rostrātus, a, um *adj*, with beaks

rostrum, i *n*, beak, snout

rŏta, ae *f*, wheel, chariot

rŏto *v.i.t.* 1, to revolve; swing round, whirl around

rŏtundĭtas, ātis *f*, rotundity

rŏtundo *v.t.* 1, to round off

rŏtundus, a, um *adj*, round, polished

rŭbĕfăcĭo, fēci, factum *v.t.* 3, to redden

rŭbens, ntis *adj*, red

rŭbĕo *v.i.* 2, to be red, blush

rŭber, bra, brum *adj*, red

ructus, ūs *m*, belching

rŭdens, ntis *m*, rope, rigging

rŭdīmentum, i *n*, first try

rŭdis, e *adj*, rough, raw, wild, awkward, inexperienced

rŭdis, is *f*, stick, wooden sword

rŭdo, īvi, ītum *v.i.* 3, to bellow

rūdus, ĕris *n*, broken stones, rubbish

rūfus, a, um *adj*, red

rūga, ae *f*, wrinkle

rūgōsus, a, um *adj*, shrivelled

ruīna, ae *f*, downfall, ruin

ruīnōsus, a, um *adj*, in ruins

rūmĭno *v.t.* 1, to chew over

rūmor, ōris *m*, rumour, general opinion, reputation

rumpo, rūpi, ruptum *v.t.* 3, to break, burst, destroy, interrupt

runcīna, ae *f*, plane

runcīno *v.t.* 1, to plane

runco *v.t.* 1, to weed

rŭo, ŭi, ŭtum *v.i.t.* 3, to fall, rush, hurry; hurl down, throw up

rūpes, is *f*, rock

rūrĭcŏla, ae *adj*, rural

rursus (rursum) *adv*, again, on the contrary, backwards

rūs, rūris *n*, countryside

Insight

If the place is a town, city or small island, the place name is usually put into the appropriate case without the preposition. The same rule applies to three common nouns: *domus* (= house), *rus* (= country) and *humus* (= ground). Moreover, the locative case expresses 'place where' (*domi* = at home).

---

rŭbesco, bŭi *v.i.* 3, to grow red

rŭbēta, ae *f*, toad

rŭbēta, ōrum *n.pl*, brambles

rŭbĭcundus, a, um *adj*, red

rŭbīgo... see rōbīgo...

rŭbor, ōris *m*, redness, blush, bashfulness

rùbrīca, ae *f*, red-chalk

rŭbus, i *m*, bramble bush

ructo *v.i.t.* 1, to belch

ructor *v.* 1, *dep*, to belch

rustĭcānus, a, um *adj*, rustic

rustĭcĭtas, ātis *f*, behaviour of country-people

rustĭcor *v.i.* 1, *dep*, to live in the country

rustĭcus, a, um *adj*, rural

rustĭcus, i *m*, countryman

rūta, ae *f*, bitter herb, rue

rŭtĭlo *v.i.* 1, to be red

rŭtĭlus, a, um *adj*, red

S

sabbăta, ōrum *n.pl*, sabbath
săbīnum, i *n*, Sabine wine
săbŭlum, i *n*, gravel
săburra, ae *f*, sand, ballast
sacchăron, i *n*, sugar
saccŭlus, i *m*, small bag
saccus, i *m*, bag
săcellum, i *n*, chapel
săcer, cra, crum *adj*, sacred, venerable, accursed
săcerdos, dōtis *c*, priest
săcerdōtālis, e *adj*, priestly
săcerdōtĭum, ii *n*, priesthood
sàcra, ōrum *n.pl*, worship, religion
sàcrāmentum, i *n*, oath
sàcrārĭum, ii *n*, sanctuary
sàcrātus, a, um *adj*, sacred
sàcrĭfĭcĭum, ii *n*, sacrifice
sàcrĭfĭco *v.i.t.* 1, to sacrifice
sàcrĭfĭcus, a, um *adj*, sacrificial
sàcrĭlĕgus, a, um *adj*, temple robbing, sacrilegious
sàcro *v.t.* 1, to consecrate, condemn, doom
sàcrōsanctus, a, um *adj*, sacred, inviolable
sàcrum, i *n*, sacred thing, religious act, religion
saecŭlum, i *n*, age, generation, century
saepe *adv*, often
saepes, is *f*, hedge, fence
saepīmentum, i *n*, fencing
saepĭo, psi, ptum *v.t.* 4, to fence in, surround
saeptum i *n*, fence, pen
saeta, ae *f*, hair, bristle
saetĭger, ĕra, ĕrum *adj*, bristly
saetōsus, a, um *adj*, bristly
saevĭo *v.i.* 4, to rage
saevĭtĭa, ae *f*, savageness
saevus, a, um *adj*, savage, violent, furious, cruel
sāga, ae *f*, fortune-teller
săgācĭtas, ātis *f*, shrewdness
săgax, ācis *adj, adv*, ĭter, keen, shrewd, acute
săgīno *v.t.* 1, to fatten
săgitta, ae *f*, arrow
săgittārĭus, ii *m*, archer
săgŭlum, i *n*, military cloak

săgum, i *n*, military cloak
sal, sălis *m*, salt, sea, wit, sarcasm
sălăco, ōnis *m*, braggart
sălārĭum, ii *n*, pension, salary (salt money)
sălax, ācis *adj*, lecherous
sălĕbra, ae *f*, roughness
sălĭāris, e *adj*, splendid
sălictum, i *n*, willow-grove
sălignus, a, um *adj*, of willow
Sălĭi, ōrum *m.pl*, priests of Mars
sălīnae, ārum *f.pl*, salt-works
sălīnum, i *n*, saltcellar
sălĭo, ŭi, saltum *v.i.* 4, to jump
sălīva, ae *f*, saliva
sălix, īcis *f*, willow tree
salmo, ōnis *m*, salmon
salsāmentum, i *n*, brine
salsus, a, um *adj, adv*, ē, salted, witty
saltātĭo, ōnis *f*, dancing
saltātor, ōris *m*, dancer
saltātrix, īcis *f*, dancing-girl
saltātus, ūs *m*, dancing
saltem *adv*, at least
salto *v.i.t.* 1, to dance
saltus, ūs *m*, leap, bound
saltus, ūs *m*, woodland, mountain pass
sălūbris, e *adj, adv*, ĭter, health-giving, beneficial
sălūbrĭtas, ātis *f*, wholesomeness
sălum, i *n*, sea
sălūs, ūtis *f*, welfare, safety
sălūtāris, e *adj, adv*, ĭter, beneficial, wholesome
sălūtātĭo, ōnis *f*, greeting
sălūtātor, ōris *m*, visitor
sălūtĭfer, ĕra, ĕrum *adj*, healing
sălūto *v.t.* 1, to greet
salvē, salvēte, salvēto *v. imperative*, how are you? welcome!
salvĭa, ae *f*, sage (herb)
salvus, a, um *adj*, safe, well; *with noun in abl*, e.g. **salvā lege** without violating the law
sambūcus, i *f*, elder tree
sānābĭlis, e *adj*, curable
sānātĭo, ōnis *f*, cure
sancĭo, xi, ctum *v.t.* 4, to appoint, establish, ratify
sanctĭfĭcātĭo, ōnis *f*, sanctification

sanctĭo, ōnis *f*, establishing
sanctĭtas, ātis *f*, sacredness, purity
sanctus, a, um *adj*, *adv*, ē, sacred, inviolable, good
sandix, īcis *f*, scarlet
sānē *adv*, certainly, very
sanguĭnārĭus, a, um *adj*, bloody, blood-thirsty
sanguĭnĕus, a, um *adj*, bloody
sanguĭnŏlentus, a, um *adj*, bloody
sanguis, ĭnis *m*, blood, bloodshed, race, stock
sănĭes, em, e *f*, bad blood
sānĭtas, ātis *f*, health, good sense, discretion
sannĭo, ōnis *m*, buffoon
sāno *v.t.* 1, to cure, restore
sānus, a, um *adj*, healthy, rational, discreet
săpĭdus, a, um *adj*, tasty
săpĭens, ntis *adj*, *adv*, nter, wise, sensible
săpĭens, ntis *m*, wise man
săpĭentĭa, ae *f*, discretion, philosophy
săpĭo, īvi *v.i.t.* 3, to be wise, discreet; to taste of savour of
sāpo, ōnis *m*, soap
săpor, ōris *m*, flavour, taste
sapphīrus, i *f*, sapphire
sarcĭna, ae *f*, pack, load
sarcĭo, si, tum *v.t.* 4, to patch
sarcŏphăgus, i *m*, sarcophagus
sarcŭlum, i *n*, light hoe
sarda, ae *f*, sardine
sarīsa, ae *f*, Macedonian lance
sarmentum, i *n*, brushwood
sarrācum, i *n*, cart
sarrānus, a, um *adj*, Tyrian
sarrĭo *v.t.* 4, to hoe
sartāto, ĭnis *f*, frying pan
sartus, a, um *adj*, repaired
sāta, ōrum *n.pl*, crops
sătelles, ĭtis *c*, attendant; *in pl*, escort
sătĭas, ātis *f*, abundance, disgust
sătĭĕtas, ātis *f*, abundance, disgust
sătĭo *v.t.* 1, to satisfy, glut
sātĭo, ōnis *f*, sowing
sătĭrĭcus, a, um *adj*, satirical
sătis (săt) *adv*, or *indecl. adj*, enough
sătisdătĭo, ōnis *f*, giving bail

sătisfăcĭo, fēci, factum *v.t.* 3, to satisfy, make amends
sătisfactĭo, ōnis *f*, excuse, reparation
sătĭus *comp. adv*, better
sător, ōris *m*, sower, creator
sătrăpes, is *m*, viceroy, satrap
sătur, ŭra, ŭrum *adj*, full, fertile
sătŭra, ae *f*, food made of various ingredients, satire
Sāturnālĭa, ōrum *n.pl*, festival in honour of Saturn (Dec. 17th)
sătŭro *v.t.* 1, to fill, glut
sătus, ūs *m*, planting
sătus, a, um *adj*, sprung from
sătȳrus, i *m*, forest god
saucĭo *v.t.* 1, to wound
saucĭus, a, um *adj*, wounded
saxĕus, a, um *adj*, rocky
saxĭfĭcus, a, um *adj*, petrifiying
saxōsus, a, um *adj*, rocky
saxum, i *n*, rock
scăbellum, i *n*, stool
scăber, bra, brum *adj*, rough, scabby
scăbĭes, em, e *f*, roughness, scab, itch
scăbo, scābi *v.t.* 3, to scratch
scaena, ae *f*, stage, scene
scaenĭcus, a, um *adj*, theatrical
scaenĭcus, i *m*, actor
scāla, ae *f*, ladder, stairs
scalmus, i *m*, rowlock
scalpo, psi, ptum *v.t.* 3, to carve
scalpellum, i *n*, lancet
scalprum, i *n*, chisel
scalptor, ōris *m*, engraver
scalptūra, ae *f*, engraving
scamnum, i *n*, bench
scando *v.i.t.* 3, to rise; climb
scăpha, ae *f*, small boat
scăpŭlae, ārum *f.pl*, shoulder blades
scărăbaeus, i *m*, beetle
scărus, i *m*, sea fish (scar)
scătĕbra, ae *f*, spring water
scătĕo *v.i.* 2, to bubble, swarm with
scaurus, a, um *adj*, with swollen ankles
scĕlĕrātus, a, um *adj*, wicked
scĕlĕro *v.t.* 1, to contaminate
scĕlestus, a, um *adj*, wicked

scĕlus, ĕris *n*, crime, scoundrel
scēna see **scaena**
scēnĭcus see **scaenĭcus**
sceptrum, i *n*, sceptre; *in pl*, dominion, authority
schĕda, ae *f*, sheet of paper
schŏla, ae *f*, lecture, school
scīens, ntis *adj, adv,* **nter**, knowing (*i.e.* purposely), expert in
scĭentĭa, ae *f*, knowledge
scīlĭcet *adv*, certainly, of course, namely
scīlla, ae *f*, sea-onion, prawn
scindo, scĭdi, scissum *v.t.* 3, to split
scintilla, ae *f*, spark
scintillans, ntis *adj*, sparkling
scintillo *v.i.* 1, to sparkle
scĭo *v.t.* 4, to know, understand
scīpĭo, ōnis *m*, staff
scirpĕus, a, um *adj*, of rushes
sciscĭtor *v.t.* 1, *dep*, to enquire
scisco, scīvi, scītum *v.t.* 3, to approve, appoint, decree
scissūra, ae *f*, tearing, rending
scītor *v.t.* 1, *dep*, to enquire
scītum, i *n*, decree, statute
scītus, a, um *adj, adv,* **ē**, shrewd, sensible, witty
scĭūrus, i *m*, squirrel

draw, compose, describe, enroll
scrīnĭum, i *n*, letter-case
scriptĭo, ōnis *f*, writing
scriptor, ōris *m*, secretary, author
scriptum, i *n*, book, writing
scriptūra, ae *f*, composition
scriptus, a, um *adj*, written
scrŏbis, is *m*, ditch
scrūpĕus, a, um *adj*, rugged
scrūpŭlus, i *m*, anxiety, embarrassment
scrūta, ōrum *n.pl*, frippery
scrūtātĭo, ōnis *f*, scrutiny
scrūtor *v.t.* 1, *dep*, to examine
sculpo, psi, ptum *v.t.* 3, to carve
sculpōnĕae, ārum *f.pl*, clogs
sculptor, ōris *m*, sculptor
sculptūra, ae *f*, sculpture
scurra, ae *m*, clown, dandy
scurrīlis, e *adj*, jeering
scūtātus, a, um *adj*, armed with oblong shields
scŭtella, ae *f*, salver
scŭtĭca, ae *f*, whip
scŭtŭla, ae *f*, wooden roller
scūtum, i *n*, oblong shield
scў̄phus, i *m*, goblet
sē *acc. or abl. of reflexive pron*, himself, herself, itself, themselves etc.

Insight

The personal pronouns 'himself', 'herself' and 'themselves' have only one form in Latin, both for the singular and plural forms, namely *se*. It declines as follows: acc. *se*, gen. *sui*, dat. *sibi*, abl. *se*. They lack the nominative and vocative forms.

---

scŏbīna, ae *f*, rasp, file
scŏbis, is *f*, sawdust
scomber, bri *m*, mackerel
scōpae, ārum *f.pl*, broom
scŏpŭlōsus, a, um *adj*, rocky
scŏpŭlus, i *m*, rock, cliff
scŏpus, i *m*, target
scorpĭo, ōnis *m*, scorpion, missile launcher
scortum, i *n*, prostitute
scrība, ae *m*, clerk
scrībo, psi, ptum *v.t.* 3, to write,

sēbum, i *n*, suet
sĕcāle, is *n*, rye
sēcēdo, cessi, cessum *v.i.* 3, to go away, withdraw
sēcerno, crēvi, crētum *v.t.* 3, to separate, part
sēcessĭo, ōnis *f*, withdrawal
sēcessus, ūs *m*, solitude
sēcĭus (sĕquĭus) *comp. adv*, differently
sēclūdo, si, sum *v.t.* 3, to separate, shut off

sēclūsus, a, um *adj*, remote
sēco, ŭi, ctum *v.t.* 1, to cut, wound, separate
sēcrētum, i *n*, solitude
sēcrētus, a, um *adj*, *adv*, ō, separate, remote, secret
secta, ae *f*, way, method, sect
sectātor, ōris *m*, follower
sectĭo, ōnis *f*, sale by auction
sector, ōris *m*, cutthroat, bidder at an auction
sector *v.t.* 1, *dep*, to pursue
sectūra, ae *f*, mine
sēcul... see saecul
sĕcundārĭus, a, um *adj*, secondary, second-rate
sĕcundo *v.t.* 1, to favour
sĕcundum *prep. with acc*, after, behind, by, next to, according to
sĕcundus, a, um *adj*, following, second, favourable
sĕcūrĭger, ĕra, ĕrum *adj*, armed with a battle-axe
sĕcūris, is *f*, axe, hatchet
sĕcūrĭtas, ātis *f*, freedom from care
sĕcūrus, a, um *adj*, carefree, tranquil
sĕcus *adv*, differently
sĕd *conj*, but
sēdātĭo, ōnis *f*, a calming
sēdātus, a, um *adj*, calm
sēdĕcim *indecl. adj*, sixteen
sĕdentārĭus, a, um *adj*, sedentary
sĕdĕo, sēdi, sessum *v.i.* 2, to sit, remain, settle, be settled
sēdes, is *f*, seat, residence, temple, bottom, foundation
sĕdīle, is *n*, seat
sēdĭtĭo, ōnis *f*, mutiny
sēdĭtĭōsus, a, um *adj*, *adv*, ē, mutinous, rebellious
sēdo *v.t.* 1, to calm, check
sēdūco, xi, ctum *v.t.* 3, to lead aside, separate
sēdŭlītas, ātis *f*, zeal
sēdŭlō *adv*, diligently, on purpose
sēdŭlus, a, um *adj*, industrious
sĕges, ĕtis *f*, cornfield, crop
segmenta, ōrum *n.pl*, trimmings
segmentum, i *n*, piece
segnis, e *adj*, *adv*, ĭter, lazy

segnĭtĭa, ae *f*, inactivity, slowness
sēgrĕgo *v.t.* 1, to separate
sēiungo, nxi, ntum *v.t.* 3, to separate, divide
sēlīgo, lēgi, lectum *v.t.* 3, to select
sella, ae *f*, seat, chair
sĕmĕl *adv*, once
sēmen, ĭtis *n*, seed, cutting, graft, offspring, instigator
sēmentis, is *f*, sowing
sēmestris, e *adj*, half-yearly
sēmēsus, a, um *adj*, half-eaten
sēmĭānĭmĭs, e *adj*, half-dead
sēmĭdĕus, a, um *adj*, half-divine
sēmĭfer, ĕra, ĕrum *adj*, half-man, half-beast
sēmĭhŏmo, ĭnis *m*, half-human
sēmĭhōra, ae *f*, half-hour
sēmĭnārĭum, ii *n*, nursery
sēmĭnātor, ōris *m*, author
sēmĭnĕcis, is *adj*, half-dead
sēmĭno *v.t.* 1, to produce
sēmĭplēnus, a, um *adj*, half-full
sēmĭrŭtus, a, um *adj*, half-ruined
sēmis, issis *m*, (coin of very low value)
sēmĭsomnus, a, um *adj*, half-asleep
sēmĭta, ae *f*, footpath
sēmĭustus, a, um *adj*, half-burned
sēmĭvir, vĭri *m*, half-man; *as adj*, effeminate
sēmĭvīvus, a, um *adj*, half-alive
sēmōtus, a, um *adj*, remote
sēmŏvĕo, mōvi, mōtum *v.t.* 2, to remove, separate
semper *adv*, always
sempĭternus, a, um *adj*, everlasting
sēmustŭlo *v.t.* 1, to half burn
sĕnātor, ōris *m*, senator
sĕnātōrĭus, a, um *adj*, senatorial
sĕnātus, ūs *m*, the Senate
sĕnecta, ae *f*, old age
sĕnectus, ūtis *f*, old age
sĕnesco, nŭi *v.i.* 3, to grow old
sĕnex, sĕnis *m*, old man
sēni, ae, a *pl. adj*, six each
sĕnīlis, e *adj*, old (of people)
sĕnĭor, ōris *c*, elderly person
sĕnĭum, ii *n*, old age, decay, trouble
sensĭlis, e *adj*, sensitive
sensim *adv*, slowly, gently

sensus, ūs *m*, perception, disposition, good taste, sense, understanding, meaning
sententĭa, ae *f*, opinion, decision, meaning, sentence, axiom; **ex mĕā sententĭā** to my liking
sententĭōsus, a, um *adj*, sententious
sentīna, ae *f*, bilge-water, dregs, ship's hold
sentĭo, sī, sum *v.t.* 4, to feel, perceive, endure, suppose
sentis, is *m*, thorn, bramble
sentus, a, um *adj*, rough
sĕorsum *adv*, separately
sēpărātim *adv*, separately
sēpărātĭo, ōnis *f*, separation
sēpărātus, a, um *adj*, separate
sēpăro *v.t.* 1, to separate
sĕpĕlĭo, līvi, pultum *v.t.* 4, to bury, overwhelm
sēpĭa, ae *f*, cuttle fish
sēpĭo see **saepĭo**
sēpōno, pŏsŭi, pŏsĭtum *v.t.* 3, to put aside, select
septem *indecl. adj*, seven
September (mensis) September
septemgĕmĭnus, a, um *adj*, sevenfold
septemplex, ĭcis *adj*, seven-fold
septendĕcim *indecl. adj*, seventeen
septēni, ae, a *pl. adj*, seven each
septentrĭōnālis, um *m.pl*, the Great Bear, the North
septĭes *adv*, seven times
septĭmus, a, um *adj*, seventh
septingenti, ae, a *pl. adj*, seven hundred
septŭāgēsĭmus, a, um *adj*, seventieth
septŭāginta *indecl. adj*, seventy
septum see **saeptum**
sĕpulcrum, i *n*, grave, tomb
sĕpultūra, ae *f*, burial
sĕquax, ācis *adj*, pursuing
sĕquens, ntis *adj*, following
sĕquester, tris *m*, agent
sĕquor, sĕcūtus *v.i.t.* 3, *dep*, to follow, attend, pursue
sĕra, ae *f*, bolt, bar
sĕrēnĭtas, ātis *f*, fair weather
sĕrēno *v.t.* 1, to brighten
sĕrēnum, i *n*, fair weather

sĕrēnus, a, um *adj*, clear, fair, cheerful, glad
sērĭa, ōrum *n.pl*, serious matters
sērĭcus, a, um *adj*, silken
sĕrĭes, em, e *f*, row, series
sērĭus, a, um *adj*, serious
sermo, ōnis *m*, talk, conversation, common talk
sĕro, sēvi, sătum *v.t.* 3, to sow, plant, cause
sĕro, ŭi, sertum *v.t.* 3, to plait, join, connect, compose
sērò *adv*, late
serpens, ntis *f*, snake
serpo, psi, ptum *v.i.* 3, to crawl
serpyllum, i *n*, thyme
serra, ae *f*, saw
serrŭla, ae *f*, small saw
serta, ōrum *n.pl*, garlands
sērum, i *n*, whey
sērus, a, um *adj*, late
serva, ae *f*, maid-servant
servātor, ōris *m*, saviour
servīlis, e *adj, adv*, **ĭter**, of a slave, servile
servĭo *v.i.* 4, to be a servant, to be of use to
servītĭum, ii *n*, slavery, slaves
servĭtus, ūtis *f*, slavery, slaves
servo *v.t.* 1, to save, protect, preserve, keep, keep watch
servus, a, um *adj*, servile
servus, i *m*, slave, servant
sescēni, ae, a *pl. adj*, six hundred each
sescenti, ae, a *pl. adj*, six hundred
sescentĭes *adv*, six hundred times
sesquĭpĕdālis, e *adj*, one foot and a half long
sessĭo, ōnis *f*, sitting, session
sestertĭum 1,000 sestertii
sestertĭus, ii *m*, small silver coin (worth about 1 p.)
sēt... see **saet...**
seu *conj*, whether, or
sĕvērĭtas, ātis *f*, sternness
sĕvērus, a, um *adj, adv*, **ē**, stern, serious, harsh, gloomy
sēvŏco *v.t.* 1, to call aside
sex *indecl. adj*, six
sexāgēnārĭus, i *m*, sexagenarian
sexāgēni, ae, a *pl. adj*, sixty each
sexāgēsĭmus, a, um *adj*, sixtieth

sexāgǐes *adv*, sixty times
sexāginta *indecl. adj*, sixty
sexennǐum, ii *n*, six years
sextans, ntis *m*, a sixth part
sextārǐus, ii *m*, a pint
Sextīlis (mensis) August
sextus, a, um *adj*, sixth
sexus, ūs *m*, sex
sī *conj*, if
sǐbi *dat. of reflexive pron*, to himself, herself, itself, etc.
sībǐlo *v.i.t.* 1, to hiss; hiss at
sībǐlus, i *m*, hissing
sībylla, ae *f*, prophetess
sīc *adv*, so, in this way
sīca, ae *f*, dagger
sīcārǐus, ii *m*, assassin
siccǐtas, ātis *f*, dryness, firmness
sicco *v.t.* 1, to dry up, drain
siccum, i *n*, dry land
siccus, a, um *adj*, dry, firm, tough, thirsty, sober
sīcǔbǐ *adv*, if anywhere
sīcut (sīcǔti) *adv*, just as
sīděrěus, a, um *adj*, starry
sīdo, di *v.i.* 3, to sit down, settle, sink
sīdus, ěris *n*, star, sky, constellation, season, weather
sīgilla, ōrum *n.pl*, little figures or images
sīgillātus, a, um *adj*, figured
signǐfer, ěri *m*, standard-bearer
signǐfǐcātǐo, ōnis *f*, sign, mark
signǐfǐco *v.t.* 1, to show, notify
signǐfǐcans, antis *adj*, significant
signo *v.t.* 1, to mark out, seal, indicate
signum, i *n*, mark, sign, military standard, watchword, statue, constellation, symptom
sǐlens, ntis *adj*, still, quiet
sǐlentǐum, ii *n*, stillness, quietness
sǐlěo *v.i.t.* 2, to be silent; to keep quiet about
sǐlesco *v.i.* 3, to grow quiet
sǐlex, ǐcis *m*, flint-stone
sǐlus, a, um *adj*, snub-nosed
silva, ae *f*, wood, forest, grove, abundance
silvestrǐa, ǐum *n.pl*, woodlands
silvestris, e *adj*, woody, rural
silvǐcǒla, ae *adj*, living in woods

sīmǐa, ae *f*, ape
sīmǐlis, e *adj, adv*, **ǐter**, similar, like
sīmǐlǐtūdo, ǐnis *f*, resemblance
sīmǐus, ii *m*, ape
simplex, ǐcis *adj, adv*, **ǐter**, unmixed, simple, frank
simplǐcǐtas, ātis *f*, honesty
sǐmul *adv*, at once, together, at the same time, as soon as
sǐmǔlac *conj*, as soon as
sǐmǔlatque *conj*, as soon as
sǐmǔlācrum, i *n*, portrait, statue, phantom
sǐmǔlātǐo, ōnis *f*, pretence
sǐmǔlātor, ōris *m*, pretender
sǐmǔlātus, a, um *adj*, feigned
sǐmǔlo *v.t.* 1, to imitate, pretend
sǐmultas, ātis *f*, animosity
sīmus, a, um *adj*, snub-nosed
sīn *conj*, but if
sǐnāpi, is *n*, mustard
sincērǐtas, ātis *f*, cleanness, purity, entirety, sincerity
sincērus, a, um *adj, adv*, **ē**, clean, pure, genuine, entire, sincere
sǐně *prep. with abl*, without
singillātim *adv*, one by one
singǔlāris, e *adj*, single, solitary, unique, remarkable
singǔlātim see **singillātim**
singǔli, ae, a *pl. adj*, one each
singultim *adv*, with sobs
singultǐo *v.i.* 4, to hiccup
singulto (no perf.) *v.i.* 1, to sob
sinultus, ūs *m*, sobbing
sǐnister, tra, trum *adj*, left, awkward, wrong, unlucky, lucky
sǐnistra, ae *f*, left hand
sǐnistrorsus *adv*, to the left
sīno, sīvi, sǐtum *v.t.* 3, to allow
sǐnum, i *n*, drinking-cup
sǐnǔo *v.t.* 1, to bend, curve
sǐnǔōsus, a, um *adj*, curved
sǐnus, ūs *m*, curve, fold, bosom, lap, hiding-place, bay
sǐpho, ōnis *m*, siphon, syringe
sīquandō *adv*, if ever
sīquǐdem *adv*, if indeed
sīquis *pron*, if any
sīrēn, ēnis *f*, siren
sisto, stǐti, stǎtum *v.i.t* 3, to stand still, resist, hold out; put, place, bring, check, establish

sīstrum, i *n*, rattle

sĭtĭens, ntis *adj*, *adv*, **nter**, thirsty

sĭtĭo *v.i.t.* 4, to thirst; long for

sĭtis, is *f*, thirst, drought

sĭtŭla, ae *f*, bucket

sĭtus, a, um *adj*, situated

sĭtus, ūs *m*, position, site, rust, mould, inactivity

sīve *conj*, whether, or

smăragdus, i *c*, emerald

sŏbŏles, is *f*, sprout, twig, offspring

sōbrĭĕtas, ātis *f*, sobriety, temperance

sōbrīnus, i *m*, cousin

sōbrĭus, a, um *adj*, *adv*, **ē**, sober, moderate, sensible

soccus, i *m*, slipper

sŏcer, ĕri *m*, father-in-law

sŏcĭālis, e *adj*, allied

sŏcĭĕtas, ātis *f*, fellowship, partnership, alliance

sŏcĭo *v.t.* 1, to unite

sŏcĭus, ii *m*, companion, ally

sŏcĭus, a, um *adj*, allied

sōcordĭa, ae *f*, laziness, folly

sōcors, cordis *adj*, lazy, careless, stupid

socrus, ūs *f*, mother-in-law

sŏdālĭcĭum, ii *n*, secret society

sŏdālis, is *c*, companion

sŏdālĭtas, ātis *f*, friendship

sōdes if you wish

sōl, sōlis *m*, sun, sunshine

sōlācĭum, ii *n*, comfort, solace

sōlāmen, ĭnis *n*, consolation

sōlārĭum, ii *n*, sundial

sōlātĭum see **sōlācĭum**

soldūrĭi, ōrum *m.pl*, retainers of a chieftain

sŏlĕa, ae *f*, sandal, sole (fish)

sŏlĕātus, a, um *adj*, wearing sandals

sŏlĕo, sŏlĭtus *v.i.* 2, *semi-dep*, to be accustomed

sŏlĭdĭtas, ātis *f*, solidity

sŏlĭdo *v.t.* 1, to strengthen

sŏlĭdum, i *n*, a solid, solidity

sŏlĭdus, a, um *adj*, compact, complete, genuine, real

sōlĭtārĭus, a, um *adj*, alone

sōlĭtūdo, ĭnis *f*, loneliness, desert

sōlĭtus, a, um *adj*, usual

sŏlĭum, ii *n*, seat, throne

sollemnis, e *adj*, established, appointed, usual, religious

sollemne, is *n*, religious ceremony, sacrifice

sollers, tis *adj*, skilled

sollertĭa, ae *f*, skill, ingenuity

sollĭcĭtātĭo, ōnis *f*, instigation

sollĭcĭto *v.t.* 1, to stir up, molest, instigate

sollĭcĭtūdo, ĭnis *f*, anxiety

sollĭcĭtus, a, um *adj*, troubled

sōlor *v.t.* 1, *dep*, to comfort, relieve

solstĭtĭālis, e *adj*, of summer

solstĭtĭum, ii *n*, summer time

sŏlum, i *n*, bottom, base, floor, sole, soil, ground, country, place

sōlum *adv*, only

sōlus, a, um *adj*, alone, only, lonely, deserted

sŏlūtĭo, ōnis *f*, unloosing, payment, explanation

sŏlūtus, a, um *adj*, *adv*, **ē**, free, loose, independent

solvendum see **solvo**

solvo, solvi, sŏlūtum *v.t.* 3, to set free, dissolve, release, open up, pay, perform, fulfil, acquit; *with* **ancŏram** to sail

somnĭcŭlūsus, a, um *adj*, drowsy

somnĭfer, ĕra, ĕrum *adj*, sleep-bringing

somnĭfĭcus, a, um *adj* sleep-bringing

somnĭo *v.t.* 1, to dream

somnĭum, ii *n*, dream

somnus, i *m*, sleep

sŏnĭpēs, pĕdis *adj*, noisy-footed

sŏnĭtus, ūs *m*, noise, sound

sŏno, ŭi, ĭtum *v.i.t.* 1, to resound; call out, utter

sŏnor, ōris *m*, noise, sound

sŏnōrus, a, um *adj*, resounding

sons, ntis *adj*, guilty

sŏnus, i *m*, noise, sound

sŏphistes, ae *m*, philosopher

sōpĭo *v.t.* 4, to lull to sleep

sŏpor, ōris *m*, sleep

sŏpōrĭfer, ĕra, ĕrum *adj*, sleep-bringing

sŏpōro *v.t.* 1, to heat, stupefy

sŏpōrus, a, um *adj*, sleep-bringing

sorbĕo *v.t.* 2, to suck in

sordĕo *v.i.* 2, to be dirty, to be despised

sordes, is *f*, dirt, mourning dress, meanness

sordĭdātus, a, um *adj*, shabbily dressed (in mourning)

sordĭdĭus, a, um *adj*, *adv*, **ē**, dirty, despicable, mean

sŏror, ōris *f*, sister

sŏrōrĭus, a, um *adj*, of a sister

sors, tis *f*, chance, lot, drawing of lots, prophesy, fortune, share, destiny

sortĭor *v.i.t.* 4, *dep*, to draw lots; to appoint by lot, obtain by lot, choose

sortītĭo, ōnis *f*, drawing of lots

sortītō *adv*, by lot

sortītus, a, um *adj*, drawn by lot

sospĕs, ĭtis *adj*, safe, lucky

spādix, īcis *adj*, nut-brown

spargo, si, sum *v.t.* 3, to sprinkle, scatter, spread

spărus, i *m*, hunting spear

spasmus, i *m*, spasm

spătĭor *v.i.* 1, *dep*, to walk about

spătĭōsus, a, um *adj*, spacious

spătĭum, ii *n*, space, room, distance, walk, track, interval

spĕcĭes, ēi *f*, sight, view, shape, appearance, pretence, display, beauty

spĕcĭmen, ĭnis *n*, mark, sign, pattern

spĕcĭōsus, a, um *adj*, handsome, plausible

spectābĭlis, e *adj*, visible, remarkable

spectācŭlum, i *n*, show, spectacle

spectātĭo, ōnis *f*, sight

spectātor, ōris *m*, onlooker

spectātus, a, um *adj*, tested, respected

speco *v.t.* 1, to watch, face, examine, consider, refer

spectrum, i *n*, image

spĕcŭla, ae *f*, look-out point

spēcŭla, ae *f*, slight hope

spĕcŭlātor, ōris *m*, spy, scout

spĕcŭlor *v.t.* 1, *dep*, to watch, observe, explore

spĕcŭlum, i *n*, mirror

spĕcus, ūs *m*, cave, pit

spēlunca, ae *f*, cave, den

sperno, sprēvi, sprētum *v.t.* 3, to despise, scorn

spēro *v.t.* 1, to hope, expect

spes, spēi *f*, hope

sphaera, ae *f*, sphere

spīca, ae *f*, ear (of corn)

spīcĕus, a, um *adj*, made of ears of corn

spīcŭlum, i *n*, point, dart

spīna, ae *f*, thorn, spine, difficulties

spīnētum, i *n*, thorn-hedge

spīnōsus, a, um *adj*, thorny

spīnus, i *f*, sloe-tree

spīra, ae *f*, coil, twist

spīrābĭlis, e *adj*, breathable

spīrācŭlum, i *n*, air-hole

spīrāmentum, i *n*, air-hole

spīrĭtus, ūs *m*, breath, breeze, pride, arrogance, soul

spīro *v.i.t.* 1, to breathe, blow, live; exhale

spisso *v.t.* 1, to condense

spissus, a, um *adj*, thick, dense

splendĕo *v.i.* 2, to shine

splendesco *v.i.* 3, to become bright

splendĭdus, a, um *adj*, *adv*, **ē**, shining, magnificent, noble

splendor, ōris *m*, brilliance, excellence

spŏlĭa see **spŏlĭum**

spŏlĭātĭo, ōnis *f*, plundering

spŏlĭo *v.t.* 1, to plunder, rob

spŏlĭum, ii *n*, skin (of an animal); *in pl*, booty, spoils

sponda, ae *f*, couch, sofa

spondĕo, spŏpondi, sponsum *v.t.* 2, to promise, pledge, betroth, warrant

spongĭa, ae *f*, sponge

spongĭōsus, a, um *adj*, spongy

sponsa, ae *f*, bride

sponsālĭa, ĭum *n.pl*, betrothal

sponsĭo, ōnis *f*, promise, guarantee, security

sponsor, ōris *m*, surety

sponsum, i *n*, covenant

sponsus, a, um *adj*, promised

sponsus, i *m*, bridegroom

spontē (*abl.*) *f*, *with* **mĕā, sŭā**, *etc.*, voluntarily

sportella, ae *f*, fruit basket

sportŭla, ae *f*, little basket

spūma, ae *f*, froth, foam

spūmĕus, a, um *adj,* foaming
spūmĭfer, ĕra, ĕrum *adj,* foaming
spūmĭger, ĕra, ĕrum *adj,* foaming
spūmo *v.i.*1, to foam, froth
spūmōsus, a, um *adj,* foaming
spŭo, ŭi, ūtum *v.i.t.* 3, to spit
spūtum, i *n,* spit
spurcus, a, um *adj,* dirty
squālĕo *v.i.* 2, to be stiff or rough, to be neglected, filthy
squālĭdus, a, um *adj,* stiff, dirty, neglected
squālor, ōris *m,* filthiness
squāma, ae *f,* scale (of fish)
squāmĕus, a, um *adj,* scaly
squāmĭger, ĕra, ĕrum *adj,* scaly
squāmōsus, a, um *adj,* scaly
stăbĭlĭo *v.t.* 4, to fix
stăbĭlis, e *adj,* firm, steadfast
stăbĭlĭtas, ātis *f,* firmness
stăbŭlo *v.i.* (stăbŭlor, *v.i. dep,*) 1, to have a home, resting-place
stăbŭlum, i *n,* stable, hut
stădĭum, ii *n,* stade (distance of 200 yds./metres approx.), racecourse
stagnans, ntis *adj,* stagnant
stagno *v.i.* 1, to stagnate
stagnum, i *n,* pool, pond
stălagmĭum, i *n,* pendant
stāmen, ĭnis *n,* thread
stătārĭus, a, um *adj,* firm, calm,
stătim *adv,* immediately
stătĭo, ōnis *f,* post, station, outposts, sentries
stătīva, ōrum *n.pl,* permanent camp
stătīvus, a, um *adj,* stationary
stător, ōris *m,* messenger
stătŭa, ae *f,* statue
stătŭo, ŭi, ūtum *v.t.* 3, to set up, place, build, establish, settle, decide
stătūra, ae *f,* stature
stătus, ūs *m,* posture, position, condition, state, circumstance

stătus, a, um *adj,* fixed
stella, ae *f,* star
stellātus, a, um *adj,* starry
stellĭger, ĕra, ĕrum *adj,* starry
stellĭo, ōnis *n,* newt
stemma, ătis *n,* garland, pedigree
stercus, ŏris *n,* manure
stĕrĭlis, e *adj,* barren
stĕrĭlĭtas, ātis *f,* sterility
sternax, ācis *adj,* bucking (horse)
sterno, strāvi, strātum *v.t.* 3, to scatter, extend, smooth, arrange, cover, overthrow, pave
sternūmentum, i *n,* sneezing
sternŭo, ŭi *v.i.t.* 3, to sneeze
sterto, ŭi *v.i.* 3, to snore
stigma, ătis *n,* brand
stillĭcĭdĭum, ii *n,* dripping rain-water
stillo *v.i.t.* 1, to drip; distil
stīlus, i *m,* pen, style
stĭmŭlo *v.t.* 1, to torment, incite
stĭmŭlus, i *m,* goad, sting, incentive
stīpātor, ōris *m,* attendant
stīpendĭārĭus, a, um *adj,* tribute paying
stīpendĭum, ii *n,* tax, dues, pay, military service campaign
stīpes, ĭtis *m,* log, post
stīpo *v.t.* 1, to compress, surround, accompany
stips, stĭpis *f,* donation
stĭpŭla, ae *f,* stalk, stem
stĭpŭlātĭo, ōnis *f,* agreement
stĭpŭlor *v.i.t.* 1, *dep,* to bargain; demand
stīria, ae *f,* icicle
stirps, pis *f,* root, stem, plant, race, family
stīva, ae *f,* plough-handle
sto, stĕti, stătum *v.i.* 1, to stand, remain, endure, persist, cost

Insight

Verbs can be transitive or intransitive. **Intransitive** verbs do not require a direct object to complete their meaning (e.g. sto = I stand). In English such intransitive verbs can be used transitively as well, when they adopt a different meaning (e.g. I cannot stand that man).

stōīcus, a, um *adj,* stoic
stŏla, ae *f,* gown, robe
stŏlīdus, a, um *adj,* dull, stupid
stŏmăchor *v.i.* 1, *dep,* to be angry
stŏmăchōsus, a, um *adj,* irritable
stŏmăchus, i *m,* gullet, stomach, taste, distaste
stŏrĕa, ae *f,* straw mat
străbo, ōnis *m,* one who squints
străges, is *f,* destruction, massacre, slaughter
străgŭlum, i *n,* rug
străgŭlus, a, um *adj,* covering
strāmen, ĭnis *n,* straw
strāmentum, i *n,* straw
strāmĭnĕus, a, um *adj,* of straw
strangŭlo *v.t.* 1, to strangle
strătēgēma, ătis *n,* stratagem
strātum, i *n,* blanket, quilt, pillow, bed
strātus, a, um *adj,* stretched out
strēnŭus, a, um *adj, adv,* ē, brisk, quick, vigorous
strĕpĭto *v.i.* 1, to rattle
strĕpĭtus, ūs *m,* din
strĕpo, ŭi *v.i.* 3, to rattle, rumble, roar
strictim *adv,* briefly
strictūra, ae *f,* iron bar
strictus, a, um *adj,* tight
strīdĕo, si (strīdo, di 3) *v.i.* 2, to creak, hiss, rattle
strīdor, ōris *m,* creaking, hissing
strīdŭlus, a, um *adj,* creaking, hissing
strĭgĭlis, is *f,* scraper used by bathers for cleaning the skin
stringo, nxi, ctum *v.t.* 3, to draw tight, graze, strip off, draw (sword)
stringor, ōris *m,* touch, shock
strix, strĭgis *f,* screech owl
structor, ōris *m,* builder
structūra, ae *f,* construction
strŭes, is *f,* heap, pile
strŭo, xi, ctum *v.t.* 3, to pile up, build, contrive
strūthĭŏcămēlus, i *m,* ostrich
stŭdĕo *v.i.t.* 2, *with dat,* to be eager about, strive; pursue, favour
stŭdĭōsus, a, um *adj, adv,* ē, eager, anxious, friendly

stŭdĭum, ii *n,* eagerness, endeavour, affection, devotion, study
stultĭtĭa, ae *f,* foolishness
stultus, a, um *adj, adv,* ē, foolish
stūpa, ae *f,* flax, tow
stŭpĕfăcĭo, fēci, factum *v.t.* 3, to stun, daze
stŭpĕfactus, a, um *adj,* stunned
stŭpĕo *v.i.t.* 2, to be stunned, amazed; be astonished at
stŭpĕus, a, um *adj,* made of tow
stŭpĭdus, a, um *adj,* amazed
stŭpor, ōris *m,* astonishment, stupidity
stupp... see stūp...
stŭpro *v.t.* 1, to ravish
stŭprum, i *n,* disgrace, lewdness
sturnus, i *m,* starling
suādĕo, si, sum *v.i.t.* 2, *with dat,* to urge, persuade, recommend
suāsĭo, ōnis *f,* recommendation
suāsor, ōris *m,* adviser
suāvĭlŏquens, ntis *adj,* pleasant speaking
suāvĭor *v.t.* 1, *dep,* to kiss
suāvis, e *adj, adv,* ĭter, agreeable, pleasant
suāvĭtas, ătis *f,* pleasantness
suāvĭum, ii *n,* kiss
sub *prep. with acc. and abl,* under, beneath, near, during, towards, just after
sŭbactĭo, ōnis *f,* preparation
sŭbausculto *v.t.* 1, to eavesdrop
subcentŭrĭo, ōnis *m,* subaltern
subdĭtīvus, a, um *adj,* counterfeit
subdo, dĭdi, dĭtum *v.t.* 3, to place under, subdue
subdŏlus, a, um *adj,* crafty
subdūco, xi, ctum *v.t.* 3, to pull up, haul up, remove, calculate, balance (accounts)
sŭbĕo *v.i.t.* 4, to come up to, spring up, occur; enter, submit to, suffer, incur
sūber, ĕris *n,* cork tree
subflāvus, a, um *adj,* yellowish
sŭbĭcĭo, iēci, iectum *v.t.* 3, to throw or place under or near, counterfeit, subject, affix, prompt
subiectĭo, ōnis *f,* placing under, forging

subiecto *v.t.* 1, to throw up

subiectus, a, um *adj*, lying near, subject

sŭbĭgo, ēgi, actum *v.t.* 3, to bring up, plough, conquer, subdue, compel, rub down

sŭbinde *adv*, immediately, now and then

sŭbĭtō *adv*, suddenly

sŭbĭtus, a, um *adj*, sudden

subiungo, nxi, nctum *v.t.* 3, to subordinate, subdue

sublābor, lapsus *v.i.* 3, *dep*, to glide away

sublātus, a, um *adj*, proud

sublĕgo, lēgi, lectum *v.t.* 3, to gather up, kidnap

sublĕvo *v.t.* 1, to lift up, support, alleviate

sublĭca, ae *f*, stake, palisade

sublĭgo *v.t.* 1, to tie on

sublīme *adv*, aloft, on high

sublīmis, e *adj*, high, eminent

sublūcĕo *v.i.* 2, to glimmer

sublŭo (*no perf.*) **lūtum** *v.t.* 3, to flow along, wash

sublustris, e *adj*, glimmering

subm... see **summ...**

subnecto, xŭi, xum *v.t.* 3, to tie on underneath

subnixus, a, um *adj*, propped up

sŭbŏles, is *f*, offspring, race

sŭborno *v.t.* 1, to equip, fit out, instigate

subr... see **surr...**

subscrībo, psi, ptum *v.t.* 3, to write underneath, note down

subscriptĭo, ōnis *f*, anything written underneath

subsĕco, ŭi, ctum *v.t.* 1, to clip

subsellĭum, ii *n*, seat, law court

subsĕquor, sĕcūtus *v.i.t.* 3, *dep*, to follow, ensue; follow closely, imitate

subsīcīvus, a, um *adj*, remaining

subsĭdĭārĭus, a, um *adj*, reserve

subsĭdĭum, ii *n*, reserve-ranks, assistance, aid, protection

subsīdo, sēdi, sessum *v.i.t.* 3, to settle down, lie in anbush; waylay

subsisto, stĭti *v.i.* 3, to stop, halt, remain, withstand

subsortĭor *v.t.* 4, *dep*, to choose as a substitute

substerno, strāvi, strātum *v.t.* 3, to spread underneath, cover

substĭtŭo, ŭi, ūtum *v.t.* 3, to put under, substitute

substringo, nxi, ctum *v.t.* 3, to tie; **aurem** prick up the ear

substructĭo, ōnis *f*, foundation

substrŭo, xi, ctum *v.t.* 3, to lay foundations

subsum, esse *v*, *irreg*, to be under or near, to be at hand

subtēmen, ĭnis *n*, texture, weft

subter *adv. and prep. with abl*, beneath, below

subterfŭgĭo, fūgi *v.t.* 3, to avoid

subterlābens, ntis *adj*, gliding under

subterlābor *v.i.* 3, *dep*, to glide under

subterrānĕus, a, um *adj*, underground

subtexo, ŭi, xtum *v.t.* 3, to veil

subtīlis, e *adj, adv*, **ĭter**, slender, delicate, precise

subtīlĭtas, ātis *f*, exactness, subtlety

subtrăho, xi, ctum *v.t.* 3, to remove stealthily, carry off

sŭbūcŭla, ae *f*, shirt

sŭbulcus, i *m*, pig-keeper

sŭburbānus, a, um *adj*, suburban

sŭburbĭum, ii *n*, suburb

subvectĭo, ōnis *f*, conveyance

subvecto *v.t.* 1, to convey

subvĕho, xi, ctum *v.t.* 3, to convey

subvĕnĭo, vēni, ventum *v.i.* 4, *with dat*, to help, aid, occur to the mind

subverto, ti, sum *v.t.* 3, to overthrow

subvŏlo *v.i.* 1, to fly up

subvolvo *v.t.* 3, to roll up

succēdo, cessi, cessum *v.i.t.* 3, to go under, advance, enter; ascend, follow after, succeed

succendo, di, sum *v.t.* 3, to kindle

succensĕo, ŭi, sum *v.t.* 2, to be angry

successĭo, ōnis *f*, succession

successor, ōris *m*, successor

successus, ūs *m*, advance, success

succĭdo, di *v.i.* 3, to sink

succīdo, di, sum *v.t.* 3, to cut down

succingo, nxi, nctum *v.t.* 3, to surround, girdle, tuck up

succlāmo *v.t.* 1, to shout out

succumbo, cŭbŭi, cŭbĭtum *v.i.* 3, to surrender

succurro, curri, cursum *v.i.* 3, *with dat,* to help, aid, occur

sūcĭnum, i *n,* amber

sūcōsus, a, um *adj,* juicy

suctus, ūs *m,* sucking

sūcus, i *m,* energy, life

sūdārĭum, i *n,* handkerchief

sŭdis, is *f,* stake, pile

sūdo *v.i.t.* 1, to sweat, toil; exude

sūdor, ōris *m,* sweat, toil

suffulcĭo, fulsi, fultum *v.t.* 4, to prop up

suffūsus, a, um *adj,* spread over

suggĕro, gessi, gestum *v.t.* 3, to carry up, supply

suggestum, i *n,* platform

suggestus, ūs *m,* platform

sūgo, xi, ctum *v.t.* 3, to suck

sŭi *genit. of reflexive pron,* of himself, herself, itself etc.

sulco *v.t.* 1, to plough

sulcus, i *m,* furrow, ditch

sulfur, ūris *n,* sulphur

sulfūrāta, ōrum *n.pl,* matches

sulfūrĕus, a, um *adj,* sulphurous

sum, esse, fŭi *v, irreg,* to be, exist, happen

Insight

The **nominative** is the case of the subject of a sentence or clause as well as the case of the complement of a verb, especially the verb 'to be' (e.g. the king is angry = *rex iratus est*).

sūdum, i *n,* clear weather

sūdus, a, um *adj,* clear, bright

sŭesco, sŭēvi, sŭētum *v.i.t.* 3, to be accustomed

sŭētus, a, um *adj,* accustomed

suffĕro, ferre, sustŭli, sublātum *v, irreg,* to undergo, suffer

sufficĭo, fēci, fectum *v.i.t.* 3, to be sufficient; impregnate, supply, substitute, elect

suffīgo, xi, xum *v.t.* 3, to fix

suffīmentum, i *n,* incense

suffĭo *v.t.* 4, to perfume

sufflāmen, ĭnis *n,* drag-chain

sufflātus, a, um *adj,* puffed up

sufflo *v.t.* 1, to inflate

suffōco *v.t.* 1, to strangle

suffŏdĭo, fōdi, fossum *v.t.* 3, to pierce underneath

suffrāgātĭo, ōnis *f,* support

suffrāgātor, ōris *m,* supporter

suffrāgĭum, ii *n,* vote, ballot

suffrāgor *v.i.* 1, *dep, with dat,* to vote for, support

suffundo, fūdi, fūsum *v.t.* 3, to spread over, tinge

summa, ae *f,* top, chief, point, perfection, amount, sum

summātim *adv,* briefly

summē *adv,* extremely

summergo, si, sum *v.t.* 3, to submerge, overwhelm

summĭnistro *v.t.* 1, to supply

summissus, a, um *adj, adv,* ē, gentle, soft, low, mean

summitto, mīsi, missum *v.t.* 3, to send up, produce, rear, raise, lower, submit, supply, send

summŏvĕo, mōvi, mōtum *v.t.* 2, to drive away, remove

summus, a, um *adj,* highest, topmost

sūmo, mpsi, mptum *v.t.* 3, to take hold of, assume, inflict, choose, claim, suppose, spend, use, buy

sumptĭo, ōnis *f,* assumption

sumptŭōsus, a, um *adj, adv,* ē, expensive, lavish

sumptus, ūs *m,* expense

sŭo, sŭi, sūtum *v.t.* 3, to sew

sŭpellex, lectīlis *f,* furniture

sŭper *adv, and prep. with acc. and abl,* above, over, on, besides, concerning

sŭpĕrābĭlis, e *adj,* able to be overcome

sŭperbĭa, ae *f,* pride, arrogance

sŭperbĭo, *v.i.* 4, to be proud

sŭperbus, a, um *adj, adv,* ē, proud, haughty, delicate, squeamish, magnificent

sŭpercĭlĭum, ii *n,* eyebrow, ridge, summit, arrogance

sŭpercresco, crēvi *v.i.* 3, to grow up

sŭpĕrēmĭnĕo *v.t.* 2, to overtop

sŭperfĭcĭes, ēi *f,* top, surface

sŭperfundo, fūdi, fūsum *v.t.* 3, to pour over

sŭpĕri, ōrum *m.pl,* the gods

sŭpĕrimmĭnĕo *v.i.* 2, to overhang

sŭpĕrimpōno (*no perf.*) **posĭtum** *v.t.* 3, to place upon

sŭpĕrīnĭcĭo (*no perf.*), **iectum** *v.t.* 3, to throw over or upon

sŭperiăcĭo, iēci, iectum *v.t.* 3, to throw over, overflow

sŭpĕrĭor, ĭus *comp. adj,* higher, previous, former, superior

sŭperlātĭo, ōnis *f,* exaggeraton, hyperbole

sŭpernus, a, um *adj, adv,* ē, upper, on high ground

sŭpĕro *v.i.t.* 1, to have the upper hand, remain; ascend, outstrip, conquer

sŭpersĕdĕo, sēdi, sessum *v.i.t.* 2, *with abl,* to refrain (from)

sŭperstĕs, ĭtis *adj,* surviving

sŭperstĭtĭo, ōnis *f,* excessive fear of the gods

sŭperstĭtĭōsus, a, um *adj,* superstitious

sŭpersto *v.i.t.* 1, to stand over

sŭpersum, esse, fŭi *v.i, irreg,* to remain, survive

sŭpĕrus, a, um *adj,* upper, higher

sŭpervăcānĕus, a, um *adj,* unnecessary

sŭpervăcŭus, a, um *adj,* unnecessary

sŭpervĕnĭo, vēni, ventum *v.i.t.* 4, to come up, arrive; fall upon

sŭpervŏlo *v.i.t.* 1, to fly over

sūpīno *v.t.* 1, to bend backwards

sūpīnus, a, um *adj,* lying on the back, sloping

suppĕdĭto *v.i.t.* 1, to be enough, plenty; to supply

suppĕto, īvi, ītum *v.i.* 3, to be at hand, to be enough

supplanto *v.t.* 1, to trip up

supplēmentum, i *n,* reinforcements

supplĕo, ēvi, ētum *v.t.* 2, to complete, fill up

supplex, ĭcis *c,* suppliant

supplex, ĭcis *adj,* beseeching

supplĭcātĭo, ōnis *f,* public thanksgiving

supplĭcĭum, ii *n,* punishment

supplĭco *v.i.* 1, to implore

supplōdo, si *v.i.t.* 3, to stamp

suppōno, pŏsŭi, pŏsĭtum *v.t.* 3, to put under, substitute

supporto *v.t.* 1, to convey

supprĭmo, pressi, pressum *v.t.* 3, to sink, suppress

suppūro *v.i.* 1, to suppurate

sùprā *adv, and prep. with acc,* above, over, beyond, before

sùprēmus, a, um *adj,* highest, last

sūra, ae *f,* calf of the leg

surcŭlus, i *m,* shoot, twig

surdĭtas, ātis *f,* deafness

surdus, a, um *adj,* deaf

surgo, surrexi, rectum *v.i.t.* 3, to rise, stand up; raise

surrēgŭlus, i *m,* subordinate ruler

surrēmĭgo *v.i.* 1, to row along

surrēpo, psi, ptum *v.i.t.* 3, to creep under

surrīdĕo, si, sum *v.i.* 2, to smile

surrĭpĭo, ŭi, reptum *v.t.* 3, to snatch away, steal

surrŏgo *v.t.* 1, to substitute

surrŭo, ŭi, ŭtum *v.t.* 3, to undermine, overthrow

sursum *adv,* upwards, on high

sūs, sŭis *c,* pig

susceptĭo, ōnis *f,* undertaking

suscĭpĭo, cēpi, ceptum *v.t.* 3, to undertake, acknowledge, undergo

suscĭto *v.t.* 1, to raise, arouse

suspectus, a, um *adj,* mistrusted

suspectus, ūs *m,* height

suspendĭum, ii *n,* hanging

suspendo, di, sum *v.t.* 3, to hang up, lift up, keep in suspense, interrupt

suspensus, a, um *adj*, raised, hesitating

suspĭcĭo, spexi, ctum *v.i.t.* 3, to look up; admire, suspect

suspĭcĭo, ōnis *f*, suspicion

suspĭcĭōsus, a, um *adj, adv, ē,* suspicious

suspĭcor *v.t.* 1, *dep*, to suspect, suppose

suspīrĭtus, ūs *m*, sigh

suspīrĭum, ii *n*, sigh

suspīro *v.i.t.* 1, to sigh; long for

sustento *v.t.* 1, to support, maintain, endure

sustĭnĕo, ŭi, tentum *v.t.* 2, to support, restrain, withstand, maintain

sŭsurro *v.i.t.* 1, to hum; mutter

sŭsurrus, i *m*, humming

sŭsurrus, a, um *adj*, whispering

sūta, ōrum *n.pl*, joints

sūtĭlis, e *adj*, sewed together

sūtor, ōris *m*, cobbler

sūtōrĭus, a, um *adj*, of a cobbler

sūtūra, ae *f*, seam

sŭus, a, um *adj*, his, hers, its, their

sўcŏmŏrus, i *f*, sycamore

sўcŏphanta, ae *m*, sycophant, cheat

syllăba, ae *f*, syllable

syllăbātim *adv*, by syllables

symphōnĭa, ae *f*, harmony

symphōnĭăcus, i *m*, chorister

sўnăgōga, ae *f*, synagogue

syngrăpha, ae *f*, promissory note

syngrăphus, i *m*, passport

syntaxis, is *f*, syntax

T

tăbānus, i *m*, gadfly

tăbella, ae *f*, small board or table, writing-tablet, letter, ballot paper, small picture

tăbellārĭus, ii *m*, letter-bearer

tābĕo *v.i.* 2, to melt away

tăberna, ae *f*, hut, shop, inn

tăbernācŭlum, i *n*, tent

tăbernārĭus, ii *m*, shopkeeper

tābes, is *f*, wasting-away, disease

tābesco, bŭi *v.i.* 3, to melt away

tābĭdus, a, um *adj*, decaying

tābŭla, ae *f*, plank, writing-tablet, letter, account book, picture, painting, map, table

tăbŭlārĭa, ae *f*, record office

tăbŭlārĭum, ii *n*, archives

tăbŭlārĭus, ii *m*, registrar

tăbŭlātum, i *n*, floor, storey

tābum, i *n*, pus, matter, infectious disease

tăcĕo *v.i.t.* 2, to be silent; to be silent about

tăcĭturnĭtas, ātis *f*, silence

tăcĭturnus, a, um *adj*, silent

tăcĭtus, a, um *adj, adv, ē,* secret, silent

tactus, ūs *m*, touch, feel, influence

taeda, ae *f*, pine tree, torch

taedet, taedŭit *v.* 2, *impers, with acc. of person*, it offends, disgusts, wearies

taedĭum, ii *n*, weariness, disgust

taenĭa, ae *f*, hair ribbon

taeter, tra, trum *adj*, hideous

taetrĭcus, a, um *adj*, harsh

tālāris, e *adj*, ankle-length

tālĕa, ae *f*, stick, stake

tălentum, i *n*, sum of money (app. £400-£500); weight ($\frac{1}{2}$ cwt.)

tālĭo, ōnis *f*, similar punishment, reprisal

tālis, e *adj*, of such a kind

talpa, ae *f*, mole

tālus, i *m*, ankle bone, heel, die (marked on four sides)

tam *adv*, so, as, equally

tamdĭū *adv*, so long

tămen *adv*, nevertheless, however, still

tămetsi *conj*, although

tamquam *adv*, as much as, just as, as if, for example

tandem *adv*, at length

tango, tĕtĭgi, tactum *v.t.* 3, to touch, taste, reach, strike, affect, impress, mention

tanquam see **tamquam**

tantisper *adv*, so long, meanwhile

tantŏpĕre *adv*, so greatly

tantŭlus, a, um *adj*, so little

tantum   *adv*, so much, only

tantummŏdo   *adv*, only, merely

tantundem   *adv*, just as much

tantus, a, um   *adj*, so great; **tanti esse** to be worth so much; **tantō** by so much

tăpēte, is   *n*, tapestry

tardĭtas, ātis   *f*, slowness

tardo   *v.i.t.* 1, to delay; hinder

tardus, a, um   *adj, adv*, **ē**, slow

tăta, ae   *m*, dad, daddy

taurĕus, a, um   *adj*, of a bull

taurīnus, a, um   *adj*, of a bull

taurus, i   *m*, bull, ox

taxus, i   *f*, yew tree

tē   *acc. or abl. of* **tū**

tector, ōris   *m*, plasterer

tectōrĭum, ii   *n*, plaster

tectum, i   *n*, roof, house

tectus, a, um   *adj, adv*, **ō**, covered, hidden, secret

tĕges, ĕtis   *f*, mat

tĕgĭmen, ĭnis   *n*, cover

tĕgo, xi, ctum   *v.t.* 3, to cover, hide, protect

tĕgŭla, ae   *f*, tile

tĕgŭmen   see **tĕgĭmen**

tĕgŭmentum, i   *n*, cover

tēla, ae   *f*, web, warp, loom

tellūs, ūris   *f*, earth, globe, land, region

tēlum, i   *n*, weapon, javelin

tĕmĕrārĭus, a, um   *adj*, rash

tĕmĕrē   *adv*, by chance, rashly

tĕmĕrĭtas, ātis   *f*, rashness

tĕmĕro   *v.t.* 1, to defile, disgrace

tēmētum, i   *n*, wine

temno   *v.t.* 3, to despise

tēmo, ōnis   *m*, pole, beam

tempĕrans, ntis   *adj*, moderate

tempĕrantĭa, ae   *f*, moderation

tempĕrātĭo, ōnis   *f*, symmetry, temperament

tempĕrātus, a, um   *adj*, moderate

tempĕrĭes, ēi   *f*, mildness

tempĕro   *v.i.t.* 1, to abstain, be moderate, be indulgent; mix properly, regulate, govern

tempestas, ātis   *f*, time, period, weather, storm

tempestīvus, a, um   *adj, adv*, **ē**, suitable, timely, early

templum, i   *n*, temple, open space

tempto   see **tento**

tempus, ŏris   *n*, time, opportunity; **tempŏra** times, temples (of the head); **ad tempus** (*adv. phr.*)   at the right time, for the time being

tēmŭlentus, a, um   *adj*, drunk

tĕnācĭtas, ātis   *f*, tenacity

tĕnax, ācis   *adj*, holding tight, firm, stingy

tendo, tĕtendi, tentum   *v.i.t.* 3, to aim, go, march, stretch, strive, encamp; stretch, extend

tĕnèbrae, ārum   *f.pl*, darkness

tĕnèbrĭcōsus, a, um   *adj*, dark, gloomy

tĕnèbrōsus, a, um   *adj*, dark, gloomy

tĕnĕo, ŭi, tentum   *v.i.t.* 2, to hold a position, sail, continue; hold, have, keep, restrain, uphold, maintain, control, comprehend, include

tĕner, ĕra, ĕrum   *adj*, tender

tĕnor, ōris   *m*, course, career

tensa, ae   *f*, triumphal chariot

tentāmentum, i   *n*, attempt

tentātĭo, ōnis   *f*, trial, attempt

tentātor, ōris   *m*, tempter

tento (tempto)   *v.t.* 1, to handle, attack, attempt, tempt, excite

tentōrĭum, ii   *n*, tent

tentus, a, um   *adj*, extended

tĕnŭis, e   *adj, adv*, **ĭter**, thin, fine, meagre, poor, subtle

tĕnŭĭtas, ātis   *f*, slenderness, poverty

tĕnŭo   *v.t.* 1, to make thin, reduce, weaken, degrade

tĕnus   *prep. with abl*, as far as, according to

tĕpĕfăcĭo, fēci, factum   *v.t.* 3, to warm

tĕpĕo   *v.i.* 2, to be warm

tĕpesco, pŭi   *v.i.* 3, to grow warm

tĕpĭdus, a, um   *adj*, warmth

tĕr   *adv*, three times

tĕrĕbinthus, i   *f*, terebinth tree

tĕrĕbra, ae   *f*, tool

tĕrĕbor   *v.t.* 1, to bore through

tĕrĕs, ĕtis   *adj*, rounded, smooth, polished

tergĕmĭnus, a, um   *adj*, triple

tergĕo

tergĕo, si, sum   *v.t.* 2, to clean, polish

tergĭbersātĭo, ōnis   *f*, backsliding

tergĭversor   *v.i.* 1, *dep*, to shuffle, refuse

tergo, si, sum   see **tergĕo**

tergum, i   *n*, back, rear, skin; a tergo (*adv. phr.*)   at the rear

termĭnālĭa, ĭum   *n.pl*, festival of Terminus (God of boundaries)

termĭnātĭo, ōnis   *f*, fixing

termĭno   *v.t.* 1, to limit, fix, define, determine, end

termĭnus, i   *m*, boundary, end

terni, ae, a   *pl. adj*, three each

tĕro, trīvi, trītum   *v.t.* 3, to rub, grind, smooth, polish, wear out, spend or waste time

terra, ae   *f*, earth, land, ground, region

terrēnus, a, um   *adj*, made of earth, terrestrial

terrĕo   *v.t.* 2, to frighten

terrestris, e   *adj*, of earth or land

terrĕus, a, um   *adj*, of earth or land

terrĭbĭlis, e   *adj*, dreadful

terrĭcŭla, ōrum   *n.pl*, scarecrow bugbear

terrĭfico   *v.t.* 1, to terrify

terrĭfĭcus, a, um   *adj*, frightful

terrĭgĕna, ae   *c*, earthborn

terrĭto   *v.t.* 1, to terrify

terror, ōris   *m*, terror, dread

tertĭus, a, um   *adj, adv*, ō, third

tĕruncĭus, ii   *m*, trifling sum

tessellātus, a, um   *adj*, tesselated, mosaic

tessĕra, ae   *f*, stone or wooden cube, die, watchword, ticket

testa, ae   *f*, jug, broken piece of pottery, shell-fish

testāmentum, i   *n*, will, testament

testātor, ōris *m*, testator

testātus, a, um   *adj*, manifest

testĭfĭcātĭo, ōnis   *f*, evidence

testĭfĭcor   *v.t.* 1, *dep*, to give evidence, demonstrate

testĭmōnĭum, ii   *n*, evidence

testis, is   *c*, witness

testor   *v.t.* 1, *dep*, to call a witness, prove, declare

testu(m), i   *n*, lid, earthen pot

testūdĭnĕus, a, um   *adj*, of a tortoise

testūdo, ĭnis   *f*, tortoise, lute, military shelter

tĕtānus, i   *m*, tetanus

tēter, tra, trum   *adj*, hideous

tĕtrarches, ae   *m*, petty princeling

tĕtrĭcus, a, um   *adj*, harsh

texo, ŭi, xtum   *v.t.* 3, to weave, build, devise

textĭle, is   *n*, fabric

textĭlis, e   *adj*, woven

textor, ōris   *m*, weaver

textum, i   *n*, web, fabric

textus, ūs   *m*, texture

thălămus, i   *m*, apartment, bedroom, marriage

thĕātrālis, e   *adj*, theatrical

thĕātrum, i   *n*, theatre

thēca, ae   *f*, envelope

thĕŏlŏgĭa, ae   *f*, theology

thĕŏlŏgus, i   *m*, theologian

thĕŏrēma, ătis   *n*, theorem

thermae, ārum   *f.pl*, warm baths

thēsaurus, i   *m*, store, hoard, treasure, treasure house

thĭăsus, i   *m*, dance in honour of Bacchus

thŏlus, i   *m*, dome

thōrax, ācis   *m*, breastplate

thunnus, i   *m*, tunny fish

thūs, thūris   *n*, incense

thymbra, ae   *f*, savory (plant)

thymum, i   *n*, thyme

thyrsus, i   *m*, stem of plant, staff carried by Bacchus

tĭāra, ae   *f*, tiara

tībĭa, ae   *f*, flute

tībĭāle, is   *n*, stocking

tībīcen, ĭnis   *m*, flute-player

tībīcĭna, ae   *f*, flute-player

tībīcĭnĭum, ii   *n*, flute-playing

tignum, i   *n*, timber, log

tīgris, is (ĭdis)   *c*, tiger

tīlĭa, ae   *f*, linden or lime tree

tĭmĕo   *v.i.t.* 2, to fear

tĭmĭdĭtas, ātis   *f*, cowardice

tĭmĭdus, a, um   *adj, adv*, ē, afraid, cowardly

tĭmor, ōris   *m*, fear, alarm, object of fear

tĭnĕa, ae   *f*, moth, bookworm

tingo, nxi, nctum   *v.t.* 3, to moisten, dye

tinnĭo   *v.i.t.* 4, to ring; tinkle
tinnītus, ūs   *m*, ringing
tinnŭlus, a, um   *adj*, tinkling
tintinnābŭlum, i   *n*, bell
tīro, ōnis   *m*, recruit, novice
tīrōcĭnĭum, ii   *n*, first campaign, inexperience
tītillātĭo, ōnis   *f*, tickling
tītillo   *v.t.* 1, to tickle
tītŭbo   *v.i.* 1, to stagger, hesitate, be perplexed
tītŭlus, i   *m*, title, placard, notice, honour, glory
tōfus, i   *m*, tufa (rock)
tŏga, ae   *f*, toga the long outer garment of the Romans
tŏgātus, a, um   *adj*, wearing the toga
tŏlĕrābĭlis, e   *adj*, endurable
tŏlĕrantĭa, ae   *f*, tolerance
tŏlĕro   *v.t.* 1, to bear, endure
tollēno, ōnis   *m*, a swing-beam
tollo, sustŭli, sublātum   *v.t.* 3, to lift, raise, remove, destroy, educate, acknowledge
tŏnans, ntis   *m*, god of thunder
tondĕo, tŏtondi, tonsum   *v.t.* 2, to shave, crop, prune, graze
tŏnĭtrus, ūs   *m*, thunder
tŏnĭtrŭum, i   *n*, thunder
tŏno, ŭi   *v.i.t.* 1, to thunder; thunder out
tonsa, ae   *f*, oar
tonsillae, ārum   *f.pl*, tonsils
tonsor, ōris   *m*, barber
tonsōrĭus, a, um   *adj*, of shaving
tonsūra, ae   *f*, shearing
tŏpĭārĭus, ii   *m*, landscape gardener
tŏreuma, ătis   *n*, embossed work
tormentum, i   *n*, missile, rope, missile-launcher, instrument of torture, rack, pain
tormĭna, um   *n.pl*, the gripes
torno   *v.t.* 1, to round off
tornus, i   *m*, lathe
tŏrōsus, a, um,   *adj*, muscular
torpĕfăcĭo, fēci, factum   *v.t.* 3, to numb
torpens, ntis   *adj*, numb
torpĕo   *v.i.* 2, to be stiff, numb, sluggish, listless
torpesco, pŭi   *v.i.* 3, to become stiff or listless

torpor, ōris   *m*, numbness
torquātus, a, um   *adj*, wearing a collar
torquĕo, torsi, sum   *v.t.* 2, to twist, bend, wield, hurl, rack, torture
torquis (torques), is   *m, f*, collar, necklace, wreath
torrens, ntis   *adj*, burning
torrens, ntis   *m*, torrent
torrĕo, ŭi, tostum   *v.t.* 2, to dry, bake, scorch, burn
torrĭdus, a, um   *adj*, parched
torris, is   *m*, firebrand
tortīlis, e   *adj*, twined
tortor, ōris   *m*, torturer
tortŭōsus, a, um   *adj*, winding, complicated
tortus, a, um   *adj*, twisted
tortus, ūs   *m*, twisting
tŏrus, i   *m*, muscle, knot, cushion, sofa, bed
torvus, a, um   *adj*, wild, grim
tŏt   *indecl. adj*, so many
tŏtĭdem   *indecl. adj*, just as many
tŏtĭens (tŏtĭes)   *adv*, so often
tōtum, i   *n*, whole
tōtus, a, um   *adj*, the whole
trăbālis, e   *adj*, of a beam
trăbĕa, ae   *f*, robe of state
trabs, trăbis   *f*, beam, timber, tree, ship
tractābĭlis, e   *adj*, manageable, pliant, flexible
tractātĭo, ōnis   *f*, handling, treatment
tractātus, ūs   *m*, handling, treatment
tractim   *adv*, little by little
tracto   *v.t.* 1, to handle, manage, practise, discuss, drag
tractus, ūs   *m*, dragging, track, district, course, progress
trādĭtĭo, ōnis   *f*, surrender
trādo, dĭdi, dĭtum   *v.t.* 3, to hand over, commit, bequeath, relate
trādūco, xi, ctum   *v.t.* 3, to bring over, degrade, spend (time)
trāductĭo, ōnis   *f*, transferring
trăgĭcus, a, um   *adj*, tragic, fearful, grand
trăgoedĭa, ae   *f*, tragedy
trăgoedus, i   *m*, tragic actor

trāgŭla, ae *f*, javelin, dart

trăhĕa, ae *f*, sledge

trăho, xi, ctum *v.t.* 3, to drag, extract, inhale, quaff, drag away, plunder, spin, influence, delay, protract

trāĭcĭo, iēci, iectum *v.t.* 3, to throw across, transport, transfix

trāiectĭo, ōnis *f*, crossing over, passage

trāiectus, ūs *m*, crossing

trāmĕs, ĭtis *m*, footpath, way

trāno *v.t.* 1, to swim across

tranquillĭtas, ātis *f*, calmness

tranquillo *v.t.* 1, to calm

tranquillum, i *n*, a calm

tranquillus, a, um *adj, adv*, **ē**, calm, placid, serene

trans *prep. with acc*, across, beyond, on the further side of

transăbĕo *v.t.* 4, to transfix

transădĭgo, ēgi, actum *v.t.* 3, to thrust through

transalpīnus, a, um *adj*, beyond the Alps

transcendo, si, sum *v.i.t.* 3, to climb over, surmount; exceed

transcrībo, psi, ptum *v.t.* 3, to transcribe, forge, transfer

transcurro, curri, cursum *v.i.t.* 3, to run across; pass through

transĕo *v.i.t.* 4, to go over or across, pass by, surpass

transfĕro, ferre, tŭli, lātum *v.t, irreg*, to bring across, carry along, transfer, translate

transfīgo, xi, xum *v.t.* 3, to pierce through

transfŏdĭo, fōdi, fossum *v.t.* 3, to pierce through

transformo *v.t.* 1, to transform

transfŭga, ae *c*, deserter

transfŭgĭo, fūgi *v.t.* 3, to desert

transfundo, fūdi, fūsum *v.t.* 3, to transfer

transgrĕdĭor, gressus *v.i.t.* 3, *dep*, to pass or climb over, across

transgressĭo, ōnis *f*, passage

transĭgo, ēgi, actum *v.t.* 3, to complete, transact, settle (a difference)

transĭlĭo, ŭi *v.i.t.* 4, to leap across

transĭtĭo, ōnis *f*, going over, passage

transĭtus, ūs *m*, going over, passage

translātīcĭus, a, um *adj*, handed down

translātĭo, ōnis *f*, transferring

translātus, a, um *adj*, transferred, copied, figurative

translūcĕo *v.i.* 2, to shine through

transmārīnus, a, um *adj*, across to sea

transmĭgro *v.i.* 1, to migrate

transmissus, ūs *m*, transferring

transmitto, mīsi, missum *v.i.t.* 3, to go across; send across, transfer, hand over

transmūto *v.t.* 1, to change

transnăto *v.i.* 1, to swim over

transpădānus, a, um *adj*, beyond the river Po

transporto *v.t.* 1, to carry across

transtrum, i *n*, rowing-bench

transvĕho, xi, ctum *v.t.* 3, to carry over

transverbĕro *v.t.* 1, to transfix

transversārĭus, a, um *adj*, crosswise

transversus, a, um *adj*, crosswise

transvŏlo *v.i.t.* 1, to fly across

trĕcēni, ae, a *pl. adj*, three hundred each

trecentensĭmus, a, um *adj*, three hundredth

trĕcenti, ae, a *pl, adj*, three hundred

trēdĕcim *indecl. adj*, thirteen

trĕmĕbundus, a, um *adj*, trembling

trĕmĕfăcĭo, fēci, factum *v.t.* 3, to cause to tremble

trĕmendus, a, um *adj*, dreadful

trĕmesco *v.i.t.* 3, to tremble; tremble at

trĕmo, ŭi *v.i.t.* 3, to tremble; tremble at

trĕmor, ōris *m*, shuddering

trĕmŭlus, a, um *adj*, trembling

trĕpĭdans, ntis *adj*, trembling

trĕpĭdātĭo, ōnis *f*, confusion

trĕpĭdo *v.i.t.* 1, to be alarmed; tremble at

trĕpīdus, a, um   *adj*, alarmed
trēs, trĭa   *adj*, three

trĭfaux, cis   *adj*, with three throats
trĭdīdus, a, um   *adj*, three-forked

Insight

The **accusative** is the usual case of a direct object. Many prepositions take the accusative; in that case the meaning of the accusative depends on the preposition. The accusative case is also used to express time throughout (tres dies = for three days) and the extent of space and its measurement (*tria milia passum* = for three miles).

trĭangŭlum, i   *n*, triangle
trĭangŭlus, a, um   *adj*, triangular
trĭārĭī, ōrum   *m.pl*, veteran soldiers who fought in the third rank
trĭbŭārĭus, a, um   *adj*, of a tribe
trĭbūlis, e   *adj*, of the same tribe
trĭbŭlum, i   *n*, threshing-platform
trĭbŭlus, i   *m*, thistle
trĭbūnal, ālis   *n*, platform, judgement seat
trĭbūnātus, ūs   *m*, position of tribune
trĭbūnĭcĭus, a, um   *adj*, of a tribune
trĭbūnus, i   *m*, tribune; 1. army officer; 2. magistrate to defend to defend the rights of the people
trĭbŭo, ŭi, ūtum   *v.t.* 3, to allot, give, attribute
trĭbus, ūs   *f*, tribe
trĭbus   see trēs
trĭbūtim   *adv*, by tribes
trĭbūtum, i   *n*, tribute, tax
trīcae, ārum   *f. pl*, tricks
trīcēni, ae, a   *pl. adj*, thirty each
trīceps, cĭpĭtis   *adj*, three-headed
trīcēsĭmus, a, um   *adj*, thirtieth
trīcĭes   *adv*, thirty times
trīclīnĭum, i   *n*, dining-couch, dining-room
trĭcorpor, ŏris   *adj*, three-bodied
trĭdens, ntis   *adj*, three-pronged; as   *nn*, trident
trīdŭum, i   *n*, three days
trĭennĭum, i   *n*, three years
trĭens, ntis   *m*, a third part
trĭĕtērĭca, ōrum   *n.pl*, festival of Bacchus

trĭfŏlĭum, i   *n*, shamrock
trĭformis, e   *adj*, three-fold
trĭgĕmĭnus, a, um   *adj*, triple
trĭgēsĭmus, a, um   *adj*, thirtieth
trīginta   *indecl. adj*, thirty
trĭgōn, ōnis   *m*, ball
trĭlībris, e   *adj*, weighing three pounds
trĭlinguis, e   *adj*, three-tongued
trĭlix, īcis   *adj*, with three thongs
trīmestris, e   *adj*, of three months
trīmus, a, um   *adj*, three years old
trīni, ae, a   *pl. adj*, three each
trīnōdis, e   *adj*, three-knotted
trĭōnes, um   *m.pl*, constellation of the Great and Lesser Bear
trĭpertītus, a, um   *adj, adv*, ō, threefold
trĭpēs, ĕdis   *adj*, three-footed
trĭplex, ĭcis   *adj*, triple
trĭplĭco   *v.t.* 1, to treble
trĭpŭdĭum, ii   *n*, religious dance, favourable omen
trĭpūs, ŏdis   *m*, tripod
trĭquĕtrus, a, um   *adj*, triangular
trīrēmis, e   *adj*, with three banks of oars
tristis, e   *adj*, sad, gloomy, harsh, disagreeable
tristĭtĭa, ae   *f*, sadness, gloominess, harshness
trĭsulcus, a, um   *adj*, three-forked
trītĭcĕus, a, um   *adj*, of wheat
trītĭcum, i   *n*, wheat
trītūra, ae   *f*, threshing (of grain)
trītus, a, um   *adj*, beaten, common, worn, familiar
trĭumphālis, e   *adj*, triumphal

trĭumpho *v.i.t.* 1, to celebrate a triumph; triumph over

trĭumphus, i *m*, triumphal procession after a victory

trĭumvĭrātus, ūs *m*, triumvirate

trĭumvĭri, ōrum *m.pl*, board of three men

trĭvĭum, ii *n*, crossroad

trŏchaeus, i *m*, metrical foot

trochlĕa, ae *f*, pulley

trŏchus, i *m*, hoop

trŏpaeum, i *n*, trophy, victory

trŏpĭcus, a, um *adj*, tropical

trŭcīdātĭo, ōnis *f*, butchery

trŭcīdo *v.t.* 1, to slaughter

trŭcŭlentus, a, um *adj*, harsh

trŭdis, is *f*, pole, pike

trŭdo, si, sum *v.t.* 3, to push, drive, put out

trulla, ae *f*, ladle

truncātus, a, um *adj*, maimed

trunco *v.t.* 1, to maim, cut off

truncus, a, um *adj*, maimed

truncus, i *m*, trunk, stem

trŭtĭna, ae *f*, pair of scales

trux, ŭcis *adj*, harsh, stern

tū *pron*, you (singular)

tŭba, ae *f*, trumpet

tŭber, ĕris *n*, swelling, tumour

tŭbĭcen, ĭnis *m*, trumpeter

tŭbŭlātus, a, um *adj*, tubular

tŭbŭlus, i *m*, tube

tŭĕor *v.t.* 2, *dep*, to look at, gaze at, consider, guard, maintain, support

tŭgŭrĭum, i *n*, cottage

tŭli see **fero**

tum *adv, and conj*, then

tŭmĕfăcio, fēci, factum *v.t.* 3, to cause to swell

tŭmĕo *v.i.* 2, to swell, be puffed up

tŭmesco, mui *v.i.* 3, to become swollen, be puffed up

tŭmĭdus, a, um *adj*, swollen, excited, enraged

tŭmor, ōris *m*, swelling, commotion

tŭmŭlo *v.t.* 1, to bury

tŭmultŭārĭus, a, um *adj*, hurried, hurriedly raised (troops)

tŭmultŭor *v.i.* 1, *dep*, to be confused

tŭmultŭōsus, a, um *adj, adv, ē*, restless, confused, turbulent

tŭmultus, ūs *m*, uproar, tempest, rebellion

tŭmŭlus, i *m*, hill, mound

tunc *adv*, then

tundo, tŭtŭdi, tunsum (tusum) *v.t.* 3, to beat, strike, pound

tŭnĭca, ae *f*, tunic, husk

tŭnĭcātus, a, um *adj*, dressed in a tunic

tŭnĭcopallĭum, i *n*, short cloak

tūrārĭus, ii *m*, a dealer

turba, ae *f*, hubbub, uproar, crowd, band, quarrel, confusion

turbātor, ōris *m*, disturber

turbātus, a, um *adj*, disturbed

turbĭdus, a, um *adj, adv, ē*, confused, troubled, violent

turbo *v.t.* 1, to confuse, disturb, make thick

turbo, ĭnis *m*, hurricane, spinning top, revolution

turbŭlentus, a, um *adj, adv, nter*, restless, boisterous, troublesome

turdus, i *m*, thrush

tūrĕus, a, um *adj*, of incense

turgĕo, rsi *v.i.* 2, to swell

turgesco *v.i.* 3, to swell up

turgĭdŭlus, a, um *adj*, swollen

turgĭdus, a, um *adj*, swollen

tūrĭbŭlum, i *n*, incense-vessel

tūrĭcrĕmus, a, um *adj*, for burning incense

tūrĭfer, ĕra, ĕrum *adj*, incense-producing

turma, ae *f*, cavalry troop, crowd

turmālis, e *adj*, of a squadron

turmātim *adv*, by squadrons

turpis, e *adj, adv, ĭter*, filthy, ugly, disgraceful, scandalous

turpĭtūdo, ĭnis *f*, disgrace, baseness

turbo *v.t.* 1, to pollute, soil

turrĭger, ĕra, ĕrum *adj*, turreted

turris, is *f*, tower

turrītus, a, um *adj*, turreted

turtur, ŭris *m*, turtle-dove

tūs, tūris *n*, incense

tussĭo *v.i.* 4, to cough

tussis, is *f*, cough

tūtāmen, ĭnis *n*, defence

tūtēla, ae *f*, safeguard, defence, position of guardian, object under guardianship

tūtō *adv*, safely
tūtor ōris *m*, guardian
tūtor *v.t.* 1, *dep*, to guard, watch
tūtus, a, um *adj*, safe, prudent
tŭus, a, um *adj*, your(s)
tympănum, i *n*, tambourine, door panel
tўrannĭcus, a, um *adj*, tyrannical
tўrannis, ĭdis *f*, despotic rule
tўrannus, i *m*, sovereign, ruler, despot

U

ūber, ĕris *n*, teat, udder, breast
ūber, ĕris *adj*, fertile, rich
ūbertas, ātis *f*, fertility, richness
ŭbĭ *adv*, where, when, as soon as
ŭbĭcumque *adv*, wherever
ŭbīque *adv*, everywhere, anywhere
ŭbĭvīs *adv*, everywhere, anywhere
ūdus, a, um *adj*, moist, wet
ulcĕrātĭo, ōnis *f*, ulceration
ulcĕro *v.t.* 1, to make sore
ulcĕrōsus, a, um *adj*, ulcerous
ulciscor, ultus *v.t.* 3, *dep*, to avenge, punish, take vengeance on
ulcus, ĕris *n*, sore, ulcer
ulex, ĭcis *m*, furze
ūlīgĭnōsus, a, um *adj*, moist, marshy
ūlīgo, ĭnis *f*, moisture
ullus, a, um *adj*, (*genit*, **ullīus**, *dat*, **ulli**), any
ulmĕus, a, um *adj*, of elm
ulmus, i *f*, elm tree
ulna, ae *f*, elbow, arm, ell
ultĕrĭor, ĭus *comp. adj*, beyond, on the farther side
ultĕrĭus *comp. adv*, beyond, farther
ultĭmus, a, um *sup. adj*, farthest, extreme, last
ultĭo, ōnis *f*, revenge
ultor, ōris *m*, avenger
ultrā *adv, and prep. with acc*, beyond, past, farther, besides
ultrix, īcis *adj*, avenging
ultrō *adv*, on the other side, moreover, spontaneously

ŭlŭla, ae *f*, screech owl
ŭlŭlātus, ūs *m*, wailing
ŭlŭlo *v.i.t.* 1, to howl; cry out to
ulva, ae *f*, sedge
umbella, ae *f*, parasol
umbĭlīcus, i *m*, navel, centre, end of rod on which Roman books were rolled
umbo, ōnis *m*, shield, knob
umbra, ae *f*, shadow, shade, ghost, trace, shelter
umbrācŭlum, i *n*, shady spot, school
umbrātĭlis, e *adj*, private, retired
umbrĭfer, ĕra, ĕrum *adj*, shady
umbro *v.t.* 1, to shade, cover
umbrōsus, a, um *adj*, shady
ūmecto *v.t.* 1, to moisten
ūmĕo *v.i.* 2, to be damp
ūmĕrus, i *m*, shoulder, arm
ūmesco *v.i.* 3, to grow wet
ūmĭdus, a, um *adj*, wet, damp
ūmor, ōris *m*, moisture, liquid
umquam *adv*, ever
ūnā *adv*, at the same time, in the same place, together
ūnănĭmus, a, um *adj*, of one mind
ūnănĭmĭtas, ātis *f*, unanimity
uncĭa, ae *f*, a twelfth, ounce
unctĭo, ōnis *f*, anointing
unctus, a, um *adj*, oiled, rich, luxurious
uncus, i *m*, hook
uncus, a, um *adj*, hooked
unda, ae *f*, wave, tide
undĕ *adv*, from where, whence
undē ... (with number)   one from ... e.g. **undēvigint i** (one from 20) 19
undĕcĭes *adv*, eleven times
undĕcĭm *indecl. adj*, eleven
undĕcĭmus, a, um *adj*, eleventh
undēni, ae, a *pl. adj*, eleven each
undĭquĕ *adv*, from all sides, everywhere
undo *v.i.* 1, to surge, undulate
undōsus, a, um *adj*, billowy
ungo (unguo), unxi, unctum *v.t.* 3, to besmear, oil
unguen, ĭnis *n*, ointment
unguentārĭus, ii *m*, perfume seller
unguentum, i *n*, ointment, perfume

unguis

unguis, is *m*, finger or toe nail
ungŭla, ae *f*, hoof, claw
ungo (3) see **ungo**
ūnĭcŏlor, ōris *adj*, of one colour
ūnĭcus, a, um *adj, adv*, ē, only, single, singular, unique
ūnĭo, ōnis *m, f*, unity
ūnĭversĭtas, ātis *f*, universe
ūnĭversum, i *n*, whole world
ūnĭversus, a, um *adj, adv*, ē, entire, all together
unquam *adv*, ever
ūnus, a, um *adj*, one, one only

urna, ae *f*, water-jar, urn (for voting tablets or ashes of the dead)
ūro, ussi, ustum *v.t.* 3, to burn, destroy by fire, scorch, nip with cold
ursa, ae *f*, she-bear
ursus, i *m*, bear
urtīca, ae *f*, nettle
ūrus, i *m*, wild fox
ūsĭtātus, a, um *adj*, usual
uspĭam *adv*, anywhere, somewhere

Insight

Cardinal **numbers** (4 to 100) do not decline except *unus* (= one), *duo* (= two) and *tres* (= three) which have their own declensions; numbers 200 to 900 decline like first-and-second-declension plural adjectives. *Mille* (= 1,000) does not decline but *milia* is a third declension noun. Ordinals decline like first-and-second-declension adjectives.

ūnusquisque *pron.* each
ūpĭlĭo, ōnis *m*, shepherd
urbānĭtas, ātis *f*, city life, elegance, courtesy, refinement
urbānus, a, um *adj, adv*, ē, of the city, refined, elegant, courteous, humorous
urbs, urbis *f*, city
urcĕus, i *m*, water jug
urgĕo, ursi *v.t.* 2, to press, push, oppress, urge, crowd
ūrīna, ae *f*, urine
ūrīnātor, ōris *m*, diver

usquam *adv*, anywhere
usquĕ *adv*, all the way, all the time, as far as, until
ustor, ōris *m*, corpse-burner
ūsūra, ae *f*, money-lending, interest
ūsurpātĭo, ōnis *f*, using, use
ūsurpo *v.t.* 1, to use, practise, exercise, acquire
ūsus, ūs *m*, using, use, practice, custom, habit, familiarity, advantage
ut (ŭti) *conj*, as, so that, that, in order to, to; *adv*, now as, when, as soon as; where

---

Insight

The conjunction **ut** can be used in several senses: *ut* + *indicative* means 'as', 'when'; *ut* + *subjunctive* is used in indirect commands, as a result (e.g. so...that) or as a purpose (e.g. in order to...). *Ut* (= as) can also be used to qualify a noun.

152

utcumquĕ (utcunquĕ) *adv*, in whatever way, however, whenever

ūter, tris *m*, bottle, bag

ūter, tra, trum *interr. pron*, which of the two

ūtercumquĕ, utrăcumque, utrumcumque *pron*, whichever of the two

ūterlībet, utrălībet, utrumlībet *pron*, which of the two you please

ūterque, utrăque, utrumque *pron*, each of the two, both

ūtĕrus, i *m*, womb, belly

ūtervīs, utrăvīs, utrumvīs *pron*, which of the two you please

ŭti see ut

ūti see ūtor

ūtĭlis, e *adj, adv*, **ĭter**, useful, suitable, advantageous

ūtĭlĭtas, ātis *f*, usefulness, advantage

ŭtĭnam *adv*, if only! would that!

ūtĭquĕ *adv*, at any rate, at least, certainly

ūtor, ūsus *v. 3, dep, with abl*, to use, practise, be familiar with

V

văcans, ntis *adj*, unoccupied

văcātĭo, ōnis *f*, exemption

vacca, ae *f*, cow

vaccīnĭum, ii *n*, whortleberry

văcĭllātĭo, ōnis *f*, vacillation

văcĭllo *v.i.* 1, to stagger, sway, hesitate

văco *v.i.* 1, to be empty, free from, have leisure (for)

văcŭĕfăcĭo, fēci, factum *v.t.* 3, to empty, clear

văcŭĭtas, ātis *f*, exemption

văcŭus, a, um *adj*, empty, free, without, unoccupied, worthless

vădīmōnĭum, i *n*, bail, security

vādo *v.i.* 3, to go, walk, rush

vādor *v.t.* 1, *dep*, to bind over by bail

vădōsus, a, um *adj*, shallow

vădum, i *n*, a shallow ford (*often in pl.*)

vae *interj*, ah! alas!

văfer, fra, frum *adj*, sly

văgātĭo, ōnis *f*, wandering

vāgīna, ae *f*, sheath, scabbard

vāgĭo *v.i.* 4, to cry, bawl

Insight

In Latin the form of a verb can be active, passive or deponent. **Deponent verbs** are those verbs which are passive in form but active in meaning (e.g. *utor* = I use).

Semi-deponent verbs take active forms in the present, future and imperfect tenses, but deponent forms in the perfect, future perfect and pluperfect.

---

utpŏtĕ *adv*, namely, as, since

ŭtrimquĕ *adv*, on both sides

ŭtrŏbīquĕ (ŭtrŭbīquĕ) *adv*, on both sides

ŭtrŏquĕ *adv*, in both directions

ŭtrum *adv, used to form an alternative question*, is it this ... or that?

ūva, ae *f*, grape, cluster

ūbĭdus, a, um *adj*, moist, damp

uxor, ōris *f*, wife

uxōrĭus, a, um *adj*, of a wife

vāgītus, ūs *m*, crying, bawling

văgor *v.i.* 1, *dep*, to wander, roam

văgus, a, um *adj*, wandering, roaming, uncertain, vague

valdē *adv*, energetically, very much, very

văle *imperative (pl, vălēte)*, farewell!

vălens, ntis *adj*, powerful, strong, healthy

vălĕo *v.i.* 2, to be strong, vigorous or healthy, to have power or influence, to be capable or effective, be worth

vălesco *v.i.* 3, to grow strong

vălētūdǐnārǐum, ii *n*, hospital

vălētūdǐnārǐus, i *m*, invalid

vălētūdo, ǐnis *f*, health (good or bad)

vălǐdus, a, um *adj*, strong, powerful, healthy

valles (vallis), is *f*, valley

vallo *v.t.* 1, to fortify with rampart, protect

vallum, i *n*, rampart, palisade

vallus, i *m*, stake, palisade

valvae, ārum *f.pl*, folding doors

vānesco *v.i.* 3, to disappear

vānǐtas, ātis *f*, emptiness, uselessness, vanity

vannus, i *f*, fan

vānus, a, um *adj*, empty, groundless, false, deceptive

văpǐdus, a, um *adj*, spoiled, flat

văpor, ōris *m*, steam, vapour

văpōro *v.t.* 1, to fumigate, warm

vappa, ae *f*, flat wine; *m*, a good-for-nothing

vāpǔlo *v.i.* 1, to be flogged

vārǐco *v.i.* 1, to straddle

vārǐcōsus, a, um *adj*, varicose

vārǐĕtas, ātis *f*, variety

vārǐo *v.i.t.* 1, to vary; diversify, change

vārǐus, a, um *adj, adv,* ē, variegated, changing, varying

vărix, ǐcis *m, f*, varicose vein

vārus, a, um *adj*, knock-kneed

văs, vădis *m*, bail, security

vās, vāsis *n*, dish, utensil, military equipment

vāsārǐum, ii *n*, expense account

vascǔlārǐus, ii *m*, metal worker

vastātǐo, ōnis *f*, devastation

vastātor, ōris *m*, destroyer

vastǐtas, ātis *f*, desert, destruction, ruin

vasto *v.t.* 1, to devastate, destroy, leave vacant

vastus, a, um *adj*, deserted, desolate, rough, devastated, enormous, vast

vātes, is *c*, forecaster, poet

vātǐcǐnātǐo, ōnis *f*, prediction

vātǐcǐnātor, ōris *m*, prophet

vātǐcǐnor *v.i.t.* 1, *dep*, to predict

vātǐus, a, um *adj*, bow-legged

vĕ *conj*, or

vēcordǐa, ae *f*, folly, madness

vēcors, dis *adj*, foolish, mad

vectīgal, ālis *n*, tax, income

vectīgālis, e *adj* tax paying

vectis, is *m*, pole, bar, lever

vecto *v.t.* 1, to convey

vector, ōris *m*, carrier, traveller, passenger

vectōrǐus, a, um *adj*, for carrying

vectūra, ae *f*, transportation, fare

vectus, a, um *adj*, conveyed, carried

vĕgĕtus, a, um *adj*, lively

vēgrandis, e *adj*, small

vĕhĕmens, ntis *adj, adv,* **nter,** violent, powerful, strong

vĕhǐcǔlum, i *n*, vehicle

vĕho, si, ctum *v.t.* 3, to convey; *in passive, or with reflexive pron,* to ride, sail, go

vĕl *conj*, either, or, indeed

vēlāmen, ǐnis *n*, cover, garment

vēlāmentum, i *n*, olive branch

vēles, ǐtis *m*, light-armed soldier

vēlǐfer, ĕra, ĕrum *adj*, carrying sails

vēlǐfǐcātǐo, ōnis *f*, sailing

vēlǐfǐcor *v.i.* 1, *dep*, to sail, gain, procure

vēlǐvǒlus, a, um *adj*, sail-winged; (**măre**) dotted with ships

vellǐco *v.t.* 1, to nip, taunt

vello, vulsi, vulsum *v.t.* 3, to tear out, pluck off

vellus, ĕris *n*, fleece, hide

vēlo *v.t.* 1, to cover, wrap up

vēlōcǐtas, ātis *f*, speed

vēlox, ōcis *adj, adv,* **ǐter,** swift, fast, fleet

vēlum, i *n*, sail, covering

vēlut *adj*, just as, like

vēna, ae *f*, vein, disposition

vēnābǔlum, i *n*, hunting spear

vēnālǐcǐum, ii *n*, slave-dealing

vēnālǐcǐus, ii *m*, slave-dealer

vēnālis, e *adj*, for sale, able to be bribed, corrupt

vēnālis, is *m*, slave for sale

vēnātĭcus, a, um *adj*, of hunting
vēnātĭo, ōnis *f*, hunting, a, hunt, combat of wild beasts
vēnātor, ōris *m*, hunter
vēnātrix, īcis *f*, huntress
vēnātus, ūs *m*, hunting
vendĭbĭlis, e *adj*, saleable
vendĭtātĭo, ōnis *f*, boasting
vendĭtĭo, ōnis *f*, sale
vendĭto *v.t.* 1, to try to sell
vendĭtor, ōris *m*, salesman
vendo, dĭdi, dĭtum *v.t.* 3, to sell, betray, praise
vĕnēfĭca, ae *f*, witch
vĕnēfĭcĭum, ii *n*, poisoning, magic
vĕnēfĭcus, a, um *adj*, poisonous, magic
vĕnēfĭcus, i *m*, poisoner, sorcerer
vĕnēnātus, a, um *adj*, poisonous
vĕnēnĭfer, ĕra, ĕrum *adj*, poisonous
vĕnēno *v.t.* 1, to poison, dye
vĕnēnum, i *n*, poison, magic charm, drug
vēnĕo, ii, ĭtum *v.i.* 4, to be sold
vĕnĕrābĭlis, e *adj*, worthy of respect
vĕnĕrābundus, a, um *adj*, devout
vĕnĕrātĭo, ōnis *f*, great respect
vĕnĕrĕus, a, um *adj*, venereal
vĕnĕror *v.t.* 1, *dep*, to worship, revere, honour, entreat
vĕnĭa, aĕ *f*, indulgence, mercy, permission, pardon
vĕnĭo, vēni, ventum *v.i.* 4, to come
vēnor *v.i.t.* 1, *dep*, to hunt
venter, tris *m*, belly
ventĭlo *v.t.* 1, to wave, fan
ventĭto *v.i.* 1, to keep coming
ventōsus, a, um *adj*, windy, swift, light, changeable, vain
ventrĭcŭlus, i *m*, ventricle
ventūrus *fut. partic.* from **vĕnĭo**
ventus, i *m*, wind
vēnūcŭla (uva) a preserving grape
vēnundo, dĕdi, dătum *v.t.* 1, to sell
vēnus, ūs *m*, (**vēnum, i**, *n*) sale
vĕnustas, ātis *f*, charm, beauty
vĕnustus, a, um *adj, adv*, ē, charming, graceful, beautiful
vĕprēcŭla, ae *f*, small thorn-bush

vĕpres, is *m*, thorn-bush
vēr, vēris *n*, spring
vēra see **vērus**
vērācĭtas, ātis *f*, veracity
vērax, ācis *adj*, true
verbēna, ae *f*, foliage, branches
verber, ĕris *n*, lash, whip, flogging, blow
verbĕrātĭo, ōnis *f*, punishment
verbĕro *v.t.* 1, to whip, strike
verbōsus, a, um *adj*, effusive
verbum, i *n*, word, language, conversation; **verba dare** to deceive
vērē *adj*, really, truly
vĕrēcundĭa, ae *f*, shyness
vĕrēcundor *v.i.* 1, *dep*, to be shy
vĕrēcundus, a, um *adj, adv*, ē, shy, modest
vĕrendus, a, um *adj*, venerable, terrible
vĕrĕor *v.i.t.* 2, *dep*, to fear, respect
verto *v.i.* 3, to turn, bend, lie, be situated
vērĭdĭcus, a, um *adj*, truthful
vērĭsĭmĭlis, e *adj*, probable
vērĭtas, ātis *f*, truth, reality
vermĭcŭlus, i *m*, worm, grub
vermĭnōsus, a, um *adj*, worm-eaten
vermis, is *m*, worm
verna, ae *c*, slave born in his master's house
vernācŭlus, a, um *adj*, domestic
vernīlĭter *adj*, slavishly
verno *v.i.* 1, to flourish, bloom
vernus, a, um *adj*, of spring
vērō *adj*, in fact, certainly, but indeed, however
verres, is *m*, pig
verro, verri, versum *v.t.* 3, to sweep, brush, impel, take away
verrūca, ae *f*, wart, blemish
versātĭlis, e *adj*, movable
versĭcŏlor, ŏris *adj*, of different colours
versĭcŭlus, i *m*, single line of verse (or prose)
verso *v.t.* 1, to turn, twist, whirl, consider
versor *v.i.* 1, *dep*, to live, stay, be situated, be engaged on

versūra, ae *f*, borrowing, loan

versus *adv*, towards

versus, ūs *m*, row, line, verse

versūtus, a, um *adj, adv, ē,* clever, shrewd, cunning, sly

vertèbra, áe *f*, vertebra

vertex, ĭcis *m*, whirlpool, whirlwind, flame, crown of the head, summit, peak

vertīcōsus, a, um *adj*, eddying

vertĭgĭnōsus, a, um *adj*, suffering from giddiness

vertīgo, ĭnis *f*, dizziness

vēro see **vērus**

verto, ti, sum *v.i.t.* 3, to turn, change; turn, change, alter overthrow, translate

vĕru, ūs *n*, roasting-spit, javelin

vĕrūcŭlum, i *n*, skewer, small javelin

vērum *adv*, but, yet, still

vērum, i *n*, truth, reality, fact

vērumtămen *conj*, nevertheless

vērus, a, um *adj, adv, ō, ē,* true, real, proper, right

vĕrūtum, i *n*, javelin

vĕrūtus, a, um *adj*, armed with a javelin

vervex, ēcis *m*, wether, sheep

vēsānĭa, ae *f*, insanity

vēsănus, a, um *adj*, mad, fierce

vescor *v.i.t.* 3, *dep. with abl*, to feed on

vescus, a, um *adj*, thin, weak

vēsīca, ae *f*, bladder

vespa, ae *f*, wasp

vesper, ĕris (ĕri) *m*, evening, the West

vespĕra, ae *f*, evening, the West

vespĕrasco, āvi *v.i.* 3, to draw towards evening

vespertīnus, a, um *adj*, of evening, western

vespillo, ōnis *m*, undertaker

vesta, ae *f*, fire

vestālis, e *adj*, of the Vesta, the Goddess of Fire, Hearth, Home

vestālis, is *f*, priestess of Vesta

vester, tra, trum *adj*, your

vestĭārĭum, i *n*, wardrobe

vestĭbŭlum, i *n*, entrance hall

vestīgĭum, i *n*, footstep, track, sole of foot, mark, moment, instant; **ē, vestīgĭo** instantly

vestīgo *v.t.* 1, to search out, investigate

vestīmentum, i *n*, clothing

vestĭo *v.t.* 4, to clothe, cover

vestis, is *f*, clothing, clothes, carpet, curtain

vestītus, ūs *m*, clothes, dresss

vĕtĕrānus, a, um *adj*, old, veteran

vĕtĕrānus, i *m*, veteran soldier

vĕtĕrātor, ōris *m*, crafty, wily or sly person

vĕtĕrātōrĭus, a, um *adj*, sly

vĕtĕres, um *m.pl*, ancestors

vĕtĕrīnārĭus, a, um *adj*, veterinary

vĕternus, i *m*, sluggishness

vĕtĭtum, i *n*, something forbidden, prohibition

vĕtĭtus, a, um *adj*, forbidden

vĕto, ŭi, ĭtum *v.t.* 1, to forbid

vĕtŭlus, a, um *adj*, old

vĕtus, ĕris *adj*, old, former

vĕtustas, ātis *f*, old age, antiquity, posterity

vĕtustus, a, um *adj*, old

vexātĭo, ōnis *f*, distress

vexillārĭus, i *m*, standard-bearer

vexillum, i *n*, standard, ensign

vexo *v.t.* 1, to shake, injure, molest, harrass, torment

vĭa, ae *f*, road, street, way, method

vĭātĭcum, i *n*, travelling expenses, soldier's savings

vĭātor, ōris *m*, traveller

vĭbex, ĭcis *f*, weal

vĭbro *v.i.t* 1, to quiver; brandish, shake

vĭcārĭus, i *m*, deputy

vĭcēni, ae, a *pl. adj*, twenty each

vĭcēsĭmus (vĭcensĭmus), a, um *adj*, twentieth

vĭcĭa, ae *f*, vetch

vĭcĭes (vĭcĭens) *adv*, twenty times

vĭcīnĭa, ae *f*, neighbourhood

vĭcīnus, a, um *adj*, neighbouring, similar

vĭcīnus, a, um *adj*, neighbouring, similar

vĭcīnus, i *m*, neighbour

vĭcis (*genitive*)**, vĭcem, vĭce** change, alternation, recompense, lot, misfortune, position, duty; in **vĭcem, per vĭces** alternately; **vĭcem, vĭce**, instead of

vīcĭssim   *adv*, in turn
vīcissĭtūdo, ĭnis   *f*, change
victĭma, ae   *f*, victim for sacrifice
victor, ōris   *m*, conqueror
victōrĭa, ae   *f*, victory
victrix, īcis   *f*, female conqueror
vitrix, īcis   *adj*, victorious
victus, ūs   *m*, nutriment, diet
vīcus, i   *m*, street, village
vīdēlīcet   *adv*, obviously
vĭdĕo, vīdi, vīsum   *v.t.* 2, to see, perceive, understand, consider, take care, see to it
vĭdĕor, vēsus   *v.* 2, *dep*, to seem; *impers*, it seems right or good
vĭdŭa, ae   *f*, widow
vĭdŭĭtas, ātis   *f*, bereavement
vĭdŭlus, i   *m*, valise
vĭdŭo   *v.t.* 1, to deprive
vĭdŭus, a, um   *adj*, robbed, widowed
vĭētus, a, um   *adj*, withered
vĭgĕo   *v.i.* 2, to flourish, thrive
vĭgesco, gŭi   *v.i.* 3, to flourish, thrive
vĭgil, ĭlis   *adj*, alert, watching
vĭgil, ĭlis   *m*, watchman
vĭgĭlans, ntis   *adj*, *adv*, **nter**, watchful, careful
vĭgĭlantĭa, ae   *f*, watchfulness
vĭgĭlĭa, ae   *f*, wakefulness, vigilance, guard, watch
vĭgĭlo   *v.i.t.* 1, to keep awake, be vigilant; spend (time) in watching
vĭginti   *indecl. adj*, twenty
vĭgor, ōris   *m*, liveliness
vīlĭco   *v.i.t.* 1, to superintend
vīlĭcus (villicus), i   *m*, superintendent
vīlis, e   *adj*, cheap, mean
vīlĭtas, ātis   *f*, cheapness
villa, ae   *f*, country house
villātĭcus, a, um   *adj*, of a villa
villicus   see **vīlicus**
villōsus, a, um   *adj*, hairy, shaggy
villŭla, ae   *f*, small villa
villus, i   *m*, tuft of hair
vīmen, ĭnis   *n*, pliant branch
Vīmĭnālis (collis)   the Viminal, one of the seven hills of Rome
vīmĭnĕus, a, um   *adj*, of wickerwork
vīnārĭum, ii   *n*, wine bottle
vīnārĭus, a, um   *adj*, of wine

vīnārĭus, i   *m*, vintner
vincĭo, nxi, nctum   *v.t.* 4, to bind, tie, surround
vinco, vīci, victum   *v.i.t.* 3, to prevail; conquer, overcome, prove conclusively
vincŭlum (vinclum), i   *n*, cord, bond fetter; *pl*, prison
vindēmĭa, ae   *f*, grape-gathering, wine
vindēmĭātor, ōris   *m*, grape-gatherer
vindex, īcis   *c*, claimant, defender, liberator, avenger
vindĭcĭae, ārum   *f.pl*, legal claim
vindĭco   *v.t.* 1, to claim, appropriate, set free, protect, avenge
vindicta, ae   *f*, rod used ot set free a slave
vīnĕa, ae   *f*, vineyard, protective shed for soldiers
vīnētum, i   *n*, vineyard
vīnītor, ōris   *m*, vine-pruner
vīnŏlentĭa, ae   *f*, wine-drinking
vīnŏlentus, a, um   *adj*, drunk
vīnōsus, a, um   *adj*, drunken
vīnum, i   *n*, wine
vĭŏla, ae   *f*, violet
vĭŏlābĭlis, e   *adj*, able to be injured or harmed
vĭŏlārĭum, ii   *n*, bed of violets
vĭŏlātĭo, ōnis   *f*, violation, profanation
vĭŏlātor, ōris   *m*, injurer
vĭŏlens, ntis   *adj*, *adv*, **nter**, impetuous, furious
vĭŏlentĭa, ae   *f*, ferocity
vĭŏlentus, a, um   *adj*, violent, impetuous
vĭŏlo   *v.t.* 1, to injure, outrage, break
vīpĕra, ae   *f*, viper
vīpĕrĕus, a, um   *adj*, of a viper or snake
vīpĕrīnus, a, um   *adj*, of a viper or snake
vĭr, vĭri   *m*, man, husband
vĭrāgo, ĭnis   *f*, female soldier, heroine
vĭrectum, i   *n*, glade, turf
vĭrĕo   *v.i.* 2, to be green, flourish
vīres   see **vis**

vīresco *v.i.* 3, to become green, flourish
vīrētum, i *n*, glade, turf
virga, ae *f*, twig, rod
virgātus, a, um *adj*, striped
virgĕus, a, um *adj*, made of rods
virgĭnālis, e *adj*, girl-like
virgĭnĕus, a, um *adj*, of a virgin
virgĭnĭtas, ātis *f*, virginity
virgo, ĭnis *f*, virgin girl
virgŭla, ae *f*, small twig
virgultum, i *n*, shrubbery
virgultus, a, um *adj*, bushy
vĭrĭdārĭum, ii *n*, park
vĭrĭdis, e *adj*, green, fresh, young, blooming
vĭrĭdĭtas, ātis *f*, greenness, freshness
vĭrĭdo *v.i.t.* 1, to be green; make green
vĭrīlis, e *adj*, male, manly, full-grown, vigorous
vĭrītim *adj*, individually
vĭrōsus, a, um *adj*, stinking
virtūs, ūtis *f*, courage, manhood, military skill, goodness, moral perfection
vīrus, i *n*, slime, poison, virus
vīs (*no genit*), **vim, vi** *f*, force, power, violence, quantity, meaning; **vīres, ĭum** *pl*, strength, power
viscātus, a, um *adj*, sprinkled with lime
viscĕra, um *n.pl*, innards, flesh, bowels
viscum, i *n*, mistletoe, birdlime
vīsĭo, ōnis *f*, idea, notion
vīsĭto *v.t.* 1, to visit
vīso, si, sum *v.t.* 3, to survey, visit
vīsum, i *n*, appearance, sight
vīsus, ūs *m*, look, sight, appearance
vīta, ae *f*, life

vītābĭlis, e *adj*, to be avoided
vītālis, e *adj*, of life, vital
vītātĭo, ōnis *f*, avoidance
vītellus, i *m*, small calf, egg yolk
vītĕus, a, um *adj*, of the vine
vĭtĭo *v.t.* 1, to spoil, mar, infect
vĭtĭōsĭtas, ātis *f*, vice
vĭtĭōsus, a, um *adj, adv*, **ē**, faulty, defective, wicked
vītis, is *f*, vine, vine branch
vītĭsātor, ōris *m*, vine planter
vĭtĭum, ii *n*, fault, defect, blemish, error, crime
vīto *v.t.* 1, to avoid
vītrĕus, a, um *adj*, made of glass, transparent, shining
vĭtrīcus, i *m*, step-father
vĭtrum, i *n*, glass, woad
vitta, ae *f*, hair-ribbon
vittātus, a, um *adj*, bound with a hair-ribbon
vĭtŭlīnus, a, um *adj*, of a calf
vĭtŭlus, i *m* (**vĭtŭla, ae**, *f*) calf
vĭtŭpĕrātĭo, ōnis *f*, blame, censure
vĭtŭpĕro *v.t.* 1, to blame, censure
vīvārĭum, ii *n*, fishpond, game reserve
vīvācĭtas, ātis *f*, vigour or length of life
vīvax, ācis *adj*, long-lived
vīvĭdus, a, um *adj*, lively, animated
vīvo, xi, ctum *v.i.* 3, to live
vīvus, a, um *adj*, alive, fresh, natural, life-like
vix *adv*, scarcely, barely
vixdum *adv*, scarcely then
vŏcābŭlum, i *n*, name
vōcālis, e *adj*, vocal
vŏcātu *abl*, at the bidding
vōcĭfĕrātĭo, ōnis *f*, outcry
vōcĭfĕror *v.i.t.* 1, *dep*, to cry out
vŏcĭto *v.i.t.* 1, to call out; name
vŏco *v.i.t.* 1, to call; summon, urge, challenge, arouse, name

Insight

The **vocative** is the case used to indicate the person or thing addressed or called to in a speech (e.g. *Quinte, veni huc* = Quintus, come here!). It has the same endings as the nominative except in the second declension.

vōcŭla, ae   *f*, feeble voice
vŏlantes, ĭum   *c, pl*, birds
vŏlātĭcus, a, um   *adj*, flighty, fleeting
vŏlātĭlis, e   *adj*, flying, swift
vŏlātus, ūs   *m*, flight
vŏlens, ntis   *adj*, willing, favourable
volg... see vulg...
vŏlĭto   *v.i.* 1, to fly about, flit, flutter
vŏlo, velle, vŏlŭi   *v.i.t, irreg*, to wish, mean
vŏlo   *v.i.* 1, to fly

vŏrāgo, ĭnis   *f*, abyss, whirlpool
vŏrax, ācis   *adj*, greedy, destructive
vŏro   *v.t.* 1, to devour, destroy
vortex   see vertes
vos   *pron, pl*, you (*plural*)
vōtīvis, a, um   *adj*, concerning a promise or vow
vōtum, i   *n*, promise, vow, offering, wish, longing
vŏvĕo, vŏvi, vōtum   *v.t.* 2, to promise, vow, dedicate
vox, vōcis   *f*, voice, sound, speech, saying, proverb

Insight

nolo (I do not want) and *malo* (I prefer) are based on the conjugation of *volo* (I want). *nolo* is a combination of *ne* + *volo*; *malo* is a combination of *magis* (more) + *volo*. All three verbs control an infinitive, as they do in English (e.g. I want to ...).

volp... see vulp...
volsella, ae   *f*, tweezers
volt... see vult...
vŏlūbĭlis, e   *adj*, turning, spinning, changeable
vŏlūbĭlĭtas, ātis   *f*, whirling motion, fluency
vŏlŭcer, cris, cre   *adj*, flying, swift, transient
vŏlūmen, ĭnis   *n*, book, roll, fold
vŏluntārĭus, a, um   *adj*, voluntary; (of soldiers) volunteers
vŏluntas, ātis   *f*, wish, choice, will, affection, good-will
vŏluptārĭus, a, um   *adj*, sensual
vŏluptas, ātis   *f*, pleasure, delight
vŏlūto   *v.i.t.* 1, to roll, twist, writhe about; ponder, consider
volva (vulva), ae   *f*, womb
volvo, volvi, vŏlūtum   *v.t.* 3, to roll, unroll, turn, ponder, consider
vōmer, ĕris   *m*, ploughshare
vŏmĭca, ae   *f*, abscess, boil
vŏmĭtĭo, ōnis   *f*, vomiting
vŏmo, ŭi, ĭtum   *v.i.t.* 3, to vomit; throw up, pour out

vulgāris, e   *adj*, general, ordinary, common
vulgātor, ōris   *m*, a gossip
vulgātus, a, um   *adj*, ordinary, notorious
vulgo   *v.t.* 1, to divulge, spread about
vulgō   *v.t.* 1, to divulge, spread about
vulgō   *adv*, everywhere, openly
vulgus, i   *n*, the public, crowd, rabble
vulnĕrātus, a, um   *adj*, wounded
vulnĕro   *v.t.* 1, to wound, hurt
vulnĭfĭcus, a, um   *adj*, wounding
vulnus, ĕris   *n*, wound, blow
vulpēcŭla, ae   *f*, small fox
vulpes, is   *f*, fox
vulsus, a, um   *adj*, hairless, effeminate
vultur, ŭris   *m*, vulture
vultŭrĭus, ii   *m*, vulture
vultus, ūs   *m*, expression, look, features, aspect, face

X

xǐphǐas, ae *m*, swordfish
xystus, i *m*, **(systum, i** *n***)**, open
colonnade

Z

zěphy̆rus, i *m*, west wind
zōdǐăcus, i *m*, zodiac
zōna, ae *f*, belt, girdle, zone

English–Latin dictionary

A

a, an (*indefinite article*), no equivalent in Latin

abandon *v.t*, rĕlinquo (3), dēsĕro (3)

abandoned dērĕlictus, dēsertus; **(person)**, perdĭtus

abandonment rĕlictĭo, *f*

abase *v.t*, dēprĭmo (3)

abasement hŭmĭlĭtas *f*, dēmĭssĭo, *f*

abash *v.t*, confundo (3), pertubo (1)

abashed pŭdōre confūsus **(perplexed with shame)**

abate *v.t*, immĭnŭo (3), rĕmitto (3)

abatement dēcessus *m*, dēcessĭo, *f*, dēmĭnūtĭo, *f*

abbot pontĭfex *m*, **(high priest)**, săcerdos, *c*

abbreviate *v.t*, immĭnŭo (3), contrăho (3)

abbreviation compendĭum *n*, contractĭo, *f*

abdicate *v.i*, se abdĭcare (1. *reflex*)

abdication abdĭcātĭo, *f*

abdomen venter, *m*, abdōmen, *n*

abduction raptus, *m*, raptĭo, *f*

abet *v.i*, adsum (*irreg. with dat. of person*), adiŭvo (1)

abettor mĭnister *m*, adiūtor, *m*

abeyance (to be in —) *v.i*, iăcĕo (2)

abhor ăbhorrĕo (2) (*with acc. or ab and abl*), ōdi. (*v. defect*)

abhorrence ŏdĭum, *n*

abide *v.i*, mănĕo (2), hăbĭto (1)

abide *v.t*, **(wait for)**, exspecto (1)

abiding *adj*, **(lasting)**, mansūrus

ability (mental —), ingĕnĭum, *n*; **(power)**, pŏtestas, *f*

abject abiectus, hŭmĭlis

abjectness hŭmĭlĭtas, *f*

abjure *v.t*, abiūro (1), ēiūro (1)

ablaze *adj*, flăgrans

able *use* possum **(be able)**, pŏtens

able (to be —) *v.i*, possum (*irreg*)

able-bodied vălĭdus

ablution lăvātĭo, *f*, ablūtĭo, *f*

ably *adv*, ingĕnĭōsē

abnegation nĕgātĭo, *f*, mŏdĕrātĭo, *f*

abnormal abnormis, ĭnūsĭtātus

aboard in nāve; **(to go —)**, *v.i*, nāvem conscendo (3); **(to put —)**, *v.t*, in nāvem impōno (3)

abode dŏmus, *f*, dŏmĭcĭlĭum, *n*, sēdes, *f*, hăbĭtātĭo, *f*

abolish *v.t*, tollo (3), ăbŏlĕo (2), dissolvo (3)

abolition dissŏlūtĭo, *f*, ăbŏlĭtĭo, *f*

abominable infandus, dētestābĭlis

abominate *v.t*, ōdī (*defect*), ăbhorrĕo (2)

abomination (hatred) ŏdĭum, *n*; **(crime)**, flāgĭtĭum, *n*

aborigines indĭgĕnae, *m.pl*

abortion ăbortus, *m*, ăbortĭo, *f*

abortive (unsuccessful) irrĭtus

abound (in) *v.i*, ăbundo (1), sŭpĕro (1), circumflŭo (3), suppĕdĭto (1)

abounding ăbundans, afflŭens, fēcundus

about *prep*, circā, circum, ăd, sŭb (*with acc*), dē (*with abl*); **(of time)**, circĭter (*with acc*)

about *adv*, **(nearly)**, circĭter, fermē, fĕrē

above *prep*, sŭper, sŭprā (*with acc*); **(more than)**, amplĭus

above *adv*, sŭprā, insŭper; **(from above)**, dēsŭper, sŭpernē

abrasion attrītus, *m*

abreast *adv*, părĭter

abridge *v.t*, contrăho (3)

abridgement ĕpĭtŏmē, *f*, ĕpĭtŏma, *f*

abroad *adv*, **(in a foreign country)**, pĕrĕgrē

abroad (to be —) *v.i*, pĕrĕgrīnor (1. *dep*)

abrogate *v.t*, abrŏgo (1); rescindo (3)

abrogation abrŏgātĭo, *f*

abrupt (sudden) sŭbĭtus; **(steep)**, praeruptus

abruptly *adv*, sŭbĭto, praerupte

abscess vŏmĭca, *f*

abscond *v.i*, lătĕo (2)

absence absentĭa, *f*

absent absens

absent (to be—) *v.i*, absum (*irreg*)

absinth absinthĭum, *n*

absolute absŏlūtus

absolute power tўrannis, *f,*
impĕrĭum, *n,* dŏmĭnātĭo, *f*
absolutely (completely) *adv,*
prorsum, prorsus
absolve *v.t,* absolvo (3), lībĕro
(1)
absorb *v.t,* bĭbo (3), haurĭo (4),
absorbĕo (2)
absorbent *adj,* bĭbŭlus
abstain *v.i,* abstĭnĕo (2)
abstemious tempĕrātus
abstinence abstĭnentĭa, *f*
abstinent abstĭnens, mŏdĕrātus
abstract *nn,* ĕpĭtŏme, *f*
abstract *adj,* abstractus
abstract *v.t,* abstrăho (3)
abstruse rĕcondĭtus, obscūrus
absurd ĭneptus, absurdus
absurdity ĭneptĭa, *f,* insulsĭtas, *f*
absurdly *adv,* ĭneptē, absurdē
abundance cōpĭa, *f,* ăbundantĭa,
f
abundant largus, fēcundus
abuse *nn,* **(insult),** contŭmelia
abuse *v.t,* mălĕdĭco (3); **(misuse),**
ăbūtor (*v. dep*)
abusive contŭmēlĭōsus
abut *v.i,* adĭăcĕo (2)
abutting adiunctus
abyss gurges, *m,* vŏrāgo, *f*
acacia ăcācĭa, *f*
academic ăcădēmĭcus
academy ăcădēmĭa, *f*
accede *v.i,* consentĭo (4)
accelerate *v.t,* accĕlĕro (1)
accent vox, *f*
accentuate *v.t,* ăcŭo (3)
accentuation accentus, *m*
accept *v.t,* accĭpĭo (3), rĕcĭpĭo (3)
acceptability suāvĭtas, *f,* făcĭlĭtas,
f
acceptable grātus
acceptance acceptĭo, *f*
access (approach) ădĭtus, *m,*
accessus, *m*
accessible făcĭlis; **(to be —),** *v.i,*
pătĕo (3)
accession **(— to the throne)**
ĭnĭtĭum (*n*) regni **(beginning of
reign);** *or use phr. with* incipio **(to
begin)** *and* regno **(to reign)**
accessory (of crime) *adj,*
conscĭus; **(helper),** auctor, *m*

accident cāsus, *m*
accidental fortŭĭtus
accidentally *adv,* cāsū, fortē
acclaim *v.t,* clāmo (1)
acclamation clāmor, *m*
acclimatized assŭētus
accommodate *v.t,* accommŏdo
(1)
accommodating obsĕquens
accommodation (lodging)
hospĭtĭum, *n;* **(loan),** commŏdum,
n
accompaniment (musical) cantus,
m
accompany *v.t,* prōsĕquor (3
dep), cŏmĭtor (1 *dep*); **(— in
singing),** oblŏquor (3 *dep*)
accomplice *adj,* conscĭus,
partĭceps
accomplish *v.t,* confĭcĭo (3)
accomplished (learned) ērŭdītus
accomplishment (completion)
confectĭo, *f*
accord (of my (your) own —) mĕā
(tŭā) spontĕ, ultrō
accord *v.t,* concēdo (3); *v.i,*
consentĭo (4)
accordance (in — with) *prep,* ex,
dē, prō (*with abl*)
according to *as above*
accordingly *adv,* ĭtăque
accost *v.t,* compello (1);
allŏquor (3 *dep*)
account *nn,* rătĭo, *f;* **(statement),**
mĕmŏrĭa, *f*
on account of *prep,* propter, ŏb
(*with acc*)
to render account for rătĭonem
reddo (3)
accountant calcŭlātor, *m,* scrība,
m
account-book tăbŭlae, *f.pl*
accoutre *v.t,* orno (1); armo (1)
accoutrements arma, *n.pl*
accredit *v.t,* **(establish),**
confirmio (1)
accrue *v.i,* accēdo (3)
accumulate *v.t,* cŭmŭlo (1),
cŏăcervo (1); *v.i,* cresco (3)
accumulation (bringing together)
collātĭo, *f*
accuracy (exactness) subtīlĭtas, *f;*
(carefulness), cūra, *f*

accurate (exact) subtīlĭs, vērus;
(careful), dīlĭgens
accursed exsĕcrābĭlĭs
accusation crīmen, *n*, accūsātĭo, *f*
accuse *v.t*, accūso (1); arcesso
(3), nōmen dēfĕro (*v. irreg*)
accused person rĕus, *m*
accuser accūsātor, dēlātor, *m*
accustom *v.t*, assŭēfacĭo (3)
to be accustomed *v.i*, sŏlĕo (2)
to become accustomed *v.i*,
assŭesco (3)
accustomed assŭētus, sŏlĭtus
ache *v.i*, dŏlĕo (2)
ache *nn*, dŏlor, *m*
achieve *v.t*. confĭcĭo (3), perfĭcĭo
(3)
achievement res gesta, *f*, făcĭnus,
n
acid *adj*, ăcerbus, ăcĭdus
acknowledge *v.t*, (confess),
confĭtĕor (2 *dep*), agnosco (3);
(accept), tollo (3)
acknowledgement confessĭo, *f*
acme summa, *f*
aconite ăcŏnītum, *n*
acorn glans, *f*
acquaint *v.t*, certĭōrem făcĭo (3)
(*with acc. of person, and* dē *with
abl*)
to become acquainted with *v.t*,
nosco (3), cognosco (3)
acquaintance (knowledge of)
scĭentĭa, *f*; (with a person),
consŭētūdo, *f*; (a person), nōtus,
m
acquiesce *v.i*, acquĭesco (3)
acquire *v.t*, acquīro (3)
acquirement (obtaining) ădeptĭo, *f*
acquit *v.t*, absolvo (3), lībĕro (1)
acquittal absŏlūtĭo, *f*, lībĕrātĭo, *f*
acre iūgĕrum, *n*
acrid asper, ācer
acrimonious ăcerbus, asper,
ămārus
acrimony ăcerbĭtas, *f*
across *prep*, trans (*with acc*)
act *v.i*, ăgo (3), gĕro (3)
act *v.t*, (a part in a play), ăgo (3)
act *nn*,factum, *n*; (law) lex, *f*
action (carrying out) actĭo, *f*,
actus, *m*, (at law) līs, *f*, (battle),
proelĭum, *n*

active impĭger, ălăcer
actively impĭgrē
activity (energy) industrĭa, *f*;
(agility, mobility) ăgĭlĭtas, *f*
actor actor, *m*
actual vērus
actually *adv*, rē vērā
actuary actŭārĭus, *m*
actuate *v.t*, mŏvĕo (2), impello
(3)
acumen ăcūmen, *n*
acute ācer, ăcūtus
acuteness ăcĭes, *f*, ăcūmen, *n*
adage dictum, *n*
adapt *v.t*, accomŏdo (1),
compōno (3)
adapted accommŏdātus, aptus
add *v.t*, addo (3), ădĭcĭo (3)
adder vīpĕra, *f*
addict *v.t*, dĕdo (3) (*with dat*)
addicted dedĭtus
addition (numerical) *use verb*
addo (3); (increase) accessĭo, *f*
additional (more, new, fresh)
nŏvus
address *v.t*, (a letter), inscrībo
(3); (person) allŏquor (3 *dep*)
address *nn*, (letter), inscriptĭo, *f*;
(speaking) allŏquĭum, *n*
adduce *v.t*, prŏdūco (3), prōfĕro
(*v. irreg*)
adept prītus
adequacy *use* sătis (enough)
(*with nn. in genit*)
adequate sătis (*with genit*)
adhere *v.i*, (cling) haerĕo (2)
adherent clĭens, *m*, sectātor, *m*
adhesive tĕnax
adjacency vīcīnĭtas, *f*
adjacent fĭnĭtĭmus, vīcīnus,
contermĭnus
adjoin *v.i*, adiăcĕo (2)
adjoin *v.t*, adiungo (3)
adjoining coniunctus, contĭgŭus
adjourn *v.t*, diffĕro (*v. irreg*)
adjournment dīlātĭo, *f*
adjudge (adjudicate) *v.t*, adiūdĭco
adjudication addictĭo, *f*
adjure *v.t*, obtestor (1 *dep*),
obsĕcro (1)
adjust *v.t*, apto (1), compōno (3)
adjustment compŏsĭtĭo, *f*
adjutant optĭo, *m*

administer *v.t*, admĭnistro (1)
administration admĭnistrātĭo, *f*,
  prōcūrātĭo, *f*
administrator procūrātor, *m*
admirable mīrābĭlis
admirably *adv*, praeclārē
admiral praefectus (*m*) classis
admiration admīrātĭo, *f*
admire *v.t*, admīror (1 *dep*),
  mīror (1 *dep*)
admirer laudātor, *m*
admissible, (letting in) ădĭtus,
  m; (acknowledgement) confessĭo, *f*
admit *v.t*, (let in) admitto (3);
  (grant) dō (1), concēdo (3);
  (confess) confĭtĕor (2 *dep*)
admonish *v.t*, mŏnĕo (2)
admonition admŏnĭtĭo, *f*
adolescence ădŏlescentĭa, *f*
adolescent ădŏlescens, *c*
adopt *v.t*, (person), ădopto (1);
  (custom) ascisco (3)
adoption ădoptĭo, *f*
adorable cŏlendus
adoration cultus, *m*, ădōrātĭo, *f*
adore *v.t*, cŏlo (3), ădōro (1)
adorn *v.t*, orno (1)
adorned ornātus
adornment (as an act) exornātĭo,
  f; (a decoration) ornāmentum, *n*
adrift *adj*, in mări iactātus (driven
  about on the sea)
adroit callĭdus, sollers
adroitness dextĕrĭtas, *f*
adulation ădūlātĭo, *f*
adult *adj*, ădultus
adulterate *v.t*, vĭtĭo (1)
adulteration adultĕrātĭo, *f*
adulterer(-ess) ădulter, *m*, (-era, *f*)
adultery ădultĕrĭum, *n*
advance *nn*, prōgressus, *m*
advance *v.i*, prōcēdo (3),
  prōgrĕdĭor (3 *dep*), incēdo (3),
  pĕdem infĕro (*irreg*)
advance *v.t*, infĕro (*irreg*),
  prōmŏvĕo (2)
in advance *adv*, prae,
  compounded with vb: e.g. send
  in advance, praemitto (3)
advance-guard prīmum agmen, *n*
advantage commŏdum, *n*
to be advantageous *v.i*, prōsum
  (*irreg*), ūsui esse (*irreg*) (*with dat*)

advantageous ūtĭlis
advantageously *adv*, ūtĭlĭter
advent adventus, *m*
adventure făcĭnus, *n*
adventurous audax
adventurously *adv*, audacter
adversary hostis, *c*
adverse adversus
adversity res adversae, *f.pl*
advert to *v.t*, attingo (3)
advertise *v.t*, prōscrībo (3),
  prōnuntĭo (1)
advertisement prōscriptĭo, *f*
advice consĭlĭum, *n*
advisable (advantageous) ūtĭlis
advise *v.t*, mŏnĕo (2), suādĕo
  (2), censĕo (2)
advisedly *adv*, consultō
adviser suāsor, *m*, auctor, *m*
advocate *nn*, patrōnus, *m*
advocate *v.t*, suādĕo (2)
adze ascĭa, *f*
aedile aedīlis, *m*
aedileship aedīlĭtas, *f*
aerial *adj*, (of the air), āĕrĭus
afar *adv*, prŏcŭl
affability cōmĭtas, *f*
affable cōmis
affably *adv*, cōmĭter
affair rēs, *f*, nĕgōtĭum, *n*
affect *v.t*, affĭcĭo (3); (the
  feelings) mŏvĕo (2)
affectation (show) sĭmŭlātĭo, *f*
affected pūtĭdus
affection (love) ămor, *m*
affectionate ămans
affiance *v.t*, spondĕo (2)
affianced sponsus
affidavit testĭmōnĭum, *n*
affiliate *v.t*, cŏ-opto (1)
affinity cognātĭo, *f*
affirm *v.t*, affirmo (1)
affix *v.t*, affīgo (3)
afflict *v.t*, affĭcĭo (3)
afflicted (with grief) mĭser
affliction (with grief etc) mĭsĕrĭa,
  f; (a bad thing), mălum, *n*
affluence dīvĭtĭae, *f.pl*
affluent dīves
afford *v.t.* (give), praebĕo (2);
  otherwise use phr. with satis
  pecuniae habere ut... (to have
  enough money to ...)

affright *v.t*, terrĕo (2)
affront contŭmēlĭa, *f*
affront *v.t*, contŭmēlĭam facio (3) (*with dat*)
afire *adj*, flăgrans
afloat (*use phr. with* in aquā **(on the water)**
afoot *adv*, pĕdĭbus
afore *adv*, sŭprā
aformentioned sŭprā scriptus
aforesaid sŭprā scriptus
afraid tĭmĭdus
afraid (to be—) *v.i. and v.t*, tĭmĕo (2), vĕrĕor (2 *dep*), mĕtŭo (3)
afresh *adv*, rursus
aft *nn*, puppis, *f*
after *prep*, post (*with acc*)
after *conj*, postquam
after *adv*, post, postĕa
after all (nevertheless) *adv*, tămen
afternoon *adv*, post mĕrīdĭem
afternoon *adj*, pōmĕrīdĭānus
afterwards *adv*, post, postĕa
again *adv*, ĭtĕrum, rursus
again and again *adv*, ĭdentĭdem
against *prep*, contra, in (*with acc*)
agape *adj*, hĭans
age aetas, *f*, aevum, *n*, (old—) sĕnectus, *f*
aged (old) sĕnex
aged (three) years nātus (tres) annos
agency (doing, action) ŏpĕra, *f*
agent actor, *m*
aggrandize *v.t*, amplĭfĭco (1)
aggrandizement amplĭfĭcātĭo, *f*
aggravate *v.t*, grăvo (1); **(annoy)** aspĕro (1); **(increase)** augĕo (2)
aggregate *nn*, summa, *f*
aggression incursĭo, *f*
aggressive hostĭlis
aggressor *use phr*. suā sponte bellum infĕrre (*irreg*), **(inflict war of one's own accord)**
aggrieve *v.t. use* afficĭo (3) **(affect)**
aghast stŭpĕfactus
agile ăgĭlis
agility ăgĭlĭtas, *f*
agitate *v.t*, ăgĭto (1), commŏvĕo (2)

agitated sollĭcĭtus
agitation (violent movement) ăgĭtātĭo, *f*; **(of the mind),** commōtĭo, *f*
agitator (political) turbātor, *m*
ago *adv*, ăbhinc (*with acc*) e.g. **two years—** ăbhinc duos annos
agonize *v.t*, crŭcĭo (1)
agony dŏlor, *m*
agrarian ăgrārĭus
agree with *v.i*, consentĭo (4) (*with* cum *and abl*); *v.t*. compōno (3); **(it is—by all)** constat inter omnes
agreeable grātus
agreeableness dulcēdo, *f*
agreed upon (it is—) constat, convĕnit, *v. impers*
agreeing congrŭens, convĕnĭens
agreement (the—itself) pactum, *n*; **(of opinions, etc)** consentsĭo, *f*
agricultural rustĭcus
agriculture agrĭcultūra, *f*
agriculturist agrĭcŏla, *m*
aground (to run—) *use phr*. in vădo haerĕo (2) **(stick fast in a shallow place)**
ague horror, *m*
ah! (alas!) ĕheu!
ahead *adv, use* prae, pro, *compounded with verbs*, e.g. **send ahead,** praemitto (3)
aid auxĭlĭum, *n*, subsĭdĭum, *n*
aid *v.t*, adiŭvo (1), subvĕnĭo (4) (*with dat*)
ail *v.i*, aegresco (3)
ailing aeger, aegrōtus
aim *v.t*. **(point a weapon, etc.)** dīrĭgo (3); **(to aim at)** pĕto (3)
aim *nn*, **(purpose)** finis, *m*; **(throwing)** coniectus, *m*
air āēr, *m*; **(manner)** spĕcĭes, *f*
air *v.t*, ventĭlo (1)
air-hoe spīrācŭlum, *n*
airy āĕrĭus
akin *adj*, **(similar)** fĭnĭtĭmus
alabaster ălăbastrītes ae, *m*
alacrity ălăcrĭtas, *f*
alarm (fear) păvor, *m*, trĕpĭdātio, *f*; **(confusion)** tŭmultus, *m*
alarm *v.t*, perturbo (1), terrĕo (2)
alarmed trĕpĭdus
alas! heu!

alcove angŭlus, *m* **(corner)**
alder alnus, *f*
alderman măgistrātus, *m*
ale cerevisia, *f*
ale-house caupona, *f*
alert ălăcer
alertness ălăcrĭtas, *f*
alien *(adj and nn)* **(foreign)**, pĕrĕgrīnus
alienate *v.t*, ălĭēno (1)
alienation ălĭēnātĭo, *f*
alight *v.i*, dēsĭlĭo (4)
alike *adj*, sĭmĭlis
alike *adv*, sĭmĭlĭter
alive vīvus
alive (to be —) vivo (3)
all *adj*, **(every)** omnis; **(the whole)** tōtus; *(with superlative*, e.g. all the best people) optĭmus quisque; **(at all, in all)** *adv*, omnīno
all-powerful omnĭpŏtens
allay *v.t*, sēdo (1)
allegation affirmātĭo, *f*
allege *v.t*. **(assert)** argŭo (3), affĕro *(irreg)*
allegiance fĭdes, *f*, officĭum, *n*
allegory allēgŏrĭa, *f*
alleviate *v.t*, lĕvo (1)
alleviation, (as an act) lĕvātĭo, *f*; **(something which brings—)** lĕvāmen, *n*
alley angĭportus, *m*
alliance sŏcĭĕtas, *f*, foedus, *n*; **(to make an—)** foedus făcĭo (3)
allied (states) foedĕrātus
allot *v.t*, distrĭbŭo (3), assigno (1)
allotment (of land) ăger assignātus, *m*
allow *v.t*. **(permit)**, pătĭor (3 *dep*), sĭno (3), concēdo (3); *or use impers. vb*. lĭcet *(with dat. of person allowed)*
allowable *use* fās, *(indecl. nn)* **(right)**
allowance (to make —) ignosco (3), rĕmitto (3)
allude to *v.t*, signĭfĭco (1)
allure *v.t*, allĭcĭo (3)
allurement blandĭtĭa, *f*, illĕcĕbra
alluring blandus
allusion signĭfĭcātĭo, *f*
alluvium allŭvĭo, *f*

ally *nn*, sŏcĭus, *m*
ally *v.t*, **(unite)**, iungo (3); **(— oneself)** se coniungere *(with dat)*
almanack fasti, *m.pl*
almighty omnĭpŏtens
almond ămygdălum, *n*; **(tree)**, ămygdăla, *f*
almost *adv*, paenĕ, prŏpĕ, fĕrē, fermē
alms stips, *f*
aloe ălŏē, *f*
aloft *adv*, sublīmĕ; *adj*, sublīmis
alone *adj*, sōlus
alone *adv*, sōlum
along *prep*, sĕcundum, praeter *(with acc)*
aloof *adv*, prŏcŭl; **(to stand — from)**, discēdo (3)
aloud *adv*, magnā vōcē
alphabet *use* litterae *f.pl* **(letters)**
already *adv*, iam
also *adv*, ĕtiam, quŏque, ĭtem; **(likewise)**, necnōn
altar āra, *f*
alter *v.t*, mūto (1), verto (3), corrĭgo (3)
alter *v.i*, mūtor (1 *dep*)
alteration mūtātĭo, *f*
altercation rixa, *f*
alternate *v.t*, alterno (1)
alternate *adj*, alternus
alternately *adv*, invĭcem
alternation vĭcissĭtūdo, *f*
alternative *use phr. with* ălĭus mŏdus **(other way)**
although *conj*, quamquam *(indicating fact)*; quamvīs *(indicating a supposition)*; etsi, tametsi
altitude altĭtūdo, *f*
altogether *adv*, omnīno
always *adv*, semper
amalgamate *v.t*, iungo (3), miscĕo (2)
amalgamation coniunctĭo, *f*
amass *v.t*, cŏăcervo (1), cŭmŭlo (1)
amatory ămātōrĭus
amaze *v.t*, obstŭpĕfăcĭo (3)
amazed stŭpĭdus, stŭpĕfactus
amazement stŭpor, *m*
amazing mīrus
amazingly *adv*, mīris mŏdis

amazon vĭrāgo, *f*
ambassador lēgātus, *m*
amber sŭcĭnum, *n*
ambiguity ambāges, *f.pl*
ambiguous ambĭgŭus, anceps
ambiguously *adv,* per ambāges
ambition glōrĭa, *f,* ambĭtĭo, *f*
ambitious *use phr.* cŭpĭdus
  glōrĭae **(keen on glory)**
amble *v.i,* lēnĭter ambŭlo (1)
  (walk quietly)
ambrosia ambrŏsĭa, *f*
ambrosial ambrŏsĭus
ambush insĭdĭae (*f.pl*) ; **(to**
  ambush) insĭdĭor (1 *dep*)
ameliorate *v.t,* mĕlĭōrem făcĭo (3)
amen! fiat! **(let it be)**
amenable obēdĭens
amend *v.t,* ēmendo (1), corrĭgo
  (3)
amendment (correction)
  ēmendātĭo, *f*
amends *use* expĭo (1) **(to make**
  —s)
amenity ămoenĭtas, *f*
amethyst ămĕthystus, *f*
amiability suāvĭtas, *f*
amiable suāvis
amiably *adv,* suāvĭter
amicable ămīcus
amid(st) *prep,* inter (*with acc*)
amiss *adv,* māle; **(to take—)**
  aegre fĕro (*irreg*)
amity ămīcĭtĭa, *f*
ammunition arma, *n.pl*
amnesty vĕnĭa, *f*
among *prep,* inter, ăpud (*with*
  acc)
amorous ămans
amount summa, *f,* finis, *m*
amount to *v.t, use* esse **(to be)**
amphitheatre amphĭthĕātrum, *n*
ample amplus, cōpĭōsus
amplify *v.t,* amplĭfĭco (1), dīlāto
  (1)
amplitude amplĭtūdo, *f*
amply *adv,* amplē
amputate *v.t,* sĕco (1), ampŭto
  (1)
amputation ampŭtātĭo, *f*
amuse *v.t,* dēlecto (1)
amusement dēlectātĭo, *f*
amusing făcētus

anaesthetic *adj,* sŏpōrĭfer
analogy (comparison) compărātĭo
analyse *v.t,* discerpo (3), explĭco
  (1)
analysis explĭcātĭo, *f*
anarchical turbŭlentus
anarchy lĭcentĭa, *f*
anathema exsecrātĭo, *f* **(curse)**
anatomy incīsĭo (*f*) corporis
  (incision of the body)
ancestor auctor, *m*; (*in pl*),
  māiōres, *m.pl*
ancestral proăvītus
ancestry (descent, origin) gĕnus, *n*
anchor ancŏra, *f*
anchor *v.i, use phr.* nāvem ad
  ancŏras dēlĭgo (1) **(fasten a ship**
  to the anchors)
anchorage stătĭo, *f*
ancient antīquus, vĕtus
and et, atque, ac; quĕ (*joined to*
  the second of two words, **e.g. I**
  and you: ego tuque) ; **(and ... not)**
  nĕque
anecdote fābella, *f*
anew *adv,* dēnŭo, dē intĕgro
anger īra, *f,* īrācundĭa, *f*
anger *v.t,* irrīto (1), lăcesso (3)
angle angŭlus, *m*
angle *v.i* **(fish),** piscor (1 *dep*)
angler piscātor, *m*
angrily *adv,* īrācundē, īrātē
angry īrātus; **(irascible)** īrācundus
anguish angor, *m,* dŏlor, *m,*
  ăcerbĭtas, *f*
angular angŭlātus, angŭlāris
animal ănĭmal, *n,* pĕcus, *f*
animal *adj,* ănĭmālis
animate *v.t,* ănĭmo, excĭto (1)
animated ănĭmans; **(lively)**
  vĕgĕtus, ălăcer, vĕhĕmens
animation (liveliness) vĭgor, *m*
animosity sĭmultas, *f*
ankle tālus, *m*
annalist annālĭum scriptor, *m*
annals annāles, *m.pl*
annex *v.t,* addo (3), iungo (3)
annihilate *v.t,* dēlĕo (2)
annihilation exĭtĭum, *n,*
  exstinctĭo, *f*
anniversary *adj,* anniversārĭus
anniversary *nn,* dĭes
  annĭversārĭus, *m*

annotate *v.t,* annŏto (1)
annotation annŏtātĭo (1)
announce *v.t,* nuntĭo (1)
announcement prōnuntĭātĭo, *f*
announcer nuntĭus, *m,*
  praeco, *m*
annoy *v.t,* irrīto (1), lăcesso (3)
annoyance mŏlestĭa, *f,*
  vexātĭo, *f*
annual anniversārĭus
annually *adv,* quŏtannis
annuity annŭa, *n.pl*
annul *v.t,* abrŏgo (1), tollo (3)
annulment ăbŏlĭtĭo, *f*
anoint *v.t,* unguo (3)
anointing *nn,* unctĭo, *f*
anomaly ănōmălĭa, *f*
anon *adv* **(immediately)**, stătim;
  (in a short time) brĕvi tempŏre
anonymously *(adv. phr)* sĭne.
  nōmĭne
another ălĭus; **(the other of two)**,
  alter; **(another's)**, *adj,* ălĭēnus
answer *nn,* responsum, *n*
answer *v.t,* respondĕo (2); **(in
  writing)** rescrībo (3); **(to — for, be
  surety for)** praesto (1)
answerable *use phr,* rătĭōnem
  reddo (3) **(to render an account)**
ant formīca, *f*
antagonism ĭnĭmīcĭtĭa, *f*
antagonist adversārĭus, *m*
antagonistic contrārĭus
antecedent *adj,* antĕcēdens
antechamber ātrĭolum, *n*
anterior prĭor
ante-room ātrĭŏlum, *n*
anticipate *v.t,* occŭpo (1),
  antĕverto (3), praecĭpĭo (3);
  (expect), exspecto (1)
anticipation (expectation)
  exspectātĭo, *f*
antics lūdi, *m.pl*
antidote rĕmĕdĭum, *n,*
  antĭdŏtum, *n*
antipathy rĕpugnantĭa, *f*; **(of
  people)** ŏdĭum, *n*
antipodes antĭpŏdes, *m.pl*
antiquarian *adj,* antĭquitatis
  stŭdĭōsus **(keen on antiquity)**
antiquated priscus
antique *adv,* vĕtus, antīquus
antiquity antīquĭtas, *f,* vĕtustas, *f*

antithesis (opposite) contrārĭum,
  n; **(in argument)**, contentĭo, *f*
antler rāmus, *m,* cornu, *n*
anvil incūs, *f*
anxiety anxĭĕtas *f,* sollĭcĭtūdo, *f,*
  cūra, *f*; **(alarm)** păvor, *m*
anxious anxĭus, sollĭcĭtus;
  (alarmed) trĕpĭdus
anxiously *adv,* anxĭē
any *adj,* ullus *(after negatives,
  and in questions, and
  comparisons)*; quisquam *(pron.
  used like ullus)*; qui, quae, quod
  (after si, nisi, ne, num)
anyone, anybody *pron,* quis
  (after si, nisi, se, num); quisquam
  (after a negative)
anything *use neuter of prons.
  given above*
anywhere *adv,* **(in any place)**,
  usquam; **(to any place)**, quō,
  quōquam; **(in any place)**, ŭbīquĕ
apace *adv,* **(quickly)**, cĕlĕrĭtĕr
apart *adv,* sĕorsum; *(adj)*
  dīversus
apartment conclāve, *n*
apathetic lentus, pĭger
apathy ignāvĭa, *f,* lentĭtūdo, *f*
ape sīmĭa, *f*
aperture fŏrāmen, *n*
apex căcūmen, *n,* ăpex, *m*
aphorism sententĭa, *f*
apiary alvĕārĭum, *n*
apiece *use distributive numeral,
  e.g.* **two each,** bīni
apologize *v.i,* excūso (1), dēfendo
  (3)
apology excūsātĭo, *f*
appal *v.t,* perterrĕo (2)
apparatus appărātus, *m*
apparel vestis, *f,* vestīmentum, *n*
apparent mănĭfestus, ăpertus
apparently *adv,* per spĕcĭem
apparition (ghost) spĕcĭes, *f,*
  ĭmāgo, *f*
appeal *v.i,* appello (1), prōvŏco
  (1), **(to —to)** *v.t,* obtestor (1 *dep*)
appeal *nn,* appellātĭo, *f,*
  obsĕcrātĭo, *f*
appear *v.i,* appārĕo (2),
  conspĭcĭor (3 *pass*); **(to seem)**
  vĭdĕor (2 *pass*); **(to come forward)**
  prōdĕo (4)

appearance (looks) spĕcĭes, *f*, aspectus, *m*; **(show)**, spĕcĭes, *f*; **(image)**, sĭmŭlācrum, *n*

appeasable plācābĭlis

appease *v.t*, **(people)**, plāco (1); **(feelings)**, sēdo (1)

appeasement plācātĭo, *f*

appellant appellātor, *m*

append *v.t*, **(attach)**, addo (3)

appendage appendix, *f*

appertain *v.i*, pertĭnĕo (2)

appetite appĕtītus, *m*; **(hunger)**, fămes, *f*

applaud *v.t*, plaudo (3), laudo (1)

applause (clapping) plausus, *m*; **(cheers)**, clāmor, *m*

apple mālum, *n*; **(−tree)**, mālus, *f*

appliance (apparatus) appărātus, *m*

applicable to commŏdus **(with dat)**

applicant pĕtītor, *m*

application (asking) pĕtītĭo, *f*; **(mental)**, stŭdĭum, *n*, dīlĭgentĭa, *f*

apply *v.t*, adhĭbĕo (2), admŏvĕo (2); **(to − oneself to)** se dēdĕre (3 *with dat*) ; *v.i*, **(refer to)**, pertĭnĕo (2); **(−for)**, flāgĭto (1)

appoint *v.t*, constĭtŭo (3) **(people to office, etc)**, crĕo (1) ; **(to appoint to a command)** praefĭcĭo (3) *(acc. of person appointed, dat. of person or thing commanded)*

appointment (office) mūnus, *n*; **(creation)**, crĕātĭo, *f* ; **(agreed meeting)**, constĭtūtum, *n*

apportion *v.t*, dīvĭdo (3), distrĭbŭo (3)

apposite aptus

appraise *v.t*, **(evaluate)**, aestĭmo (1)

appraisement aestĭmātĭo, *f*

appreciate *v.t*, **(value)**, aestĭmo (1) magni

appreciation aesĭmātĭo, *f*

apprehend *v.t*, **(arrest)**, comprĕhendo (3) ; **(understand)**, intellĕgo (3), percĭpĭo (3)

apprehension (fear) formīdo, *f*; **(arrest)** comprĕhensĭo, *f*; **(understanding)**, intellĕgentĭa, *f*

apprehensive (fearful) tĭmĭdus

apprentice tīro, *m*

approach *v.i*, apprŏpinquo (1) *(with* ad *and acc. or dat)*, accēdo (3)

approach *nn*, ădĭtus, *m*, adventus, *m*, accessus, *m*

approbation apprŏbātĭo, *f*, laus, *f*

appropriate *adj*, aptus, accommŏdātus *(with dat)*

appropriate *v.t*, sūmo (3)

appropriately *adv*, aptē

approval apprŏbātĭo, *f*

approve (of) *v.t*, apprŏbo (1)

approved spectātus, prŏbātus

approximate proxĭmus

approximate *v.i*, accēdo (3)

April Aprīlis (mensis)

apron ŏpĕrīmentum, *n*

apt aptus, ĭdŏnĕus; **(inclined)**, prōnus, prōpensus

aptitude (ability) ingĕnĭum, *n*

aptly *adv*, aptē

aptness *use adj*, aptus **(suitable)**

aquatic ăquātĭlis

aqueduct ăquae ductus *m*

aquiline ăquĭlīnus, ăduncus

arable land arvum, *n*

arbiter arbĭter, *m*

arbitrarily *adv*, **(according to whim)**, ad lĭbīdĭnem

arbitrary (capricious) lĭbīdĭnōsus

arbitrate *v.t*, discepto (1)

arbitration arbĭtrĭum, *n*

arbitrator arbĭter, *m*

arbour umbrācŭlum, *n*

arc arcus, *m*

arcade portĭcus, *f*

arch fornix *m*, arcus, *m*

arch *adj*, **(playful)**, lascīvus

archaeology investīgātĭo, *(f)* rērum antīquārum **(search for ancient things)**

archaism verbum obsŏlētum, *n*

archer săgittārĭus, *m*

archipelago *use phr*, măre, *(n)* insŭlis consĭtum **(sea set with islands)**

architect archĭtectus, *m*, ŏpĭfex, *c*

architecture archĭtectūra, *f*

archives tăbŭlae, *f. pl*

arctic septentrĭōnālis

ardent ardens, fervĭdus

ardently *adv,* ardenter, věhěmenter
ardour ardor, *m,* cǎlor, *m,* fervor, *m*
arduous ardǔus
area spǎtǐum, *n*
arena hǎrēna, *f,* ǎrēna, *f*
argue *v.i,* discepto (1), dissěro (3)
argument (quarrel) rixa, *f,* argūmentum, *n;* **(discussion),** dispǔtātǐo, *f*
arid ārǐdus, siccus
aridity ārǐdǐtas, *f,* siccǐtas, *f*
aright *adv,* rectē
arise *v.i,* surgo (3); **(heavenly bodies),** ǒrǐor (4 *dep*)
aristocracy (aristocratic party) optǐmātes, *c. pl;* **(govt.)** optǐmātǐum dǒmǐnātus, *m*
aristocratic patrǐcǐus
arithmetic ǎrithmētǐca, *n.pl*
ark arca, *f*
arm (fore—) brācchǐum, *n;* **(upper—),** lǎcertus, *m;* **(weapon),** telum, *n*
arms (weapons) arma, *n.pl,* tēla, *n.pl;* **(call to —),** ad arma vǒco (1); **(to take —s)** arma cǎpǐo (3); **(to lay down —s),** arma dēdo (3)
arm *v.t,* armo (1); **(to take —s),** arma cǎpǐo (3)
armament (forces) cōpǐae, *f.pl;* **(weapon),** tēlum, *n*
armed armātus
armistice indūtǐae *f.pl*
armour arma *n.pl*
armour-bearer armǐger, *m*
armourer fǎber, *m*
armoury armāmentārǐum, *n*
army exercǐtus, *m;* **(marching —),** agmen, *n;* **(drawn up for battle),** ǎcǐes, *f*
around *adv, and prep. with acc,* circā, circum
arouse *v.t,* suscǐto (1), excǐto (1)
arraign *v.t,* accūso (1)
arrange *v.t,* compōno (3), constǐtǔo (3), collǒco (1), instrǔo (3)
arrangement (as an act) collǒcātǐo, *f* **(order),** ordo, *m*
array *nn,* **(clothing)** vestis, *f,* vestǐmenta, *n.pl;* **(battle—),** ǎcǐes, *f*

array *v.t,* compōno (3)
arrears rělǐquae pěcūnǐae, *f.pl* **(money remaining)**
arrest *v.t,* comprěhendo (3)
arrest *nn,* comprěhensǐo, *f*
arrival adventus, *m*
arrive *v.i,* advěnǐo (4), pervěnǐo (4)
arrogance arrǒgantǐa, *f*
arrogant arrǒgans
arrogate *v.t,* arrǒgo (1) *(with dat)*
arrow sǎgitta, *f*
arsenal armāmentārǐum, *n*
art ars, *f*
artery vēna, *f*
artful callǐdus, vǎfer
artfully *adv,* callǐde
artfulness callǐdǐtas, *f*
article (thing) rēs, *f;* **(term of a treaty, etc.),** condǐcǐo, *f*
articulate *adj,* clārus, distinctus
articulate *v.t,* exprǐmo (3)
articulation explānātǐo, *f*
artifice ars, *f*
artificer (craftsman) artǐfex, *m,* ǒpǐfex, *c*
artificial artǐfǐcǐōsus
artificially *adv,* mǎnu, artē
artillery tormenta, *n.pl*
artisa fǎber, *m,* ǒpǐfex, *c*
artist artǐfex, *m;* **(painter),** pictor, *m*
artistic artǐfǐcǐōsus
artless (person) simplex; **(work),** incomptus
artlessness simplǐcǐtas, *f*
as *conj,* **(because),** quod, cum, quǐa; *(in a comparative phr, e.g.* **as strong as)** tam fortis quam; **(the same as)** īdem atque; **(as ... as possible)** quam *with the superlative, e.g.* **as quickly as possible;** quam cělerrime; **(as if)** tamquam, quǎsǐ, vělut
ascend *v.t,* ascendo (3)
ascendant (to be in the—) *v.i,* praesto (1)
ascendancy praestantǐa, *f*
ascent ascensus, *m*
ascertain *v.t.* **(find out),** cognosco (3), compěrǐo (4)
ascetic *adj,* abstǐnens

ascribe *v.t*, ascrībo (3), assigno (1), attrĭbuo (3)

ash (tree) fraxĭnus, *f*, *(adj)*, fraxĭnĕus

ashamed (to be —) pŭdet; *impers. with acc. and genit*, *(e.g.* **I am ashamed of my brother)** pŭdet me frātris

ashes cĭnis *m*

ashore *adv*, **(on shore)**, in lītŏre; **(to shore)**, in lītus

aside *use* se, *compounded with verb*, **e.g. to put aside**, sēcerno (3)

ask *v.t*, rŏgo (1) *(with 2 accs)* **e.g. I ask you for a sword**, tē glădĭum rŏgo

askance (to look — at) līmis ŏcŭlis aspĭcĭo (3) **(look with a sidelong glance)**

aslant *adv*, oblīque

asleep (to be —) *v.i*, dormĭo (4); **(to fall—)** obdormĭo (4)

asp aspis, *f*

aspect (appearance) aspectus, *m*, făcĭes, *f*

asperity ăcerbĭtas, *f*

asperse *v.t*, aspergo (3)

aspersion călumnĭa, *f*

asphalt bĭtūmen, *n*

aspirate *nn*, aspīrātĭo, *f*

aspiration (desire) affectātĭo, *f*; **(hope)** spes, f

aspire to affecto (1)

ass ăsĭnus, *m*

assail *v.t*, appĕto (3), oppugno (1)

assailant oppugnātor, *m*

assassin percussor, *m*, sīcārĭus, *m*

assassinate *v.t*, trŭcīdo (1)

assassination caedes, *f*

assault *nn*, impĕtus, *m*, oppugnātĭo, *f*

assault *v.t*, oppugno (1), ădŏrĭor (4 *dep*)

assemble *v.i*, convĕnĭo (4); *v.t*, cōgo (3)

assembly coetus, *m*, conventus, *m*; **(— of the Roman people)**, cŏmĭtĭa, *n.pl*

assent *nn*, assensĭo, *f*

assent to *v.i*, assentĭor (4 *dep*) *(with dat)*

assert *v.t*, affirmo (1), confirmo (1)

assertion affirmātĭo, *f*, dēfensĭo, *f*

assess *v.t* **(evaluate)**, aestĭmo (1)

assessment (valuation) aestĭmātĭo, *f*

assessor censor, *m*

assets bŏna, *n.pl*

assiduity assĭdŭĭtas, *f*, sēdŭlĭtas, *f*

assiduous assĭdŭus, sēdŭlus

assiduously *adv*, assĭdŭe, sēdŭlō

assign *v.t*, assigno (1), trĭbŭo (3)

assignation constĭtūtum, *n*

assimilate *v.t*, sĭmĭlem făcĭo (3)

assist *v.t*, iŭvo (1), auxĭlĭor (1 *dep*), subvĕnĭo (4) *(with dat)*

assistance auxĭlĭum, *n*, ŏpem *(no nomin)*, *f*

assistant adiŭtor, *m*

assize (provincial law court) conventus, *m*

associate *nn*, sŏcĭus, *m*

associate *v.t* **(join)**, coniungo (3); *v.i*, ūtor (3 *dep. with abl*)

association sŏcĭĕtas, *f*, consortĭo, *f*

assort *v.t* **(arrange)**, dīgĕro *(irreg)*

assortment (heap) ăcervus *m*

assuage *v.t*, lĕvo (1), mītĭgo (1)

assume *v.t*, pōno (3), sūmo (3); **(take on)** suscĭpĭo (3)

assumption (hypothesis) sumptĭo, *f*

assurance (promise) fĭdes, *f*; **(confidence)** fīdūcĭa, *f*

assure *v.t*, confirmo (1)

assured (certain) explōrātus

assuredly *adv*, **(certainly)** prōfecto

astern *adv*, ā puppi

asthma dyspnoea, *f*

astonish *v.t*, obstŭpĕfăcĭo (3)

astonished stŭpĕfactus; **(to be —)**, *v.i*, obstŭpesco (3)

astonishing mīrĭfĭcus, admīrābĭlis

astonishingly *adv. phr*, mīrum in mŏdum

astonishment stŭpor *m*

astound *v.t*, obstŭpĕfăcĭo (3)

astray (to go —) *v.i*, erro (1); **(to lead —)**, *v.t*, indūco (3)

astrologer măthēmătĭcus, *m*

aunt

astrology astrŏlŏgĭa, *f*
astronomy astrŏlŏgĭa, *f*
astute callĭdus
astuteness callĭdĭtas, *f*
asylum (refuge) perfŭgĭum, *n*
at (*of place*) in (*with abl*), a, ăpŭd
(*with acc*); *with proper names
and* dŏmus *use locative case, e.g.*
at Rome, Rōmae, at home, dŏmi;
(*of time*) *use abl. case, e.g.* at the
third hour, tertĭa hōra; *or
sometimes* ăd *with the acc. case*
atheist ăthĕŏs, *m*
athlete āthlēta, *c*
athletic (strong) fortis
athwart *prep*, (across), trans
(*with acc*)
Atlantic Ocĕănus, *m*
atmosphere āēr, *m*
atom ătŏmus, *f*, sēmĭna (*n.pl*)
rērum (seeds of things)
atone for *v.t*, expĭo (1)
atonement expĭātĭo, *f*
atrocious nĕfārĭus
atrociousness fĕrĭtas, *f*
atrocity nĕfas, *n*
atrophy tābes, *f*
atrophy *v.i*, tābesco (3)
attach *v.t*, (fasten), affĭgo (3),
applĭco (1); (connect) adiungo (3)
attached (fastened) fixus, aptus;
(fond) dēvinctus, ămans
attachment (affection) stŭdĭum,
n, ămor, *m*
attack *nn*, impĕtus, *m*,
oppugnātĭo, *f*
attack *v.t*, oppugno (1),
aggrĕdĭor (3 *dep*), ădŏrĭor (4
dep), invādo (3), pĕto (3)
attacker oppugnātor, *m*
attain *v.i*. (reach), pervĕnĭo (4)
(*with* ad *and acc*); *v.t*. (obtain),
consĕquor (3 *dep*)
attainable impĕtrābĭlis
attainment (obtaining) ădeptĭo, *f*;
(learning) ērŭdītĭo, *f*
attempt *nn*, inceptum, *n*,
cōnātum, *n*
attempt *v.i*, cōnor (1 *dep*)
attend *v.i*. (be present at),
intersum (*irreg. with dat*); *v.t*.
(accompany), cŏmĭtor (1 *dep*),
prōsĕquor, (3 *dep*); (pay

attention) ŏpĕram do (1),
ănĭmadverto (3)
attendance (being present) *use
vb*. adsum (*irreg*) (to be present);
(of crowds), frĕquentĭa, *f*;
(service), appārĭtĭo, *f*
attendant *nn*, (servant) mĭnister,
m; (of a nobleman) sectātor, *m*,
sătellĕs, *c*
attention (concentration) attentĭo
(*f*) ănĭmi; (to pay —); ŏpĕram, (*f*)
do (1)
attentive (alert) intentus, attentus;
(respectful), observans
attentively *adv*, sēdŭlo
attenuate *v.t*, attĕnŭo (1)
attest *v.t*, testor (1 *dep*)
attestation testĭfĭcātĭo, *f*
attire *nn*, vestis, *f*
attire *v.t*, vestĭo (4)
attitude (of mind) ănĭmus, *m*; (of
body), gestus *m*, hăbĭtus, *m*
attract *v.t*, attrăho (3), allĭcĭo (3)
attraction (charms) illĕcĕbrae
(*f.pl*)
attractive blandus, iūcundus
attribute *v.t*, attrĭbŭo (3), assigno
(1)
attune *v.t*, (adjust) consŏnum
(aptum) reddo (3) (make
harmonious (suitable))
auburn flāvus
auction auctĭo, *f*; (to sell by
public —), sub hastā vendo (3)
(sell under the spear)
auctioneer praeco, *m*
audacious audax
audacity audācĭa, *f*, confĭdentĭa, *f*
audibly *use phr*. quod audīri
pŏtest (that can be heard)
audience (of people) audītōres,
m.pl (hearing), ădĭtus, *m*
audit *v.t*, inspĭcĭo (3)
auditorium auditorĭum, *n*
augment *v.t*, augĕo (2)
augur *nn*, augur, *c*
augur *v.t*, vātĭcĭnor (1 *dep*)
augury augŭrĭum, *n*, auspĭcĭum, *n*
August Sextīlis or Augustus
(mensis)
august *adj*, augustus
aunt (paternal) ămĭta, *f*;
(maternal), mātertĕra, *f*

auspices auspĭcĭum, *n*
auspicious faustus, sĕcundus
auspiciously *adv,* fēlīcĭter
austere (severe) sĕvērus
austerity sĕvērĭtas, *f*
authentic vērus, certus
authentically *adv,* certō
authenticate *v.t,* rĕcognosco (3)
authenticity auctōrĭtas, *f*
author (writer) scriptor, *m*;
 (instigator), auctor, *m*
authoritative grăvis, impĕrĭosus
authority auctōrĭtas, *f,* pŏtestas, *f,*
 impĕrĭum, *n*
authorize (give permission to) *v.i,*
 pŏtestātem (auctōrĭtātem), făcĭo
 (3) *(with dat)*
autocracy tўrannis, *f*
autocrat dŏmĭnus, *m*
autograph mănus, *f*
autumn auctumnus, *m*
autumnal auctumnālis
auxiliary *adj,* auxĭlĭāris,
 auxĭlĭārĭus; *nn* adiūtor, *m*;
 (—forces) auxĭlĭa, *n.pl*
avail *v.t* **(assist)**, prōsusm *(irreg)*
 (with dat.); **(make use of)**, ūtor (3
 dep. with abl)
available (ready) expēdītus,
 părātus
avarice ăvārĭtĭa, *f*
avaricious ăvārus
avenge *v.t,* ulciscor (3 *dep)*
avenger ultor, *m*
avenging *adj,* ultrix
avenue xystus, *m*
aver *v.t* **(affirm)**, affirmo (1)
average *adj,* mĕdĭus **(middle)**
averse āversus
aversion ŏdĭum, *n*
avert *v.t,* āverto (3), dēpello (3)
aviary ăvĭārĭum, *n*
avid ăvĭdus
avidity ăvĭdĭtas, *f*
avoid *v.t,* vīto (1), fŭgĭo (3)
avoidance vītātĭo, *f,* fŭga, *f*
avow *v.t,* fătĕor (2 *dep)*
avowal confessĭo, *f*
avowed prŏfessus, ăpertus
await *v.t,* exspecto (1)
awake *adj,* vĭgĭlans; **(to be —)**,
 v.i, vĭgĭlo (1); **(to awake)**, *v.t,*
 excĭto (1)

award *nn,* **(judicial decision)**;
 arbĭtrĭum, *n* **(prize)**, palma,*f*
award *v.t,* trĭbŭo (3), adiūdĭco
 (1)
aware gnārus; **(to be —)**, sentĭo
 (4); **(know)**, scĭo (4)
away *use* a, ab *compounded
 with a verb, e.g.* (ăbĕo) **go
 away** (4)
awe formīdo, *f,* mĕtus, *m,*
 rĕvĕrentĭa, *f*
awe (be in —) vĕrĕor (2 *dep)*
awful vĕrendus
awestruck păvĭdus
awhile *adv,* paulisper, părumper
awkward rŭdis, impĕrītus
awkwardness inscītĭa, *f*
awning vēlum, *n*
awry *adj,* perversus; *adj,* perversē
axe sĕcūris, *f*
axiom sententia, *f*
axis, axle axis, *m*
ay, aye *adv,* ĭta, vērō; **(forever)** in
 perpĕtŭum
azure *adj,* caerŭlĕus

B

babble *v.i,* garrĭo (4), blătĕro (1)
babbler, babbling *adj,* garrŭlus
baby infans, *c*
babyhood infantĭa, *f*
bacchanalian bacchānālis
bachelor *adj,* caelebs
back *nn,* tergum, *n,* dorsum, *n*;
 (at the —) a tergo; **(to move
 something—)**, rĕtro mŏvĕo (2),
 rĕĭcĭo (3); **(to go —)** se rĕcĭpĕre
 (3 *reflex)*
backbite *v.t,* obtrecto (1)
backwards *adj,* **(dull)** pĭger
backwards *adv,* rĕtro
bacon lārĭdum, *n*
bad mălus; **(of health)**, aeger; **(of
 weather)**, ādversus
badge insigne, *n*
badger mēles,*f*
badly *adv,* mălē, prāvē, imprŏbē
badness (worthlessness) nēquĭtĭa,*f*
baffle *v.t,* ēlūdo (3)
bag saccus, *m*
baggage (military) impĕdīmenta,
 n.pl; **(individual packs)**, sarcĭnae,
 f.pl

bail *nn,* (person), vǎs, *m;*
(security) vǎdǐmōnǐum, *n*
bail (to give — for) *v.t,* sponděo
(2) prō (*with abl*)
bailiff (estate manager) villǐcus,
m; (official), appārǐtor, *m*
bait *nn,* esca, *f*
bait *v.t,* (tease), lǎcesso (3),
illūdo (3)
bake *v.t,* torrěo (2), cǒquo (3)
baker pistor, *m*
bakery pistrīnum, *n*
balance *nn,* (scales), lībra, *f;*
(equilibrium), lībrāmentum, *n*
balance *v.t,* lībro (1), compenso
(1)
balcony maenǐāna, *n.pl*
bald calvus, glǎber; (unadorned),
ārǐdus
baldness calvǐtǐum, *n*
bale out *v.t,* (discharge), ēgěro
(3)
bale (bundle) fascis, *m*
baleful pernǐcǐōsus
balk (beam) trabs, *f*
balk *v.t,* frustror (1 *dep*)
ball (for play) pǐla, *f;* (globe,
sphere), glǒbus, *m*
ballad carmen, *n*
ballad-singer cantātor, *m*
ballast sǎbura, *f*
ballet *use vb.* salto (1) (dance)
ballista ballista, *f*
ballot suffrāgǐum, *n*
ballot-box cista, *f,* urna, *f*
balm balsāmum, *n,* unguentum, *n*
balmy (soothing) mollis, lēnis
balustrade (railings) cancelli, *m.pl*
bamboo hǎrundo, *f* (reed)
ban *v.t,* věto (1)
band (bond) vincǔlum, *n;* (of
people), mǎnus, *f,* grex, *m*
band together *v.i,* conǐūro (1)
bandage fascǐa, *f*
bandage *v.t,* lǐgo (1)
bandit lǎtro, *m*
bandy (to — words) *v.i,* altercor
(1 *dep*)
bandy-legged lōrǐpes
bane (injury) pernǐcǐes, *f;* (poison),
věnēnum, *n*
baneful pernǐcǐōsus
bang crěpǐtus, *m*

bang *v.t.* (beat) tundo (3)
banish *v.t, use phr.* ǎquā et igni
interdīco (3) (*with dat*) (forbid on
the use of fire and water), expello
(3)
banishment rělēgātǐo, *f,* exsǐlǐum, *n*
bank *nn,* (of earth), tǒrus, *m;* (of
a river) rīpa, *f;* (for money)
argentārǐa tǎberna (money shop)
banker argentārǐus, mensārǐus, *m*
bankrupt *nn,* dēcoctor, *m* (to
be —), *v.i,* solvendo non esse
bankruptcy (personal) rūīna, *f*
(downfall)
banner vexillum, *n*
banquet convīvǐum, *n,* ěpǔlae,
f.pl
banter *nn,* cǎvǐllātǐo, *f*
banter *v.i,* cǎvillor (1 *dep*)
bar (wooden) asser, *m;* (lock),
claustra, *n.pl;* (bolt), sěra, *f;*
(barrier) rěpāgǔla, *n.pl*
bar *v.t* (fasten), obsěro (1);
(— the way), obsto (1) (*with dat*)
barb (hook) uncus, *m*
barbarian barbǎrus, *m*
barbaric (barbarous) barbǎrus,
crūdēlis, immānis
barbarity barbǎrǐa, *f*
barbarously *adv,* (cruelly),
crūdēlǐter
barbed hāmātus
barber tonsor, *m*
bard (poet, etc.) poēta, *m*
bare nūdus; (to make —), *v.t,*
ǎpěrǐo (4), nūdo (1)
barefaced (shameless) impǔdens
barefoot *adv,* nūdo pěde
barely *adv,* vix
bargain *nn,* pactum, *n*
bargain *v.i,* (make a — with),
paciscor (3 *dep*) (*with* cum *and
abl. of person*)
barge linter, *f;* (— man), nauta, *m*
bark *nn,* (of trees), cortex, *m;* (of
dogs), lātrātus, *m;* (boat), rǎtis, *f*
bark *v.i,* lātro (1)
barley horděum, *n*
barley-water ptǐsǎna, *f*
barn horrěum, *n*
baron princeps, *m*
barque rǎtis, *f*

barracks   castra *n.pl*
barrel   dōlĭum, *n*
barren   stĕrĭlis
barrenness   stĕrĭlĭtas, *f*
barricade   *nn*, agger, *m*
barricade   *v.t*, obsaepĭo (4)
barrier   impĕdĭmentum, *n*, claustra, *n.pl*
barrister   pătrōnus, *m*
barrow   fercŭlum, *n*
barter   *v.t*, (exchange), mūto (1)
barter   *nn*, permūtātĭo, (*f*) mercĭum (exchange of goods)
base   *nn*, băsis, *f*, fundāmentum, *n*
base   *adj*, (worthless), turpis; (lowborn), hŭmĭlis
baseless   *adj*, falsus
basely   *adv*, turpĭter
basement   băsis, *f*
baseness   turpĭtūdo, *f*
bashful   vĕrēcundus
bashfulness   vĕrēcundĭa, *f*
basin   pelvis, *f*
basin   băsis, *f*, fundāmentum, *n*
bask   *v.i*, ăprīcor (1 *dep*)
basket   călăthus, *m*, corbis, *f*, quālum, *n*
bass   *adj*, grăvis
bastard   *adj*, nŏthus
bastion   turris, *f*
bat (animal)   vespertīlĭo, *m*; (club, stick), clāva, *f*
bath   *nn*, balnēum, *n*; (public —) balneae, *f.pl*
bath, bathe   *v.i*, lăvor (1 *pass*); *v.t*, lăvo (1)
bathing   *nn*, lăvātĭo, *f*
baton   scīpĭo, *m*
battalion   cŏhors, *f*
batter   *v.t*, pulso (1), verbĕro (1)
battering-ram   ărĭes, *m*
battery (assault)   vīs, *f*; (cannon), tormenta *n.pl*
battle   proelĭum, *n*; (— line), ăcĭes, *f* (— cry), clāmor, *m*; (— field), lŏcus (*m*) pugnae
battlement   pinna, *f*, mūnītĭōnes, *f.pl*
bawd   lēna, *f*
bawl   *v.i*, clāmĭto (1)
bawling   *nn*, clāmor, *m*

bay (of the sea)   sĭnus, *m*; (tree) laurus, *f*; (at bay) (*adj*) părātus ad pugnam (ready for a fight)
bay   *v.i*, lātro (1)
bayonet   pŭgĭo, *m*
be   *v.i*, sum (*irreg*)
beach   lītus, *n*
beacon (fire)   ignis, *m*
bead   bāca, *f*
beak   rōstrum, *n*
beaker   pōcŭlum, *n*
beam (of timber)   tignum, *n*, trabs, *f*; (cross —), transtrum, *n*; (ray) rădĭus, *m*
bean   făba, *f*
bear   *nn*, ursus, *m*, ursa, *f*; (constellation), septentrĭōnes, *m.pl*; (The Great —), ursa maior; (The Little —) septentrio minor
bear   *v.t*, fĕro (*irreg*), gĕro (3); (carry), porto (1); (produce), părĭo (3); (— away) aufĕro (*irreg*)
bearable   *adj*, tŏlĕrābĭlis
beard   barba, *f*; (bearded), barbātus
bearer (carrier)   bāiŭlus, *m*, portĭtor, *m*
bearing (posture)   gestus, *m*
beast (wild)   bestĭa, *f*, fĕra, *f*; (domestic), pĕcus, *f*
beastly (filthy)   obscēnus
beat (in music, poetry)   ictus, *m*
beat   *v.t*, caedo (3), fĕrĭo (4), vervĕro (1); (conquer), sŭpĕro (1), vinco (3); (— back), rĕpello (3); (— down) sterno (3); (be beaten), *v.i*, văpŭlo (1)
beating   *nn*, verbĕra, *n.pl*
beautiful   pulcher
beautifully   *adv*, pulchrē
beautify   *v.t*, orno (1)
beauty   pulchrĭtūdo, *f*, forma, *f*
beaver   castor, *m*
becalmed   vento dēstĭtūtus (deserted by the wind)
because   *conj*, quod, quĭa, cum; (because of) *prep*, propter, ŏb (*with acc*)
beckon   *v.t*, innŭo (3) (*with dat*)
become   *v.i*, fīo (*irreg*); *v.t* (to suit, adorn) dĕcet (2 *impers. with acc. of person*)
becoming   *adj*, dĕcōrus

bed lectus, *m*; **(go to —)**, cŭbĭtum ĕo (4)
bedroom cŭbĭcŭlum, *n*
bedaub *v.t*, lĭno (3)
bedeck *v.t*, orno (1); **(bedecked)**, ornātus
bedew *v.t*, irrōro (1)
bee ăpis, *f*
bee-hive alvĕārĭum, *n*
beech (tree) fāgus, *f*
beef caro būbŭla, *f*, **(ox flesh)**
beer cervisia, *f*
beetle scărăbaeus, *m*
befall *v.i*, accĭdo (3)
befit *v.i* **(suit)**, convĕnĭo (4)
before *prep*, **(time and place)**, antĕ (*with acc*); **(place)**, prae, prō (*with abl*); **(in the presence of)**, cōram (*with abl*)
before *adv*, **(time)**, antĕ, prĭus; **(space)** prae; **before** *conj*, antĕquam, prĭusquam
befoul *v.t*, inquĭno (1)
befriend *v.t*, adiŭvo (1)
beg *v.t* **(request)**, pĕto (3), ōro (1); **(be a beggar)**, *v.i*, mendĭco (1)
beget *v.t*, gigno (3)
begetter gĕnĭtor, *m*
beggar mendĭcus, *m*
begin *v.i*, incĭpĭo (3), coepi (3 *defect*)
beginner (originator) auctor, *m* **(learner)**, tīro, *m*
beginning *nn*, ĭnĭtĭum, *n*, princĭpĭum, *n*, inceptum, *n*
begone! ăpăgĕ!
begrudge *v.t* **(envy)**, invĭdĕo (2) (*with dat*)
beguile *v.t*, fallo (3), dēcĭpĭo (3)
behalf (on — of) (*prep*), prō (*with abl*)
behave oneself *v. reflex*, se gĕrĕre (3)
behaviour (manners) mōres, *m.pl*
behead *v.t*, sĕcŭri fĕrĭo (4) **(strike with an axe)**
behest (command) iussum, *n*
behind *prep*, post (*with acc*)
behind *adv*, post, ā tergo
behold *v.t*, conspĭcĭo (3)
behold! (exclamation) eccĕ!
being (human —) hŏmo, *c*
belabour *v.t*, verbĕro (1)

belated sērus
belch *v.i*, *and v.t*, ructo (1)
belch *nn*, ructus, *m*
beleaguer *v.t*, obsĭdĕo (2)
belfry turris, *f*
belie *v.t*, **(conceal)**, dissĭmŭlo (1)
belief fĭdes, *f*; **(impression)**, ŏpīnĭo, *f*, persuāsĭo, *f*
believe *v.t*, crēdo (3) (*with dat. of person*) pŭto (1), arbĭtror (1 *dep*), censĕo (2)
believer crēdens, *c*
bell tintinnābŭlum, *n*
belligerent bellans, belli cŭpĭdus **(keen on war)**
bellow *v.i*, mūgĭo (4)
bellowing *nn*, mūgĭtus, *m*
bellows (pair of —) follis, *m*
belly venter, *m*, abdōmen, *n*
belong to *v.i*, use esse (*irreg*) **(to be)** *with genit. of person*
beloved cārus, dīlectus
below *prep*, infrā, subter (*with acc*), sub (*with abl. or acc*)
below *adv*, infrā, subter
belt baltĕus, *m*
bemoan *v.t*, gĕmo (3)
bench scamnum, *n*; **(for rowers)** transtrum, *n*
bend *v.t*, flecto (3), curvo (1); *v.i*, se flectĕre (3 *pass*)
bend, bending *nn*, flexus, *m*
beneath see below
benefactor *phr*, qui bĕnĕfĭcĭa confert **(who confers favours)**
beneficence bĕnĕfĭcentĭa, *f*
beneficent bĕnĕfĭcus
beneficial sălūtāris, ūtĭlis; **(to be —)** *v.i*, prōsum (*irreg*) (*with dat*)
benefit *v.i* prōsum (*irreg*) (*with dat*), adiŭvo (1)
benefit *nn*, bĕnĕfĭcĭum, *n*
benevolence bĕnĕfĭcentĭa, *f*, bĕnĕvŏlentĭa, *f*
benevolent bĕnĕfĭcus, bĕnĕvŏlus
benign bĕnignus
benignity bĕnignĭtas, *f*
bent *adj*, curvus; **(—on)** attentus; **(—back)** rĕsŭpīnus; **(—forward)** prōnus
benumb *v.t*, *phr* torpōre affĭcĭo (3) **(affect with numbness)**

bequeath *v.t*, lēgo (1)
bequest lēgātum, *n*
bereave *v.t*, orbo (1)
bereaved orbus
bereavement orbĭtas, *f*, damnum, *n*
berry bāca, *f*
berth (for a ship) stătĭo, *f*
beseech ōro (1), obsĕcro (1), quaeso (3)
beseem (become) dĕcet (2 *impers. with acc. of person*)
beset *v.t*, obsĭdĕo (2), circumvĕnĭo (4)
beside *prep*, **(near)**, prŏpĕ (*with acc*); **(except)**, praeter (*with acc*)
besides *adv or conj*, praeterquam
besides *adv*, **(further)**, praetĕrĕā, insŭper
besiege *v.t*, obsĭdĕo (2), circum sĕdĕo (2)
besieger obsessor, *m*
besmear *v.t*, illĭno (3)
bespatter *v.t*, aspergo (3)
bespeak *v.t*, **(hire)** condūco (3)
besprinkle *v.t*, aspergo (3)
best *adj*, optĭmus; **(to the best of (one's) ability)** prō (vĭrīli) parte;
best *adv*, optĭmē
bestial *use phr*, bestĭārum mōre **(after the manner of beasts)**
bestir (to — oneself) *v.i*, expergiscor (3 *dep*)
bestow *v.t*, do (1), trĭbŭo (3), confĕro (*irreg*)
bestowal largītĭo, *f*
bet *nn*, pignus, *n*
bet *v.t*, pignŏre contendo (3)
betake *v.t*, conferre (*irreg*)
betimes *adv*, mātūrē
betray *v.t*, prōdo (3)
betrayal prōdĭtĭo, *f*
betrayer prōdĭtor, *m*
betroth *v.t*, spondĕo (2)
betrothal sponsālĭa, *n.pl*
better *adj*, mĕlĭor; **(of health)**, sānus; **better** *adv*, mĕlĭus
better *v.t*, **(improve)**, corrĭgo (3); ēmendo (1)
between *prep*, inter (*with acc*)
beverage pōtĭo, *f*, pōtus, *m*
bevy căterva, *f*

bewail *v.t*, dēplōro (1), lūgeo (2)
beware *v.i and v.t*, căvĕo (2)
bewilder *v.t*, perturbo (1), distrăho (3)
bewildered turbātus, distractus
bewitch *v.t*, fascĭno (1); **(charm)**, căpĭo (3)
beyond *prep*, ultrā, trans, sŭprā, extrā (*with acc*)
beyond *adv*, ultrā, sŭprā
bias inclīnātĭo, *f*
bias *v.t*, inclīno (1)
Bible *use phr*. scripta săcra, *n.pl* **(sacred writings)**
bicker *v.i*, altercor (1 *dep*)
bid *nn*, **(of a price)** lĭcĭtātĭo, *f*
bid *v.t* **(tell, order)**, iŭbĕo (2)
bide *v.i* **(stay)**, mănĕo (2)
bier fĕrĕtrum, *n*, fercŭlum, *n*
big magnus, vastus, ingens
bigotry obstĭnātĭo, *f*
bile bīlis, *f*
bilge-water sentīna, *f*
bilious bīlĭōsus
bill (written, financial) lĭbellus, *m*, rătĭo, *f*, syngrăpha, *f*; **(proposal in Parliament)**, rŏgātĭo, *f*; **(a law)**, lex, *f* **(of a bird)**, rōstrum, *n*
billet (of wood) lignum, *n*; **(lodging of soldiers)**, hospĭtĭum, (*n*) mīlĭtum
billet *v.t* **(soldiers)**, per hospĭtĭa dispōno (3) **(distribute through lodgings)**
billow fluctus, *m*
billowy fluctŭosus
bind *v.t*, lĭgo (1), vincĭo (4); **(oblige)**, oblĭgo (1); **(— together)**, collĭgo (1)
biographer scriptor rērum gestārum **(writer of exploits)**
biography vīta, *f*
birch (tree) bĕtŭla, *f*
bird ăvis, *f*; **(— cage)**, căvĕa, *f*; **(— nest)**, nīdus, *m*
birth ortus, *m*, gĕnus, *n*
birthday (dĭes) nātālis
birth place sŏlum, (*n*) nātāle
bishop pontĭfex, *m*
bit (bite) offa, *f*; **(small piece of food)**, frustum, *n*; **(for a horse)**, frēnum, *n*

bitch cănis, *f*
bite *nn*, morsus, *m*
bite *v.t*, mordĕo (2)
biting *adj*, mordax, asper
bitter ămārus, ăcerbus, asper
bitterness ăcerbĭtas, *f*
bitumen bĭtūmen, *n*
bivouac *nn*, excŭbĭae, *f.pl*
bivouac *v.i*, excŭbo (1)
blab *v.i*, blătĕro (1)
black nĭger; (— art), măgĭce, *f*
blackberry mōrum, *n*, rŭbus, *m*
blackbird mĕrŭla, *f*
blacken *v.t*, nigrum reddo (3)
blackguard nĕbŭlo, *m*
Black Sea Pontus Euxīnus, *m*
blacksmith făber, *m*
bladder vēsīca, *f*
blade (of grass) herba, *f*; (of sword, knife), lāmĭna, *f*
blame *nn*, culpa, *f*
blame *v.t*, culpo (1)
blameable culpandus
blameless innŏcens, intĕger
blamelessness innocentĭa, *f*
bland blandus
blandishment blandītĭa, *f*, blandīmentum, *n*
blank *adj*, (empty), văcŭus; (paper), pūrus
blank *nn*, ĭnāne, *n*
blanket lōdix, *f*
blaspheme *v.t*, blasphēmo (1)
blast *nn*, ĭnāne, *n*
blanket lōdix, *f*
blaspheme *v.t*, blasphēmo (1)
blast *nn*, flāmen, *n*, flātus, *m*
blast *v.t*, ūro (3)
blatant *adj*, (manifest), ăpertus
blaze *nn*, flamma, *f*
blaze *v.i*, ardĕo (2), flăgro (1)
bleach candĭdum reddo (3)
bleak algĭdus, frīgĭdus
blear-eyed lippus
bleat, bleating bālātus, *m*
bleat *v.i*, bālo (1)
bleed *v.i*, sanguĭnem effundo (3); *v.t*, sanguĭnem mitto (3)
bleeding *adj*, (wound), crūdus
bleeding *nn*, use phr effūsĭo, (*f*), sanguĭnis (shedding of blood)
blemish *nn*, (physical), vĭtĭum, *n*, (moral), măcŭla, *f*

blemish *v.t*, măcŭlo (1)
blend *v.t*, miscĕo (2)
bless *v.t*, (favour, make successful), sĕcundo (1), bĕnĕdīco (3)
blessed beātus; (of the dead), pĭus
blessedness bĕātĭtūdo, *f*, fēlīcĭtas, *f*
blessing *nn*, bĕnĕdictĭo, *f*, bŏnum, *n*
blight *nn*, rōbīgo, *f*
blight *v.t*, ūro (3); (—of hopes) frustror (1 *dep*)
blind *adj*, caecus
blind *v.t*, caeco (1)
blindly (rashly) *adv*, tĕmĕre
blindness caecitas, *f*
blink *v.i*, connīvĕo (2)
bliss fēlīcĭtas, *f*
blissful *adj*, fēlix
blister pustŭla, *f*
blithe hĭlăris
blizzard imber, *m*
bloated sufflātus
block *nn*, (of wood), stīpes, *m*, massa, *f*
block *v.t*, obstrŭo (3), obsaepĭo (4)
blockade *nn*, obsĭdĭo, *f*
blockade *v.t*, obsĭdĕo (2)
blockhead caudex, *m*
blood sanguis, *m*; (gore), crŭor, *m*
blood-letting *nn*, missĭo, (*f*) sanguĭnis
bloodshed caedes, *f*
bloodshot crŭōre suffusus (spread over with blood)
blood-stained crŭentus
bloodthirsty sanguĭnārĭus
bloody crŭentus, sanguĭnĕus
bloom *nn*, flōs, *m*
bloom *v.i*, flōrĕo (2)
blooming flōrens
blossom, etc. see bloom
blot *v.t*, măcŭlo (1); (—out, obliterate), dēlĕo (2)
blot *nn*, măcŭla, *f*
blow *nn*, (stroke), plāga, *f*, ictus, *m*
blow *v.i. and v.t*, flo (1)

blowing *nn*, flātus, *m*
bludgeon fustis, *m*
blue *adj*, caerŭlĕus
bluff *v.t*, illūdo (3)
blunder *nn*, mendum, *n*, error, *m*
blunder *v.i*, offendo (3), erro (1)
blunt *adj*, hĕbes; **(frank)**, līber
blunt *v.t*, hĕbĕto (1), obtundo (3)
bluntly *adv*, lībĕrē, plāne
blush *nn*, rŭbor, *m*
blush *v.i*, ērŭbesco (3)
bluster *v.i*, dēclāmo (1)
bluster *nn*, dēclāmātĭo, *f*
blusterer iactātor, *m*
boar verres, *m*, ăper, *m*
board *nn*, tăbŭla, *f*; **(council)**, concĭlĭum, *n*
board *v.t* **(ship)**, conscendo (3); **(to — up)**, contăbŭlo (1); **(provide food)**, victum praebĕo (2)
boast *v.i*, glōrĭor (1 *dep.*), se iactāre (1 *reflex*)
boasting *nn*, glōrĭātĭo, *f*, iactātĭo, *f*
boat scăpha, *f*, linter, *f*
boatsman nauta, *m*
bode *v.t* **(predict)**, praesāgĭo (4)
bodily *adj*, corpŏrĕus
bodkin ăcus, *f*
body corpus, *n*; **(— of soldiers, etc.)**, mănus, *f*, nŭmĕrus, *m*, multĭtūdo, *f*
bodyguard stīpātōres, *m.pl*
bog pălus, *f*
boggy păluster
boil *nn*, vŏmĭca, *f*
boil *v.t*, cŏquo (3); *v.i*, fervĕo (2)
boiled *adj*, ēlixus
boiler caldārĭum, *n*
boisterous prŏcellōsus, turbĭdus
bold audax, ănĭmōsus, fortis
boldly *adv*, audacter, anĭmōse, fortĭter
boldness audācĭa, *f*, fĭdentĭa, *f*
bolster cervīcal, *n*, pulvīnus, *m*
bolt *nn*, **(door, etc.)**, ŏbex, *m*, rĕpāgŭla, *n.pl*
bolt *v.t* **(door, etc.)**, obsĕro (1), claudo (3); **(food)**, obsorbĕo (2)

bombastic inflātus
bond vincŭlum, *n*, cătēna, *f*; **(legal)**, syngrăpha, *f*
bondage servĭtus, *f*
bone ŏs, *n*
book lĭber, *m*, lĭbellus, *m*
bookbinder glūtĭnātor, *m*
bookcase armārĭum, *n*
book-keeper actŭārĭus, *m*
bookseller biblĭŏpōla, *m*
boom *v.i*, sŏno (1)
boon (good thing) bŏnum, *n*
boor hŏmo ăgrestis
boorish agrestis
boot calcĕus, *m*; **(heavy —)**, călĭga, *f*
bootless (unsuccessful) *adj*, irrĭtus
booth tăberna, *f*
booty praeda, *f*, spŏlĭa, *n.pl*
booze *v.i. and v.t*, pōto (1)
border margo, *m*, *f*; **(of a country)**, finis, *m*
border *v.i*, attingo (3)
bordering *adj*, fīnĭtĭmus
bore (person) use, *adj*, importūnus **(rude)**
bore *v.t*, perfŏro (1), tĕrĕbro (1); **(— someone)**, fătĭgo (1)
boredom taedĭum, *n*
born *adj*, nātus; **(to be —)**, *v.i*, nascor (3 *dep*)
borough mūnĭcĭpĭum, *n*
borrow mūtŭor (1 *dep.*)
bosom sĭnus, *m*, pectus, *n*
boss (of a shield) umbo, *m*
botany ars herbārĭa, *f*
botch *v.t*, măle sarcĭo (4), **(patch badly)**
both ambo; **(each of two)** ŭterquĕ; **(both ... and)**, et ... et
bother *nn*, use *adj*, mŏlestus **(troublesome)**
bother *v.t*, lăcesso (3), vexo (1)
bottle ampulla, *f*, lăgēna, *f*
bottom fundus, *m*, *or use adj*, īmus *in agreement with noun*, *e.g.* **at the bottom of the tree,** ad īmam arbŏrem
bottomless (very deep) prŏfundus
bough rāmus, *m*
boulder saxum, *n*
bounce *v.i*, rĕsĭlĭo (4)

bride

bound (limit) fīnis, *m*, mŏdus, *m*; **(leap)**, saltus, *m*

bound *v.i*, **(leap)**, sălĭo (4); *v.t*, **(limit)**, contĭnĕo (2)

boundary fīnis, *m*

boundless infīnītus

bountiful largus, bĕnignus

bounty largĭtas, *f*, bĕnignĭtas, *f*

bouquet serta, *n.pl*

bout (contest) certāmen, *n*

bow (archery) arcus, *m*; **(of a ship)**, prōra, *f*; **(of salutation)**, sălūtātĭo, *f*

bow *v.t*, inclīno (1), dēmitto (3); *v.i*, se dēmittĕre (3 *reflex*)

bow-legged vătĭus

bowman săgittărĭus, *m*

bowels viscĕra, *n.pl*

bower umbrācŭlum, *n*

bowl crātēra, *f*

box arca, *f*, cista, *f*; **(tree)**, buxus, *f*; **(slap)**, cŏlăphus, *m*

box *v.i*, pugnis certo (1), **(fight with the fists)**

boxer pŭgil, *m*

boxing *nn*, pŭgĭlātĭo, *f*

boy pŭer, *m*

boyhood pŭĕrītĭa, *f*

boyish pŭĕrīlis

brace (support) fascĭa, *f*; **(in architecture)**, fībŭla, *f*

brace *v.t*, lĭgo (1), firmo (1)

bracelet armilla, *f*

bracket mūtŭlus, *m*

brackish ămārus

brag *v.i*, glōrĭor (1 *dep.*)

braggart iactātor, *m*

braid *nn*, **(of hair)**, grădus, *m*

braid *v.t*, necto (3)

brain cĕrĕbrum, *n*

brainless (stupid) sōcors

bramble dūmus, *m*

bran furfur, *m*

branch rāmus, *m*

branch *v.i*, **(separate)**, dīvĭdor (3 *pass*)

branching *adj*, rāmōsus

brand (fire —) fax, *f*, torris, *m*; **(burn-mark)**, nŏta, *f*; **(stigma)**, stigma, *n*

brand *v.t*, ĭnūro (3), nŏto (1)

brandish *v.t*, vibro (1)

brass ŏrĭchalcum, *n*

brave fortis, ănĭmōsus, ăcer

bravely *adv*, fortĭter, ănĭmōsē

bravery fortĭtūdo, *f*

brawl *v.i*, rixor (1 *dep*)

brawl *nn*, rixa, *f*

brawny lăcertōsus

bray *v.i*, rŭdo (3)

brazen (made of brass) aēnĕus, aerĕus; **(impudent)**, impŭdens

breach rŭīna, *f*, *or use vb.* rumpo (3) **(to burst)**; **(— in a treaty, etc.)** *use* vĭŏlo (1) **(to violate)**

bread pānis, *m*

breadth lātĭtūdo, *f*

break *v.t*, frango (3); **(treaty, etc.)** vĭŏlo (1); **(— promise)**, fĭdem fallo (3); **(— down)**, *v.t*, rēscindo (3); **(— in)**, *v.t*, **(horses)**, dŏmo (1); **(— into)**, *v.t*, irrumpo (3); **(— loose)** ērumpo (3)

break (of day) prīma lux, *f*, **(first light)**; **(fracture)**, fractūra, *f*

breakfast ientācŭlum, *n*

breakfast *v.i*, iento (1)

breakwater mōles, *f*

breast pectus, *n*, mamma, *f*

breast-plate lōrīca, *f*

breath spīrĭtus, *m*, ănĭma, *f*; **(out of —)**, exănĭmātus; **(to hold one's —)**, ănĭmam comprĭmo (3)

breathe *v.i*, spīro (1); **(— out)**, exspīro (1)

breathing *nn*, aspīrātĭo, *f*

breathless exănĭmātus

breed *v.t*, gĕnĕro (1); *v.i*, nascor (3 *dep.*) **(to be born)**

breed *nn*, gĕnus, *n*

breeding *nn*, **(giving birth)** partus, *m*; **(manners)**, hūmānĭtas, *f*

breeze aura, *f*

breezy ventōsus

brevity brĕvĭtas, *f*

brew *v.t*, cŏquo (3); *v.i* **(overhang)** impendĕo (2)

bribe *nn*, praemĭum, *n*

bribe *v.t*, corrumpo (3)

bribery ambĭtus, *m*

brick lăter, *m*; **(made of —)**, *adj*, lătĕrīcĭus

bricklayer structor, *m*

bridal nuptĭālis

bride (before marriage) sponsa, *f* **(after marriage)**, nupta, *f*

English–Latin   181

bridegroom (before marriage)
sponsus, *m* **(after marriage),**
nuptus, *m*, mărītus, *m*
bridge pons, *m*
bridle frēnum, *n*
brief *adj*, brĕvis
briefly *adv*, brĕvĭter
briar dūmus, *m*
brigade lĕgĭo, *f*
bright clārus
brighten *v.t*, illustro (1); *v.i,*
clāresco (3)
brightly *adv*, clāre
brilliance splendor, *m*, nĭtor, *m*
brilliant splendĭdus; **(famous),**
praeclārus
brim margo, *m*, *f*, labrum, *n*
brimstone sulfur, *n*
brine salsāmentum, *n*
bring, *v.t*, fĕro, affĕro (*irreg*),
addūco (3) apporto (1);
(— about), confĭcĭo (3); **(— back,**
— before), rĕfĕro (*irreg*);
(—down), dēfĕro (*irreg*);
(—forward), prōfĕro (*irreg*);
(— in), infĕro (*irreg*); **(— out),**
ēffĕro (*irreg*); **(— over),** perdūco
(3); **(—together),** cōgo (3); **(— up)**
(children), ēduco (1)
brink (river, etc.) rīpa, *f*; **(of cliff,**
etc.) *use adj*, summus **(highest)**
brisk ălăcer
briskness ălacrĭtas, *f*
bristle saeta, *f*
bristle *v.i.* horrĕo (2)
brittle frăgĭlis
broach *v.t*, ăpĕrĭo (4), prōfĕro
(*irreg*)
broad lātus
broadly (widely) *adv*, lātē
broil (quarrel) rixa, *f*
broil *v.t*, torrĕo (2)
broken fractus; **(disabled),**
confectus
broker interpres, *c* **(agent)**
bronze aes, *n*; *(adj)*, aēnĕus,
aerĕus
brooch fĭbŭla, *f*
brood *v.i.* incŭbo (1)
brood (of young, etc.) fētus, *m*
brook rīvus, *m*
brook (no interference etc) pătĭor
(3 *dep*)

broom scōpae, *f.pl*
broth ius, *n*
brothel gānĕa, *f*
brother frāter, *m*
brotherhood sŏcĭĕtas, *f*
brow (forehead) frons, *f*; **(eye-**
brow), sŭpercĭlĭum, *n*; **(of hill),**
căcūmen, *n*
brown fuscus
browse *v.t* **(read),** perlĕgo (3)
bruise *nn*, contūsum, *n*
bruise *v.t*, contundo (3)
brunt (bear the — of) *use* sustĭnĕo
(2) **(to bear)**
brush *nn*, pēnĭcŭlus, *m*
brush *v.t*, dētergĕo
brushwood sarmenta, *n.pl*
brutal fĕrus, ătrox
brutality immānĭtas, *f*
brutally *adv*, immānĭter
brute bestĭa, *f*, fĕra, *f*
bubble bulla, *f*
bubble *v.i*, bullo (1)
buccaneer pīrāta, *m*
buck (male stag) cervus, *m*
bucket sĭtŭla, *f*
buckle fĭbŭla, *f*
buckle *v.t*, fĭbŭlā necto (3)
(fasten with a buckle)
buckler (shield) scūtum, *n*
bud *nn*, gemma, *f*
bud *v.i*, gemmo (1), germĭno (1)
budge *v.i*, cēdo (3); *v.t*, mŏvĕo (2)
budget rătĭo, *f* **(reckoning,**
account)
buff lŭtĕus
buffet (blow) cŏlăphus, *m*
buffoon scurra, *m*
bug cīmex, *m*
bugbear terrĭcŭla, *n.pl*
bugle būcĭna, *f*
build *v.t*, aedĭfĭco (1)
builder aedĭfĭcātor, *m*
building (act of —) aedĭfĭcātĭo, *f*,
(structure itself), aedĭfĭcĭum, *n*
bulb bulbus, *m*
bulk magnĭtūdo, *f*, mōles, *f*
bulky ingens, grandis
bull taurus, *m*
bullet glans, *f*
bullion aurum, *n*
bullock iŭvencus, *m*
bulrush iuncus, *m*

bulwark mūnīmentum, *n*
bump *nn*, tūber, *n*, tŭmor, *m*
bump *v.i*, offendo (3)
bumpkin rustĭcus, *m*
bunch ūva, *f*, rācēmus, *m*
bundle fascis, *m*
bung (stopper) obtūrāmentum, *n*
bungle *v.i*, inscītē, ăgo (3) (do unskilfully)
bungler *adj*, impĕrītus
buoyancy lĕvĭtas, *f*
buoyant lĕvis
burden ŏnus, *n*
burden *v.t*, ŏnĕro (1)
burdensome grăvis
bureau scrīnĭum, *n*, armārĭum, *n*
burgess cīvis, *c*
burglar fūr, *m*
burglary furtum, *n*
burgle *v.t*, fūror (1 *dep*.) (steal)
burial fūnus, *n*, sĕpultūra, *f*
burial-place lŏcus, (*m*) sĕpultūrae
burly lăcertōsus
burn *v.t*, ūro (3), incendo (3); *v.i*, ardĕo (2), flagro (1)
burn *nn*, ambustum, *n*
burning *adj*, ardens
burnish *v.t*, pŏlĭo (4)
burrow cŭnīcŭlum, *n*
burst *v.t*, rumpo (3); *v.i*, rumpor (3 *pass*)
burst out *v.i*, ērumpo (3)
bursting out *nn*, ēruptĭo (3)
bursting out *nn*, ēruptĭo, *f*
bury *v.t*, sĕpĕlĭo (4), abdo (3)
bush dūmus
bushel mĕdimnum, *n*
bushy frŭtĭcōsus
busily *adv*, sēdŭlō
business nĕgōtĭum, *n*, res, *f*
bust (statue) ĭmāgo, *f*
bustle *nn*, festīnātĭo, *f*
bustle *v.i*, festīno (1)
busy occŭpātus
but *conj*, sed, vērum, at (*first word in clause*) autem, vēro (*second word in clause*); (except), praeter (*with acc*)
butcher lănĭus, *m*
butcher *v.t* (murder), trŭcīdo (1)
butchery trŭcīdātĭo, *f*
butler prōmus, *m*
butt (laughing stock) lūdĭbrĭum, *n*

butt *v.t*, cornū fĕrĭo (4) (strike with the horn)
butter būtŷrum, *n*
butterfly pāpĭlĭo, *m*
buttock clūnis, *m*, *f*
buttress antēris, *f*
buxom vĕnustus
buy *v.t*, ĕmo (3)
buyer emptor, *m*
buying *nn*, emptĭo, *f*
by *prep* (of place, near), ad, prŏpe (*with acc*); (of time) often expressed by abl. of noun, e.g. by night, nocte; (— means of), per (*with acc*) (by an agent, e.g. by a spear, abl. case alone), hastā; (—chance), *adv*, fortĕ
bygone *adj*, praetrītus
bystander spectātor, *m*
byway trāmes, *m*

C

cab raeda, *f*, cĭsĭum, *n*
cabal (faction) factĭo, *f*
cabbage brassĭca, *f*
cabin (hut) căsa, *f*
cabinet (furniture) armārĭum, *n*; (council) summum consĭlĭum, *n*
cable (anchor —) ancŏrāle, *n*
cackle, cackling *nn*, strĕpĭtus, *m*
cackle *v.i*, strĕpo (3)
cadaverous cădāvĕrōsus
cadence cursus, *m*
cadet discĭpŭlus, *m*, tīro, *m*
cage căvĕa, *f*
cajole *v.t*, blandĭtor (4 *dep. with dat*)
cajolery blandĭtĭae, *f.pl*
cake *nn*, plăcenta, *f*, lībum, *n*
calamitous exĭtĭōsus
calamity clādes, *f*, mălum, *n*
calculate *v.t*, compŭto (1), aestīmo (1)
calculation rătĭo, *f*
calendar fasti, *m.pl*
calf vĭtŭlus, *m*; (of the leg), sūra, *f*
call *v.t*, (name), vŏco (1), appello (1); dīco (3); (— back), rĕvŏco (1); (— to, summon), advŏco (1); (— together), convŏco (1); (— up or out), suscĭto (1)

call *nn* **(cry)**, clāmor, *m*; **(visit)**
   sălūtātĭo, *f*
caller sălūtātor, *m*
calling *nn*, **(vocation)**, ars, *f*,
   artĭfĭcĭum, *n*
calling *nn*, **(vocation)**, ars, *f*,
   artĭfĭcĭum, *n*
callous callōsus
callow implūmis
calm *adj*, plăcĭdus, tranquilius
calm *nn*, tranquillĭtas, *f*, mălăcĭa
calm *v.t*, sēdo (1), plāco (1)
calmly *adv*, tranquille, plăcĭde
calumniate *v.t*, crīmĭnor (1 *dep*)
calumnious crīmĭnōsus
calumny crīmĭnātĭo, *f*
camel cămēlus, *m*
camp castra, *n.pl*; **(to pitch —)**,
   castra pōno (3); **(to move —)**,
   castra mŏvĕo (2); **(a winter ...)**,
   hīberna, *n.pl*
campaign stīpendĭum, *n*
campaign *v.i*, stīpendĭum mĕrĕor
   (2 *dep*)
can *nn*, urcĕus, *m*
can *v.i*, **(to be able)**, possum
   (*irreg*)
canal fossa, *f*
cancel *v.t*, dēlĕo (2), abrŏgo (1)
cancer **(sign of zodiac)** cancer, *m*
candid ăpertus, līber
candidate candĭdātus, *m*
candle candēla, *f*
candlestick candēlābrum, *n*
candour lībertas, *f*
cane hărundo, *f*, băcŭlum, *n*,
   virga, *f*
cane *v.t*, verbĕro (1)
canister arca, *f*, pyxis, *f*
canker rōbīgo, *f*
canker *v.t*, corrumpo (3)
cannibal anthrōpŏphăgus, *m*
cannon tormentum, *n*
canoe scăpha, *f*
canon **(rule)** rēgŭla, *f*
canopy vēla, *n.pl*
cant ostentātĭo, *f*
canter *v.i*, lēnĭter curro (3) **(run
   smoothly)**
canton păgus, *m*
canvas vēla, *n.pl*, carbăsus, *f*
canvass *v.i*, ambĭo (4)
canvass *nn*, ambĭtĭo, *f*; **(illegal)**,
   ambĭtus

cap pillĕus, *m*
capability făcultas, *f*
capable căpax
capacious căpax
capacity căpăcĭtas, *f*; **(mental —)**,
   ingĕnĭum, *n*
cape prōmontŭrĭum, *n*
caper *v.i*, exsulo (1), salĭo (4)
capital *nn*, **(city)**, căput, *n*
capital *adj*, **(crime, etc.)**, căpĭtālis;
   (chief), princeps
capitulate *v.t*, dēdo (3); *v.i*, se
   dēdĕre (3 *reflex*)
caprice lībīdo, *f*
capricious lĕvis
captain dux, *m*, princeps, *m*; **(of
   a ship)**, măgister, *m*, nauarchus, *m*
captivate *v.t*, căpĭo (3), dēlēnĭo
   (4)
captive *adj. and nn*, captīvus, *m*.
captivity captīvĭtas, *f*
capture *nn*, **(of city, camp, etc.)**,
   expugnātĭo, *f*; **(of persons)**, *use
   vb*, căpĭo (3) **(to capture)**
capture *v.t*, căpĭo (3)
car currus, *m*, plaustrum, *n*
caravan **(convoy)** commĕātus, *m*,
   (vehicle), raeda, *f*
carbuncle fūruncŭlus, *m*
carcass cădāver, *n*, corpus, *n*
card charta, *f*
cardinal *adj*, prīmus, princeps
care cūra, *f*, sollĭcĭtūdo, *f*
care *v.t* **(to — about or for)** cūro
   (1)
career currĭcŭlum, *n*
careful dīlĭgens; **(carefully
   prepared)** accūrātus; **(cautious)**
   cautus
carefully *adv*, dīlĭgenter
careless neglĕns, indīlĭgens
carelessly *adv*, neglegenter
carelessness neglēgentĭa, *f*
caress blandīmenta *n.pl*,
   complexus, *m*
caress *v.t*, blandĭor (4 *dep*.)
   (*with dat*.)
caressing *adj*, blandus
cargo ŏnus, *n*
caricature imāgo, *f*
caricature *v.t*, *use phr*. vultum
   dētorquĕo (2) **(distort the
   features)**

carnage caedes, *f*, strāges, *f*
carnal corpŏrĕus
carnival fērĭae, *f.pl*
carnivorous carnĭvŏrus
carol cantus, *m*
carousal cōmissātĭo, *f*
carouse *v.i*, cōmissor (1 *dep.*)
carp at *v.t*, carpo (3), mordĕo (2)
carpenter făber, *m*
capet strāgŭlum, *n*
carriage (vehicle) raeda, *f*, carpentum, *n*; (transportation), vectūra, *f*; (poise), incessus, *m*
carrier vector, *m*
carrion căro, *f*, cădāver, *n*
carrot pastĭnăca, *f*
carry *v.t*, porto (1), fĕro (*irreg.*), vĕho (3), gĕro (3); (— away or off), aufĕro (*irreg.*); (— back) rēfĕro (*irreg.*); (— in) infĕro (*irreg.*); (— on) gĕro (3); (— over) transporto (1); (— out, perform) exsĕquor (3 *dep*); (— through a law, etc.) perfĕro (*irreg.*)
cart plaustrum, *n*
cart *v.t*, vĕho (3)
cart-horse iūmentum, *n*
cartilage cartĭlāgo, *f*
carve *v.t*, caelo (1), sĕco (1), sculpo (3)
carver sculptor, *m*
carving *nn*, caelātūre, *f*
case (in law) causa, *f* (circumstances), cāsus, *m* (cover), thēca, *f*
casement fĕnestra, *f*
cash nummus, *m*, pĕcūnĭa nŭmĕrāta, *f*
cashier *nn, use phr.* qui nummos dispensat (who dispenses the cash)
cashier *v.t*, (from the army), exauctoro (1)
cask cūpa, *f*
casket arcŭla, *f*
cast *nn*, (throw), iactus, *m*
cast *v.t*, iăcĭo (3), mitto (3); (— down) dēĭcĭo (3); (— off) dēpōno (3); (— out) expello (3)
castaway perdĭtus, *m*
caste ordo, *m*
castigate *v.t*, castīgo (1)

castle castellum, *n*
castor oil cĭcĭnum ŏlĕum, *n*
castrate *v.t*, catro (1)
casual fortŭĭtus
casually *adv*, neglĕgenter
casualty (accident) cāsus, *m*; (killed) *adj*, interfectus
cat fēles, *f*
catalogue index, *c*
catapault cătăpulta, *f*
cataract (waterfall) cătăracta, *f*
catarrh grăvēdo, *f*
catastrophe rŭīna, *f*
catch căpĭo (3), comprĕhendo (3); (a disease), contrăho (3)
categorical (absolute) simplex, plānus
category nŭmĕrus, *m*
cater *v.t*, obsōno (1)
caterpillar ērūca, *f*
catgut chorda, *f*
cattle pĕcus, *n*
cauldron cortīna, *f*
cause *nn*, causa, *f*
cause *v.t*, făcĭo (3), effĭcĭo (3)
causeway agger, *m*
caustic *adj*, mordax (biting)
caution cautĭo, *f*
caution *v.t*, mŏnĕo (2)
cautious cautus
cavalry ĕquĭtātus, *m*, ĕquĭtes, *m.pl*
cave spēlunca, *f*, căverna, *f*, antrum, *n*
caw *v.i*, crōcĭo (4)
cease *v.i*, dēsĭno (3) (*with infin*)
ceaseless perpĕtŭus
cedar cefrus, *f*
ceiling tectum, *n*
celebrate *v.t*, căno (3), cĕlĕbro (1)
celebrated clārus, illustris
celebration cĕlĕbrātĭo, *f*
celebrity fāma, *f*, glōrĭa, *f*; (person), vir praeclārus
celerity cĕlĕrĭtas, *f*
celestial caelstis
celibacy caelĭbātus, *m*
cell, cellar cella, *f*
cement ferrūmen, *n*
cement *v.t*, glūtĭno (1), ferrūmĭno (1)

cemetery sĕpulcrētum, *n*
censor censor, *m*
censure vĭtŭpĕrātĭo, *f*
censure *v.t*, vĭtŭpĕro (1)
reprĕhendo (3)
census census, *m*
per cent *use nn*, centēsĭma, *f* **(one hundredth part)**
centaur centaurus, *m*
central mĕdĭus
centre (of) mĕdĭus, *in agreement with noun, e.g.* **in the centre of the line,** in mĕdĭā ăcĭe
centre on *v.i* **(depend on)**, pendĕo (2) *(with* ab *and* abl*)*
centurion centŭrĭo, *m*
century saecŭlum, *n*
ceremonial rītus, *m*, caerĭmōnĭa, *f*
ceremonious sollemnis
certain certus, explōrātus;
(a — person) *use pron*, quĭdam
certainly *adv*, certo, certē, prŏfecto
certainty res certa; *or use adj*, certus **(certain)**
certificate scriptum testĭmōnĭum **(written proof)**
certify *v.i*, rĕcognosco (3), confirmo (1)
cessation intermissĭo, *f*
chafe *v.t*, fŏvĕo (2), călĕfăcĭo (3·); *v.i*, stŏmăchor (1 *dep.*) **(be irritated)**
chaff pălĕa, *f*
chaffinch fringilla
chagrin stŏmăchus, *m*
chain cătēna, *f*, vincŭlum, *n*
chain *v.t*, cătēnas īnĭcĭo (3) *(with dat)*
chair sella, *f*
chairman măgister, *m*
chalk crēta, *f*
chalk out (mark out) *v.t*, dēsigno (1)
challenge *nn*, prōcŏcātĭo, *f*
challenge *v.t*, prōvŏco (1)
chamber conclāve, *n*; **(bed —),** cŭbĭcŭlum, *n*
chamberlain cŭbĭcŭlārĭus, *m*
chamois căprĕŏlus, *m*
champ *v.t*, mando (3)
champion victor *m*; **(defender),** prōpugnātor, *m*

chance *nn*, cāsus, *m*, fors, *f*, fortūna, *f*
by chance *adv*, **(happen),** forte, cāsu
chance *v.i*, accĭdo (3)
chandelier candēlābrum, *n*
change, changing *nn*, mūtātĭo, *f*, permūtātĭo, *f*
change *v.t*, mūto (1), converto (3); *v.i*, mūtor (1 *pass*)
changeable mūtābĭlis
channel cănālis, *m*, alvĕus, *m*
chant *v.i and v.t*, canto (1)
chaos pertubātĭo, *f*
chaotic perturbātus
chapel săcellum, *n*
chapter căpŭt, *n*
char *v.t*, ambūro (3)
character mōres, *m.pl*, ingĕnĭum *n*; **(reputation),** existĭmātĭo, *f*, ŏpīnĭo, *f*; **(in a play),** persōna, *f*
characteristic *adj*, prōprĭus
charcoal carbo, *m*
charge *nn*, **(attack),** impĕtus, *m*; **(accusation),** crīmen, *n*; **(price),** prĕtĭum, *n*; **(care of),** cūra, *f*
charge *v.t*, **(attack),** impĕtum făcĭo (3); signa infĕro *(irreg)*; **(accuse),** accūso (1); **(of price),** vendo (3) **(sell)** (3); **(put in —)** praefĭcĭo (3) *(with dat)*; **(be in —)** praesum *(irreg.) (with dat)*
chariot currus, *m*, essĕdum, *n*
charioteer aurīga, *c*
charitable bĕnignus, mītis
charity ămor, *m*, bĕnĕfĭcentĭa, *f*
charm blandīmentum, *n*, grātĭa, *f* **(trinket),** bulla, *f*
charm *v.t*, fascīno (1), dēlēnĭo (4), dēlecto (1)
charming vĕnustus, lĕpĭdus
chart tăbŭla, *f*
charter *v.t*, **(hire),** condūco (3)
chase *nn*, **(hunt),** vēnātĭo, *f*, vēnātus, *m*
chase *v.t*, sector (1 *dep.*), vēnor (1 *dep.*)
chasm hĭātus, *m*
chaste castus
chastise *v.t*, castīgo (1), pūnĭo (4)
chastisement castīgātĭo, *f*
chastity castĭtas, *f*

chat *v.i,* fābŭlor (1 *dep.*)
chat *nn,* sermo, *m*
chatter *v.i,* garrĭo (4); **(of teeth),** crĕpĭto (1)
chatter *nn,* garrŭlĭtas, *f*
chattering *adj,* garrŭlus
cheap vīlis
cheapness vīlĭtas, *f*
cheat *nn,* **(person),** fraudātor, *m*
cheat *v.t,* fraudo (1)
cheating *nn,* fraudātĭo, *f*
check *nn,* **(hindrance),** impedīmentum, *n,* incommŏdum, *n;* **(set back),** incommŏdum, *n*
check *v.t,* cŏhĭbĕo (2), contĭnĕo (2), comprĭmo (3), cŏercĕo (2)
cheek gĕna, *f*
cheer *nn,* **(shout),** clāmor, *m*
cheer *v.i,* **(applaud),** plaudo (3), clāmo (1)
cheerful hĭlăris
cheerfulness hĭlărĭtas, *f*
cheerless tristis
cheese cāsĕus, *m*
cheque perscriptĭo, *f,* **(written entry)**
chequered vărĭus
cherish *v.t,* fŏvĕo (2), cŏlo (3)
cherry, cherry tree cĕrăsus, *f*
chess latruncŭli, *m.pl*
chest (box) amārĭum, *n,* cista, *f;* **(body),** pectus, *n,* thorax, *m*
chestnut glands, *f;* **(— tree),** castănĕa, *f*
chew mando (3)
chicken pullus, *m*
chide *v.t,* obiurgo (1), incrĕpĭto (1), rĕprĕhendo (3)
chiding rĕprĕhensĭo, *f*
chief *nn,* princeps, *m,* prōcer, *m*
chief *adj,* prīmus, princeps
chieftain see **chief**
child pŭer, *m,* infans, *c;* (*pl.*) lībĕri, *m.pl*
childbirth partus, *m*
childhood pŭĕrĭtĭa, *f*
childish pŭĕrīlis
childless orbus
chill, chilly *adj,* frīgĭdus
chill *v.t,* rĕfrīgĕro (1)
chime *nn,* concentus, *m*
chime *v.i,* **(sound),** căno (3)
chimney cămīnus, *m*

chin mentum, *n*
chine tergum, *n*
chink rīma, *f*
chip assŭla, *f*
chirp, chirping *nn,* pīpātus, *m*
chirp *v.i,* pīpĭo (4)
chisel scalprum, *n*
chisel *v.t,* sculpo (3)
chivalrous magnănĭmus
chivalry magnănĭmĭtas, *f*
choice *nn,* dēlectus, *m;* **(— between),** optĭo, *f*
choice *adj,* ēlectus
choir chŏrus, *m*
choke *v.t,* suffōco (1); *v.i,* suffōcor (1 *pass*)
choose *v.t,* lĕgo (3), ēlĭgo (3)
chop *v.t,* caedo (3); **(cut off),** abscīdo (3)
chord *use* nervus, *m,* **(string)**
chorus chŏrus, *m*
Christ Christus, *m*
Christian Christĭānus
chronic (long-lasting) dĭūturnus
chronicle annāles, *m.pl*
chuckle *v.i,* căchinno (1)
church templum, *n*
churchyard ārĕa, *f*
churl hŏmo rusticus
churlish rustĭcus
churn *v.t,* **(stir),** ăgĭto (1)
cinder cĭnis, *m,* făvilla, *f*
cipher (a nonentity) nŭmĕrus, *m;* **(secret writing),** nŏta, *f*
circle orbis, *m*
circuit circŭĭtus, *m*
circuitous (route, etc.), flexŭōsus
circular rŏtundus
circulate *v.t,* spargo (3), dīvulgo (1); *v.i,* diffundor (3 *pass*), percrēbresco (3)
circulation, (to be in —) (of books etc.) in mănĭbus esse (*irreg*)
circumcise *v.t,* circumcīdo (3)
circumference ambĭtus, *m*
circumscribe *v.t,* circumscrībo (3)
circumstance res, *f; or use neuter of an adj, e.g.* adversa **(adverse circumstances)**
circumstantial evidence coniectūra, *f*
circumvent *v.t,* circumvĕnĭo (4)
circus circus, *m*

cistern cisterna, *f*
citadel arx, *f*
cite *v.t*, (quote), prōfĕro (*irreg*)
citizen cīvis, *c*
citizenship cīvĭtas, *f*
city urbs, *f*
civic cīvīlis
civil (polite) urbānus; (civic) cīvīlis; (— war), bellum dŏmestĭcum
civilian (opp. military) tŏgātus, *m*
civilization cultus, *m*, hūmānĭtas, *f*
civilize *v.t*, excŏlo (3), expŏlĭo (4)
civilized hūmānus, cultus
claim *v.t*, postŭlo (1), rĕposco (3)
claim *nn*, postŭlātio, *f*
claimant pĕtītor, *m*
clammy lentus
clamorous clāmans
clamour *nn*, clāmor, *m*, strĕpĭtus, *m*
clamour *v.i*, vōcĭfĕror (1 *dep*)
clandestine clandestīnus
clang *nn*, clangor, *m*
clang *v.i. and v.t*, strĕpo (3)
clank crĕpĭtus, *m*
clank *v.i*, crĕpo (1)
clap *nn*, (hands), plausus, *m*; (thunder), frăgor, *m*
clap *v.i. and v.t*, plaudo (3)
clash *v.i*, concrĕpo (1), crĕpĭto (1); (opinions) rĕpugno (1); (fight), conflīgo (3)
clash *nn*, (noise), crĕpĭtus, *m*; (collision), concursus, *m*
clasp *nn*, (embrace), complexus, *m*; (fastener), fĭbŭla, *f*
clasp *v.t*, (fasten), fĭbŭlo (1); (embrace), complector (3 *dep.*)
class classis, *f*, gĕnus, *n*
classic, classical (well-established), prŏbus
classify *v.t*, dēscrībo (3) ordĭne
clatter *nn*, strĕpĭtus, *m*
clatter *v.i*, increpo (1)
clause membrum, *n*, căpŭt, *n*
claw unguis, *m*
clay argilla, *f*, lŭtum, *n*
clean *adj*, mundus, pūrus
clean *v.t*, purgo (1), mundo (1)
cleanliness mundĭtĭa, *f*
cleanse *v.t*, purgo (1)
clear clārus; (weather), sĕrēnus; (matter), mănĭfestus

clear *v.t*, (open up), expĕdĭo (4); (— oneself), sē purgāre (1 *reflex*); *v.i*, (of the weather), dissĕrēnat (1 *impers*)
clearing *nn*, (open space), lŏcus ăpertus
clearly *adv*, clārē, ăpertē, plānē
clearness clārĭtas, *f*
cleave *v.t*, (split), findo (3); *v.i* (stick to), adhaerĕo (2)
cleft hĭātus, *m*, rīma, *f*
clemency clēmentĭa, *f*
clement clēmens, lēntis
clench (the fist) *v.t*, comprĭmo (3)
clerk scrība, *m*
clever callĭdus, astūtus
cleverness *f*, callĭdĭtas, *f*
client clĭens, *m*, consultor, *m*
cliff cautes, *f*, scŏpŭlus, *m*, rūpes
climate caelum, *n*
climax grădātĭo, *f*
climb *v.i. and v.t*, ascendo (3), scando (3)
climb *nn*, ascensus, *m*
cling to *v.i*, ădhaerĕo (2) (*with dat*)
clip *v.t*, tondĕo (2)
cloak pallĭum, *n*, lăcerna, *f*
cloak *v.t*, (hide), dissĭmŭlo (1)
clock hŏrŏlŏgĭum, *n*
clod glaeba, *f*
clog (hindrance) impĕdīmentum, *n*; (shoe), sculpōnĕa, *f*
clog *v.t*, (impede), impĕdĭo (4)
close *adj*, (near), vīcīnus; (packed together) confertus, densus; (at close quarters), commĭnus, *adv*
close *nn*, (end), fīnis, *m*, termĭnus, *m*
close *adv*, prŏpe, iuxta
close *v.t*, claudo (3); *v.i*, claudor (3 *pass*)
close in on *v.t*, prĕmo (3) (press)
closely *adv*, prŏpe; (accurately), exacte
closeness prŏpinquĭtas, *f*
closet cella, *f*
clot (of blood) crŭor, *m*
cloth textum, *n*
clothe *v.t*, vestĭo (4), indŭo (3)
clothes vestis, *f*, vestīmenta, *n.pl*
cloud nūbes, *f*
cloudy nūbĭlus

cloven bĭsulcus
clown scurra, *m*
club (cudgel) clāva, *f*; (association), sŏdālĭtas, *f*
cluck *v.i*, singultĭo (4)
clump massa, *f*
clumsy ĭnhăbĭlis, rustĭcus
cluster *nn*, răcēmus, *m*; (people), glŏbus, *m*
clutch *v.t*, arrĭpĭo (3)
coach carpentum, *n*, raeda, *f*
coachman raedārĭus, *m*
coagulate *v.i*, concresco (3)
coal carbo, *m*
coalition coniunctĭo, *f*, conspīrātĭo, *f*
coarse crassus; (manners), incultus
coarseness crassĭtūdo, *f*, ĭnhūmānĭtas, *f*
coast ōra, *f*, lītus, *n*
coast *v.i*, praetervĕhor (3 *pass*)
coat tŭnĭca, *f*, ămictus, *m*; (animal's), pellis, *f*
coat *v.t*, illĭno (3)
coax *v.t*, mulcĕo (2), blandĭor (4 *dep*)
cobble *v.t*, sarcĭo (4)
cobbler sūtor, *m*
cock gallus, *m*
code (method, system) rătĭo, *f*
coerce *v.t*, cōgo (3), cŏercĕo (2)
coercion cŏercĭtĭo, *f*
coffin arca, *f*
cog dens, *m*
cogent vălĭdus
cogitate *v.i*, cōgĭto (1)
cognizance cognĭtĭo, *f*
cohabit *v.i*, consŭesco (3)
cohere *v.i.* cŏhaerĕo (2)
coherent cŏhaerens
cohesion cŏhaerentĭa, *f*
cohort cŏhors, *f*
coil *nn*, spīra, *f*
coil *v.t*, glŏmĕro (1)
coin *nn*, nummus, *m*
coin *v.t*, cūdo (3)
coinage nummi, *m.pl*
coincide *v.i*, compĕto (3), concurro (3)
coincidence consursātĭo, *f*, concursus, *m*
cold *adj*, frīgĭdus, gĕlĭdus
cold (to be —) *v.i*, algĕo (2)

coldness frīgus, *n*
collapse *v.i*, collābor (3 *dep*)
collar torques, *m and f*
collation (comparison) collātĭo, *f*
colleague collēga, *m*
collect *v.t*, collĭgo (3), cōgo (3)
collection (act of —) collātĭo, *f*; (heap, etc.), congĕrĭes, *f*
collector (of taxes, etc.) exactor, *m*
college collēgĭum, *n*
collide *v.i*, conflīgo (3), concurro (3)
collision concursus, *m*
colloquial (speech) *use* sermo, *m*
collusion collūsĭo, *f*
colon cōlon, *n*
colonel praefectus, *m*
colonist cŏlōnus, *m*
colony cŏlōnĭa, *f*
colonnade portĭcus, *f*
collossal igens
colour cŏlor, *m*; (flag), vexillum, *n*; (— bearer), signĭfer, *m*
colour *v.t*, cŏlōro (1)
coloured pictus
colourful fūcātus
colt equŭlĕus, *m*
column (pillar) columna, *f*; (military), agmen, *n*
comb *nn*, pecten, *m*
comb *v.t*, pecto (3)
combat *nn*, proelĭum, *n*
combat *v.i*, pugno (1), luctor (1 *dep*)
combat *v.t*, (oppose) obsto (1)
combatant pugnātor, *m*
combination coniunctĭo, *f*
combine *v.t*, coinungo (3)
come *v.i*, vĕnĭo (4); (— about, happen), ēvĕnĭo (4); (— across, find), *v.t*, invĕnĭo (4); (— back), *v.i*, rĕvĕnĭo (4); (— by, obtain), *v.t*, ădĭpiscor (3 *dep*); (— in) incēdo (3); (— near) apprŏpinquo (1); (— on, advance), prōgrĕdĭor (3 *dep*); (— out) exĕo (4); (— to) advĕnĭo (4) (regain consciousness) ad se rĕdire (4); (— together) convĕnĭo (4); (—upon), *v.t*, sŭpervĕnĭo (4) (attack) incīdo (3)
comedian cōmoedus, *m*

comedy cōmoedĭa, *f*

comely pulcher

comet cŏmētes, *m*

comfort sōlācĭum, *n*, consōlātĭo, *f*

comfort *v.t*, consōlor (1 *dep*.)

comfortable commŏdus

comforter consōlātor, *m*

comic, comical cōmĭcus

coming *adj*, ventūrus

coming *nn*, adventus, *m*

command *nn*, **(power)**, impĕrĭum, *n*; **(an order)** iussum, *n*, mandātus, *m*; **(to be in —)** *v.i*, praesum (*with dat*)

command *v.t*, impĕro (1) (*with dat*.), iŭbĕo (2)

commander dux, *m*, impĕrātor, *m*

commemorate *v.t*, cĕlĕbro (1)

commemoration cĕlĕbrātĭo, *f*

commence *v.i*, incĭpĭo (3)

commencement ĭnĭtĭum, *n*

commend *v.t*, commendo (1); **(praise)**, laudo (1)

commendable laudābĭlis

comment *v.i*, dīco (3), sententĭas dīco (3) **(declare one's opinion)**

comment *nn*, dicta, *n.pl*

commentary commentărĭi, *m.pl*

commerce commercĭum, *n*

commercial traveller instĭtor, *m*

commiserate *v.i. and v.t*, mĭsĕror (1 *dep*.)

commisariat praefecti (*m.pl*) rĕi frūmentārĭae **(superintendents of corn supply)**; **(provisions)**, commĕātus, *m*

commissary prōcūrātor, *m*, lēgātus, *m*

commission **(task)** mandātum, *n*

commission *v.t*, **(give a task to)**, mando (1) (*dat. of person*)

commit *v.t*, **(crime, etc.)** admitto (3); **(entrust)**, committo (3), mando (1)

committee dēlecti, *m.pl*, **(selected ones)**

commodious **(opportune)** commŏdus; **(capacious)**, amplus

commodity **(thing)** res, *f*

common *adj*, commūnis; **(belonging to the public)**, pūblĭcus; **(ordinary)**, vulgāris; **(common land)**, ăger pūblĭcus, *m* **(usual)**, ūsĭtātus

commonplace *adj*, vulgāris, trītus

commonly *adv*, **(mostly)**, plērumque

commonwealth respublĭca, *f*

commotion mōtus, *m*, tŭmultus, *m*, commōtĭo, *f*

communicate *v.t*, commūnĭco (1); **(report)**, dēfĕro (*irreg*)

communication commūnĭcātĭo, *f*; **(reporting)**, nuntĭus, *m*

communicative līber, lŏquax

communion sŏcĭĕtas, *f*

community cīvĭtas, *f*, sŏcĭĕtas, *f*

commute *v.t*, mūto (1)

compact *adj*, confertus, pressus

compact *nn*, pactum, *n*, foedus, *n*

companion sŏcĭus, *m*, cŏmes, *c*

companionable făcĭlis

companionship sŏdālĭtas, *f*

company coetus, *m*, sŏcĭĕtas, *f* **(military body)**, mănĭpŭlus, *m*

comparable confĕrendus

comparative compărātīvus

compare *v.t*, compăro (1), confĕro (*irreg*)

comparison compărātĭo, *f*

compartment lŏcŭlus, *m*

compass **(range)** fīnes, *m.pl*; **(pair of compasses)**, circĭnus, *m*

compass *v.t*, complector (3 *dep*)

compassion mĭsĕrĭcordĭa, *f*

compassionate mĭsĕrĭcors

compatability congrŭentĭa, *f*

compatible congrŭens

compatriot cīvis, *c*

compel *v.t*, cōgo (3), compello (3)

compensate for *v.t*, compenso (1)

compensation compensātĭo, *f*

compete *v.i*, certo (1) **(struggle)**

competent căpax; **(to be — to)**, *v.i*, suffĭcĭo (3)

competition certāmen, *n*

competitor compĕtītor, *m*

complacent sĭbi plăcens **(pleasing to oneself)**

complain *v.i*, gĕmo (3); *v.t*, quĕror (3 *dep*.)

complaint questus, *m*, quĕrēla, *f*; **(disease)**, morbus, *m*

complement complēmentum, *n*

complete plēnus, perfectus

complete *v.t*, complĕo (2), confĭcĭo (3)

completely *adv*, omnīno

completion perfectĭo, *f*, confectĭo, *f*

complex multĭplex

complexion cŏlor, *m*

compliance obsĕquĭum, *n*

compliant obsĕquens

complicated invŏlūtus

complication implĭcātĭo, *f*

compliment *nn*, **(esteem)**, hŏnor, *m*; **(praise)** laus, *f*; **(greeting)**, sălūtātĭo, *f*

compliment *v.t*, **(praise)**, laudo (1)

complimentary hŏnōrĭfĭcus

comply with *v.i*, concēdo (3) (*with dat*)

component *nn*, **(part)**, ĕlĕmentum, *n*

compose *v.t*, compōno (3)

composed (calm) sēdātus

composer scriptor, *m*

composition (act of —) compŏsĭtĭo, *f*; **(a literary —)**, ŏpus scriptum, *n*

composure tranquillĭtas, *f*

compound *adj*, compŏsĭtus

compound *v.t*, compōno (3), miscĕo (2)

comprehend *v.t*, **(understand)** intellĕgo (3)

comprehension comprĕhensĭo, *f*

comprehensive *use phr*, ad omnĭa pertĭnens **(extending to everything)**

compress *v.t*, comprĭmo (3)

comprise *v.t*, contĭnĕo (2)

compromise *nn*, **(agreement)**, compŏsĭtĭo, *f*

compromise *v.t*, compōno (3); **(implicate)**, implĭco (1)

compulsion nĕcessĭtas, *f*

compunction paenĭtentĭa, *f*

compute *v.t*, compŭto (1)

comrade sŏcĭus, *m*, cŏmes, *c*

concave căvus

conceal *v.t*, cēlo (1), abdo (3)

concede *v.t*, cēdo (3)

conceit arrŏgantĭa, *f*

conceited arrŏgans

conceive *v.t*, concĭpĭo (3)

concentrate (mentally) *v.i*, ălĭmum intendo (3); **(bring together)**, *v.t*, contrăho (3), cōgo (3)

conception (mental) nōtĭo, *f*; **(physical)**, conceptĭo, *f*

concern *nn*, **(affair, circumstance)**, rēs, *f*; **(worry)**, sollĭcĭtūdo, *f*

concern *v.t*, pertĭnĕo (2); **(it concerns)**, rēfert (*irreg. impers*)

concerned (to be —) *v.i*, sollĭcĭtus esse

concerning *prep*, dē (*with abl. of nn. etc*)

concern *v.t*, **(plans, etc.)**, confĕro (*irreg*), compōno (3)

concession concessĭo, *f*

conciliate *v.t*, concĭlĭo (1)

conciliation concĭlĭātĭo, *f*

conciliatory pācĭfĭcus

concise brĕvis

conciseness brĕvĭtas, *f*

conclude *v.t*, **(decide)**, stătŭo (3); **(end)**, perfĭcĭo (3)

conclusion (end) exĭtus, *m*, finis, *m* **(decision)**, decrētum, *n*

conclusive certus

concord concordĭa, *f*

concourse concursus, *m*

concubine pellex, *f*

concupiscence lĭbīdo, *f*

concur *v.i*, consentĭo (4)

concurrence consensus, *m*

concurrent *use adv*, sĭmŭl **(at the same time)**

concurrently *adv*, sĭmŭl

condemn *v.t*, damno (1) (*with acc of person and genit. of crime or punishment*)

condemnation damnātĭo, *f*

condense *v.t*, denso (1), comprĭmo (3)

condensed densus

condescend *v.i*, dēscendo (3)

condescension cōmĭtas, *f*, **(friendliness)**

condition condĭcĭo, *f*, stătus, *m*

condole *v.i*, dŏlĕo (2) cum (*with abl*)

condone *v.t*, condōno (1)

conduce *v.t*, condūco (3)

conductive ūtĭlis **(advantageous)**

conduct *nn*, **(personal, etc.)**, mōrēs, *m.pl*; **(administration)**, admĭnistrātĭo, *f*

conduct *v.t*, **(lead)**, dūco (3); **(administer)**, admĭnistro (1); **(— oneself)**, sē gĕrĕre (3 *reflex*)

conductor dux, *m*

conduit cănālis, *m*

cone cōnus, *m*

confectionery crustum, *n*

confederacy sŏcĭĕtas, *f*

confederate foedĕrātus

confer *v.t*, confĕro (*irreg*); **(—with)**, collŏquor (3 *dep*); **(—about)**, ăgo (3) dē

conference collŏquĭum, *n*

confess *v.t*, confĭtĕor (2 *dep*)

confession confessĭo, *f*

confide *v.t*, confīdo (3), fīdo (3), (*with dat.*)

confidence fĭdes, *f*, fĭdūcĭa, *f*

confident fīdens

confidential **(trusty)** fīdus; **(one's own, special)**, prŏprĭus; **(secret)**, arcānus

confine *v.t*, inclūdo (3), contĭnĕo (2)

confinement inclūsĭo, *f*, custōdĭa, *f*; **(childbirth)**, partus, *m*; pŭerpĕrĭum, *n*

confirm *v.t*, confirmo (1)

confiscate *v.t*, pūblĭco (1), ădĭmo (3)

confiscation pūblĭcātĭo, *f*

conflagration incendĭum, *n*

conflict *nn*, certāmen, *n*

conflict *v.i*, certo (1); dissentĭo (4)

confluence conflŭens, *m*

conform to *v.i*, obtempĕro (1) (*with dat*); *v.t*, accommŏdo (1)

conformity convĕnĭentĭa, *f*

confound *v.t*, **(disturb)**, turbo (1); **(amaze)**, obstŭpĕfăcĭo (3); **(bring to nothing, thwart)**, frustor (1 *dep.*)

confront *v.i*, obvĭam ĕo (*irreg.*) (*with dat*)

confuse *v.t*, turbo (1)

confused perturbātus

confusion perturbātĭo, *f*

congeal *v.i. and v.t*, congĕlo (1)

congenial concors

congested frĕquens

congratulate *v.t*, grātŭlor (1 *dep*)

congratulation grātŭlātĭo, *f*

congregate *v.i*, sē congrĕgare (1 *reflex*)

congress concĭlĭum, *n*, conventus, *m*

congruous congrŭens

conjecture *nn*, coniectūra, *f*

conjecture *v.i*, cōnĭcĭo (3)

conjugate *v.t*, dēclīno (1)

conjunction **(grammar)** coniunctĭo, *f*

conjure *v.i*, **(perform tricks)**, praestigĭis ūtor (3 *dep.*); **(image)** cōgĭto (1)

conjurer măgus, *m*

connect *v.t*, coniungo (3)

connected coniunctus

connection coniunctĭo, *f*; **(by marriage)**, affīnĭtas, *f*

connive at *v.i*, connīvĕo (2) in (*with abl*)

connoisseur use *vb*, stŭdĕo (2) **(to be keen on)**

conquer *v.t*, vinco (3), sŭpĕro (1)

conqueror victor, *m*

conquest victōrĭa, *f*

conscience conscĭentĭa, *f*

conscientious rēlĭgĭōsus

conscientiousness fĭdes, *f*

conscious conscĭus

consciously *adv*, use *adj*, scĭens **(knowingly)**

consciousness conscĭentĭa, *f*, sensus, *m*

conscript **(recruit)** tīro, *m*

consecrate *v.t*, conscĕro (1)

consecrated săcer

consecutive contĭnŭus

consent *nn*, consensus, *m*; **(by the — of)**, consensu;

consent to *v.i*, assentĭo (4)

consequence **(result)** exĭtus, *m*; **(importance)**, mōmentum, *n*; **(in — of)**, *prep*, propter (*with acc*)

consequent sĕquens

consequently *adv*, ĭgĭtur, ĭtăque

conserve *v.t*, conservo (1)

consider *v.t*, cōgĭto (1), dēlībĕro (1), existĭmo (1); **(— with respect)**, respĭcĭo (3)

considerable ălĭquantus

considerate hūmānus

considerateness hūmānĭtas, *f*
consideration consīdĕrātĭo, *f*;
(regard), rătĭo, *f*
considering *conj*, ut
consign *v.t*, mando (1), committo
(3)
consignment (of goods)   merces,
f.pl
consist of *v.i*, consisto (3) in (*with
abl*)
consistency constantĭa, *f*
consistent (constant) constans;
(consistent with), consentānĕus
console *v.t*, consōlor (1 *dep.*)
consolidate *v.t*, firmo (1), sōlĭdo
(1)
consonant consŏnans littĕra
consort (husband)   mărītus, *m*;
(wife), mărīta, *f*
consort with *v.i*, ūtor (3 *dep*) (*with
abl*)
conspicuous mănĭfestus, insignis
conspiracy coniūrātĭo, *f*
conspirator coniūrātus, *m*
conspire *v.i*, coniūro (1)
constable dĕcŭrĭo, *m*, lictor, *m*
constancy fĭdes, *f*; (steadiness),
constantĭa, *f*, fĭdēlĭtas, *f*
constant fĭdēlis, constans
constellation sīdus, *n*
consternation păvor, *m*
constituent parts ĕlĕmenta, *n.pl*
constitute *v.t*, constĭtŭo (3),
compōno (3), crĕo (1)
constitution (of a state)
respūblĭca, *f*; (of a body), hăbĭtus,
m
constitutional lēgĭtĭmus
constrain *v.t*, cōgo (3), compello
(3)
construct *v.t*, făbrĭcor (1 *dep*)
exstrŭo (3)
construction *v.t*, făbrĭcor (1 *dep*)
exstrŭo (3)
construction (act of —)   făbrĭcātĭo,
f; (method) fĭgūra, *f*, structūra, *f*
construe *v.t*, interprĕtor (1 *dep*)
consul consul, *m*
consulship consŭlātus, *m*
consult *v.t*, consŭlo (3); *v.i*,
dēlībĕro (1); (— someone's
interests), consŭlo (3) (*with dat*)

consultation collŏquĭum, *n*
consume *v.t*, consumo (3),
confĭcĭo (3)
consummate *v.t*, consummo (1),
perfĭcĭo (3)
consummate *adj* summus
consummation connsummātĭo, *f*
consumption consumptĭo, *f*
contact tactus, *m*
contagion contāgĭo, *f*
contain *v.t*, contĭnĕo (2)
contaminate *v.t*, contāmĭno (1)
contamination contāgĭo, *f*, măcŭla,
f
contemplate *v.t*, contemplor (1
dep)
contemplation (study) mēdĭtātĭo, *f*
contemporary aequālis
contempt contemptus, *m*
contemptible contemnendus
contend *v.i*, contendo (3), certo
(1), pugno (1); (argue), *v.t*,
affirmo (1)
content contentus
content *v.t*, sătisfăcĭo (3) (*with
dat.*); *v.i*, (be content) sătis hăbĕo
(2)
contentment aequus ănĭmus, *m*
contest *nn*, certāmen, *n*, pugna, *f*
contest *v.t*, certo (1), contendo (3)
contestant pugnātor, *m*, pĕtītor, *m*
contiguous contĭgŭus, confinis
continent *adj*, contĭnens
continent *nn*, contĭnens, *f*
contingency cāsus, *m*
continual perpĕtŭus, contĭnens
continually *adv*, perpĕtŭo,
contĭnenter
continuation perpĕtŭĭtas, *f*
continue *v.t*, prōdūco (3), prōrŏgo
(1), *v.i*, mănĕo (2)
continuity perpĕtŭĭtas, *f*
continuous contĭnens
contort *v.t*, torquĕo (2)
contour fĭgūra, *f*
contraband *adj*, vĕtĭtus
contract *nn*, pactum, *n*
contract *v.i*, (grow smaller), sē
contrăhĕre (3 *reflex*); *v.t*,
contrăho (3)
contraction contractĭo, *f*
contractor conductor, *m*

contradict *v.t*, contrādīco (3) (*with dat*)
contradiction contrādictĭo, *f*; (inconsistency), rĕpugnantĭa, *f*
contradictory rĕpugnans
contrary *adj*, adversus, contrārĭus; (— to), *prep*, contrā (*with acc*); the contrary, *nn*, contrārĭum, *n*; (on the —), *adv*, contrā
contrast *v.t*, confĕro (*irreg*); *v.i*, discrĕpo (1)
contravene *v.t*, vĭŏlo (1)
contribute *v.t*, confĕro (*irreg*)
contribution collātĭo, *f*, trĭbūtum, *n*
contrivance (gadget) māchĭna, *f*
contrive *v.t*, (think out), excōgĭto (1)
control *v.t*, mŏdĕror (1 *dep*) (*with dat*); (guide), rĕgo (3)
control *nn*, pŏtestas, *f*, tempĕrantĭa, *f*
controversy contrōversĭa, *f*
contumacious pertĭnax
contumacy pertĭnācĭa, *f*
contumely contŭmēlĭa, *f*
convalescent convălescens
convenience commŏdĭtas, *f*, opportūnĭtas, *f*
convenient commŏdus, opportūnus
convention (meeting) conventus, *m*; (agreement), conventĭo, *f*
converge *v.i*, ĕōdem vergo (3)
conversation sermo, *m*, collŏquĭum, *n*
converse *v.i*, collŏquor (3 *dep*)
conversion commūtātĭo, *f*
convert *v.t*, mūto (1), converto (3)
convex convexus
convey *v.t*, vĕho (3), porto (1)
conveyance (act of —) vectūra, *f*; (vehicle), vĕhĭcŭlum, *n*
convict *v.t*, damno (1)
conviction (belief) *use phr*, persuāsum est (*with dat. of person*) e.g. persuāsum est mĭhi (it is my conviction); (convicting), damnātĭo, *f*
convince *v.t*, persuādĕo (2) (*with dat.*)
conviviality hĭlărĭtas, *f*
convoke *v.t*, convŏco (1)
convoy *nn*, commĕātus, *m*;

(escort), praesĭdĭum, *n*
convulse *v.t*, concŭtĭo (3), ăgĭto (1)
convulsion tŭmultus, *m*, mōtus, *m*; (medical), convulsĭo, *f*
cook *nn*, cŏquus, *m*
cook *v.t*, cŏquo (3)
cool frīgĭdus; (of mind), lentus
cool *v.t*, rĕfrīgĕro (1); *v.i*, rĕfrīgĕror (1 *pass*)
cooly *adv*, frīgĭde, lentē
coolness frīgus, *n*
co-operate with *v.t*, adiŭvo (1)
co-operation auxĭlĭum, *n*, (help)
cope with *v.i*. congrĕdĭor (3 *dep.*)
copious largus, cōpĭōsus
copper aes, *n*
copper *adj*, aēnĕus
coppice dūmētum, *n*
copy exemplum, *n*
copy *v.t*, ĭmĭtor (1 *dep*), dēscrībo (3)
coral cŏrălĭum, *n*
cord fūnis, *m*
cordial *adj*, bĕnignus
cordiality bĕnignĭtas, *f*
cordon cŏrōna, *f*
core nuclĕus, *m*
cork *nn*, cortex, *m*, *f*
corn frūmentum, *n*; (crop), sĕges, *f*; (on the foot), clāvus, *m*
corner angŭlus, *m*
cornice cŏrōna, *f*
coronation *use* crĕo (1) (elect to office)
coroner quaesĭtor, *m*
corporal *adj*, corpŏrĕus
corporal *nn*, dĕcŭrĭo, *m*
corps (company) mănus, *f*
corpse cădāver, *n*, corpus, *n*
corpulence ŏbēsĭtas, *f*
corpulent ŏbēsus
correct rectus, pūrus
correct *v.t*, corrĭgo (3), ēmendo (1)
correction ēmendātĭo, *f*; (chastisement), castĭgātĭo, *f*
correctly *adv*, rectē
correctness vērĭtas, *f*
correspond *v.i*, (agree with), convĕnĭo (4) (*with dat*); (write), littĕras mitto (3) et accĭpĭo (3) (send and receive letters)

correspondence missĭo et acceptĭo ĕpistŏlārum **(sending and receiving of letters)**
corresponding par, gĕmellus
corroborate *v.t*, confirmo (1)
corrode *v.t*, rōdo (3), ĕdo (3)
corrosive mordax
corrupt *v.t*, corrumpo (3)
corrupt *adj*, corruptus
corruption dēprāvātĭo, *f*
corselet lōrīca, *f*
cost *nn*, prĕtĭum, *n*, sumptus, *m*
cost *v.i*, sto (1) *(with dat. of person and abl. or genit. of price)* e.g. **the victory cost the Carthaginians much bloodshed:** victōrĭa stĕtit Poenis multo sanguĭne
costly *adj*, prĕtĭōsus
costume hăbĭtus, *m*
cot lectŭlus, *m*
cottage căsa, *f*
cotton gossypĭum, *n*
couch lectus, *m*
couch *v.i*, subsīdo (3); *v.t*, **(—a weapon)**, intendo (3)
cough *nn*, tussis, *f*
cough *v.i*, tussĭo (4)
council concĭlĭum, *n*
counsel (advice) consĭlĭum, *n*; **(lawyer)**, pătrōnus, *m*
count *v.t*, nŭmĕro (1); **(— upon, trust)**, confīdo (3) *(with dat)*
countenance *nn*, vultus, *m*
countenance *v.t*, permitto (3), făvĕo (2), indulgĕo (2)
counter (in shop) mensa, *f*; **(for counting)** calcŭlus, *m*
counter *adv*, contra
counteract *v.t*, obsisto (3) *(with dat.)*
counterbalance *v.t*, exaequo (1)
counterfeit *adj*, ădultĕrīnus, fictus
counterfeit *v.t*, sĭmŭlo (1), fingo (3)
counterpart res gĕmella **(paired, twin thing)**
countless innŭmĕrābĭlis
country (fatherland) pătrĭă, *f*; **(countryside)**, rūs, *n*; **(region)**, rĕgĭo, *f*
country house villa, *f*

countryman (of the same country) cīvis, *c*; **(living in the countryside)**, rustĭcus, *m*
couple *nn*, **(pair)**, pār *n*
couple *v.t*, coniungo (3)
courage virtus, *f*, ănĭmus, *m*
courageous fortis, ācer, fĕrox
courier (messenger) nuntĭus, *m*
course (motion) cursus, *m*; **(route)**, vĭa, *f*, ĭter *n*; **(plan)**, rătĭo, *f*; **(race —)**, circus, *m*; **(of —)**, *adv*, nīmīrum, certē
court (— of justice) iūdĭcĭum, *n*; **(judges themselves)**, iūdĭces, *m.pl*; **(palace)**, aula, *f*, dŏmus, *(f)* rĕgis **(the house of the king)**; **(courtyard)**, ārĕa, *f*
court *v.t*, cŏlo (3)
court martial *use phr*. in castris iudĭcare (1) **(to try in camp)**
courteous cōmis, hūmānus
courtesy cōmĭtas, *f*, hūmānĭtas, *f*
courtier aulĭcus, *m*
courtship ămor, *m*
cousin consōrbrīnus, *m* (...a), *f*
covenant pactum, *n*
cover *v.t*, tĕgo (3); **(conceal)** occulto (1)
cover, covering *nn*, tĕgŭmen, *n*; **(lid)**, ŏpĕrīmentum, *n*
coverlet strāgŭlum, *n*
covert *nn*, dūmētum, *n*
covet *v.t*, cŭpĭo (3)
covetous ăvārus, ăvĭdus, cŭpĭdus
covetousness ăvārĭtĭa, *f*, cŭpĭdĭtas, *f*
cow vacca, *f*
cow *v.t*, terrĕo (2), dŏmo (1) **(tame)**
coward ignāvus, *m*
cowardice ignāvĭa, *f*
cowardly *adj*, ignāvus
cowl cŭcullus, *m*
coy (bashful) vĕrēcundus
crab cancer, *m*
crabbed mōrōsus
crack *nn*, **(noise)**, crĕpĭtus, *m*; **(chink)**, rīma, *f*
crack *v.t*, findo (3), frango (3); *v.i*, **(open up)**, dĕhisco (3); **(sound)**, crĕpo (1)

cradle cūnae, *f.pl*
craft (deceit) dŏlus, *m*; **(skill)**, artĭfĭcĭum, *n*; **(boat)**, rătis, *f*, nāvis, *f*
craftsman ŏpĭfex, *m*
crafty callĭdus
crag scŏpŭlus, *m*
cram *v.t*, confercĭo (4)
cramp *v.t*, comprĭmo (3)
crane (bird) grus, *m, f*; **(machine)**, tollēno, *f*
crank uncus, *m*
cranny rīma, *f*
crash *nn*, frăgor, *m*
crash *v.i*, **(noise)**, strĕpo (3); **(bring into collision)**, *v.t*, collīdo (3)
crate corbis, *m*
crater crāter, *m*
crave for *v.t*, ōro (1), appĕto (3)
craving *nn*, dēsīdĕrĭum, *n*
crawl *v.i*, rēpo (3)
crayon crēta, *f*
crazy cerrītus, dēmens
creak *v.i*, crĕpo (1)
creaking *nn*, strīdor, *m*, crĕpĭtus, *m*
crease *nn*, rūga, *f*
crease *v.t*, rūgo (1)
create *v.t*, crĕo (1)
creation (act of —) crĕātĭo, *f*; **(making)**, făbrĭcātĭo, *f*; **(universe)**, mundus, *m*
creator auctor, *m*, crĕātor, *m*
creature ănĭmal, *n*
credence (belief) fĭdes, *f*
credible crēdĭbĭlis
credit (belief or commercial credit) fĭdes, *f*; **(reputation)**, existĭmātĭo, *f*
credit *v.t*, **(believe)**, crēdo (3); **(—an account, person, etc.)**, acceptum rĕfĕro (*irreg*) (*with dat. of person*)
creditable (honourable) hŏnestus
creditor crēdĭtor, *m*
credulous crēdŭlus, *m*
creek sĭnus, *m*
creep *v.i*, serpo (3), rēpo (3)
crescent lūna, *f*, **(crescent moon)**
crescent-shaped lūnatus
crest crista, *f*
crested cristātus
crestfallen dēmissus
crevice rīma, *f*

crew nautae, *m.pl*, rēmĭges, *m,pl*
crib (child's bed) lectŭlus, *m*
cricket (insect) cĭcāda, *f*
crime făcĭnus, *n*, scĕlus, *n*
criminal *nn*, hŏmo sons, hŏmo nŏcens
criminal *adj*, nĕfārĭus, scĕlestus
crimson *adj*, coccĭnĕus
cringe to *v.i*, ădūlor (1 *dep*)
cripple *nn*, hŏmo claudus
cripple *v.t*, dēbĭlĭto (1); **(— a person)**, claudum reddo (3)
crippled dēbĭlis, claudus
crisis discrīmen, *n*
crisp frăgĭlis
critic existĭmātor, *m*, censor, *m*
critical ēlĕgans; **(of a crisis, etc.)**, *use* discrīmen, *n* **(crisis)**
criticize *v.t*, **(find fault)** rĕprĕhendo (3), iŭdĭco (1)
croak *v.i*, căno (3), crōcĭo (4)
crockery fictĭlĭa, *n.pl*
crocodile crŏcŏdīlus, *m*
crocus crŏcus, *m*
crook (shepherd's —) pĕdum, *n*
crooked curvus; **(bad, etc.)**, prāvus
crop (of corn) sĕges, *f*, frŭges, *f.pl*; **(of a bird)**, inglŭvĭes, *f*
crop *v.t*, tondĕo (2)
cross *nn*, crux, *f*
cross *adj*, transversus; **(annoyed)**, īrātus
cross *v.i. and v.t*, transĕo (4 *irreg*)
cross-examine *v.t*, interrŏgo (1)
crossing (act of —) transĭtus, *m*; **(cross-road)**, compĭtum, *n*
crouch *v.i*, sē dēmittĕre (3 *reflex*)
crow (bird) cornix, *f*
crow *v.i*, **(of a cock)**, căno (3); **(boast)**, sē iactare (1 *reflex*)
crowd turba, *f*
crowd together *v.i*, congrĕgor (1 *dep*); *v.t*, stīpo (1), frĕquento (1)
crowded confertus, cĕlĕber
crown cŏrōna, *f*; **(royal)** dĭădēma, *n*; **(of head, etc.)** vertex, *m*
crown *v.t*, crōno (1)
crucifixion *use phr. with* crux, *f*, **(cross)**
crucify *v.t*, crŭce affĭcĭo (3)
crude rŭdis
cruel crūdēlis, atrox

cruelty crūdēlĭtas, *f*
cruet gutus, *m*
cruise *nn*, nāvĭgātĭo
cruise *v.i.* nāvĭgo (1)
crumb mīca, *f*
crumble *v.t*, tĕro (3); *v.i*, corrŭo (3)
crumple *v.t*, rūgo (1)
crush *v.t*, contundo (3), opprĭmo (3)
crust crusta, *f*
crutch băcŭlum, *n*
cry *nn*, clāmor, *m*, vox, *f*
cry *v.i*, clāmo (1); **(weep)**, lacrĭmo (1)
crystal *nn*, crystallum, *n*
cub cătŭlus, *m*
cube tessĕra, *f*
cubic cŭbĭcus
cuckoo cŭcŭlus, *m*, coccyx, *m*
cucumber cŭcŭmis, *m*
cudgel fustis, *m*
cudgel *v.t*, verbĕro (1), mulco (1)
cue signum, *n*
cuff *nn*, **(blow)**, cŏlăphus, *m*, ălăpa
cuff *v.t*, incŭtĭo (3)
cuirass lōrīca, *f*, thōrax, *m*
culminate *use adj*, summus **(topmost)**
culpable culpandus, nŏcens
culprit hŏmo nŏcens
cultivate *v.t*, cŏlo (3)
cultivation cultus, *m*, cultūra, *f*
cultivator cultor, *m*
culture cultus, *m*, cultūra, *f*
cumbersome inhăbĭlis
cunning *adj*, callĭdus, dŏlōsus
cunning *nn*, callĭdĭtas, *f*, dŏlus, *m*
cup pōcŭlum, *n*
cupboard armārĭum, *n*
cupidity cŭpĭdĭtas, *f*
cupola thŏlus, *m*
curate săcerdos, *c*, **(priest)**
curator cūrātor, *m*
curb *v.t*, frēno (1), cŏhĭbĕo (2)
curdle *v.t*, cōgo (3), cŏāgŭlo (1); *v.i*, concresco (ī)
cure *nn*, sānātĭo, *f*
cure *v.t*, mĕdĕor (2 *dep*) **(with dat.)**
curiosity stŭdĭum, *n*
curious (inquisitive) cūrĭōsus; **(rare)**, rārus

curl *v.t*, crispo (1)
curl *nn*, cincinnus, *m*
curly cincinnātus
currant ăcĭnus, *m*
currency mŏnēta, *f*, nummi, *m.pl*
current *nn*, **(of river)**, flūmen, *n*
current *adj*, **(present)**, hic; **(general)**, ūsĭtātus
curse *nn*, imprĕcātĭo, *f*, dīrae, *f.pl*
curse *v.t*, exsĕcror (1 *dep.*)
cursed exsĕcrābĭlis
cursorily *adv*, summātim, brĕvĭter
curt brĕvis
curtail *v.t*, arto (1)
curtain aulaeum, *n*
curve *nn*, flexus, *m*
curve *v.t*, flecto (3), curvo (1)
curved curvātus
cusion pulvīnar, *n*
custodian cūrātor, *m*
custody (keeping) custōdĭa, *f*; **(imprisonment)**, vincŭla, *n.pl*
custom mos, *m*, consŭētŭdo, *f*; **(— duty)**, portōrĭum, *n*
customary ūsĭtātus, sŏlĭtus
customer emptor, *m*
cut *nn*, **(incision)**, incīsĭo, *f*; **(blow)**, ictus, *m*, plāga, *f*
cut *v.t*, sĕco (1), caedo (3); **(—away)**, abscīdo (3); **(— down)**, succīdo (3); **(— off)**, praecīdo (3); **(— off from communications, supplies, etc.)** interclūdo (3); **(— out)**, excīdo (3); **(— short)**, praecīdo (3); **(— to pieces)** concīdo (3), trŭcīdo (1)
cutaneous *use genit. of* cŭtis **(skin)**
cutlass glădĭus, *m*
cutlery cultri *m.pl* **(knives)**
cutter (boat) phăsēlus, *m*, cĕlox, *f*
cutting *adj*, **(biting)**, mordax
cuttlefish sēpĭa, *f*
cycle (circle) orbis, *m*
cygnet pullus, *m*
cylinder cȳlindrus, *m*
cymbal cymbălum, *n*
cynic cȳnĭcus, *m*
cynical mordax, diffĭcĭlis
cynicism dūrĭtĭa, *f*
cypress cupressus, *f*

dab

D

dab *v.t*, illīdo (3)
dabble in *v.t*, attingo (3)
daffodil narcissus, *m*
dagger pŭgĭo, *m*
daily *adj*, quŏtīdĭānus
daily *adv*, quŏtīdĭē
daintiness (of manners)
  fastīdĭum, *n*
dainty (things) dēlĭcātus; **(people)**,
  fastīdĭōsus
daisy bellis, *f*
dale valles, *f*
dalliance lūsus, *m*
dally *v.i*, **(delay)** mŏror (1 *dep.*)
dam (breakwater) mōles, *f*
dam *v.t*, obstrŭo (3)
damage *nn*, dētrīmentum, *n*,
  damnum, *n*
damage *v.t*, laedo (3), afflīgo (3)
dame dŏmĭna, *f*, mātrōna, *f*
damn *v.t*, damno (1)
damp *adj*, hūmĭdus
damp *v.t*, hūmecto (1);
  (enthusiasm, etc.) immĭnŭo (3)
  (lessen)
damp *nn*, hūmor, *m*
dance *v.i*, salto (1)
dance *nn*, saltātus, *m*
dancer saltātor, *m* (...trix, *f*)
dandy hŏmo lĕpĭdus, ēlĕgans,
  bellus
danger pĕrīcŭlum, *n*
dangerous pĕrīcŭlōsus
dangle *v.i*, pendĕo (2)
dank hūmĭdus, ūvĭdus
dapper (spruce) nĭtĭdus
dappled măcŭlōsus
dare *v.i*, audĕo (2 *semi-dep*)
  mōlĭor (4 *dep*)
daring *adj*, audax
daring *nn*, audācĭa, *f*
dark *adj*, obscūrus tĕnĕbrōsus; **(in
  colour)**, fuscus
dark, darkness *nn*, tĕnĕbrae, *f.pl*
darken *v.t*, obscūro (1), occaeco
  (1)
darling *nn*, dēlĭcĭae, *f.pl*; *adj*,
  mellītus
darn *v.t*, sarcĭo (4)
dart *nn*, tēlum, *n*, iăcŭlum, *n*
dart *v.i*, **(rush)**, *use compound of*

vŏlo (1) **(to fly)**
dash *nn*, **(rush)**, *use vb*, vŏlo (1)
  (to fly)
dash *v.i*, prōvŏlo (1), rŭo (3); *v.t*,
  afflīgo (3), impingo (3)
dashing *adj*, ălăcer
dastardly *adj*, ignāvus
date (fruit) palmŭla, *f*; **(time)**,
  dĭes, *f*
date *v.t*, **(something)**, dĭem ascrībo
  (3) in *(with abl.)*
daub *v.t*, oblĭno (3)
daughter fīlĭa, *f*; **(— in-law)**, nŭrus
daunt *v.t*, percello (3)
dauntless impăvĭdus
dawdle *v.i*, cesso (1)
dawn prīma lux, aurōra, *f*
dawn *v.i*, dīlūcesco (3)
day dĭes, *m*, *f*; **(at — break)**, *adv.
  phr*, prīma lūce; **(by —)**, *adv*,
  interdĭu; **(every —)**, *adv*, quŏtīdĭē;
  (late in the —), multo dĭe; **(on the
  — before)**, prīdĭe; **(on the
  next —)**, postrīdĭe; **(— time)**,
  tempus dĭurnum, *n*
daze *v.t*, stŭpĕfăcĭo (3)
dazzle *v.t*, perstringo (3)
dazzling splendĭdus
dead *adj*, mortŭus; **(the dead or
  departed)**, mānes, *m.pl*; **(a —
  body)**, corpus, *n*
deaden *v.t*, **(senses, etc.)**, hĕbēto
  (1)
deadly *adj*, mortĭfer, pernĭcĭōsus,
  fūnestus
deaf surdus
deafen *v.t*, exsurdo (1), obtundo
  (3)
deafness surdĭtas, *f*
deal (a good —) ălĭquantum,
  (business) nĕgōtĭum, *n*
deal *v.t*, **(distribute)**, distrĭbŭo (3);
  mētĭor (4 *dep.*); *v.i*, **(deal with)**,
  ăgo (3) cum *(with abl)*
dealer mercātor, *m*
dealings *nn*, ūsus, *m*,
  commercĭum, *n*
dear cārus; **(of price)**, prĕtĭōsus
dearly *adv* **(at a high price)** magni
death mors, *f*
deathbed (on his —) *use adj*,
  mŏrĭens **(dying)**
deathless immortālis

debar *v.t,* exclūdo (3)
debase *v.t,* dēmitto (3), vĭtĭo (1)
debate contrōversĭa, *f*
debate *v.t,* dispŭto (1), discepto (1)
debater dispŭtātor, *m*
debauch *v.t,* corrumpo (3)
debauchery stŭprum, *n*
debit *nn,* expensum, *n*
debit *v.t,* expensum fĕro (*irreg*) (*with dat*)
debt aes ălĭēnum, *n*
debtor dēbĭtor, *m*
debut ĭnĭtĭum, *n*
decamp *v.i,* castra mŏvĕo (2); discēdo (3)
decant *v.t,* diffundo (3)
decanter lăgēna, *f*
decapitate *v.t,* sĕcūri fĕrĭo (4)
decay *nn,* tābes, *f,* dēmĭnūtĭo, *f*
decay *v.i,* dīlābor (3 *dep*), tābesco (3)
decease dēcessus, *m*
deceased *adj,* mortŭus
deceit fraus, *f,* dŏlus, *m*
deceitful fallax
deceive *v.t,* dēcĭpĭo (3), fallo (3)
December Dĕcember (mensis)
decency dĕcōrum, *n,* hŏnestas, *f*
decent dĕcōrus, hŏnestus
deception fraus, *f,* dŏlus, *m*
deceptive fallax
decide *v.t,* constĭtŭo (3), stătŭo (3), dēcerno (3)
decided (persons) firmus; **(things),** certus
decidedly *adv,* **(assuredly),** plānē, vēro
decimate *v.t,* dĕcĭmo (1)
decision arbĭtrĭum, *n,* dēcrētum, *n*
deck pons, *m*
deck *v.t,* orno (1)
declaim *v.t,* dēclāmo (1)
declaration prŏfessĭo, *f* (**— of war),** dēnuntĭātĭo, *f,* (belli)
declare *v.i,* prŏfĭtĕor (2 *dep*), affirmo (1); *v.t,* dēclāro (1); (**— war),** dēnuntĭo (1) (bellum)
decline *nn,* dēmĭnūtĭo, *f* **(diminution)**
decline *v.t,* **(refuse),** rĕcūso (1); *v.i,* inclīno (1), dēcresco (3)
declivity clīvus, *m*

decompose *v.t,* solvo (3); *v.i,* solvor (3 *pass*)
decomposition sŏlūtĭo, *f*
decorate *v.t,* orno (1), dĕcŏro (1)
decoration (ornament) ornāmentum, *n,* dĕcus, *n*; **(badge),** insigne, *n*
decorous dĕcōrus
decorum dĕcōrum, *n,* pŭdor, *m*
decoy illex, *m*; **(bait),** esca, *f*
decrease *nn,* dēmĭnūtĭo, *f*
decrease *v.i,* dēcresco (3); *v.t,* mĭnŭo (3)
decree *nn,* dēcrētum, *n*; **(— of the Senate),** consultum, *n*
decree *v.t,* dēcerno (3), censēo (2)
decrepit dēcrĕpĭtus, dēbĭlis
decry *v.t,* vĭtŭpĕro (1), obtrecto (1)
dedicate *v.t,* consĕcro (1)
deduce *v.t,* conclūdo (3)
deduct *v.t,* dēdūco (3)
deduction (taking away) dēductĭo, *f*
deed factum, *n,* făcĭnus, *n*; **(legal),** tăbŭla, *f*
deem *v.t,* pŭto (1)
deep *nn,* **(the sea),** altum, *n*
deep altus **(of sound),** grăvis
deepen *v.t,* altĭōrem reddo (3)
deeply *adv,* altē, pĕnĭtus **(deep within)**
deer cervus, *m,* cerva, *f*
deface *v.t,* dēformo (1)
defame *v.t,* mălĕdīco (3) (*with dat*)
default *v.i,* dēfĭcĭo (3) **(fail to answer bail),** vădĭmōnĭum dēsĕro (3)
defeat *nn,* clādes, *f*
defeat *v.t,* vinco (3), sŭpĕro (1)
decect vĭtĭum, *n*
defective vĭtĭōsus
defence (protection) praesĭdĭum, *n*; **(legal),** dēfensĭo, *f*
defenceless ĭnermis
defend *v.t,* dēfendo (3)
defendant (in a trial) rĕus, *m*
defender dēfensor, *m*; **(in court),** pătrōnus, *m*
defer *v.t,* **(put off),** diffĕro (*irreg*); *v.i,* **(show deference to),** cēdo (3)

deference observantĭa, *f*
defiance prŏvŏcātĭo, *f*
defiant fĕrox
deficiency dēfectĭo, *f*
deficient ĭnops, mancus
deficit lăcūna, *f*
defile *v.t*, contāmĭno (1)
defile *nn*, augustĭae, *f.pl*
define *v.t*, circumscrībo (3)
definite constĭtūtus, certus
definition dēfinītĭo, *f*
deflect *v.t*, dēflecto (3)
deform *v.t*, dēformo (1)
deformity dēformĭtas, *f*
defraud *v.t*, fraudo (1)
defray *v.t*, suppĕdĭto (1) **(supply)**
deft doctus **(skilled)**
defy *v.t*, obsto (1), prŏvŏco (1)
degenerate *v.i*, dēgĕnĕro (1)
degenerate *adj*, dēgĕner
degradation ignōmĭnĭa, *f*
degrade *v.t*, mŏvĕo (2), dē *or* ex
   (*with abl*), **(move down from)**;
   dēhŏnesto (1)
degree (interval, stage, rank)
   grădus, *m*; **(to such a degree)**,
   adv, ădĕo; **(by degrees)**, *adv*,
   (gradually), grădātim
deify *v.t*, consĕcro (1)
deign *v.t*, dignor (1 *dep*)
deity dĕus, *m*
deject *v.t*, afflīgo (3)
dejected dēmissus, afflictus
dejection maestĭtĭa, *f*
delay *nn*, mŏra, *f*
delay *v.i*, mŏror (1 *dep*.), cunctor
   (1 *dep*.); *v.t*, mŏror (1 *dep*.),
   tardo (1)
delegate *nn*, lēgātus, *m*
delegate *v.t*, **(depute)**, lēgo (1),
   mando (1) (*with acc. of thing and
   dat. of person*)
delegation lēgātĭo, *f*
deliberate *adj*, consīdĕrātus
deliberate *v.t*, consŭlo (3), dēlībĕro
   (1)
deliberately *adv*, consultō
deliberation dēlībĕrātĭo, *f*
delicacy subtīlĭtas, *f*, suāvĭtas, *f*;
   (food), cūpēdĭa, *n.pl*
delicate subtīlis, tĕnĕr; **(of health)**,
   infirmus

delicious suāvis
delight *nn*, **(pleasure)**, vŏluptas, *f*
delight *v.t*, dēlecto (1), *v.i*, gaudĕo
   (2)
delightful iūcundus, ămoenus
delineate *v.t*, dēscrībo (3)
delinquency dēlictum, *n*
delinquent *nn*, peccātor, *m*
delirious dēlīrus
delirium dēlīrĭum, *n*
deliver *v.t*, **(set free)**, lībĕro (1);
   (hand over), do (1), trādo (3),
   dēdo (3); **(— a speech)**, hăbĕo
   (2), ōrātĭonem
deliverance (freeing) lībĕrātĭo, *f*;
   (childbirth) partus, *m*; **(of
   a speech)**, ēlŏcūtĭo, *f*
delude *v.t*, dēcĭpĭo (3)
deluge dīlŭvĭum, *n*, ĭnundātĭo, *f*
delusion error, *m*; **(trick)**, fallācĭa,
   f, fraus, *f*
delusive (deceitful) fallax;
   (empty), vānus
demagogue plēbĭcŏla, *c*
demand *nn*, postŭlātĭo, *f*
demand *v.t*, posco (3), postŭlo (1)
demean oneself dēmittor (3 pass),
   sē dēmĭttĕre (3 *reflex*)
demeanour mōres, *m.pl*, hăbĭtus,
   m
demented dēmens
demise *nn*, **(death)**, dēcessus, *m*,
   mors, *f*
democracy cīvĭtas pŏpŭlāris, *f*
democrat plēbĭcŏla, *c*
demolish *v.t*, dīrŭo (3), dēlĕo (2),
   dēmōlĭor (4 *dep*)
demolition ēversĭo, *f*, rŭīna, *f*
demon daemŏnĭum, *n*
demonstrate *v.t*, dēmonstro (1)
demonstration dēmonstrātĭo, *f*
demur *v.i*, haesĭto (1)
demure *adj*, vĕrēcundus
den lătĭbŭlum, *n*
denial nĕgātĭo, *f*
denominate *v.t*, nōmĭno (1)
denote *v.t*, indĭco (1), signĭfĭco (1),
   nŏto (1)
denounce *v.t*, (nōmen) dēfĕro
   (*irreg*)
dense densus, confertus
density crassĭtūdo, *f*
dent nŏta, *f*

dentist dentĭum mĕdĭcus, *m*

denude *v.t*, nūdo (1)

deny *v.t*, nĕgo (1), abnŭo (3)

depart *v.i*, ăbĕo (4), discēdo (3)

departed (dead) mortŭus

department (of administration, etc.) prōvincĭa, *f*; **(part)**, pars, *f*

departure discessus, *m*

depend on *v.i*, pendĕo (2) ex *or* in (*with abl*); **(rely on)**, confido (3 *semi-dep*) (*with dat*)

dependant *nn*, clĭens, *c*

dependence on clĭentēla, *f*; **(reliance)**, fĭdes, *f*

dependency (subject state) prōvincĭa, *f*

depict *v.t*, dēscrībo (3), effingo (3)

deplorable mĭsĕrābĭlis

deplore *v.t*, dēplōro (1)

deploy *v.t*, explĭco (1)

depopulate *v.t*, pŏpŭlor (1 *dep*); vasto (1)

deport *v.t*, dēporto (1); **(behave oneself)**, se gĕrĕre (3 *reflex*)

deportment hăbĭtus, *m*

depose *v.t*, mŏvĕo (2) (*with abl*)

deposit *v.t*, dēpōno (3)

deposit *nn*, dēpŏsĭtum, *n*

deprave *v.t*, dēprāvo (1), corrumpo (3)

depravity prāvĭtas, *f*

deprecate *v.t*, dēprĕcor (1 *dep*)

depreciate *v.t*, dētrăho (3); *v.i*, mĭnŭor (3 *pass*) **(grow less)**

depreciation (decrease) dēmĭnūtĭo, *f*; **(disparagement)** obtrectātĭo, *f*

depredation expīlātĭo, *f*, praedātĭo, *f*

depress *v.t*, dēprĭmo (3); **(spirits, etc.)**, infringo (3)

depression (sadness) tristĭtĭa, *f*

deprive *v.t*, prīvo (1) (*with acc. of person deprived, and abl. of thing*)

depth altĭtūdo, *f*

deputation lēgātĭo, *f*

depute *v.t*, lēgo (1), mando (1) (*with dat*)

deputy lēgātus, *m*

deputy-governor prōcūrātor, *m*

derange *v.t*, perturbo (1)

deride *v.t*, dērīdĕo (2)

derision irrīsĭo, *f*, rīsus, *m*

derive (from) *v.t*, **(deduce)** dūco (3), ab (*and abl*)

derogate from *v.i*, dērŏgo (1) dē (*with abl*)

derogatory (remark) noxĭus

descend *v.i*, dēscendo (3)

descendant prōgĕnĭes, *f*

descent (lineage) prōgĕnĭes, *f*; **(movement)**, dēscensus, *m*; **(slope)**, dēclīve, *n*

describe *v.t*, dēscrībo (3), expōno (3)

description dēscriptĭo, *f*, narrātĭo, *f*

descry *v.t*, conspĭcor (1 *dep*)

desecrate *v.t*, prŏfāno (1)

desert (wilderness) sōlĭtūdo, *f*

desert *v.t*, dēsĕro (3), rĕlinquo (3)

deserted dēsertus

deserter perfŭga, *m*, transfŭga, *m*

deserve *v.t*, mĕrĕor (2 *dep*); dignus esse (*irreg*) (*with abl*)

deservedly *adv*, mĕrĭto

design dēscriptĭo, *f*; **(plan)**, consĭlĭum, *n*

design *v.t*, dēscrībo (3); **(intend)**, in ănĭmo hăbĕo (2)

designate *v.t*, dēsigno (1)

designing *adj*, callĭdus, dŏlōsus

desirable optābĭlis

desire *nn*, dēsĭdĕrĭum, *n*, cŭpĭditas

desire *v.t*, cŭpĭo (3), opto (1)

desirous cŭpĭdus

desist *v.i*, dēsisto (3), dēsĭno (3)

desk scrīnĭum, *n*

desolate dēsertus, sōlus

despair *nn*, dēspērātĭo, *f*

despair *v.i*, dēspēro (1)

despatch *v.t*, mitto (3); **(kill)**, interfĭcĭo (3)

despatch *nn*, **(sending)**, dīmissĭo, *f*; **(letter)**, littĕrae, *f.pl*; **(speed)**, cĕlĕrĭtas, *f*

desperate dēspērātus; **(situation)**, extrēmus

desperate despĕrātĭo, *f*

despicable contemptus

despise *v.t*, dēspĭcĭo (3), sperno (3)

despite *prep*, contrā (*with acc*)

despoil *v.t*, spŏlĭo (1)

despond

despond *v.i*, ănĭmum dēmitto (3)
despondent *use adv. phr*, ănĭmo dēmisso
despot dŏmĭnus, *m*
despotic tўrannĭcus, *m*
despotism dŏmĭnātus, *m*
dessert mensa sĕcunda **(second table)**
destination *often* quo? **(whither)**, *or* ĕo **(to that place)**
destine *v.t*, dēstĭno (1), dēsigno (1)
destiny fātum, *n*
destitute ĭnops
destroy *v.t*, perdo (3), dēlĕo (2), ēverto (3)
destroyer vastātor, *m*
destruction pernĭcĭes, *f*, ēversĭo, *f*, exĭtĭum, *n*
destructive pernĭcĭōsus
desultory inconstans
detach *v.t*, sēiungo (3), sēpăro (1)
detached sēpărātus
detachment **(of troops, etc.)** mănus
details singŭla, *n.pl*
detail *v.t*, explĭco (1)
detain *v.t*, rĕtĭnĕo (2)
detect *v.t*, dēprĕhendo (3), compĕrĭo (4)
deter *v.t*, dēterrĕo (2), dēpello (3)
deteriorate *v.i*, corrumpor (3 *pass*)
determinate *adj*, certus
determination **(resolution)** constantĭa, *f*; **(intention)**, consĭlĭum, *n*
determine *v.i and v.t*, constĭtŭo (3)
determined **(resolute)** firmus; **(fixed)** certus
detest *v.t*, ōdi (*v. defect*)
detestable ŏdĭōsus
dethrone *v.t*, regno pello (3) **(expel from sovereignty)**
detour circŭĭtus, *m*
detract from *v.t*, dētrăho (3) dē (*with abl*)
detriment dētrīmentum, *n*
detrimental **(to be —)** *v.i*, esse (*irreg*) dētrīmento (*with dat*)
devastate *v.t*, vasto (1)
devestation vastātĭo, *f*
develop *v.t*, explĭco (1), ēdŭco (1); *v.i*, cresco (3) **(grow)**
development prōlātĭo, *f*; **(unfolding)**, explĭcātĭo, *f*

deviate *v.i*, dēclīno (1), discēdo (3)
deviation dēclīnātĭo, *f*
device **(contrivance)** artĭfĭcium, *n*; **(emblem)**, insigne, *n*; **(plan)**, dŏlus, *m*
devil daemŏnĭum, *n*
devilish nēfandus
devious dēvĭus
devise *v.t*, excōgĭto (1), fingo (3)
devoid expers, văcŭus
devolve *v.i*, obvĕnĭo (4); *v.t*, dēfĕro (*irreg*)
devote *v.t*, dēdico (1), dēdo (3); **(consecrate)**, dēvŏvĕo (2)
devoted dēdĭtus, dēvōtus
devotion stŭdĭum, *n*; **(love)**, ămor, *m*
devour *v.t*, dēvŏro (1), consūmo (3)
devouring ĕdax
devout pĭus, vĕnĕrābundus, rēlĭgĭōsus
dew rōs, *m*
dexterity sollertĭa, *f*, callĭdĭtas, *f*
dexterous sollers, callĭdus
diadem dĭădēma, *n*
diagonal *adj*, dĭăgōnālis
diagram forma, *f*
dial sōlārĭum, *n*
dialect dĭălectus, *f*
dialectics dĭălectĭca, *n.pl*
dialogue sermo, *m*; **(written)**, dĭălŏgus, *m*
diameter crassĭtūdo, *f*
diamond ădămas, *m*
diaphragm praecordĭa, *n.pl*
diarrhoea prōflŭvĭum, *n*
diary commentārii dĭurni, *m.pl*
dice tāli, *m.pl*; **(the game)**, ălĕa, *f*
dictate *v.t*, dicto (1); *v.i*, impĕro (1) (*with dat*)
dictation dictātĭo, *f*
dictator dictātor, *m*
dictatorial impĕrĭōsus
dictatorship dictātūra, *f*
dictionary glossārĭum, *n*
die *v.i*, mŏrĭor (3 *dep*), cădo (3)
diet victus, *m*
differ *v.i*, discrĕpo (1), diffĕro (*irreg*)
difference discrīmen, *n*, dīversĭtas, *f*; **(— of opinion)**, discrĕpantĭa, *f*
different ălĭus, dīversus

difficult diffĭcĭlis
difficulty dĭffĭcultas, f; (to be in—),
 lăbōro (1); (with —), adv, aegrē
diffidence diffīdentĭa, f
diffident diffīdens
diffuse v.t, diffundo (3)
dig v.t, fŏdĭo (3)
digest v.t, concŏquo (3)
digestion concoctĭo, f
dignified grăvis
dignify v.t, hŏnesto (1)
dignity (of character) grăvĭtas, f,
 dignĭtas, f
digress v.i, dīgrĕdĭor (3 dep)
digression dīgressĭo, f
dike (ditch) fossa, f; (mound)
 agger, m
dilapidated rŭīnōsus
dilate v.i, sē dīlātāre (1 reflex); v.t,
 (— upon), dīlāto (1)
dilatory ignāvus, lentus
dilemma (difficulty) angustĭae, f.pl
diligence dīlĭgentĭa, f
dilute v.t, dīlŭo (3), miscĕo (2)
dim adj, (light, etc.), obscūrus;
 (dull, stupid), hĕbes
dim v.t, obscūro (1)
dimension mŏdus, m
diminish v.t, mĭnŭo (3); v.i,
 mĭnŭor (3 pass)
diminution dēmĭnūtĭo, f
diminutive parvus, exĭgŭus
dimness obscūrĭtas, f
dimple lăcūna, f
din strĕpĭtus, m
dine v.i, cēno (1)
dingy sordĭdus
dining room trīclīnĭum, n, cēnātĭo,
 f
dinner cēna, f
by dint of prep, per (with acc)
dip v.t, mergo (3); v.i, mergor (3
 pass)
diploma dĭplōma, n
diplomacy (by —) per lĕgātos (by
 means of diplomats)
diplomat(ist) lēgātus, m
direct adj, rectus
direct v.t, dīrĭgo (3); (order),
 praecĭpĭo (3) (with dat. of
 person); (show), monstro (1)

direction (of motion) cursus, m;
 (pointing out), monstrātĭo, f;
 (affairs), admĭnĭstrātĭo, f; (in
 different —s), (pl. adj), dīversi
director cūrātor, m
dirt sordes, f
dirty sordĭdus, spurcus
dirty v.t, inquĭno (1), foedo (1)
disable v.t, dēbĭlĭto (1)
disabled inhăbĭlis, confectus
disadvantage incommŏdum, n
disadvantageous incommŏdus
disaffected ălĭēnātus
disaffection ănĭmus āversus, m
disagree v.i, discrēpo (1), dissentĭo
 (4)
disagreeable (unpleasant)
 iniūcundus
disagreement discrĕpantĭa, f,
 dissensĭo, f
disappear v.i, ēvānesco (3),
 diffŭgĭo (3)
disappearance exĭtus, m
disappoint v.t, frustror (1 dep)
disappointment incommŏdum, n
disapproval rĕprĕhensĭo, f
disapprove v.t, imprŏbo (1)
disarm v.t, armis exŭo (3) (strip of
 arms)
disaster clādes, f
disastrous pernĭcĭōsus
disavow v.t, diffĭtĕor (2 dep)
disavowal infĭtĭātĭo, f
disband v.t, dīmitto (3)
disbelieve v.t, non crēdo (3),
 diffīdo (3) (with dat)
disburse v.t, expendo (3)
disc orbis, m
discard v.t, rĕpŭdĭo (1)
discern v.t, cerno (3)
discerning adj, perspĭcax
discernment intellĕgentĭa, f
discharge v.t, (missiles, etc.),
 ēmitto (3), iăcŭlor (1 dep);
 (soldiers, etc.), dīmitto (3);
 (duties, etc.), fungor (3 dep) (with
 abl)
discharge nn, ēmissĭo, f, dīmissĭo,
 f
disciple discĭpŭlus, m

discipline

discipline disciplīna, *f*
discipline *v.t*, instĭtŭo (3)
disclaim *v.t*, nĕgo (1), rĕpŭdĭo (1)
disclose *v.t*, ăpĕrĭo (4)
disclosure indĭcĭum, *n*
discolour *v.t*, dēcŏlōro (1)
discomfiture clādes, *f*
discomfort incommŏdum, *n*
disconcert *v.t*, perturbo (1)
disconnect *v.t*, sēiungo (3)
disconsolate maestus
discontented măle contentus
discontinue *v.t*, intermitto (3)
discord (strife) discordĭa, *f*,
  dissensĭo, *f*
discount *nn*, dēcessĭo, *f* (decrease)
discourage *v.t*, ănĭmum dēmitto
  (3)
discouragement ănĭmi infractĭo, *f*,
  or dēmissĭo, *f*
discourse *v.i*, dissĕro (3)
discourse *nn*, sermo, *m*, contĭo, *f*
discover *v.t*, invĕnĭo (4), rĕpĕrio
  (4), cognosco (3)
discovery inventĭo, *f*; (thing
  discovered), inventum, *n*
discredit *v.t*, fĭdem abrŏgo (1)
discreditable ĭnhŏnestus
discreet consīdĕrātus, prūdens
discretion prūdentĭa, *f*
discriminate *v.t*, discerno (3)
discuss *v.t*, discepto (1), dispŭto
  (1)
discussion dispŭtātĭo, *f*
disdain *v.t*, sperno (3), dēspĭcĭo (3)
disdain *nn*, fastīdĭum, *n*
disdainful fastīdĭōsus
disease morbus, *m*
diseased aeger
disembark *v.t*, expōno (3); *v.i*,
  ēgrĕdĭor (3 *dep*)
disengage *v.t*, (release), solvo (3)
disengaged (at leisure) ōtĭōsus;
  (free, loose) sŏlūtus
disentangle *v.t*, explĭco (1)
disfigure *v.t*, dēformo (1)
disgrace *nn*, dēdĕcus, *n*,
  ignōmĭnĭa, *f*
disgrace *v.t*, dēdĕcoro (1)
disgraceful turpis, flāgĭtĭōsus
disguise *nn*, persōna, *f*,
  intĕgŭmentum, *n*

disguise *v.t*, vestem mūto (1)
  (change the clothes); dissĭmŭlo
  (1) (pretend, hide)
disgust *nn*, fastīdĭum, *n*, taedĭum,
  n
disgust *v.t*, taedĭum mŏvĕo (2)
  (*with dat*)
disgusted (to be —) *use
  impersonal vb*, pĭget (2) (it
  disgusts)
disgusting foedus
dish *nn*, pătĭna, *f*
dishearten *v.t*, exănĭmo (1),
  percello (3)
dishonest imprŏbus, perfĭdus
dishonesty *f*, imprŏbĭtas, *f*
dishonour *nn*, dēdĕcus, *n*
dishonour *v.t*, dēdĕcŏro (1)
dishonourable inhŏnestus
disinclination dēclīnātĭo, *f*
disinherit *v.t*, exhērēdo (1)
disintegrate *v.t*, solvo (3); *v.i*,
  solvor (3 *pass*)
disinterested neutri făvens
  (favouring neither side)
disjointed ĭnordĭnātus
disk orbis, *m*
dislike *nn*, ŏdĭum, *n*
dislike *v.t*, ăbhorrĕo (2) ab (*with
  abl*); displĭcĕo (2)
dislocate *v.t*, extorquĕo (2)
dislodge *v.t*, dēĭcĭo (3), pello (3)
disloyal infĭdēlis
dismal āter, maestus
dismantle *v.t*, dĭrĭpĭo (3)
dismay *nn*, păvor, *m*
dismay *v.t*, consterno (1), pertubo
  (1)
dismiss *v.t*, dīmitto (3)
dismissal dīmissĭo, *f*
dismount *v.i*, ex ĕquo dēscendo
  (3)
disobedience *use phr. with vb*,
  pārĕo (obey)
disobedient măle pārens
disobey *v.t*, măle pārĕo (*with
  dat*)
disoblige *v.t*, offendo (3)
disorder *nn*, perturbātĭo, *f*
disorderly *adv*, turbātus; (crowd),
  turbŭlentus
disown *v.t*, infĭtĭor (1 *dep*)

disparage *v.t*, dētrăho (3), obtrecto (1)

dispatch *v.t*, (see **despatch**)

dispel *v.t*, dēpello (3), discŭtĭo (3)

dispense *v.t*, dispertĭor (4 *dep*) distrĭbŭo (3); (— **with**), dīmitto (3)

dispersal dissĭpātĭo, *f*

disperse *v.t*, dispergo (3), dissĭpo (1), *v.i*, diffŭgĭo (3)

dispirited *use adv. phr*, dēmisso ănĭmo

display *nn*, ostentātĭo, *f*

display *v.t*, ostento (1)

displease *v.t*, displĭcĕo (2) (*with dat*)

displeasing ŏdĭōsus

displeasure offensĭo, *f*

disposal ēmissĭo, *f*; (**power**), arbĭtrĭum, *n*

dispose *v.t*, (**arrange**), constĭtŭo (3), dispōno (3); (**induce**), inclīno (1); (**get rid of**) ēlŭo (3)

disposed inclīnātus

disposition (**arrangement**) dispŏsĭtĭo, *f*, (**of mind, etc.**), nātūra, *f*, ingĕnĭum, *n*

dispossess *v.t*, dēturbo (1), dētrūdo (3)

disproportion dissĭmĭlĭtūdo, *f*; (**of parts, etc.**) inconcinnĭtas, *f*

disprove *v.t*, rĕfello (3), rĕfūto (1)

dispute *nn*, contrōversĭa, *f*

dispute *v.t*, dispŭto (1)

disqualify *v.t*, (**prevent**), prŏhĭbĕo (2)

disregard *nn*, neglĕgentĭa, *f*

disregard *v.t*, neglĕgo (3)

disreputable infāmis

disrespectful contŭmax, insŏlens

dissatisfaction mŏlestĭa, *f*

dissatisfied (— **to be**) *use impers. vb*, paenĭtet (*with acc. of subject and genit of object*)

dissect *v.t*, insĕco (1), persĕco (1)

dissemble *v.i*, dissĭmŭlo (1)

dissension discordĭa, *f*, dissensĭo, *f*

dissent *v.i*, dissentĭo (4)

dissimilar dissĭmĭlis

dissipate *v.t*, dissĭpo (1)

dissipated dissŏlūtus, lĭbīdĭnōsus

dissipation lĭcentĭa, *f*

dissolute dissŏlūtus, lĭbīdĭnōsus

dissolve *v.t*, solvo (3), lĭquĕfăcĭo (3), *v.i*, solvor (3 *pass*), lĭquesco (3)

dissuade *v.t*, dissuādĕo (2) (*with dat*)

distaff cŏlus, *f*

distance spătĭum, *n*; (**remoteness**), longinquĭtas, *f*; (**at a —**), *adv*, longē, prŏcul

distant rĕmōtus, distans; (**to be —**), absum (*irreg*)

distaste fastīdĭum, *n*

distasteful inĭūcundus

distemper (**malady**) morbus, *m*

distend *v.t*, tendo (3)

distil *v.t*, stillo (1)

distinct (**separate**) sēpărātus; (**clear**), clārus, mănĭfestus

distinction (**difference**) discrīmen, *n*; (**mark of honour**), hŏnor, *m*, dĕcus, *n*

distinctive prŏprĭus

distinguish *v.t*, distinguo (3); *v.i*, (— **oneself**), clāresco (3), ēmĭnĕo (2)

distinguished insignis, clārus

distort *v.t*, dētorquĕo (2)

distortion distortĭo, *f*

distract *v.t*, distrăho (3)

distracted (**mentally**) āmens, turbātus

distraction (**mental**) āmentĭa, *f*

distress mĭsĕrĭa, *f*, dŏlor, *m*

distress *v.t* sollĭcĭto (1)

distressed sollĭcĭtus

distribute *v.t*, distrĭbŭo (3), partĭor (4 *dep*)

distributioon partītĭo, *f*

district rĕgĭo, *f*

distrust *nn*, diffĭdentĭa, *f*

distrust *v.t*, diffīdo (3) (*with dat*)

distrustful diffīdens

disturb *v.t*, turbo (1)

disturbance mōtus, *m*, tŭmulus, *m*

disunion discordĭa, *f*

disunite *v.t*, sēiungo (3), dissŏcĭo (1)

disused dēsŭētus

ditch fossa, *f*

ditty carmen, *n*

divan lectŭlus, *m*

dive *v.i*, sē mergĕre (3 *reflex*)

diver

diver ūrīnātor, *m*
diverge *v.i*, discēdo (3)
divergence dēclīnātĭo, *f*
diverse ălĭus, dīversus
diversion dērīvātĭo, *f*; (of thought, etc.), āvŏcātĭo, *f*
divert *v.t*, āverto (3), āvŏco (1); (amuse), oblecto (1), prōlecto (1)
divide *v.t*, dīvĭdo (3); (share out), partĭor (4 *dep*); *v.i*, sē dīvĭdĕre (3 *reflex*)
divine dīvīnus
divine *v.t*, dīvīno (1), augŭror (1 *dep*)
diviner augur, *m*
divinity dīvīnĭtas, *f*
divisible dīvĭdŭus
division (act of —) dīvīsĭo, *f*; (a section), pars, *f*; (discord), discĭdĭum, *n*
divorce dīvortĭum, *n*
divorce *v.i*, dīvortĭum făcĭo (3), cum (*and abl*)
divulge *v.t*, pătĕfăcĭo (3), ăpĕrĭo (4)
dizziness vertīgo, *f*
dizzy vertīgĭnōsus
do *v.t*, făcĭo (3), ăgo (3); (to be satisfactory), *v.i*, sătis esse; (—away with) ăbŏlĕo (2); (—without), cărĕo (2) (*with abl*)
docile făcĭlis, dŏcĭlis
dock nāvālĭa, *n.pl*
doctor mĕdĭcus, *m*
doctor *v.t*, cūro (1)
doctrine dogma, *n*, rătĭo, *f*
document tăbŭla, *f*, littĕrae, *f.pl*
dodge dŏlus, *m*
dodge *v.t*, (elude), ēlūdo (3)
doe cerva, *f*
dog cănis, *c*
dog *v.t*, insĕquor (3 *dep*)
dogged (stubborn) pertĭnax, pervĭcax
dogged (by ill-luck, etc.) ăgĭtātus
dogma dogma, *n*
dogmatic arrŏgans
dole (small allowance) dĭurna, *n.pl*
dole out *v.t*, dīvĭdo (3)
doleful tristis, maestus
dolefulness tristĭtĭa, *f*
doll pūpa, *f*

dolphin delphīnus, *m*
dolt caudex, *m*
dome thŏlus, *m*
domestic dŏmestĭcus, fămĭlĭāris; (animals) villātĭcus
domestic *nn*, (servant), fămŭlus, *m*
domicile dŏmĭcĭlĭum, *n*
dominant pŏtens
dominate *v.t*, dŏmĭnor (1 *dep*)
domination dŏmĭnātus, *m*
domineering impĕrĭōsus
dominion impĕrĭum, *n*, regnum, *n*
donation dōnum, *n*
donkey ăsĭnus, *m*
doom fātum, *n*
doom *v.t*, damno (1)
door iănŭa, *f*; (out of —s) *adv*, fŏrīs
doorkeeper iānĭtor, *m*
doorpost postis, *f*
dormitory cŭbĭcŭlum, *n*
dormouse glīs, *m*
dot *nn*, punctum, *n*
dotage sĕnĭum, *n*
dotard sĕnex, *m*
dote upon *v.i*, dēpĕrĕo (4)
double *adj*, dŭplex, gĕmĭnus
double *v.t*, dŭplĭco (1); *v.i*, dŭplex fīo (*irreg*), ingĕmĭno (1)
double-dealing *nn*, fraus, *f*
double-faced fallax
doubt *v.i*, dŭbĭto (1)
doubt *nn*, dŭbĭum, *n*, dŭbĭtātĭo
doubtful dŭbĭus, incertus
doubtless *adv*, sĭne dŭbĭo, nīmīrum
dough fărīna, *f*
dove cŏlumba, *f*
dove-coloured cŏlumbīnus
dovecot cŏlumbārĭum, *n*
dowager vĭdŭa, *f*
down *prep*, dē (*with abl*); *adv, use* dē *in a coumpound verb, e.g.* run down dēcurro (3)
down *nn*, (feathers, etc.) plūma, *f*
down *v.t*, (put down) dēpōno (3)
downcast dēiectus, dēmissus
downfall occāsus, *m*, rŭīna, *f*
down-hearted *adv*, dēmisso ănĭmo
downpour imber, *m*
downright dīrectus; (sheer), mĕrus
downward *adj*, dēclīvis

downwards *adv,* dĕorsum
downy *adj,* plūmĕus
dowry dos, *f*
doze *v.i,* dormīto (1)
dozen (twelve) dŭŏdĕcim
dozing *adj,* somnĭcŭlōsus
drab cĭnĕrĕus **(ash-coloured)**
drag *v.t,* trăho (3)
dragon drăco, *m*
drain *nn,* clŏāca, *f,* fossa, *f*
drain *v.t,* **(land),** sicco (1); **(a drink),**
  haurĭo (4)
dram cўăthus, *m*
drama fābŭla, *f,* scēna, *f*
dramatic (theatrical) scēnĭcus
dramatist pŏēta, *m*
drapery vēlāmen, *n*
draught (of air) spīrĭtus, *m;* **(water,**
  etc.) haustus, *m;* **(game of −s),**
  lătruncŭli, *m.pl*
draw *v.t,* **(pull)** trăho (3); **(portray),**
  dēscrībo (3); **(− a sword),**
  glădĭum stringo (3);
  (−aside), sēdūco (3); **(− water,**
  etc.) haurĭo (4); *v.i* **(− back),**
  pĕdem rĕfĕro *(irreg);* **(− lots),**
  sortes dūco (3); **(− up troops,**
  etc.) *v.t,* instrŭo (3)
drawback, *nn,* incommŏdum, *n*
drawbridge pontĭcŭlus, *m*
drawing (picture) pictūra, *f*
drawl *v.i,* lentē prōnuntĭo (1)
  (pronounce slowly)
dray plaustrum, *n*
dread *nn,* formīdo *f,* păvor, *m*
dread *v.t,* tĭmĕo (2), formīdo (1)
dreadful terrĭbĭlis, ātrox
dream *nn,* somnĭum, *n*
dream *v.t,* somnĭo (1)
dreamy somnĭcŭlōsus
dreary tristis
dregs faex, *f*
drench *v.t,* mădĕfăcĭo (3)
dress *nn,* vestis, *f,* hăbĭtus, *m*
dress *v.t,* **(clothe);** vestĭo (4); **(− a**
  wound) cūro (1) **(care for)**
dressing *nn,* **(of wound)**
  fōmentum, *n*
drift *nn,* **(heap),** agger, *m;*
  (tendency), *use phr. with* quōrsus
  (to what end?)
drift *v.i,* dēfĕror *(irreg. pass)*

drill (military) exercĭtātĭo, *f;* **(tool),**
  tĕrĕbra, *f*
drill *v.t,* **(pierce),** tĕrĕbro (1);
  (train), exercĕo (2)
drill (military) exercĭtātĭo, *f;* **(tool),**
  tĕrĕbra, *f*
drill *v.t,* **(pierce),** tĕrĕbro (1);
  (train), exercĕo (2)
drink *v.t,* bĭbo (3), pōto (1)
drink *nn,* pōtĭo, *f*
drinker pōtātor, *m*
drinking pōtĭo, *f;* **(− party),**
  cōmissātĭo, *f*
drip *v.i,* stillo (1)
dripping *adj,* mădĭdus
drive *nn,* gestātĭo, *f*
drive *v.t,* ăgo (3); **(− away),** fŭgo
  (1) pello (3); **(− back),** rĕpello
  (3); **(− out),** expello (3)
drive *v.i,* **(on horse-back, etc.)**
  vĕhor (3 *pass*)
drivel ĭneptĭae, *f.pl*
drivel *v.i,* dēlīro (1)
driver aurīga, *c*
drizzle *v.i,* rōro (1)
droll rīdĭcŭlus, lĕpĭdus
drollery făcētĭae, *f.pl*
dromedary drŏmas, *m*
drone *nn,* **(bee),** fūcus, *m;* **(sound),**
  murmur, *n*
drone *v.i,* murmŭro (1)
droop *v.i,* pendĕo (2), languesco
  (3)
drooping *adj,* pendŭlus; **(of spirits,**
  etc.), dēmissus
drop *nn,* gutta, *f*
drop *v.t,* dēmitto (3); **(leave off),**
  omitto (3); *v.i,* cădo (3)
dropsy hydrops, *m*
drought siccĭtas, *f*
drove (flock) grex, *m*
drown *v.t,* submergo (3); **(of noise)**
  obstrĕpo (3)
drowsy somnĭcŭlōsus
drudge *nn,* servus, *m*
drudge *v.i,* servĭo (4); **(weary**
  oneself) *v.i,* sē fătīgăre (1 *reflex*)
drudgery lăbor servīlis **(servile**
  labour)
drug *nn,* mĕdĭcāmentum, *n*
drug *v.t,* mĕdĭco (1)
drum tympănum, *n*

drunk

drunk *adj*, ēbrĭus
drunkenness ēbrĭĕtas, *f*
dry siccus, ārĭdus; **(thirsty)**, sĭtĭens
dry (up) *v.t*, sicco (1); *v.i*, āresco (3)
dryness sĭccĭtas, *f*, ārĭdĭtas, *f*
dubious dŭbĭus
duck *nn*, ănas, *f*
duck *v.t*, mergo (3)
duckling ănătĭcŭla, *f*
duct fŏrāmen, *n*
due *adj*, **(owed)**, dēbĭtus; **(just)**, iustus; **(suitable)**, ĭdōnĕus, aptus
due *nn*, **(a right)**, ius, *n*; **(taxes)**, vectīgal, *n*, portōrĭum, *n*
duel certāmen, *n*
dull **(person)** hĕbes, obtūsus; **(colour)**, obscūrus; **(blunt)**, hĕbes; **(weather)**, subnūbĭlus
dullness **(of mind)** tardĭtas, *f*
duly *adv*, **(established by precedent)** rītĕ
dumb mūtus
dumbfound *v.t*, obstŭpĕfăcĭo (3)
dump *v.t*, cŏăcervo (1)
dun fuscus
dunce hŏmo stŭpĭdus
dung stercus, *n*
dungeon carcer, *m*
dupe *nn*, hŏmo crēdŭlus
dupe *v.t*, dēcĭpĭo (3)
duplicate exemplum, *n*
duplicity fallācĭa, *f*
durability firmĭtas, *f*
durable firmus
duration spătĭum, *n*; **(long —)**, dĭŭturnĭtas, *f*
during *prep*, per (*with acc*)
dusk crēpuscŭlum, *n*
dusky fuscus, nĭger
dust *nn*, pulvis, *m*
dust *v.t*, dētergĕo (2)
duster pēnĭcŭlus, *m*
dusty pulvĕrŭlentus
dutiful pĭus
dutifulness pĭĕtas, *f*
duty **(moral)** offĭcĭum, *n*; **(given)**, mūnus, *n*; **(tax)** vectīgal, *n*; **(it is my —)** *use vb.* dēbĕo (2) **(ought)**
dwarf pūmĭlĭo, *c*
dwarfish pŭsillus

dwell *v.i*, hăbĭto (1), incŏlo (3); **(— on a theme)**, commŏror (1 *dep*), haerĕo (2) in (*with abl*)
dweller incŏla, *c*
dwelling (place) dŏmĭcĭlĭum, *n*
dwindle *v.i*, dēcresco (3)
dye *nn*, fūcus, *m*
dye *v.t*, tingo (3), infĭcĭo (3)
dyer infector, *m*
dying *adj*, mŏrĭens
dynasty dŏmus, *f*
dysentry dўsentĕrĭa, *f*
dyspeptic crūdus

E

each ūnusquisque; **(— of two)**, ŭterque; **(one —)**, *use distributive num*, singŭli, bīnī
eager cŭpĭdus, ăvĭdus (*with genit*)
eagerness cŭpĭdĭtas, *f*, ăvĭdĭtas, *f*
eagle ăquĭla, *f*
ear auris, *f*; **(— of corn)**, spīca, *f*
early *adj*, **(in the morning)** mātūtīnus; **(of time, etc.)**, mātūrus
early *adv*, **(in the morning)** māne; **(in time, etc.)**, mātūrē
earn *v.t*, mĕrĕo (2), mĕrĕor (2 *dep*)
earnest intentus, ācer
earnestly *adv*, intentē
earth **(land)** terra, *f*; **(ground)**, sŏlum, *n*; **(globe)**, orbis (*m*) terrārum
earthenware fictīlĭa, *n.pl*
earthly *adj* **(terrestrial)** terrestris
earthquake terrae mōtus, *m*, **(movement of the earth)**
earthwork agger, *m*
ease quĭes, *f*, ōtĭum, *n*
ease *v.t*, **(lighten)**, lĕvo (1), exŏnĕro (1)
easily *adv*, făcĭlĕ
easiness făcĭlĭtas, *f*
east *nn*, ŏrĭens, *m*
eastern *use genit.* of ŏrĭens **(east)**
eastward *adv. phr*, ăd ŏrĭentem
easy făcĭlis
eat *v.t*, ĕdo (3); **(— away)**, rōdo (3)
eatable escŭlentus
eating-house pŏpīna, *f*
eaves prōtectum, *n*
eavesdropper auceps, *c*

ebb *v.i*, rĕcēdo (3)
ebb-tide rĕcessus aaestus **(receding of the tide)**
ebony ĕbĕnus, *f*
eccentric **(of persons)** nŏvus
echo *nn*, ĭmāgo, *f*, ēcho, *f*
echo *v.t*, rĕfĕro (*irreg*), rĕsŏno (1)
echoing *adj*, rĕsŏnus
eclipse *nn*, dēfectĭo, *f*
eclipse *v.t*, obscūro (1)
economical parcus, dīlĭgens
economy parsĭmōnĭa, *f*, **(frugality)**
ecstasy fŭror, *m*
ecstatic fŭrens
eddy vertex, *m*
edge **(of knife etc.)** ăcĭes, *f*; **(margin)**, margo, *c*, ōra, *f*
edible escŭlentus
edict ēdictum, *n*
edifice aedĭfĭcĭum, *n*
edify *v.t*, instĭtŭo (3)
edit *v.t*, ēdo (3)
edition ēdĭtĭo, *f*
educate *v.t*, ēdŭco (1)
education ēdŭcātĭo, *f*, doctrīna, *f*
eel anguilla, *f*
efface *v.t*, dēlĕo (2)
effect *v.t*, effĭcĭo (3)
effect *nn*, **(influence, impression)**, vīs, *f*; **(result)**, effectus, *m*; **(consequence)**, ēventus, *m*; **(without —)**, (*adv*), nēquīquem
effective **(impressive)** grăvis; *or use phr. with* confĭcĭo (3) **(to bring to a conclusion)**
effectual effĭcax
effeminate effēmĭnātus
effervescence **(of spirit, etc.)** fervor, *m*
efficacy vīs, *f*
efficiency vīs, *f*
efficient hăbĭlis, effĭcĭens
effigy ĭmāgo, *f*
effort ŏpĕra, *f*
effrontery ōs, *n*
effulgent fulgens
effusion effūsĭo, *f*
egg ōvum, *n*
egg on *v.t*, incĭto (1)
egoism ămor (*m*) sŭi **(fondness of oneself)**
egoist ămātor (*m*) sŭi
egregious insignis

egress exĭtus, *m*
eight octo; **(— each)**, octōni; **(—times)**, *adv*. octĭens; **(— hundred)** octingenti
eighteen dŭŏdēvīginti
eighteenth dŭŏdēvīcensimus
eight octāvus
eightieth octōgēsĭmus
eighty octōginta
either *pron*, altĕrŭter; *conj*, aut
either ... or aut ... aut, vel ... vel
ejaculate *v.t*, ēmitto (3)
ejaculation **(cry)** vox, *f*, clāmor, *m*
eject *v.t*, ēĭcĭo (3)
eke out *v.t*, parco (3) **(*with dat*)**
elaborate *adj*, ēlăbōrātus
elaborate *v.t*, ēlăbōro (1)
elapse *v.i*, **(of time)**, intercēdo (3)
elate *v.t*, effĕro (*irreg*)
elated **(joyful)** laetus
elbow cŭbĭtum, *n*
elder *adj*, māior nātu **(greater by birth)**
elder tree sambūcus, *f*
elderly *adj*, prōvectus aetāte **(advanced in age)**
elect *v.t*, crĕo (1), dēlĭgo (3)
elect *adj*, dēsignātus
election ēlectĭo, *f*, cŏmĭtĭa, *n.pl*
elector suffrāgātor, *m*
elegance ēlĕgantĭa, *f*, vĕnustas, *f*
elegant ēlĕgans, vĕnustus
elegy ĕlĕgīa, *f*
element ēlĕmentum, *n*, prĭncĭpĭa, *n.pl*
elementary prīmus, simplex
elephant ĕlĕphantus, *m*
elevate *v.t*, tollo (3)
elevated ēdĭtus; **(mind)** ēlātus
elevation altĭtūdo, *f*, ēlātĭo, *f*
eleven undĕcim; **(— each)**, undēni
eleventh undĕcĭmus
elicit *v.t*, ēlĭcĭo (3)
eligible ĭdōnĕus, opportūnus
elk alces, *f*
ell ulna, *f*
elm ulmus, *f*
elocution prōnuntĭātĭo, *f*
elope *v.i*, aufŭgĭo (3) **(run away)**
eloquence ēlŏquentĭa, *f*
eloquent ēlŏquens, dĭsertus
else *adj*, ălĭus
else *adv*, ălĭter

elsewhere *adv,* ălĭbī
elude *v.t,* ēlūdo (3)
emaciate *v.t,* attĕnŭo (1)
emaciated măcer
emaciation măcĭes, *f*
emanate *v.i,* ēmāno (1)
emancipate *v.t,* lībĕro (1),
    mănŭmitto (3)
embalm *v.t,* condĭo (4)
embankment mōles, *f*
embark *v.t,* in nāvem impōno (3);
    v.i, nāvem conscendo (3)
embarrass *v.t,* **(entangle),** impĕdĭo
    (4); **(confuse),** turbo (1)
embarrassment scrūpŭlus, *m;*
    (difficulty), diffĭcultas, *f*
embassy (delegation) lēgāti, *m.pl,*
    (ambassadors)
embedded sĭtus
embellish *v.t,* orno (1)
embellishment ornāmentum, *n*
embers cĭnis, *m*
embezzle *v.t,* āverto (3), pĕcŭlor
    (1 *dep)*
embezzlement pĕcūlātus, *m*
embezzler āversor *(m)* pĕcūnĭae
embitter *v.t,* exăcerbo (1)
emblem insigne, *n,* indĭcĭum, *n*
embody *v.t,* inclūdo (3)
embolden *v.t,* confirmo (1)
embrace *nn,* amplexus, *m,*
    complexus, *m*
embrace *v.t,* amplector (3 *dep),*
    complector (3 *dep);* **(— an**
    opportunity) arrĭpĭo (3)
embroidered (clothing, etc.)
    pictus
embroil *v.t,* **(entangle),** implĭco (1)
emerald smăragdus, *c*
emerge *v.i,* ēmergo (3), prōdĕo (4)
emergency discrīmen, *n,* tempus,
    n
emigrate *v.i,* mĭgro (1)
emigration mĭgrātĭo, *f*
eminence (high ground) tŭmŭlus,
    m; **(of rank, etc.)** lŏcus
    amplissĭmus
eminent ēgrĕgĭus, insignis
emissary lēgātus, *m*
emit *v.t,* ēmitto (3)
emolument lŭcrum, *n*
emotion mōtus *(m)* ănĭmi
    (movement of the mind)

emperor impĕrātor, *m,* princeps,
    m
emphasize *v.t,* prĕmo (3)
emphatic grăvis
empire impĕrĭum, *n*
empirical empīrĭcus
employ *v.t,* ūtor (3 *dep)* **(with abl)**
employed (of persons) occŭpātus
employer conductor, *m*
employment (occupation)
    quaestus, *m;* **(business),**
    nĕgōtĭum, *n;* **(using),** ūsurpātĭo, *f*
emporium empŏrĭum, *n*
empower (someone to do ...) *v.i,*
    pŏtestātem făcĭo (3) **(with dat. of**
    person and genit. of gerund(ive))
empty *adj,* văcŭus, ĭnānis
empty *v.t,* exĭnānĭo (4)
emulate *v.t,* aemŭlor (1 *dep)*
emulous aemŭlus
enable *v.t,* făcultātem do (1) **(with**
    dat)
enact *v.t,* **(law)** sancĭo (4),
    constĭtŭo (3)
enactment lex, *f*
enamoured (to be — of someone)
    v.t, ămo (1)
encamp *v.i,* castra pōno (3)
enchant *v.t,* fascĭno (1), dēlecto (1)
enchantment (allurement)
    blandīmentum, *n*
encircle *v.t,* circumdo (1)
enclose *v.t,* inclūdo (3), saepĭo (4)
enclosure saeptum, *n*
encounter *v.t,* incĭdo (3) in **(with**
    acc); concurro (3), obvĭam ĕo (4)
    (irreg) **(with dat)**
encounter *nn,* congressus, *m*
encourage *v.t,* hortor (1 *dep)*
encouragement hortātus, *m,*
    confirmātĭo, *f,* hortātĭo, *f*
encroach upon *v.t,* occŭpo (1)
encumber *v.t,* ŏnĕro (1), impĕdĭo
    (4)
encumbrance impĕdīmentum, *n*
end fĭnis, *m; or use* extrēmus, *adj,*
    agreeing with a noun; e.g. **at the**
    end of the bridge, in extrēmo
    ponte
end *v.t,* confĭcĭo (3), fĭnĭo (4); *v.i,*
    use phr. with extrēmum, *n,* **(end);**
    (turn out, result) cēdo (3), ēvĕnĭo
    (4)

endanger *v.t*, in pĕrīcŭlum addūco (3)
endear *v.t*, dēvincĭo (4)
endeavour *nn*, cōnātus, *m*
endeavour *v.t*, cōnor (1 *dep*)
endless infīnītus, perpĕtŭus
endorse *v.t*, confirmo (1)
endow *v.t*, dōno (1)
endowed praedĭtus
endurable tŏlĕrābĭlis
endurance pătĭentĭa, *f*
endure *v.t*, pătĭor (3 *dep*), fĕro (*irreg*); *v.i*, dūro (1)
enemy (public) hostis, *c*; **(private)**, ĭnĭmīcus, *m*
energetic ācer, strēnŭus, impĭger
energy vīs, *f*, vĭgor, *m*
enervate *v.t*, ēnervo (1)
enervation dēbĭlĭtātĭo, *f*
enfeeble *v.t*, dēbĭlĭto (1)
enforce *v.t*, **(carry out)** exsĕquor (3 *dep*)
enfranchise *v.t*, **(give the right of voting)** suffrāgĭum do (1) (*with dat*)
enfranchisement cīvĭtātis dōnātĭo, *f*, **(granting of citizenship)**
engage *v.t*, **(join)** iungo (3); **(hire)** condūco (3); **(— in battle)**; signa conferre (*irreg*); **(enter into)**, ingrĕdĭor (3 *dep*)
engaged occŭpātus; **(betrothed)**, sponsus
engagement (battle) proelĭum, *n*; **(agreement)**, pactum, *n*; **(promise)**, sponsĭo, *f*
engender *v.t*, gigno (3), părĭo (3)
engine māchĭna, *f*; **(military —)**, tormentum, *n*
engineer făber, *m*
England Brĭtannĭa, *f*
English Brĭtannus, Brĭtannĭcus
engrave *v.t*, scalpo (3)
engraver scalptor, *m*
engraving *nn*, scalptūra, *f*
engross *v.t*, occŭpo (1)
enhance *v.t*, augĕo (2), orno (1)
enigma aenigma, *n*, ambāges, *f.pl*
enigmatic ambĭgŭus
enjoin *v.t*, iŭbĕo (2), mando (1)
enjoy *v.t*, frŭor (3 *dep*) (*with abl*)

abl); **(possess)**, ūtor (3 *dep*) (*with abl*)
enjoyment (pleasure) gudĭum, *n*, lĭbīdo, *f*
enlarge *v.t*, augĕo (2), amplĭfĭco (1)
enlargement prōlātĭo, *f*
enlighten *v.t*, **(instruct)**, dŏcĕo (2)
enlist *v.t*, **(troops)**, conscrībo (3); **(bring over)**, concĭlĭo (1); *v.i*, nōmen do (1) **(give one's name)**
enliven *v.t*, excĭto (1)
enmity ĭnĭmīcĭtĭa, *f*
ennoble *v.t*, **(make honourable)**, hŏnesto (1)
enormity immānĭtas, *f*; **(crime)**, scĕlus, *n*
enormous ingens
enough *nn. and adv*, sătis; **(foll. by** *genit*), e.g. **enough water**, sătis ăquae
enquire *v.t*, quaero (3) ab (*with abl*)
enrage *v.t*, irrīto (1), inflammo (1)
enrapture *v.t*, oblecto (1)
enrich *v.t*, lŏcŭplēto (1)
enroll *v.t*, scrībo (3)
ensign signum, *n*; **(— bearer)**, signĭfer, *m*
enslave *v.t*, servĭtūtem iniungo (3) (*with dat*)
ensue *v.i*, sĕquor (3 *dep*)
entail *v.t*, affĕro (*irreg*)
entangle *v.t*, impĕdĭo (4)
enter *v.i, and v.t*, intro (1), ingrĕdĭor (3 *dep*), ĭnĕo (4 *irreg*); *v.t*, **(write in)**, inscrībo (3)
enterprise (undertaking) inceptum, *n*
enterprising promptus, strēnŭus
entertain *v.t*, **(people)**, excĭpĭo (3) **(receive)**; **(amuse)**, oblecto (1); **(an idea, etc.)** hăbĕo (2)
entertainment (of guests) hospĭtĭum, *n*
enthusiasm stŭdĭum, *n*, fervor, *m*
enthusiastic fānātĭcus, stŭdĭōsus
entice *v.t*, illĭcĭo (3)
entire tōtus, intĕger
entirely *adv*, omnīno

entitle *v.t*, **(give the right to)** ius do (1) (*with dat*); **(name)**, inscrĭbo (3)
entitled **(to be — to)** *v.i*, ius hăbĕo (2)
entrails viscĕra, *n.pl*
entrance **(act of —)** ingressĭo, *f*; **(door, etc.)** ădĭtus, *m*, ostĭum, *n*
entreat *v.t*, obsĕcro (1), ōro (1)
entreaty obsĕcrātĭo, *f*
entrust *v.t*, crēdo (3) (*with dat*) committo (3) (*with dat*)
enumerate *v.t*, nŭmĕro (1)
envelop *v.t*, involvo (3)
envelope *nn*, invŏlūcrum, *n*
enviable fortūnātus
envious invĭdus
envoy lēgātus, *m*
envy invĭdĭa, *f*
envy *v.t*, invĭdĕo (2) (*with dat*)
ephemeral brĕvis
epic *adj*, ĕpĭcus
epidemic pestĭlentĭa, *f*
epigram ĕpĭgramma, *n*
epigrammatic ĕpĭgrammătĭcus, a, um, *adj*
epilepsy morbus cŏmĭtĭālis, *m*
episode **(digression)** excursus, *m*; res, *f*
epitaph ĕlŏgĭum, *n*
epoch aetas, *f*
equable aequus
equal *adj*, aequus, pār
equal *nn, use adj*, pār
equal *v.i and v.t*, aequo (1)
equality aequālĭtas, *f*
equanimity aequus ănĭmus, *m*
equator aequĭnoctĭālis circŭlus, *m*
equestrian ĕquester
equilibrium aequĭlībrĭum, *n*
equinox aequĭnoctĭum, *n*
equip *v.t*, orno (1), armo (1)
equipment arma, *n.pl*, armāmenta, *n.pl*
equitable aequus
equity aequĭtas, *f*; **(justice)**, iustĭtĭa, *f*
equivalent *adj*, **(equal)**, pār; **(to be —)**, *v.i, use* vălĕo (2) **(to be worth)** tanti
equivocal ambĭgŭus
era tempus, *n*, aetas, *f*

eradicate *v.t*, ēvello (3), exstirpo (1)
erase *v.t*, dēlĕo (2)
ere **(before)** *conj*, prĭusquam
erect *v.t*, ērĭgo (3); **(build)**, exstrŭo (3)
erect *adj*, rectus
erection **(act of —)** aedĭfĭcātĭo, *f*; **(a building)** aedĭfĭcĭum, *n*
err *v.i*, erro (1), pecco (1)
errand mandātum, *n*
erratic văgus
erroneous falsus
error error, *m*
erudite doctus
eruption ēruptĭo, *f*
escape *nn*, fŭga, *f*
escape *v.i, and v.t*, effŭgĭo (3), ēlābor (3 *dep*)
escarpment praeruptus lŏcus, *m*
escort *nn*, comĭtātus, *m*; **(protective)**, praesĭdĭum, *n*
escort *v.t*, cŏmĭtor (1 *dep*)
especial praecĭpŭus
especially *adv*, praecĭpŭē
espouse *v.t*, **(betroth)**, spondĕo (2); **(marry)** dūco (3), nūbo (3)
essay **(attempt)** cōnātus, *m*; **(composition)**, lĭbellus, *m*
essence **(nature)** nātūra, *f*, vīs, *f*
essential **(necessary)** nēcessārĭus
establish *v.t*, constĭtŭo (3), confirmo (1)
establishment constĭtŭo, *f*
estate **(property)** rēs, *f*, fundus, *m*
esteem *nn*, existĭmātĭo, *f*
esteem *v.t*, **(think)** aestĭmo (1), pŭto (1); **(think highly of)** magni aestĭmo (1)
estimable laudātus
estimate *nn*, aestĭmātĭo, *f*
estimate *v.t*, aestĭmo (1)
estimation **(opinion)** ŏpīnĭo, *f*
estrange *v.t*, ălĭĕno (1)
estrangement ălĭēnātĭo, *f*
estuary aestŭārĭum, *n*
eternal aeternus
eternally *adv. phr*, in aeternum
eternity aeternĭtas, *f*
ether aether, *m*
ethereal aethĕrĭus
ethical **(moral)** mōrālis
eulogy laudātĭo, *f*

evacuate *v.t,* (— troops from a
place), dēdūco (3); *v.i,* (depart
from), excēdo (3), ex (*with abl*)
evade *v.t,* ēlūdo (3)
evaporate *v.i,* discŭtĭor (3 *pass*)
evasion lătĕbra, *f*
evasive ambĭgŭus
eve (evening) vesper, *m*
even *adv,* ĕtĭam, *often use
emphatic pron, e.g.* even
Caesar, Caesar ipse; (not —),
nĕ...quĭdem
even *adj,* (level, equable), aequus;
(— number), pār
even if *conj,* etsi
evening vesper, *m* (in the —), sub
vespĕrum
event (occurrence) rēs, *f*;
(outcome), exĭtus, *m*
eventually *adv,* ălĭquando
ever *adv,* (at any time) umquam;
(always), semper; (if —), si
quando
evergreen *adj,* semper vĭrĭdis
everlasting aeternus
every (all) omnis; (each), quisque;
(— day), *adv,* cottīdĭe; (— one),
omnes, *m.pl*; (— thing), omnĭa,
n.pl; (— where), *adv,* ŭbīque
evict *v.t,* expello (3)
evidence testĭmōnĭum, *n*; (factual),
argūmentum, *n*
evident mănĭfestus, perspĭcŭus;
(it is —), appāret (2 *impers*)
evil *adj,* mălus, prāvus
evil *nn,* mălum, *n*
evil-doer hŏmo nĕfārĭus
evoke *v.t,* ēvŏco (1)
evolve *v.t,* ēvolvo (3)
ewe ŏvis, *f*
exact *adj,* (number, etc.), exactus;
(persons), dīlĭgens
exact *v.t,* exĭgo (3)
exactness subtīlĭtas, *f*
exaggerate *v.t,* augĕo (2)
exaggeration sŭperlātĭo, *f*
exalt *v.t,* tollo (3), augĕo (2)
exalted celsus
examination (test, etc.) prŏbātĭo,
f; (enquiry) investīgātĭo, *f*
examine *v.t,* investīgo (1),
interrŏgo (1); (test), prŏbo (1)
example exemplum *n*; (for —),

verbi causā
exasperate *v.t,* exăcerbo (1)
excavate *v.t,* căvo (1)
excavation (cavity) căvum, *n*
exceed *v.t,* sŭpĕro (1), excēdo (3)
exceedingly *adv,* admŏdum; *or
use superlative of adj, e.g.*
(— large), maxĭmus
excel *v.t,* praesto (1) (*with dat*)
excellence praestantĭa, *f*
excellent praestans, ēgrĕgĭus
except *prep,* praeter (*with acc*)
except *v.t,* excĭpĭo (3)
exception (everyone, without —)
omnes ad ūnum; (take — to)
aegre fĕro (*irreg*)
exceptional rārus, insignis
excess (over-indulgence)
intempĕrantĭa, *f*
excessive nĭmĭus
exchange *nn,* permūtātĭo, *f*
exchange *v.t,* permūto (1)
exchequer aerārĭum, *n*
excitable fervĭdus, fĕrox
excite *v.t,* excĭto (1), incendo (3)
excited commōtus, incensus
excitement commōtĭo, *f*
exclaim *v.i,* clāmo (1), conclāmo
(1)
exclamation exclāmātĭo, *f*
exclude *v.t,* exclūdo (3)
exclusion exclūsĭo, *f*
exclusive (one's own) prŏprĭus
excrescence tūber, *n*
excruciating (pain, etc.) ācer
excursion ĭter, *n*
excusable excūsābĭlis
excuse *nn,* excūsātĭo, *f*
excuse *v.t,* excūso (1); (pardon),
ignosco (3) (*with dat*)
execrable nĕfārĭus
execrate *v.t,* dētestor (1 *dep*)
execute *v.t,* (carry out), exsĕquor
(3 *dep*); (inflict capital
punishment), nĕco (1)
execution (carrying out) *use vb*
exsĕquor; (capital punishment),
supplĭcĭum, *n*
executioner carnĭfex, *m*
exemplary ēgrĕgĭus
exempt *v.t,* excĭpĭo (3)
exempt *adj* immūnis
exemption immūnĭtas, *f*

exercise

exercise exercĭtātĭo, f; (set task), ŏpus, n
exercise v.t, exercĕo (2)
exert v.t, contendo (3), ūtor (3 dep) (with abl); (to — oneself), v.i, nītor (3 dep)
exertion contentĭo, f, lăbor, m
exhale v.t, exhālo (1)
exhaust v.t, exhaurĭo (4); (weary), confĭcĭo (3), dēfătīgo (1)
exhausted (tired out) confectus
exhaustion vīrĭum dēfectĭo, f, (failing of strength)
exhibit v.t, expōno (3)
exhibition (spectacle) spectācŭlum, n
exhilarate v.t, hĭlăro (1)
exhilaration hĭlărĭtas, f
exhort v.t, hortor (1 dep)
exhume v.t, ērŭo (3)
exile nn, (person), exsul, c; (banishment), exsĭlĭum, n; (to be in —), v.i, exsŭlo (1)
exist v.i, in exsĭlĭum pello (3) (drive into exile)
exist v.i, sum (irreg), existo (3)
existence (life) vīta, f
exit exĭtus, m
exonerate v.t, lībĕro (1)
exorbitant nĭmĭus
exotic externus
expand v.t, extendo (3); v.i, extendor (3 pass)
expanse spătĭum, n
expatiate (on a theme etc.) v., permulta dissĕro (3) dē (with abl.)
expatriate v.t, ēĭcĭo (3)
expect v.t, exspecto (1)
expectation exspectātĭo, f
expediency ūtĭlĭtas, f
expedient adj, ūtĭlis
expedient nn, rătĭo, f
expedite v.t, expĕdĭo (4)
expedition (military, etc.) expĕdītĭo, f
expeditious cĕler
expel v.t, expello (3)
expend v.t, expendo (3)
expenditure ērŏgātĭo, f
expense impensa, f, sumptus, m
expensive sumptŭōsus, prĕtĭōsus

experience ūsus, m, pĕrītĭa, f
experience v.t, expĕrĭor (4 dep), pătĭor (3 dep)
experienced pĕrītus
experiment expĕrīmentum, n
expert adj, scĭens
expiate v.t, expĭo (1)
expiation expĭātĭo, f
expiatory pĭācŭlāris
expiration (breathing out) exsspīrātĭo, f; (time), use partic. confectus (completed)
expire v.i, (persons), exspīro (1); (time), exĕo (4), confĭcĭo (3)
explain v.t, explĭco (1), expōno (3)
explanation explĭcātĭo, f
explicit ăpertus
explode v.i, dīrumpor (3 pass)
explore v.t, explōro (1)
export v.t, exporto (1)
exports merces, f, pl
expose v.t, expōno (3), dētĕgo (3), nūdo (1); (— to danger, etc.), offĕro (irreg)
exposition (statement) expŏsĭtĭo, f
expostulate v.i, expostŭlo (1)
expound v.t, explĭco (1), expōno (3)
express v.t, exprĭmo (3); (— in writing), dēscrībo (3)
expression (verbal) vox, f, verba, n.pl; (facial), vultus, m
expressive use phr, multam vim hăbens (having much significance)
expulsion exactĭo, f
expunge v.t, dēlĕo (2)
exquisite conquīsītus
extant (to be —) v.i, exsto (1)
extemporary extempŏrālis
extemporize v.i, sŭbĭta dīco (3)
extend v.t, extendo (3), distendo (3); v.i, pătĕo (2); (— to), pertĭnĕo (2) ad (with acc)
extension (act of) porrectĭo, f; (of boundaries etc.) prŏpāgātĭo, f
extensive amplus
extent spătĭum, n
extenuate v.t, lĕvo (1), mītĭgo (1)
exterior adj, externus
exterior nn, spĕcĭes, f

214

exterminate *v.t*, interfĭcĭo (3), dēlĕo (2)
extermination internĕcĭo, *f*
external externus
extinct exstinctus
extinguish *v.t*, exstinguo (3)
extirpate *v.t*, exstirpo (1), excīdo (3)
extol *v.t*, laudo (1)
extort *v.t*, (by force), extorquĕo (2)
extortion res rĕpĕtundae, *f.pl*
extra *adv*, praetĕrĕā
extract *nn*, (from a book, etc.), exceptĭo, *f*
extract *v.t*, extrăho (3), ēvello (3)
extraction (pulling out) ēvulsĭo, *f*
extraordinary extraordinārĭus, insŏlĭtus
extravagance sumptus, *m*, luxŭrĭa, *f*, intempĕrantĭa, *f*
extravagant immŏdĭcus, sumptŭōsus
extreme *adj*, extrēmus, ultĭmus
extremity extrēmum, *n*; (top), căcūmen, *n*, vertex, *m*; *or use adj*, extrēmus (extreme)
extricate *v.t*, expĕdĭo (4), solvo (3)
exuberance luxŭrĭa, *f*
exuberant luxŭrĭōsus, effūsus
exude *v.i*, māno (1)
exult *v.i*, exsulto (1), laetor (1 *dep*)
exultant laetus, ēlātus
eye ŏcŭlus, *m*; (− lash), palpĕbrae pĭlus, *m*; (− lid), palpĕbra, *f*; (− sight), ăcĭes, *f*; (− witness), arbĭter, *m*

F

fable fābŭla, *f*
fabric (woven) textum, *n*; (building), aedĭfĭcĭum, *n*
fabricate *v.t*, fabrĭcor (1 *dep*)
fabrication mendācĭum, *n*
fabulous fictus, falsus
face făcĭes, *f*, vultus, *m*, ōs, *n*
face *v.t*, (confront), obvĭam ĕo (4) (*with dat*); (look towards), specto (1) ad (*with acc*)
facetious făcētus
facilitate *v.t*, făcĭlĭorem reddo (3) (make easier)

facility (possibility) făcultas, *f*; (dexterity), făcĭlĭtas, *f*
facing *prep*, adversus (*with acc*)
fact rēs, *f*; (in −, truly), *conj*, ĕnim; *adv*, vēro
faction factĭo, *f*
factious factĭōsus
factory offĭcīna, *f*
faculty făcultas, *f*, vīs, *f*
fade *v.i*, pallesco (3)
faggot sarmenta *n.pl*
fail *v.i*, cădo (3), dēfĭcĭo (3), dēsum (*irreg*) (*with dat*)
failing *nn*, (defect) vĭtĭum, *n*
failure (of supplies, strength, etc.), dēfectĭo, *f*, *otherwise use* irrĭtus (vain, unsuccessful)
faint *v.i*, collābor (3 *dep*), languesco (3)
faint *adj*, (exhausted) dēfessus
faint-hearted tĭmĭdus, imbellis
faintness (of body) languor, *m*
fair *nn*, (market), nundĭnae, *f.pl* (ninth day)
fair *adj*, (beautiful), pulcher; (just), aequus; (colour), candĭdus; (weather), sĕrēnus; (wind, etc.), sĕcundus; (fairly good), mĕdĭocris
fairly *adv* (justly), iustē; (moderately), mĕdĭŏcrĭter
fairness (justice) aequĭtas, *f*; (of complexion, etc.) candor, *m*
faith fĭdes, *f*; (to keep −), *v.i*, fĭdem servo (1)
faithful fĭdēlis, fidus
faithfulness fĭdēlĭtas, *f*
faithless infĭdus, perfĭdus
faithlessness perfĭdĭa, *f*
falcon falco, *m*
fall *nn*, cāsus, *m*, rŭīna, *f*
fall *v.i*, cădo (3); (− back) rĕcĭdo (3); (retreat), pĕdem rĕfĕro (*irreg*); (− headlong), praecĭpĭto (1); (− in love with) ădămo (1); (− off), dēlābor (3 *dep*); (− out, happen), cădo (3); (− upon, attack), *v.t*, invādo (3)
fallacious fallax, falsus
fallacy vĭtĭum, *n*
falling off *nn*, (revolt), dēfectĭo, *f*
fallow nŏvālis, ĭnărātus
false falsus; (not genuine), fictus; (person), perfĭdus

falsehood mendācĭum, *n*
falsify *v.t*, vĭtĭo (1)
falter *v.i*, haerĕo (2), haesĭto (1)
faltering *adj*, haesĭtans
fame glōrĭa, *f*, fāma, *f*
familiar nōtus, fămĭlĭāris; **(usual)**, consŭētus, *f*
familiarity fămĭlĭārĭtas, *f*
familiarize *v.t*, consŭesco (3)
family *nn*, fămĭlĭa, *f*, dŏmus, *f*, gens, *f*
family *adj*, fămĭlĭāris, gentīlis
famine fămes, *f*
famished făme confectus **(exhausted from hunger)**
famous clārus
fan flābellum, *n*
fan *v.t*, ventĭlo (1)
fanatical fānātĭcus
fanaticism sŭperstĭtĭo, *f*
fancied (imaginary) fictus
fancy *nn*, **(notion)** ŏpīnĭo, *f*; **(liking for)**, lĭbīdo, *f*
fancy *v.t*, **(imagine)**, fingo (3); **(think)**, ŏpinor (1 *dep*); **(want)** cŭpĭo (3)
fang dens, *m*
far *adv*, **(of distance)** prŏcul, longē **(as — as)** *prep*, tĕnus; *with comparatives*, multō, *e.g*, **far bigger**, multō māior; **(how —)** quātĕnus; **(— and wide)**, longē lātēque
far-fetched quaesītus
farce mĭmus, *m*
farcical mĭmĭcus
fare (food) cĭbus, *m*; **(charge)**, vectūra, *f*
farewell!! ăvē; *(pl)* ăvete; vălē, vălete; **(to bid —)**, vălēre iŭbĕo (2)
farm *nn*, fundus, *m*
farm *v.t*, cŏlo (3)
farmer agrĭcŏla, *m*, cŏlōnus, *m*
farming agrĭcultūra, *f*
farther *adj*, ultĕrĭor
farther *adv*, longĭus
farthest *adj*, ultĭmus
farhtest *adv*, longissĭme
fascinate *v.t*, fascīno (1)
fascination fascĭnātĭo, *f*
fashion *nn*, mōs, *m*
fashion *v.t*, fingo (3)
fashionable ēlĕgans

fast *nn*, iēiūnĭum, *n*
fast *v.i*, iēiūnus sum *(irreg)* **(be hungry)**
fast *adj*, **(quick)** cĕler; **(firm)**, firmus; **(make —)**, *v.t*, firmo (1), dēlĭgo (1)
fast *adv*, **(quickly)**, cĕlĕrĭter; **(firmly)**, firme
fasten *v.t*, fīgo (3), dēlĭgo (1); **(doors etc.)** obtūro (1)
fastening *nn*, vincŭlum, *n*
fastidious dēlĭcātus
fat *adj*, pinguis
fat *nn*, ădeps, *c*
fatal (deadly) pernĭcĭōsus
fatality cāsus, *m*
fate fātum, *n*
fated fātālis
father păter, *m*; **(-in-law)**, sŏcer, *m*
fatherland pătrĭa, *f*
fatherless orbus
fathom *nn*, ulna, *f*
fatigue *nn*, dēfătīgātĭo, *f*
fatigue *v.t*, fătīgo (1)
fatigued fătīgātus
fatten *v.t*, săgīno (1)
fault culpa *f*, vĭtĭum, *n*
faultless intĕger, perfectus
faulty mendōsus, vĭtĭōsus
favour *nn*, grātĭa, *f*, **favour**, *m*, stŭdĭum, *n*; **(a benefit)**, grātĭa, *f*, bĕnĕfĭcĭum, *n*
favour *v.t*, făvĕo (2) *(with dat)*
favourable commŏdus; **(of wind)**, sĕcundus
favourite *nn*, dēlĭcĭae, *f.pl*
favourite *adj*, grātus
fawn *nn*, hinnŭlĕus, *m*
fawn upon *v.t*, ădūlor (1 *dep*)
fear *nn*, tĭmor, *m*, mĕtus, *m*
fear *v.t*, tĭmĕo (2), mĕtŭo (3), vĕrĕor (2 *dep*)
fearful *adj*, **(afraid)**, tĭmĭdus; **(terrible)**, terrĭbĭlis
fearless intrĕpĭdus
fearlessness audācĭa, *f*
feasible *use phr. with vbs*, posse **(to be able)** *and* effĭcĕre **(to bring about)**
feast *nn*, daps, *f*, ĕpŭlae, *f.pl*; **(— day)** dĭes festus, *m*
feast *v.i*, ĕpŭlor (1 *dep*); *v.t*, pasco (3)

feat făcĭnus, *n*

feather penna, *f*, plūma, *f*

feature (of face, etc.) līnĕāmentum, *n*; **(peculiarity)** *use adj*, prŏprĭus **(one's own)**

February Fĕbrŭārĭus (mensis)

fecundity fēcundĭtas, *f*

federal foedĕrātus

fee merces, *f*, hŏnor, *m*

feeble infirmus, imbēcillus

feebleness infirmĭtas, *f*

feed *v.t*, pasco (3), ălo (3); *v.i*, vescor (3 *dep.*), pascor (3 *dep*)

feel *v.t*, sentĭo (4); **(with the hands)**, tempto (1)

feeler cornĭcŭlum, *n*

feeling *nn*, **(sensation or emotion)**, sensus, *m*, tactus, *m*; **(spirit, etc.)**, ănĭmus, *m*

feign *v.t*, sĭmŭlo (1)

feigned sĭmŭlātus

feint sĭmŭlātĭo, *f*

felicitous fēlix

felicity fēlĭcĭtas, *f*

fell *v.t*, excīdo (3), sterno (3)

fellow (companion) cŏmĕs, *c*; **(— citizen)**, cīvis, *c*; **(— feeling)**, consensĭo, *f*; **(— soldier)**, commīlĭto, *m*; **(worthless —)**, nēbŭlo, *m*

fellowship (companionship), sŏcĭĕtas, *f*

felt *nn*, cŏactum, *n*

female *nn*, fēmĭna, *f*

female *adj*, mŭlĭĕbris

fen pălus, *f*

fence *nn*, saeptum, *n*, cancelli, *m,pl*

fence *v.t*, saepĭo (4); **(with swords)**, *v.i*, băttŭo

fencing (art of —) ars, *(f)* glădĭi

ferment *nn*, **(excitement)**, aestus, *m*

ferment *v.i*, fervĕo (2)

fern fīlix, *f*

ferocious saevus, fĕrus

ferocity saevĭtĭa, *f*

ferry *nn*, trāiectus, *m*; **(— boat)**, cymba, *f*

ferry *v.t*, trāĭcĭo (3)

fertile fēcundus, fertĭlis

fertility fēcundĭtas, *f*

fervent ardens, fervĭdus

fervour ardor, *m*, fervor, *m*

festival (holidays) fērĭae, *f.pl*; **(religious —, etc.)** sollemne, *n*

festive (gay) hĭlăris

festivity (gaiety) hĭlărĭtas, *f*

fetch *v.t*, peto (3), affĕro (*irreg*)

fetter *nn*, vincŭlum, *n*

fetter *v.t*, vincŭla inĭcĭo (3) (*with dat*)

feud (quarrel) sĭmultas, *f*

fever fēbris, *f*

feverish fĕbrĭcŭlōsus; **(excited)** commōtus

few *adj*, pauci (*pl*)

fewness paucĭtas, *f*

fib mendācĭum, *n*

fibre fibra, *f*

fickle inconstans

fickleness inconstantĭa, *f*

fiction commentum, *n*, fābŭla, *f*

fictitious commentĭcĭus

fiddle (instrument) fĭdes, *f.pl*

fidelity fĭdēlĭtas, *f*

fidgety inquĭētus

field ăger *m*; **(plain)**, campus, *m*; **(— of battle)**, lŏcus, (*m*) pugnae; **(scope)**, lŏcus, *m*

fiendish nĕfandus

fierce fĕrox, fĕrus

fierceness fĕrōcĭtas

fiery (of temper, etc.) ardens

fifteen quindĕcim; **(— times)**, *adv*, quindĕcĭes

fifteenth quintus dĕcĭmus

fifth quintus

fiftieth quinquāgēsĭmus

fifty quinquāginta

fig, fig tree fīcus, *f*

fight *nn*, pugna, *f*

fight *v.i*, pugno (1)

fighter pugnātor, *m*

figurative translātus

figure fĭgŭra, *f*, forma, *f*

figure *v.t*, **(imagine)**, fingo (3)

figured sĭgillātus

filch *v.t*, surrĭpĭo (3)

file (tool) scŏbīna, *f*; **(rank)**, ordo, *m*

file *v.t*, **(wood, metal)**, līmo (1)

filial (dutiful, respectful) pĭus

fill *v.t*, implĕo (2), complĕo (2); **(a post, etc.)** fungor (3 *dep*) (*with abl*)

fillet (for the hair) vitta, *f*
film membrāna, *f*
filter *v.t,* cōlo (1)
filth caenum, *n*
filthy sordĭdus, foedus
fin pinna, *f*
final ultĭmus
finally *adv,* postrēmo, dēnĭque, tandem
finance (of the state) aerārĭum, *n*
find *v.t,* invĕnĭo (4), rĕpĕrĭo (4); **(— out)**; cognosco (3), compĕrĭo (4); **(— fault with)**, culpo (1); accūso (1)
fine *v.t,* multo (1)
fine *nn,* multa, *f*
fine *adj,* **(of texture)**, subtīlis; **(handsome, etc.)** praeclārus; **(weather)**, sĕrēnus
finery mundĭtĭa, *f*
finger dĭgĭtus, *m*; **(fore —)**, index dĭgitus
finger *v.t,* tango (3)
finish *nn,* **(perfection)**, perfectĭo, *f*
finish *v.t,* confĭcĭo (3); **(limit)**, finĭo (4)
finished (complete, perfect) perfectus
fir, fir tree ăbĭes, *f*
fire ignis, *m*; **(ardour)**, vīs, *f*, ardor, *m*; **(to be on —)**, *v.i,* ardĕo (2); **(to set on —)** *v.t,* incendo (3)
fire *v.t,* incendo (3); **(missiles)**, cōnĭcĭo (3)
firebrand fax, *f*
fireplace fŏcus, *m*
firewood lignum, *n*
firm firmus; **(constant)**, constans; **(to make —)**, *v.t,* confirmo (1)
first *adj,* prīmus
first *adv,* prīmum, prīmō
fish *nn,* piscis, *m*
fish *v.i,* piscor (1 *dep*)
fisherman piscātor, *m*
fishing *nn,* piscātus, *m*
fishing boat hŏrĭŏla, *f*
fishing net rēte, *n*
fishmonger cētārĭus, *m*
fishpond piscīna, *f*
fissure rīma, *f*
fist pugnus, *m*
fit (violent seizure) accessĭo, *f*, impĕtus, *m*

fit, fitted aptus, ĭdōnĕus, accommŏdātus
fit *v.t,* accommŏdo (1), apto (1); **(— out)**, exorno (1)
five quinque; **(— each)**, quīni; **(— times)** *adv,* quinquĭes
five hundred quingenti
fix *v.t,* fīgo (3); **(determine)**, stătŭo (3), constĭtŭo (3)
fixed certus
flabby flaccĭdus
flag vexillum, *n*
flag *v.i* **(become weak)**, languesco (3)
flagrant (clear) mănĭfestus; **(heinous)**, nĕfandus
flail pertĭca, *f*
flame *nn,* flamma, *f*
flame *v.i,* flagro (1)
flame-coloured flammĕus
flank (of army, etc.) lătus, *n*; **(of animal)** īlĭa, *n.pl*
flap (of dress, etc.) lăcĭnĭa, *f*
flare *v.i,* flăgro (1)
flash *nn,* fulgor, *m*
flash *v.i,* fulgĕo (2)
flask ampulla, *f*
flat aequus, plānus
flatness plānĭtĭes, *f*
flatter *v.t,* ădūlor (1 *dep*)
flatterer ădūlātor, *m*
flattering ădūlans
flattery ădūlātĭo, *f*
flaunt *v.t,* iacto (1)
flavour săpor, *m*
flaw vĭtĭum, *n*
flawless ēmendātus
flax līnum, *n*
flaxen *adj,* līnĕus
flea pūlex, *m*
flee *v.i* **(flee from, *v.t.*)**, fŭgĭo (3)
fleece *nn,* vellus, *n*
fleece *v.t,* **(rob)**, spŏlĭo (1)
fleecy lānĭger
fleet *nn,* classis, *f*
fleet *adj,* cĕler
fleeting fŭgax
flexh căro, *f*
flesh-coloured, fleshy carnōsus
flexibility făcĭlĭtas, *f*
flexible flexĭbĭlis
flicker *v.i,* trĕpĭdo (1), cŏrusco (1)

flickering trĕpĭdans, trĕmŭlus
flight (flying) cŏlātus, *m*; **(escape)** fŭga, *f*
flighty mōbĭlis, lĕvis
fling *v.t*, cōnĭcĭo (3)
flint sĭlex, *m*
flippant făcētus
flirt *v.i*, blandĭor (4 *dep*)
flit *v.i*, vŏlĭto (1); **(— in, or upon)**, inno (1) *(with dat)*
float *v.i*, năto (1); **(in the air)**, vŏlĭto (1)
flock grex, *m*, pĕcus, *n*
flock *v.i*, conflŭo (3), concurro (3)
flog *v.t*, verbĕro (1)
flogging verbĕra, *n.pl*
flood dīlŭvĭes, *f*, *n*
flood *v.t*, ĭnundo (1)
floor sŏlum, *n*; **(upper —)** contăbŭlātĭo, *f*
florid flōrĭdus
flotilla classis, *f*
flounder *v.i*, vŏlūtor (1 *pass*)
flour fărīna, *f*
flourish *v.i*, flōrĕo (2); *v.t*, vĭbro (1)
flourishes (of style) călămistri, *m.pl*
flow *nn*, cursus, *m*, fluxĭo, *f*; **(of the tide)**, accessus, *m*
flow *v.i*, flŭo (3); **(— past)**, praeterflŭo (3); **(— together)**, conflŭo (3); **(trickle)**, māno (1)
flower *nn*, flos, *m*
flower *v.i*, flōrĕo (2)
flowing flŭens; **(hair)**, fūsus
fluctuate *v.i*, iacto (1 *pass*); aestŭo (1)
fluctuation mūtātĭo, *f*
fluency vŏlūbĭlĭtas, *f*
fluent vŏlūbĭlĭs
fluid *nn*, hūmor, *m*, lĭquor, *m*
fluid *adj*, lĭquĭdus
flurry concĭtātĭo, *f*
flush *nn*, rŭbor, *m*
flush *v.i*, ērŭbĕsco (3)
fluster *v.i*, ăgĭto (1)
flute tībĭa, *f*; **(— player)**, tībĭcen, *m*
flutter *nn*, trĕpĭdātĭo, *f*
flutter *v.i*, vŏlĭto (1), **(in fear)**, trĕpĭdo (1)
flux (flow) fluctus, *m*, fluxus, *m*
fly *nn*, musca, *f*

fly *v.i*, vŏlo (1)
flying *adj*, vŏlātĭlis, vŏlŭcer
flying *nn*, vŏlātus,
foal ĕquŭlĕus, *m*, pullus, *m*
foam *nn*, spūma, *f*
foam *v.i*, spūmo (1)
foaming, foamy spūmōsus
fodder pābŭlum, *n*
foe hostis, *c*
fog cālīgo, *f*
foggy cālīgĭnōsus
foil (sword) rŭdis, *f*; **(metal leaf)**, lāmĭna, *f*
foil *v.t*, **(parry a blow, delude)**, ēlūdo (3)
fold *nn*, **(of garment, etc.)** sĭnus, *m*
fold *v.t*, plĭco (1)
folding-doors valvae *f.pl*
foliage frons, *f*
folk (people) hŏmĭnes, *c.pl*
follow *v.i. and v.t*, sĕquor (3 *dep*); sector (1 *dep*); **(succeed)**, succēdo (3) *(with dat)*
follower (attendant) assectātor, *m*; or use *adj*, e.g. **(— of Ceasar)** Caesărĭānus
following sĕquens, proxĭmus, sĕcundus
folly stultĭtĭa, *f*
foment *v.t*, fŏvĕo (2); **(— trouble, etc.)** sollĭcĭto (1)
fond ămans *(with genit)*
fondle *v.t*, mulcĕo (2)
fond cĭbus, *m*; **(fodder)**, pābŭlum, *n*
fool hŏmo stultus; **(to act the —)**, *v.i*, dēsĭpĭo
fool *v.t*, lūdo (3)
foolhardy tĕmĕrārĭus
foolish stultus
foot pes, *m*; **(on —)**, *adj*, pĕdester; **(— in length)**, *adj*, pĕdālis; **(bottom of)**, use *adj*, īmus, *in agreement with noun*, e.g. īma quercus **(foot of an oak)**
footing stătus, *m*, or use *vb*, consisto (3), **(to stand)**
footman pĕdĭsĕquus, *m*
footpath sēmĭta, *f*
footprint vestīgĭum, *n*
footsoldier pĕdes, *m*

for *prep* **(on behalf of)**, prō (*with abl*); **(on account of)**, propter, ŏb (*with acc*); **(during a certain time)**, *use acc, e.g.* **for two hours**, dŭas hōras, *or* per (*with acc*); **(expressing purpose)**, *use* ad (*with acc*)

for *conj*, nam, namque; ĕnim (*second word in clause*); **(because)**, quippe, quod

forage *nn*, pābŭlum, *n*

forage *v.i, and v.t*, pābŭlor (1 *dep*)

forbear *v.i, and v.t*, parco (3)

forbearance contĭnentĭa, *f*

forbid *v.t*, vĕto (1)

force *nn*, vīs, *f*; **(military forces)**, cōpĭae, *f.pl*

force *v.t*, **(compel)**, cōgo (3); **(break through)**, perrumpo (3)

forced (unnatural) quaesītus; **(a — march)**, magnum ĭter, *n*

forcible, forcibly *use adv. phr*, per vim

ford *nn*, vădum, *n*

ford *v.i. and v.t*, vădo transĕo (4) **(cross by a ford)**

forearm bracchĭum, *n*

forebode *v.t*, paresāgĭo (4), portendo (3)

foreboding *nn*, praesensĭo, *f*

forecast *v.t*, praevĭdĕo (2)

forefather prŏăvus, *m*; (*pl*) māiōres *m.pl*

forehead frons, *f*

foreign externus, pĕrĕgrīnus

foreigner pĕrĕgrīnus, *m*

foreman qui (servis) praeest **(who is in charge of (slaves))**

foremost prīmus

forensic fŏrensis

forerunner praenuntĭus, *m*

foresee *v.t*, prŏvĭdĕo (2)

foresight prŏvĭdentĭa, *f*

forest silva, *f*

foretell *v.t*, praedīco (3)

forethought prŏvĭdentĭa, *f*

forewarn *v.t*, preaemŏnĕo (2)

forfeit *nn*, poena, *f*

forfeit *v.t*, āmitto (3)

forge *nn*, fornax, *f*

forge *v.t*, făbrĭcor (1 *dep*), excūdo (3); **(strike counterfeit coins)**, nummos ădultĕrīnos cūdo (3); **(documents)**, suppōno (3)

forgery *use phr*. subiectĭo falsārum littĕrāum **(substitution of counterfeit letters)**

forget *v.t*, ovlīviscor (3 *dep*) (*with genit*)

forgetful immĕmor

forgetfulness oblīvĭo, *f*

forgive *v.t*, ignosco (3) (*with dat of person*)

forgiveness vĕnĭa

fork furca, *f*

forked bĭfurcus

forlorn destĭtūtus, perdĭtus

form forma, *f*, fĭgūra, *f*

form *v.t*, **(shape)**, formo (1), fingo (3); **(— a plan)**, ĭnĕo (4), căpĭo (3); **(troops, etc.)** instrŭo (3)

formality rītus, *m*

formally *adv*, rītĕ

formation conformātĭo, *f*

former prĭor, sŭpĕrĭor; **(the — and the latter)**, ille … hic

formerly *adv*, antĕā, ōlim

formidable grăvis, mĕtŭendus

formula formŭla, *f*

forsake *v.t*, rĕlinquo (3), dēsĕro (3)

forswear *v.t*, **(renounce)**, abiūro (1); **(swear falsely)**, periūro (1)

fort castellum, *n*

forth *adv, use compound vb. with* e *or* ex, *e.g.* exĕo, **go forth**; **(of time)**, inde

forthwith, *adv*, stătim, extemplo

fortification mūnītĭo, *f*

fortify *v.t*, mūnĭo (4)

fortitude fortĭtūdo, *f*

fortuitous fortŭĭtus

fortunate fēlix, fortūnātus

fortune fortūna, *f*, **(property, etc.)**, rēs, *f*, ŏpes, *f.pl*

fortune-teller hărĭolŭs, *m*

forty quădrāginta

forum fŏrum, *n*

forward, forwards *adv*, porro, prorsum, ante; *or use compound verb with* pro *e.g.* prōdūco **(lead forward)**

forward *adj*, praecox

forward *v.t*, **(send on)**, perfĕro (*irreg*)

foster *v.t*, nūtrĭo (4)

foster-brother collactĕus, *m*; **(— child)**, ălumnus, *m*; **(— father)**, altor, *m*; **(— mother)**, nūtrix, *f*; **(— sister)**, collactĕa, *f*

foul *adj*, foedus

found *v.t*, condo (3); **(metal)**, fundo (3)

foundation fundāmenta, *n.pl*

founder condĭtor, *m*

founder *v.i*, submergo (3 *pass*)

fountain fons, *m*

four quattŭor; **(— times)**, *adv*, quătĕr; **(— each)**, quăterni

fourteen quattŭordĕcim; **(-teenth)**, quartus dĕcĭmus

fourth quartus; **(— part, quarter)**, quădrans, *m*

fowl ăvis, *f*, gallīna, *f*

fowler auceps, *c*

fox vulpes, *f*

fraction (part) pars, *f*

fractious diffĭcĭlis

fracture *nn*, fractūra, *f*

fracture *v.t*, frango (3)

fragile frăgĭlis

fragment fragmentum, *n*

fragile frăgĭlis

fragment fragmentum, *n*

fragrance dulcis ŏdōr, *m*, **(pleasant smell)**

fragrant dulcis, suāvis

frail frăgĭlis, dēbĭlis

frailty frăgĭlĭtas, *f*, dēbĭlĭtas

frame forma, *f*, compāges, *f*; **(— of mind)** ănĭmus, *m*, affectĭo, *f*

frame *v.t*, **(shape)**, făbrĭcor (1 *dep*), fingo (3); **(form)**, compōno (3)

franchise (citizenship) cīvĭtas, *f*; **(right of voting)**, suffrāgĭum, *n*

frank līber, ăpertus

frantic āmens

fraternal frăternus

fraternity (association of men) sŏdālĭtas, *f*

fratricide (the person) frātrĭcīda, *m*; **(the crime)**, fraternum parrĭcīdĭum, *n*

fraud fraus, *f*, dŏlus, *m*

fraudulent fraudŭlentus, dŏlōsus

fraught opplētus **(filled)**

fray certāmen, *n*, pugna, *f*

freak (prodigy) prōdĭgĭum, *n*

freckle lentīgo, *f*

free līber; **(generous)**, lībĕrālis; **(of one's will)**, sŭă sponte (*abl*)

free *v.t*, lībĕro (1), solvo (3)

free-born ingĕnŭus

freedman lībertus, *m*

freedom lībertas, *f*; **(— from a burden, tax, etc.)**, immūnĭtas, *f*

freehold *nn*, praedĭum lībĕrum, *n*, **(free estate)**

freely *adv*, lībĕrē; **(generously)**, mūnĭfĭcē, largē; **(of one's own free will)**, sŭă sponte

free-will vŏluntas, *f*

freeze *v.t*, glăcĭo (1); *v.i*, congĕlo (1)

freight *nn*, ŏnus, *n*

freight *adj*, ŏnustus

French *adj*, Gallĭcus; **(The French)**, Galli, *pl*

frenzied fŭrens, āmens

frenzy fŭror, *m*, āmentĭa, *f*

frequent *adj*, crēber, frĕquens

frequent *v.t*, cĕlĕbro (1)

frequently *adv*, saepe

fresh (new) rĕcens, nŏvus; **(wind)**, incrēbresco (3)

freshness vĭrĭdĭtas, *f*

fret *v.i*, dŏlĕo (2)

fretful mōrōsus

fretfulness mōrōsĭtas, *f*

friction trītus, *m*

friend ămīcus, *m*

friendless ĭnops ămīcōrum **(destitute of friends)**

friendliness cōmĭtas, *f*

friendly ămīcus, cōmis

friendship ămīcĭtĭa, *f*

fright terror *m*, păvor, *m*; **(to take —)**, *v.i*, păvesco (3)

frighten *v.t*, terrĕo (2)

frightful terrĭbĭlis, horrĭbĭlis

frigid frīgĭdus

frill segmenta, *n.pl*

fringe fimbrĭae, *f.pl*

frippery nūgae, *f.pl*

frisk *v.i*, lascīvĭo (4)

fritter away *v.t*, dissĭpo (1)

frivolity lĕvĭtas, *f*

frivolous lĕvis; **(opinion, etc.)** fūtĭlis

fro (to and —) *adv, phr*, hūc et illūc

frock stŏla, *f*
frog rāna, *f*
frolic *nn,* lūdus, *m*
frolic *v.i,* lūdo (3)
from ā, ab, dē, ē, ex (*all with abl*) (*with expressions of place, time and cause*)
front *nn,* frons, *f,* prĭor pars; **(in —)** ā fronte, *or use adj,* adversus; **(in — of)** *prep,* prō (*with abl*)
front *adj,* prĭor
frontage frons, *f*
frontier fīnis, *m*
frost gĕlu, *n;* **(— bitten),** *adj,* ambustus
frosty gĕlĭdus
froth *nn,* spūma, *f*
froth *v.i,* spūmo (1)
frown *nn,* contractĭo (*f*) frontis **(contraction of the forehead)**
frown *v.i,* frontem contrăho (3)
frowsy incultus
frozen rĭgĭdus, glăcĭālis
fructify *v.t,* fēcundo (1)
frugal frūgi, *indecl*
frugality parsĭmōnĭa, *f*
fruit fructus, *m,* pōmum, *n*
fruitful fēcundĭtas, *f*
fruition fructus, *m*
fruitless (without result) irrĭtus
fruit tree pōmum, *n,* pōmus, *f*
frustrate *v.t,* **(an undertaking, etc.)** ad vānum rĕdĭgo (3)
frustrated (to be —) *v.i,* frustrā esse
frustration frustrātĭo, *f*
fry *v.t,* frīgo (3)
frying pan sartāgo, *f*
fuel ligna, *n.pl*
fugitive *nn,* prŏfŭgus, *m,* fŭgĭtīvus, *m*
fugitive *adj,* fŭgĭtīvus
fulfil *v.t,* explĕo (2), exsĕquor (3 *dep*), fungor (3 *dep*) (*with abl*)
full plēnus, replētus; **(with people),** frĕquens, crēber
full-grown ădultus
fulminate *v.i,* fulmĭno (1), intŏno (1)
fulness (abundance) ūbertas, *f*
fulsome pūtĭdus
fumble *v.t,* **(handle),** tento (1)
fume *nn,* hālĭtus, *m*

fume *v.i,* **(with anger etc.),** fŭro (3)
fumigate *v.t,* suffĭo (4)
fun iŏcus, *m,* lūdus, *m*
function offĭcĭum, *n,* mūnus, *n*
fund (of knowledge, etc.) cōpĭa, *f,* with *nn.* in *genit.*
fundamental prīmus
funeral fūnus, *n,* exsĕquĭae, *f.pl*
funeral, funereal *adj,* fŭnĕbris
fungus fungus, *m*
funnel infundĭbŭlum, *n*
funny rīdĭcŭlus
fur pĭlus, *m*
furbish *v.t,* interpŏlo (1)
furious fŭrens, saevus; **(to be —),** *v.i,* saevĭo (4), fŭro (3)
furl *v.t,* contrăho (3), lĕgo (3), subdūco (3)
furlough commĕātus, *m*
furnace fornax, *f*
furnish *v.t,* suppĕdĭto (1), orno (1)
furniture sŭpellex, *f*
furrow *nn,* sulcus, *m*
furrow *v.t,* sulco (1)
further *adj,* ultĕrĭor; *adv,* ultĕrĭus
further *v.t,* **(help),** adiŭvo (1)
furthermore *adv,* porro, praetĕrĕa
furthest *adj,* ultĭmus
furtive furtīvus
fury fŭror, *m*
fuse *v.t,* **(melt),** lĭquĕfăcĭo (3); **(— together),** miscĕo (2)
fuss *nn,* perturbātĭo, *f*
fussy nĭmis stŭdĭōsus
fusty mūcĭdus
futile vānus, fūtĭlis
futility fūtĭlĭtas, *f*
future *adj,* fŭtūrus
future *nn,* fŭtūra, *n.pl;* **(in —),** *adv,* in fēlĭquum tempus
futurity tempus fŭtūrum, *n*

G

gabble *v.i,* blătĕro (1)
gabbler blătĕro, *m*
gable fastīgĭum, *n*
gad about *v.i,* văgor (1 *dep*)
gadfly tăbānus, *m*
gag *v.t,* ōs obvolvo (3) (*with dat*) **(muffle the mouth)**
gage pignus, *n*

gaiety hĭlărĭtas, *f*

gaily *adv*, hĭlăre

gain *nn*, lŭcrum, *n*, quaestus, *m*

gain *v.t*, (profit, etc.) lŭcror (1 *dep*); (obtain), consĕquor (3 *dep*), pŏtĭor (4 *dep*) (*with abl*); (— a victory), victōrĭam rĕporto (1) or părĭo (3)

gainsay *v.t*, contrā dīco (3)

gait incessus, *m*

gaiters ŏcrĕae, *f.pl*

galaxy *use* vĭa lactĕa, *f*. (milky way)

gale ventus, *m*, prŏcella, *f*

gall *nn*, fel, *n*

gall *v.t*, (chafe), ūro (3); (annoy), sollĭcĭto (1); or pĭget (2 *impers*) (it irks)

gallant fortis

gallant *nn*, (lover), ămātor, *m*

gallantry virtus, *f*

gallery portĭcus, *f*

galley (ship) nāvis, *f*

galling mordax

gallon congĭus, *m*

gallop *v.i*, ĕquo cĭtāto vĕhi (3 *pass*) (to be carried by a swift horse)

gallows furca, *f*, crux, *f*

gamble *v.i*, ālĕa lūdo (3) (play with dice)

gambler ālĕātor, *m*

gambling *nn*, ālĕa, *f*

gambol *v.i*, lascĭvĭo (4)

game lūdus, *m*; (wild beasts), fĕrae, *f.pl*

gamester ālĕātor, *m*

gammon perna, *f*

gander anser, *m*

gang grex, *m*, căterva, *f*

gangrene gangraena, *f*

gangway fŏrus, *m*

gaol carcer, *m*

gaoler custos, *m*

gap lăcūna, *f*, hĭātus, *m*

gape *v.i*, hĭo (1)

gaping *adj*, hĭans

garb vestītus, *m*

garbage quisquĭlĭae, *f.pl*

garden hortus, *m*

gardening cūra (*f*) hortōrum (care of gardens)

gargle *v.i*, gargărĭzo (1)

garland serta, *n.pl*

garlic ālĭum, *n*

garment vestīmentum, *n*

garner *v.t*, (store), condo (3)

garnish *v.t*, dĕcŏro (1)

garret cēnācŭlum, *n*

garrison praesĭdĭum, *n*

garrison *v.t*, praesĭdĭum collŏco (1) in (*with abl*)

garrulity lŏquācĭtas, *f*

garrulous lŏquax

gas spīrĭtus, *m*

gash *nn*, plāga, *f*

gash *v.t*, percŭtĭo (3)

gasp *nn*, ănhēlĭtus, *m*

gasp *v.i*, ănhēlo (1)

gastric *use genitive* stŏmăchi (of the stomach)

gate porta, *f*, iānŭa, *f*; (— keeper), iānĭtor, *m*

gather *v.t*, lĕgo (3), collĭgo (3); (pluck), carpo (3); *v.i*, convĕnĭo (4), congrĕgor (1 *dep*)

gathering coetus, *m*

gaudy fūcātus

gauge *v.t*, mētĭor (4 *dep*)

gauge *nn*, mŏdŭlus, *m*

gaunt măcer

gay hĭlăris

gaze at *v.t*, tŭĕor (2 *dep*)

gaze *nn*, obtūtus, *m*

gazelle dorcas, *f*

gazette acta dĭurna, *n.pl*, (daily events)

gear appărātus, *m*

geld *v.t*, castro (1)

gelding cantērĭus, *m*

gem gemma, *f*

gender gĕnus, *n*

geneology (lineage) ŏrīgo, *f*, gĕnus, *n*

general *adj*, (opp. to particular), gĕnĕrālis; (common, widespread), vulgāris, commūnis

general *nn*, dux, *m*, impĕrātor, *m*

generality (majority) plērīque

generally (for the most part) *adv*, plērumque

generalship ductus, *m*

generate *v.t*, gĕnĕro (1), gigno (3)

generation saecŭlum, *n*

generosity bĕnignĭtas, *f*

generous (with money, etc.) lībĕrālis

genial cōmis
geniality cōmĭtas, f
genius (ability) ingĕnĭum, n;
 (guardian spirit), gĕnĭus, m
genteel urbānus
gentle (mild) mītis; (of birth),
 gĕnĕrōsus
gentleman hŏmo ingĕnŭus
gentlemanly adj, lībĕrālis, hŏnestus
gentleness lēnĭtas, f
gently adv, lēnĭter
gentry nōbĭles, m.pl
genuine sincērus
geography gĕōgraphĭa, f
geometry gĕōmĕtrĭa, f
germ germen, n
German Germānus
germane affīnis
germinate v.i, germĭno (1)
gesticulate v.i, sē iactāre (1 reflex)
gesture gestus, m
get v.t, (obtain), ădĭpiscor (3 dep),
 nanciscor (3 dep); (a request),
 impĕtro (1); (become), v.i, fio
 (irreg); (— about, or spread, etc.),
 percrēbesco (3); (— away),
 effŭgĭo (3); (— back), v.t, rĕcĭpĭo
 (3); (— the better of), sŭpĕro (1);
 (— down), v.i, dēscendo (3); (—
 out), exĕo (4); (— ready) v.t, păro
 (1); (— rid of), āmŏvĕo (2) in or
 ad (with acc); (— up, rise), surgo
 (3)
ghastly exsanguis
ghost mānes, m.pl
giant vir ingenti stătūra (man of
 huge stature)
gibbet crux, f
giddy vertīgĭnōsus
gift dōnum, n
gifted (mentally, etc.) ingĕnĭōsus
gigantic ingens
giggle v.i, use rīdĕo (2), (to laugh)
gild v.t, ĭnauro (1)
gills (of fish) branchĭae, f.pl
gimlet tĕrĕbra, f
gin pĕdĭca, f
giraffe cămēlŏpardălis, f
gird v.t, cingo (3); (— oneself), sē
 accingĕre (3 reflex)
girder trabs, f
girdle cingŭlum, n

girl pŭella, f, virgo, f
girlhood aetas, (f) pŭellāris
girth ambĭtus, m
give v.t, do (1), dōno (1); (render),
 reddo (3); (— an opportunity),
 făcultātem do (1); (— back),
 reddo (3); (— in), v.i, cēdo (3); (—
 up, deliver), trādo (3); (abandon),
 dīmitto (3); (— up hope), v.i,
 dēspēro (1); (— orders), iŭbĕo (2)
glad laetus, hĭlăris
gladden v.t, hĭlăro (1)
glade nĕmus, n, saltus, m
gladiator glădĭātor, m
gladness laetĭtĭa, f
glance at v.t, aspĭcĭo (3); (graze)
 stringo (3)
glance nn, aspectus, m
gland glans, f
glare nn, fulgor, m
glare v.i, fulgĕo (2); (look with
 stern glance) torvis ŏcŭlis tŭĕor
 (2 dep)
glaring (conspicuous) mănĭfestus
glass nn, vĭtrum, n; (drinking —),
 pōcŭlum, n
glass adj, vĭtrĕus
gleam nn, fulgor, m
gleam v.i, fulgĕo (2)
glean v.t, spīcas collĭgo (3) (collect
 ears of corn)
glee laetĭtĭa, f
glen valles, f
glib (of tongue) vŏlūbĭlis
glide lābor (3 dep)
glimmer v.i, sublūcĕo (2)
glimmering adj, sublustris
glimpse (get a — of) v.t, dispĭcĭo
 (3)
glitter v.i, fulgĕo (2)
glittering adj, fulgĭdus, cŏruscus
gloat over v.t, gaudens aspĭcĭo (3)
globe glŏbus, m; (the earth) orbis,
 m
gloom tĕnebrae, f.pl, tristĭtĭa, f
gloomy tĕnebrōsus, tristis
glorify v.t, laudo (1), extollo (3)
glorious praeclārus, illustris
glory glōrĭa, f, dĕcus, n, laus, f
gloss n, nĭtor, m
gloss over v.t, praetĕrĕo (4)
glossy nĭtĭdus

gloves mănĭcae, *f.pl*
glow *nn*, ardor, *m*
glow *v.i*, ardĕo (2), candĕo (2)
glue *nn*, glūten, *n*
glut *nn*, sătĭĕtas, *f*
glut *v.t*, explĕo (2), sătĭo (1)
glutton hellŭo, *m*
gluttonous ĕdax
gluttony ĕdācĭtas, *f*
gnarled nōdōsus
gnash (the teeth) *v.t*, frendĕo (2),
   (dentibus)
gnat cŭlex, *m*
gnaw *v.t*, rōdo (3)
gnawing *adj*, mordax
go *v.i*, ĕo (*irreg*), vādo (3);
   (depart), ăbĕo (4), prŏfĭciscor (3
   dep); (— abroad), pĕrĕgre exĕo (4
   irreg); (— away), ăbĕo (4 *irreg*);
   (— by, past), praetĕrĕo (4 *irreg*);
   (— down), dēscendo (3); (— in)
   ĭnĕo (4 *irreg*); (— over), transĕo
   (4 *irreg*); (— round), circumĕo (4
   irreg); (— through) ŏbĕo (4 *irreg*);
   (— up), ascendo (3); (— without)
   cărĕo (2) (*with abl*)
goad *v.t*, stĭmŭlo (1)
goal mēta, *f*
goat căper, *m*
go-between *nn*, interpres, *c*
goblet pōcŭlum, *n*
god dĕus, *m*
goddess dĕa, *f*
godless impĭus
godlike dīvīnus
godly *adj*, pĭus
gold aurum, *n*
golden aurĕus
goldsmith aurĭfex, *m*
good *adj*, bŏnus, prŏbus,
   hŏnestus, aptus, commŏdus
good *nn*, bŏnum, *n*; (advantage),
   commŏdum, *n*; (goods,
   possessions), bŏna, *n.pl*; (— for
   nothing), *adj*, nēquam; (to do —),
   prōdesse (*irreg*)(*with dat*)
goodbye! vălē! (*pl*, vălete!)
good-humour cōmĭtas, *f*
good-humoured cōmis
good-looking spĕcĭōsus
good-nature cōmĭtas, *f*
good-natured cōmis

goodness (virtue) virtus, *f*,
   prŏbĭtas, *f*; (excellence) bŏnĭtas, *f*
good-tempered mītis
goose anser, *m*
gore *nn*, crŭor, *m*
gorge (throat) guttur, *n*, fauces,
   f.pl; (mountain pass), angustĭae,
   f.pl
gorge oneself *v.i*, sē ingurgĭtāre (1
   reflex)
gorgeous spĕcĭōsus, splendĭdus
gorgeousness magnĭfĭcentĭa, *f*
gory crŭentus
gossip *v.i*, garrĭo (4)
gossip *nn*, (talk), rūmor, *m*;
   (person), garrŭlus, *m*
gouge *v.t*, (— out eyes), ŏcŭlos
   ērŭo (3)
gourd cŭcurbĭta, *f*
gout morbus (*m*) artĭcŭlōrum
   (disease of the joints)
gouty arthrītĭcus
govern *v.t*, gŭberno (1), impĕro
   (1), tempĕro (1), mŏdĕror (1 *dep*)
government (act of —)
   admĭnistrātĭo, *f*, cūra, *f*;
   (persons), *use phr*, ii qui
   summum impĕrĭum hăbent
   (those who hold supreme
   authority)
governor (supreme) gŭbernātor,
   m; (subordinate), prōcūrātor, *m*,
   lēgātus, *m*
gown (woman's) stŏla, *f*; (man's)
   tŏga, *f*
grace grātĭa, *f*; (pardon), vĕnĭa, *f*;
   (charm), vĕnustas, *f*; (to say —),
   grātĭas ăgo (3)
grace *v.t*, (adorn), dĕcŏro (1)
graceful vĕnustus, lĕpĭdus
gracious prŏpĭtĭus, bĕnignus
grade grădus, *m*
gradient clīvus, *m*
gradually *adv*, paulātim
graft *v.t*, insĕro (3)
grain frumentum, *n*
grammar grammătĭca, *f*
granary horrĕum, *n*
grand magnĭfĭcus, grandis
grandchild nĕpos, *m*, *f*
granddaughter neptis, *f*
grandeur magnĭfĭcentĭa, *f*
grandfather ăvus, *m*

grandiloquent grandĭlŏquus
grandmother ăvĭa, *f*
grandson nĕpos, *m*
granite (hard rock) *use*, sĭlex, *m*, (flint stone)
grant, granting *nn*, concessĭo, *f*
grant *v.t*, concēdo (3), do (1)
grape ăcĭnus, *m*, ūva, *f*
graphic expressus
grapple *v.i*, luctor (1 *dep*)
grappling-iron harpăgo, *m*
grasp *nn*, mănus, *f*; (of the mind), captus, *m*
grasp *v.t*, prěhendo (3); (mentally), intellěgo (3); (snatch at, aim at), capto (1)
grass grāmen, *n*, herba, *f*
grasshopper gryllus, *m*
grassy grāmĭnĕus
grate crātīcŭla, *f*
grate *v.t*, těro (3); *v.i*, strīdĕo (2)
grateful grātus
gratification explētĭo, *f*, vŏluptas, *f*
gratify *v.t*, grātĭfĭcor (1 *dep*) (*with dat*)
grating *nn*, (noise), strīdor, *m*
gratitude grātĭa, *f*, grātus ănimus, *m*
gratuitous grātuītus
gratuity congĭārĭum, *n*
grave *nn*, sěpulcrum, *n*
grave *adj*, grăvis
gravel glārĕa, *f*
gravity grăvĭtas, *f*
gravy iūs, *n*
gray see grey
grayness see grey, greyness
graze *v.t*, (animals), pasco (3); *v.i*, pascor (3 *dep*.); (touch lightly), *v.t*, stringo (3)
grease *nn*, ădeps, *c*
grease *v.t*, ungo (3)
greasy unctus
great magnus, grandis, amplus; (distinguished), illustris
greatcoat lăcerna, *f*
great-grandfather prŏăvus, *m*
great-grandson prŏněpos, *m*
greatness magnĭtūdo, *f*
greaves ŏcrĕae, *f.pl*
Greece Graecĭa, *f*
greed ăvārītĭa, *f*
greedy ăvārus

Greek Graecus
green *adj*, vĭrĭdis; (unripe), crūdus; (to become —), *v.i*, vĭresco (3)
greet *v.t*, sălūto (1)
greeting sălūtātĭo, *f*
gregarious grěgālis
grey caesĭus, rāvus; (of hair), cānus
greyness (of hair) cānĭtĭes, *f*
gridiron crātīcŭla, *f*
grief dŏlor, *m*, luctus, *m*
grievance quěrĭmōnĭa, *f*
grieve *v.i, and v.t*, dŏlěo (2)
grievous grăvis, ăcerbus
grim trux
grin *v.i*, rīdĕo (2)
grind *v.t*, contěro (3); mŏlo (3) (— down, oppress), opprĭmo (3);
grindstone cōs, *f*
grip *nn, use* mănus, *f*, (hand)
grip *v.t*, arrĭpĭo (3)
gripes tormĭna, *n.pl*
grisly horrendus
grist fărīna, *f*
gristle cartĭlāgo, *f*
grit glārĕa
groan *nn*, gěmĭtus, *m*
groan *v.i*, gěmo (3)
grocer tūrārĭus, *m*
groin inguen, *n*
groom *nn*, ăgāso, *m*
groom *v.t*, (look after), cūro (1)
groove cănālis, *m*
grope *v.i*, praetento (1)
gross *adj*, crassus; (unseemly), inděcōrus
grotto antrum, *n*
grotesque monstrŭōsus
ground (earth) hŭmus, *f*, sŏlum, *n*, terra, *f*; (cause, reason), causa, *f*; (to give —), pědem rěfěro (*irreg*)
ground *v.i*, (of ships) sīdo (3)
groundless vānus
groundwork (basis) fundāmentum, *n*
group glŏbus, *m*
group *v.t*, dispōno (3)
grouse lăgōpūs, *f*
groove lūcus, *m*
grovel *v.i*, serpo (3)
grow *v.i*, cresco (3), augesco (3); (— up), ădŏlesco (3); (become), fīo (*irreg*); *v.t*, cŏlo (3)
growl *nn*, frěmĭtus, *m*

growl *v.i*, frĕmo (3)
growth incrēmentum, *n*
grub *nn*, vermĭcŭlus, *m*
grudge *nn*, sĭmultas, *f*
grudge *v.t*, invĭdĕo (2) (*with dat*)
grudgingly *adv, use adj*, invītus
gruel ptĭsāna, *f*
gruff asper
grumble *v.i*, frĕmo (3)
grunt *nn*, grunnītus, *m*
grunt *v.i*, grunnĭo (4)
guarantee *nn*, fĭdes, *f*
guarantee *v.t*, fĭdem do (1) (*with dat*)
guarantor vas, *m*
guard (person) custos, *c*; (defence), custōdĭa, *f*, praesĭdĭum, *n*; (to keep —) *v.i*, custōdĭam ăgo (3)
guard *v.t*, custōdĭo (4)
guarded (cautious) cautus
guardian custos, *c*; (of child), tūtor, *m*
guardianship custōdĭa, *f*; (of child), tūtēla, *f*
guess *nn*, coniectūra, *f*
guess *v.t*, cōnĭcĭo (3), dīvīno (1)
guest hospes, *m*, hospĭta, *f*; (at a party, etc.) convīva, *c*
guidance (advice) consĭlĭum, *n*
guide *nn*, dux, *c*
guide *v.t*, dūco (3)
guild collēgĭum, *n*
guile dŏlus, *m*
guileful dŏlōsus
guileless simplex
guilt culpa, *f*
guiltless innŏcens, insons
guilty sons, nŏcens
guise hăbĭtus, *m*, spĕcĭes, *f*
gulf (bay) sĭnus, *m*; (abyss), gurges, *m*, vŏrāgo, *f*
gullet guttur, *n*
gullible crēdŭlus
gully (channel) cănālis, *m*, fossa, *f*
gulp *v.t*, haurĭo (4)
gum (of the mouth) gingīva, *f*; (of plants etc.) gummi, *n*
gurgle *v.i*, singulto (1)
gush *v.i*, prŏfundor (3 *pass*)
gust flātus, *m*
gut intestīna, *n.pl*

gutter fossa, *f*, clŏāca, *f*
gutteral grăvis
gymnasium gymnăsĭum, *n*
gymnastics pălaestra, *f*

H

haberdasher lintĕo, *m*
habit consŭētūdo, *f*, mōs, *m*
habitable hăbĭtābĭlis
habitation dŏmĭcĭlĭum, *n*
habitual ūsĭtātus
habituate *v.t*, consŭēfăcĭo (3)
hack căballus, *m*
hack *v.t*, concīdo (3)
hackneyed trītus
haft mănūbrĭum, *n*
hag ănus, *f*
haggard măcĭe corruptus (marred by leanness)
haggle *v.i*, dē prētĭo căvillor (1 *dep*) (to quibble about price)
hail *nn*, grando, *f*
hail *v.i*, (weather), grandĭnat (*impers.*); *v.t*, (greet), sălūto (1)
hair căpillus, *m*, crīnis, *m*, caesărĭes, *f*
hairdresser tonsor, *m*
hairless (bald) calvus
hairy pĭlōsus
halcyon *adj*, alcўōnēus
hale (healthy) vālĭdus
half *nn*, dīmĭdĭum, *n*; *adj*, dīmĭdĭus; *adv, use prefix* sēmi-, *e.g.* half-asleep, sēmĭsomnus; (half-dead), sēmĭănĭmis, mŏrĭbundus; (— hour) sēmĭhōra, *f*; (— moon), lūna dīmĭdĭāta, *f*; (— yearly), sēmestris
hall (of house) ātrĭum, *n*; (public), concĭlĭābŭlum, *n*
hallo! heus!
hallow *v.t*, consĕcro (1)
hallucination somnĭa, *n.pl*
halo cŏrōna, *f*
halt *nn, use vb*, consisto (3)
halt *v.i*, consisto (3)
halter (horse) căpistrum, *n*; (noose), lăquĕus, *m*
halve *v.t*, ex aequo dīvĭdo (3)
ham perna, *f*

hamlet vīcus, *m*
hammer *nn*, mallĕus, *m*
hammer *v.t*, contudo (3)
hamper quălum, *n*
hamper *v.t*, impĕdĭo (4)
hamstring *v.t*, poplĭtem succīdo
  (3) (*with dat*)
hand mănus, *f*; (left —), mănus
  sĭnistra; (right —), dextra mănus;
  (to shake — s) detras coniungĕre
  (3); (— cuffs), mănĭcae, *f.pl*;
  (— writing), chīrgrăphum, *n*; (on
  the one—, on the other —) et...et,
  or quĭdem (*second word in
  clause*) ...autem (*second word in
  clause*); (— to — fighting, etc.)
  commĭnus, *adv*; (at hand),
  praesto, *adv*
hand *v.t*, do (1), trādo (3);
  (— down or over), trādo (3)
handful (few) *use adj*, pauci
handicraft artĭfĭcĭum, *n*
handiwork ŏpus, *n*
handkerchief sūdārĭum, *n*
handle mănūbrĭum, *n*
handle *v.t*, tracto (1)
handling (treatment) tractātĭo, *f*
handsome spĕcĭōsus, pulcher
handy (manageable) hăbĭlis
hang *v.t*, suspendo (3); (— the
  head) dēmitto (3); *v.i*, pendĕo (2);
  (— back, hesitate), dŭbĭto (1);
  (overhang) impendĕo (2)
hanger-on assecla, *c*
hanging (death by —)
  suspendĭum, *n*
hangman carnĭfex, *m*
hanker after *v.t*, opto (1)
haphazard *use adv. phr.* nullo
  ordĭne (in no order)
happen *v.i*, accĭdo (3), ēvĕnĭo (4)
happiness fēlīcĭtas, *f*
happy fēlix, bĕātus
harangue *nn*, contĭo, *f*
harangue *v.t*, contĭōnor (1 *dep.*)
harass *v.t*, sollĭcĭto (1)
harbour portus, *m*; (— dues),
  portōrĭum, *n*
harbour *v.t*, (shelter), excĭpĭo (3)
hard dūrus; (difficult), difficĭlis
hard *adv*, (strenuously), strēnŭē
harden *v.t*, dūro (1); *v.i*, dūresco
  (3)

hard-hearted dūrus
hardiness rōbur, *n*
hardly *adv*, vix; (harshly),
  crūdēlĭter
hardness dūrĭtĭa, *f*
hardship lăbor, *m*
hardware ferrāmenta, *n.pl*
hardy dūrus
hare lĕpus, *m*
hark! heus!
harlot mĕrĕtrix, *f*
harm *nn*, damnum, *n*
harm *v.t*, nŏcĕo (2) (*with dat*)
harmful noxĭus
harmless innŏcŭus, innŏcens
harmonious concors
harmonize *v.i*, concĭno (3)
harmony concentus, *m*, consensus,
  m
harness *nn*, ĕquestrĭa arma, *n.pl*,
  (horse equipment), frēnum, *n*
harness *v.t*, iungo (3)
harp fĭdes, *f.pl*; (harpist), fĭdĭcen,
  m
harrow *nn*, irpex, *m*
harrow *v.t*, occo (1)
harrowing *adj*, horrendus, terrĭbĭlis
harsh asper, ăcerbus
harshness aspĕrĭtas, *f*
hart cervus, *m*
harvest messis, *f*
hasp fībŭla, *f*
haste *nn*, festīnātĭo, *f*
hasten *v.i*, prŏpĕro (1), festīno (1);
  v.t, mātūro (1), accĕlĕro (1)
hastily *adv*, prŏpĕrē
hastiness (of temper) īrācundĭa, *f*
hasty prŏpĕrus; (of temper)
  īrācundus
hat pĕtăsus, *m*
hatch *v.t*, (eggs), exclūdo (3);
  (plans etc.) ĭnĕo (4)
hatchet sĕcūris, *f*
hate *nn*, ŏdĭum, *n*
hate *v.t*, ōdi (*v. defect*)
hateful ŏdĭōsus
haughtiness sŭperbĭa, *f*
haughty sŭperbus, arrŏgans
haul *v.t*, trăho (3)
haunt *nn*, lătĕbrae, *f.pl*
haunt *v.t*, (visit frequently), cĕlĕbro
  (1); (trouble), sollĭcĭto (1)

have *v.t*, hăbĕo (2); *or use* esse
(*irreg*) *with dat. of possessor, e.g.*
I have a brother, est mĭhĭ frāter
haven portus, *m*
haversack saccus, *m*
havoc strāges, *f*, vastātĭo
hawk *nn*, accĭpĭter, *m*, *f*
hay faenum, *n*
hazard *nn*, pĕrīcŭlum, *n*
hazardous pĕrīcŭlōsus
haze nĕbŭla, *f*
hazel *nn*, cŏrȳlus, *f*
hazy nĕbŭlōsus
he *pron, if not emphatic, use 3rd
pers. of verb; otherwise,* ille, hic,
is
head căput, *n*, vertex, *m*; (chief),
princeps, *m*; (to be at the — of)
praesum (*irreg*) (*with dat*)
heat *adj*, (of wind) adversus
head *v.t*, (be in charge), praesum
(*irreg*) (*with dat*)
headache căpĭtĭs dŏlor, *m*
headband vitta, *f*
headland promontūrĭum, *n*
headlong *adj*, praeceps
headquarters praetōrĭum, *n*
headstrong *adj*, pervĭcax
heal *v.t*, sāno (1), mĕdĕor (2 *dep*)
(*with dat*); *v.i*, consānesco (3)
healing *nn*, sānātĭo, *f*
healing *adj*, sălūtāris
health vălētūdo, *f*
healthy sānus, vălĭdus; (of place or
climate), sălūbris
heap *nn*, ăcervus, *m*
heap *v.t*, cŭmŭlo (1), congĕro (3)
hear *v.t*, audĭo (4); (learn),
cognosco (3)
hearer audītor, *m*
hearing *nn*, (sense of —), audītus,
m
hearsay rūmor, *m*
heart cor, *n*; (interior), *use adj*,
intĭmus (inmost); (feelings, etc.),
pectus, *n*, mens, *f*; (courage),
ănĭmus, *m*; (— ache), sollĭcĭtūdo,
f; (— break), dŏlor, *m*; (— broken)
adj. phr, ănĭmo afflictus
hearth fŏcus, *m*
heartiness stŭdĭum, *n*
heartless dūrus
heartlessness crūdēlĭtas, *f*

hearty ălăcer
heat *nn*, călor, *m*, ardor, *m*,
aestus, *m*, fervor, *m*
heat *v.t*, călĕfăcĭo (3); (excite),
incendo (3)
heath lŏca obsĭta, *n.pl*, lŏca
inculta, *n.pl*
heave *v.t*, tollo (3); *v.i*, tŭmesco
(3)
heaven caelum, *n*; (— dwelling)
adj, caelĭcŏla
heavenly *adj*, dīvīnus
heaviness grăvĭtas, *f*; (— of mind),
tristĭtĭa, *f*
heavy grăvis; (sad), tristis; (air,
etc.) crassus
hectic (agitated, confused)
turbŭlentus
hedge saepes, *f*
hedge in *v.t*, saepĭo (4)
hedgehog ĕchīnus, *m*
heed *v.t*, (obey) pārĕo (2) (*with
dat*); (to take —), *v.i*, căvĕo (2)
heedless incautus
heedlessness neglĕgentĭa, *f*
heel calx, *f*; (take to one's —s)
fŭgĭo (3)
heifer iŭvenca, *f*
height altĭtūdo, *f*; (high ground)
sŭpĕrĭor lŏcus, *m*
heighten *v.t*, *use* augĕo (2)
(increase)
heinous ătrox
heir, heiress hēres, *c*
hell infĕri, *m.pl*. Orcus, *m*
hellish infernus
helm gŭbernācŭlum, *n*
helmet cassis, *f*, gălĕa, *f*
helmsman gŭbernātor, *m*
help *nn*, auxĭlĭum, *n*
help *v.t*, iŭvo (1), subvĕnĭo (4)
(*with dat*); (I cannot help coming),
non possum făcĕre quīn vĕnĭam
helper adiūtor, *m*
helpful ūtĭlis
helpless ĭnops
helplessness ĭnŏpĭa, *f*
helpmate consors *m*, *f*
hem *nn*, limbus, *m*
hem in *v.t*, circumsĕdĕo (2), saepĭo
(4)
hemisphere hēmisphaerĭum, *n*
hemp cannăbis, *f*

hen gallīna, *f*; (— house),
gallīnārĭum, *n*
hence *adv*, (place or cause), hinc;
(time), posthāc
henceforth *adv*, posthāc
her *pron, adj*, eius; (*if it refers to
the subject of the sentence*), sŭus,
a, um
herald praeco, *m*
herb herba, *f*, hŏlus, *n*
herd grex, *m*
herd together *v.i*, congrĕgor (1
pass)
herdsman pastor, *m*
here hīc; (hither), hūc; (to be —),
v.i, adsum (*irreg*)
hereafter *adv*, posthāc
hereby *adv*, ex hōc
hereditary hērēdĭtārĭus
heredity gĕnus, *n*
heretical prāvus
hereupon *adv*, hīc
heritage hērēdĭtas, *f*
hermit hŏmo sōlĭtārĭus
hernia hernĭa, *f*
hero vir fortissĭmus
heroic (brave) fortis
heroine fēmĭna fortis, *f*
heroism virtus, *f*
heron ardĕa, *f*
hers see her
herself *pron. reflexive*, sē; (*pron.
emphatic*) ipsa
hesitancy, hesitation haesĭtātĭo, *f*
hesitate *v.i*, dŭbĭto (1), haesĭto (1)
hew *v.t*, caedo (3)
heyday (youth) iŭventus, *f*
hibernate *v.i*, condor (3 *pass*)
hiccough singultus, *m*
hidden occultus
hide *nn*, (skin), cŏrĭum, *n*, pellis, *f*
hide *v.t*, abodo (3), cēlo (1)
hideous foedus
hideousness foedĭtas, *f*
hiding-place lătĕbrae, *f.pl*
high altus, celsus; (of rank),
amplus; (of price), magnus,
magni; (— born), gĕnĕrōsus;
(— handed), impĕrĭōsus;
(— lands), montes, *m.pl*; (—
landers), montāni, *m.pl*;
(— spirited), ănĭmōsus;

(— treason), măiestas, *f*; (— way),
vĭa, *f*; (— wayman) lătro, *m*
hilarity hĭlărĭtas, *f*
hill collis, *m*
hillock tŭmŭlus, *m*
hilly montŭōsus
hilt căpŭlus, *m*
himself *pron, reflexive*, sē; *pron.
emphatic*, ipse
hind *adj*, postĕrĭor
hinder *v.t*, impĕdĭo (4), obsto (1)
(*with dat*)
hindrance impĕdīmentum, *n*
hinge *nn*, cardo, *m*
hinge on *v.i*, vertor (3 *dep*), versor
(1 *dep*) in (*with abl*)
hint *nn*, signĭfĭcātĭo, *f*
hint at *v.t*, signĭfĭco (1)
hip coxendix, *f*
hippopotamus hippŏpŏtămus, *m*
hire (wages) merces, *f*
hire *v.t*, condūco (3)
hired conductus
his *pron*, ēius, hūius, illĭus; *or* sŭus
(*referring to the subject of the
sentence*)
hiss *nn*, sībĭlus, *m*
hiss *v.i. and v.t*, sībĭlo (1)
historian scriptor (*m*) rērum
historic(al) *use nn*, historĭa, *f*,
(history)
history historĭa, *f*, rēs gestae, *f.pl*
hit *nn*, (blow) plāga, *f*
hit *v.t*, (strike) fērĭo (4); (— upon),
incĭdo (3)
hitch impĕdīmentum, *n*
hitch *v.t*, necto (3)
hither *adv*, hūc; (— and thither),
hūc illūc
hitherto *adv*, ădhūc
hive alvĕārĭum, *n*
hoard *nn*, ăcervus, *m*
hoard *v.t*, collĭgo (3), condo (3)
hoarfrost prŭīna, *f*
hoarse raucus
hoary cānus
hoax *nn*, lūdus, *m*
hoax *v.t*, lūdĭfĭcor (1 *dep*), lūdo (3)
hobble *v.i*, claudĭco (1)
hobby stŭdĭum, *n*
hobnail clāvus, *m*
hoe *nn*, sarcŭlum, *n*

hoe *v.t*, sarrĭo (4)

hog porcus, *m*

hogshead dōlĭum, *n*

hoist *v.t*, tollo (3)

hold *nn*, (grasp) *use* comprĕhendo (3), *or* mănus, *f*

hold *v.t*, tĕnĕo (2), obtĭnĕo (2), hăbĕo (2); (— an office), obtĭnĕo (2), fungor (3 *dep*); (— elections, etc.), hăbĕo (2); (— back), *v.i*, cunctor (1 *dep*), *v.t*, rĕtĭnĕo (2); (— fast), rĕtĭnĕo (2); (— out), *v.t*, porrĭgo (3); (endure), sustĭnĕo (2), perfĕro (*irreg*); (— up, lift), tollo (3)

hold-fast *nn*, fībŭla, *f*

hole fŏrāmen, *n*, căvum, *n*

holiday fērĭae, *f.pl*

holiness sanctĭtas, *f*

hollow *nn*, căvum, *n*, lăcūna, *f*; (— of the hand), căva mănus, *f*

hollow *adj*, căvus; (false), vānus

hollow *v.t*, căvo (1)

holm-oak īlex, *f*

holy săcer

homage (respect) observantĭa, *f*

home *adj*, dŏmestĭcus; (homely), rustĭcus

home dŏmus, *f*; (at —), dŏmi; (homewards), dŏmum; (from —), dŏmo (— less), cărens tecto (lacking shelter)

homicide (deed) caedes, *f*; (person), hŏmĭcīda, *c*

honest prŏbus

honesty prŏbĭtas, *f*, intĕgrītas, *f*

honey mel, *n*

honeycomb făvus, *m*

honorary hŏnōrārĭus

honour hŏnos, *m*; (glory), dĕcus, *n*; (integrity), hŏnestas, *f*, intĕgrĭtas, *f*; (repute), fāma, *f*

honour *v.t*, cŏlo (3), hŏnesto (1)

honourable hŏnōrātus, hŏnestus

hood cŭcullus, *m*

hoof ungŭla, *f*

hook hāmus, *m*

hook *v.t*, hāmo căpĭo (3) (catch by a hook)

hooked hāmātus

hoop circŭlus, *m*

hoot *nn*, cantus, *m*

hoot *v.i*, căno (3); *v.t*, (hoot at), explōdo (3)

hop *v.i*, sălĭo (4)

hope *nn*, spes, *f*

hope *v.i. and v.t*, spēro (1)

hopeful (promising) *use genit*. *phr*, bŏnae spĕi

hopefully *adj*, *phr*, multa spĕrans

hopeless (desperate) dēspērātus

hopelessness dēspērātĭo, *f*

horizon orbis (*m*) fīnĭens (limiting circle)

horizontal lībrātus

horn cornu, *n*; (made of —), *adj*, cornĕus

hornet crābro, *m*

horrible horrĭbĭlis, horrendus, ătrox, foedus

horrid horrĭbĭlis, horrendus, ătrox, foedus

horrify *v.t*, (dismay), percello (3), terrĕo (2)

horror horror, *m*

horse ĕquus, *m*

horseback (to ride on —) in ĕquo vĕhor (3 *pass*); (to fight on —), ex ĕquo pugno (1)

horsefly tăbānus, *m*

horserace certāmen ĕquestre, *n*

horseshoe sŏlĕa, *f*

horsewhip flăgellum, *n*

horticulture hortōrum cultus, *m*

hospitable hospĭtālis

hospital vălētūdĭnārĭum, *n*

hospitality hospĭtĭum, *n*

host (one who entertains) hospes, *m*; (innkeeper), caupo, *m*; (large number), multĭtūdo, *f*

hostage obses, *c*

hostess hospĭta, *f*

hostile hostīlis, infestus

hostility ĭnĭmīcĭtĭa, *f*; (hostilities, war), bellum, *n*

hot călĭdus, fervens; (of temper), ācer; (to be —), *v.i*, călĕo (2), fervĕo (2); (to become —), *v.i*, călesco (3); (— headed), *adj*, fervĭdus, fervens; (hotly), *adv*, ardenter

hotel hospĭtĭum, *n*

hound cănis, *m*, *f*

hound on *v.t*, (goad on), instīgo (1), ăgĭto (1)

hour hōra, *f*

hourly *adv*, in hōras

hourglass hōrārĭum, *n*

house dŏmus, *f*, aedes, *f.pl*; **(family)**, gens, *f*; **(— hold)** dŏmus, *f*, fămĭlĭa, *f*; **(— keeper)**, prōmus, *m*; **(— maid)**, ancĭlla, *f*; **(— wife)**, māterfămĭlĭas, *f*

house *v.t*, **(store)** condo (3), rēpōno, (3)

hovel tŭgŭrĭum, *n*, căsa, *f*

hover *v.i*, vŏlĭto (1), impendĕo (2)

how (in what way?) quōmŏdŏ?; *with adj. or adv*, quam?; **(— many)**, quot?; **(— often)**, quŏtĭes?; **(— great or big)**, quantus?

however *conj*, tămen; *adv*, quamvis; **(how big or great)**, quantumvis

howl *nn*, ŭlŭlātus, *m*

howl *v.i*, ŭlŭlo (1)

hubbub tŭmulus, *m*

huddle *v.i*, **(— together)**, congrĕgor (1 *dep*), confĕror (*irreg. pass*)

hue (colour) cŏlor, *m*

huff (to be in a — about) *v.t*, aegrē fĕro (*irreg*)

hug *nn*, complexus, *m*

hug *v.t*, amplector (3 *dep*)

huge ingens, immānis

hull (of a ship) alvĕus, *m*

hum *nn*, frĕmĭtus, *m*

hum *v.i*, frĕmo (3), strĕpo (3)

human *adj*, hūmānus; **(— being)**, hŏmo, *c*

humane (compassionate) mĭsĕrĭcors

humanity hūmānĭtas, *f*; **(human race)** hŏmĭnes, *c.pl*; **(compassion)**, mĭsĕrĭcordĭa, *f*

humble hŭmĭlis, vĕrēcundus

humble *v.t*, dēprĭmo (3); **(— in war)**, dēbello (1); **(— oneself)**, sē summittĕre (3 *refles*)

humdrum *adj*, mĕdĭŏcris, tardus

humid hūmĭdus

humidity hūmor, *m*

humiliate *v.t*, dēprĭmo (3)

humility mŏdestĭa, *f*

humorous rīdĭcŭlus

humour făcētĭae, *f.pl*; **(disposition)**, ingĕnĭum, *n*. lĭbīdo, *f*; **(to be in the — to)**, *use* lĭbet (*v. 2 impers*)

(with dat. of person)

humour *v.t*, obsĕquor (3 *dep*) *(with dat. of person)*

hump gibber, *m*

humpbacked *adj*, gibber

hunch, hunchbacked see **humpbacked**

hundred *adj*, centum; **(— times)**, *adv*, centies; **(— fold)**, *adj*, centŭplex

hundredth centēsĭmus

hundredweight centumpondĭum, *n*

hunger fămes, *f*

hunger *v.i*, ēsŭrĭo (4)

hungry ēsŭrĭens, ăvĭdus (cĭbi)

hunt *v.t*, vēnor (1 *dep*)

hunt, hunting *nn*, vēnātĭo, *f*

hunter vēnātor, *m*

huntress vēnātrix, *f*

hurdle crātes, *f.pl*

hurl *v.t*, iăcŭlor (1 *dep*), cōnĭcĭo (3)

hurricane tempestas, *f*, prŏcella, *f*

hurried praeceps

hurriedly *adv*, raptim

hurry *v.i*, festīno (1), prŏpĕro (1); *v.t*, răpĭo (3); **(an action, etc.)**, mātūro (1)

hurt *nn*, **(wound)** vulnus, *n*

hurt *v.t*, laedo (3), nŏcĕo (2) *(with dat)*

hurt *adj*, **(wounded)**, saucĭus

hurtful nŏcens, noxĭus

husband vir, *m*, mărītus, *m*

husbandry agrĭcultūra, *f*

hush! tăcē; *pl*, tăcētē *(from tăcĕo)*

hush up *v.t*, **(conceal)**, tĕgo (3), cēlo (1)

husk follĭcŭlus, *m*

husky fuscus, raucus

hustle *v.t*, pulso (1), trūdo (3)

hut căsa, *f*, tūgūrĭum, *n*

hutch căvĕa, *f*

hyacinth hўăcinthus, *m*

hybrid hybrĭda, ae, *c*

hymn carmen, *n*

hyperbole hўperbŏlē, *f*

hyperchondriac mĕlanchŏlĭcus

hypocrisy sĭmŭlātĭo, *f*

hypocrite sĭmŭlātor, *m*

hypocritical sĭmŭlātus

hypothesis coniectūra, *f*, condĭcĭo, *f*

hysteria āmentĭa, *f*, perturbātĭo, *f*

I

I *pron*, (*emphatic*), ĕgo; *otherwise use 1st pers. sing. of verb, e.g.*
I love, ămo
iambic *adj*, ĭambēus
ice glăcĭes, *f*
icicle stīrĭa, *f*
icy gĕlĭdus, glăcĭālis
idea nōtĭo, *f*, imāgo, *f*, sententĭa, *f*; **(to form an —)** *v.i*, cōgĭtātĭōne fingo (3)
ideal *adj*, **(perfect)** perfectus, summus, optĭmus
ideal *nn*, exemplar, *n*
identical īdem **(the same)**
identify *v.t*, agnosco (3)
identity (to find the — of) cognosco (3) quis sit …
ides īdūs, *f.pl*
idiocy fătŭĭtas, *f*
idiom prŏprĭĕtas, *f*. (linguae) **(peculiarity of language)**
idiot fătŭus, *m*
idiotic fătŭus
idle (unemployed) ōtĭōsus; **(lazy)**, ignāvus; **(useless)**, vānus; **(to be —)**, *v.i*, cesso (1)
idleness ignāvĭa, *f*, cessātĭo, *f*
idler cessātor, *m*, cessātrix, *f*
idol (statue) sĭmŭlăcrum, *n*; **(something loved)** dēlĭcĭae, *f.pl*
idolatry vĕnĕrātĭo, (*f*) sĭmŭlācrōrum **(worship of images)**
idolize *v.t*, cŏlo (3)
idyl īdyllĭum, *n*
if *conj*, sī; **(— not)**, sīn; *after a vb. of asking* **(— whether)** num, ŭtrum; **(whether … or if)** sīve … sīve; **(— only)**, dummŏdo
ignite *v.i*, ardesco (3); *v.t*, accendo (3)
ignoble (of birth) ignōbĭlis; **(dishonourable)** tupis
ignominious turpis
ignominy ignōmĭnĭa, *f*, infāmĭa, *f*
ignorance inscĭentĭa, *f*
ignorant ignārus, inscĭus
ignore *v.t*, praetĕrĕo

ill *adj*, aeger; **(evil)**, mălus; **(to be —)**, *v.i*, asgrōto (1); **(to fall —)**, *v.i*, in morbum incĭdo (3)
ill *adv*, mălē
ill *nn*, **(evil)** mălum, *n*
ill-advised (reckless) temĕrārĭus
ill-bred inhūmānus
ill-disposed mălĕvŏlus
illegal illĭcĭtus
illegitimate non lēgĭtĭmus
ill-favoured dēformis, turpis
ill-health vălētūdo, *f*
illicit illĭcĭtus
illiterate illittĕrātus
ill-natured mălĕvŏlus
ill-omened dīrus
ill-starred infēlix
ill-temper īrācundĭa
illness morbus, *m*
illogical absurdus, rĕpugnans
illuminate *v.t*, illustro (1)
illusion error, *m*
illusive vānus
illustrate *v.t*, illustro (1)
illustration exemplum, *n*
illustrious clārus, *llustris*
image ĭmāgo, *f*, effĭgĭes, *f*
imaginable *use phr*, quod concĭpi pŏtest **(that can be imagined)**
imaginary commentĭcĭus
imagination cōgĭtātĭo, *f*
imagine *v.t*, ănĭmo concĭpĭo (3) *or* fingo (3)
imbecile fătŭus
imbecility imbēcillĭtas (*f*) ănĭmi
imbibe *v.t*, bĭbo (3), haurĭo (4)
imbue *v.t*, inficĭo (3)
imitate *v.t*, ĭmĭtor (1 *dep*)
imitation ĭmĭtātĭo, *f*; **(likeness)**, effĭgĭes, *f*
imitator ĭmĭtātor, *m*
immaculate intĕger
immaterial (unimportant) *use phr*, nullo mōmento
immature immātūrus
immeasurable immensus
immediate praesens, proxĭmus
immediately *adv*, stătim, confestim
immemorial (from time —), ex hŏmĭnum mĕmōrĭa
immense immensus, ingens

immensity immensĭtas, *f*
immerse *v.t*, immergo (3)
immigrant advĕna, *m. f*
immigrate *v.i*, immĭgro (1)
imminent praesens; **(to be —)** *v.i*,
  immĭnĕo (2)
immobility immōbĭlĭtas, *f*
immoderate immŏdĕrātus,
  immŏdĭcus
immodest impŭdĭcus
immodesty impŭdīcĭtĭa, *f*
immolate *v.t*, immŏlo (1)
immoral prāvus, turpis
immorality mōres māli, *m.pl*
immortal immortālis, aeternus
immortality immortālĭtas, *f*
immovable immōbĭlis
immunity immūnĭtas, *f*, văcātĭo, *f*
immutable immūtābĭlis
impair *v.t*, mĭnŭo (3)
impale *v.t*, transfīgo (3)
impart *v.t*, impertĭo (4)
impartial aequus, iustus
impartiality aequĭtas, *f*
impassable insŭpĕrābĭlis
impassioned concĭtātus, fervens
impassive pătĭens
impatience (haste) impătĭentĭa, *f*,
  festīnātĭo, *f*
impatient ăvĭdus
impeach *v.t*, accūso (1)
impeachment accūsātĭo, *f*
impeccable impeccābĭlis
impede *v.t*, impĕdĭo (4)
impediment impĕdīmentum, *n*; **(of
  speech)**, haesĭtantĭa, *f*
impel *v.t*, impello (3), incĭto (1)
impend *v.i*, impendĕo (2),
  immĭnĕo (2)
impending fŭtūrus
impenetrable impĕnĕtrābĭlis
imperfect imperfectus
imperfection (defect) vĭtĭum, *n*
imperial (kingly) rēgĭus *or use
  genit. of* impĕrĭum, *n*, **(empire)**,
  or impĕrātor, *m*, **(emperor)**
imperil *v.t*, in pĕrīcŭlum addūco
  (3)
imperious impĕrĭōsus
impermeable impervĭus

impersonate *v.t*, partes sustĭnĕo
  (2) **(keep up a part)**
impertinence insŏlentĭa, *f*
impertinent insŏlens
imperturbable immōtus, immōbĭlis
impetuosity vīs, *f*
impetuous vĕhĕmens
impetus vīs, *f*, impĕtus, *m*
impious impĭus
implacable implācābĭlis
implant *v.t*, insĕro (3)
implement instrūmentum, *n*
implicate *v.t*, implĭco (1)
implicit *adj*, tăcĭtus; **(absolute)**,
  omnis, tōtus
implore *v.t*, implōro (1), ōro (1)
imply *v.t*, signĭfĭco (1); **(involve)**,
  hăbĕo (2)
impolite ĭnurbānus
import *nn*, **(meaning)**, signĭfĭcātĭo,
  f
import *v.t*, importo (1)
importance mōmentum, *n*; **(of
  position)** amplĭtūdo, *f*
important grăvis; **(people)**, amplus
importunate mŏlestus
importune *v.t*, flāgĭto (1)
impose *v.t*, impōno (3)
imposition (fraud) fraus, *f*
impossible *use phr*, quod fĭĕri nōn
  pŏtest **(which cannot be done)**
imposter fraudātor, *m*
impotence imbēcillĭtas, *f*
impotent imbēcillus, infirmus
impoverish *v.t*, in paupertātem
  rĕdĭgo (3)
impoverishment paupertas, *f*
imprecation exsēcrātĭo, *f*
impregnable ĭnexpugnābĭlis
impregnate *v.t*, īnĭcĭo (3)
impress *v.t*, imprĭmo (3); **(the
  mind)**, mŏvĕo (2)
impression (mental) mōtus, *(m)*
  ănĭmi; **(idea, thought)** ŏpīnĭo, *f*,
  ŏpīnātĭo, *f*; **(mark)**, vestīgĭum, *n*
impressive grăvis
imprint *nn*, signum, *n*; **(of a foot)**,
  vestīgĭum, *n*
imprison *v.t*, in vincŭla cōnĭcĭo (3)
  (throw into chains)

imprisonment vincŭla, *n.pl*
improbable nōn vērĭsĭmĭlis **(not likely)**
improper indĕcōrus
improve *v.t*, mĕlĭōrem făcĭo (3) *or* reddo; *v.i*, mĕlĭor fīo (*irreg*)
improvement ēmendātĭo, *f*
improvident neglĕgens, imprōvĭdus
imprudence imprūdentĭa, *f*
imprudent inconsultus, imprūdens
impudence impŭdentĭa, *f*
impudent impŭdens
impulse impĕtus, *m*, impulsus, *m*
impulsive vĕhĕmens
impunity (with —) *adv*, impūnĕ
impure impūrus, foedus
impurity impūrĭtas, *f*, incestus, *m*
impute *v.t*, attrĭbŭo (3)
in *prep*, **(place)**, in (*with abl.*) *or use locative case if available, e.g.* Londīnĭi, **in London; (time)**, *use abl. or* in (*with abl.*)
inability (weakness) imbēcillĭtas, *f*
inaccessible ĭnaccessus
inaccuracy (fault) error, *m*
inaccurate (things) falsus
inactive ĭners
inactivity cessātĭo, *f*, ĭnertĭa, *f*
inadequate impar
inadmissible *use phr*, quod nōn lĭcet **(which is not allowed)**
inadvertent imprūdens
inane ĭnānis
inanimate ĭnănĭmus
inappropriate nōn aptus **(not suitable)**
inasmuch as *conj*, quŏnĭam, quandōquĭdem
inattention neglĕgentĭa, *f*
inattentive neglĕgens
inaudible *use phr*, quod audīri nōn pŏtest **(which cannot be heard)**
inaugurate *v.t*, ĭnaugŭro (1)
inauguration consĕcrātĭo, *f*
inauspicious infēlix
inborn insĭtus
incalculable *use phr*, quod aestĭmāri nōn pŏtest **(which cannot be estimated)**
incapable inhăbĭlis
incarcerate *v.t*, in vincŭla cōnĭcĭo (3) **(throw into chains)**

incarnate spĕcĭe hūmānā indūtus **(clothed with human form)**
incautious incautus
incendiary incendĭārĭus, *m*
incense *nn*, tūs, *n*
incense *v.t*, ad īram mŏvĕo (2) **(arouse to anger)**
incentive stĭmŭlus, *m*
incessant perpĕtŭus, assĭdŭus
incest incestum, *n*
inch uncĭa, *f*
incident rēs, *f*
incidental (casual) fortŭĭtus
incipient *use vb*. incĭpĭo **(begin)**
incision incīsūra, *f*
incisive mordax, ācer
incite *v.t*, incĭto (1)
inclemency aspĕrĭtas, *f*, sĕvērĭtas, *f*
inclement asper, sĕvērus
inclination (desire) stŭdĭum, *n*, vŏluntas, *f*; **(leaning, bias)** inclīnātĭo, *f*
incline *v.t*, inclīno (1); *v.i*, inclīnor (1 *pass*)
incline *nn*, **(slope)** acclīvĭtas, *f*
inclined (disposed) prōpensus
include *v.t*, rĕfĕro (*irreg*), comprĕhendo (3)
including (together with) cum (*with abl*)
incoherent *use vb. phr. with* nōn *and* cŏhaerĕo (2) **(to hold together)**
income fructus, *m*, stīpendĭum, *n*
incomparable singŭlāris
incompatibility rĕpugnantĭa, *f*
incompatible rĕpugnans
incompetent ĭnhăbĭlis
incomplete imperfectus
incomprehensible *use phr*, quod intellĕgi nōn pŏtest
inconceivable *use phr*, quod ănĭmo fingi nōn pŏtest **(that cannot be conceived)**
inconclusive (weak) infirmus
incongruous rĕpugnans
inconsiderable parvus
inconsiderate inconsīdĕrātus
inconsistency inconstantĭa, *f*
inconsistent inconstans; **(to be —)**, *v.i*, rĕpugno (1)
inconsolable inconsōlābĭlis
inconspicuous obscūrus

inconstancy inconstantĭa, *f*
inconstant inconstans
inconvenience incommŏdum, *n*
inconvenient incommŏdus
incorporate *v.t*, constĭtŭo (3),
  iungo (3)
incorrect falsus
incorrigible perdĭtus
incorruptible incorruptus
increase *nn*, incrēmentum, *n*
increase *v.t*, augĕo (2), *v.i*, cresco
  (1)
incredible incrēdĭbĭlis
incredulous incrēdŭlus
incriminate *v.t*, implĭco (1)
inculcate *v.t*, inculco (1)
incumbent upon (it is —) ŏportet
  (*v. 2 impers. with acc. of person*)
incur *v.t*, sŭbĕo (4)
incurable insānābĭlis
indebted obnoxĭus
indecency turpĭtūdo, *f*
indecent turpis, obscēnus
indecisive dŭbĭus, anceps
indeed *adv, emphatic*, prŏfecto;
  (yes —), vēro; *concessive;* quĭdem
indefatigible assĭdŭus
indefensible *use phr*, quod nōn
  pŏtest făcĭlē dēfendi (that cannot
  be defended easily)
indefinite incertus
indemnify *v.t*, damnum rēstĭtŭo (3)
  (restore a loss)
indentation lăcuna, *f*
independence lībertas, *f*
independent līber
indescribable ĭnēnarrābĭlis
indestructible (unfailing) pĕrennis
indeterminate incertus
index index, *m*
indicate *v.t*, indĭco (1), signĭfĭco
  (1)
indication indĭcĭum, *n*
indict *v.t*, accūso (1)
indictment accūsātĭo, *f*
indifference lentĭtūdo, *f*
indifferent neglĕgens; (middling)
  mĕdĭŏcris
indifferently *adv* (moderately)
  mĕdĭŏcrĭter
indigenous *adj*, indĭgĕna
indigestible *adv*, grăvis
indigestion crūdĭtas, *f*

indignant īrātus; (to be —), *v.i*,
  indignor (1 *dep*), īrātus ess
indignation indignātĭo, *f*, īra, *f*
indignity contŭmēlĭa, *f*
indirect oblīquus (path, etc.) dēvĭus
indiscreet inconsultus
indiscriminate prōmiscŭus
indispensable nĕcessārĭus
indispose *v.t*, ălĭēno (1)
indisposed (not inclined) āversus;
  (ill), aegrōtus
indisposition (unwillingness)
  ănĭmus āversus; (sickness),
  vălētūdo, *f*
indisputable certus
indistinct obscūrus
individual *nn*, hŏmo, *c*
individual *adj*, prŏprĭus
indivisible indīvĭdŭus
indolence ignāvĭa, *f*
indolent ignāvus
indomitable indŏmĭtus
indoor *adj*, umbrātĭlis (in the
  shade)
indoors (motion) in tectum
indubitable certus
induce *v.t*, addūco (3)
inducement praemĭum, *n*
indulge *v.i and v.t*, indulgĕo (2)
indulgence indulgentĭa, *f*
indulgent indulgens
industrious industrĭus, dīlĭgens
industry (diligence) industrĭa, *f*,
  dīlĭgentĭa, *f*
inebriated ēbrĭus
ineffective ĭnūtĭlis
inefficient *use phr*, qui rem
  cĕlĕrĭter confĭcĕre nōn pŏtest
  (who cannot complete a matter
  quickly)
inelegant ĭnēlĕgans
inept ĭneptus
inequality dissĭmĭlĭtūdo, *f*
inert ĭners, segnis
inertly *adv*, segnĭter
inestimable ĭnaestĭmābĭlis
inevitable nĕcessārĭus
inexcusable *use phr*, quod
  praetermitti nōn pŏtest (that
  cannot be overlooked)
inexhaustible infīnītus, sĭne fine
inexorable ĭnexōrābĭlis

inexperience impĕrītĭa, *f*,
    insciĕntĭa, *f*
inexperienced impĕrītus
inexplicable ĭnexplĭcābĭlis
inexpressible ĭnēnarrābĭlis, *or phr*,
    quod exprĭmi nōn pŏtest **(that
    cannot be expressed)**
infallible qui falli nōn pŏtest **(who
    cannot be mistaken)**
infamous infāmis
infamy infāmĭa, *f*
infancy infantĭa, *f*
infant *adj, and nn*, infans
infantry pĕdĭtātus, *m*
infatuate *v.t*, infătŭo (1)
infatuated dēmens
infect *v.t*, infĭcĭo (3)
infection contāgĭo, *f*
infer *v.t*, collĭgo (3)
inference coniectūra, *f*
inferior *adj*, infĕrĭor, dētĕrĭor
infernal infernus
infested infestus
infidelity perfĭdĭa, *f*
infinite infinĭtus
infinity infinĭtas, *f*
infirm invălĭdus, infirmus
infirmity infirmĭtas, *f*
inflame *v.t*, accendo (3)
inflammable *use phr*, quod făcĭlĕ
    incendi pŏtest **(that can be set on
    fire easily)**
inflammation inflammātĭo, *f*
inflate *v.t*, inflo (1)
inflexible rĭgĭdus
inflict *v.t*, inflīgo (3); **(war, etc.)**,
    infĕro *(irreg) (with dat of person)*
infliction mălum, *n*, **(trouble)**
influence *nn*, vīs, *f*, mōmentum, *n*;
    (authority), auctōrĭtas, *f*; **(to have
    —)** *v.i*, vălĕo (2)
influence *v.t*, mŏvĕo (2)
influential grăvis
inform *v.t*, certĭōrem făcĭo (3);
    (— against someone), nōmen
    dēfĕro *(irreg) (with genit)*
information (news) nuntĭus, *m*
informer dēlātor, *m*
infrequency rārĭtas, *f*
infrequent rārus
infringe *v.t*, vĭŏla, (1)
infringement vĭŏlātĭo, *f*
infuriate *v.t*, effĕro (1)

infuriated īrā incensus
infuse *v.t*, infudo (3), īnĭcĭo (3)
ingenious subtīlis
ingenuity *f*, ars, *f*, callĭdĭtas, *f*
ingenuous ingĕnŭus
inglorious inglōrĭus
ingot lăter, *m*
ingrained insĭtus
ingratiate oneself with *v.t*,
    conncĭlĭo (1), sē grātum reddere
    (with dat)
ingratitude ănĭmus ĭngrātus, *m*
ingredient pars, *f*
inhabit *v.t*, incŏlo (3), hăbĭto (1)
inhabitant incŏla, *c*
inhale *v.t*, (spīrĭtum) haurĭo (4)
inherent insĭtus
inherit *v.t, use phr. with*, hēres
    (heir), *and* accĭpĭo **(to receive)**
inheritance hērēdĭtas, *f*
inherited hērēdĭtārĭus
inhibit *v.t*, interdīco (3)
inhospitable ĭnhospĭtālis
inhuman immānis, crūdēlis
inhumanity immānĭtas, *f*,
    crūdēlĭtas, *f*
inimitable nōn ĭmĭtābĭlis
iniquitous ĭnīquus, imprŏbus
iniquity imprŏbĭtas, *f*
initial *adj*, prīmus
initiate *v.t*, ĭnĭtĭo (1)
initiative (take the —) *v.i*, occŭpo
    (1)
inject *v.t*, īnĭcĭo (3)
injudicious inconsultus
injure *v.t*, nŏcĕo (2) *(with dat)*
injurious noxĭus, nŏcens
injury (of the body) vulnus, *n*;
    (disadvantage), dētrīmentum, *n*,
    iniūrĭa, *f*
injustice ĭnīquĭtas, *f*, iniūrĭa, *f*
ink ātrāmentum, *n*
inland mĕdĭterrānĕus
inlay *v.t*, insĕro (3)
inlet aestŭārĭum, *n*
inn dēversōrĭum, *n*, caupōna, *f*; **(—
    keeper)** caupo, *m*
innate insĭtus, innātus
inner intĕrĭor
innocence innŏcentĭa, *f*
innocent innŏcens, insons
innocuous innŏcŭus
innovate *v.t*, nŏvo (1)

innumerable innŭmĕrābĭlis
inobservant nōn perspĭcax
inoffensive innŏcens
inopportune ĭnopportūnus
inordinate immŏdĕrātus
inquest quaestĭo, *f*
inquire *v.i*, quaero (3) ab (*with abl*) *or* dē (*with abl*)
inquiry interrŏgātĭo, *f*; **(official),** quaestĭo, *f*
inquisitive cūrĭōsus
inquisitor quaesītor, *m*
inroad incursĭo, *f*
insane insānus, dēmens
insanity insānĭa, *f*, dēmentĭa, *f*
insatiable insătĭābĭlis
inscribe *v.t*, inscrībo (3) in (*with abl*)
inscription inscriptĭo, *f*
inscrutable obscūrus
insect bestĭŏla, *f*
insecure intūtus **(unsafe)**
insecurity *use adj*, intūtus
insensible (unfeeling) dūrus
inseparable *use phr*, quod sēpărāri nōn pŏtest **(that cannot be separated)**
insert *v.t*, insĕro (3)
inside *prep*, intrā (*with acc*)
inside *adv*, intus
inside *nn*, interĭor pars *f*
insidious insĭdĭōsus
insight (understanding) intellĕgentĭa, *f*
insignia insignĭa, *n.pl*
insignificant exĭgŭus, nullĭus mōmenti
insincere sĭmŭlātus
insincerity fallācĭa, *f*, sĭmŭlātĭo, *f*
insinuate *v.t*, insĭnŭo (1); **(hint),** signĭfĭco (1)
insinuating (smooth) blandus
insipid insulsus
insist *v.i*, insto (1); *v.t*, **(— on, demand)** posco (3), flāgĭto (1)
insolence contŭmācĭa, *f*, insŏlentĭa, *f*
insolent contŭmax, insŏlens
insoluble *use phr*, quod explĭcāri non pŏtest **(that cannot be explained)**
insolvent (to be —) *v.i*, nōn esse solvendo

inspect *v.t*, inspĭcĭo (3)
inspection *use vb,* inspĭcĭo (3), *or* lustro (1)
inspector (superintendent) cūrātor, *m*
inspiration (divine, poetic, etc) instinctus, *m*, afflātus, *m*
inspire *v.t*, īnĭcĭo (3) (*with acc. of thing inspired and dat. of person*); **(rouse),** accendo (3)
inspired (of persons) incensus
instal *v.t*, ĭnaugŭro (1)
instalment pensĭo, *f*
instance (example) exemplum, *n*; **(for—),** verbi grātĭā
instant *adj*, praesens
instant *nn*, mōmentum, *n*
instantly (at once) *adv*, stătim
instantaneous praesens
instead *adv*, măgis **(rather)**
instead of *prep*, prō (*with abl*); *with a clause, use* tantum ăbĕrat (ăbest) ut … ut
instigate *v.t*, instīgo (1)
instill *v.t*, instillo (1), īnĭtĭo (3)
instinct nātūra, *f*
instinctive nātūrālis
institute *v.t*, instĭtŭo (3)
institute, institution collĕgĭum, *n*; instĭtūtum, *n*
instruct *v.t*, dŏcĕo (2), ērŭdĭo (4); **(order),** praecĭpĭo (3)
instruction dĭscĭplīna, *f*, institutio, *f*; **(command),** mandātum, *n*
instructor măgister, *m*
instrument instrūmentum, *n*
instrumental (in doing something) ūtĭlis
insubordinate sēdĭtĭōsus
insufferable intŏlĕrābĭlis
insufficiency ĭnŏpĭa, *f*
insufficient haud sătis (*with genit*) **(not enough …)**
insult *nn*, contŭmēlĭa, *f*
insult *v.t*, contŭmēlĭam impōno (3) (*with dat*)
insulting contŭmēlĭōsus
insuperable *use phr*, quod sŭpĕrāri nōn pŏtest **(that cannot be overcome)**
insure against *v.t*, praecăvĕo (2)
insurgent rĕbellis, *m*
insurrection mōtus, *m*

intact intĕger
integral nĕcessārĭus **(necessary)**
integrity intĕgrĭtas, *f*
intellect mens, *f*, ingĕnĭum, *n*
intellectual ingĕnĭōsus
intelligence ingĕnĭum, *n*; **(news)**, nuntĭus, *m*
intelligent săpĭens, intellĕgens
intelligible perspĭcŭus
intemperate intempĕrans
intend *v.t*, in ănĭmo hăbĕo (2) (*with infinitive*)
intense ācer
intensify *v.t*, augĕo (2), incendo (3) **(inflame, rouse)**
intensify vīs, *f*
intent *adj*, intentus; **(to be — on)**, ănĭmum intendo (3) in (*with acc*)
intention consĭlĭum, *n*, prōpŏsĭtum, *n*
intentionally *adv*, consultō
inter *v.t*, sĕpĕlĭo (4)
intercede (on behalf of) dēprĕcor (1 *dep*) pro (*with abl*)
intercept *v.t*, **(catch)** excĭpĭo (3); **(cut off)**, interclūdo (3)
intercession dēprĕcātĭo, *f*
interchange *nn*, permūtātĭo, *f*
interchange *v.t*, permūto (1)
intercourse commercĭum, *n*, ūsus, *m*
interest *nn*, **(zeal)**, stŭdĭum, *n*; **(it is in the — of)**, intĕrest (*v.impers. with genit*); **(financial)**, fēnus, *n*, ūsūra, *f*
interest *v.t*, tĕnĕo (2), plăcĕo (2); **(— oneself in)**, stŭdĕo (2) (*with dat*)
interested attentus
interesting *use vb*. **to interest**
interfere *v.i*, sē interpōnĕre (3 *reflex*)
interim *adv*, **(in the —)** intĕrim
interior *adj*, intĕrĭor; *nn*, pars intĕrĭor, *f*
interject *v.t*, intericĭo (3)
interlude embŏlĭum, *n*
intermarriage connūbĭum, *n*
intermediate mĕdĭus
interminable infīnītus
intermingle *v.t*, miscĕo (2); *v.i*, sē miscēre (2 *reflex*)
intermission intermissĭo, *f*

internal intestīnus
international *use genit*, gentĭum **(of nations)**
internecine internĕcīnus
interpose *v.t*, interpōno (3)
interpret *v.t*, interprĕtor (1 *dep*)
interpretation interprĕtātĭo, *f*
interpreter interpres, *c*
interregnum interregnum, *n*
interrogate *v.t*, interrŏgo (1)
interrupt *v.t*, interpello (1), interrumpo (3)
interruption interpellātĭo, *f*
intersect *v.t*, sĕco (1) **(cut)**
interval intervallum, *n*, spătĭum, *n*
intervene *v.i*, intercēdo (3), sē interpōnĕre (3 *reflex*) (*both with dat*)
intervention intercessĭo, *f*
interview collŏquĭum, *n*
interview *v.t*, collŏquor (3 *dep*) cum (*with abl*) **(speak with)**
interweave *v.t*, intertexo (3), implĭco (1)
intestines intestīna, *n.pl*
intimacy consŭētūdo, *f*, fămĭlĭārĭtas, *f*
intimate *adj*, fămĭlĭāris
intimate *v.t*, signĭfĭco (1)
intimidate *v.t*, dēterrĕo (2)
intimidation terror, *m*, mĭnae, *f.pl*
into *prep*, in (*with acc*)
intolerable intŏlĕrābĭlis
intolerance sŭperbĭa, *f*
intolerant sŭperbus
intone *v.t*, căno
intoxicate *v.t*, ēbrĭum reddo (3) **(make drunk)**
intoxicate ēbrĭus
intoxication ēbrĭĕtas, *f*
intractable diffĭcĭlis
intrepid intrĕpĭdus
intricacy (difficulty) diffĭcultas
intricate diffĭcĭlis
intrigue dŏlus, *m*
intrigue *v.i*, dŏlīs ūtor (3 *dep*)
introduce *v.t*, intrōduco (3)
introduction intrōductĭo, *f*; **(letter of —)** littĕrae commendātĭcĭae, *f.pl*
intrude *v.i*, sē inculcāre (1 *reflex*)
intrusive *use phr*, qui interpellāre sŏlet **(who usually disturbs)**

intuition cognĭtio, *f*
inundate *v.t*, ĭnundo (1)
inundation ĭnundātĭo, *f*
inure *v.t*, assuēfăcĭo (3)
invade *v.t*, bellum infĕro (*irreg*)
  (*with dat*), invādo (3) in (*with*
  acc)
invader hostis, *c*
invalid *nn*, aeger, *m*
invalid *adj*, (of no avail), irrĭtus,
  infirmus
invalidate *v.t*, infirmo (1)
invariable constans
invasion incursĭo, *f*
invective convĭcĭum, *n*
inveigh against *v.i*, invĕhor (3 *dep*)
  in (*with acc.*)
inveigle *v.t*, illĭcĭo (3)
invent *v.t*, invĕnĭo (4)
invention (faculty) inventĭo, *f*;
  (thing invented), inventum, *n*
inventor inventor, *m*
inverse inversus
invert *v.t*, inverto (3)
invest *v.t*, (money), collŏco (1);
  (besiege) obsĭdĕo (2);
  (— someone with an office)
  măgistrātum committo (3) (*with*
  dat)
investigate *v.t*, exquīro (3),
  cognosco (3)
investigation investĭgātĭo, *f*,
  cognĭtĭo, *f*
investiture consĕcrātĭo, *f*
inveterate invĕtĕrātus
invidious (envious, hateful)
  invĭdĭōsus
invigorate *v.t*, vīres rĕfĭcĭo (3)
invincible invictus
inviolability sanctĭtas, *f*
  (sacredness)
inviolable invĭŏlātus
invisible caecus
invitation invītātĭo, *f*; (at your —),
  tŭo invītātu
invite *v.t*, invīto (1)
inviting blandus
invoke *v.t*, invŏco (1)
involuntary nōn vŏluntārĭus
involve *v.t*, involvo (3), illĭgo (1),
  hăbĕo (2)
invulnerable *use phr*, quod
  vulnĕrāri nōn pŏtest (that cannot
  be wounded)

inward *adj*, intĕrĭor
inwardly, inwards *adv*, intus
irascibility īrācundĭa, *f*
irascible īrācundus
iris īris, *f*
irk (it —s) pĭget (*v. 2 impers.*)
  (*with acc. of person*)
irksome grăvis, mŏlestus
iron *nn*, ferrum, *n*
iron *adj*, ferrĕus
ironical *use nn*, īrōnĭa, *f*, (irony)
ironmongery ferrāmenta, *n.pl*
irony īrōnĭa, *f*, dissĭmŭlātĭo, *f*
irradiate *v.t*, illustro (1)
irrational rătĭōnis expers (devoid of
  reason)
irreconcilable rĕpugnans
irrefutable firmus
irregular (out of the ordinary)
  ĭnūsĭtātus, extrăordĭnārĭus; (not
  well regulated) nōn ordĭnātus
irregularity vĭtĭum, *n*; *otherwise*
  use adjs. above
irrelevant ălĭēnus
irreligious ĭmpĭus
irremediable insānābĭlis
irreparable *use phr*, quod rĕfĭci
  nōn pŏtest (that cannot be
  repaired)
irreproachable intĕger, invictus
irresistible invicus
irresolute dubĭus
irretrievable irrĕpĕrābĭlis
irreverance ĭmpĭĕtas, *f*
irreverent ĭmpĭus
irrevocable irrĕpĕrābĭlis
irrigate *v.t*, irrĭgo (1)
irrigatin irrĭgātĭo, *f*
irritable stŏmăchōsus
irritate *v.t*, irrīto (1); (make worse),
  pēius reddo (3)
irruption (attack) incursĭo, *f*
island insŭla, *f*
islander insŭlānus, *m*
isolate *v.t*, sēpăro (1)
isolation sōlĭtŭdo, *f*
issue *nn*, (result), ēventus, *m*;
  (topic), rēs, *f*; (offspring),
  prōgĕnĭes, *f*
issue *v.i*, (proceed), ēgrĕdĭor (3
  dep); (turn out), ēvĕnĭo (4); *v.t*
  (give out), ēdo (3); (edicts, etc.)
  ēdīco (3)

isthmus isthmus, *m*
it *pron*, id, hoc, illud; *often expressed by 3rd person sing. of verb, e.g.* **it is,** est
itch *nn*, prūrītus, *m*; **(disease),** scăbĭes, *f*
itch *v.i*, prūrĭo (4)
item rēs, *f*
itinerant circumfŏrānĕus
itinerary ĭter, *n* **(route)**
itself see **himself**
ivory *nn*, ĕbur, *n*; *adj*, ēburnĕus
ivy hĕdĕra, *f*

J

jab *v.t*, fŏdĭo (3)
jabber *v.i*, blătĕro (1)
jackass ăsĭnus, *m*
jacket tŭnĭca, *f*
jaded dēfessus
jagged asper
jail carcer, *m*
jailer custos, *c*
janitor iānĭtor, *m*
January Iānŭārĭus (mensis)
jar olla, *f*, amphŏra, *f*, dōlĭum, *n*
jarring dissŏnus
jaunt excursĭo, *f*
javelin pīlum, *n*
jaws faucēs *f.pl*
jealous invĭdus
jealousy invĭdĭa, *f*
jeer at *v.t*, dērīdĕo (2)
jeering *nn*, irrīsĭo, *f*
jejune iēiūnus
jeopardize *v.t*, pĕrīclĭtor (1 *dep*)
jeopardy pĕrīcŭlum, *n*
jerk *v.t*, quătĭo (3)
jerkin tŭnĭca, *f*
jest *nn*, iŏcus, *m*
jest *v.i*, iŏcor (1 *dep*)
jester scurra, *m*
jetty mōles, *f*
Jew *nn*, Iūdaeus, *m*
jewel gemma, *f*
jeweller gemmārĭus, *m*
  jibe convīcĭum, *n*
jilt *v.t*, rĕpŭdĭo (1)
jingle *nn*, tinnītus, *m*
jingle *v.i*, tinnĭo (4)
job ŏpus, *n*
jockey ăgāso, *m*

jocose iŏcōsus
jocular iŏcŭlāris
jocund hĭlăris, iūcundus
jog *v.t*, fŏdĭco (1) **(nudge)**
join *v.t*, iungo (3); *v.i*, sē coniungĕre (3 *reflex*); **(— battle)** committo (3)
joiner lignārĭus, *m*
joint commissūra, *f*
joist tignum transversum, *n*
joke *nn*, iŏcus, *m*
joke *v.i*, iŏcor (1 *dep*)
joker iŏcŭlātor, *m*
jollity hĭlărĭtas, *f*
jolly hĭlăris
jolt *v.t*, concŭtĭo (3)
jostle *v.t*, pulso (1)
jot *v.t*, adnŏto (1)
journal commentārĭi dĭurni, *m.pl*
journey *nn*, ĭter, *n*
journey *v.i*, ĭter făcĭo (3)
journey-man ŏpĭfex, *c*
jovial hĭlăris
jowl gĕnae, *f.pl*
joy (outward) laetĭtĭa, *f*; **(inner),** gaudĭum, *n*
joyful laetus
joyless tristis
jubilant gaudĭo (*or* laetĭtĭā) exsultans **(exultant with joy)**
judge *nn*, iūdex, *m*
judge *v.t*, iūdĭco (1), aestĭmo (1)
judgement iūdĭcĭum, *n*
judicature iūdĭces, *m.pl*
judicial iūdĭcĭālis
judicious săpĭens
judiciously săpĭenter
judiciousness prūdentĭa, *f*
jug urcĕus, *m*
juggling tricks praestĭgĭae, *f.pl*
juice sūcus, *m*
juicy sūcōsus
July (before Caesar) Quintīlis (mensis); **(after Caesar),** Iūlĭus (mensis)
jumble *nn*, congĕrĭes, *f*
jumble *v.t*, confundo (3)
jump *nn*, saltus, *m*
jump *v.i*, sălĭo (4)
junction coniunctĭo, *f*
juncture tempus, *n*
June Iūnĭus (mensis)
junior mĭnor nātu, iūnĭor

juniper iūnĭpĕrus, *f*
jurisconsult iūrisconsultus, *m*
jurisdiction iūrisdictĭo, *f*
juror iūdex, *m*
jury iūdĭces, *m.pl*
just iustus
justice iustĭtĭa, *f*
justification sătisfactĭo, *f*
justify *v.t,* purgo (1), excūso (1)
justly *adv,* iustē
jut *v.i,* exsto (1)
juvenile iūvĕnīlis

K

keel cărīna, *f*
keen ācer; (mentally), perspĭcax
keenness (eagerness) stŭdĭum,
   n; (sagacity), săgācĭtas, *f*;
   (sharpness, etc.) ācerbĭtas, *f*
keep *nn,* arx, *f*
keep *v.t,* (hold), tĕnĕo (2), hăbĕo
   (2); (preserve), servo (1); (store),
   condo (3); (support, rear), ălo (3);
   (— apart), distĭnĕo (2); (— back),
   rĕtĭnĕo (2), dētĭnĕo (2); (— off),
   arcĕo (2); *v.i,* (remain), mănĕo (2)
keeper custos, *c*
keeping (protection) tūtēla, *f,*
   custōdĭa, *f*
keg dōlĭum, *n,* amphŏra, *f*
kennel stăbŭlum, *n*
kerb (stone) crĕpīdo, *f*
kernel nŭclĕus, *m*
kettle lĕbes, *m*
key clāvis, *f*
kick *nn,* calcĭtrātus, *m*
kick *v.i,* calcĭtro (1)
kid haedus, *m*
kidnap *v.t,* surrĭpĭo (3)
kidney rēn, *m*
kidney bean phăsēlus, *m, f*
kill *v.t,* nĕco (1), interfĭcĭo (3)
kiln fornax, *f*
kind *nn,* gĕnus, *n*; (of such a —),
   adj, tālis
kind *adj,* bĕnignus
kindle *v.t,* accendo (3), excĭto (1)
kindliness bĕnignĭtas, *f*
kindness bĕnĕfĭcĭum, *n*; (of
   disposition) bĕnignĭtas, *f*
kindred (relatives) consanguĭnĕi,
   m.pl; cognāti, *m.pl*

king rex, *m*
kingdom regnum, *n*
kingfisher alcēdo, *f*
kinsman nĕcessārĭus, *m*
kiss *nn,* oscŭlum, *n*
kiss *v.t,* oscŭlor (1 *dep*)
kitchen cŭlīna, *f*
kitten fēlis cătŭlus, *m* (the young of
   a cat)
knapsack sarcĭna, *f*
knave scĕlestus, *m*
knavery nēquĭtĭa, *f,* imprŏbĭtas, *f*
knavish nēquam (*indeclinable*);
   imprŏbus
knead *v.t,* sŭbĭgo (3)
knee gĕnu, *n*; (knock-kneed), *adj,*
   vārus
kneecap pătella, *f*
kneel gĕnu (gĕnĭbus) nītor (3 *dep*)
   (rest on the knee(s))
knife cutler, *m*
knight ĕques, *m*
knighthood dignĭtas ĕquestris, *f*
knit *v.t,* texo (3); (— the forehead)
   frontem contrăho (3)
knob bulla, *f,* nōdus, *m*
knock *v.t,* pulso (1); (— against),
   offendo (3); (— down), dēpello
   (3), dēĭcĭo (3)
knock, knocking pulsus, *m,*
   pulsātĭo, *f*
knoll tŭmŭlus, *m*
knot *nn,* nōdus, *m*
knot *v.t,* nōdo (1)
knotty nōdōsus
know *v.t,* scĭo (4); (get to —),
   cognosco (3); (person,
   acquaintance), nosco (3); (not
   to —), nescĭo (4)
knowing *adj,* (wise) prūdens
knowingly *adv,* consultō
knowledge scĭentĭa, *f*
known nōtus; (to make —), dēclāro
   (1)
knuckle artĭcŭlus, *m*

L

label tĭtŭlus, *m,* pittăcĭum, *n*
laborious lăbōrĭōsus
labour lăbor, *m,* ŏpus, *n*; (to be
   in —) *v.i,* partŭrĭo (4)

labour *v.i*, lăbōro (1), ēnītor (3 *dep*)
labourer ŏpěrārĭus, *m*
labyrinth lăbўrinthus, *m*
lace rētĭcŭlāta texta, *n.pl* **(net-like fabric)**
lacerate *v.t*, lăcĕro (1)
laceration lăcĕrātĭo, *f*
lack *nn*, ĭnōpĭa, *f*
lack *v.i*, ĕgĕo (2), cărĕo (*both with abl*)
lackey pĕdĭsĕquus, *m*
laconic brĕvis
lad pŭer, *m*
ladder scālae, *f.pl*
ladle trulla, *f*
lady mātrōna, *f*, dŏmĭna, *f*
ladylike lībĕrālis **(gracious)**
lag *v.i*, cesso (1)
laggard cessātor, *m*
lagoon lăcus, *m*
lair lătĭbŭlum, *n*
lake lăcus, *m*
lamb agnus, *m*; (agna, *f*)
lame claudus; **(argument, etc.)** lĕvis; **(to be —)** *v.i*, claudĭco (1)
lameness claudĭcātĭo, *f*
lament lāmentātĭo, *f*, complōrātĭo, *f*, ŭlŭlātus, *m*
lament *v.i, and v.t*, lāmentor (1 *dep*), dēplōro (1), lūgĕo (2)
lamentable lāmentābĭlis
lamented dēplōrātus, flēbĭlis
lamp lŭcerna, *f*
lampoon carmen rīdĭcŭlum et fāmōsum **(facetious defamatory verse)**
lance lancĕa, *f*, hasta, *f*
lancet scalpellum, *n*
land (earth, etc.) terra, *f*; **(region of country)**, rĕgĭo, *f*, fines, *m.pl*; **(native —)** pătrĭa, *f*
land *v.t*, expōno (3); *v.i*, ēgrĕdĭor (3 *dep*)
landing *nn*, ēgressus, *m*
landlord (innkeeper) caupo, *m*; **(owner)**, dŏmĭnus, *m*
landmark lăpis, *m*
landslide lapus (*m*) terrae
lane sēmĭta, *f*
language lingua, *f*; **(speech, style)**, ōrātĭo, *f*
languid languĭdus, rĕmissus

languish *v.i*, langueo (2), tabesco (3)
languor languor, *m*
lank (hair) prōmissus; **(persons)**, prōcerus
lantern lanterna, *f*
lap grĕmĭum, *n*, sĭnus, *m*
lap up *v.t*, lambo (3)
lapse *nn*, **(mistake)** peccātum, *n*; **(of time)**, fŭga, *f*
lapse *v.i*, **(err)** pecco (1); **(time)**, praetĕrĕo (4)
larcerny furtum, *n*
larch lărix, *f*
lard ădeps, *c*, lārīdum, *n*
larder *use* cella, *f*, **(store-room)**, *or* armārĭum, *n* **(food cupboard)**
large magnus
largeness magnĭtūdo, *f*
largess largītĭo, *f*
lark ălauda, *f*
larynx *use* guttur, *n* **(throat)**
lascivious lībīdĭnōsus
lash (whip) lōrum, *n*, flăgellum, *n*; **(eye —)**, pilus, m
lash *v.t*, **(whip)**, verbĕro (1); **(bind)**, allĭgo (1)
lass pŭella, *f*
last *adj*, ultĭmus, postrēmus, extrēmus; **(most recent)**, nŏvissĭmus, proxĭmus; **(at —)**, *adv*, tandem
last *v.i*, dūro (1), mănĕo (2)
lasting *adj*, dĭūturnus
lastly *adv*, postrēmo, dēnīque
latch pessŭlus, *m*
late sērus, tardus; **(dead)**, mortŭus; *adv*, sēro; **(— at night)** (*adv. phr.*), multā nocte
lately *adv*, nūper
latent occultus
lathe tornus, *m*
Latin Lătīnus; **(— language)**, lingua Lătīna, *f*
latitude (freedom, scope) lībertas, *f*
latter (the —) hic
lattice cancelli, *m. pl*
laud *v.t*, laudo (1)
laudable laudābĭlis
laugh *nn*, rīsus, *m*; **(loud —)**, căchinnus, *m*
laugh *v.i*, cachinno (1)

laughing-stock lŭdībrĭum, *n*
launch *v.t*, (a ship), dēdūco (3);
v.i, (launch out), insĕquor (3 *dep*)
laurel laurus; *f*; *adj*, laurĕus
lava massa lĭquĕfacta, *f*, (molten mass)
lavish *adj*, prōdĭgus, prŏfūsus
lavish *v.t*, prŏfundo (3)
law (a law) lex, *f*; (the law), iūs, *n*
lawful lēgĭtĭmus
lawless nĕfārĭus
lawn prātum, *n*
lawsuit līs, *f*
lawyer iūrisconsultus, *m*
lax dissŏlūtus
laxness rĕmissĭo, *f*, neglĕntĭa, *f*
laxity rĕmissĭo, *f*, neglĕgentĭa, *f*
lay *v.t*, pōno (3); (— aside), pōno
(3); (— foundations), iăcĭo (3);
(— an ambush), insĭdĭs collŏco (1);
(— down arms), ab armis discēdo
(3); (— eggs), ōva părĭo (3)
layer cŏrĭum, *n*, tăbŭlātum, *n*
laziness ignāvĭa, *f*
lazy ignāvus, pĭger
lead *nn*, plumbum, *n*; *adj*,
plumbĕus
lead *v.t*, dūco (3); (— a life, etc.),
ăgo (3); (— on, persuade),
addūco (3)
leader dux, *c*
leadership ductus, *m*; *or use phr.
in abl*, e.g. **under the — of
Brutus**, Brūto dŭce (with Brutus
leader)
leading *adj*, princeps
leaf frons, *f*, fŏlĭum, *n*; (paper)
schĕda, *f*
leafy frondōsus
league foedus, *n*, sŏcĭĕtas, *f*
league together *v.i*, coniūro (1)
leak *nn*, rīma *f*
leak (let in water) ăquam per
rīmas accĭpĭo (3)
leaky rīmōsus
lean *adj*, măcer, exīlis
lean *v.i*, innītor (3 *dep*); *v.t*,
inclīno (1)
leanness măcĭes, *f*
leap *nn*, saltus, *m*
leap *v.i*, sălĭo (4); (— down)
dēsĭlĭo (4)
leap year bĭsextĭlis annus, *m*

learn *v.t*, disco (3); (ascertain)
cognosco (3)
learned doctus
learning doctrīna, *f*, ērŭdītĭo, *f*
lease *nn*, conductĭo, *f*
lease *v.t*, condūco (3)
leash cōpŭla, *f*
least *adj*, mĭnĭmus; *adv*, mĭnĭmē;
(at —), *adv*, saltem
leather cŏrĭum, *n*
leave *nn*, (permission), pŏtestas,
f, permissĭo, *f*; (— of absence)
commĕātus, *m*
leave *v.i*, discēdo (3); *v.t*, rĕlinquo
(3), dēsĕro (3)
leave off *v.i. and v.t*, dēsĭno (3)
leavings *nn*, rĕlĭquĭae, *f. pl*
lecture *nn*, audītĭo, *f*, (hearing)
lecture *v.i*, schŏlas hăbĕo (2)
lecture-room schŏla, *f*
ledge *use adj*, ĕmĭnens
(projecting) *in agreement with a
noun*
ledger cōdex, *m*
leech hĭrūdo, *f*
leek porrum, *n*
leering *adj*, līmus
left *adj*, (opp. to right), sĭnister,
laevus; (remaining), rĕlĭquus
leg crus, *n*
legacy lēgātum, *n*
legal lēgĭtĭmus
legalize *v.t*, sancĭo (4)
legate lēgātus, *m*
legation lēgātĭo, *f*
legend fābŭla, *f*
legendary fābŭlōsus
leggings ŏcrĕae, *f. pl*
legible *use phr*, făcĭlis ad
lĕgendum (easy for reading)
legion lĕgĭo, *f*
legislate *v.i*, lēges făcĭo (3) (make
laws)
legislator lātor, (*m*) lēgum
(proposer of laws)
legitimate lēgĭtĭmus
leisure ōtĭum, *n*; (to be at —), *v.i*,
ōtĭor (1 *dep*)
leisurely *adj*, lentus
lend *v.t*, mūtŭum do (1) (give a
loan), commŏdo (1)
length longĭtūdo, *f*; (of time),
dĭūturnĭtas, *f*; (at —), *adv*, tandem

lengthen *v.t*, prōdūco (3), longĭōrem reddo (3)
leniency clēmentĭa, *f*
lenient mītis, clēmens
lentil lens, *f*
leper hŏmo lĕprōsus, *m*
leprosy lĕprae, *f. pl*
less *adj*, mĭnor; *adv*, mĭnus
lessen *v.i. and v.t*, mĭnŭo (3)
lesson dŏcŭmentum, *n*
lest *conj*, nē
let *v.t*, sĭno (3) permitto (3) (*with dat of person*); **(lease)**, lŏco (1); **(— go)**, dīmitto (3); **(— in)**, admitto (3); **(— out)**, ēmitto (3)
lethal mortĭfer
lethargic lentus
letter (of the alphabet) littĕra, *f*; **(epistle)**, littĕrae, *f. pl*, ĕpistŏla, *f*
lettering *nn*, littĕrae, *f. pl*
letters (learning) littĕrae, *f. pl*
lettuce lactūca, *f*
level *adj*, plānus; **(— place)**, *nn*, plānĭtĭes, *f*
level *v.t*, aequo (1); **(— to the ground)**, sterno (3)
lever vectis, *m*
levity lĕvĭtas, *f*
levy *nn*, dēlectus, *m*
levy *v.t*, **(troops)**, scrībo (3); **(taxes, etc.)**, impĕro (1), ĕxĭgo (3)
lewd incestus, impŭdīcus
lewdness incestum, *n*
liable obnoxĭus
liar hŏmo mendax
libellous fāmōsus
liberal lībĕrālis, largus
liberality lībĕrālĭtas, *f*, largĭtas, *f*
liberate *v.t*, lībĕro (1)
liberation lībĕrātĭo, *f*
liberty lībertas, *f*
librarian bĭblĭŏthēcārĭus, *m*
library bĭblĭŏthēca, *f*
licence lĭcentĭa, *f*; **(permission)**, pŏtestas, *f*
licentious dissŏlūtus
lick *v.t*, lambo (3)
lid ŏpercŭlum, *n*
lie *nn*, mendācĭum, *n*
lie *v.i*, **(tell a —)**, mentĭor (4 *dep*)
lie *v.i*, iăcĕo (2); **(rest)**, cŭbo (1); **(— ill)**, iăcĕo (2); **(— in wait)**, insĭdĭor (1 *dep*)

lieutenant lēgātus, *m*
life vīta, *f*, ănĭma, *f*; **(vivacity)**, vĭgor, *m*; **(— blood)**, sanguis, *m*
lifeless exănĭmis, exanguis
lifelike *use* sĭmĭlis **(similar)**
lifetime aetas, *f*
lift *v.t*, tollo (3)
ligament lĭgāmentum, *n*
light *nn*, lux, *f*, lūmen, *n*; **(to bring to —)**, in mĕdĭum prōfĕro (*irreg*)
light *adj* **(not dark)**, illustris; **(in weight)**, lĕvis; **(— armed)**, expĕdītus; **(trivial, of opinions, etc.)**, lĕvis
light *v.t*, **(illuminate)**, illustro (1); **(kindle)**, accendo (3)
lighten *v.t*, **(burden, etc.)**, lĕvo (1); *v.i*, **(of lightning)**, fulgĕo (2)
lighthouse phārus, *f*
lightly *adv*, lĕvĭter
lightning fulmen, *n*
like *v.t*, ămo (1)
like *adj*, sĭmĭlis (*with genit. or dat*), par (*with dat*)
like *adv*, sĭmĭlĭter; **(just as)**, sīcut
likelihood sĭmĭlĭtūdo, (*f*), vĕri
likely sĭmĭlis vĕri; *often use future participle, e.g.* **likely to come**, venturus
liken *v.t*, compăro (1)
likeness sĭmĭlĭtūdo (1)
likewise *adv*, ĭtem
liking *nn*, ămor, *m*, lĭbīdo, *f*
lily līlĭum, *n*
limb membrum, *n*, artus, *m. pl*
lime calx, *f*; **(tree)**, tĭlĭa, *f*
limit *nn*, finis, *m*, termĭnus, *m*
limit *v.t*, finĭo (4)
limitation finis, *m*
limited (small) parvus
limitless infīnītus
limp *adj*, **(slack)**, rĕmissus
limp *v.i*, claudĭco (1)
limping *adj*, claudus
limpid limpĭdus
linden tree tĭlĭa, *f*
line līnĕa, *f*; **(boundary —)**, finis, *m*; **(of poetry)**, versus, *m*; **(of battle)**, ăcĭes, *f*; **(front —)**, prīma ăcĭes, *f*; **(second —)**, princĭpes, *m. pl*; **(third —)**, trĭārĭi, *m. pl*; **(— of march)**, agmen, *n*

line *v.t*, **(put in —)**, instrŭo (3)
lineage stirps, *f*, gĕnus, *n*
linen *nn*, lintĕum, *n*; *adj*, lintĕus
linger *v.i*, mŏror (1 *dep*); cunctor (1 *dep*)
lingering *nn*, mŏra, *f*
link *nn*, **(of chain)**, ănŭlus, *m*
link *v.t*, coniungo (3)
lint līnāmentum, *n*
lintel līmen sŭpĕrum, *n*
lion lĕo, *m*; **(lioness)**, lĕaena
lip lābrum, *n*
liquefy *v.t*, lĭquĕfăcĭo (3)
liquid *nn*, lĭquor, *m*
liquid *adj*, lĭquĭdus
liquidate *v.t*, solvo (3)
liquor lĭquor, *m*
lisping *adj*, blaesus
list tăbŭla, *f*
listen (to) *v.t*, audĭo (4)
listener auscultātor, *m*
listless languĭdus
listlessness languor, *m*
literal *use*, prŏprĭus **(its own)**
literally *adv. phr*, ad verbum
literary (person) littĕrātus
literature littĕrae, *f. pl*
lithe flexĭbĭlis, ăgĭlis
litigation līs, *f*
litter (of straw, etc.) strāmentum, *n*; **(sedan)**, lectīca, *f*; **(of young)**, fĕtus, *m*
little *adj*, parvus, exĭgūus; **(for a — while)**, *adv*, părumper, paulisper
little *adv*, paulum
little *nn*, paulum, *n*, nonnīhil, *n*; **(too little)**, părum, *n*; *with comparatives*, paulo; *e.g.* **a little bigger**, paulo māior
littleness exĭgŭĭtas, *f*
live *v.i*, vīvo (3); **(— in or at)**, hăbĭto (1), incŏlo (3); **(— on)**, vescor (3 *dep*) **(**with *abl*); **(— one's life, etc.)**, vītam ăgo (3)
live *adj*, vīvus
livelihood victus, *m*
liveliness ălăcrĭtas, *f*
lively *adj*, ălăcer
liver iĕcur, *n*
livery vestītus, *m*
livid līvĭdus
living *adj*, vīvus

lizard lăcerta, *f*
load ŏnus, *n*
load *v.t*, ŏnĕro (1)
loaded ŏnustus
loaf pănis, *m*
loam lŭtum, *n*
loan mūtŭum, *n*, *or use adj*, mūtuus **(borrowed, lent)**
loathe *v.t*, ōdi **(defect)**
loathing *nn*, ŏdĭum, *n*
loathesome tēter
lobby vestĭbŭlum, *n*
local *use genit*. of lŏcus **(place)**
locality lŏcus, *m*
lock (bolt) claustra, *n. pl*; **(hair)**, crīnis, *m*
lock *v.t*, obsĕro (1)
locker capsa, *f*, armārĭum, *n*
locust lŏcusta, *f*
lodge *v.i*, dēversor (1 *dep*); **(stick fast)**, adhaerĕo (2) fixus; *v.t* **(accommodate temporarily)**, excĭpĭo (3)
lodger inquĭlīnus, *m*
lodgings dēversōrĭum, *n*
loft cēnācŭlum, *n*
loftiness altĭtūdo, *f*
lofty celsus, altus
log tignum, *n*
logic dĭălectĭca, *f*
logical dĭălectĭcus
loin lumbus, *m*
loiter *v.i*, cesso (1), cunctor (1 *dep*)
loiterer cessātor, *m*
loneliness sōlĭtūdo, *f*
lonely *adj*, sōlus
long *adj*, longus (*with acc. of extent of length*), *e.g.* **three feet long**, longus tres pĕdes; **(a — way)**, *adv*, prŏcul, longē; **(of time)**, dĭūtĭnus, dĭūturnus; **(how — ?)**, quam dĭū? **(for a — time)**, *adv*, dĭū
long *adv*, **(time)**, dĭū
long for *v.t*, dēsīdĕro (1), cŭpĭo (3)
longevity vīvācĭtas, *f*
longing *nn*, dēsīdĕrĭum, *n*
long-suffering *adj*, pătĭens
look at *v.t*, aspĭcĭo (3); **(— back)**, rēspĭcĭo (3); **(— down (upon))**, dēspĭcĭo (3); **(— for)**, quaero (3);

(**— round**), circumspĭcĭo (3); *v.i*
(**— towards**), specto (1); (**seem**),
vĭdĕor (2 *pass*)
look *nn*, aspectus, *m*;
(**appearance**), spĕcĭes, *f*;
(**expression**), vultus, *m*
looking glass spĕcŭlum, *n*
loom tēla, *f*
loop (winding) flexus, *m*
loophole fĕnestra, *f*
loose *adj*, laxus; (**at liberty**),
sŏlūtus; (**hair**), passus, prŏmissus;
(**dissolute**), dissŏlūtus
loose *v.t*, laxo (1), solvo (3)
loosely *adv*, sŏlūtē
loot *nn*, praeda, *f*
loot *v.t*, praedor (1 *dep*)
lop off *v.t*, ampŭto (1)
loquacious lŏquax
loquacity lŏquācĭtas, *f*
lord dŏmĭnus, *m*
lordly *adv*, rēgālis, sŭperbus
lordship (supreme power)
impĕrĭum, *n*
lore doctrīna, *f*
lose *v.t*, āmitto (3), perdo (3); (**—
heart**), ănĭmo dēfĭcĭo (3)
loss (act of losing) āmissĭo, *f*; (**the
loss itself**), damnum, *n*,
dētrīmentum, *n*; (**to be at a —**),
v.i, haerĕo (2)
lost (*adj*) āmissus, perdĭtus
lot (chance) sors, *f*; (**to draw — s**),
sortĭor (4 *dep*); (**much**), multum,
n
loth (unwilling) invītus
lottery sortītĭo, *f*
loud clārus, magnus
loudness magnĭtūdo, *f*
lounge *v.i*, (**recline**), rĕcŭbo (1)
louse pĕdīcŭlus, *m*
lousy pĕdīcŭlōsus
lout hŏmo agrestis
love *nn*, ămor, *m*
love *v.t*, ămo (1), dīlĭgo (3)
loveliness vĕnustas, *f*
lovely vĕnustus
lover ămātor, *m*, ămans, *c*
loving *adj*, ămans
low hŭmĭlis; (**sounds**); grăvis; (**—
born**), hŭmĭli lŏco nātus; (**price**),
vīlis; (**conduct, etc.**), sordĭdus; (**in
spirits**), *adv. phr*, ănĭmo dēmisso

low *v.i*, mūgĭo (4)
lower *comp. adj*, infĕrĭor
lower *v.t*, dēmitto (3); (**—
oneself**), sē ăbĭcĕre (3 *reflex*)
lowering mĭnax
lowest infĭmus
lowing mūgĭtus, *m*
lowlands lŏca, plāna, *n. pl*
lowness, lowliness hŭmĭlĭtas, *f*
lowly hŭmĭlis, obscūrus
loyal fĭdēlis
loyalty fĭdes, *f*
lozenge pastillus, *m*
lubricate *v.t*, ungo (3)
lucid lūcĭdus
lucidity perspĭcŭĭtas, *f*
luck fortūna, *f*, fors, *f*; (**good —**),
fēlīcĭtas, *f*; (**bad —**), infēlīcĭtas
luckily *adv*, fēlīcĭter
luckless infēlix
lucky fēlix, fortūnātus
lucrative quaestŭōsus
ludicrous rīdĭcŭlus
lug *v.t*, trăho (3)
luggage impĕdīmenta, *n. pl*
lugubrious lūgŭbris
lukewarm tĕpĭdus
lull *v.t*, sēdo (1); *v.i*, (**of wind**),
sēdor (1 *pass*)
lull *nn*, *use vb.* intermitto (3)
lumber scrūta, *n. pl*
luminary lūmen, *n*
luminous illustrus, lūcĭdus
lump massa, *f*
lunacy insānĭa, *f*, ălĭēnātĭo, *f*
lunar lūnāris
lunatic hŏmo insānus
lunch *nn*, prandĭum, *n*
lunch *v.i*, prandĕo (2)
lung pulmo, *m*
lurch *v.i*, ăgĭtor (1 *pass*) (**leave in
the —**), rĕlinquo (3)
lure *nn*, illex, *c*, illĕcĕbrae, *f. pl*
lure *v.t*, allĭcĭo (3)
lurid lūrĭdus
lurk *v.i*, lătĕo (2)
lurking in wait *use* insĭdĭor (1
dep) (**lie in ambush**)
luscious dulcis
lust *nn*, lĭbīdo, *f*
lust after *v.t*, concŭpisco (3)
lustful lĭbīdĭnōsus
lustiness vĭgor, *m*

lustre splendor, *m*
lusty vălĭdus
lute cĭthăra, *f*
luxuriance luxŭrĭa, *f*
luxuriant luxŭrĭōsus
luxurious luxŭrĭōsus, lautus
luxury luxus, *m*, luxŭrĭa, *f*
lying *adj*, **(telling lies)**, mendax
lynx lynx, *c*
lyre cĭthăra, *f*, fĭdes, *f. pl*
lyrical lўrĭcus

M

macebearer lictor, *m*
macerate *v.t*, măcĕro (1)
machination dŏlus, *m*
machine māchĭna, *f*
machinery māchĭnātĭo, *f*
mackerel scomber, *m*
mad insānus, vēcors, fŭrĭōsus; **(to
 be —)**, *v.i*, fŭro (3)
madden *v.t*, mentem ălĭēno (1)
 (with dat); **(excite)**, accendo (3)
maddening *adj*, fŭrĭōsus
madman hŏmo vēcors
madness insānĭa, *f*
magazine horrĕum, *n*; **(arsenal)**,
 armāmentārĭum, *n*
maggot vermĭcŭlus, *m*
magic *adj*, măgĭcus
magic *nn*, ars măgĭca, *f*
magician măgus, *m*
magistracy măgistrātus, *m*
magistrate măgistrātus, *m*
magnanimity magnănĭmĭtas, *f*
magnanimous magnănĭmus
magnet lăpis magnes, *m*
magnetic magnētĭcus
magnificence magnĭfĭcentĭa, *f*
magnificent magnĭfĭcus,
 splendĭdus
magnify *v.t*, amplĭfĭco (1),
 exaggĕro (1)
magnitude magnĭtūdo, *f*
magpie pīca, *f*
maid, maiden virgo, *f*; **(servant)**,
 ancilla, *f*
maiden *adj*, virgĭnālis
mail (letters) littĕrae, *f. pl*,
 ĕpistŏlae, *f. pl*; **(armour)**, lōrĭca, *f*
maim *v.t*, mŭtĭlo (1)
main *adj*, prīmus, praecĭpŭus

mainland contĭnens terra, *f*
maintain *v.t*, servo (1), sustĭnĕo
 (2); **(with food, etc.)**, ălo (3); **(by
 argument)**, affirmo (1)
maintenance *use vb*. servo (1) **(to
 maintain)**
majestic augustus
majesty māiestas, *f*
major *nn*, **(officer)**, praefectus, *m*
major *adj*, māior
majority māior pars, *f*
make *v.t*, făcĭo (3), effĭcĭo (3),
 fingo (3), reddo (3); **(compel)**,
 cōgo (3); **(appoint)**, crĕo (1); **(—
 for, seek)**, pĕto (3); **(— haste)**, *v.i*,
 festīno (1), accĕlĕro (1); **(—
 good)**, *v.t*, rĕpăro (1), sarcĭo (1);
 (— ready), praepăro (1); **(— up, a
 total, etc.)**, explĕo (2); **(— use of)**,
 ūtor (3 *dep*) *(with abl)*
maker făbrĭcātor, *m*
maladministration măla
 admĭnistrātĭo, *f*
malady morbus, *m*
malcontent cŭpĭdus nŏvārum
 rērum **(eager for innovations)**
male *adj*, mascŭlus, mās
male *nn*, mās, *m*
malediction dīrae, *f. pl*, **(curses)**
malefactor hŏmo mălĕfĭcus,
 nŏcens
malevolence mălĕvŏlentĭa, *f*
malevolent mălĕvŏlus
malice mălĕvŏlentĭa, *f*; **(envy)**,
 invĭdĭa, *f*
malicious mălĕvŏlus
malignant mălĕvŏlus
maligner obtrectātor, *m*
malignity mălĕvŏlentĭa, *f*
malleable ductĭlis
mallet mallĕus, *m*
maltreat *v.t*, vĕxo (1)
maltreatment vexātĭo, *f*
man (human being) hŏmo, *c*; **(opp.
 to woman, child)**, vĭr, *m*;
 (mankind), hŏmĭnes, *c. pl*; **(chess,
 etc.)**, latruncŭlus, *m*; **(fighting —)**,
 mīles, *c*
man *v.t*, **(ships, etc.)**, complĕo (2)
man-of-war (ship) nāvis longa, *f*
manacle *nn*, mănĭcae, *f. pl*,
 vincŭla, *n. pl*
manage *v.t*, admĭnistro (1), cūro
 (1), gĕro (3)

manageable tractābĭlis, hăbĭlis
management cūra, *f*,
   admĭnistrātĭo, *f*
manager prōcūrātor, *m*,
   admĭnistrātor, *m*
mandate impĕrātum, *n*,
   mandātum, *n*
mane (of horse) iŭba, *f*
manful vĭrīlis
manger praesēpe, *n*
mangle *v.t*, lăcĕro (1), lănĭo (1)
mangled truncus
mangy scăber
manhood pūbertas, *f*, tŏga vĭrīlis,
   f **(manly dress)**
mania insānĭa, *f*
maniac hŏmo vēcors, āmens
manifest *v.t*, ostendo (3), ăpĕrĭo
   (4)
manifest *adj*, mănĭfestus, ăpertus
manifestation ostentātĭo, *f, or use*
   vbs. above
manifold multĭplex
maniple (of a legion) mănĭpŭlus,
   m
manipulate *v.t*, tracto (1)
mankind hŏmĭnes, *c. pl*
manliness virtus, *f*
manly vĭrīlis
manner (way) mŏdus, *m*, rătĭo, *f*;
   (custom), mos, *m*; **(type)**, gĕnus,
   n; **(good manners)**, dĕcōrum, *n*
mannerism gestus prŏprĭus
manoeuvre (military) dēcursus, *m*;
   (trick), dŏlus, *m*
manoeuvre *v.i*, dēcurro (3)
manor praedĭum, *n*
manservant servus, *m*
mansion dŏmus magna, *f*
manslaughter hŏmĭcīdĭum, *n*
mantle palla, *f*, lăcerna, *f*
manual *adj, use* mănus **(hand)**
manual *nn*, **(book)**, lĭbellus, *m*
manufacture *nn*, făbrĭca, *f*
manufacture *v.t*, făbrĭcor (1 *dep*)
manufacturer făbrĭcātor, *m*
manumission mănūmissĭo, *f*
manure stercus, *n*
manuscript lĭber, *m*
many *adj*, multi (*pl*); **(very —)**,
   plūrĭmi; **(a good —)**, plērīque,
   complūres; **(as — as)**, tŏt ...
   quŏt; **(how — ?)**, quŏt?; **(so —)**,
   tŏt; **(— times)**, *adv*, saepĕ

map tăbŭla, *f*
map (to — out) *v.t*, dēsigno (1)
maple ăcer, *n; adj*, ăcernus
mar *v.t*, dēformo (1)
marauder praedātor, *m*
marble marmor, *n; adj*,
   marmŏrĕus
March Martĭus (mensis)
march *nn*, ĭter, *n*; **(forced —)**,
   magnum ĭter; **(on the —)**, *adv.*
   phr, in ĭtĭnĕre
march *v.i*, ĭter făcĭo (3); **(—**
   quickly), contendo (3); **(advance)**,
   prōgrĕdĭor (3 *dep*)
mare ĕqua, *f*
margin margo, *m, f*
marine *nn*, mīles classĭcus, *m*
marine *adj*, mărīnus
mariner nauta, *m*
maritime mărĭtĭmus
mark nŏta, *f*, signum, *n*,
   vestĭgĭum, *n*; **(characteristic)**, *use*
   genit. case of nn. with esse; e.g. it
   is the — of a wise man, est
   săpĭentis ...
mark *v.t*, nŏto (1); **(indicate)**,
   dēsigno (1); **(notice, observe)**,
   ănĭmădverto (3)
market fŏrum, *n*, măcellum, *n*;
   (cattle —), fŏrum bŏārĭum, *n*
market *v.t*, nundĭnor (1 *dep*)
market-day nundĭnae, *f. pl*, **(ninth**
   day)
marketing *nn, use vb.* vendo (3)
   (sell)
marketplace fŏrum, *n*
marriage conĭŭgĭum, *n*; **(—**
   feast), nuptĭae, *f. pl*; **(—**
   contract), pactĭo nuptĭālis, *f*
marriageable nŭbĭlis
marrow mĕdulla, *f*
marry *v.t*, **(— a woman)**, dūco
   (3); **(— a man)**, nūbo (3) (*with*
   dat)
marsh pălus, *f*
marshal appărĭtor, *m*
marshal *v.t*, **(troops, etc.)**,
   dispōno (3)
marshy păluster
martial bellĭcōsus; **(court —)**,
   castrense iūdĭcĭum, *n*
martyr martyr, *c*

martyrdom martўrĭum, *n*
marvel (miracle, etc.) mīrācŭlum, *n*
marvel at *v.t* mīror (1 *dep*)
marvellous mīrus, mīrābĭlis
masculine vĭrīlis
mash *nn*, farrāgo, *f*
mash *v.t* contundo (3)
mask *nn*, persōna, *f*; **(disguise)**, intĕgūmentum, *n*
mask *v.t*, **(oneself)**, persōnam indŭo (3); **(disguise)**, dissĭmŭlo (1)
mason structor, *m*
masonry structūra, *f*
mass mōles, *f*; **(of people)**, multĭtūdo, *f*
mass *v.t*, cŭmŭlo (1), ăcervo (1)
massacre *nn*, caedes, *f*
massacre *v.t*, trŭcīdo (1), caedo (3)
massive sŏlĭdus; **(huge)**, ingens
mast mālus, *m*
master dŏmĭnus, *m*; **(— of the household)**, păterfămĭlĭas, *m*; **(school —)**, măgister, *m*; **(skilled in …)**, use *adj*, pĕrītus
master *v.t*, **(subdue)**, dŏmo (1); **(knowledge, etc.)**, bĕne scĭo (4), disco (3)
masterful impĕrĭoūsus
masterly *adj*, bŏnus; **(plan, etc.)**, callĭdus
masterpiece ŏpus summā laude dignum **(work worthy of the highest praise)**
masterly (rule) dŏmĭnātus, *m*
masticate *v.t*, mandūco (1)
mastiff cănis Mŏlussus **(Molossian hound)**
mat stŏrĕa, *f*
mat *v.t*, implĭco (1)
match (contest) certāmen, *n*; **(equal)**, *adj*, pār; **(marriage —)**, nuptĭae, *f. pl*
match *v.t*, **(equal)**, aequo (1)
matchless ēgrĕgĭus
matching *adj*, **(equal)** pār
mate sŏcĭus, *m*; **(— in marriage)**, coniunx, *m*, *f*.
mate *v.i*, coniungor (3 *pass*)
material *nn*, mātĕrĭa, *f*
material *adj*, corpŏrĕus

materially *adv*, **(much)**, multum
maternal maternus
maternity māter, *f*, **(mother)**
mathematician măthēmătĭcus, *m*
mathematics măthēmătĭca, *f*
matter (substance) corpus, *n*, mātĕrĭa, *f*; **(affair)**, res, *f*; **(what is the — ?)**, quid est?; **(it matters, it is important)**, rēfert (*v. impers*)
mattress culcĭta, *f*
mature *adj*, mātūrus, ădultus
mature *v.t*, mātūro (1); *v.i*, mātūresco (3)
maturity mātūrĭtas, *f*
maudlin ĭneptus
maul *v.t*, mulco (1), lănĭo (1)
maw inglŭvĭes, *f*
maxim praeceptum, *n*
maximum *use adj*, maxĭmus **(biggest)**
May Māius (mensis)
may *v. auxiliary*, **(having permission to)**, lĭcet (2 *impers. with dat. of person allowed*), e.g. **you may go**, lĭcet tĭbĭ īre; **(having ability to)**, possum (*irreg*); *often expressed by subjunctive mood of verb*
maybe (perhaps) *adv*, fortassĕ
May Day Kălendae Māiae (first day of May)
mayor praefectus, *m*
maze *nn*, lăbўrinthus, *m*
meadow prātum, *n*
meagre măcer, iēiūnus
meagreness iēiūnĭtas, *f*
meal (flour) fārīna, *f*; **(food)**, cĭbus, *m*
mean *nn*, mŏdus, *m*
mean *adj*, **(middle, average)**, mĕdĭus; **(of low rank)**, hŭmĭlis; **(miserly)**, sordĭdus
mean *v.t*, signĭfĭco (1); **(intend)**, in ănĭmo hăbĕo (2)
meander *v.i*, **(of a river)**, sĭnŭōso cursu flŭo (3) **(flow on a winding course)**
meaning *nn*, signĭfĭcātĭo, *f*
meanness hŭmĭlĭtas, *f*; **(of disposition)**, sordes, *f. pl*
means (method) mŏdus, *m*; **(opportunity)**, făcultas, *f*; **(resources)**, ŏpes, *f. pl*; **(by no**

—), *adv*, haudquāquam, nullo mŏdo

meantime, meanwhile (in the —) *adv*, intĕrĕā, intĕrim

measure mensūra, *f*, mŏdus, *m*; **(plan)**, consĭlĭum, *n*; **(music)**, mŏdi, *m. pl*

measure *v.t*, mētĭor (4 *dep*)

measureless immensus

meat căro, *f*

mechanic făber, *m*, ŏpĭfex, *c*

mechanical māchĭnālis

mechanism māchĭnātĭo, *f*

medal, medallion phălĕrae, arum, *f. pl*

meddle *v.i*, sē interpōnĕre (3 *reflex*)

mediate *v.i*, sē interpōnĕre (3 *reflex*), intervĕnĭo (4)

mediator dēprĕcātor, *m*

medical mĕdĭcus

medicine (art of —) ars mĕdĭcīna, *f*; **(the remedy itself)**, mĕdĭcāmentum, *n*

mediocre mĕdĭŏcris

mediocrity mĕdĭŏcrĭtas, *f*

meditate *v.t*, cōgĭto (1)

Mediterranean Sea măre nostrum, *n*, **(our sea)**

medium *use adj*, mĕdĭus **(middle)**; **(through the — of)** per

medley farrāgo, *f*

meek mītis

meekness ănĭmus summissus, *m*

meet *v.t*, obvĭam fĭo (*irreg*) *(with dat)*; **(go to — , encounter)**, obvĭam ĕo (*irreg*) *(with dat)*; *v.i*, convĕnĭo (4); concurro (3)

meeting *nn*, conventus, *m*

melancholy *nn*, tristĭtĭa, *f*

melancholy *adj*, tristis

mellow mītis

mellow *v.i*, mātūresco (3)

melodious cănōrus

melody mĕlos, *n*

melon mēlo, *m*

melt *v.t*, lĭquĕfăcĭo (3); **(people, etc.)**, mŏvĕo (2); *v.i*, lĭquesco (3)

member (of a society) sŏcĭus, *m*; **(of the body)**, membrum, *n*

membrane membrāna, *f*

memoirs commentārĭi, *m. pl*

memorable mĕmŏrābĭlis

memorandum lĭbellus mĕmŏrĭālis

memorial mŏnŭmentum, *n*

memory mĕmŏrĭa, *f*

menace mĭnae, *f. pl*

menace *v.t*, mĭnor (1 *dep*)

menacing *adj*, mĭnax

mend *v.t*, rĕfĭcĭo (3), sarcĭo (4); *v.i*, **(in health)**, mĕlĭor fĭo (*irreg*) **(get better)**

mendacious mendax

mendicant mendīcus, *m*

menial *adj*, servīlis

mensuration rătĭo (*f*) mētĭendi **(system of measuring)**

mental *use genitive of* mens, *or* ănĭmus **(mind)**

mention *nn*, mentĭo, *f*

mention *v.t*, mĕmŏro (1), dīco (3)

mercantile mercātōrum **(of merchants)**

mercenary *adj*, mercēnārĭus

merchandise merx, *f*

merchant mercātor, *m*

merchant-ship nāvis ŏnĕrĭa, *f*

merciful mĭsĕrĭcors

merciless crūdēlis, inclēmens

mercury (quick silver) argentum vīvum, *n*; **(god)**, Mercŭrĭus

mercy mĭsĕrĭcordĭa, *f*

mere *adj*, sōlus, *or use emphathic pron*, ipse

merely *adv*, tantummŏdo

merge *v.i*, miscĕor (2 *pass*)

meridian circŭlus mĕrĭdĭānus, *m*

meridian *adj*, mĕrīdĭānus

merit *nn*, mĕrĭtum, *n*

merit *v.i*, mĕrĕor (2 *dep*)

meritorious dignus laude **(worthy of praise)**

merriment hĭlărĭtas, *f*

merry hĭlăris

mesh măcŭla, *f*

mess (confused state) turba, *f*; **(dirt)**, squālor, *m*

message nuntĭus, *m*

messenger nuntĭus, *m*

metal mĕtallum, *n*

metallic mĕtallĭcus

metamorphosis *use vb*, transformo (1) **(to change in shape)**

metaphor translātĭo, *f*

metaphorical translātus

meteor fax, *f*

method rătĭo, *f*

methodically ex ordĭne, *or use adv phr*, rătĭōne et vĭā **(by reckoning and method)**

metre nŭmĕrus, *m*

metrical mĕtrĭcus

metropolis căpŭt, *n*

mettle fĕrōcĭtas, *f*

mettlesome ănĭmōsus, fĕrox

mew *v.i*, **(cat)**, quĕror (3 *dep*)

mica phengītes, *m*

mid *adj*, mĕdĭus

midday *nn*, mĕrīdĭes, *m*

midday *adj*, mĕrīdĭānus

middle *adj*, mĕdĭus

middle *nn, use* mĕdĭus *in agreement with noun, e.g.* **the middle of the river**, mĕdĭus flŭvĭus

middling *adj*, mĕdĭŏcris

midnight mĕdĭa nox, *f*

midst *nn, use adj*, mĕdĭus

midsummer mĕdĭa aestas, *f*

midwife obstĕtrix, *f*

might (power) vīs, *f*

mighty fortis, vălĭdus, magnus

migrate *v.t*, ăbĕo (4)

migratory bird advĕna ăvis, *f*

mild mītis, clēmens, lēvis

mildew rōbīgo, *f*

mildness lēnĭtas, *f*

mile mille passus (*or* passŭum) **(a thousand paces)**

milestone mīlĭărĭum, *n*

military adj, mīlĭtāris; **(— service)**, stīpendĭa, *n. pl*

militate against *v.t*, făcĭo (3) contrā (*with acc*)

milk lac, *n*

milk *v.t*, mulgĕo (2)

milky lactĕus

mill mŏla, *f*, pistrīnum, *n*

miller mŏlĭtor, *m*

million dĕcĭēs centēna mīlĭa

millstone mŏla, *f*

mimic *v.t*, ĭmītor (1 *dep*)

mince *v.t*, concīdo (3)

mincemeat mĭnūtal, *n*

mind ănĭmus, *m*, mens, *f*; **(intellect)**, ĭngĕnĭum, *n*; **(to make up one's —)** constĭtŭo (3)

mind *v.t*, **(I — my own business)**, nĕgōtĭum mĕum ăgo (3)

mindful mĕmor (*with genit*)

mine *adj*, mĕus

mine *nn*, mĕtallum, *n*, cŭnīcŭlus, *m*

mine *v.i*, fŏdĭo (3)

miner fŏdĭens, *m*

mineral *nn*, mĕtallum, *n*

mineral *adj*, mĕtallĭcus

mingle *v.i*, sē miscēre (2 *reflex*)

miniature *nn*, parva tăbella, *f*

minimum *adj*, mĭnĭmus **(smallest)**

minister mĭnister, *m*, admĭnĭster, *m*

ministry (office) mĭnĭstĕrĭum, *n*

minor *nn*, pūpillus, *m*

minority mĭnor pars, *f*

minstrel tībīcen văgus **(wandering —)**

mint (plant) menta, *f*; **(coinage)**, mŏnēta, *f*

mint *v.t*, cūdo (3)

minute *adj*, exĭgŭus, mĭnūtus

minute *nn*, **(of time)**, mōmentum (*n*) tempŏris

miracle mīrăcŭlum, *n*

miraculous mīrus

mire lŭtum, *n*

mirror spĕcŭlum, *n*

mirth hĭlărĭtas, *f*

mirthful hĭlăris

misadventure cāsus, *m*

misanthropy *use phr*. ŏdĭum, (*n*) ergā hŏmĭnes **(hatred towards mankind)**

misapply *v.t*, ăbūtor (3 *dep with abl*)

misbehave *v.i*, mălĕ sē gĕrĕre (3 *reflex*)

miscalculate *v.i*, fallor (3 *pass*), erro (1)

miscalculation error, *m*

miscarriage (childbirth) ăbortus, *m*; **(— of justice)** error, (*m*) iūdĭcum

miscarry *v.i*, **(child)**, ăbortum făcĭo (3); **(fail)** frustrā *or* irrĭtum ēvĕnĭo (4)

miscellaneous vărĭus

mischief (injury, wrong) mălĕfĭcĭum, *n*

mischievous mălĕfĭcus; **(playful)**, lascīvus

misconduct *nn*, dēlictum, *n*

miscreant hŏmō scĕlestus

misdeed dēlictum, *n*

misdemeanour   dēlictum, *n*,
   peccātaum, *n*
miser   hŏmŏ ăvārus
miserable   mīser, infēlix
miserliness   ăvārītĭa, *f*
miserly   *adj*, ăvārus, sordĭdus
misery   mīsĕrĭa, *f*, angor, *m*
misfortune   rēs adversae, *f. pl*
misgiving   praesāgĭum, *n*
misgovern   v.*t*, mălĕ rĕgo (3)
misguided (deceived)   dēceptus
misinterpret   *v.t*, mălĕ interprĕtor (1
   dep)
misjudge   *v.t*, mălĕ iūdĭco (1)
mislay   *v.t*, ămitto (3)
mislead   *v.t*, dēpĭcĭo (3)
misplace   *v.t*, ălĭēno lŏco pōno (3)
   (put in an unsuitable place)
misprint   *nn*, mendum, *n*
misrepresent   *v.t*, verto (3);
   (disparage), obtrecto (1)
misrule   *v.t*, mălĕ rĕgo (3)
miss   *v.i*, (fail to hit or meet), ăberro
   (1), frustrā mittor (3 *pass*); *v.t*,
   (want), dēsīdĕro (1)
misshapen   dēformis
missile   tēlum, *n*
mission (embassy)   lēgātĭo, *f*; (task),
   ŏpus, *n*
misspend   *v.t*, perdo (3)
mist   nĕbŭla, *f*
mistake   error, *m*; (make a —), *v.i*,
   erro (1)
mistake   *v.t*, (for someone else)
   crēdĕre ălĭum esse
mistaken   falsus; (to be —), *v.i*, erro
   (1)
mistletoe   viscum, *n*
mistress (of the house, etc.)
   dŏmĭna, *f*; (sweetheart), pŭella, *f*,
   concŭbīna, *f*
mistrust   *v.t*, diffīdo (3 *semi-dep.*
   with dat)
misty   nĕbŭlōsus
misunderstand   *v.t*, haud rectē, *or*
   mălĕ, intellĕgo (3)
misunderstanding   error, *m*
misuse   *v.t*, ăbūtor (3 *dep. with*
   abl)
mitigate   *v.t*, mītĭgo (1), lēnĭo (4)
mitigation   mītĭgātĭo, *f*
mittens   mănĭcae, *f. pl*
mix   *v.t*, miscĕo (2); (— up

together), confundo (3); *v.i*,
   miscĕor (2 *pass*)
mixed   *adj*, mixtus; (indiscriminate),
   prōmiscŭus
mixture   mixtūra, *f*
moan   *nn*, gĕmĭtus, *m*
moan   *v.i*, gĕmo (3)
moat   fossa, *f*
mob   turba, *f*, vulgus, *m*
mobile   mōbĭlis
mock   *v.t*, illūdo (3) (*with dat*);
   dērīdĕo (2)
mockery   irrīsus, *m*, lūdĭbrĭum, *n*
mode   mŏdus, *m*, rătĭo, *f*
model   exemplum, *n*, exemplar, *n*
model   *v.t*, fingo (3)
moderate   mŏdĕrātus, mŏdĭcus
moderate   *v.t*, tempĕro (1)
moderation   mŏdus, *m*, mŏdĕrātĭo, *f*
modern   rēcens, nŏvus
modest   vērēcundus
modesty   vērēcundĭa, *f*, pŭdor, *m*
modify   *v.t*, immūto (1)
modulate   *v.t*, flecto (3)
moist   hūmĭdus
moisten   *v.t*, hūmecto (1)
moisture   hūmor, *m*
molar   dens gĕnŭīnus
mole (animal)   talpa, *f*; (dam, etc.),
   mōles, *f*; (on the body), naevus, *m*
molest   *v.t*, vexo (1), sollĭcĭto (1)
mollify   *v.t*, mollĭo (4)
molten   lĭquĕfactus
moment   punctum, (*n*) tempŏris; (in
   a —), *adv*, stătim; (importance),
   mōmentum, *n*
momentary   brĕvis
momentous   magni mōmenti (of
   great importance)
momentum   impĕtus, *m*
monarch   rex, *m*
monarch   regnum, *n*
monastery   mŏnastērĭum, *n*
money   pĕcūnĭa, *f*; (coin), nummus,
   m; (profit), quaestus, *m*
moneybag   fiscus, *m*
moneyed   pĕcūnĭōsus
moneylender   faenĕrātor, *m*
moneymaking   quaestus, *m*
mongrel   *nn*, hibrĭda, *c*
monkey   sīmĭa, *f*
monopolize   *v.i*, use *phr. with* sōlus
   (alone), *and* hăbĕo (2)

monopoly mŏnŏpōlĭum, *n*
monotonous *use phr. with* mŏlestus **(laboured)**, *or* sĭmĭlis **(similar)**
monster monstrum, *n*
monstrous **(huge)** immuanis; **(shocking)**, infandus
month mensis, *m*
monthly *adj*, menstrŭus
monument mŏnŭmentum, *n*
mood affectĭo (*f*) ănĭmi
moody mōrōsus
moon lūna, *f*
moonlight lūmen (*n*) lūnae; **(by —)**, ad lūnam
moonlit *adj*, illustris lūnā **(lighted up by the moon)**
moor lŏca dēserta, *n. pl*, **(a lonely place)**
moor *v.t*, **(ship, etc.),** rĕlĭgo (1)
moorhen fūlĭca, *f*
moot **(it is a — point)** nondum convĕnit … **(it is not yet decided …)**
mop *nn*, pēnĭcŭlus, *m*
mop *v.t*, dētergĕo (2)
moral *adj*, mōrālis; **(of good character)**, hŏnestus
moral *nn*, **(of a story)**, *use phr. wih* sĭgnĭfĭco (1) **(to indicate)**, *e.g.* haec fābŭla sĭgnĭfĭcat … **(this story indicates …)**
morale ănĭmus, *m*
morals, morality mōres, *m. pl*
moralize *v.i*, dē mōrĭbus dissĕro (3) **(discuss conduct)**
morbid aeger, aegrōtus
more *nn*, plus, *n* (*with genit*), *e.g.* **more corn**, plus frūmenti; (*adv. before adjs. or advs*) *use comparative of adj. or adv, e.g.* **more quickly**, cĕlĕrĭus; *otherwise use* măgis **(to a higher degree)** *or* pŏtĭus; **(in addition)**, amplĭus
moreover *adv*, praetĕrĕă
moribund mŏrĭbundus
morning *nn*, tempus mātūtīnum, *n*; **(in the —)**, *adv*, mānĕ
morning *adj*, mātūtīnus
morose tristis
morrow **(following day)** postĕrus dĭes, *m*
morsel offa, *f*
mortal *adj*, mortālis; **(causing death)**, mortĭfer
mortality mortālĭtas, *f*
mortar mortārĭum, *n*
mortgage pignus, *n*
mortgage *v.t*, oblĭgo (1)
mortification offensĭo, *f*
mortify *v.t*, **(vex)** offendo (3)
mosaic *adj*, tessellātus
mosquito cŭlex, *m*
moss muscus, *m*
mossy muscōsus
most *adj*, plūrĭmus *or* plūrĭmum, *n*, *with genit, of noun, e.g.* **most importance**, plūrĭmum grăvĭtātis; **(for the — part)**, *adv*, plērumque
most *adv*, *with adjs. and advs. use superlative*; *e.g.* **most quickly**, cĕlerrĭmē; *with vbs*, maxĭmē
mostly **(usually)** *adv*, plērumque
moth blatta, *f*
mother māter, *f*; **(-in-law)**, socrus, *f*
motherly *adj*, māternus
motion **(movement)** mōtus, *m*; **(proposal)**, rŏgātĭo, *f*
motion *v.t*, gestu indĭco (1) **(indicate by a gesture)**
motionless immōtus
motive cause, *f*
mottled măcŭlōsus
motto sententĭa, *f*
mould **(soil)** sŏlum, *n*; **(shape)**, forma, *f*
mould *v.t*, formo (1)
mouldiness sĭtus, *m*
mouldy mūcĭdus
moult *v.i*, plūmas exŭo (3) **(lay down feathers)**
mound tŭmŭlus, *m*
mount *v.t*, **(horse, ship, etc.),** conscendo (3); *otherwise*, scando (3)
mounted **(on horseback)** *adj*, ĕquo vectus
mountain mons, *m*, iŭgum, *n*
mountaineer hŏmŏ montānus
mountainous montŭōsus
mourn *v.t. and v.i*, lūgĕo (2)
mournful luctŭōsus; **(of sounds, etc.)**, lūgŭbris
mourning luctus, *m*, maeror, *n*
mouse mūs, *c*
mousetrap muscĭpŭlum, *n*
mouth ōs, *n*; **(of river)**, ostĭum, *n*

mouthful bucca, *f*, **(filled out cheek)**
mouth-piece interpres, *c*, ōrātor, *m*
movable mōbĭlis
move *v.t*, mŏvĕo (2); *v.i*, sē mŏvēre (2 *reflex*)
movement mōtus, *m*
moving *adj*, **(of pity, etc.)**, mĭsĕrābĭlis
mow *v.t*, sĕco (1)
much *adj*, multus; **(too —)**, nĭmĭus
much *adv*, multum; *with comparative adj. or adv*, multo, *e.g.* **much bigger**, multo māior
muck stercus, *n*
mucous *adj*, mūcōsus
mud, muddiness lŭtum, *n*
muddle *v.t*, confundo (3)
muddle *nn*, turba, *f*
muddy lŭtĕus
muffle *v.t*, obvolvo (3)
mug pōcŭlum, *n*
muggy ūmĭdus
mulberry (tree) mōrus, *f*; **(fruit)**, mōrum, *n*
mule mūlus, *m*
mullet mullus, *m*
multifarious vărĭus
multiplication multĭplĭcātĭo
multiply *v.t*, multĭplĭco (1)
multitude multĭtūdo, *f*
multitudinous plūrĭmus, crēber
mumble *v.i. and v.t*, murmŭro (1)
munch *v.t*, mandūco (1)
mundane *use genit. of* mundus **(world)**
municipal mūnĭcĭpālis
municipality mūnĭcĭpĭum, *n*
munificence mūnĭficentĭa, *f*
munificent mūnĭficus
munition appārātus (*m*) belli **(war-equipment)**, arma, *n. pl*
murder *nn*, caedes, *f*
murder *v.t*, nĕco (1), interfĭcĭo (3)
murderer hŏmĭcīda, *c*, sīcārĭus, *m*
murky cālĭgĭnōsus
murmur *nn*, murmur, *n*
murmur *v.i*, murmŭro (1)
muscle tŏrus, *m*, lăcertus, *m*
muscular lăcertōsus
muse *nn*, mūsa, *f*
muse *v.i*, mĕdĭtor (1 *dep*)
museum mūsēum, *n*
mushroom fungus, *m*

music mūsĭca, *f*, cantus, *m*
musical mūsĭcus; **(person)**; stŭdĭōsus mūsĭcōrum **(keen on music)**
musician mūsĭcus, *m*
muslim byssus, *f*
must *v.i*, **(obligation)**, *use gerundive: e.g.* **Carthage must be destroyed**, Carthāgo dēlenda est; **(duty)**, ŏportet (2 *impers*) *with acc. of person and infinitive, e.g.* **we must go**, nōs ŏportet īre
mustard sĭnāpi, *n*
muster *nn*, dēlectus, *m*
muster *v.t*, convŏco (1), rĕcensĕo (2); *v.i*, convĕnĭo (4)
musty mūcĭdus
mutable mūtābĭlis
mute *adj*, mūtus, tăcĭtus
mutilate *v.t*, mŭtĭlo (1), trunco (1)
mutilated mŭtĭlus, truncātus
mutiny sēdĭtĭo, *f*
mutiny *v.i*, sēdĭtĭōnem făcĭo (3)
mutter *v.i. and v.t*, musso (1)
muttering *nn*, murmur, *n*
mutton ŏvilla căro, *f*, **(sheep's flesh)**
mutual mūtŭus
muzzle (for the mouth) fiscella, *f*
my mĕus
myriad (10,000) dĕcem mīlĭa (*with genit*)
myrrh murra, *f*
myrtle myrtus, *f*
myself (*emphatic*), ipse; (*reflexive*) mē
mysterious occultus
mystery rēs abdĭta, *f*; **(religious, etc.)**, mystērĭa, *n. pl*
mystic mystĭcus
mystification ambāges, *f. pl*
mystify *use adv. phr*, per ambāges **(in an obscure way)**
myth fābŭla, *f*
mythology fābŭlae, *f. pl*

N

nab *v.t*, **(catch)**, apprĕhendo (3)
nag *nn*, căballus, *m*
nag *v.t*, incrĕpĭto (1), obiurgo (1)
nail (finger, toe) unguis, *m*; **(of metal)**, clāvus, *m*

nail *v.t*, clāvīs affīgo (3) **(fix on with nails)**

naive simplex

naked nūdus

nakedness *use adj*, nūdus **(naked)**

name nōmen, *n*; **(personal — , equivalent to our Christian name)**, praenōmen, *n*; **(— of a class of things)**, vŏcābŭlum, *n*; **(reputation)**, existīmātĭo, *f*

name *v.t*, nŏmĭno (1), appello (1)

nameless nōmĭnis expers **(without a name)**

namely (I mean to say) dīco (3)

namesake *use phr*, cui est ĭdem nōmen **(who has the same name)**

nap *v.i*, **(sleep)**, paulisper dormĭo (4)

napkin mappa, *f*

narcissus narcissus, *m*

narcotic miedĭcāmentum somnĭfĕrum, *n*, **(sleep-bringing drug)**

narrate narro (1)

narrative narrātĭo, *f*; *adj, use vb*, narro (1) **(narrate)**

narrator narrātor, *m*

narrow angustus

narrow *v.t*, cŏarto (1); *v.i*, sē cŏartāre (1 *reflex*)

narrowly (nearly, scarcely) *adj*, vix

narrow-minded anĭmi angusti **(of narrow mind)**

narrowness angustĭae, *f. pl*

nasal nārĭum **(of the nose)**

nastiness foedĭtas, *f*

nasty foedus

natal nātālis

nation gens, *f*

national dŏmestĭcus *or use genit. of* gens

nationality pŏpŭlus, *m*, cīvĭtas, *f*

native *adj*, indĭgĕna; **(— land)**, pătrĭa, *f*

native *nn*, indĭgĕna, *c*

nativity (birth) gĕnus, *n*, ortus, *m*

natural nātūrālis; **(inborn)**, nātīvus, innātus; **(genuine)**, sincērus

naturalize *v.t*, cīvĭtātem do (1) **(with dat) (grant citizenship)**

naturally sĕcundum nātūram **(according to nature)**

nature nātūra, *f*; **(character of persons)**, ingĕnĭum, *n*

naught nĭhil, *n*

naughty imprŏbus, lascīvus

nausea nausĕa, *f*

nauseate *v.t*, fastīdĭo (4)

nautical nāvālis, nautĭcus

navel umbĭlĭcus, *m*

navigable nāvĭgābĭlis

navigate *v.i*, nāvĭgo (1)

navigation nāvĭgātĭo, *f*

navy classis, *f*

nay (no) nōn

neaptide mĭnĭmus aestus, *m*

near *adv*, prŏpĕ, iuxtā

near *prep, adv*, prŏpĕ

nearly *adv*, prŏpĕ, fermē

nearness prŏpinquĭtas, *f*, vīcīnĭtas, *f*

neat nĭtĭdus, mundus

neatly *adv*, mundē

neatness mundĭtĭa, *f*

nebulous nĕbŭlōsus

necessarily *adv*, nĕcessārĭo

necessary nĕcessārĭus, nĕcesse

necessitate *v.t*, **(compel)**, cōgo (3)

necessity (inevitableness) nĕcessĭtas, *f*; **(something indispensable)**, rēs nĕcessārĭa, *f*

neck collum, *n*, cervix, *f*

necklace mŏnĭle, *n*

need *nn*, ŏpus, *n*, **(with abl. of thing needed or infinitive)**; **(lack)**, ĭnŏpĭa, *f*

need *v.t*, ĕgĕo (2) **(with abl)**

needful nĕcessārĭus, *or use nn*, ŏpus, *n*, **(necessity)**

needle ăcus, *f*

needless nōn nĕcessārĭus

needy ĕgens

nefarious nĕfārĭus

negation nĕgātĭo, *f*

negative *adj, use* nōn **(not)**, *or* nēgo (1) **(to deny)**

neglect *v.t*, neglĕgo (3), praetermitto (3)

neglect *nn*, neglĕgentĭa, *f*

negligent neglĕgens

negotiate *v.t*, ăgo (3) dē **(with abl. of thing)** cum **(with abl. of person)**

negotiation *use vb*, ăgo (3), **(to negotiate)**

negress Aethĭŏpissa, *f*

negro Aethĭops, *m*

neigh *v.i*, hinnĭo (4)

neigh, neighing   hinnītus, *m*

neighbour   vīcīnus, *m*; (of nations), *adj*, finĭtĭmus

neither   *pron*, neuter

neither   *conj*, nĕque, nĕc; neither ... nor, neque ... neque, *or* nec ... nec

nephew   fīlĭus, (*m*) frātris (*or* sŏrōris)

nerve   nervi, *m. pl*

nervous (afraid)   tĭmĭdus

nervousness   tĭmĭdĭtas, *f*, formīdo, *f*

nest   nīdus, *m*

nestle   *v.i*, haerĕo (2), ĭacĕo (2)

nestlings   nīdi, *m. pl*

net   rētĕ, *n*

net   *v.t*, plăgīs căpĭo (3) (catch with a net)

nettle   urtīca, *f*

network   rētĭcŭlum, *n*

neuter   neuter

neutral   mĕdĭus; (to be or remain —), neutri parti făvĕo (2) (to favour neither side)

neutralize   *v.t*, aequo (1), compenso (1)

never   *adv*, numquam

nevertheless   nĭhĭlōmĭnus, tămen

new   nŏvus; (fresh), rĕcens

newcomer   advĕna, *c*

newly   *adv*, nūper, mŏdo

newness   nŏvĭtas, *f*

news   nuntĭus, *m*

newspaper   acta dĭurna, *n. pl*

newt   lăcertus, *m*

next   *adj*, proxĭmus; (on the — day), *adv*, postrīdĭē

next   *adv*, (of time), dĕinceps, dĕinde; (of place), iuxtā, proxĭmē

nibble   *v.t*, rōdo (3)

nice (pleasant)   dulcis; (particular), fastīdĭōsus; (precise), subtīlis

nicety (subtlety)   subtīlĭtas, *f*

niche   aedĭcŭla, *f*

in the nick of time   in ipso artĭcŭlo tempŏris

nickname   agnōmen, *n*, (an additional name)

niece   fīlĭa (*f*) frātris (*or* sŏrōris)

niggardly   ăvārus, parcus

night   nox, *f*; (by, at —), *adv*, noctu, nocte; (at mid —), mĕdĭā nocte; (at the fall of —), prīmis tĕnĕbris

nightingale   luscĭnĭa, *f*

nimble   ăgĭlis

nine   nŏvem; (— times), *adv*, nŏvĭens; (— each), nŏvēni; (— hundred), nongenti

nineteen   undēvīginti

ninety   nōnāginta

ninth   nōnus

nip   *v.t*, vellĭco (1); (with frost), ūro (3)

nipple   păpilla, *f*

no   *adj*, nullus, nĭhil (*foll. by genit*)

no   *adv*, nōn, mĭnĭmē; (to say —), *v.i*, nĕgo (1)

nobility (of birth)   nōbĭlĭtas, *f*; (people of noble birth), nōbĭles, *m. pl*

noble (of birth)   nōbĭlis; (of birth or character), gĕnĕrōsus

nobody   nēmo, *m, f*

nocturnal   nocturnus

nod   *v.i*, nūto (1); (assent), annŭo (3)

nod   *nn*, nūtus, *m*

noise   strĕpĭtus, *m*, sŏnĭtus, *m*; (of shouting), clāmor, *m*; (to make a —), *v.i*, strĕpo (3)

noiseless   tăcĭtus

noisily   *adv*, cum strĕpĭtu

noisy   use a *phr. with* strĕpo (to make a noise)

nomadic   văgus

nominal   use nōmen (name)

nominally   *adv*, nōmĭne

nominate   *v.t*, nōmĭno (1)

nomination   nōmĭnātĭo, *f*

nominee   use vb. nōmĭno, (name)

nonchalant   aequo ănĭmo (with unruffled mind)

nondescript   non insignis

none   nullus

nonentity   nĭhil, *n*

nonsense   nūgae, *f. pl*, ĭneptĭae, *f. pl*

nonsensical   ĭneptus, absurdus

nook   angŭlus, *m*

noon   mĕrīdĭes, *m*; (at —), *adv*, mĕrīdĭē; *adj*. mĕrīdĭanus

noose   lăquĕus, *m*

nor   *conj*, nĕc, nĕque

normal (usual)   ūsĭtātus

north   *nn*, septentrĭōnes, *m. pl*

north, northern, northerly   *adj*, septentrĭonālis

north-east wind ăquĭlo, *m*
North Pole arctos, *f*
northwards versus ad
  septentrĭōnes
north wind ăquĭlo, *m*
nose nāsus, *m*, nāres, *f. pl*
  (nostrils)
not nōn, haud; (— at all), *adv*,
  haudquāquaml **(not even ...)**, nĕ
  ... quĭdem; **(and not)**, nĕc, nĕque;
  (in commands), e.g. do not go,
  nōli īre
notable insignis, mĕmŏrăbĭlis
notary scrība, *m*
notch *nn*, incīsŭra, *f*
notch *v.t*, incīdo (3)
note (explanatory, etc.) adnŏtātĭo,
  f; **(mark)**, nŏta, *f*; **(letter)**, littĕrae,
  f. pl
note v.t, **(notice)**, ănĭmadverto (3);
  (down), ēnŏto (*i*)
notebook commentārĭi, *m. pl*
noted (well-known) insignis
nothing nĭhil, *n*; **(good for —)**,
  nēquam
nothingness nĭhĭlum, *n*
notice *v.t*, ănĭmadverto (3)
notice *nn*, **(act of noticing)**,
  ămĭmadversĭo, f; **(written —)**,
  prōscriptĭo, *f*
noticeable insignis
notification dēnuntĭātĭo, *f*
notify *v.t*, dēnuntĭo (1)
notion nōtĭo, *f*
notoriety infāmĭa, *f*
notorious nōtus, fāmōsus
notwithstanding *adv*, nĭbĭlōmĭnus,
  tămen
nought nĭhil
noun nōmen, *n*, **(name)**
nourish *v.t*, ălo (3)
nourishment ălĭmentum, *n*
novel *nn*, **(story)**, fābŭla, *f*
novel *adj*, **(new)**, nŏvus
novelist fābŭlārum, scriptor, *m*,
  (writer of stories)
novelty (strangeness) nŏvĭtas, *f*
November Nŏvember (mensis)
novice tīro, *m*
now (at the present time) *adv*.
  nunc; **(at the time of the action)**,
  iam; **(just —)**, mŏdŏ; **(now ...
  now)**, mŏdŏ ... mŏdŏ; **(— and**

then), ălĭquandŏ
nowadays *adv*, nunc
nowhere *adv*, nusquam
noxious nŏcens
nozzle nāsus, *m*
nude nūdus
nudge *v.t*, fŏdĭco (1)
nuisance incŏmmŏdum, *n*, or use
  adj, mŏlestus **(troublesome)**
null irrĭtus, vānus
nullify *v.t*, irrĭtum făcĭo (3)
numb torpens; **(to be —)**, *v.i*,
  torpĕo (2)
numb *v.t*, torpĕfăcĭo (3)
number *nn*, nŭmĕrus, *m*; **(what —,
  how many?)**, quot?; **(a large —)**,
  multĭtūdo, *f*
number *v.t*, nŭmĕro (1)
numbering (in number) ad *(with
  acc)*
numberless innŭmĕrābĭlis
numbness torpor, *m*
numerically *adv*, nŭmĕro
numerous plūrĭmi, crēber
nun mŏnăcha, *f*
nuptial nuptĭālis, iŭgālis
nuptials nuptĭae, *f.pl*
nurse nūtrix, *f*
nurse *v.t*, **(the sick)**, cŭro (1);
  (cherish), fŏvĕo (2)
nursery (for plants) sēmĭnārĭum, *n*
nurture ēdūcātĭo, *f*
nut, nut tree nux, *f*
nutriment ălĭmentum, *n*
nutrition ălĭmentum, *n*
nutritious vălens
nutshell pŭtāmen, *n*
nymph nympha, *f*

O

o! oh! o! oh!; **(Oh that ...)** ŭtĭnam
  ...
oak quercus, *f*; **(holm —)**, īlex, *f*;
  (oak-wood), rōbur, *n*
oak, oaken *adj*, quernus
oakum stuppa, *f*
oar rēmus, *m*
oarsmen rēmĭges, *m. pl*
oats ăvēna, *f*
oath iusiūrandum; *n*; **(to take an —
)**, *v.i*, iusiūrandum accĭpĭo (3);
  (military —), săcrāmentum, *n*

oatmeal fărīna, ăvēnācĕa, *f*
obdurate obstĭnātus, dūrus
obedience ŏbēdĭentĭa, *f*; *or use vb*, pārĕo (2) **(to obey, *with dat*)**
obeisance (to make an —) ădōro (1) **(reverence)**
obelisk ŏbĕliscus, *m*
obese ŏbēsus
obey *v.i. and v.t*, pārĕo (2) (*with dat*), ŏbēdĭo (4) (*with dat*)
object *nn*, **(thing)**, rēs, *f*; **(aim)**, consĭlĭum, n. fīnis, m; **(to be an — of hatred)** ŏdĭo esse (*irreg*)
object *v.t*, rĕcūso (1), nōlo (*irreg*)
objection *use vb*, rĕcūso (1) **(object to)**
objectionable ingrātus, *m*
objective *nn*, quod petitur **(that is sought)**
obligation (moral) offĭcĭum, *n*; **(legal)**, oblĭgātĭo *f*; **(religious — , conscientiousness)**, rēlĭgĭo, *f*; **(to put someone under an —)**, *v.t*, obstringo (3); **(to be under an —)**, *v.i*, dēbĕo (2)
obligatory (it is —) ŏportet (2 *impers*) *or use gerundive of vb*
oblige *v.t*, obstringo (3); **(compel)**, cōgo (3)
obliging cōmis
oblique (slanting) oblīquus
obliterate *v.t*, dēlĕo (2)
oblivion oblīvĭo, *f*
oblivious immĕmor
oblong *adj*, oblongus
obloquy vĭtŭpĕrātĭo, *f*
obnoxious invīsus, noxĭus
obscene obscēnus
obscenity obscēnĭtas, *f*
obscure obscūrus, caecus, rĕcondĭtus; **(of birth, etc.)**, hŭmĭlis
obscure *v.t*, obscūro (1)
obscurity obscūrĭtas, *f*
obsequies exsĕquĭae, *f*, *pl*
obsequious obsĕquens, offĭcĭōsus
observance observantĭa, *f*, conservātĭo *f*; **(practice)**, rītus, *m*
observant attentus, dīlĭgens
observation observātĭo, *f*; **(attention)**, ănĭmadversĭo, *f*; **(remark)**, dictum, *n*
observatory spĕcŭla, *f*
observe *v.t*, observo (1),

ănĭmadverto (3); **(remark)**, dīco (3); **(maintain)**, conservo (1)
observer spectātor, *m*
obsolete obsŏlētus; **(to become —)**, *v.i*, obsŏlesco (3), sĕnesco (3)
obstacle impĕdīmentum, *n*
obstinacy pertĭnācĭa, *f*
obstinate pertĭnax
obstreperous (noisy) vŏcĭfĕrans
obstruct *v.t*, obstrŭo (3), obsto (1) (*with dat*)
obstruction impĕdīmentum, *n*
obtain *v.t*, ădĭpiscor (3 *dep*), nanciscor (3 *dep*), consĕquor (3 *dep*), **(— possession of)**, pŏtĭor (4 *dep*, *with abl*)
obtrude *v.t*, inculco (1)
obtrusive mŏlestus
obtuse hĕbes
obviate *v.t*, **(meet)**, obvĭam ĕo (4 *irreg*) (*with dat*)
obvious ăpertus, mănĭfestus
occasion (opportunity) occāsĭo, *f*; **(cause)**, causa, *f*; **(on that —)**, illo tempŏre
occasion *v.t*, mŏvĕo (2), fĕro (*irreg*)
occasionally *adv*, interdum, rāro
occult occultus, arcānus
occupancy possessĭo, *f*
occupant possessor, *m*
occupation (act of —) *use vb*, occŭpo (1); **(employment)**, quaestus, *m*; nĕgōtĭum, *n*
occupy *v.t*, occŭpo (1), obtĭnĕo (2); **(to be occupied with something)**, *v.b*, tĕnĕor (2 *pass*)
occur *v.i*. **(take place)**, accĭdo (3); **(come into the mind)**, in mentem vēnĭo (4), sŭbĕo (4) (*with dat*)
occurrence rēs, *f*
ocean ōcĕănus, *m*
ochre ōchra, *f*
octagon octōgōnum, *n*
October Octōber (mensis)
oculist ŏcŭlārĭus mĕdĭcus, *m*
odd (numbers, etc.) impar; **(strange)**, nŏvus
odds (to be at — with) *v.i*, dissĭdĕo (2) ab (*with abl*)
odious ŏdĭōsus, invīsus
odium invĭdĭa, *f*, ŏdĭum, *n*
odorous ŏdōrātus

odour ŏdor, *m*

of *usually the genit. of the noun,* e.g. **the head of the boy,** căput pŭĕri; **(made —),** ex *(with abl)*; **(about, concerning)** dē *(with abl)*

off *adv, often expressed by prefix* ab- *with vb,* e.g. **to cut off,** abscīdo (3); **(far —),** *adv,* prŏcul; **(a little way —),** *prep and adv,* prŏpe

offal (waste) quisquĭlĭae, *f.pl*

offence offensĭo, *f;* **(crime, etc.)** dēlictum, *n;* **(to take — at),** aegrē fĕro *(irreg.)*

offend *v.t,* offendo (3), laedo (3); **(to be offended),** aegrē fĕro (irreg) **(tolerate with displeasure)**

offensive *adj,* ŏdĭōsus, grăvis

offensive *nn,* **(military),** *use phr,* bellum infĕro *(irreg)* **(to inflict war)**

offer *nn,* condĭcĭo, *f*

offer *v.t,* offĕro *(irreg)*; **(stretch out),** porrĭgo (3); **(give),** do (1)

offering (gift) dōnum, *n*

office (political power) măgistrātus m; **(duty),** offĭcĭum, *n;* **(place of business),** fŏrum, *n*

officer (military) praefectus, *m*

official *nn,* măgistrātus, *m,* mĭnister, *m*

official *adj.* **(state),** pūblĭcus

officiate *v.i,* **(perform),** fungor (*3 dep*)

officious mŏlestus

offing, (in the —) *use* longē **(far off),** *or* prŏpe **(near)** *acc. to sense*

offshoot surcŭlus, *m*

offspring prōgĕnĭes, *f* lībĕri, *m, pl*

often *adv,* saepĕ; **(how — ?),** quŏtĭes?; **(so —),** *adv,* tŏtĭes

ogle *v.t,* ŏcŭlis līmis intŭĕor (*2 dep*) **(look at with sidelong glances)**

oil ŏlĕum, *n*

oily ŏlĕācĕus

ointment unguentum, *n*

old vĕtus; **(of persons),** sĕnex; **(so many years — , of persons),** nātus *(with acc. of extent of time),* e.g. **three years old,** tres annos nātus; **(— age),** sĕnectus, *f;* **(— man),** sĕnex, *m;* **(— woman),** ănus, *f*

olden priscus

oldness vĕtustas, *f*

oligarchy dŏmĭnātĭo, *(f)* paucōrum **(rule of a few)**

olive (tree) ŏlĕa, *f*

Olympic *adj,* Ōlympĭcus; **(— Games),** Ōlympĭa, *n. pl*

omelette lăgănum, *n*

omen omen, *n*

ominous infaustus

omission praetermissĭo, *f*

omit *v.t,* ŏmitto (3), praetermitto (3)

omnipotent omnĭpotens

on *prep,* in *(with abl)*; **(in the direction of,** e.g. **on the right),** ā, āb *(with abl)*; **(— everyside),** *adv,* undĭque; **(of time),** *abl case,* e.g. **on the Ides of March,** Īdĭbus Martĭis; **(about a subject)** dē *(with abl)*

once *num. adv,* sĕmel; **(— upon a time),** ōlim, ălĭquandŏ; **(at — , immediately),** stătim; **(at the same time),** sĭmul

one *num. adj.* ūnus; **(in — s, singly),** *adv,* singillātim, *adj,* singŭli; **(at — time),** *adv,* ălĭquandŏ; **(one ... another),** ălĭus ... ălĭus **(one ... the other),** alter ... alter; **(a certain),** quīdam; **(indefinite),** *use 2nd pers sing. of the vb*

onerous grăvis

oneself *(emphatic)* ipse; *(reflexive),* sē

one-sided ĭnaequālis

onion caepa, *f*

onlooker circumstans, *m*

only *adj,* ūnus, sōlus, ūnĭcus

only *adv,* sōlum, tantum, mŏdŏ; **(not only ...),** non mŏdŏ ...

onset impĕtus, *m*

onwards *adv,* porro, *often use compound vb. with* pro, e.g. prōcĕdĕre (3) **(to go onwards)**

ooze *nn,* ūlīgo, *f*

ooze *v.i,* māno (1)

oozy ūlīgĭnōsus

opal ŏpălus, *m*

opaque caecus

open *v.t,* ăpĕrĭo (4), pătĕfăcĭo (3), pandi (3); **(inaugurate),** consĕcro

(1); *v.i*, sē ăpĕrīre (*4 reflex*); **(gape open)**, hisco (3)
open *adj*, ăpertus; **(wide** — **),** pătens, hĭans; **(to lie, stand or be** — **)** pătĕo (2); **(— handed),** *adj*, lībĕrālis
opening (dedication) consĕcrātĭo, *f*; **(hole),** fŏrāmen, *n*; **(opportunity),** occāsĭo, *f*
openly *adv*, pălam
operate *v.t*, **(set in motion),** mŏvĕo (2); *v.i*, **(in war),** rem gĕro (3)
operation (task) ŏpus, n; **(military** — **),** rēs bellĭca, *f*; **(naval** — **),** rēs mărītĭma, *f*
operative *adj*, effĭcax
opiate mĕdĭcāmentum somnĭfĕrum, *n*, **(sleep-bringing drug)**
opinion sententĭa, *f*, ŏpīnĭo, *f*, existĭmātĭo, *f*
opium ŏpĭum, *n*
opponent adversārĭus, *m*
opportune opportūnus
opportunity occāsĭo, *f*, cŏpĭa, *f*, făcultas, *f*
oppose *v.t*, oppōno (3); **(resist),** rĕsisto (*3 with dat*), adversor (*1 dep*)
opposite *adj*, adversus, contrārĭus, dīversus
opposite (to) *prep*, contrā (*with acc*)
opposition (from people) *use partic*, adversans *or* rĕsistens; **(from a party),** *use* factĭo, *f*, **(party)**
oppress *v.t*, opprĭmo (3)
oppression (tyranny) iniūrĭa, *f*
oppressive grăvis, mŏlestus
oppressor tўrannus, *m*
opprobrious turpis
optical *adj*, *use genit, case of* ŏcŭlus, *m*, **(eye)**
option optĭo, *f*
opulence ŏpŭlentĭa, *f*, ŏpes, *f*, *pl*
opulent dīves, lŏcŭples
or aut, vel; **(either ... or),** aut ... aut, vel ... vel; **(whether ... or)** (*questions*), ŭtrum ... an; **(or not)** (*direct questions*), annon, (*indirect questions*), necne
oracle ōrācŭlum, *n*

oral *use* vox **(voice)**
oration ōrātĭo, *f*
orator ōrātor, *m*
oratory ars ōrātōrĭa, *f*
orb, orbit orbis, *m*
orchard pōmārĭum, *n*
orchid orchis, *f*
ordain *v.t*, ēdīco (3), stătŭo (3)
ordeal discrīmen, *n*
order *nn*, **(arrangement),** ordo, *m*; **(in** — **),** *adv*, ordĭne; **(command, direction),** iussum, *n*; **(class, rank),** ordo, *m*; **(in** — **to),** ut
order *v.t*, **(command),** iŭbĕo (2); **(arrange),** dispōno (3)
orderly *adj*, **(behaviour),** mŏdestus; **(arrangement),** ordĭnātus dispŏsĭtus
orderly *nn*, stător, *n*
ordinary ūsĭtātus, mĕdĭŏcris
ordnance tormenta, *n. pl*
ore aes, *n*
organ (of the body) membrum, *n*
organization dispŏsĭtĭo, *f*
organize *v.t*, ordĭno (1)
orgies orgĭa, *n. pl*; **(revelry),** cōmissātĭo, *f*
orient ŏrĭens, *m*
oriental *use genit. of* ŏrĭens **(orient)**
orifice fŏrāmen, *n*, os, *n*
origin ŏrīgo, *f*, princĭpĭum, *n*
original principālis, antīquus, (one's own), prŏprĭus
originally *adv*, princĭpĭo, ĭnĭtĭo
originate *v.i*, ŏrĭor (*4 dep*)
originator auctor, *m*
ornament *nn*, ornămentum, *n*
ornament *v.t*, orno (1)
ornate *adj*, ornātus, pictus
orphan orbus, *m*
oscillate *v.i*, quătĭor (3 pass)
oscillation *use vb*. quătĭor (*above*) (*3 pass*)
osier *nn*, vīmen, *n*
osier *adj*, vīmĭnĕus
osprey ossĭfrăgus, *m*
ostensible *use adv. below*
ostensibly *adv*, per spĕcĭem
ostentation ostentātĭo, *f*
ostentatious glōrĭōsus
ostler ăgāso, *m*
ostracize *v.t*, vīto (1) **(avoid)**

ostrich strūthĭŏcămēlus, *m*

other *adj*, ălĭus; (the — of two), alter; (the others, the rest) cētĕri

others *adj*, (belonging to —), ălĭēnus

otherwise *adv*, (differently), ălĭter; (in other respects also), ălĭoqui

otter lūtra, *f*

ought *v. auxil*, dēbĕo (2), ŏportet (2 *impers, with acc. of person*), e.g. I ought, ŏportet mē

ounce uncĭa, *f*

our, ours noster

ourselves (*in apposition to subject*), ipsi; (*reflexive*), nos

out *adv*, (being out), fŏris; (going out), fŏras

out of *prep*, ē, ex, dē (*with abl*); extrā (with acc); (on account of), propter (*with acc*)

outbid *v.t, use phr*, plūs offĕro quam ... (offer more than ...)

outbreak use *vb*. ŏrĭor (4 *dep*) (to arise); (beginning), ĭnĭtĭum, *n*

outcast prŏfŭgus, *m*

outcome (result) exĭtus, *m*

outcry clāmor, *m*

outdo *v.t*, sŭpĕro (1)

outdoors *adv*, fŏras

outer *adj*, extĕrĭor

outfit (equipment) appărātus, *m*

outflank *v.i*, circŭmĕo (4)

outgrow *v.t, use phr*, magnĭtūdĭne sŭpĕro (1) (surpass in size)

outhouse tŭgŭrĭum, *n*

outlast *v.t*, dĭuturnĭtāte sŭpĕro (surpass in duration)

outlaw *nn*, prōscriptus, *m*

outlaw *v.t*, prōscrībo (3)

outlay *nn*, sumptus, *m*

outlet exĭtus, *m*

outline finis, *m*, ădumbrātĭo, *f*

outlive *v.i*, sŭperstĕs sum (*irreg*) (to be a survivor)

outlook (future) fŭtūra, *n.pl*

outnumber *v.t*, plūres nŭmĕro esse quam ... (to be more in number than ...)

outpost stătĭo, *f*

outrage *nn*, iniūrĭa, *f*

outrage *v.t*, vĭŏlo (1)

outrageous indignus

outright *adv*, prorsus; (immediately), stătim

outset ĭnĭtĭum, *n*

outside *nn*, extĕrna pars, *f*; (on the —), *adv*, extrinsĕcus; (appearance), spĕcĭes, *f*, frons, *f*

outside *adj*, externus

outside *adv*, extrā

outside of *prep*, extrā (*with acc*)

outskirts *use adj*. sūburbānus (near the city)

outspoken (frank) līber

outstretched porrectus

outstrip *v.t*, sŭpĕro (1)

outward *adj*, externus

outwardly *adv*, extrā

outweigh *v.t*, grăvĭtāte sŭpĕro (1) (surpass in weight)

outwit *v.t*, dēcĭpĭo (3)

oval *adj*, ōvātus

oven furnus, *m*

over *prep*, (above, across, more than), sŭper (*with acc*)

over *adv*, (above), sŭper, suprā; (left —), *adj*, rĕlĭquus; (it is — , all up with), actum est; (— and — again), *adv*, ĭdentĭdem

overawe *v.t*, percello (3)

overbearing sŭperbus

overboard *adv*, ex nāvi

overcast (sky) nūbĭlus

overcoat lăcerna, *f*

overcome *v.t*, vinco (3), sŭpĕro (1)

overdone *use adv*, nĭmis (too much)

overdue *use adv*, dĭūtĭus (too long), *and* dĭffĕro (*irreg*), (to put off)

overflow *v.i*, effundor (3 *pass*); v.t, ĭnundo (1)

overgrown obsĭtus

overhang *v.i*, immĭnĕo (2), impendĕo (2) (*both with dat*)

overhanging impendens

overhasty praeceps

overhaul *v.t*, (repair), rĕsarcĭo (4)

overhead *adv*, insŭper

overhear *v.t*, excĭpĭo (3)

overjoyed laetĭtĭā ēlātus (elated with joy)

overland *adv*, terrā, per terram

overlap *v.t*, (overtake), sŭpervĕnĭo (4)

overlay *v.t*, indūco (3)

overload *v.t*, grăvo (1)

overlook *v.t*, prōspǐcǐo (3); **(forgive)**; ignosco (3) (*with dat*); **(neglect)**, praetermitto (3)
overmuch *adv*, nǐmis
overpower *v.t*, opprǐmo (3)
overrate *v.t*, plūris aestǐmo (1) **(value too highly)**
override *v.t*, praeverto (3)
overrule *v.t*, vinco (3)
overrun *v.t*, pervǎgor (1 *dep*)
oversea *v.t*, cūro (1), inspǐcǐo (3)
overseer cūrātor, *m*
overshadow *v.t*, officǐo (3) (*with dat*)
oversight (omission) error, *m*, neglĕgentǐa, *f*, *or use vb*, praetermitto (3) **(overlook)**
overspread *v.t*, obdūco (3)
overt ǎpertus, plānus
overtake *v.t*, consĕquor (3 *dep*)
over tax (strength etc.) v.t, nǐmis ūtor (3 *dep*) (*with abl*)
overthrow *nn*, rūīna, *f*
overthrow *v.t*, ēverto (3), opprǐmo (3)
overtop *v.t*, sǔpĕro (1)
overture (to make — s) *use vb*. instǐtǔo (3) **(to begin)**
overweening sǔperbus
overwhelm *v.t*, opprǐmo (3), obrǔo (3)
overwork *v.i*, nǐmis lǎbōro (1)
overwrought (exhausted) confectus
owe *v.t*, dēbĕo (2)
owing to prep, **(on account of)**, propter, ob (*both with acc*)
owl būbo, *m*, strix, *f*
own *adj*, prǒprǐus; *often expressed by possessive pron, e.g.* **my own**, mĕus
own *v.t*, **(possess)**, tĕnĕo (2), possǐdĕo (2); **(confess)**, fǎtĕor (2 *dep*)
owner possessor *m*, dǒmǐnus, *m*
ox bōs, *c*
oxherd armentārǐus, *m*
oyster ostrĕa, *f*

P

pace *nn*, passus, *m*
pace (step) spǎtǐor (1 *dep*), grǎdǐor (3 *dep*)
pacific pācǐfǐcus
pacification pācǐfǐcātǐo, *f*
pacify *v.t*, plāco (1), sēdo (1)
pack (bundle) sarcǐna, *f*; **(— of people)**, turna, *f*
pack *v.t*, **(gather together)**, collǐgo (3); **(— close together)**, stǐpo (1)
package sarcǐna, *f*
packet fascǐcǔlus, *m*
packhorse iūmentum, *n*
pact pactum, *n*, foedus, *n*
padding *nn*, fartūra, *f*
paddle *nn* **(oar)**, rēmus, *m*
paddle *v.t*, rēmǐgo (1), **(to row)**
paddock saeptum, *n*
padlock sĕra, *f*
pagan pāgānus
page (book) pāgǐna, *f*; **(boy)**, pǔer, *m*
pageant spectācǔlum, *n*, pompa, *f*
pageantry spĕcǐes (*f*) atque pompa *f* **(display and public procession)**
pail sǐtǔla, *f*
pain dǒlor, *m*; **(to be in —)**, *v.i*, dǒlĕo (2)
pain *v.t*, dǒlōre affǐcǐo (3) **(inflict pain)**
painful ǎcerbus
painless *use adv. phr*, sǐne dǒlōre **(without pain)**
pains (endeavour) ǒpĕra, *f*; **(to take — over)**, ǒpĕram do (1) (*with dat*)
painstaking ǒpĕrōsus
paint *v.t*, pingo (3); **(colour)**, fūco (1)
paint *nn*, pigmentum, *n*
paintbrush pēnǐcullus, *m*
painter pictor, *m*
painting pictūra, *f*
pair pār, *m*
pair *v.t*, iungo (3); *v.i*, iungor (3 *pass*)
palace rēgǐa, *f*
palatable iūcundus
palate pǎlātum, *n*

palatial

palatial rēgĭus

pale *adj*, pallĭdus; (to be —), *v.i*, pallĕo (2); (to become —), *v.i*, pallesco (3)

pale *nn*, (stake), pālus, *m*

paleness pallor, *m*

palisade vallum, *n*

pall *nn*, pallĭum, *n*

pall *v.i*, (it —s), taedet (2 *impers*)

pallet lectŭlus, *m*

palliate *v.t*, extĕnŭo (1)

palliation *use vb*, extĕnŭo (1) (palliate)

palliative lēnĭmentum, *n*

pallid *adj* pallĭdus

pallor pallor, *m*

palm (of hand, tree) palma, *f*

palm (to — off) *v.t*, suppōno (3)

palpable (obvious) mănĭfestus

palpitate *v.t*, palpĭto (1)

palpitation palpĭtatĭo, *f*

palsy părălysis, *f*

paltry vīlis

pamper *v.t*, nĭmĭum indulgĕo (2) (*with dat*) (to be too kind to ...)

pamphlet lĭbellus, *m*

pamphleteer scriptor (*m*) lĭbellorum

pan pătĭna, *f*; (frying —), sartāgo, *f*

panacea pănăcēa, *f*

pancake lăgănum, *n*

pander *v.i*, lēnōcĭnor (1 dep)

panegyric laudātĭo, *f*

panel (of door, etc.) tympānum, *n*

panelled lăquĕātus

pang dŏlor, *m*

panic păvor, *m*

panic-stricken păvĭdus

pannier clītellae, *f, pl*

panorama prōspectus, *m*

pant *v.i*, ănhēlo (1)

panther panthēra, *f*

panting *nn*, ănhēlĭtus, *m*

pantomime mīmus, *m*

pantry cella pĕnarĭa, *f*

pap (nipple) păpilla, *f*

paper charta, *f*; (sheet of —), schĕda, *f*; (newspaper), acta dīurna, *n.pl*

papyrus păpyrus, *m, f*

par (on a — with) *adj*, pār

parable părăbŏla, *f*

parade (military) dēcursus, *m*; (show), appărātus, *m*, pompa, *f*

parade *v.i*, (of troops), dēcurro (3); *v.t* (display), ostento (1)

paradise Ēlysĭum, ĭi, *n*

paragon spĕcĭmen, *n*

paragraph căput, *n*

parallel *adj*, părallēlus; (like), sĭmĭlis

paralysis părălysis, *f*, dēbĭlĭtas, *f*

paralyze *v.t*, dēbĭlĭto (1)

paralyzed dēbĭlis

paramount summus

paramour ădulter, *m*, ămātor, *m*

parapet lōrīca, *f*, mūnītĭo, *f*

paraphernalia appărātus, *m*

parasite assecla, *c*

parasol umbella, *f*

parcel fascĭcŭlus, *m*

parcel out *v.t*, partĭor (4 dep)

parch *v.t*, torrĕo (2)

parched (dry) ārĭdus; (scorched), torrĭdus

parchment membrāna, *f*

pardon *nn*, vĕnĭa, *f*

pardon *v.t*, ignosco (3) (*with dat*)

pardonable *use phr*, cui ignoscendum est (who should be pardoned)

pare *v.t*, (circum)sĕco (1) (cut around)

parent părens, *m, f*

parentage gĕnus, *n*

parental pătrĭus, *or use genit pl*, părentum (of parents)

parenthesis interpŏsĭtĭo, *f*

parish păroecĭa, *f*

park horti, *m. pl*

parley collŏquĭum, *n*

parley *v.i*, collŏquor (3 dep)

parliament sĕnātus, *m*

parliamentary *use genit. case of* sĕnātus

parlour conclāve, *n*

parody versus rīdĭcŭli, *m, pl*

parole fĭdes *f* (promise)

paroxysm *use* accessus, *m*, (approach)

parricide (person) parrĭcīda, *c*; (act), parrĭcīdĭum, *n*

parrot psittăcus, *m*

parry *v.t*, prōpulso (1)

parse *v.t, use phr*, verba singŭlātim percĭpĭo (**understand the words one by one**)
parsimonious parcus
parsimony parsĭmōnĭa, *f*
parsley ăpĭum, *n*
parson (priest) săcerdos, *c*
part pars, *f*; **(in a play)**, persōna, *f*, partes, *f, pl*; **(side, faction)**, partes, *f. pl*; **(duty)**, officĭum, *n*; **(region)**, lŏca, *n.pl*; **(from all — s)**, *adv*, undĭque; **(for the most —)**, *adv*, plērumque; **(to take — in)**, intersum *(irreg) (with dat)*
part *v.t*, dīvĭdo (3), sēpăro (1); *v.i*, discēdo (3)
partake of *v.t*, partĭceps sum *(irreg) (with genit)*; **(food)**, gusto (1)
partaker partĭceps, *adj*
partial (affecting only a part) *use adv. phr*, ex ălĭquā parte; **(unfair)**, ĭnīquus
partiality stŭdĭum, *n*
participate *v.i*, partĭceps sum *(irreg) (with genit)*
participation sŏcĭĕtas, *f*
particle partĭcŭla, *f*
particular (characteristic) prŏprĭus; **(special)**, singŭlāris; **(exacting)**, dēlĭcātus
particularly (especially) *adv*, praecĭpŭē
parting *nn*, dīgressus, *m*
partisan fautor, *m*
partition (act of —) partītĭo, *f*; **(wall)**, părĭes, *m*
partly *adv*, partim
partner sŏcĭus, *m* (sŏcĭa, *f*)
partnership sŏcĭĕtas, *f*
partridge perdix, *c*
party (political, etc.) factĭo, *f*; **(of soldiers)**, mănus, *f*; **(for pleasure)**, convīvĭum, *n*
pasha sătrăpes, *m*
pass *nn* **(mountain)**, angustĭae, *f. pl*
pass *v.t.* **(go beyond)**, praetergrĕdĭor (3 dep); **(surpass)**, excēdo (3); **(— on, — down)**, trādo (3); **(of time)**, ăgo (3), tĕro (3); **(— over, omit)**, praetĕrĕo (4); **(— a law)**, sancĭo (4); **(approve)**,

prŏbo (1); v.i, praetĕrĕo (4); **(of time)**, transĕo (4); **(give satisfaction)**, sătisfăcio (3); **(— over, cross over)**, transĕo (4); **(come to — , happen)**, fīo *(irreg)*
passable (road, etc.) pervĭus
passage (crossing) transĭtus, *m*, trāiectĭo, *f*; **(route, way)**, ĭter, *n*, vīa, *f*; **(in a book)**, lŏcus, *m*
passenger vector, *m*
passion mōtus (*m*) ănĭmi **(impulse of the mind)**; **(love)**, ămor, *m*
passionate fervĭdus, ardens, īrācundus
passive pătĭens
passivity pătĭentĭa
passport dĭplōma, *n*
password tessĕra, *f*
past *adj*, praetĕrītus; **(just —)**, proxĭmus
past *nn*, praetĕrĭtum tempus, *n*
past *prep*, praeter *(with acc)*; **(on the far side of)**, ultrā *(with acc)*
past *adv, use compound vb. with* praeter, e.g. praetĕrĕo (4) **(go past)**
paste fărīna, *f*
paste *v.t*, glūtĭno (1)
pastime oblectāmentum, *n*
pastor pastor, *m*
pastoral pastōrālis
pastry crustum, *n*
pastry-cook crustŭlărĭus, *m*
pasture pascŭum, *n*
pasture *v.t*, pasco (3)
pat *v.t*, **(caress)**, permulcĕo (2)
patch *nn*, pannus, *m*
patch *v.t*, sarcĭo (4)
patent *adj*, ăpertus
paternal păternus
path sēmĭta, *f*, vĭa, *f*
pathetic mĭsĕrandus
pathless invĭus
pathos *f*, affectĭo (*f*) ănĭmi
pathway sēmĭta, *f*
patience pătĭentĭa, *f*
patient *adj*, pătĭens
patient *nn, use* aeger **(ill)**
patiently *adv*, pătĭenter
patrician *nn. and adj*, pătrĭcĭus
patrimony pătrĭmōnĭum, *n*
patriot *use phr*, qui pătrĭam ămat **(who loves his country)**

patriotic ămans pătrĭae
patriotism ămor (*m*) pătrĭae
patrol *nn*, use custŏdes, *m. pl*,
(guards)
patrol *v.t*, circŭmĕo (4)
patron pătrōnus, *m*
patronage pătrōcĭnĭum, *n*
patronzie *v.t*, făvĕo (2) (*with dat*)
patter *nn*, crĕpĭtus, *m*
patter *v.i*, crĕpo (1)
pattern exemplum, *n*, exemplar, *n*
paucity paucĭtas, *f*
pauper pauper *c*, ĕgens (needy)
pause *nn*, mŏra, *f*
pause *v.i*, intermitto (3)
pave *v.t*, sterno (3)
pavement păvīmentum, *n*
pavilion *use* praetōrĭum, *n*,
(general's tent), *or* tăbernācŭlum,
n, (tent)
paw *nn*, pes, *m*
paw *v.t*, pĕdĭbus calco (1) (tread
with the feet)
pawn (chess) lătruncŭlus, *m*;
(security), pignus, *n*
pawn *v.t*, pignĕro (1)
pay *nn*, stĭpendĭum, *n*
pay *v.t*, solvo (3), pendo (3),
nŭmĕro (1); *v.i* (— attention),
ŏpĕram do (1); (— the penalty),
poenas do (1)
paymaster (in army) trĭbūnus
aerārius, *m*
payment sŏlūtĭo, *f*
pea pīsum, *n*, cĭcer, *n*
peace pax, *f*, ōtĭum, *n*
peaceable plăcĭdus
peaceful plăcĭdus, pācātus
peacefulness transquillĭtas, *f*
peace offering pĭācŭlum, *n*
peacock pāvo, *m*
peak ăpex, *m*; (mountain),
căcūmen, *n*
peal (thunder) frăgor, *m*; *otherwise*
use sŏnus, *m*, (sound)
peal *v.i*, sŏno (1)
pear pyrum, *n*; (— tree), pyrus, *f*
pearl margărīta, *f*
peasant rustĭcus, *m*, ăgrestis, *m*
peasantry ăgrestes, *m. pl*
pebble lăpillus, *m*
peck (measure) mŏdĭus, *m*

peck *v.t*, vellĭco (1)
peculation pĕcūlātus, *m*
peculiar (to one person,
etc.) prŏprĭus; (remarkable),
singŭlāris
peculiarity prŏprĭetas, *f*
pecuniary pĕcūnĭārĭus
pedagogue măgister, *m*
pedant hŏmo ĭneptus
pedantic (affected — of style,
etc.) pūtĭdus
peddle *v.t*, vendĭto (1)
pedestal băsis, *f*
pedestrian *nn*, pĕdes, *m*
pedestrian *adj* pĕdester
pedigree stemma, *n*
pedlar instĭtor, *m*
peel *nn*, cūtis, *f*
peel *v.i*, cŭtem rĕsĕco (1)
peep *nn*, aspectus, *m*
peep *nn*, aspectus, *m*
peep at *v.t*, inspicio (3); *v.i*, sĕ
prōferre (*irreg*)
peer (equal) par, *m*
peer at *v.t*, rīmor (1 *dep*)
peerless ūnĭcus
peevish stŏmăchōsus
peevishness stŏmăchus, *m*
peg clāvus, *m*
pelt *v.t*, *use* intorquĕo (2) (hurl at);
v.i, (of rain, etc.) *use* plŭit (it rains)
pen călămus, *m*; (for cattle),
saeptum, *n*
pen *v.t*, (write), scrībo (3)
penal poenālis
penalty poena, *f*, damnum, *n*; (to
pay the —), poenas do (1)
penance (do —) *use vb*. expĭo (1)
(to make amends)
pencil pēnĭcillum, *n*
pending *prep*, inter, per (*with acc*)
pendulous pendŭlus
penetrate *v.i*, and *v.t*, pĕnĕtro (1)
pervādo (3)
penetrating *adj*, ăcūtus, ācer
(mentally), săgax
penetration ăcūmen, *n*
peninsula paenīnsŭla, *f*
penitence paenĭtentĭa, *f*
penitent *use vb*, paenĭtet (2
impers) (*with acc. of person*), *e.g.*
I am penitent, mĕ paenĭtet

pennant vexillum, *n*
penny as, *m*
pension annŭa, *n.pl*
pensive multa pŭtans **(thinking many things)**
penthouse vīnĕa, *f*
penultimate paenultĭmus
penurious parcus
penury ĕgestas, *f*, ĭnŏpĭa, *f*
people (community) pŏpŭlus, *m*; (persons), hŏmĭnes, *c. pl*; (the common —), plebs, *f*, vulgus, *n*
people *v.t*, frĕquento (1); (inhabit), incŏlo (3)
pepper pĭper, *n*
perambulate *v.t*, pĕrambŭlo (1)
perceive *v.t*, sentĭo (4), percĭpĭo (3), ănĭmadverto (3), intellĕgo (3)
percentage pars, *f*
perception perspĭcācĭtas, *f*, *or use adj*, perspĭcax **(sharp-sighted)**
perceptive perspĭcax
perch *nn*, pertĭca, *f*; (fish), perca, *f*
perch *v.i*, insīdo (3)
perchance *adv*, fortĕ
percolate *v.i*, permāno (1)
percussion ictus, *m*
perdition exĭtĭum, *n*
peremptory *use vb.* obstringo (3) **(to put under obligation)**
perennial pĕrennis
perfect perfectus, absŏlūtus
perfect *v.t*, perfĭcĭo (3), absolvo (3)
perfection perfectĭo, *f*, absŏlūtĭo, *f*
perfidious perfĭdus
perfidy perfĭdĭa, *f*
perforate *v.t*, perfŏro (1)
perform *v.t*, fungor (3 *dep. with abl*); pĕrăgo (3), praesto (1), exsĕquor (3 *dep*)
performance functĭo, *f*
performer actor, *m*
perfume ŏdor, *m*
perfume *v.t*, ŏdōro (1)
perfunctory neglĕgens
perhaps *adv*, fortĕ, fortassĕ, forsĭtan
peril pĕrīcŭlum, *m*
perilous pĕrīcŭlōsus
period spătĭum, *n*
periodical *adv*, stătus
perish *v.i*, pĕrĕo (4)

perishable frăgĭlis
perjure *v.t*, perĭūro (1)
perjured perĭūrus
perjury perĭūrĭum, *n*
permanence stăbĭlĭtas, *f*
permanent stăbĭlis
permanently *adv*, perpĕtŭo
permeate *v.i*, permāno (1)
permissible (it is —) lĭcet (2 *impers*)
permission (to give —) permitto (3) (*with dat*); (without your —), tē invīto
permit *v.t*, sĭno (3), permitto (3)
pernicious pernĭcĭōsus
perpendicular *adj*, dīrectus
perpetrate *v.t*, admitto (3)
perpetual sempĭternus
perpetuate *v.t*, contĭnŭo (1)
perplex *v.t*, distrăho (3), sollĭcĭto (1)
perplexed dŭbĭus
perquisite pĕcūlĭum, *n*
persecute *v.t*, insector (1 *dep*)
persecution insectātĭo, *f*
persecutor insectātor, *m*
perseverance persĕvērantĭa, *f*
persevere *v.i*, persĕvēro (1)
persist *v.i*, persto (1)
persistence pertĭnācĭa, *f*
person hŏmo, *c*; (body), corpus, *n*; (in person), *use pron*, ipse **(self)**
personal (opp. to public) prīvātus
personality ingĕnĭum, *n*
perspicacious perspĭcax
perspicacity perspĭcācĭtas, *f*
perspiration sūdor, *m*
perspire *v.i*, sūdo (1)
persuade *v.t*, persuādĕo (2) (*with dat of person*)
persuasion persuāsĭo, *f*
persuasive suāvĭlŏquens
pert prŏcax
pertain *v.i*, attĭnĕo (2)
pertainacious pertĭnax
pertinacity pertĭnācĭa, *f*
perturb *v.t*, turbo (1)
perusal perlectĭo, *f*
peruse *v.t*, perlĕgo (3)
pervade *v.t*, permāno (1), perfundo (3)
perverse perversus

perversion dēprāvātĭo, *f*
pervert *v.t*, dēprāvo (1)
pervious pervĭus
pest pestis, *f*
pester *v.t*, sollĭcĭto (1)
pestilence pestĭlentĭa, *f*
pestilential pestĭlens
pestle pistillum, *n*
pet *nn*, dēlĭcĭae, *f. pl*
pet *v.t*, dēlĭcĭis hăbĕo (2) **(regard among one's favourites)**, indulgĕo (2)
petition *use vb*. pĕto (3) **(seek)**
petition *v.t*, rŏgo (1)
petitioners pĕtentes, *c.pl*
petrify v.t, **(with fear, etc.)**, terrōrem īnĭcĭo (3), (*with dat*)
pettifogging vīlis
petty mĭnūtus
petulance pĕtŭlantĭa, *f*
petulant pĕtŭlans
phantom sĭmŭlācrum, *n*, ĭmāgo, *f*
phases (alternations) vĭces, *f. pl*
pheasant āles (*c*) Phāsĭdis **(bird of Phasis)**
phenomenon rēs, *f*; **(remarkable occurrence)**, rēs mīrābĭlis
phial lăguncŭla, *f*
philanthropic hūmānus
philanthropy hūmānĭtas, *f*
philologist phĭlŏlŏgus, *m*
philology phĭlŏlŏgĭa, *f*
philosopher phĭlŏsŏphus, *m*
philosophical phĭlŏsŏphus
philosophy phĭlŏsŏphĭa, *f*
philtre philtrum, *n*
phlegm pītŭīta, *f*; **(of temperament)**, aequus ănĭmus, *m*
phoenix phoenix, *m*
phrase *nn*, lŏcūtĭo, *f*
phraseology *use* verba, *n.pl*, **(words)**
phthisis phthĭsis, *f*
physic mĕdĭcāmentum, *n*
physical (relating to the body) *use nn*, corpus, *n*, **(body)**; **(natural)**, *use* nātūra, *f*, **(nature)**
physician mĕdĭcus, *m*
physics phўsĭca, *n.pl*
physiology phўsĭŏlŏgĭa, *f*
pick (axe) dŏlābra, *f*; **(choice)**, *use adj*, dēlectus **(chosen)**
pick *v.t*, **(pluck)**, lĕgo (3), carpo

(3); **(choose)**, ēlĭgo (3); **(— up, seize)**, răpĭo (3)
picked (chosen) dēlectus
picket stătĭo, *f*
pickle mŭrĭa, *f*
pickle *v.t*, condĭo (4)
pickpocket fūr, *c*
picnic *use phr*, fŏrīs ĕpŭlor (1 *dep*) **(to eat out of doors)**
picture tăbūla, *f*
picture *v.t*, expingo (3)
picturesque ămoenus
pie crustum, *n*
piebald bĭcŏlor
piece (part) pars, *f*; **(of food)**, frustrum, *n*; **(to pull or tear to — s)**, discerpo (3), dīvello (3); **(to fall to — s)**, dīlābor (3 *pass*)
piecemeal *adv*, membrātim
piece together *v.t*, compōno (3)
pier mōles, *f*
pierce *v.t*, perfŏdĭo (3)
piercing *adj*, ăcūtus
piety pĭĕtas, *f*
pig porcus, *m*, sūs, *c*
pigeon cŏlumba, *f*
pigheaded obstĭnātus, difficĭlis
pigsty hăra, *f*
pike hasta, *f*
pile (heap) ăcervus, *m*; **(building)**, mōles, *f*; **(supporting timber)**, sublĭca, *f*
pile *v.t*, ăcervo (1), congĕro (3)
pilfer *v.t*, surrĭpĭo (3)
pilfering *nn*, furtum, *n*
pilgrim pĕrĕgrīnātor, *m*
pilgrimage pĕrĕgrinātĭo, *f*
pill pĭlŭla, *f*
pillage *nn*, răpīna, *f*, dīreptĭo, *f*
pillage *v.t*, praedor (1 *dep*) dīrĭpĭo (3)
pillar cŏlumna, *f*
pillory vincŭla, *n.pl*
pillow pulvīnus, *m*
pillow *v.t*, suffulcĭo (4)
pilot gŭbernātor, *m*
pilot *v.t*, gŭberno (1)
pimp lēno, *m*
pimple pustŭla, *f*
pin ăcus, *f*
pin *v.t*, ăcu fīgo (3) **(fix with a pin)**
pincers forceps, *m, f*
pinch *nn*, **(bite)**, morsus, *m*

pine *nn*, pīnus, *f*; *adj*, pīněus
pine *v.i*, tābesco (3); *v.t*, (— for), dēsīděro (1)
pinion (nail) clāvus, *m*; **(bond)**, vincŭla, *n.pl*
pinion *v.t*, rěvincĭo (4)
pink rŭbor, *m*
pinnace lembus, *m*
pinnacle fastīgĭum, *n*
pint sextārĭus, *m*
pioneer explōrātor, *m*
pious pĭus
pip (seed) sēmen, *n*, grānum, *n*
pipe cănālis, *m*; **(musical)**, fistŭla, *f*
pipe *v.i*, căno (3)
piper tībīcen, *m*
piquant ăcerbus
pique *nn*, offensĭo, *f*
pique *v.t*, laedo (3)
piracy lătrōcĭnĭum, *n*
pirate praedo, *m*, pīrāta, *m*
pit fŏvěa, *f*; **(arm —)**, āla, *f*; **(theatre)**, căvěa, *f*
pit (— one's wits, etc.) *use* ūtor (3 *dep*) **(to use)**
pitch *nn*, pix, *f*; **(in music)**, sŏnus, *m*
pitch *v.t*, **(camp, tent, etc.)**, pōno (3); **(throw)**, cōnĭcĭo (3); **(ships)**, *use* ăgĭtor (1 *pass*) **(to be tossed about)**
pitcher urcěus, *m*
pitchfork furca, *f*
piteous, pitiable mĭsěrăbĭlis
pitfall fŏvěa, *f*
pith mědulla, *f*
pitiful mĭser, mĭsěrĭcors
pitifulness mĭsěrĭa, *f*
pitiless immĭsěrĭcors
pittance (small pay) tips, *f*
pity *v.t*, mĭsěret (2 *impers*) *(with acc. of subject and genit. of object, e.g.* **I pity you**); mē mĭsěret tŭi
pity *nn*, mĭsěrĭcordĭa, *f*
pivot cardo, *m*
placard inscriptum, *n*
placate *v.t*, plāco (1)
place lŏcus, *m*; **(in this —)**, *adv*, hīc; **(in that —)**, illīc, ĭbĭ; **(in what — ?)** ŭbĭ?; **(in the same —)**, ĭbīdem; **(to this —)** hūc; **(to that —)**, illūc; **(to the same —)**, ěōdem; **(to what — ?)**, quō; **(from this —)**. hinc; **(from that —)**, inde; **(from the same —)**, indĭdem; **(from what — ?)**, unde? **(in the first —)**, prīmum; **(to take —, happen)**, *v.i*, accĭdo (3)
place *v.t*, pōno (3), lŏco (1); **(— in command)**, praefĭcĭo (3); **(— upon)** impōno (3)
placid plăcĭdus, tranquillus
plague *nn*, pestĭlentĭa, *f*, pestis, *f*
plague *v.t*, **(trouble)**, sollĭcĭto (1)
plain *nn*, campus, *m*, plānĭtĭes, *f*
plain *adj*, **(clear)**, clārus, plānus; **(unadorned)**, subtīlis, simplex; **(frank, candid)**, sincērus
plainness perspĭcŭĭtas, *f*, simplĭcĭtas, *f*, sincērĭtas, *f*
plaintiff pětītor, *m*
plaintive *adj*, mĭsěrăbĭlis
plait *v.t*, intexo (3)
plan *nn*, consĭlĭum, *n*; **(drawing)**, dēscriptĭo, *f*; **(to make a —)**, consĭlĭum căpĭo (3)
plan *v.i*, **(intend)**, in ănĭmo hăběo (2); *v.t*, **(design)**, dēscrībo (3)
plane *nn*, **(tool)**, runcīna, *f*; **(tree)**, plătănus, *f*
plane *v.t*, runcīno (1)
planet sīdus (*n*) errans **(moving constellation)**
plank tăbŭla, *f*
plant *nn*, herba, *f*
plant (seeds, etc.) sěro (3); **(otherwise)**, pōno (3), stătŭo (3)
plantation plantārĭum, *n*, arbustum, *n*
planter sător, *m*
planting *nn*, sătus, *m*
plaster *nn*, tectōrĭum, *n*; **(medical)**, emplastrum
plaster *v.t*, gypso (1)
plasterer tector, *m*
plate (dish) cătĭllus, *m*; **(thin layer of metal)**, lāmĭna, *f*; **(silver, gold)**, argentum, *n*
plate *v.t*, indūco (3)
platform suggestus, *m*
Platonic Plătōnĭcus
platoon děcŭrĭa, *f*
plausible spěcĭōsus
play *nn*, lūdus, *m*, lūsus, *m*; **(theatre)**, fābŭla, *f*; **(scope)**, camous, *m*

play *v.i*, lūdo (3) (*with abl. of game played*); (musical), căno (3); (a part in a play), partes ăgo (3); (a trick), lūdĭfĭco (1)

player (stage) historĭo, *m*; (flute —), tībīcen, m; (strings —), fĭdĭcen, *m*; (lute, guitar —), cĭthărista, *m*

playful (frolicsome) lascīvus

playfulness lascīvĭa, *f*

playground ārĕa, *f*

playwright fābŭlārum scriptor, *m*

plea (asking) obsĕcrātĭo, *f*; (excuse), excūsātĭo, *f*

plead *v.t*, ōro (1), ăgo (3); (as an excuse), excūso (1); (beg earnestly), obsĕcro (1); (law), dīco (3)

pleader (in law) ōrātor, *m*

pleasing, pleasant iūcundus

pleasantness iūcundĭtas, *f*

please *v.t*, plăcĕo (2) (*with dat*); (if you —), si vis

pleasureable iūcundus

pleasure vŏluptas, *f*; (will), arbĭtrĭum, *n*; (— gardens), horti, *m. pl*

plebeian plēbēius

pledge *nn*, pignus, *n*; (to make a — , promise), sē obstringĕre (3 reflex)

pledge *v.t*, oblĭgo (1), prōmitto (3)

plenipotentiary lēgātus, *m*

plenitude plēnĭtūdo, *f*

plentiful largus, cōpĭōsus

plenty cōpĭa, *f*; (enough), sătis (*with genit*)

pleurisy pleurītis, *f*

pliable flexĭbĭlis, lentus

plight angustĭae, *f.pl* (difficulties)

plight *v.t*, spondĕo (2), oblĭgo (1)

plinth plinthus, *m*, *f*

plod v.i, lentē prōcēdo (3)

plot (of ground) ăgellus, *m*; (conspiracy), coniūrātĭo, *f*; (story), argūmentum, *n*

plot *v.i*, coniūro (1)

plough *nn*, ărātrum, *n*; (— share), vōmer, *m*

plough *v.t*, ăro (1)

ploughman ărātor, *m*, bŭbulcus, *m*

pluck *nn*, fortĭtūdo, *f*, ănĭmus, *m*

pluck *v.t*, carpo (3); (— up courage), ănĭmum rĕvŏco (1)

plug *nn*, obtūrāmentum, *n*

plum prūnum, *n*

plum tree prūnus, *f*

plumage plūmae, *f*, *pl*

plumb line līnĕa, *f*

plume penna, *f*

plump pinguis

plumpness nĭtor, *m*, pinguĭtūdo, *f*

plunder *nn*, praeda, *f*; (act of plundering), răpĭna, *f*, dīreptĭo, *f*

plunder *v.t*, praedor (1 dep), dīrĭpĭo (3)

plunderer praedātor, *m*

plunge *v.i*, sē mergĕre (3 *reflex*); *v.t*, mergo (3)

plural *adj*, plūrālis

plurality multĭtūdo, *f*

ply *v.t*, exercĕo (2)

poach *v.t*, use răpĭo (3), (to seize); (cook), cŏquo (3)

poacher fur, *c*, raptor *m*

pocket sĭnus, *m*

pocket *v.t*, (money), āverto (3)

pocketbook pŭgillāres, *m*, *pl*

pocket money pĕcūlĭum, *n*

pod sĭlĭqua, *f*

poem pŏēma, *n*, carmen, *n*

poet pŏēta, *m*

poetical pŏētĭcus

poetry pŏēsis, *f*, carmĭna, *n. pl*

poignant ăcerbus

point ăcūmen, *n* (of a sword), mūcro, *m*; (spear), cuspis, *f*; (place), lŏcus, *m*; (issue), res, *f*; (on the — of), *use fut. participle of vb*, *e.g.* on the point of coming; ventūrus

point *v.t* (make pointed), praeăcŭo (3); (direct), dīrĭgo (3)

point out *or* at *v.t*, monstro (1)

pointed praeăcūtus; (witty) salsus

pointer index, *m*, *f*

pointless insulsus

poison vĕnēnum, *n*, vīrus, *n*

poison *v.t*, vĕnēno nĕco (1) (kill by poison)

poisoning *nn*, vĕnēfĭcĭum, *n*

poisonous vĕnēnātus

poke *v.t*, fŏdĭco (1)

polar septentrĭōnālis

pole (rod, staff) contus, *m*, longŭrĭus, *m*; (earth), pŏlus, *m*

polemics contrōversĭae, *f. pl*

police (men) vĭgĭles, *m, pl*
policy rătĭo, *f*
polish *nn,* (brightness), nĭtor, *m*
polish *v.t,* pŏlĭo (4)
polished pŏlītus
polite cōmis, urbānus
politeness cōmĭtas, *f,* urbānĭtas, *f*
politic *adj,* prūdens
political cīvĭlis, pūblĭcus
politician qui reĭpūblĭcae stŭdet
   (who pursues state affairs)
politics rēs pūblĭca, *f*
poll (vote) suffrāgĭum, *n*
pollute *v.t,* inquĭno (1)
pollution collŭvĭio, *f*
polytheism *use phr,* crēdĕre multos
   esse dĕos (believe that there are
   many gods)
pomade căpillāre, *n*
pomegranate mālum grānātum, *n*
pommel *v.t,* verbĕro (1)
pomp appărātus, *m*
pompous magnĭfĭcus
pompousness magnĭfĭcentĭa, *f*
pond stagnum, *n;* (fish —),
   piscīna, *f*
ponder *v.t,* rĕpŭto (1)
ponderous gravis
poniard pūgĭo, *m*
pontiff pontĭfex, *m*
pontoon pons, *m*
pony mannus, *m*
pool lăcūna, *f*
poop puppis, *f*
poor pauper, ĭnops; (worthless),
   vīlĭs; (wretched), mĭser
poorly *adj,* (sick, ill), aeger
poorly *adv,* tĕnŭĭter, mălĕ
pop *v.i,* crĕpo (1)
pope Pontĭfex Maxĭmus, *m*
poplar pōpŭlus, *f*
poppy păpāver, *n*
populace vulgus, *n,* plebs, *f*
popular grātĭōsus; (of the people),
   pŏpŭlāris
popularity făvor (*m*) pŏpŭli
   (goodwill of the people)
population cīves, *c.pl*
populous frĕquens
porch vestībŭlum, *n*
porcupine hystrix, *f*
pore fŏrāmen, *n*

pore over *v.i,* ănĭmum intendo (3)
   (direct the mind)
pork porcīna, *f*
porker porcus, *m*
porous rārus
porpoise porcŭlus mărīnus, *m*
porridge puls, *f*
port portus, *m*
portable quod portāri pŏtest (that
   can be carried)
portal porta, *f,* iānŭa, *f*
portcullis cătăracta, *f*
portend *v.t,* portendo (3)
portent portentum, *n*
portentous monstrŭōsus
porter (doorkeeper) iānĭtor, *m;*
   (baggage carrier) bāiŭlus, *m*
portfolio lĭbellus, *m*
portico portĭcus, *f*
portion pars, *f*
portion out *v.t,* partĭor (4 *dep*)
portrait ĭmāgo, *f*
portray *v.t,* dēpingo (3)
pose *nn,* stătus, *m*
position lŏcus, *m;* (site), sĭtus, *m*
positive certus
possess *v.t,* hăbĕo (2), possĭdĕo
   (2)
possession possessĭo, *f;* (to take —
   of), pŏtĭor (4 *dep. with abl*);
   (property), *often use possessive
   pron. e.g.* mĕa (my — s), *or* bŏna
   n.pl
possessor possessor, *m,* dŏmĭnus,
   m
possibility *use phr. with* posse; (to
   be possible)
possible *use vb,* posse (*irreg*) (to
   be possible); (as ... as possible),
   use quam *with superlative, e.g.* as
   large as possible, quam
   maxĭmus; (as soon as —), quam
   prīmum
post cippus, *m,* pālus, *m;* (military),
   stătĭo, *f,* lŏcus, *m;* (letter),
   tăbellārĭi pūblĭci, *m. pl* (state
   couriers)
post *v.t,* (in position), lŏco (1);
   (letter), tăbellārĭo do (1) (give to a
   courier)
posterior *nn,* nătes, *f. pl*
posterity postĕri, *m. pl*

postern postīcum, *n*

posthumous *use phr*, post mortem (*with genit*) **(after the death of ...)**

postman tăbellārĭus, *m*

postpone *v.t*, differo (*irreg*)

postscript verba subiecta, *n. pl*, **(words appended)**

posture stătus, *m*

pot olla, *f*

potent pŏtens, effĭcax

potentate tўrannus, *m*

potion pōtĭo, *f*

potsherd testa, *f*

potter fĭgŭlus, *m*

pottery (articles) fictīlĭa, *n. pl*

pouch saccŭlus, *m*

poultice mălagma, *n*

poultry ăves cŏhortāles, *f. pl*

pounce upon v.t, invŏlo (1)

pound *nn*, **(weight)**, lībra, *f*

pound *v.t*, tundo (3), tĕro (3)

pour *v.t*, fundo (3); *v.i*, fundor (3 *pass*)

pouring *adj.* effūsus

pout *v.i*, lăbellum extendo (3) **(stretch a lip)**

poverty paupertas, *f*, ĕgestas, *f*, ĭnŏpĭa, *f*; **(— stricken)**, *adj*, ĭnops

powder *nn*, pulvis, *m*

power vīres, *f. pl*; **(dominion)**, pŏtestas, *f*; **(authority)**, ius, *n*, impĕrĭum, *n*; **(inconstitutional —)**, pŏtentĭa, *f*

powerful pŏtens; **(of body)**, vălĭdus

powerless invălĭdus; **(to be —)**, *v.i*, mĭnĭmum posse (*irreg*)

practicable *use phr*, quod fĭĕri pŏtest **(that can be done)**

practical (person) făbrĭcae pĕrītus **(skilled in practical work)**

practically (almost) *adv.*, paene

practice ūsus, *m*; **(custom)**, mos, *m*, consŭētŭdo, *f*

practise *v.t*, exercĕo (2), factĭto (1)

practitioner (medical) mĕdĭcus, *m*

praetor praetor, *m*

praetorship praetūra, *f*

praise *nn*, laus, *f*

praise *v.t*, laudo (1)

praiseworthy laudābĭlis

prance *v.i*, exsulto (1)

prank *use* lūdĭfĭcor (1 dep) **(to make fun of)**

prattle *v.i*, garrĭo (4)

pray *v.i*, and *v.t*, ōro (1) prĕcor (1 *dep*)

prayer prĕces, *f. pl*

preach *v.t*, contĭōnor (1 *dep*)

preamble exordĭum, *n*

precarious incertus

precaution (to take — s (against)) *v.i*, and *v.t*, praecăvĕo (2)

precede *v.t*, antēcēdo (3), antĕĕo (4)

precedence (to give —) *use vb*, cēdo (3); **(to take —)**, prĭor esse (*irreg*)

precedent exemplum, *n*

preceding *adj*, prĭor, proxĭmus

precept praeceptum, *n*

precious (of great price) magni prĕtĭi; **(dear)**, dīlectus

precipice lŏcus praeceps, *m*

precipitate *adj*, praeceps

precipitate *v.t*, praecĭpĭto (1)

precipitous praeceps

precise subtīlis

precision subtīlĭtas, *f*

preclude *v.t*, prŏhĭbĕo (2)

precocious praecox

preconceived praeiūdĭcātus

precursor praenuntĭus, *m*

predatory praedātōrĭus

predecessor (my —) *use phr*, qui ante me ... **(who before me ...)**

predicament angustĭae, *f. pl*

predict *v.t*, praedīco (3)

prediction praedictĭo, *f*

predilection stŭdĭum, *n*

predisposed inclĭnātus

predominant pŏtens

predominate *v.i*, *use phr*, qui in pŏtentĭā sunt **(who are in authority)**

pre-eminent praestans

preface praefātĭo, *f*

preface *v.t*, praefor (1 *dep*)

prefer *v.t*, with infinitive, mālo (*irreg*); **(put one thing before another)**, antĕpōno (3); **(— a charge)**, dēfĕro (*irreg*)

preferable pŏtĭor

preference (desire) vŏluntas, *f*; **(in**

—), *adv*, pŏtĭus

preferment hŏnor, *m*

pregnant praegnans, grăvĭda

prejudge *v.t*, praeiūdĭco (1)

prejudice praeiūdĭcāta ŏpīnĭo, *f*

prejudice *v.t*, (**impair**), immĭnŭo (3)

prejudicial noxĭus; (**to be — to**), obsum (*irreg*) (*with dat*)

prelate săcerdos, *c*

preliminary *use compound word with* prae, *e.g.* **to make a — announcement**, praenuntĭo (1)

prelude prŏoemĭum, *n*

premature immātūrus

premeditate *v.t*, praemĕdĭtor (1 *dep*)

premeditation praemĕdĭtātĭo, *f*

premier princeps, *m*

premise prōpŏsĭtĭo, *f*

premises (buildings) aedĭfĭcĭa, *n.pl*

premium praemĭum, *n*

premonition mŏnĭtĭo, *f*

preoccupy (to be — with) stŭdĕo (2) (*with dat*)

preparation compărātĭo, *f*, appărātus, *m*; (**to make — s**), compăro (1)

prepare *v.t*, păro (1), compăro (1)

prepossess *v.t*, commendo (1)

prepossessing *adj*, suāvis, blandus

preposterous praepostĕrus

prerogative iūs, *n*

presage praesāgĭum, *n*

presage *v.t*, portendo (3)

prescribe *v.t*, praescrībo (3)

presence praesentĭa, *f*; (**in the — of**), prep, cōram (*with abl*)

present *nn* (**gift**), dōnum, *n*; (**time**), praesentĭa, *n.pl*

present *adj*, praesens; (**to be —)**, *v.i*, adsum (*irreg*)

present *v.t*, offĕro (*irreg*); (**give**), dōno (1) (*with acc. of person and abl. of gift*)

presentation dōnātĭo, *f*

presentiment augŭrĭum, *n*

presently *adv*, (**soon**), mox

preservation conservātĭo, *f*

preserve *v.t*, servo (1)

preserver servātor, *m*

preside *v.i*, praesĭdĕo (*with dat*)

presidency praefectūra, *f*

president praefectus, *m*

press *nn*, (**machine**), prēlum, *n*

press *v.t*, prĕmo (3); (**urge**), urgĕo (2)

pressure nīsus, *m*

prestige fāma, *f*, ŏpīnĭo, *f*

presume *v.t*, (**assume**), crēdo (3); (**dare**), *v.i*, audĕo (2)

presumption (**conjecture**) coniectūra, *f*; (**conceitedness**), arrŏgantĭa, *f*

presumptuous arrŏgans

pretence sĭmŭlātĭo, *f*; (**under — of**), per sĭmŭlātĭōnem

pretend *v.t*, sĭmŭlo (1)

pretended *adj*, sĭmŭlātus

pretender (claimant) *use vb*, pĕto (3) (**aspire to**)

pretension postŭlātĭo, *f*

pretext spĕcĭes, *f*; (**on the — of**), *use vb*. sĭmŭlo (1) (**to pretend**)

prettily *adv*, bellē, vĕnustē

prettiness concinnĭtas, *f*, vĕnustas, *f*

pretty *adj*, pulcher

pretty *adv*, sătis (**enough**)

prevail *v.i*, obtĭnĕo (2), sŭpĕrĭor esse (*irreg*); (**to — upon**), *v.t*, persuādĕo (2) (*with dat*)

prevalent vulgātus

prevaricate *v.t*, tergĭversor (1 *dep*)

prevent *v.t*, prŏhĭbĕo (2)

prevention *use vb*, prŏhĭbĕo (**prevent**)

previous prŏxĭmus

previously *adv*, antĕā

prey *nn*, praeda, *f*

prey *v.t*, praedor (1 *dep*)

price *nn*, prĕtĭum, *n*; (**— of corn**), annōna, *f*

price *v.t*, prĕtĭum constĭtŭo (3) (**fix the price**)

priceless inaestĭmābĭlis

prick *nn*, punctum, *n*

prick *v.t*, pungo (3); (**spur**), stĭmŭlo (1)

prickly *adj*, ăcŭlĕātus

pride sŭperbĭa, f; (**honourable —)**, spīrĭtus, *m*

priest săcerdos, *c*

priesthood săcerdōtĭum, *n*
prim mōrōsĭor
primarily *adv*, princĭpĭō
primary prīmus
prime *nn*, (of life, etc.), *use vb*, flōrĕo (2) (flourish); (best part), flŏs, *m*
prime *adj*, ēgrĕgĭus
primeval prīmĭgenĭus
primitive prīmĭgĕnĭus
prince (king) rēgŭlus, *m*; (king's son), filĭus (*m*) rēgis
princess (king's daughter) filĭa (*f*) rēgis
principal *adj*, princĭpālis, praecĭpŭus
principal *nn*, măgister, *m*
principality regnum, *n*
principle princĭpĭum, *n*; (element), ĕlĕmentum, *n*, prīmordĭa, *n. pl*; (rule, maxim), praeceptum, *n*
print *nn*, (mark), nŏta, *f*
print *v.t*, imprĭmo (3)
prior *adj*, prĭor
priority *use adj*, prĭor
prism prisma, *n*
prison carcer, *m*
prisoner captīvus, *m*
privacy sōlĭtūdo, *f*
private prīvātus, sēcrētus
private soldier mīles grĕgārĭus, *m*
privately *adv*, prīvātim, clam
privation ĭnōpĭa, *f*
privet lĭgustrum, *n*
privilege iūs, *n*
privy *adj*, (acquainted with), conscĭus; (secret), prīvātus
privy *nn*, fŏrĭca, *f*
privy-council consĭlĭum, *n*
privy-purse fiscus, *m*
prize, praemĭum, *n*; (booty), praeda, *f*
prize *v.t*, (value), magni aestĭmo (1)
probability sĭmĭlĭtūdo (*f*) vēri
probable sĭmĭlis vēri
probation prŏbātĭo, *f*
probe *v.t*, tento (1)
problem quaestĭo, *f*
problematical (doubtful) dŭbĭus
procedure rătĭo, *f*
proceed *v.i*, (move on), pergo (3); (originate) prŏfīciscor (3 dep);

(take legal action against) lītem intendo (3) (*with dat*)
proceedings (legal) actĭo, *f*; (doings), acta, *n.pl*
proceeds fructus, *m*
process rătĭo, *f*; (in the — of time), *adv*, *use phr*, tempŏre praetĕreunte (with time going by)
procession pompa, *f*
proclaim *v.t*, praedīco (1), prōnuntĭo (1)
proclamation prōnuntĭātĭo, *f*, ēdictum, n
proconsul prōconsul, *m*
procrastinate *v.t*, diffĕro (*irreg*)
procrastination tardĭtas, *f*, mŏra, *f*
procreate *v.t*, prōcrĕo (1)
procreation prōcrĕātĭo, *f*, partus, *m*
procure *v.t*, compăro (1)
procurer lēno, *m*
prodigal *adj*, prōdĭgus
prodigality effūsĭo, *f*
prodigious immānis
prodigy prōdĭgĭum, *n*
produce *nn*, fructus, *m*
produce *v.t*, (into view) prōfĕro (*irreg*); (create), părĭo (3); (— an effect), mŏvĕo (2)
productive fĕrax
profanation vĭŏlātĭo, *f*
profane impĭus, prŏfānus
profane *v.t*, vĭŏlo (1)
profanity impĭĕtas, *f*
profess *v.t*, prŏfĭtĕor (2 dep)
profession (occupation) mūnus, n, offĭcĭum, n; (avowal), prŏfessĭo, *f*
professor prŏfessor, *m*
proffer *v.t*, pollĭcĕor (2 dep)
proficient (skilled) pĕrītus
profile oblīqua făcĭes, *f*
profit *nn*, ēmŏlŭmentum, *n*, lŭcrum, *n*, quaestus, *m*
profit *v.t*, (benefit), prōsum (*irreg. with dat*)
profitable fructŭōsus
profitless īnūtĭlis
profligacy nēquĭtĭa, *f*
profligate perdĭtus
profound altus
profuse effūsus
profusion effūsĭo, *f*
progeny prōgĕnĭes, *f*

prognostic signum, *n*

programme lĭbellus, *m*

progress (improvement, etc.) prōgressus, *m*; **(to make —)**, prōfĭcĭo (3), prōgrĕdĭor (3 dep)

progress *v.i*, prōgrĕdĭor (3 dep)

prohibit *v.t*, vĕto (1)

prohibition interdictum, *n*

project *nn*, **(plan)**, consĭlĭum, *n*

project *v.t*, prōĭcĭo (3); *v.i*, ēmĭnĕo (2)

projectile tēlum, *n*

projecting ēmĭnens

proleteriat vulgus, *n*

prolific fēcundus

prolix verbōsus

prologue prŏlŏgus, *m*

prolong *v.t*, prōdūco (3); **(— a command)**, prōrŏgo (1)

prolongation prōpāgātĭo, *f*

promenade ambŭlātĭo, *f*

prominence ēmĭnentĭa, *f*

prominent ēmĭnens; **(person)**, praeclārus

promiscuous prōmiscŭus

promise *nn*, prōmissum, *n*, fĭdes, *f*

promise *v.i*, prōmitto (3), pollĭcĕor (2 *dep*)

promising *adj, use adv. phr*, bŏnā spe **(of good hope)**

promissory note chīrogrăphum, *n*

promontory prōmontōrĭum, *n*

promote *v.t*, prōmŏvĕo (2); **(favour, assist)**, iŭvo (1), prōsum (*irreg*) (*with dat*)

promoter auctor, *m*

promotion (act of —) *use vb.* prōmŏvĕo (2); **(honour)**, hŏnor, *m*

prompt *adj*, promptus

prompt *v.t*, **(assist in speaking)**, sūbĭcĭo (3) (*with dat. of person*); **(incite)**, incĭto (1)

promptitude, promptness cĕlĕrĭtas, *f*

promulgate *v.t*, prōmulgo (1)

prone prōnus; **(inclined to)**, prōpensus

prong dens, *m*

pronoun prōnōmen, *n*

pronounce *v.t*, prōnuntĭo (1)

pronunciation appellātĭo, *f*

proof argūmentum, *n*, dŏcŭmentum *n*, prŏbātĭo, *f*

prop *nn*, admĭnĭcŭlim, *n*

prop *v.t*, fulcĭo (4)

propagate *v.t*, prōpāgo (1)

propel *v.t*, prōpello (3)

propensity ănĭmus inclīnātus, *m*

proper dĕcōrus, vērus, aptus

properly *adv*, **(correctly)**, rectē

property (possessions) bŏna, *n. pl*, rēs, *f*; **(characteristic quality)**, prŏprĭĕtas, *f*

prophecy praedictĭo, *f*, praedictum, *n*

prophesy *v.t*, praedīco (3), vātĭcĭnor (1 *dep*)

prophet vātes, *c*

prophetic dīvīnus

propitiate *v.t*, plāco (1)

propitious prŏpĭtĭus, praesens

proportion portĭo, *f*; **(in —)**, prōportĭōne

proportional *use adv. phr*, prō portĭōne

proposal condĭcĭo, *f*

propose *v.t*, fĕro (*irreg*), rŏgo (1)

proposer lātor, *m*

proposition condĭcĭo, *f*

proprietor dŏmĭnus, *m*

propriety (decorum) dĕcōrum, *n*

prorogation prōrŏgātĭo, *f*

prosaic (flat) iēiūnus

proscribe *v.t*, prōscrībo (3)

proscription prōscriptĭo, *f*

prose ōrātĭo, sŏlūta, *f*

prosecute *v.t*, **(carry through)**, exsĕquor (3 *dep*); **(take legal proceedings)** lītem intendo (3)

prosecution exsĕcuutĭo, *f*; **(legal)**, accuusātĭo, *f*

prosecutor accūsātor, *m*

prospect (anticipation) spes fŭtūra, *f*; **(view)**, prospectus, *m*

prospective fūtūrus

prosper *v.i*, flōrĕo (2)

prosperity res sĕcundae, *f. pl*

prosperous sĕcundus

prostitute *nn*, mĕrĕtrix, *f*

prostitute *v.t*, vulgo (1)

prostitution mĕrĕtricĭus quaestus, *m*

prostrate (in spirit, etc.) fractus; **(lying on the back)**, sŭpīnus; **(lying on the face)**, prōnus

prostrate *v.t*, sterno (3), dēĭcĭo (3)

protect *v.t*, tĕgo (3), tŭĕor (2 *dep*), dēfendo (3)

protection tūtēla, *f*, praesĭdĭum, *n*

protector dēfensor, *m*

protest against *v.t*, intercēdo (3)

prototype exemplar, *n*

protract *v.t*, dūco (3)

protrude *v.t*, prōtrūdo (3); *v.i*, ēmĭnĕo (2)

protuberance tūber, *n*

proud sŭperbus

prove v.t, prŏbo (1); **(to — oneself)** sē praestāre (1 *reflex*); **(test)**, pĕrīclītor (1 *dep*); v.i, **(turn out (of things))**, fīo (*irreg*), ēvĕnĭo (4)

proverb prōverbĭum, *n*

proverbial *use nn*, prōverbĭum, *n*, **(proverb)**

provide *v.t*, **(supply)**, păro (1), praebĕo (2); v.i, **(make provision for)**, prōvĭdĕo (2); **(— against)**, căvĕo (2) ne (*with vb. in subjunctive*)

provided that *conj*, dum, dummŏdo

providence prōvĭdentĭa, *f*

provident prōvĭdus

province prōvincĭa, f

provincial prōvincĭālis

provision (to make —) prōvĭdĕo (2)

provisional *use adv. phr*, ad tempus **(for the time being)**

provisions cĭbus, *m*

provocation *use vb*, irrīto (1) **(to provoke)**

provoke *v.t*, irrīto (1); **(stir up)**, incĭto (1)

prow prōra, *f*

prowess virtus, *f*

prowl *v.i*, văgor (1 *dep*)

proximity prōpinquĭtas, *f*

proxy prōcūrātor, *m*

prudence prūdentĭa, *f*

prudent prūdens

prune *nn*, prūnum, *n*, **(plum)**

prune *v.t*, ampŭto (1)

prurient lĭbīdĭnōsus

pry *v.t*, rīmor (1 *dep*)

psalm carmen, *n*

psychological *use genit. of* mens, **(mind)**

puberty pūbertas, *f*

public *adj*, pūblĭcus; **(of the state)**, *use nn*, respublĭca, *f*, **(state)**, *or* pŏpŭlus, *m*, **(people)**

public *nn*, hŏmĭnes, c. pl

publican (innkeeper) caupo, *m*

publication *use* ēdo (3), **(publish)**

publicity cĕlĕbrĭtas, *f*

publicly *adv*, pălam

publish *v.t*, effĕro (*irreg*), prōfĕro (*irreg*); **(book)**, ēdo (3)

pucker *v.t*, corrūgo (1)

puddle lăcūna, *f*

puerile (silly) īnseptus

puff *v.i*, **(pant)**, ănhēlo (1); v.t, **(inflate)** inflo (1); **(puffed up)**, inflātus

pugilist pŭgil, *m*

pull *v.t*, trăho (3); **(— down, demolish)**, dēstrŭo (3)

pulley trochlĕa, *f*

pulp cāro, *f*

pulpit suggestus, *m*

pulsate *v.i*, palpīto (1)

pulse vēnae, *f. pl.* **(veins)**

pulverize *v.t*, in pulvĕrem contĕro (3) **(pound into dust)**

pumice pūmex, *m*

pump *nn*, antlĭa, *f*

pump *v.t*, haurĭo (4)

pumpkin pĕpo, *m*

pun făcētĭae, *f. pl*

punch ictus, *m*, pugnus, *m*

punch *v.t*, percŭtĭo (3)

punctilious mōrōsus

punctual, punctuality *use adv. phr*, ad tempus **(at the right time)**

punctuate *v.t*, distinguo (3)

punctuation interpunctĭo, *f*

puncture *nn*, punctum

puncture *v.t*, pungo (3)

pungency morsus, *m*, ăcerbĭtas, *f*

pungent ācer

punish *v.t*, pūnĭo (4), ănĭmadverto (3) in (*with acc*), poenas sūmo (3); **(to be — ed)**, poenas do (1)

punishment poena, *f*, supplĭcĭum, *n*; **(to undergo —)**, poenam sŭbĕo (4)

punitive *use vb*, pūnĭo **(punish)**

puny pŭsillus
pup, puppy cătŭlus, *m*
pupil (scholar) discĭpŭlus, *m*; **(of the eye)** pūpilla, *f*
puppet pūpa, *f*
purchase *nn*, emptĭo, *f*
purchase *v.t*, ĕmo (3)
pure pūrus, mĕrus; **(morally)**, intĕger
purgative *use phr. with* mĕdĭcămentum, *n*, **(medicine)**
purge *nn, use vb*, purgo (1)
purge *v.t*, purgo (1)
purification purgātĭo, *f*
purify *v.t*, purgo (1), lustro (1)
purity castĭtas, *f*, intĕgrĭtas, *f*
purloin *v.t*, surrĭpĭo (3)
purple *nn*, purpŭra, *f*
purple *adj*, purpŭrĕus
purport *nn*, **(meaning)**, signĭfĭcātĭo, *f*
purport *v.t*, **(mean)**, signĭfĭco (1)
purpose *nn*, prōpŏsĭtum, *n*, consĭlĭum, *n*; **(for the — of doing something)**, ĕo consĭlĭo ut (*with vb in subjunctive*); **(on —)**, *adv*, consulto; **(to no —, in vain)**, *adv*, frustrā; **(for what —?)** quāre
purpose *v.t*, **(intend)**, in ănĭmo hăbĕo (2)
purr *v.i*, murmŭro (1)
purse saccŭlus, *m*
in pursuance of ex (*with abl*)
pursue *v.t*, sĕquor (3 *dep*)
pursuit (chase) *use vb*, sĕquor **(to pursue)**; **(desire for)**, stŭdĭum, *n*
purvey *v.t*, obsōno (1)
purveyor obsōnātor, *m*
pus pūs, *n*
push, pushing *nn*, impulsus, *m*, impĕtus, *m*
push *v.t*, pello (3), trūdo (3); **(— back)**, rĕpello (3); **(— forward)**, prōmŏvĕo (2)
pushing *adj*, mŏlestus
pusillanimity ănĭmus, hŭmĭlis, *m*
pusillanimous hŭmĭlis
pustule pustŭla, *f*
put *v.t*, **(place)**, pōno (3), do (1), impōno (3); **(— aside)**, sĕpōno (3); **(— away)**, abdo (3), condo (3); **(— back)**, rĕpōno (3); **(— down)**, dĕpōno (3); **(suppress)**,

exstinguo (3); **(— forward)**, praepōno (3), prōfĕro (*irreg*); **(— in)**, immitto (3); **(— into land, port, etc.)**, *v.i*, portum căpĭo (3); **(— off)**, *v.t*, pōno (3); **(delay)**, differo (*irreg*); **(— on)**, impōno (3); **(— clothes)**, indŭo (3); **(— out)**, ēĭcĭo (3); **(quench)**, exstinguo (3); **(— to drive to)**, impello (3); **(— together)**, collĭgo (3), confĕro (*irreg*); **(— under)**, sūbĭcĭo (3); **(— up, erect)**, stătŭo (3); **(offer)**, prōpōno (3); **(put up with, bear)**, fĕro (*irreg*); **(— upon)**, impōno (3); **(— to flight)** fŭgo (1)
putrefy *v.i*, pūtesco (3)
putrid pŭtrĭdus
putty glūten, *m or n*
puzzle *nn*, **(riddle)**, nōdus, *m*; **(difficulty)**, diffĭcultas, *f*, angustĭae, *f, pl*
puzzling *adj*, perplexus; **(in a — way)**, *adv. phr*, per ambāges
pygmy nānus, *m*
pyramid pȳrămis, *f*
pyre rŏgus, *m*
Pyrenees Montes Pȳrēnaei, *m. pl*
python pȳthon, *m*

Q

quack *nn*, **(medicine)**, pharmăcŏpōla, *m*
quadrangle ārĕa, *f*
quadrant quădrans, *m*
quadrilateral quădrĭlătĕrus
quadruped quădrŭpes
quadruple *adj*, quădruplex
quaff *v.t*, haurĭo (4)
quagmire pălus, *f*
quail *nn*, cŏturnix, *f*
quail *v.i*, trĕpĭdo (1)
quaint nŏvus
quake *nn*, trĕmor, *m*
quake *v.i*, trĕmo (3)
qualification iūs, *n*; **(condition)**, condĭcĭo, *f*
qualified (suitable) aptus, ĭdōnĕus
quality *v.t*, **(fit someone for something)**, aptum reddo (3); **(restrict)**, circumscrībo (3), mītĭgo (1)

quality nātūra, *f*
qualm (doubt) dŭbĭtātĭo, f
quantity nŭmĕrus, *m*, magnĭtūdo, *f*; (a certain —), ălĭquantum, *n* (*nn*); (a large —) cōpĭa, *f*, multum, *n*; (what — ?), use *adj*, quantus (how great)
quarrel iurgĭum, *n*, rixa, *f*
quarrel *v.i*, iurgo (1), rixor (1 *dep*)
quarrelsome lītĭgĭōsus
quarry (stone) lăpĭcīdīnae, *f. pl*; (prey), praeda, *f*
quarry *v.t*, caedo (3)
quart (measure) dŭo sextărĭī, *m. pl*
quarter quarta pars, *f*, quădrans, *m*; (district), rĕgĭo, f; (surrender), dēdĭtĭo, *f*
quarter *v.t*, quădrĭfărĭam dīvĭdo (3), (divide into four parts)
quarter-deck puppis, *f*
quartermaster quaestor mīlĭtāris, *m*
quarterly *adj*. trĭmestris
quarters (lodging) hospĭtĭum, *n*; (at close —), *adv*, commĭnus; (to come to close —), signa confĕro (*irreg*)
quash *v.t*, opprĭmo (3); (sentence, verdict), rēscindo (3)
quaver *v.i*, trĕpĭdo (1)
quay crēpīdo, *f*
queen rēgīna, *f*
queer rīdĭcŭlus
queerness insŏlentĭa, *f*
quell *v.t*, opprĭmo (3)
quench *v.t*, exstinguo (3)
quenchless ĭnexstinctus
querulous quĕrŭlus
query quaestĭo, *f*
query *v.t*, quaero (3)
quest inquīsītĭo, *f*
question *nn*, rŏgātĭo, *f*, interrŏgātum, *n*, quaestĭo, *f*; *or use vb*, rŏgo (1) (to ask —s); (doubt), dŭbĭum, *n*
question *v.t*, rŏgo (1), quaero (3); (doubt), dŭbĭto (1)
questionable incertus
questioner interrŏgātor, *m*
quibble *nn*, captĭo, *f*
quibble *v.i*, căvillor (1 *dep*)
quick *adj*, cĕler; (sprightly), ăgĭlis; (— witted), săgax

quickly *adv*, cĕlĕrĭter, cĭto
quicken *v.t*, accĕlĕro (1), stĭmŭlo (1); v.i, (move quicker), sē incĭtāre (1 *reflex*)
quickness vēlōcĭtas, *f*; (— of wit), săgăcĭtas, *f*
quicksilver argentum vīvum, *n*
quick-tempered īrācundus
quiescent quĭescens
quiet *nn*, quĭes, *f*
quiet *adj*, quĭētus, tranquillus
quiet, quieten *v.t*, sēdo (1)
quietly *adv*, quĭētē, tranquillē
quill penna, *f*; (for writing), *use* stĭlus, *m*, (pen)
quilt *nn*, strāgŭlum, *n*
quinquennial quinquennālis
quinsy angĭna, *f*
quintessence vīs, *f*, flōs, *m*
quip *nn*, rēsponsum (salsum) ((witty) reply)
quirk căvillātĭo, *f*
quit *v.t*, rĕlinquo (3)
quite *adv*, admŏdum, prorsus; (— enough), sătis
quiver *nn*, phărĕtra, *f*
quiver *v.i*, trĕmo (3)
quoit discus, *m*
quota răta pars, *f*
quotation prōlātĭo, *f*
quote *v.t*, prōfĕro (*irreg*)
quotidian cottīdĭānus

R

rabbit cŭnīculus, *m*
rabble turba, *f*
rabid răbīdus
race (family) gĕnus, *n*, prōgĕnĭes, *f*; (running), cursus, *m*, certāmen, *n*
race *v.i*, cursu certo (1) (contend by running)
racecourse stădĭum, *n*, currĭcŭlum, *n*
racehorse ĕquus cursor, *m*
rack (for torture) ĕquŭlĕus, m
rack *v.t*, (torture), torquĕo (2)
racket (bat) rētĭcŭlum, *n*; (noise), strĕpĭtus, *m*
racy (smart) salsus
radiance fulgor, *m*
radiant clārus, fulgens
radiate *v.i*, fulgĕo (2)

radiation rădĭātĭo, *f*
radical (fundamental) tōtus; **(original),** innātus; **(keen on change),** cŭpĭdus rērum nŏvārum
radically *adv*, pĕnĭtus, fundĭtus
radish rădix
radius rădĭus, *m*
raffle ālĕa, *f*
raft rătis, *f*
rafter cantērĭus, *m*
rag pannus, *m*
rage fŭror, *m*
rage *v.i*, fŭro (3)
ragged pannōsus
raging *adj*, fŭrens
raid incursĭo, *f*; **(to make a —),** invādo (3) in (*with acc.*)
rail longŭrĭus, *m*
rail at (abuse) mălĕdīco (3) (*with dat.*)
railing cancelli, *m.pl*
raillery căvillātĭo, *f*
raiment vestīmenta, *n.pl*
rain *nn*, plŭvĭa, *f*, imber, *m*
rain *v.i*, **(it rains),** plŭit (3 impers.)
rainbow arcus, *m*
rainy plŭvĭus
raise v.t, **(lift),** tollo (3); **(forces),** compăro (1); **(rouse),** ērĭgo (3); **(— a seige),** obsĭdĭōnem solvo (3)
raisin ăcĭnus passus, *m*, **(dried berry)**
rake *nn*, **(tool),** rastellus, *m*; **(person)** nĕpos, *c*
rake *v.t*, rādo (3)
rally *v.t*, **(troops)** mīlĭtes in ordĭnes rĕvŏco (1), **(call back the soldiers to their ranks);** v.i, se collĭgĕre (3 reflex)
ram (or battering —) ărĭes m; (beak of a ship), rostrum, n
ram *v.t*, fistūco (1); **(ship)** rostro laedo (3)
ramble *v.i*, erro (1)
rambler erro, *m*
rammer fistūca, *f*
rampart agger, *m*, vallum, *n*
rancid rancĭdus
rancorous infestus
rancour ŏdĭum, *n*
random *adj*, fortŭĭtus; **(at —),** *adv*, fortŭĭto

range ordo, *m*; **(— of mountains),** iŭga, *n.pl*; **(of a missile),** iactus, *m*; **(scope),** campus, *m*
rank *nn*, ordo, *m*
rank *v.i*, sē hăbere (2 *reflex*)
rank *adj*, **(smell, etc.),** fētĭdus
rankle *v.t*, exulcĕro (1), mordĕo (2)
ransack *v.t*, dīrĭpĭo (3)
ransom *nn*, rĕdemptĭo, *f*; **(— money),** prĕtĭum, *n*
ransom *v.t*, rĕdĭmo (3)
rant *v.t*, dēclāmo (1)
ranting *nn*, sermo tŭmĭdus, *m*, **(bombastic speech)**
rap *nn*, pulsātĭo, *f*
rap *v.t*, pulso (1)
rapacious răpax
paracity răpācĭtas, *f*
rape *nn*, raptus, *m*
rapid răpĭdus, cĕler
rapidity cĕlĕrĭtas, *f*
rapier glădĭus, *m*
rapine răpīna, *f*
rapture laetĭtĭa, *f*
rapturous laetus
rare rārus
rarefy v.t, extĕnŭo (1)
rareness, rarity rārĭtas, *f*
rascal scĕlestus, *m*
rascality scĕlĕra, *n.pl*
rase (to the ground) *v.t*, sŏlo aequo (1)
rash *adj*, tĕmĕrārĭus
rash *nn*, ēruptĭo, *f*
rashness tĕmĕrĭtas, *f*
rasp *nn*, **(file),** scŏbīna, *f*
rasp *v.t*, rādo (3)
rat mūs, *c*
rate (price) prĕtĭum, *n*; **(tax)** vectīgal, *n*; **(speed),** cĕlĕrĭtas, *f*; **(at any —),** *adv*, ŭtĭque
rate *v.t*, **(value),** aestĭmo (1); **(chide),** increpo (1); **(tax),** censĕo (2)
rather *adv*, **(preferably),** pŏtĭus; **(somewhat),** ălĭquantum; **(a little),** *with comparatives, e.g.* **rather (more quickly),** paulo (cĕlĕrĭus)
ratification sanctĭo, *f*
ratify *v.t*, rătum făcĭo (3)

ratio portĭo, *f*

ration *nn*, dēmensum, *n*, cĭbārĭa, *n.pl*

rational (a — being), partĭceps rătĭonis **(participant in reason)**

rationally *adv*, rătĭōne

rattle *nn*, crĕpĭtus, *m*; **(toy)**, crĕpĭtācŭlum, *n*

rattle *v.i*, crĕpo (1)

ravage *v.t*, pŏpŭlor (1 dep.)

ravaging *nn*, pŏpŭlātĭo, *f*

rave *v.i*, fŭro (3)

raven corvus, *m*

ravening, ravenous răpax

ravine fauces, *f.pl*

raving *adj*, fŭrens, insānus

raving *nn*, fŭror, *m*

ravish *v.t*, răpĭo (3), stŭpro (1)

ravishing suāvis

raw crūdus; **(inexperienced, unworked)**, rŭdis

ray rădĭus, *m*

razor nŏvācŭla, *f*

reach *nn*, **(range)**, iactus, *m*; **(space)**, spătĭum, *n*

reach *v.i*, **(extend)**, pertĭnĕo (2), attingo (3); *v.t*, **(come to)**, pervĕnĭo (4) ad (*with acc.*)

react v.t, **(be influenced)**, affĭcĭor (3 pass.)

reaction (of feeling) *use vb*, commŏvĕo (2) (to make an impression on)

read v.t, lĕgo (3); **(— aloud)**, rĕcĭto (1)

readable făcĭlis lectu

reader lector, *m*

readily *adv*, **(willingly)**, lĭbenter

readiness (preparedness) *use adj*, părātus **(ready); (willingness)**, ănĭmus lĭbens, *m*

reading *nn*, lectĭo, *f*, rĕcĭtātĭo, *f*

reading-room bĭblĭŏthēca, *f*

ready părātus, promptus; **(to be —)**, părātus, praesto esse (*irreg.*); **(to make, get —)**, păro (1)

real *adj*, vērus

realism vērĭtas, *f*

reality rēs, *f*

realization (getting to know) cognĭtĭo, *f*; **(completion)**, confectĭo, *f*

realize *v.t*, intellĕgo (3); **(a project)**, perfĭcĭo (3), perdūco (3)

really *adv*, rēvērā; **(is it so?)**, ĭtăne est?

realm regnum, *n*

reap *v.t*, mĕto (3); **(gain)**, compăro (1)

reaper messor, *m*

reaping-hook falx, *f*

reappear *v.i*, rĕdĕo (*irreg.*)

rear *nn*, **(of a marching column)**, agmen nŏvissĭmum, n; **(of an army)**, ăcĭes nŏvissĭma, *f*; **(in the —)** *adv*, ā tergo

rear *v.t*, **(bring up)**, ēdŭco (1), ălo (3); v.i, **(of horses)**, sē ērĭgĕre (3 *reflex.*)

reason (faculty of thinking) mens, *f*; **(cause)**, causa, *f*; **(for this —)**, *adv*, ĭdĕo, idcirco; **(for what —, why?)**, cur, quārē; **(without —, heedlessly)**, *adv*, tĕmĕre

reason *v.t*, rătĭōcĭnor (1 dep.); **(— with)**, dissĕro (3), cum (*with abl.*)

reasonable (fair) aequus, iustus; **(in size)**, mŏdĭcus

reasonable (fairness) aequĭtas, *f*

reasoning *nn*, rătĭo, *f*

reassemble *v.t*, cōgo (3), in ūnum lŏcum collĭgo (3), **(collect into one place)**; *v.i*, rĕdĕo (4)

reassert *v.t*, rēstĭtŭo (3)

reassure *v.t*, confirmo (1)

rebel *nn*, sēdĭtĭōsus, *m*

rebel rĕbello (1), dēfĭcĭo (3)

rebellion sēdĭtĭo, *f*

rebellious sēdĭtĭōsus

rebound *v.i*, rĕsĭlĭo (4)

rebuff *v.t*, rĕpello (3)

rebuff *nn*, rĕpulsa, *f*

rebuke *nn*, rĕprĕhensĭo, *f*

rebuke *v.t*, rĕprĕhendo (3)

recall *nn*, rĕvŏcātĭo, *f*

recall *v.t*, rēvŏco (1); **(— to mind)**, rĕpĕto (3)

recapitulate *v.t*, ēnŭmĕro (1)

recapitulation ēnŭmĕrātĭo, *f*

recapture *v.t*, rĕcĭpĭo (3)

recede *v.i*, rĕcēdo (3)

receipt (act of receiving) acceptĭo, *f*; **(document)**, ăpŏcha, *f*

receipts (proceeds) rĕdĭtus, *m*

receive *v.t*, accĭpĭo (3), excĭpĭo (3)

receiver (of stolen goods) rĕceptor, *m*

recent rĕcens

recently *adv*, nūper

receptacle rĕceptācŭlum, *n*

reception ădĭtus, *m*

receptive dŏcĭlis

recess rĕcessus, *m*; **(holidays)**, fērĭae, *f. pl*

reciprocal mūtŭus

reciprocate *v.t*, rĕfĕro (*irreg.*)

recital narrătĭo, *f*

recite v.t, rĕcĭto (1), prōnuntĭo (1)

reckless tĕmĕrārĭus

recklessness tĕmĕrĭtas, *f*

reckon *v.t*, **(count)**, nŭmĕro (1); **(— on, rely on)**, confīdo (3) (*with dat.*); **(consider)**, dūco (3)

reckoning rătĭo, *f*

reclaim *v.t*, rĕpĕto (3)

recline *v.i*, rĕcŭbo (1)

recluse hŏmo sōlĭtārĭus

recognizable *use phr*, quod agnosci pŏtest **(that can be recognized)**

recognize *v.t*, agnosco (3), cognosco (3); **(acknowledge)**, confĭtĕor (2 *dep.*)

recognition cognĭtĭo, *f*

recoil *v.i*, rĕsĭlĭo (4)

recollect v.t, rĕmĭniscor (3 *dep. with genit*)

recollection mĕmŏrĭa, *f*

recommence *v.t*, rĕdintĕgro (1)

recommend *v.t*, commendo (1)

recommendation commendātĭo, *f*

recompense *v.t*, rĕmūnĕror (1 *dep*)

reconcile *v.t*, rĕconcĭlĭo (1)

reconciliation rĕconcĭlĭātĭo, *f*

reconnoitre *v.t*, explōro (1)

reconsider *v.t*, rĕpŭto (1)

record *v.t*, in tăbŭlas rĕfĕro (*irreg*)

records tăbŭlae, *f. pl*, fasti, *m. pl*

recount *v.t*, **(expound)**, ēnarro (1)

recourse (to have — to) v.i, confŭgĭo (3) ad (*with acc*)

recover *v.t*, rĕcŭpĕro (1) rĕcĭpĭo (3); *v.i*, **(from illness, etc.)**, rĕvălesco (3), rĕfĭcĭor (3 *pass*), sē collĭgĕre (3 reflex)

recovery rĕcŭpĕrātĭo, *f*; **(from illness)**, sălus, *f*

recreate *v.t*, rĕcrĕo (1)

recreation rĕmissĭo, *f*

recruit *nn*, tīro, *m*

recruit *v.t*, **(enrol)**, conscrībo (3)

recruiting *nn*, dēlectus, *m*

rectify *v.t*, corrĭgo (3)

rectitude prŏbĭtas, *f*

recumbent rĕcŭbans

recur *v.i*, rĕdĕo (4)

red rŭber, rūfus; **(redhanded)**, *adj*, mănĭfestus

redden *v.t*, rŭbĕfăcĭo (3); *v.i.* rŭbesco (3)

redeem *v.t*, rĕdĭmo (3)

redeemer lībĕrātor, *m*

redemption rĕdemptĭo, *f*

red-lead mĭnĭum, *n*

redness rŭbor, *m*

redouble *v.t*, ingĕmĭno (1)

redound rĕdundo (1)

redress *v.t*, rēstĭtŭo (3)

reduce *v.t*, rĕdĭgo (3)

reduction dēmĭnūtĭo, *f*; **(taking by storm)**, expugnātĭo, *f*

redundancy rĕdundantĭa, *f*

redundant sŭpervăcŭus

re-echo *v.i*, rĕsŏno (1)

reed ărundo, *f*

reef saxa, *n.pl*

reek *v.i*, fūmo (1)

reel v.i, **(totter)**, văcillo (1)

re-elect *v.t*, rĕcrĕo (1)

re-establish *v.t*, rēstĭtŭo (3)

refectory cēnācŭlum, *n*

refer *v.t*, rĕfĕro or dēfĕro (*irreg*) ad (*with* acc); **(to — to)**, perstringo (3), specto (1) ad (*with acc*)

referee arbĭter, *m*

reference rătĭo, *f*

refill *v.t*, rĕplĕo (2)

refine *v.t*, **(polish)**, expŏlĭo (4)

refined pŏlītus, hūmānus

refinement hūmānĭtas, *f*

refinery officīna, *f*

reflect *v.t*, rĕpercŭtĭo (3), reddo (3); *v.i*, **(ponder)**, rĕpŭto (1) (ănĭmo) **(in the mind)**

reflection (image) ĭmāgo, *f*; **(thought)**, cōgĭtātĭo, *f*

reform ēmendātĭo, *f*

reform *v.t*, rēstĭtŭo (3); **(correct)**, corrĭgo (3); *v.i*, sē corrĭgĕre (3 *reflex*)

reformer ēmendātor, *m*
refract *v.t*, infringo (3)
refractory contŭmax
refrain from *v.i*, sē contĭnēre (2 *reflex*) ad (*with abl*)
refresh *v.t*, rĕcrĕo (1), rĕfĭcĭo (3)
refreshment (food) cĭbus, *m*
refuge perfŭgĭum, *n*; **(to take —)**, *v.i*, confŭgĭo (3) ad (*with acc*)
refugee *adj*, prŏfŭgus
refulgent splendĭdus
refund *v.t*, reddo (3)
refusal rĕcūsātĭo, *f*
refuse *nn*, purgāmentum, *n*
refuse *v.t*, rĕcūso (1); **(to — to do)** nōlo (*irreg*) (*with infin*); **(say no)**, nĕgo (1)
refute *v.t*, rĕfello (3)
regain *v.t*, rĕcĭpĭo (3)
regal rēgālis
regale *v.t*, excĭpĭo (3)
regalia insignĭa, *n.pl*
regard *nn*, **(esteem)**, studĭum, *n*, hŏnor, *m*; **(consideration)**, rēspectus, *m*
regard v.t, **(look at)**, intŭĕor (2 *dep*); **(consider)**, hăbĕo (2); **(esteem)**, aestĭmo (1)
regardless neglĕgens
regency interregnum
regent interrex, *m*
regicide caedes (*f*) rēgis **(killing of a king)**
regiment lĕgĭo, *f*
region rĕgĭo, *f*, tractus, *m*
register tăbŭlae, *f.pl*
register *v.t*, perscrībo (3)
registrar tăbŭlārĭus, *m*
regret *nn*, dŏlor, *m*
regret *v.t*, **(repent of)**, *use* paenĭtet (2 *impers*) (*with acc. of subject*), e.g. **I repent of**, mē paenĭtet (*with genit*)
regular (correctly arranged) ordĭnātus, compŏsĭtus; **(customary)**, sollemnis
regularity ordo, *m*
regularly *adv*, **(in order)**, ordĭne; **(customarily)**, sollemnĭter
regulate *v.t*, ordĭno (1)
regulation (order) iussum, *n*; **(rule)**, praeceptum, *n*
rehabilitate *v.t*, rēstĭtŭo (3)

rehearsal (practice) exercĭtātĭo, *f*
rehearse *v.t*, **(premeditate)**, praemĕdĭtor (1 *dep*)
reign *nn*, regnum, *n*
reign *v.i*, regno (1)
reimburse *v.t*, rĕpendo (3)
rein *nn*, hăbēna, *f*
rein *v.t*, **(curb)**, frēno (1)
reinforce *v.t*, confirmo (1)
reinforcement (help) auxĭlĭum, *n*
reinstate *v.t*, rēstĭtŭo (3)
reiterate *v.t*, ĭtĕro (1)
reject *v.t*, rĕĭcĭo (3)
rejection rĕiectĭo, *f*
rejoice *v.i*, gaudĕo (2)
rejoicing *nn*, laetĭtĭa, *f*
rejoin *v.i*, rĕdĕo (4)
relapse *v.i*, rĕcĭdo (3)
relate *v.t*, **(tell)**, narro (1), expōno (3); *v.i*, pertĭnĕo (2)
related (by birth) cognātus; **(by marriage)**, affĭnis; **(by blood)**, consanguĭnĕus; **(near)**, prŏpinquus
relation (relative) cognātus, *m*, affĭnis *m*; **(connection)**, rătĭo, *f*
relationship cognātĭo, *f*, affĭnĭtas, *f*
relative *nn*, cognātus, *m*, affĭnis, *m*
relative *adj*, compărātus **(compared)**
relax *v.t*, rĕmitto (3); *v.i*, rĕlanguesco (3)
relaxation rĕmissĭo, *f*
relay *v.t*, **(send)**, mitto (3)
relays of horses ĕqui dispŏsĭti, *m.pl* **(horses methodically arranged)**
release *nn*, lībĕrātĭo, *f*
release *v.t*, exsolvo (3) lībĕro (1)
relent *v.t*, rĕmitto (3)
relentless immĭsĕrĭcors
relevant *use vb*, pertĭnĕo (2) **(to concern)**
reliance fidūcĭa, *f*
relic rĕlĭquĭae, *f, pl*
relief (alleviation) lĕvātĭo, *f*; **(help)**, auxĭlĭum, *n*
relieve *v.t*, lĕvo (1), rĕmitto (3); **(help)**, subvĕnĭo (4) (*with dat*); **(of command, etc.)**, succĕdo (3) (*followed by in and acc. or by dat*)
religion rĕlĭgĭo, *f*, săcra, *n.pl*

religious rĕlĭgĭōsus, pĭus
relinquish *v.t*, rĕlinquo (3)
relish *nn*, stŭdĭum, *n*, săpor, *m*
relish *v.t*, frŭor (*3 dep. with abl*)
reluctance *use adj*, invītus
  (unwilling)
reluctant invītus
rely on *v.t*, confīdo (3) (*with dat. of person or abl. of thing*)
relying on *adj*, frētus (*with abl*)
remain *v.i*, mănĕo (2); **(be left over)**, sūpersum (*irreg*)
remainder rĕlĭquum, *n*
remaining *adj*, rĕlĭquus
remains rĕlĭquĭae, *f*, *pl*
remand *v.t*, amplĭo (1)
remark *nn*, dictum, *n*
remark *v.t*, **(say)**, dīco (3); **(observe)**, observo (1)
remarkable insignis
remedy rĕmĕdĭum, *n*, mĕdĭcāmentum, *n*
remedy *v.t*, sāno (1); **(correct)**; corrĭgo (3)
remember *v.i*, mĕmĭni (*v. defect. with genit*), rĕcordor (1 *dep. with acc*)
remembrance rĕcordātĭo, *f*, mĕmŏrĭa, *f*
remind *v.t*, mŏnĕo (2)
reminiscence rĕcordātĭo, *f*
remiss neglĕgens
remission (forgiveness) vĕnĭa, *f*; **(release)**, sŏlūtĭo, *f*
remit *v.t*, rĕmitto (3)
remittance pĕcūnĭa, *f*
remnant rĕlĭquĭae, *f. pl*
remonstrate *v.i*, rĕclāmo (1) (*with dat*)
remorse conscĭentĭa, *f*
remorseless immĭsĕrĭcors, dŭrus
remote rĕmōtus
remoteness longinquĭtas, *f*
removal (driving away) āmōtĭo, *f*; **(sending away)**, rĕlēgātĭo, *f*; **(— by force)**, raptus, *m*
remove *v.t*, rĕmŏvĕo (2); **(send away)**, rĕlēgo (1); *v.i*, migro (1)
remunerate *v.t*, rĕmūnĕror (1 dep)
remuneration rĕmūnĕrātĭo, f
rend *v.t*, scindo (3)
render *v.t*, reddo (3)

rendezvous (to fix a —) lŏcum (et dĭem) constĭtŭo (3), **(place (and day))**
rending (severing) discĭdĭum, *n*
renegade (deserter) transfŭga, *c*
renew *v.t*, rĕnŏvo (1), rĕdintĕgro (1)
renewal rĕnŏvātĭo, *f*
renounce *v.t*, rĕnuntĭo (1), rĕmitto (3)
renovate *v.t*, rĕnŏvo (1)
renovation rēstĭtūtĭo, *f*
renown fāma, *f*, glōrĭa, *f*
renowned clārus
rent *nn*, scissūra, *f*; **(of houses, etc.)**, merces, *f*
rent *v.t*, **(let)**, lŏco (1); **(hire)**, condūco (3)
renunciation rĕpŭdĭātĭo, f
repair *v.t*, rĕfĭcĭo (3), sarcĭo (4)
repaired sartus
reparation sătisfactĭo, *f*
repast cĭbus, *m*
repay *v.t*, (grātĭam) rĕfĕro (*irreg*)
repayment sŏlūtĭo, *f*
repeal *nn*, abrŏgātĭo, *f*
repeal *v.t*, abrŏgo (1), rēscindo (3)
repeat *v.t*, ĭtĕro (1), reddo (3)
repeatedly *adv*, ĭdentĭdem
repel *v.t*, rĕpello (3)
repent *v.i*, paenĭtet (2 *impers*) (*with acc. of person and genit. of cause*), *e.g.* **I repent of this deed**, mē paenĭtet huius facti
repentance paenĭtentĭa, *f*
repentant paenĭtens
repetition ĭtĕrātĭo, *f*
replace *v.t*, rĕpōno (3); **(substitute)**, substĭtŭo (3)
replenish *v.t*, rĕplĕo (2)
replete rĕplētus
reply *nn*, rēsponsum, *n*
reply *v.i*, rēspondĕo (2)
report *nn*, nuntĭus, *m*; **(rumour)**, fāma, *f*; **(bang)**, crĕpĭtus, *m*
report *v.t*, rĕfĕro (*irreg*), nuntĭo (1)
repose *nn*, quĭes, *f*
repose *v.i*, **(rest)** quĭesco (3)
repository rĕceptācŭlum, *n*
reprehend *v.t*, rĕprĕhendo (3)
reprehensible culpandus

represent

represent *v.t*, exprĭmo (3), fingo (3); **(take the place of)**, persōnam gĕro (3)

representation ĭmāgo, *f*

representative (deputy) prōcūrātor, *m*

repress *v.t*, cŏhĭbĕo (2)

reprieve *nn*, **(respite)**, mŏra, *f*

reprieve *v.t*, **(put off)**, diffĕro (*irreg*)

reprimand *nn*, rĕprĕhensĭo, *f*

reprimand *v.t*, rĕprĕhendo (3)

reprisal *use* poena, *f*, **(punishment)**

reproach *nn*, exprŏbrātĭo, *f*, opprŏbrĭum, *n*

reproach *v.t*, exprŏbro (1), ōbĭcĭo (3) (*both with acc. of thing and dat. of person*)

reproachful obiurgātōrĭus

reprobate *nn*, perdĭtus, *m*, nĕbŭlo, *m*

reproduce *v.t*, rĕcrĕo (1)

reproof rĕprĕhensĭo, *f*, obiurgātĭo, *f*, vĭtŭpĕrātĭo, *f*

reprove *v.t*, rĕprĕhendo (3), obiurgo (1), vĭtŭpĕro (1)

reptile serpens, *f*

republic respublĭca, *f*

republican *adj*, pŏpŭlāris

repudiate *v.t*, rĕpŭdĭo (1)

repudiation rĕpŭdĭatĭo, *f*

repugnance ŏdĭum, *n*

repugnant āversus; **(it is — to me, I hate it)**, *use phr*, ŏdĭo esse **(to be hateful)**, *with dat. of person*

repulse *v.t*, rĕpello (3)

repulsive foedus, ŏdĭōsus

reputable hŏnestus

reputation, repute fāma, *f*; **(good —)**, existĭmātĭo, *f*; **(bad —)**, infāmĭa, *f*

request nn, rŏgātĭo, *f*

request *v.t*, rŏgo (1), prĕcor (1 dep)

require *v.t*, **(demand)**, postŭlo (1) **(need)**, ĕgĕo (2) (*with abl*)

requirement (demand) postŭlātĭo, *f*; *or use adj*, nĕcessārĭus

requisite *adj*, nĕcessārĭus

requisition postŭlātĭo, *f*

requite *v.t*, rĕpōno (3)

rescind *v.t*, rēscindo (3)

rescue *v.t*, ērĭpĭo (3)

rescue *nn*, lībĕrātĭo, *f*

research investīgātĭo, *f*

resemblance sĭmĭlĭtŭdo, *f*

resemble *v.t*, rĕfĕro (*irreg*), sĭmĭlis esse (*irreg*) (*with genit. or dat*)

resembling *adj*, sĭmĭlis

resent *v.t*, aegrē fĕro (*irreg*) **(tolerate with displeasure)**

resentful īrācundus

resentment īra, *f*

reservation (restriction) exceptĭo, *f*

reserve *nn*, **(military)**, subsĭdĭum, *n*; **(of disposition)**, grăvĭtas, *f*

reserve *v.t*, servo (1); **(put aside)**, sēpōno (3)

reserved (of disposition) grăvis

reservoir lăcus, *m*

reside *v.i*, hăbĭto (1)

residence sēdes, *f.pl*, dŏmĭcĭlĭum, *n*

resident incŏla, *c*

resign *v.i*, and *v.t*, concēdo (3); **(to — oneself to)**, sē committĕre (3 *reflex. with* in *and acc*)

resignation (of office, etc.) abdĭcātĭo, *f*; **(of mind)** aequus ănĭmus, *m*

resin rēsīna, *f*

resist *v.t*, rĕsisto (3) (*with dat*)

resistance rĕpugnantĭa, *f*, *or use* *vb*, rĕsisto (3) **(to resist)**

resolute firmus, fortis

resolution obstĭnātĭo, *f*, constantĭa, *f*; **(decision)**, *use vb*, plăcet **(it is resolved)**

resolve *v.t*, **(determine)**, stătŭo (3); **(solve)**, dissolvo (3)

resort to *v.t*, **(a place)**, cĕlĕbro (1); **(have recourse to)**, confŭgĭo (3) ad (*with acc*)

resort *nn*, **(plan)**, consĭlĭum, *n*; **(last —)**, extrēma, *n.pl*

resound *v.i*, rĕsŏno (1)

resource (help) auxĭlĭum, *n*; **(wealth, means)** ŏpes, *f*, *pl*

respect *nn*, **(esteem)**, observantĭa, *f*; **(in all — s)**, omnĭbus partĭbus; **(in — of)**, *use abl. case*, e.g. **stronger in respect of number**, sŭpĕrĭor nŭmĕro

respect *v.t*, **(esteem)**, observo (1); **(reverence)**, sispĭcĭo (3)

respectability hŏnestas, *f*

respectable hŏnestus

respectful observans
respecting *prep*, dē (*with abl*)
respective *use* quisque (**each**) with
  sŭus (**his own**)
respiration respīrātĭo, *f*
respite (delay) mŏra, *f*
resplendent splendĭdus
respond *v.i*, rēspondĕo (2)
response rēsponsum, *n*
responsibility (duty,
  function) officĭum, *n; or use imp.*
  vb, ŏportet (**it behoves**)
responsible (to be — for) praesto
  (1)
rest *nn*, (**repose**), quĭes, *f*, ōtĭum,
  n; (**remainder**), *use adj*, rĕlĭquus,
  e.g. **the — of one's life**, rĕlĭqua
  vīta, *f*
rest *v.i*, quĭesco (3); (**— on, depend**
  on), nītor (3 *dep*)
resting-place cŭbīle, *n*
restitution (to make —) *v.t*, rēstĭtŭo
  (3)
restive *use phr*, qui nōn făcĭle
  dŏmāri pŏtest (**that cannot easily**
  be subdued)
restless inquĭētus
restlessness ĭnquĭes, *f*
restoration rēstĭtūtĭo, *f*
restore *v.t*, rēstĭtŭo (3)
restrain *v.t*, cŏercĕo (2), rĕprĭmo
  (3), cŏhĭbĕo (2)
restraint mŏdĕrātĭo, *f*
restrict *v.t*, circumscrību (3)
restriction (bound) mŏdus, *m*
result *nn*, ēventus, *m*
result *v.i*, ēvĕnĭo (4)
resume *v.t*, rĕpĕto (3)
resurrection rēsurrectĭo, *f*
resuscitate *v.t*, rēsuscĭto (1)
retail *v.t*, dīvendo (3)
retailer caupo, *m*
retain *v.t*, rĕtĭnĕo (2)
retainer sătelles, *c*; (*pl*) soldūrĭi, *m.*
  pl
retake *v.t*, rĕcĭpĭo (3)
retaliate *v.t*, ulciscor (3 *dep*)
retaliation ultĭo, *f*
retard *v.t*, mŏror (1 *dep*)
reticent tăcĭturnus
retinue (companions) cŏmĭtes, *c.pl*
retire *v.i*, (**go away**), rĕcēdo (3),
  ăbĕo (4); (**from a post, etc.**),

dēcēdo (3); (**retreat**), sē rĕcĭpĕre (3
  reflex)
retired rĕmōtus
retirement (act of —) rĕcessus, *m*;
  (**leisure**), ōtĭum, *n*
retiring *adj*, vĕrēcundus
retort *v.t*, rĕfero (*irreg*)
retrace *v.t*, rĕpĕto (3)
retract *v.t*, rĕnuntĭo (1)
retreat *nn*, rĕceptus, *m*; (**place of**
  refuge), rĕfŭgĭum, *n*
retreat *v.i*, sē rĕcĭpĕre (3 *reflex*)
retrench *v.t*, mĭnŭo (3)
retribution poena, *f*
retrieve *v.t*, rĕcŭpĕro (1)
retrograde *adj, use comp. adj*,
  pēĭor (**worse**)
retrogression rĕgressus, *m*
retrospect *use vb*, rēspĭcĭo (3) (**to**
  look back)
return *nn*, (**coming back**), rĕdĭtus,
  m; (**giving back**), rēstĭtūtĭo, *f*;
  (**profit**), quaestus, *m*
return *v.t*, (**give back**), reddo (3),
  rĕfĕro (*irreg*), v.i, (**go back**), rĕdĕo
  (4)
reunite *v.t*, rĕconcĭlĭo (1)
reveal *v.t*, pătĕfăcĭo (3)
revel *nn*, cōmissātĭo, *f*
revel *v.i*, cōmissor (1 *dep*)
revelation pătĕfactĭo, *f*
revenge *nn*, ultĭo, *f*
revenge oneself on *v.t*, ulciscor (3
  dep)
revengeful cŭpĭdus ulciscendi
  (**keen on revenge**)
revenue vectīgal, *n*
reverberate *v.i*, rĕsŏno (1)
revere, reverence *v.t*, vĕnĕror (1
  dep)
reverence vĕnĕrātĭo, *f*
revered vĕnĕrābĭlis
reverend vĕnĕrābĭlis
reverent rĕvĕrens
reverse (contrary) *adj*, contrārĭus
  (**opposite**); (**defeat**), clādes
reverse *v.t*, inverto (3)
revert *v.i*, rĕdĕo (4)
review *nn*, rĕcognĭtĭo, *f*, rĕcensĭo, *f*
review *v.t*, rĕcensĕo (2)
revile *v.t*, mălĕdīco (3) (*with dat*)
reviling *nn*, mălĕdictĭo, *f*
revise *v.t*, ēmendo (1)

revision ēmendātĭo, *f*
revisit *v.t*, rĕvīso (3)
revival rĕnŏvātĭo, *f*
revive *v.t*, rĕcrĕo (1), excĭto (1);
v.i, rĕvīvisco (3)
revocable rĕvŏcābĭlis
revoke *v.t*, abrŏgo (1)
revolt *nn*, dēfectĭo, f, sēdĭtĭo, f
revolt *v.i*, dēfĭcĭo (3)
revolting *adj*, (disgusting), foedus
revolution (turning
round) conversĭo, *f*; (political),
nŏvae res, *f. pl*
revolutionize *v.t*, nŏvo (1)
revolutionary sēdĭtĭōsus
revolve *v.i*, sē volvĕre (3 *reflex*)
reward *nn*, praemĭum, *n*
reward *v.t*, rĕmŭnĕror (1 *dep*)
rewrite *v.t*, rēscrībo (3)
rhetoric rhētŏrĭca, *f*
rhetorical rhētŏrĭcus
Rhine Rhēnus, *m*
rhinoceros rhīnŏcĕros, *m*
rhubarb rādix Pontĭca, *f* (Black
Sea root)
rhyme (verse) versus, *m*
rhythm nŭmĕrus, *m*
rhythmical nŭmĕrōsus
rib costa, *f*
ribald obsēnus
ribbon taenĭa, *f*
rice ŏrўza, *f*
rich dīves, lŏcŭples; (fertile),
pinguis
riches dīvĭtĭae, *f. pl*
richness ūbertas, *f*
rick (heap) ăcervus, *m*
rid *v.t*, lībĕro (1); (to get — of),
dēpōno (3), dēpello (3)
riddle aenigma, *n*; (in — s), per
ambāges
riddle *v.t*, (sift), cerno (3); (— with
holes), confŏdĭo (3)
ride *v.i*, vĕhor (3 *dep*); (— at
anchor), consisto (3)
ride (horseman) ĕquĕs, *m*
ridge (mountain —), iŭgum, *n*
ridicule *nn*, rīdĭcŭlum, *n*
ridicule *v.t*, irrīdĕo (2)
ridiculous rīdĭcŭlus
riding *nn*, ĕquĭtātĭo, *f*
rife frĕquens, crēber
rifle *v.t*, praedor (1 *dep*.)

rift rīma, *f*
rig *v.t*, armo (1)
rigging armāmentum, *n.pl*
right *adj*, (direction), dexter; (true),
rectus, vērus; (correct), rectus;
(fit), ĭdōnĕus; (— hand), dextra
(manus)
right *nn*, (moral), fas, *n*; (legal), iūs,
n
rightly adv, rectē, vērē
right *v.t*, rēstĭtŭo (3)
righteous iustus
righteousness prŏbĭtas, *f*
rightful iustus
rigid rĭgĭdus, dūrus
rigorous dūrus
rigour dūrĭtĭa, *f*
rill rīvŭlus, *m*
rim ōra, *f*, lābrum, *n*
rime prŭīna, *f*
rind crusta, *f*
ring (finger, etc.), ānŭlus, *m*;
(circle), orbis, *m*
ring *v.i*, tinnĭo (4); (surround)
circŭmĕo (4)
ringing *nn*, tinnītus, *m*
ringing *adj*, tinnŭlus
ringleader auctor, *m*
ringlet cincinnus, *m*
rinse *v.t*, collŭo (3)
riot turba, *f*, tŭmultus, *m*; (to make
a —), tŭmultum făcĭo (3)
riotous turbŭlentus; (extravagant),
luxŭrĭōsus
rip *v.t*, scindo (3)
ripe mātūrus
ripen *v.i*, mātūresco (3); *v.t*,
mātūro (1)
ripeness mātūrĭtas, *f*
ripple *v.i*, (tremble), trĕpĭdo (1)
rise *nn*, (of sun, etc., *or* origin),
ortus, *m*
rise *v.i*, surgo (3); (of sun, etc.),
ŏrĭor (4 *dep*); (in rank), cresco
(3); (in rebellion), consurgo (3)
rising *nn*, ortus, *m*; (in rebellion),
mōtus, *m*
rising (ground) *nn*, clīvus, *m*
risk *nn*, pĕrīcŭlum, *n*
risk *v.t*, pĕrīclĭtor (1 *dep*)
ritual rītus, *m*
rival *nn*, aemŭlus, *m*, rīvālis, *c*
rival *v.t*, aemŭlor (1 *dep*)

rivalry aemŭlātĭo, *f*
river *nn*, flūmen, *n*, flŭvĭus, *m*
riverbank rīpa, *f*
riverbed alvĕus, *m*
rivet clāvus, *m*
rivulet rīvŭlus, *m*
road vĭa, *f*, ĭter, *n*; **(to make a —)**, vĭam mūnĭo (4)
road-making mūnītĭo, *(f)* vĭārum
roadstead (for ships) stătĭo, *f*
roam *v.i*, văgor (1 *dep*), erro (1)
roaming *adj*, văgus
road *nn*, frĕmĭtus, *m*
road *v.i*, frĕmo (3)
roast *v.t*, torrĕo (2)
roasted assus
rob *v.t*, spŏlĭo (1) *(with acc. of person robbed, abl. of thing taken)*
robber lătro, *m*
robbery lătrōcĭnĭum, *n*
robe vestis, *f*, vestīmentum, *n*; **(woman's —)**, stŏla, *f*; **(— of state)**, trăbĕa, *f*; **(— of kings)**, purpŭra, *f*
robe *v.t*, vestĭo (4), indŭo (3)
robust rōbustus
rock rūpes, *f*
rock *v.t*, ăgĭto (1)
rocky scŏpŭlōsus
rod virga, *f*; **(fishing —)**, ărundo, *f*
roe căprĕa, *f*; **(of fish)**, ōva, *n.pl* **(eggs)**
rogue scĕlestus, *m*
roguery nēquĭtĭa, *f*
roll *nn*, **(something rolled up)**, vŏlūmen, *n*; **(names)**, album, *n*
roll *v.t*, volvo (3); *v.i*, volvor (3 *pass*)
roller cўlindrus, *m*
rolling *adj*, vŏlūbĭlis
Roman Rōmānus
romance (story) fābŭla, *f*
romance *v.i*, fābŭlor (1 *dep*)
romantic (fabulous) commentĭcĭus
Rome Rōma, *f*
romp *v.i*, lūdo (3)
romp *nn*, lūsus, *m*
roof *nn*, tectum, *n*
roof *v.t*, tĕgo (3)
rook (raven) corvus, *m*

room conclāve, *n*; **(space)**, spătĭum, *n*; **(bed —)**, cŭbĭcŭlum, *n*; **(dining —)** trīclīnĭum, *n*
roomy căpax
roost *nn*, pertĭca, *f*
root rādix, *f*; **(to strike — s, become rooted)**, rādīces ăgo (3); **(— ed to the spot)**, dēfixus
rope fūnis, *m*, restis, *f*, rŭdens, *m*
rosary (garden) rŏsārĭum, *n*
rose rŏsa, *f*
rosemary ros mărīnus, *m*
rostrum rostra, *n.pl*
rosy rŏsĕus
rot *nn*, tābes, *f*
rot *v.i*, pūtesco (3)
rotate *v.i*, sĕ volvĕre (3 *reflex*)
rotation turbo, *m*
rotten pŭtrĭdus
rotundity rŏtundĭtas, *f*
rouge *nn*, fūcus, *m*
rouge *v.t*, fūco (1)
rough asper; **(weather)**, ătrox; **(of sea)**, turbĭdus; **(of manner)**, incultus
roughness aspĕrĭtas, *f*
round *adj*, rŏtundus
round *adv*, circum
round *prep*, circum *(with acc)*
round *v.t*, **(to make —)**, rŏtundo (1), curvo (1); **(to — off)**, conclūdo (3); *v.i*, **(to go —)**, circummăgor (3 *pass*)
roundabout *adj*, dēvĭus
rouse *v.t*, excĭto (1)
rout *nn*, **(flight, defeat)**, fŭga, *f*
rout *v.t*, fŭgo (1)
route ĭter, *n*
routine ūsus, *m*
rove *v.i*, văgor (1 *dep*)
roving *nn*, văgātĭo, *f*
row (line) ordo, *m*; **(quarrel)**, rixa, *f*; **(noise)**, strĕpĭtus, *m*
row *v.i*, rēmĭgo (1)
rowing *nn*, rēmĭgĭum, *n*
royal rēgĭus
royalty regnum, *n*
rub *v.t*, tĕro (3), frĭco (1); **(— out)**, dēlĕo (2)
rubbish quisquĭlĭae, *f. pl*
rubicund rŭbĭcundus

ruby *nn*, carbuncŭlus, *m*
ruby *adj*, purpŭrĕus
rudder gŭbernācŭlum, *n*
ruddy rŭbĭcundus
rude (person)   asper, ĭnurbānus
rudeness ĭnhūmānĭtas, *f*
rudimentary incŏhātus
   (incomplete)
rudiments ĕlĕmenta, *n.pl*
rue *nn*, rūta, *f*
rueful maestus
ruff torquis, *m. or f*
ruffian perdĭtus, *m*, lătro, *m*
ruffianly *adj*, scĕlestus
ruffle *v.t*, ăgĭto (1)
rug strāgŭlum, *n*
rugged asper
ruin exĭtĭum, *n*, rŭīna, *f*; (building),
   părĭĕtĭnae, *f. pl*
ruin *v.t*, perdo (3)
ruinous exĭtĭōsus, damnōsus
rule *nn*, (law), lex, *f*; (precept),
   praeceptum, *n*; (pattern), norma,
   f; (for measuring), rēgŭla, *f*;
   (government), impĕrĭum, *n*
rule *v.t*, rĕgo (3); *v.i*, regno (1)
ruler (person)   dŏmĭnus, *m*;
   (measurement), rēgŭla, *f*
rumble *nn*, mumur, *n*
rumble *v.i*, murmŭro (1), mūgĭo
   (4)
ruminate *v.t*, cōgĭto (1)
rummage *v.t*, rīmor (1 *dep*)
rumour *nn*, rūmor, *m*, fāma, *f*
rump clūnes, *f. pl*
rumple *v.t*, corrūgo (1)
run *v.i*, curro (3); (— about), hūc
   illūc curro (3); (— after),
   persĕquor (3 *dep*); (— away),
   fŭgio (3); (— aground), impingor
   (3 *pass*), inflīgor (3 *pass*); (—
   back), rĕcurro (3); (— down),
   dēcurro (3); (— forward),
   prōcurro (3); (— into), incurro
   (3); (— out), excurro (3); (—
   over, with vehicle, etc.), obtĕro
   (3); (— through), percurro (3)
runaway *adj*, fŭgĭtīvus
runner cursor, *m*
running *nn*, cursus, *m*
running *adj*, (water), vīvus
rupture (disease)   hernĭa, *f*

rupture *v.t*, rumpo (3)
rural rustĭcus
rush *nn*, (plant), iuncus, *m*;
   (rushing, running), impĕtus, *m*
rush *v.i*, rŭo (3); (— forward), sē
   prōrĭpĕre (3 *reflex*); (— into),
   irrŭo (3); (— out), sē effundĕre (3
   reflex)
rusk crustum, *n*
russet rūfus
rust *nn*, rōbīgo, *f*
rustic *adj*, rustĭcus
rusticate *v.i*, rustĭcor (1 *dep*); *v.t*,
   rēlēgo (1)
rusticity rustĭcĭtas, *f*
rustle *v.i*, crĕpo (1)
rustle, rustling *nn*, sŭsurrus, *m*
rusty rōbīgĭnōsus
rut orbĭta, *f*
ruthless immītis, sĕvērus
rye sĕcāle, *n*

S

Sabbath sabbăta, *n.pl*
sable *adj*, (black), āter
sabre glădĭus, *m*
sack (bag)   saccus, *m*; (pillage),
   dīreptĭo, *f*
sack *v.t*, (pillage), dīrĭpĭo (3)
sackcloth saccus, *m*
sacrament săcrāmentum, *n*
sacred săcer, sanctus
sacredness sanctĭtas, *f*
sacrifice săcrĭfĭcĭum, *n*; (the
   victim), hostĭa, *f*
sacrifice *v.i*, săcrĭfĭco (1); *v.t*,
   immŏlo (1)
sacrificial săcrĭfĭcus
sacrilege săcrĭlĕgĭum, *n; or use vb*,
   dīrĭpĭo (3) (to plunder)
sad tristis
sadden *v.t*, tristĭtĭā afficĭo (3)
   (affect with sadness)
saddle *nn*, ĕphhippĭum, *n*
saddle *v.t*, sterno (3); (impose),
   impōno (3)
sadness tristĭtĭa, f
safe (free from danger)   tūtus;
   (having escaped from danger),
   incŏlŭmis

safe-conduct fīdes, *f*
safeguard (act of —) cautǐo, *f*;
  (defence), prōpugnācǔlum, *n*
safely *adv*, tūtō
safety sǎlus, *f*
saffron *nn*, crǒcus, *m*
saffron *adj*, crǒcěus
sagacious prūdens, sǎgax
sagacity prūdentǐa, *f*, sǎgācǐtas, *f*
sage (wise man) sǎpǐens, *m*;
  (plant), salvǐa, *f*
sail *nn*, vēlum, *n*; (to set —), vēla
  do (1)
sail *v.i*, nāvǐgo (1), vēhor (3 *pass*);
  (to go by means of sails), vēla
  fǎcǐo (3)
sailing *nn*, nāvǐgātǐo, *f*
sailor nauta, *m*
saint sanctus, *m*
saintly sanctus
sake (for the — of), *prep*, causā
  (*with genit*); (on behalf of), prō
  (*with abl*), ǒb, propter (*with acc*)
salad ǎcētārǐa, *n.pl*
salary merces, *f*
sale vendǐtǐo, *f*; (auction), hasta, *f*
salient *adj*, prīmus (first)
saline salsus
saliva sǎlīva, *f*
sallow pallǐdus
sally *nn*, ēruptǐo, *f*
sally *v.i*, ēruptǐōnem fǎcǐo (3)
salmon salmo, *m*
saloon ātrǐum, *n*
salt *nn*, sal, *m*
salt *adj*, salsus
salt *v.t*, sǎle condǐo (4) (season
  with salt)
saltcellar sǎlīnum, *n*
saltmines sǎlīnae, *f. pl*
salubrious sǎlūbris
salutary sǎlūtāris; (useful), ūtǐlis
salutation sǎlūtātǐo, *f*
salute *v.t*, sǎlūto (1)
salvation sǎlus, *f*
salve unguentum, *n*
salver scǔtella, *f*, pǎtella, *f*
same *prep*, īdem; (the same as),
  īdem qui, īdem atque; (in the —
  place), *adv*, ǐbīdem (at the —
  time), sǐmǔl; (fixed, constant),
  constans

sample exemplum, *n*
sanctification sanctǐfǐcātǐo, *f*
sanctify *v.t*, consěcro (1)
sanction auctōrǐtas, *f*; (penalty)
  poena, *f*
sanction *v.t*, fǎtum fǎcǐo (3)
sanctity sanctǐtas, *f*
sanctuary fānum, *n*, templum, *n*:
  (refuge), rěfǔgǐum, *n*
sand hǎrēna, *f*
sandal sǒlěa, *f*
sandstone tōfus, *m*
sandy hǎrēnōsus
sane sānus
sanguinary crǔentus, sanguǐnārǐus
sanguine *use* spēs, *f*, (hope)
sanity mens sāna, *f*
sap *nn*, sūcus, *m*
sap *v.t*, subrǔo (3)
sapient *adj*, sǎpǐens
sapless ārǐdus
sapling arbor nǒvella
sappers (military) mūnītōres, *m.
  pl*
sapphire sapphīrus, *f*
sarcasm cǎvillātǐo, *f*, (scoffing)
sarcastic ǎcerbus
sarcophagus sarcǒphǎgus, *m*
sash cingǔlum, *n*
satanic něfandus
satchel lǒcǔlus, *m*
satellite (star) stella, *f*;
  (attendant), sǎtelles, *c*
satiate *v.t*, sǎtǐo (1)
satiety sǎtǐětas, *f*
satire sǎtǔra, *f*
satirical (bitter) ǎcerbus
satirize *v.t*, perstringo (3)
satirist scriptor sǎtǐrǐcus, *m*
satisfaction (inner) vǒluptas, *f*;
  (compensation, punishment),
  poena,
satisfactorily *adv*, ex sententǐā
satisfactory ǐdōněus, *or* sǎtis
  (enough)
satisfied contentus
satisfy *v.t*, (a need), explěo (2),
  (*with dat*); (convince), persuāděo
  (2)
satrap sǎtrǎpes, *m*
saturate *v.t*, sǎtǔro (1)

satyr sătÿrus, *m*
sauce condīmentum, *n*
saucepan cācăbus, *m*, cortīna
saucer pătella, *f*
saucy pĕtŭlans
saunter *v.i*, văgor (1 *dep*)
sausage farcīmen, *n*
savage *adj*, fĕrus, ătrox, effĕrātus
savageness, savagery fĕrĭtas, *f*,
    saevĭtĭa, *f*
save *v.t*, servo (1); **(defend)**, tŭĕor
    (2 *dep*); **(lay by)**, rĕservo (1)
save *prep*, praeter (*with acc*)
saving *nn*, conservātĭo, *f*
savings pĕcūlĭum, *n*
saviour servātor, *m*
savour *nn*, săpor, *m*
savour *v.t*, săpĭo (3)
savoury *adj*, condītus
saw serra, *f*
saw *v.t*, serrā sĕco (1) **(cut with a**
    saw)
sawdust scŏbis, *f*
say *v.t*, dīco (3), lŏquor (3 *dep*);
    (to — that something will not ...),
    use nĕgo (1) **(to deny); (it is said),**
    fertur
saying *nn*, dictum, *n*
scab crusta, *f*
scabbard văgīna, *f*
scabby scăber
scaffold (frame) māchĭna, *f*;
    (execution), supplĭcĭum, *n*
scald *nn*, ădusta, *n.pl*
scale (pair of —s) lībra, *f*; **(of**
    fish), squāma, *f*; **(gradation),**
    grădus, *m*
scale *v.t*, **(climb with ladders),**
    scālis ascendo (3)
scaling-ladders scālae, *f. pl*
scallop pecten, *m*
scalp cŭtis, *f*, **(skin)**
scalpel scalpellum, *n*
scamp scĕlestus, *m*
scamper *v.i*, fŭgĭo (3)
scan *v.t*, contemplor (1 *dep*)
scandal opprŏbrĭum, *n*;
    (disparagement) obtrectātĭo, *f*
scandalous infāmis
scanty exĭgŭus
scantiness exĭgŭĭtas, *f*
scapegrace nĕbŭlo, *m*
scar cĭcātrix, *f*

scarce rārus
scarcely *adv*, vix, aegrĕ
scarcity (of supplies, etc.) ĭnŏpĭa,
    f
scare *v.t*, terrĕo (2)
scarecrow formīdo, *f*
scarf chlămys, *f*
scarlet *nn*, coccum, *n*
scarlet *adj*, coccĭnĕus
scathing ăcerbus
scatter *v.t*, spargo (3); *v.i*, sē
    spargĕre (3 *reflex*)
scene (of play) scēna, *f*;
    (spectacle), spectācŭlum, *n*
scenery (natural —) *use* rĕgĭo, *f*,
    (region)
scent (sense of smell) ŏdōrātus,
    m; **(the smell itself)**, ŏdor, *m*
scent *v.t*, **(discern by smell),**
    ŏdōror (1)
scented ŏdōrātus
sceptical dŭbĭtans
sceptre sceptrum, *n*
schedule tăbŭla, *f*
scheme *nn*, consĭlĭum, *n*
scheme *v.t*, consĭlĭum căpĭo (3)
    (make a plan)
scholar (pupil) discĭpŭlus, *m*;
    (learned man), doctus, *m*
scholarly doctus
scholarship littĕrae, *f. pl*
school lūdus, *m*, schŏla
school *v.t*, ērŭdĭo (4)
schoolmaster măgister, *m*
schoolmistress măgistra, *f*
schooner phăsēlus, *m*
sciatica ischĭas, *f*
science scĭentĭa, *f*, discĭplīna, *f*,
    rătĭo, *f*
scientific *use genit. of nouns*
    above
scimitar ăcīnăces, *m*
scintillate *v.i*, scintillo (1)
scion prōles, *f*
scissors forfīces, *f. pl*
scoff at *v.t*, irrīdĕo (2)
scoffer irrīsor, *m*
scoffing *nn*, irrīsĭo, *f*
scold *v.t*, obiurgo (1), incrĕpo (1)
scoop out *v.t*, căvo (1)
scoop *nn*, trulla, *f*
scope (room) campus, *m*
scorch *v.t*, ambūro (3)

scorched torrĭdus

scorching torrĭdus

score (total) summa, *f*; **(account, reckoning)**, rătĭo, *f*; **(mark)**, nŏta, *f*

score *v.t*, **(note, mark)**, nŏto (1); **(— a victory)**, victōrĭam rĕporto (1)

scorn *nn*, contemptus, *m*

scorn *v.t*, sperno (3), contemno (3)

scornful sŭperbus

scorpion scorpĭo, *m*

scoundrel nēbŭlo, *m*

scour *v.t*, **(clean)**, tergĕo (2); **(run over)** percurro (3)

scourge *nn*, **(whip)**, flăgellum, *n*; **(pest)**, pestis, *f*, pernĭcĭes, *f*

scourge *v.t*, verbĕro (1)

scourging *nn*, verbĕra, *n.pl*

scout explōrātor, *m*

scout *v.t*, **(spy out)**, spĕcŭlor (1 *dep*)

scowl *nn*, frontis contractĭo, *f*

scowl *v.i*, frontem contrăho (3), **(contract the brow)**

scramble for *v.t*, *use phr*, inter sē certāre **(struggle among themselves)**

scrap frustrum, *n*

scrape *v.t*, rādo (3)

scraper strĭgĭlis, *f*

scratch *v.t*, rādo (3), scalpo (3)

scream *nn*, vōcĭfĕrātĭo, *f*

scream *v.i*, vōcĭfĕror (1 *dep*)

screech owl ŭlŭla, *f*

screen tĕgĭmen, *n*

screen *v.t*, tĕgo (3)

screw *nn*, clāvus, *m*

scribble *v.t*, scrībo (3)

scribe scrība, *m*

Scripture Scriptūra, *f*

scroll vŏlūmen, *n*

scrub *v.t*, tergĕo (2)

scruple (religious, etc.) rĕlĭgĭo, *f*

scrupulous rĕlĭgĭōsus, dīlĭgens

scrutinize *v.t*, scrūtor (1 *dep*)

scrutiny scrūtātĭo, *f*

scuffle *nn*, rixa, *f*

scull (oar) rēmus, *m*; **(***v.i*, rēmĭgo (1)

sculptor sculptor, *m*

sculpture (art of —) sculptūra, *f*; **(the work itself)**, ŏpus, *n*

scum spūma, *f*

scurf furfur, *m*

scurrility prŏcācĭtas, *f*

scurrilous scurrīlis, prŏcax

scurvy foedus

scuttle *v.t*, **(a ship)**, *use phr*, nāvem ultro dēprĭmo (3) **(sink the ship of their own accord)**

scythe falx, *f*

sea măre, *n*, **(to be at —)**, nāvĭgo (1)

sea *adj*, mărĭtĭmus, mărīnus

seacoast ōra mărĭtĭma, *f*

seafaring *adj*, mărĭtĭmus

seafight pugna nāvālis, *f*

seagull lărus, *m*

seal *nn*, **(of letter)**, signum, *n*; **(animal)**, phōca, *f*

seal *v.t*, **(letter)**, signo (1); **(close up)**, comprĭmo (3)

sealing-wax cēra, *f*

seam sūtūra, *f*

seaman nauta, *m*

sear *v.t*, ădūro (3)

search for *v.t*, quaero (3); **(explore)**, rīmor (1 *dep*)

search *nn*, investīgātĭo, *f*

seasick *adj*, nausĕābundus; **(to be —)**, *v.i*, nausĕo (1)

seasickness nausĕa, *f*

season tempus, *n*, tempestas, *f*; **(right time)**, tempus, *n*

season *v.t*, condĭo (4)

seasonable tempestīvus

seasoned (flavoured) condītus; **(hardened)**, dūrātus

seasoning *nn*, condīmentum, *n*

seat sēdes, *f*, sĕdīle, *n*, sella, *f*; **(home)**, dōmĭcĭlĭum, *n*: *v.t*. collŏco (1)

seaweed alga, *f*

secede *v.i*, dēcēdo (3)

secession dēfectĭo, *f*

secluded sēcrētus

seclusion sōlĭtūdo, *f*

second *adj*, sĕcundus; **(— of two)**, alter; **(for the — time)**, *adv*, ĭtĕrum; **(— ly)**, *adv*, de inde

second *nn*, **(time)**, mōmentum, *n*

second *v.t*, adĭŭvo (1)

secondary infĕrĭor

second-hand ūsu trītus **(worn with usage)**

secrecy sēcrētum, *n*
secret arcāna, *n.pl*
secret *adj*, occultus, arcānus; (hidden), clandestīnus; (to keep something —), *v.t*, cēlo (1)
secretary scrība, *m*
secrete *v.t*, cēlo (1), abdo (3)
secretly *adv*, clam
sect secta, *f*
section pars, *f*
secular (not sacred), prŏfānus
secure *v.t*, mūnĭo (4), firmo (1), lĭgo (1) (tie up)
secure *adj*, tūtus
security sălus, *f*; (guarantee), pignus, *n*; (to give —), căvĕo (2)
sedate grăvis
sedative mĕdĭcāmentum sŏpōrĭfĕrum
sedentary sĕdentārĭus
sedge ulva, *f*
sediment faex, *f*
sedition sēdĭtĭo, *f*
seditious sēdĭtĭōsus
seduce *v.t*, tento (1), sollĭcĭto (1)
seducer corruptor, *m*
seduction corruptēla, *f*
sedulous assĭdŭus
see *v.t* vĭdĕo (2), cerno (3), aspĭcĭo (3); (to — to it that ...), cūro (1) ad (*with gerund phr*); (understand), intellĕgo (3)
seed sēmen, *n* (literal and metaphorical)
seedling arbor nŏvella, *f*
seedy grānōsus
seeing that *conj*, cum
seek *v.t*, quaero (3), pĕto (3), affecto (1)
seem *v.i*, vĭdĕor (2 *pass.*)
seeming *nn*, spĕcĭes, *f*
seemly *adj*, dĕcōrus, (it is —), dĕcet (2 *impers*)
seer vātes, *c*
seethe *v.i*, fervĕo (2)
segment segmentum, *n*
segregate *v.t*, sēcerno (3)
seize *v.t*, răpĭo (3), corrĭpĭo (3), prendo (3), occŭpo (1); (of illness, passion, etc.), affĭcĭo (3)
seizure comprĕhensĭo, *f*
seldom *adv*, rārō
select *v.t*, lĕgo (3)

select *adj*, lectus
selection dēlectus, *m*
self *pron*, (emphatic), ipse; (reflexive), sē
self-confident confĭdens
self-satisfied contentus
selfish, selfishness, (to be —) sē ămāre (1 *reflex*)
sell *v.t*, vendo (3)
seller vendĭtor, *m*
semblance ĭmāgo, *f*
semicircle hēmĭcyclĭum, *n*
senate sĕnātus, *m*
senate house cūrĭa, *f*
senator sĕnātor, *m*
send *v.t*, mitto (3); (— away), dīmitto (3); (— back), rĕmitto (3); (— for), arcesso (3); (— forward), praemitto (3); (— in), immitto (3)
senile sĕnīlis
senior, (in age) nātu maior
sensation (feeling) sensus, *m*; mōtus (*m*) ănĭmi (impulse)
sensational nŏtābĭlis
sense (feeling) sensus, *m*; (understanding), prūdentĭa, *f*; (meaning), sententĭa, *f*
senseless (unconscious) *use adv. phr*, sensu ablāto (with feeling withdrawn); (stupid), sōcors
sensible prūdens
sensitive sensĭlis
sensitiveness mollĭtĭa
sensual lĭbīdĭnōsus
sensuality lĭbīdo, *f*
sentence (criminal) iūdĭcĭum, *n*; (writing, etc.), sententĭa, *f*
sentence *v.t*, damno (1)
sententious sententĭōsus
sentiment (feeling) sensus, *m*; (opinion), ŏpīnĭo, *f*
sentimental mollis
sentimentality mollĭtĭa, *f*
sentinel vĭgil, *m*; (to be on — duty), in stătĭōne esse (*irreg*)
separable dīvĭdŭus
separate *v.t*, sēpăro (), dīvĭdo (3), sēiungo (3), sēcerno (3)
separate *adj*, sēpărātus, sēcrētus
separately *adv*, sēpărātim
separation sēpărātĭo, *f*
September September (mensis)

sepulchre sĕpulcrum, *n*
sequel (outcome) exĭtus, *m*
sequence ordo, *m*
serene tranquillus
serf servus, *m*
series sĕrĭes, *f*
serious grăvis
seriousness grăvĭtas
sermon ōrātĭo, *f*
serpent serpens, *f*
serried confertus
servant mĭnister, *m*, fămŭlus, *m*,
  servus, *m*
serve *v.t*, servĭo (4), (*with dat*); (at
  table, etc.), mĭnistro (1); (in the
  army), stīpendĭa mĕrĕor (2 *dep*);
  (to — as), esse (*irreg*) (*with prō
  and abl*)
service mĭnistĕrĭum, *n*, ŏpĕra,
  (military), mīlĭtĭa, *f*
serviceable ūtĭlis
servile servīlis
servitude servĭtus, *f*
session (assembly) conventus, *m*
set *nn*, (of people), glŏbus, *m*
set *adj*, stătus
set *v.t*, (place), stătŭo (3), pōno
  (3); *v.i*, (of the sun), occĭdo (3);
  (— about, begin), incĭpĭo (3);
  (— aside), *v.t*, sēpōno (3);
  (— down in writing), nŏto (1);
  (— free), lībĕro (1); (set off *or*
  out), *v.i*, prŏfīciscor (3 *dep*);
  (— up), *v.t*, stătŭo (3)
settee lectŭlus, *m*
setting (of sun) occāsus, *m*
settle *v.t*, constĭtŭo (3); (a dispute),
  compōno (3); (debt), solvo (3);
  v.i, (in a home, etc.), consīdo (3)
settled certus
settlement (colony) cŏlōnĭa, *f*;
  (— of an affair), compŏsĭtĭo, *f*
settle cŏlōnus, *m*
seven septem; (— hundred),
  septingenti; (— times), *adv*,
  septĭes
seventeen septendĕcim
seventeenth septĭmus dĕcĭmus
seventh septĭmus
seventieth septŭăgēsĭmus
seventy septŭăginta
sever *v.t*, sēpăro (1), sēiungo (3)

several complūres, ălĭquot
severe sĕvērus, dūrus
severity sĕvērĭtas, *f*, ăcerbĭtas, *f*
sew *v.t*, sŭo (3)
sewer (drain) clŏāca, *f*
sex sexus, *m*
sexagenarian sexāgēnārĭus, *m*
sexual *use nn*, sexus, *m*, (sex)
shabbiness sordes, *f. pl*
shabby sordĭdus
shackle *v.t*, vincŭlis constringo (3)
  (bind with chains)
shackle(s) *nn*, vincŭla, *n.pl*
shade *nn*, umbra, *f*; (the —s of the
  dead), mānes, *m. pl*
shade *v.t*, ŏpāco (1)
shadow umbra, *f*
shadowy ŏpācus, ĭnānis
shady ŏpācus
shaft (of a weapon) hastīle, *n*; (an
  arrow), săgitta, *f*; (of a mine),
  pŭtĕus, *m*
shaggy hirtus, hirsūtus
shake *v.t*, quătĭo (3), ăgĭto (1)
  lăbĕfăcĭo (3); *v.i*, trĕmo (3),
  trĕpĭdo (1); (— hands), dextras
  iungo (3) (join right hands)
shaking *nn*, quassātĭo, *f*
shallow *adj*, (sea), vădōsus, brĕvis
shallows *nn*, văda, *n.pl*
sham *adj*, sĭmŭlātus
sham *nn*, sĭmŭlātĭo, *f* (pretence)
sham *v.t*, sĭmŭlo (1)
shamble *use* turba, *f*
shame *nn*, (feeling), pŭdor, *m*;
  (disgrace), dēdĕcus, *n*
shame *v.t*, rŭbōrem incŭtĭo (3)
  (*with dat*)
shamefaced vĕrēcundus
shameful turpis
shamefulness turbĭtūdo, *f*
shameless impŭdens
shamelessness impŭdentĭa, *f*
shamrock trĭfŏlĭum, *n*
shank crus, *n*
shape *nn*, forma, *f*
shape *v.t*, formo (1)
shapeless informis
shapely formōsus
share (part) pars, *f*; (plough —),
  vōmer, *m*
share *v.t*, partĭor (4 *dep*)
sharer partĭceps, *c*

shark pistrix, *f*
sharp ăcūtus, ācer
sharp-sighted perspĭcax
sharp-witted ăcūtus
sharpen *v.t*, ăcŭo (3)
sharply *adv*, ăcūte, ācrĭter
sharpness (of tongue) aspĕrĭtas, *f*; (mental), ăcūmen, *n*
shatter *v.t*, frango (3)
shave *v.t*, rādo (3)
shawl ămĭcŭlum, *n*
she *pron*, illa, ĕa, haec, ista
sheaf mănĭpŭlus, *m*
shear *v.t*, tondĕo (2)
shearing *nn*, tonsūra, *f*
shears forfex, *f*
sheath vāgīna, *f*
sheathe *v.t*, in vāgīnam rĕcondo (3) (put back into the sheath)
shed *nn*, tŭgŭrĭum, *n*
shed *v.t*, fundo (3)
sheen fulgor, *m*
sheep ŏvis, *f*
sheepfold saeptum, *n*
sheepskin pellis ŏvilla, *f*
sheepish sŏcors, *or use adv. phr*, dēmisso vultu (with downcast face)
sheer (steep) abruptus; (pure, absolute), mĕrus
sheet (cloth) lintĕum, *n*; (paper), schĕda, *f*; (— of a sail), pes, *m*
shelf plŭtĕus, *m*
shell concha, *f*, crusta, *f*
shellfish conchȳlĭum, *n*
shelter *nn*, perfŭgĭum, *n*, tectum, *n*
shelter *v.t*, tĕgo (3); *v.i, use phr*, ad perfŭgĭum sē conferre (*irreg*) (betake oneself to shelter)
shelving *adj*, dēclīvis
shepherd pastor, *m*
shield *nn*, scūtum, *n*
shield *v.t*, tĕgo (3), dēfendo (3)
shift (change) vīcissĭtūdo, *f*.
shift *v.t*, mūto (1); *v.i*, mūtor (1 *pass*)
shifty versūtus
shin crūs, *n*
shine *v.i*, lūcĕo (2), fulgĕo (2)
ship *nn*, nāvis, *f*; (war —), nāvis longa, *f*; (transport —), nāvis ŏnĕrārĭa, *f*

ship *v.t*, (put on board), in nāvem impōno (3); (transport), nāve transporto (1)
ship-owner nāvĭcŭlārĭus, *m*
shipping nāvĭgĭa, *n.pl*
shipwreck naufrăgĭum, *n*
shipwrecked naufrăgus
shirt sŭbūcŭla, *f*
shiver *v.i*, horrĕo (2)
shivering *nn*, horror, *m*
shoal (water) vădum, *n*; (fish), exāmen, *n*
shock offensĭo, *f*, ictus, *m*; (of battle), concursus, *m*
shock *v.t*, offendo (3), percŭtĭo (3)
shocking *adj*, ătrox
shoe *nn*, calcĕus, *m*
shoe *v.t*, calcĕo (1)
shoemaker sūtor, *m*
shoot *nn*, (sprout), surcŭlus, *m*
shoot *v.t*, (a missile), mitto (3); *v.i*, (— along, across), vŏlo (1)
shooting-star fax caelestis, *f*
shop tăberna, *f*
shopkeeper tăbernārĭus, *m* (*pl. only*)
shore lītus, *n*, ōra, *f*
shore-up *v.t*, fulcĭo (4)
short brĕvis, ĕxĭgŭus; (— cut), via compendĭārĭa, *f*; (in —), *adv*, dēnĭque
shortage ĭnŏpĭa, *f* (lack)
shortcoming dēlictum, *n*
shorten *v.t*, contrăho (3)
shortly *adv*, (of time), brĕvi; (briefly), brĕvĭter
shortness brĕvĭtas, *f*
shot (firing) ictus, *m*
shoulder hŭmĕrus, *m*; (— blade), scăpŭlae, *f. pl*
shoulder *v.t*, fĕro (*irreg*) (to bear)
shout *nn*, clāmor, *m*
shout *v.i*, clāmo (1)
shove *v.t*, trūdo (3)
shovel pāla, *f*
show *nn*, (appearance), spĕcĭes, *f*; (spectacle), spectācŭlum, *n*; (procession, etc.), pompa, *f*
show *v.t*, monstro (1), praebĕo (2), ostendo (3); (— off), *v.t*, ostento (1); *v.i*, sē ostentare (1 *reflex*)

shower imber, *m*
shower *v.t*, fundo (3)
showery plŭvĭus
showy spĕcĭōsus
shred pannus, *m*
shrew fēmĭna prŏcax
shrewd ăcūtus, săgax
shrewdness săgācĭtas, *f*
shriek *nn*, ŭlŭlātus, *m*
shriek *v.i* ŭlŭlo (1)
shrill ăcūtus, ācer
shrine dēlūbrum, *n*
shrink *v.t*, contrăho (3); *v.i,*
(— from), ăbhorrĕo (2)
shrinking *nn*, contractĭo, *f*
shrivel *v.t*, corrūgo (1)
shrivelled rūgōsus
shroud *use* lintĕum, *n*, (cloth)
shroud *v.t*, involvo (3)
shrub frŭtex, *m*
shrubbery frŭtĭcētum
shudder *v.i*, horrĕo (2)
shudder *nn*, horror, *m*
shuffle *v.t*, miscĕo (2); *v.i, use phr,*
lentē ambŭlo (1) (walk slowly)
shun *v.t*, fŭgĭo (3), vīto (1)
shut *v.t*, claudo (3); (— in or up),
inclūdo (3); (— out), exclūdo (3)
shutters fŏrĭcŭlae, *f. pl*
shuttle rădĭus, *m*
shy vĕrēcundus
shy *v.i*, (of horses), consternor (1
pass)
shyness vĕrēcundĭa, *f*
sick aeger; (to be —), *v.i*, aegrōto
(1); (vomit), *v.i, and v.t*, vŏmo
(3)
sicken *v.t*, fastīdĭum mŏvĕo (2);
v.i, aeger fīo (*irreg*)
sickle falx, *f*
sickly infirmus
sickness morbus, *m*
side (of the body) lătus, *n*; (part,
region), pars, *f*; (party, faction),
pars, *f*; (from (or on) all —s), *adv,*
undĭque; (on both —s), ŭtrimque;
(on this —), hinc; (on that —),
illinc; (on this — of), *prep*, citra
(*with acc*); (on that — of), ŭltra
side *adj*, (sidelong), oblīquus
sideboard ăbăcus, *m*
sideways *adv*, oblīquē
siege *nn*, obsĭdĭo, *f*

siege-works ŏpĕra, *n.pl*
sieve crībrum, *n*
sift *v.t*, crībro (1); (— evidence,
etc.), scrūtor (1 *dep*)
sigh *nn*, suspīrĭum, *n*
sigh *v.i*, suspīro (1)
sight (sense or act) vīsus, *m*;
(view), conspectus, *m*;
(spectacle), spectācŭlum, *n*
sight *v.t*, conspĭcor (1 *dep*)
sightly formōsus, vĕnustus
sign *nn*, signum, *n*; (mark), nŏta, *f*;
(trace, footprint), vestīgĭum, *n*;
(portent), portentum, *n*
sign *v.t*, subscrībo (3); (give a —),
v.i, signum do (1)
signal signum, *n*
signal *v.i*, signum do (1)
signature nōmen, *n*
signet signum, *n*
significance signĭfĭcātĭo, *f*
significant signĭfĭcans
signify *v.t*, signĭfĭco (1)
silence sĭlentĭum, *n*
silent tăcĭtus, (to be —), *v.i*, tăcĕo
(2), sĭlĕo (2)
silk *nn*, bombyx, *m*
silk, silken *adj*, sērĭcus
silkworm bombyx, *m*
silky mollis
sill līmen, *n*
silliness stultĭtĭa, *f*
silly stultus
silt *nn*, līmus, *m*, sentīna, *f*
silver *nn*, argentum, *n*
silver *adj*, argentĕus
silver-mine argentārĭum metallum
similar sĭmĭlis (*with genit. or dat*)
similarity sĭmĭlĭtūdo, *f*
similarly *adv*, sĭmĭlĭter
simmer *v.i*, lentē fervĕo (3) (boil
slowly)
simper *v.i*, subrīdĕo (2)
simple simplex; (weak-minded),
ĭneptus
simpleton stultus, *m*
simplicity simplĭcĭtas, *f*
simplify *v.t*, făcĭlem reddo (3)
simulation sĭmŭlātĭo, *f*
simultaneous *use adv*, sĭmul (at
the same time)
sin *nn*, peccātum, *n*

sin *v.i*, pecco (1)

since *conj*, cum (*foll. by vb. in subjunctive*); **(temporal)** postquam

since *adv*, ăbhinc

since *prep*, ē, ex, ā, ăb (*with abl*)

sincere sincērus, simplex

sincerity sincērĭtas, *f*, simplĭcĭtas, *f*

sinew nervus, *m*

sinful impĭus

sinfulness impĭĕtas, *f*

sing *v.i. and v.t*, căno (3)

singe *v.t*, ădūro (3)

singer cantātor, *m*

singing *nn*, cantus, *m*

single *adj*, **(one, sole)**, ūnus, sŏlus; **(unmarried)**, caelebs

single out *v.t*, ēlĭgo (3)

singly *adv*, singŭlātim

singular, **(one)** singŭlaris; **(strange)**, nŏvus

singularly *adv*, ūnĭcē

sinister sĭnister

sink *v.t*, mergo (3); *v.i*, sīdo (3), consīdo (3)

sinner peccātor, *m*

sinuous sĭnŭōsus

sip *v.t*, dēgusto (1), lībo (1)

sir **(respectful address)** bŏne vir

sire păter, *m*

siren sīrēn, *f*

sister sŏror, *f*

sit *v.i*, sĕdĕo (2); **(— down)**, consīdo (3); **(— up, stay awake)**, vĭgĭlo (1)

site sĭtus, *m*

sitting *nn*, sessĭo, *f*

situated sĭtus

situation sĭtus, *m*

six sex; **(— each)**, sēni; **(— times)**, *adv*, sexĭens

sixteen sēdĕcim

sixteenth sextus dĕcĭmus

sixth sextus

sixtieth sexāgēsĭmus

sixty sexāginta

size magnĭtūdo, *f*; **(of great —)**, *adj*, magnus; **(of small —)**, parvus; **(of what — ?)**, quantus?

skeleton ossa, *n.pl*, **(bones)**

sketch *nn*, ădumbrātĭo, *f*

sketch *v.t*, ădumbro (1)

skewer vĕrūcŭlum, *n*

skiff scăpha, *f*

skilful, skilled pĕrītus

skilfulness, skill pĕrītĭa, *f*

skim *v.t*, **(— off)**, dēspūmo (1); **(— over)**, percurro (3)

skin cŭtis, *f*, pellis, *f*

skin *v.t*, pellem dīrĭpĭo (3) **(tear away the skin)**

skip *v.i*, exsulto (1); **(— over)**, *v.i. and v.t*, praetĕrĕo (4)

skipper nauarchus, *m*

skirmish *nn*, lĕve certāmen, *n*

skirmish *v.i*, parvŭlis proelĭis contendo (3) **(fight in small engagements)**

skirmisher vēlĕs, *m*

skirt *nn*, limbus, *m*

skirt *v.t*, **(scrape past)**, rādo (3)

skittish lascīvus

skulk *v.i*, lătĕo (2)

skull calvārĭa, *f*

sky caelum, *n*

sky-blue caerŭlĕus

skylark ălauda, *f*

slab **(of stone)** ăbăcus, *m*

slack rĕmissus

slacken *v.t*, rĕmitto (3); *v.i*, rĕmittor (3 *pass*)

slackness rĕmissĭo, *f*; **(idleness)**, pĭgrĭtĭa, *f*

slake **(thirst)** *v.t*, (sĭtim) exstinguo (3)

slander *nn*, călumnĭa, *f*

slander *v.t*, călumnĭor (1 *dep*)

slanderer obtrectātor, *m*

slanderous fāmōsus

slanting *adj*, oblīquus

slap *nn*, ălăpa, *f*

slap *v.t*, fĕrĭo (4)

slash *nn*, **(blow)**, ictus, *m*

slash *v.t*, caedo (3)

slate **(roofing)** tēgūlae, *f. pl*.

slate *v.t*, rĕprĕhendo (3)

slaughter *nn*, caedes, *f*, strāges, *f*

slaughter *v.t*, caedo (3)

slaughterhouse *use* lănĭēna, *f* **(butcher's stall)**

slave servus, *m*

slave-dealer vēnālĭcĭus, *m*

slavery servĭtus, *f*

slave-trade vēnālĭcĭum, *n*

slavish servīlis

slay *v.t*, interfĭcĭo (3)

slayer interfector, *m*
slaying *nn*, trŭcīdātĭo, *f*
sledge trăhĕa, *f*
sleek nĭtĭdus
sleep *nn*, somnus, *m*
sleep *v.i*, dormĭo (4), quĭesco (3);
  (to go to —), obdormisco (3)
sleepless insomnis
sleeplessness insomnĭa, *f*
sleepy somnĭcŭlōsus
sleeve mănĭcae, *f. pl*
sleigh trăhĕa, *f*
sleight-of-hand praestīgĭae, *f. pl*
slender grăcĭlis
slenderness grăcĭlĭtas, *f*
slice segmentum, *n*, frustum, *n*
slice *v.t*, concīdo (3)
slide *v.i*, lābor (3 *dep*)
slight *adj*, lĕvis, exĭgŭus
slight *v.t*, neglĕgo (3)
slim grăcĭlis
slime līmus, *m*
slimy līmōsus
sling *nn*, (for throwing), funda, *f*;
  (bandage), mĭtella, *f*
sling *v.t*, mitto (3)
slinger fundĭtor, *m*
slip *v.i*, lābor (3 *dep*); (— away), sē
  subdūcĕre (3 *reflex*); (— out
  from), ēlābor (3 *dep*)
slip *nn*, lapsus, *m*; (mistake), error,
  m
slipper sŏlĕa, *f*
slippery lūbrĭcus
slipshod neglĕgens
slit *nn*, scissūra, *f*
slit *v.t*, incīdo (3)
sloop nāvis longa, *f*
slope *nn*, clīvus, *m*
slope *v.i*, sē dēmittĕre (3 *reflex*),
  vergo (3)
sloping *adj*, (down), dēclīvis; (up),
  acclīvis
sloth segnĭtĭa, *f*, ignāvĭa, *f*
slothful segnis
slough (mire) pălus, *f*
slovenliness cultus neglectus
  (neglected dress)
slow tardus, lentus
slowly *adv*, tardē, lentē
slowness tardĭtas, *f*
slug līmax, *f*
sluggish pĭger, segnis

sluggishness pigrĭtĭa, *f*
sluice ductus (*m*) ăquărum
  (bringing of water)
slumber *nn*, somnus, *m*
slumber *v.i*, dormĭo (4)
slur *nn*, măcŭla, *f*
sly astūtus, callĭdus
smack *nn*, (blow), ălăpa, *f*; (taste),
  săpor, *m*
smack *v.t*, (slap), verbĕro (1)
small parvus, exĭgŭus
smallness exĭgŭitas, *f*
smart *adj*, ācer; (clothes, etc.),
  nĭtĭdus; (witty), făcētus
smart *nn*, dŏlor, *m*
smart *v.i*, dŏlĕo (2), ūror (3 *pass*)
smartness (alertness) ălăcrĭtas, *f*
smash *nn*, fractūra, *f*
smash *v.t*, confringo (3)
smattering lĕvis cognĭtĭo, *f*, (slight
  knowledge)
smear *v.t*, līno (3)
smell *nn*, (sense of —), ŏdōrātus,
  m; (scent), ŏdor, *m*
smell *v.t*, olfăcĭo (3); *v.i*, ŏlĕo (2)
smelt *v.t*, cŏquo (3)
smile *nn*, rīsus, *m*
smile *v.i*, subrīdĕo (2)
smirk *nn*, rīsus, *m*
smite *v.t*, fĕrĭo (4)
smith făber, *m*
smithy făbrĭca, *f*
smock indūsĭum, *n*
smoke *nn*, fūmus, *m*
smoke *v.i*, fūmo (1)
smoky fūmōsus
smooth lĕvis, (of the sea), plăcĭdus;
  (of temper), aequus
smooth *v.t*, lēvo (1)
smoothness lēvĭtas, *f*, lēnĭtas, *f*
smother *v.t*, suffōco (1), opprĭmo
  (3)
smoulder *v.i*, fūmo (1)
smudge *nn*, lābes, *f*
smuggle *v.t*, furtim importo (1)
  (bring in secretly)
snack cēnŭla, *f*
snail cochlĕa, *f*
snake anguis, *m*, *f*
snaky vīpĕrĕus
snap *v.t*, rumpo (3); (— the
  fingers), *v.i*, concrĕpo (1); (— up),
  v.t, corrĭpĭo (3)

snare lăquĕus, *m*

snarl *nn*, gannĭtus, *m*

snarl *v.i*, gannĭo (4)

snatch *v.t*, răpĭo (3)

sneak *v.i*, corrēpo (3)

sneer *nn*, obtrectātĭo, *f*

sneer at *v.t*, dērīdĕo (2)

sneeze *v.i*, sternŭo (3)

sneezing sternūmentum, *n*

sniff at (smell at) *v.t*, ŏdōror (1 *dep*)

snip *v.t*, (cut off), ampŭto (1)

snob nŏvus hŏmo (upstart)

snore *v.i*, sterto (3)

snore, snoring *nn*, rhonchus, *m*

snort *v.i*, frĕmo (3)

snorting *nn*, frĕmĭtus, *m*

snout rostrum, *n*

snow *nn*, nix, *f*

snow (it —s) ningit (*v. impers*)

snowy nĭvĕus

snub *v.t*, rĕprĕhendo (3)

snub-nosed sĭlus

snuff *v.t*, (extinguish), exstinguo (3)

snug commŏdus

so *adv*, (in such a way), sīc, ĭtă; (to such an extent), ădĕo; (*with adj and adv*) tam, *e.g.* so quickly, tam cĕlĕrĭter; (*with a purpose or consecutive clause*, so that ...) ut; (— big, — great), tāntus; (— many), tot; (— much), tantum; (— often), tŏtĭes

soak *v.t*, mădĕfăcĭo (3)

soaking mădens; (of rain), largus

soap *nn*, sāpo, *m*

soar *v.i*, sublīme fĕror (*irreg pass*) (be borne aloft)

sob *nn*, singultus, *m*

sob *v.i*, singulto (1)

sober sōbrĭus

sobriety sōbrĭĕtas, *f*, mŏdĕrātĭo, *f*

sociability făcĭlĭtas, *f*

sociable făcĭlis

social commūnis

society (in general) sŏcĭĕtas, *f*; (companionship), sŏdālĭtas, *f*

sock tībĭāle, *n*

sod caespes, *m*

soda nĭtrum, *n*

sodden mădĭdus

sofa lectŭlus, *m*

soft mollis

soften *v.t*, mollĭo (4); *v.i*, mollĭor (4 *pass*)

softness mollĭtĭa, *f*

soil sŏlum, *n*

soil *v.t*, inquĭno (1)

sojourn *nn*, commŏrātĭo, *f*

sojourn *v.i*, commŏror (1 *dep*)

solace *nn*, sōlātĭum, *n*

solace *v.t*, consōlor (1 *dep*)

solar *use genit. case of* sōl, *m*, (sun)

solder *nn*, ferrūmen, *n*

solder *v.t*, ferrūmĭno (1)

soldier mīles, *c*; (foot —), pĕdes, *m*; (cavalry —), ĕques, *m*; *v.i*, (serve as a —), stĭpendĭa mĕrĕor (2 *dep*)

soldierly *adj*, mīlĭtāris

sole *adj*, sōlus

sole *nn*, sŏlum, *n*; (fish), sŏlĕa, *f*

solely *adv*, sōlum

solemn (serious) grăvis; (festivals, etc.), sollemnis

solemnity grăvĭtas, *f*; (religious —), sollemne, *n*

solemnize *v.t*, cĕlĕbro (1)

solicit *v.t*, pĕto (3), osĕcro (1), sollĭcĭto (1)

solicitation flāgĭtātĭo, *f*

solicitor advŏcātus, *m*

solicitude anxĭĕtas, *f*

solid *adj*, sŏlĭdus

solid *nn*, sŏlĭdum, *n*

solidity sŏlĭdĭtas, *f*

soliloquize *v.i*, sēcum lŏquo (3 *dep*) (speak with oneself)

solitary sōlus, sōlĭtārĭus; (places), dēsertus

solitude sōlĭtūdo, *f*

solstice (summer —) solstĭtĭum, *n*; (winter —), brūma, *f*

solution *use vb.* solvo (3) (to solve), *or nn*, explĭcātĭo, *f*

solve *v.t*, explĭco (1)

solvent (to be —) solvendo esse (*irreg*)

sombre obscūrus

some *adj*, ălĭquis, nonnullus; (a certain), quīdam

somebody, someone *pron*, ălĭquis, nonnullus; (a certain one), quīdam; (— or other), nescĭo quis; **(some . . . others)**, ălĭi . . . ălĭi

somehow *adv*, nescĭŏ quōmŏdŏ

something *pron*, ălĭquid

sometime *adv*, ălĭquandŏ

sometimes *adv*, ălĭquandŏ, interdum; **(occasionally)**, sŭbinde; **(sometimes . . . sometimes . . .)**, mŏdŏ . . . mŏdŏ . . .

somewhat *adv*, ălĭquantum

somewhere *adv*, ălĭcŭbi; **(to —)**, ălĭquo

somnolent sēmĭsomnus

son fīlĭus, *m*; **(— in-law)**, gĕner, *m*

song carmen, *n*

sonorous sŏnōrus

soon *adv*, mox; **(as — as)**, sĭmul ac, sĭmŭl atque, cum prīmum; **(as — as possible)**, quam prīmum

sooner (earlier) mātūrĭus; **(rather)**, pŏtĭus

soot fūlīgo, *f*

soothe *v.t*, mulcĕo (2), lēnĭo (4)

soothing *adj*, lēnis

soothsayer auspex, *c*, hăruspex, *m*

sooty fūlīgĭnōsus

sop offa, *f*

sophist sŏphistes, *m*

soporific sŏpōrĭfer

sorcerer vĕnēfĭcus, *m*

sorcery vĕnēfĭcĭa, *n.pl*

sordid sordĭdus

sore ăcerbus

sore *nn*, ulcus, *n*

sorrel lăpăthus, *f*

sorrow *nn*, dŏlor, *m*, maeror, *m*

sorrow *v.i*, dŏlĕo (2)

sorrowful maestus, tristis

sorry (to be —) mĭsĕret (2 *impers*) (*with acc. of subject and genit. of object*), *e.g.* **I am sorry for you**, me mĭsĕret tŭi

sort gĕnus, *n*; **(what — of?)**, quālis?

sort *v.t*, dīgĕro (3)

sot pōtātor, *m*

soul ănĭma, *f*, ănĭmus, *m*, spīrĭtus, *m*

sound *nn*, sŏnus, *m*, sŏnĭtus, *m*

sound *adj*, sānus; **(of sleep)**, artus; **(of arguments)**, firmus

sound *v.i*, sŏno (1); *v.t*, inflo (1); **(— the trumpet)**, būcĭnam inflo (1), căno (3)

soundness sānĭtas, *f*, intgĕrĭtas, *f*

soup iūs, *n*

sour ăcerbus, ăcer, ămārus

source fons, *m*, căput, *n*

sourness ăcerbĭtas, *f*

south *nn*, mĕrīdĭes, *m*

south, southern *adj*, mĕrīdĭānus

southwards *adv. phr*, in mĕrīdĭem

sovereign *nn*, princeps, *m*, rex, *m*, tўrannus, *m*

sovereign (independent) *adj, use phr* sŭi iūris **(of one's own authority)**

sovereignty impĕrĭum, *n*

sow *nn*, sūs, *f*

sow *v.t*, sĕro (3)

sower sător, *m*

space spătĭum, *n*; **(— of time)**, spătĭum, (*n*) tempŏris

spacious amplus

spaciousness amplĭtūdo, *f*

spade pāla, *f*

span palmus, *m*

span *v.t*, **(river, etc.)**, *use vb*, iungo (3) **(join)**

spangled distinctus

Spanish Hispānus

spar (of timber) asser, *m*

spare *adj*, exīlis **(thin)**

spare *v.t*, parco (3) (*with dat*)

sparing *adj*, **(frugal)**, parcus

spark *nn*, scintilla, *f*

sparkle *v.i*, scintillo (1)

sparkling *adj*, scintillans

sparrow passer, *m*

sparse rārus

spasm spasmus, *m*

spatter *v.t*, aspergo (3)

spawn *nn*, ōva, *n.pl*

spawn *v.i*, ōva gigno (3) **(produce eggs)**

speak *v.t*, lŏquor (3 *dep*), dīco (3); **(— out)**, ēlŏquor (3 *dep*); **(— to)**, allŏquor (3 *dep*)

speaker ōrātor, *m*

spear hasta, *f*

special (one in particular) pĕcūlĭāris; **(one's own)**, prŏprĭus; **(outstanding)**, praecĭpŭus

speciality *use adj*, prŏprĭus **(one's own)**

specially *adv*, praecĭpŭē, praesertim

species gĕnus, *n*

specific dīsertus; *or use emphatic pron*, ipse

specify *v.t*, ēnŭmĕro (1)

specimen exemplum, *n*

specious prŏbābĭlis

speck măcŭla, *f*

spectacle spectācŭlum, *n*

spectator spectātor, *m*

spectre ĭmāgo, *f*

spectrum spectrum, *n*

speculate *v.i*, cōgĭto (1); **(guess)**, cōnĭcĭo (3)

speculation cōgĭtātĭo, *f*; **(guess)**, coniectūra, *f*

speech ōrātĭo, *f*

speechless (literally so) mūtus; **(struck with fear, etc.)**, stŭpĕfactus

speed cĕlĕrĭtas, *f*

speed *v.t*, mātūro (1); *v.i*, festīno (1)

speedy cĕler, cĭtus

spell (charm) carmen, *n*

spell *v.t, use phr. with* littĕra, *f*, **(letter)**

spellbound obstŭpĕfactus

spend *v.t*, **(money)**, impendo (3), insūmo (3); **(time)**, ăgo (3)

spendthrift nĕpos, *m, f*

spew *v.t*, vŏmo (3)

sphere glŏbus, *m*; **(— of responsibility, etc.)**, prōvincĭa, *f*

spherical glŏbōsus

sphinx sphinx, *f*

spice condĭmentum, *n*

spice *v.t*, condĭo (4)

spicy condītus

spider ărānĕa, *f*

spider's web ărānĕa, *f*

spike clāvus, *m*

spill *v.t*, effundo (3)

spin *v.t*, **(thread, etc.)**, nĕo (2); **(turn rapidly)**, verso (1); *v.i*, versor (1 *pass*)

spinster virgo, *f*

spiral *nn*, cochlĕa, *f*

spiral *adj*, invŏlūtus

spire turris, *f*

spirit (breath of life) ănĭma, *f*; **(mind, soul)**, ănĭmus, *m*; **(disposition)**, ingĕnĭum, *n*; **(character)**, mōres, *m. pl*; **(courage)**, ănĭmus, *m*; **(departed —)**, mānes, *m. pl*

spirited ănĭmōsus

spiritual (of the mind) *use* ănĭmus, *m*

spit *nn*, **(for roasting)**, vĕru, *n*

spit *v.t*, spŭo (3)

spite mălĕvŏlentĭa, *f*; **(in — of)**, *often use abl. phr. with* obstans **(standing in the way)**

spiteful mălignus

spittle spūtum, *n*

splash *v.t*, aspergo (3)

spleen lĭēn, *n*; **(vexation)**, stŏmăchus, *m*

splendid splendĭdus

splendour splendor, *m*

splint fĕrŭlae, *f. pl*

splinter fragmentum, *n*

split *v.t*, findo (3); *v.i*, findor (3 *pass*)

split *nn*, fissūra, *f*

splutter *v.i*, balbūtĭo (4)

spoil *nn*, praeda, *f*, spŏlĭa, *n.pl*

spoil *v.t*, corrumpo (3), vĭtĭo (1)

spokesman ōrātor, *m*

sponge *nn*, spongĭa, *f*

spongy spongĭōsus

sponsor auctor, *c*

spontaneous *use adv. phr*, sŭā (mĕā), sponte **(of his (my) own accord)**

spoon coclĕar, *n*

sporadic rārus

sport *nn*, lūdus, *m*, lūsus, *m*; **(ridicule)**, lūdĭbrĭum, *n*

sport *v.i*, lūdo (3)

sportive (playful) lascīvus

sportsman vēnātor, *m*

spot *nn*, **(stain)**, măcŭla, *f*; **(place)**, lŏcus, *m*

spot *v.t*, **(look at)**, aspĭcĭo (3); **(stain)**, măcŭlo (1)

spotless (of character, etc.) intĕger, pūrus

spotted măcŭlōsus

spouse coniunx, *c*

spout *nn*, ōs, *n*

spout *v.i*, ēmĭco (1); *v.t*, **(pour out)**,

effundo (3)
sprain *v.t*, intorquĕo (2)
sprawl *v.i*, fundor (3 *pass*)
spray *nn*, aspergo, *f*
spread *v.t*, extendo (3), pando (3), diffundo (3); **(— about, publish)**, diffĕro (*irreg*) dīvulgo (1); *v.i*, diffundor (3 *pass*), incrēbresco (3)
sprightly ălăcer
spring *nn*, **(season)**, vēr, *n*; **(leap)**, saltus, *m*; **(fountain)**, fons, *m*
spring *adj*, vernus
spring *v.i*, **(leap)**, sălĭo (4); **(— from, proceed from)**, ŏrĭor (4 *dep*) **(— upon, assault)**, ădŏrĭor (4 *dep*)
sprinkle *v.t*, spargo (3)
sprout *nn*, surcŭlus, *m*
sprout *v.i*, pullŭlo (1)
spruce *adj*, nĭtĭdus
spruce *nn*, **(fir)**, pīnus, *f*
spur *nn*, calcar, *n*
spur *v.t*, concĭto (1)
spurious ădultĕrīnus
spurn *v.t*, aspernor (1 *dep*)
spurt *v.i*, ēmĭco (1)
spy *nn*, explōrātor, *m*, dēlātor, *m*
spy *v.t*, spĕcŭlor (1 *dep*)
squabble *nn*, rixa, *f*
squabble *v.i*, rixor (1 *dep*)
squadron (of cavalry) turma, *f*; **(of ships)**, classis, *f*
squalid sordĭdus
squall (storm) prŏcella, *f*
squall *v.i*, **(cry)**, vāgĭo (4)
squalor sordes, *f. pl*
squandor effundo (3)
squanderer nĕpos, *m*, *f*
square *adj*, quădrātus; *nn*, quădrātum, *n*
square *v.t*, quădro (1); **(accounts, etc.)**, subdūco (3), constĭtŭo (3)
squash *v.t*, contĕro (3)
squat *v.i*, subsīdo (3)
squat *adj*, **(of figure)**, brĕvis
squeak *nn*, strīdor, *m*
squeak *v.i*, strīdĕo (2)
squeamish fastīdĭōsus
squeeze *v.t*, prĕmo (3)
squint *v.i*, strābo esse (*irreg*)
squirrel scĭūrus, *m*
squirt *v.t*, ēĭcĭo (3); *v.i*, ēmĭco (1)

stab *v.t*, fŏdĭo (3)
stab *nn*, ictus, *m*
stability stăbĭlĭtas, *f*
stable *adj*, stăbĭlis
stable *nn*, stăbŭlum, *n*
stack *nn*, ăcervus, *m*
stack *v.t*, cŏăcervo (1)
staff băcŭlum, *n*; **(advisers)**, consĭlĭārĭi, *m. pl*
stag cervus, *m*
stage (theatre) proscaenĭum, *n*; **(step)**, grădus, *m*
stagger *v.i*, văcillo (1); *v.t*, concŭtĭo (3), commŏvĕo (2)
stagnant stagnans
stagnate *v.i*, stagno (1)
staid grăvis
stain *nn*, măcŭla, *f*
stain *v.t*, măcŭlo (1)
stainless pūrus, intĕger
stairs scālae, *f. pl*
stake (post, etc.) pālus, *m*, sŭdis, *f*, stīpes, *m*; **(pledge, wager)**, pignus, *n*
stake *v.t*, **(wager)**, dēpōno (3)
stale vĕtus
stalk stirps, *f*
stalk *v.i*, incēdo (3); **(game, etc.)**, *use phr*, cautē sĕquor (3 *dep*) **(follow cautiously)**
stall (cattle) stăbŭlum, *n*; **(shop, etc.)**, tăberna, *f*
stallion admissārĭus, *m*
stalwart *adj*, fortis
stamina vīres, *f. pl*
stammer *nn*, haesĭtantĭa (*f*) linguae **(hesitation of speech)**
stammer *v.i*, balbūtĭo (4)
stamp (mark) nŏta, *f*; **(with a ring, etc.)**, signum, *n*
stamp *v.t*, **(mark)**, signo (1); **(— with the foot)**, supplōdo (3)
stand *nn*, **(halt)**, mŏra, *f*; **(to make a —)** consisto (3) rēsisto (3), **(with dat.)**; **(platform)**, suggestus, *m*; **(stall)**, mensa, *f*
stand *v.i*, sto (1), consisto (3); **(— back)**, rĕcēdo (3), **(— by, help)**, adsum (*irreg with dat*); **(— for, seek a position)**, *v.t*, pĕto (3); **(endure)**, pătĭor (3 *dep*); **(— out, project)** exsto (1); **(— up)**, surgo (3)

standard

standard signum, *n*; **(of the legion)**, ăquĭla, *f*; **(measure)**, norma, *f*; **(— bearer)**, signĭfer, *m*

standing *nn*, **(position)**, stătus, *m*

staple products merces, *f, pl*

star stella, *f*, sīdus, *n*

starboard *use adj*, dexter **(right)**

starch *nn*, ămўlum, *n*

stare *nn*, obtūtus, *m*

stare *v.t*, **(— at)**, intŭĕor (2 *dep*)

stark **(stiff)** rĭgĭdus; **(— naked)**, nūdus; **(— mad)**, āmens

starling sturnus, *m*

start *nn*, **(movement)**, trĕmor, *m*; **(beginning)**, ĭnĭtĭum, *n*; **(setting out)**, prŏfectĭo, *f*; **(starting point)**, carcĕres, *m. pl*

start *v.i*, **(make a sudden movement)**, trĕmo (3), horrĕo (2); **(— out)**, prŏfĭciscor (3 *dep*); *v.t*, **(establish)**, instĭtŭo (3)

startle *v.t*, terrĕo (2)

startling *adj*, terrĭbĭlis

starvation fămes, *f*

starve *f.t*, făme nĕco (1) **(kill by starvation)**; *v.i*, făme nĕcor (1 *pass*)

state **(condition)** stătus, *m*, condĭcĭo, *f*; **(the —)**, respublĭca, *f*, cīvĭtas, *f*

state *v.t*, prŏfĭtĕor (2 *dep*)

stately magnĭfĭcus, cĕlĕber

statement dictum, *n*

statesman *use phr. with* respublĭca **(state)**, *and* admĭnistro (1), **(to manage)**

station **(standing)** stătus, *m*; **(occupied place)**, stătĭo, *f*

station *v.t*, lŏco (1)

stationary *adj*, immōtus

stationer bĭblĭŏpōla, *m*

statistics census, *m*

statue stătŭa, *f*

stature stătūra, *f*

status stătus, *m*

statute lex, *f*

staunch *adj*, firmus

stave off *v.t*, arcĕo (2)

stay *nn*, **(prop)**, firmāmentum, *n*; **(rest, etc.)**, mansĭo, *f*, commŏrātĭo, *f*

stay *v.i*, mănĕo (2), mŏror (1 *dep*); *v.t*, **(obstruct, stop)**, mŏror (1 *dep*)

steadfast firmus, stăbĭlis

steady firmus, stăbĭlis

steadfastness stăbĭlĭtas, *f*

steadiness stăbĭlĭtas, *f*

steak offa, *f*

steal *v.t*, fūror (1 *dep*); *v.i*, **(— upon)**, surrēpo (3) **(with dat)**

stealing *nn*, **(theft)**, furtum, *n*

stealth **(by —)**, **(adv)** furtim

stealth furtīvus

steam văpor, *m*

steam *v.i*, exhālo (1)

steed ĕquus, *m*

steel chălybs, *m*; **(iron, sword, etc.)**, ferrum, *n*

steel *v.t*, **(strengthen)**, confirmo (1)

steep praeruptus

steep *v.t*, **(soak)**, mădĕfăcĭo (3)

steeple turris, *f*

steer *nn*, iŭvencus, *m*

steer *v.t*, gŭberno (1)

steersman gŭbernātor, *m*

stem stirps, *f*, **(— literal and metaphorical)**

stem *v.t*, **(check)**, sisto (3), rĕsisto (3) **(with dat)**

stench fētor, *m*

step *nn*, grădus, *m*, passus, *m*; **(foot —)**, vestīgĭum, *n*; **(— by —)**, pĕdētentim; **(steps, stairs)**, scālae, *f.pl*

step *v.i*, grădĭor (3 *dep*); **(— forward)**; prōgrĕdĭor (3 *dep*)

step-brother **(father's side)** filĭus vĭtrĭci; **(mother's side)**, filĭus nŏvercae; **(— daughter)**, prīvigna, *f*; **(— father)**, vĭtrĭcus, *m*; **(— mother)**, nŏverca, *f*; **(— sister)**, filĭa vĭtrĭci *or* nŏvercae; **(— son)**, prīvignus, *m*

sterile stĕrĭlis

sterility stĕrĭlĭtas, *f*

sterling *adj*, **(genuine)**, vērus

stern *nn*, puppis, *f*

stern *adj*, dūrus

sternness sĕvērĭtas, *f*

stew *v.t*, cŏquo (3)

steward vīlĭcus, *m*

stick *nn*, băcŭlum, *n*

stick *v.t*, **(fix)**, fīgo (3); *v.i*, haerĕo (2)

sticky *adj*, tĕnax
stiff rĭgĭdus; **(to be —)**, *v.i*, rĭgĕo (2)
stiffen *v.i*, rĭgĕo (2); *v.t*, rĭgĭdum făcĭo (3)
stiffness rĭgor, *m*
stifle *v.t*, suffŏco (1); **(suppress)**, opprĭmo (3)
stigma stigma, *n*
stigmatize *v.t*, nŏto (1)
still *adj*, immōtus, tranquillus
still *adv*, **(nevertheless)**, tămen; **(up to this time)**, ădhuc; **(even)**, ĕtĭam
still *v.t*, sēdo (1)
stillness quĭes, *f*
stilts grallae, *f. pl*
stimulant (incentive) stĭmŭlus, *m*
stimulus (incentive) stĭmŭlus, *m*
stimulate *v.t*, stĭmŭlo (1)
sting *nn*, ăcūlĕus, *m*
sting *v.t*, pungo (3)
stinging *adj*, mordax
stingy sordĭdus
stink *nn*, fētor, *m*
stink *v.i*, fētĕo (2)
stipend merces, *f*
stipulate *v.i*, stĭpŭlor (1 *dep*)
stir *nn*, mōtus, *m*
stir *v.t*, mŏvĕo (2); *v.i* mŏvĕor (2 *pass*)
stitch *v.t*, sŭo (3)
stock (of tree, family, etc.) stirps, *f*; **(amount)**, vīs, *f*
stock *v.t*, complĕo (2)
stockbroker argentārĭus, *m*
stocking tībĭāle, *n*
stoic *nn. and adj*, stŏĭcus
stoical dūrus
stoicism rătĭo Stŏĭca, *f*
stolen furtīvus
stomach stŏmăchus, *m*
stomach *v.t*, **(put up with)**, perfĕro (*irreg*)
stone lăpis, *m*; **(precious —)**, gemma, *f*; **(fruit —)**, nūclĕus, *m*
stone *adj*, lăpĭdĕus
stone *v.t*, **(— to death)**, lăpĭdĭbus cŏŏpĕrĭo (4) **(overwhelm with stones)**
stone-quarry lăpĭcīdīnae, *f. pl*
stony lăpĭdōsus; **(of heart)**, asper
stool scăbellum, *n*

stoop *v.i*, sē dēmittĕre (3 *reflex*); **(condescend)**, dēscendo (3)
stop *nn*, intermissĭo, *f*
stop *v.t*, sisto (3); **(— up a hole, etc.)**, obtūro (1); *v.i*, **(pause)**, sisto (3); **(desist)**, dēsĭno (3); **(remain)**, mănĕo (2)
stoppage (hindrance) impĕdīmentum, *n*
stopper obtūrāmentum, *n*
store (supply) cōpĭa, *f*; **(place)**, rĕceptācŭlum, *n*
store *v.t*, condo (3)
storey tăbŭlātum, *n*
stork cĭcōnĭa, *f*
storm *nn*, tempestas, *f*
storm *v.t*, **(attack)**, expugno (1)
storming *nn*, expugnātĭo, *f*
stormy (weather) turbĭdus
story fābŭla, *f*
story-teller narrātor, *m*
stout (fat) pinguis; **(strong)**, vălĭdus; **(— hearted)**, fortis
stove fŏcus, *m*
stow *v.t*, rĕpōno (3)
straddle *v.i*, vārĭco (1)
straggle *v.i*, văgor (1 *dep*)
straight *adj*, rectus
straight *adv*, rectā
straight away *adv*, stătim
straighten *v.t*, corrĭgo (3)
straightforward simplex
strain *nn*, contentĭo, *f*
strain *v.t*, **(stretch)**, tendo (3); **(liquids, etc.)**, cōlo (3); *v.i*, **(strive)**, nītor (3 *dep*)
strait *adj*, angustus
strait *nn*, **(a narrow place or a difficulty)**, angustĭae, *f. pl* **(sea)** frētum, *n*
strand (shore) lītus, *n*
stranded rĕlictus
strange insōlĭtus, nŏvus
strangeness insōlentĭa, *f*
stranger hospes, *m*
strangle *v.t*, strangŭlo (1)
strap *nn*, lōrum, *n*
stratagem dŏlus, *m*
strategist *use phr. with* pĕrītus **(skilled in)**, *with phr. below*
strategy ars (*f*) bellandi **(the art of making war)**
straw strāmentum, *n*

strawberry frāgum, *n*
stray *v.i*, erro (1)
stray *adj*, errābundus
streak *nn*, līnĕa, *f*
streak *v.t*, līnĕis vărĭo (1), **(variegate with streaks)**
streaky virgātus
stream *nn*, flūmen, *n*
stream *v.i*, effundor (3 *pass*)
street vĭa, *f*
strength vīres, *f. pl*, rōbur, *n*
strengthen *v.t*, firmo (1)
strenuous impĭger
stress **(importance)** mōmentum, *n*
stretch *nn*, **(extent)**, spătĭum, *n*
stretch *v.t*, tendo (3); **(— out)**, extendo (3); *v.i*, sē tendĕre (3 *reflex*)
stretcher lectīca, *f*
strew *v.t*, sterno (3)
strict **(severe)** dūrus; **(careful)** dīlĭgens
strictness sĕvērĭtas, *f*
stricture rĕprĕhensĭo, *f*
stride *nn*, passus, *m*
strife certāmen, *n*, discordĭa, *f*
strike *v.t*, fĕrĭo (4), percŭtĭo (3), pulso (1); **(— the mind, occur to)**, subvĕnĭo (4)
striking *adj*, insignis
string līnĕa, *f*; **(of bow or instrument)**, nervus, *m*
stringent sĕvērus
strip *v.t*, spŏlĭo (1), nūdo (1)
strip *nn*, **(flap, edge)**, lăcĭnĭa, *f*
stripe līmes, *m*; **(blow)**, verber, *n*
stripling ădŏlescentŭlus, *m*
strive *v.i*, nītor (3 *dep*), contendo (3)
striving *nn*, contentĭo, *f*
stroke *nn*, verber, *n*, ictus, *m*; **(line)**, līnĕa, *f*
stroke *v.t*, mulcĕo (2)
stroll *nn*, ambŭlātĭo, *f*
stroll *v.i*, ambŭlo (1)
strong vălĭdus, firmus; **(powerful)**, fortis; **(to be —)**, *v.i*, vălĕo (2)
stronghold arx, *f*
structure **(building)** aedĭfĭcĭum, *n*
struggle *nn*, certāmen, *n*

struggle *v.i*, luctor (1 *dep*), nītor (3 *dep*)
strumpet mĕrĕtrix, *f*
strut *v.i*, incēdo (3)
stubble stĭpŭla, *f*
stubborn pertĭnax
stucco tectōrĭum, *n*
stud clāvus, *m*; **(horses)**, ĕquārĭa, *f*
stud *v.t*, insĕro (3)
student *use adj*, stŭdĭōsus **(devoted to)**, *with a suitable noun*
studied mĕdĭtātus
studious stŭdĭōsus
study *nn*, stŭdĭum, *n*; **(room, library)**, bĭblĭŏthēca, *f*
study *v.t*, stŭdĕo (2) *(with dat)*
stuff **(material)** mātĕrĭa, *f*; **(woven-)**, textĭle, *n*
stuff *v.t*, farcĭo (4)
stuffing *nn*, fartum, *n*
stumble *nn*, **(fall)**, lapsus, *m*
stumble *v.i*, offendo (3)
stumbling block impĕdīmentum, *n*
stump **(post)** stīpes, *m*
stun *v.t*, obstŭpĕfăcĭo (3)
stupefaction stŭpor, *m*
stupefy *v.t*, obstŭpĕfăcĭo (3)
stupendous mīrābĭlis
stupid stŏlĭdus, stultus
stupidity stultĭtĭa, *f*
stupor stŭpor, *m*
sturdiness firmĭtas, *f*
sturdy firmus, vălĭdus
sturgeon ăcĭpenser, *m*
stutter *v.i*, balbūtĭo (4)
sty hăra, *f*; **(in the eye)**, hordĕŏlus, *m*
style *nn*, gĕnus, *n*
style *v.t*, **(name)**, appello (1)
stylish spĕcĭōsus
suave suāvis
subaltern sucentŭrĭo, *m*
subdivide *v.t*, dīvĭdo (3)
subdue *v.t*, sūbĭcĭo (3)
subject *adj*, subiectus
subject *nn*, **(of a state, etc.)**, cīvis, *c*; **(matter)**, rēs, *f*
subject *v.t*, sūbĭcĭo (3)
subjection **(slavery)** servĭtus, *f*
subjoin *v.t*, subiungo (3)
subjugate *v.t*, sŭbĭgo (3)

sublime ēlātus

sublimity ēlātĭo, *f*

submerge *v.t*, submergo (3)

submission (compliance) obsĕquĭum, *n*

submissive ŏbēdĭens

submit *v.t*, sūbĭcĭo (3); **(present)**, rĕfĕro (*irreg*); *v.i*, **(yield)**, cēdo (3)

subordinate *adj*, subiectus

subordination (obedience) obsĕquĭum, *n*

subscribe *v.t*, **(give money, etc.)**, confĕro (*irreg*); **(signature)**, subscrībo (3)

subscription (of money, etc.) collātĭo, *f*

subsequent sĕquens

subsequently *adv*, postĕā

subservient obsĕquens

subside *v.i*, rĕsīdo (3)

subsidize *v.t*, pĕcūnĭam suppĕdĭto (1), **(furnish with money)**

subsidy subsĭdĭum, *n*

subsist *v.i*, consto (1)

subsistence victus, *m*

substance (essence) nātūra, *f*; **(being)**, rēs, *f*; **(goods)**, bŏna, *n.pl*

substantial (real) vērus; **(important)**, grăvis

substitute *nn*, vĭcārĭus, *m*

substitute *v.t*, suppōno (3)

subterfuge lătĕbra, *f*

subterranean subterrānĕus

subtle (crafty) astūtus; **(refined)**, subtīlis

subtlety (craftiness) astūtĭa, *f*; **(fineness)**, subtīlĭtas, *f*

subtract *v.t*, dēdūco (3)

subtraction detractĭo, *f*

suburb sŭburbĭum, *n*

suburban sŭburbānus

subvert *v.t*, ēverto (3)

succeed *v.t*, **(in, do well)**, bĕnĕ effĭcĭo (3); **(of things)**, *v.i*, prospĕrē ēvĕnĭo (4); *v.t*, **(follow)**, sĕquor (3 *dep*); **(to an office)**, succēdo (3)

success res sĕcundae, *f.pl*

successful (persons) fēlix; **(things)**, prospĕrus

succession (to an office, etc.) successĭo, *f*; **(series)**, contĭnŭātĭo, *f*

successive contĭnŭus

successor successor, *m*

succinct brĕvis

succour *nn*, auxĭlĭum, *n*

succour *v.t*, succurro (3) **(with dat)**

succulent sūcōsus

succumb *v.i*, cēdo (3)

such *adj*, tālis, hūius mŏdi **(of this kind)**

suck *v.t*, sūgo (3)

sucket planta, *f*

suckle *v.t*, ūbĕra do (1) **(with dat)**

suction suctus, *m*

sudden sŭbĭtus

suddenly *adv*, sŭbĭto, rĕpentē

sue *v.t*, **(in law)**, in ius vŏco (1); **(— for, beg for)**, rŏgo (1)

suet sēbum, *n*

suffer *v.t*, pătĭor (3 *dep*), fĕro (*irreg*); **(permit)**, permitto (3) **(with dt)**; *v.i*, affĭcĭor (3 *pass*)

sufferance pătĭentĭa, *f*

sufferer (of illness) aeger, *m*

suffering *nn*, dŏlor, *m*

suffice *v.i*, sătis esse (*irreg*)

sufficiency *use adv*, sătis **(enough)**

sufficient *use* sătis, *adv*, **(with genit. of noun)**

suffocate *v.t*, suffōco (1)

suffrage suffrāgĭum, *n*

sugar sacchăron, *n*

suggest *v.t*, sūbĭcĭo (3) **(with acc. of thing and dat. of person)**

suggestion admŏnĭtus, *m*

suicide mors vŏluntārĭa, *f*; **(to commit —)**, sĭbĭ mortem conscisco (3) **(inflict death upon oneself)**

suit (law —) līs, *f*; **(clothes)**, vestīmenta, *n.pl*

suit *v.i*, convĕnĭo (4); *or use impers. vb*, dĕcet **(it —s)**

suitable aptus, ĭdōnĕus

suite (retinue) cŏmĭtes, *c, pl*

suitor prŏcus, *m*

sulky mōrōsus

sullen torvus

sully *v.t*, inquĭno (1)

sulphur sulfur, *n*

sultry aestŭōsus

sum (total) summa, *f*; **(— of money)**, pĕcūnĭa, *f*

sum up *v.t*, compŭto (1); **(speak briefly)**, summātim dīco (3)

summarily *adv*, **(immediately)**, sĭne mŏrā

summary *nn*, ĕpĭtŏme, *f*

summary *adj*, **(hasty)**, sŭbĭtus

summer *nn*, aestas, *f*; *adj*, aestīvus

summit căcūmen, *n*, *or use adj*, summus **(top of)**

summon *v.t*, arcesso (3)

summon up *v.t*, excĭto (1)

summons vŏcātĭo, *f*, accītu (*abl. case only*: **at the — of**)

sumptuous sumptŭōsus

sumptuousness appărātus, *m*

sun sōl, *m*

sun *v.i*, **(— oneself)**, ăprīcor (1 *dep*)

sunbeam rădĭus (*m*) sōlis

sunburnt ădustus

sundial sōlārĭum, *n*

sunny aprīcus

sunrise ortus (*m*) sōlis

sunset occāsus (*m*) sōlis

sunshine sōl, *m*

sup *v.i*, cēno (1)

superabound *v.i*, sŭpersum (*irreg*)

superb magnĭfĭcus

supercilious sŭperbus

superficial lĕvis

superfluous sŭpervăcānĕus

superhuman dīvīnus

superintend *v.t*, prōcūro (1)

superintendent cūrātor, *m*, praefectus, *m*

superior sŭpĕrĭor; **(to be —)**, *v.i*, sŭpĕro (1)

superiority *use adj*, sŭpĕrĭor

superlative exĭmĭus

supernatural dīvīnus

supernumerary ascriptīvus

superscription tĭtŭlus, *m*

supersede *v.t*, succēdo (3) (*with dat*)

superstition sŭperstĭtĭo, *f*

superstitious sŭperstĭtĭōsus

supervise *v.t*, prōcūro (1)

supper cēna, *f*

supplant *v.t*, **(surpass)**, praeverto (3)

supple flexĭbĭlis

supplement supplēmentum, *n*

suppliant supplex, *c*

supplication obsĕcrātĭo, *f*

supply *nn*, cōpĭa, *f*; **(supplies, esp. military)**, commĕātus, *m*

supply *v.t*, suppĕdĭto (1); afféro (*irreg*)

support *nn*, **(bearing)**, firmāmentum, *n*; **(military)**, subsĭdĭa, *n.pl*; **(sustenance)**, ălĭmentum, *n*

support *v.t*, sustĭnĕo (2); **(aid)**, adiŭvo (1); **(nourish)**, ălo (3)

supportable tŏlĕrābĭlis

supporter adiŭtor, *m*

suppose *v.t*, pŭto (1), ŏpīnor (1 *pass*)

supposition ŏpīnĭo, *f*

suppress *v.t*, opprĭmo (3)

suppurate *v.i*, suppūro (1)

supremacy impĕrĭum, *n*

supreme sŭprēmus

sure ertus; **(reliable)**, fĭdēlis; **(I am —)**, compertum hăbĕo (2)

surely *adv*, prŏfecto; **(no doubt)**, nīmīrum; (*in questions; if an affirmative answer is expected*) nonne; (*if a negative answer*), num

surety vas, *m*, sponsor, *m*

surf fluctus, *m*

surface sŭperfĭcĭes, *f*

surge *v.i*, surgo (3)

surgeon chīrurgus, *m*

surgery chīrurgĭa, *f*

surly mōrōsus

surmise *nn*, coniectūra, *f*

surmise *v.t*, suspĭcor (1 *dep*)

surmount *v.t*, sŭpĕro (1)

surname cognōmen, *n*

surpass *v.t*, sŭpĕro (1)

surplus rĕlĭquum, *n*

surprise *nn*, mīrātĭo, *f*

surprise *v.t*, admīrātĭōnem mŏvĕo (2) (*with dat*); **(to attack)**, ădŏrĭor (4 *dep*)

surrender *nn*, dēdĭtĭo, *f*

surrender *v.t*, dēdo (3), trādo (3); *v.i*, sē dēdĕre (3 *reflex*)

surround *v.t*, cingo (3), circumdo (1)

survey *v.t*, contemplor (1 *dep*); **(land)**, mētĭor (4 *dep*)

surveyor fīnītor, *m*
survive *v.i*, sŭpersum (*irreg*)
survivor sŭperstes, *m*, *f*
susceptibility mollĭtĭa, *f*
susceptible mollis
suspect *v.t*, suspĭcor (1 *dep*)
suspend *v.t*, suspendo (3);
  (interrupt), intermitto (3);
  (— from office), dēmŏvĕo (2)
suspense dŭbĭtātĭo, *f*
suspension (interruption)
  intermissĭo, *f*
suspicion suspīcĭo, *f*
suspicious suspīcĭōsus
sustain *v.t*, sustĭnĕo (2)
sustenance ălĭmentum, *n*
swaddling clothes incūnābŭla, *n.pl*
swagger *v.i*, sē iactāre (1 *reflex*)
swallow *nn*, hĭrundo, *f*
swallow *v.t*, gluttĭo (4), sorbĕo (2)
swamp *nn*, pălus, *f*
swamp *v.t*, opprĭmo (3)
swampy pălūdōsus
swan cycnus, *m*
swarm (people)   turba, *f*; (bees),
  exāmen, *n*
swarm *v.i*, glŏmĕror (1 *pass*)
swarthy fuscus
swathe *v.t*, collĭgo (1)
sway *nn*, impĕrĭum, *n*
sway *v.t*, (rule), rĕgo (3); *v.i*,
  (— to and fro), văcillo (1)
swear *v.i*, iūro (1); (— allegiance
  to), iūro in nōmen (*with genit. of
  person*)
sweat *nn*, sūdor, *m*
sweat *v.i*, sūdo (1)
sweep *v.t*, verro (3)
sweet dulcis
sweeten *v.t*, dulcem reddo (3)
  (make sweet)
sweetheart dēlĭcĭae, *f. pl*
sweetness dulcĭtūdo, *f*
swell *nn*, (wave), fluctus, *m*
swell *v.i*, tŭmĕo (2); *v.t*, augĕo (2)
swelling tŭmor, *m*
swerve *v.i*, dēclīno (1)
swift *adj*, cĕler
swiftness cĕlĕrĭtas, *f*
swill *v.t*, (drink), pōto (1)
swim *v.i*, năto (1)
swimmer nătātor, *m*

swimming *nn*, nătātĭo, *f*
swindle *nn*, fraus, *f*
swindle *v.t*, fraudo (1)
swindler fraudātor, *m*
swine sūs, *m*, *f*
swineherd sŭbulcus, *m*
swing *nn*, oscillātĭo, *f*
swing *v.t*, ăgĭto (1); *v.i*, pendĕo (2)
switch (cane)   virga, *f*
switch *v.t*, mūto (1)
swollen tŭmĭdus
swoon *v.i*, *use phr*, ănĭmus
  rĕlinquit . . . (sensibility leaves ...)
swoop *nn*, *use vb*, advŏlo (1)
swoop on *v.i*, advŏlo (1)
sword glădĭus, *m*
sword-edge ăcĭes, *f*
swordfish xĭphĭas, *m*
sworn (treaty, etc.)   confirmātus
  iūrĕiūrando (confirmed by
  swearing)
sycamore sўcămōrus, *f*
sycophant sўcŏphanta, *m*
syllable syllăba, *f*
symbol signum, *n*
symmetrical congrŭens
symmetry convĕnĭentĭa, *f*
sympathetic mĭsĕrĭcors
sympathize *v.t*, consentĭo (4)
sympathy consensus, *m*
symphony symphōnĭa, *f*
symptom signum, *n*
synagogue sўnăgōga, *f*
syndicate sŏcĭĕtas, *f*
synonym verbum ĭdem signĭfĭcans
  (word expressing the same thing)
synopsis ēpĭtŏma, *f*
syntax syntaxis, *f*
syringe sīpho, *m*
syringe *v.t*, aspergo (3) (sprinkle)
system formŭla, *f*, rătĭo, *f*
systematic ordĭnātus

T

table mensa, *f*, tăbŭla, *f*; (list),
  index, *m*
tablecloth mantēle, *n*
tablet tăbŭla, *f*
tacit tăcĭtus
taciturn tăcĭturnus
tack clāvŭlus, *m*

tack

tack *v.t*, **(fix)**, fīgo (3); *v.i*, **(ships)**, rĕcīprŏcor (1 *pass*)
tackle **(fittings)** armāmenta, *n.pl*
tact dextĕrĭtas, *f*, urbānĭtas, *f*
tactician pĕrītus (*m*) rĕi mīlĭtāris
tactics **(military)** rătĭo (*f*) bellandi **(method of making war)**
tadpole rānuncŭlus, *m*
tag *v.t, use* fīgo (3) **(fix)**
tail cauda, *f*
tailor vestītor, *m*
taint *nn*, contāgĭo, *f*
taint *v.t*, infĭcĭo (3)
take *v.t*, căpĭo (3); **(grasp)**, prĕhendo (3); **(receive)**, accĭpĭo (3); **(seize)**, răpĭo (3); **(take possession of)**, occŭpo (1); **(— by storm)**, expugno (1); **(— away)**, aufĕro (*irreg*) ădĭmo (3); **(— in)**, excĭpĭo (3); **(— off)**, dēmo (3); **(— on)**, suscĭpĭo (3); **(— up)**, sūmo (3)
taking **(capture of a city)** expugnātĭo, *f*
tale fābŭla, *f*
talent **(ability)** ingĕnĭum, *n*; **(money)**, tălentum, *n*
talk *nn*, sermo, *m*
talk *v.i*, lŏquor (3 *dep*)
talkative lŏquax
tall prōcērus
tallness prōcērĭtas, *f*
tallow sēbum, *n*
tally *v.i*, convĕnĭo (4)
talon unguis, *m*
tamable dŏmābĭlis
tame *v.t*, dŏmo (1), mansŭēfăcĭo (3)
tame *adj*, mansŭēfactus, dŏmĭtus
tameness mansŭētūdo, *f*
tamer dŏmĭtor, *m*
tamper with *v.t*, tempto (1)
tan *v.t*, **(leather, etc.)**, confĭcĭo (3)
tangent *use* līnĕa, *f*, **(line)**
tangible tractābĭlis
tangle *nn*, implĭcātĭo, *f*
tangle *v.t*, implĭco (1)
tank lăcus, *m*
tanner cŏrĭārĭus, *m*
tantalize *v.t*, **(torment)**, fătīgo (1)
tap *nn*, **(blow)**, ictus, *m*
tap *v.t*, **(hit)**, fĕrĭo (4), pulso (1); *with* lĕvĭter **(lightly)**

tape taenĭa, *f*
taper cērĕus, *m*
taper *v.i*, fastīgor (1 *pass*)
tapestry *use* vēlum, *n*, **(curtain)**
tar pix lĭquĭda, *f*
tardiness tardĭtas, *f*
tardy tardus
tare lŏlĭum, *n*
target scŏpus, *m*
tarnish *v.i*, hĕbesco (3); *v.t*, inquĭno (1)
tarry *v.i*, mŏror (1 *dep*)
tart *nn*, crustŭlum, *n*
tart *adj*, ăcĭdus
task ŏpus, *n*
taste *nn*, **(sense of —)**, gustātus, *m*; **(flavour)**, săpor, *m*; **(judgement)**, iūdĭcĭum, *n*
taste *v.t*, gusto (1); *v.i*, **(have a flavour)**, săpĭo (3)
tasteful **(elegant)** ēlĕgans
tasteless insulsus
tasty săpĭdus
tattered pannōsus
tatters pannus, *m*
tattle *v.i*, garrĭo (4)
taunt *nn*, convīcĭum, *n*
taunt *v.t*, ŏbĭcĭo (3) (*dat. of person and acc. of thing*)
taunting *adj*, contŭmēlĭōsus
tavern caupōna, *f*
tavern-keeper caupo, *m*
tawdry fūcōsus
tawny fulvus
tax *nn*, vectīgal, *n*
tax *v.t*, **(impose —)**, vectīgal impōno (3) (*with dat*)
taxable vectīgālis
tax collector exactor, *m*, pūblĭcānus, *m*
teach *v.t*, dŏcĕo (2) (*with acc. of person and acc. of thing*)
teacher doctor, *m*, măgister, *m*
teaching *nn*, doctrīna, *f*
team **(— of horses)** iŭgum, *n*
tear *nn*, lăcrĭma, *f*; **(to shed —s)**, lăcrĭmas fundo (3); **(rent)**, scissūra, *f*
tear *v.t*, scindo (3); **(— away)**, abscindo (3); **(— down, open)**, rēscindo (3); **(— up, in pieces)**, distrăho (3)
tearful flēbĭlis

tease *v.t*, obtundo (3)

teat mamma, *f*

technical *use phr*, prŏprĭus artis (particular to a skill)

tedious lentus

teem with *v.i*, scătĕo (2)

teethe *v.i*, dentĭo (4)

teething *nn*, dentĭtĭo, *f*

tell *v.t*, (give information), dīco (3); narro (1) (*with acc. of thing said and dat. of person told*), certĭōrem făcĭo (3) (*acc. of person told, foll. by* dē *with abl. of thing said*); (order), iŭbĕo (2)

teller (counter) nŭmĕrātor, *m*

temerity tĕmĕrĭtas, *f*

temper (of mind) ănĭmus, *m*; (bad —), īrācundĭa, *f*

temper *v.t*, tempĕro (1)

temperament nātūra, *f*, ingĕnĭum, *n*

temperance tempĕrantĭa, *f*

temperate tempĕrātus

temperate climate tĕmpĕrĭes, *f*

temperateness mŏdĕrātĭo, *f*

tempest tempestas, *f*

tempestuous prŏcellōsus

temple templum, *n*, aedes, *f*; (of the head), tempus, *n*

temporal hūmānus

temporary *use adv. phr*, ad tempus (for the time being)

tempt *v.t*, tento (1)

temptation (allurement) illĕcĕbra, *f*

tempter tentātor, *m*

tempting *adj*, illĕcĕbrōsus

ten dĕcem; (— each), dēni; (— time), *adv*, dĕcĭes

tenacious tĕnax

tenacity tĕnācĭtas, *f*

tenant inquĭlīnus, *m*

tend *v.t*, (care for), cŏlo (3); *v.i*, (go, direct oneself), tendo (3); (incline to), inclīno (1); (be accustomed), consŭesco (3)

tendency inclīnātĭo, *f*

tender *adj*, tĕner, mollis

tender *v.t*, (offer), dēfĕro (*irreg*)

tenderness mollĭtĭa, *f*, indulgentĭa, *f*

tenement conductum, *n*

tenor (course) tĕnor, *m*, cursus, *m*

tense *adj*, tentus, intentus

tense *nn*, tempus, *n*

tension intentĭo, *f*

tent tăbernācŭlum, *n*; (general's —), praetōrĭum, *n*

tentacle cornĭcŭlum, *n*

tenth dĕcĭmus

tepid ēgĕlĭdus, tĕpĭdus; (to be —), *v.i*, tĕpĕo (2)

term (period of time) spătĭum, *n*; (limit), fīnis, *m*; (word), verbum, *n*; (condition), condĭcĭo, *f*

term *v.t*, vŏco (1)

terminate *v.t*, termĭno (1)

termination fīnis, *m*

terrace sōlārĭum, *n*

terrestrial terrestris

terrible terrĭbĭlis

terrify *v.t*, terrĕo (2)

territory fines, *m. pl*, ăger, *m*

terror terror, *m*, păvor, *m*

terse brĕvis

terseness brĕvĭtas, *f*

test *nn*, expĕrīmentum, *n*

test *v.t*, expĕrĭor (4 *dep*)

testament testāmentum, *n*

testator testātor, *m*

testify *v.t*, testĭfĭcor (1 *dep*)

testimony testĭmōnĭum, *n*

testy stŏmăchōsus

text scriptum, *n*

textile textĭle, *n*

texture textus, *m*

than *conj*, quam

thank *v.t*, grātĭas ăgo (3) (*with dat. of person*)

thankfulness grātus ănĭmus, *m*

thankless ingrātus

thanks grātĭas, *f. pl*

thanksgiving actĭo (*f*) grātĭārum

that *demonstrative pron*, ille, is, iste

that *relative pron*, qui, quae, quod

that *conj*, (*with purpose or consecutive clauses*) ut (ne *if negative*); (*after vbs introducing statements*) *no separate word, but rendered by the expression itself*: *e.g.* **he said that the king was coming**, rēgem vĕnīre dixit

thatch strāmentum, *n*

thaw

thaw *v.t*, solvo (3); *v.i*, sē rĕsolvĕre (3 *reflex*)
the *no equivalent in Latin*
theatre thĕătrum, *n*
theatrical thĕātrālis
theft furtum, *n*
their *reflexive*, sŭus; *otherwise* ĕōrum, (*f*, ĕārum)
them *use appropriate case of pron*, is, ille, iste
theme prōpŏsĭtĭo, *f*
themselves *reflexive pron*, sē; *(pron. emphatic)* ipsi, ae, a
then *adv. of* **(time)**, tum; **(therefore)**, ĭgĭtur
thence *adv*, inde, illinc
theologian thĕŏlŏgus, *m*
theology thĕŏlŏgĭa, *f*
theorem thĕōrēma, *n*
theoretical rătĭōnālis
theory rătĭo, *f*
there (in *or* **at that place)**, ĭbĭ; **(to that place)**, ĕō; **(— is)**, est; **(— are)**, sunt (*from* esse)
thereabouts *adv*, circā
thereafter *adv*, dĕinde
therefore *adv*, ĭgĭtur, ergo
thereupon *adv*, sŭbinde
thesis prōpŏsĭtum, *n*
they *as subject of vb. usually not rendered; otherwise use* ĭi, illi, isti
thick crassus, densus, confertus
thicken *v.t*, denso (1); *v.i*, concresco (3)
thicket dūmētum, *n*
thick-headed crassus
thickness crassĭtūdo, *f*
thick-set (of body) compactus
thick-skinned (indifferent) neglĕgens
thief fur, *c*
thieve *v.t*, fūror (1 *dep*)
thieving *nn*, **(theft)**, furtum, *n*
thigh fĕmur, *n*
thin tĕnŭis, grăcĭlis
thin *v.t*, tĕnŭo (1)
thing rēs, *f*
think *v.t*, cōgĭto (1); **(believe, suppose)**, crēdo (3), arbĭtror (1 *dep*), pŭto (1), existĭmo (1)
thinker phĭlŏsŏphus, *m*
thinness tĕnŭĭtas, *f*

third *adj*, tertĭus; **(a — part)**, tertĭa pars, *f*; **(thirdly)**, *adv*, tertĭo
thirst *v.i*, sĭtĭo (4)
thirst *nn*, sĭtis, *f*
thirsty sĭtĭens
thirteen trĕdĕcim
thirteenth tertĭus dĕcĭmus
thirtieth trīgēsĭmus
thirty trīginta
this *demonstrative pron*, hĭc, haec, hōc
thistle cardŭus, *m*
thither *adv*, ĕō, illūc; **(hither and —)**, hūc atque illūc
thong lōrum, *n*
thorn sentis, *m*, spīna, *f*
thorn-bush vĕpres, *m*
thorny spīnōsus
thorough perfectus; **(exact)**, subtīlis
thoroughbred gĕnĕrōsus
thoroughfare pervĭum, *n*
those *demonstrative pron*, illi
though *conj*, etsi
thought (act or faculty of thinking) cōgĭtātĭo, *f*; **(opinion)**, cōgĭtātum, *n*; **(plan, intention)**, consĭlĭum, *n*
thoughtful (careful) prōvĭdus; **(deep in thought)**, multa pŭtans
thoughtfulness cūra, *f*, cōgĭtātĭo, *f*
thoughtless tĕmĕrārĭus, inconsultus
thoughtlessness nĕglegentĭa, *f*, tĕmĕrĭtas, *f*
thousand mille (*indeclinable adj*); *in pl*, mīlĭa (*n.pl*, *nn*)
thrash *v.t*, tundo (3); **(corn)**, tĕro (3)
thrashing *nn*, trītūra, *f*; **(chastisement)**, verbĕrātĭo, *f*
thrashing-floor ārĕa, *f*
thread fĭlum, *n*
thread *v.t*, **(— one's way)**, sē insĭnŭāre (1 *reflex*)
threadbare obsŏlētus
threat mĭnae, *f. pl*
threaten *v.t*, mĭnor (1 *dep*) (*with acc. of thing and dat. of person*); *v.i*, **(impend)**, immĭnĕo (2)
threatening *adj*, mĭnax
three tres; **(— each)**, terni; **(— times)**, *adv*, ter
threefold (triple) trĭplex
threehundred trĕcenti**

threehundredth trĕcentensĭmus

thresh *v.t*, tĕro (3)

threshold līmen, *n*

thrice *adj*, ter

thrift frūgālĭtas, *f*

thrifty parcus

thrill *v.t, use* affĭcĭo (3) **(affect)**

thrill (of pleasure) hĭlărĭtas, *f*; **(a shock)**, stringor, *m*

thrilling *adj, use vb*, affĭcĭo (3) **(to affect)**

thrive *v.i*, vĭgĕo (2)

throat fauces, *f. pl*

throb *v.i*, palpĭto (1)

throbbing *nn*, palpĭtātĭo, *f*

throne sŏlĭum, *n*; **(regal, imperial power)**, regnum, *n*

throng *nn*, multĭtūdo, *f*

throng *v.t*, cĕlĕbro (1)

throttle *v.t*, strangŭlo (1)

through *prep*, per *(with acc)*; **(on account of)**, propter *(with acc)*

through *adv, often expressed by a compount vb, with* per; *e.g.* perfĕro **(carry through)**

throughout *prep*, per; *adv*, pĕnĭtus **(entirely, wholly)**

throw *nn*, iactus, *m*

throw *v.t*, iăcĭo (3), cōnĭcĭo (3) **(— away)**, ăbĭcĭo (3); **(— back)**, rēĭcĭo (3); **(— down)**, dēĭcĭo (3); **(— oneself at the feet of)**, se prōĭcĕre ad pĕdes *(with genit. of person)*; **(— out)**, ēĭcĭo (3)

thrush turdus, *m*

thrust *nn*, pĕtītĭo, *f*

thrust *v.t*, trūdo (3); **(— forward)**, prōtrūdo (3)

thumb pollex, *m*

thump *nn*, cŏlăphus, *m*

thump *v.t*, tundo (3)

thunder *nn*, tŏnĭtrus, *m*; **(— bolt)**, fulmen, *n*

thunder *v.i*, tŏno (1)

thunderstruck attŏnĭtus

thus *adv*, īta, sīc

thwart *nn*, **(seat)**, transtrum, *n*

thwart *v.t*, obsto (1) *(with dat. of person)*, impĕdĭo (4)

tiara tĭăra, *f*

ticket tessĕra, *f*

tickle *v.t*, tītillo (1)

tickling *nn*, tītillātĭo, *f*

ticklish lūbrĭcus

tide aestus, *m*

tidiness mundĭtĭa, *f*

tidings nuntĭus, *m*

tidy mundus

tie *nn*, vincŭlum, *n*

tie *v.t*, lĭgo (1), nōdo (1)

tier ordo, *m*

tiger tigris, *c*

tight strictus

tighten *v.t*, stringo (3)

tile tēgŭla, *f*

till *prep*, usque ad *(with acc)*

till *conj*, dum, dōnĕc

till *nn*, arca, *f*

till *v.t*, cŏlo (3)

tillage, tilling *nn*, cultus, *m*

tiller (boat) clāvus, *(m)* gŭbernācŭli **(handle of the rudder)**

tilt *v.t*, **(bend)**, dēclīno (1)

timber mātĕrĭa, *f*

time tempus, *n*; **(period, space of —)**, intervallum, *n*, spătĭum, *n*; **(generation, age)**, aetas, *f*; **(— of day)**, hōra, *f*; **(at the right —)**, *adv, phr*, ad tempus; **(at —s)**, *adv*, interdum; **(once upon a —)**, *adv*, ōlim; **(at the same —)**, *adv*, sĭmŭl; **(at that —)**, *adv*, tum

timely *adj*, opportūnus

timid tĭmĭdus

timidity tĭmĭdĭtas, *f*

tin plumbum album, *n*

tincture cŏlor, *m*

tinder fōmes, *m*

tinge *v.t*, tingo (3)

tingle *v.i*, prūrĭo (4)

tinker făber, *m*, **(artificer)**

tinkle *v.i*, tinnĭo (4)

tiny exĭgŭus, parvŭlus

tip căcūmen, *n*

tip *v.t*, **(put a point on)**, praefĭgo (3); **(tip over)**, verto (3)

tire *v.t*, fătīgo (1); *v.i*, dēfătīgor (1 *dep*)

tired fessus

tiresome mŏlestus

tissue textus, *m*

titbits cūpēdĭa, *n.pl*

tithe dĕcŭma, *f*

title tītŭlus, *m*

titled (of nobility) nōbĭlis
titter nn, rīsus, m
to prep, (motion towards a place, and expressions of time), ad (with acc); (sometimes, e.g. names of towns, acc. of nn. alone); often dat. case can be used, e.g. indirect object after vb. to give; (before a clause expressing purpose), ut; (sometimes indicates the infinitive of a vb), e.g. **to love**, ămāre
toad būfo, m
toast v.t, torrĕo (2); (a person's health), prōpīno (1) (with dat. of person)
today adv, hŏdĭē
toe dĭgĭtus, m
together adv, sĭmŭl, ūnā
toil nn, lăbor, m
toil v.i, lăbōro (1)
toilet (care of person, etc.), cultus, m
token signum, n
tolerable tŏlĕrābĭlis
tolerance tŏlĕrantĭa, f
tolerate v.t, tŏlĕro (1)
toll nn, vectīgal, n
tomb sĕpulcrum, n, tŭmŭlus, m
tombstone lăpis, m
tomorrow adv, crās
tomorrow nn, crastīnus dĭes, m
tone sŏnus, m
tongs forceps, m
tongue lingua, f
tonight adv, hŏdĭē nocte
tonsils tonsillae, f. pl
too (also) ĕtĭam; (− little), părum; (− much), nĭmis; comparative adj. or adv. can be used, e.g. **too far**, longĭus
tool instrūmentum, n
tooth dens, m
toothache dŏlor (m) dentĭum
toothed dentātus
toothless ēdentŭlus
toothpick dentiscalpĭum, n
top use adj, summus in agreement with nn, e.g. **the top of the rock**, summum saxum, n; (summit), căcūmen, n
top v.t, sŭpĕro (1)
topic rēs, f

topmost summus
topography use phr, nātūra (f) lŏci (nature of the land)
torch fax, f
torment nn, crŭcĭātus, m
torment v.t, crŭcĭo (1)
tornado turbo, m
torpid torpens, pĭger
torpor torpor, m
torrent torrens, m
tortoise testūdo, f
tortuous sĭnŭōsus
torture nn, crŭcĭātus, m
torture v.t, crŭcĭo (1)
torturer carnĭfex, m
toss nn, iactus, m
toss v.t, iacto (1)
total nn, summa, f
total adj, tōtus
totally adv, omnīno
totter v.i, lăbo (1)
touch nn, tactus, m; (contact), contāgĭo, f
touch v.t, tango (3), attingo (3); (move), mŏvĕo (2)
touchy stŏmăchōsus
tough adj, lentus
toughness dūrĭtĭa, f
tour pĕrĕgrīnātĭo, f, ĭter, n
tourist pĕrĕgrīnātor, m
tournament use certāmen, n, (contest)
tow v.t, trăho (3)
tow nn, (hemp), stuppa, f
towards prep, (of direction, position), ad (with acc); (of time), sub (with acc); (emotions), ergā, in (with acc); (with names of towns), versus (placed after the noun)
towel mantēle, n
tower nn, turris, f
tower v.i, exsto (1)
town urbs, f, oppĭdum, n
townsman oppĭdānus, m
toy (child's rattle) crĕpundĭa, n.pl
toy with v.i, illūdo (3)
trace nn, vestīgĭum, n, signum, n
trace v.t, sĕquendo invĕnĭo (4) (find by following)
track nn, (path), callis, m; (footsteps, etc.), vestīgĭum, n
track v.t, (− down), investīgo (1);

(pursue), sĕquor (3 *dep*)
trackless āvĭus
tract (region) rĕgĭo, *f*; **(booklet)**, lĭbellus, *m*
tractable dŏcĭlis
trade mercātūra, *f*; **(a particular —)** , ars, *f*
trade *v.i*, mercātūram făcĭo (3)
trade mercātor, *m*
tradition mĕmŏrĭa, *f*
traditional *use phr*, trādĭtus ā māĭōrĭbus **(handed down from our ancestors)**
traffic (trade, etc.) commercĭum, *n*; **(streets, etc.)**, *use phr. with* frĕquento (1) **(to crowd)**
tragedy trăgŏedĭa, *f*
tragic trăgĭcus; **(unhappy)**, tristis
trail (path) callis, *m*
train ordo, *m*; **(procession)**, pompa, *f. pl*; **(of a dress)**, pēnĭcŭlāmentum, *n*
train *v.t*, instĭtŭo (3), exercĕo (2)
trainer exercĭtor, *m*
training *nn*, disciplīna, *f*
traitor prōdĭtor, *m*
traitorous perfĭdus
tramp *v.i*, ambŭlo (1)
trample on *v.t*, obtĕro (3)
trance (elation, exaltation) ēlātĭo, *f*
tranquil tranquillus, plăcĭdus
transact *v.t*, ăgo (3)
transaction rēs, *f*, nĕgōtĭum, *n*
transcend *v.t*, sŭpĕro (1)
transcribe *v.t*, transcrībo (3)
transfer *nn*, **(of property)**, mancĭpĭum, *n*
transfer *v.t*, transfĕro (*irreg*)
transfix *v.t*, transfīgo (3)
transform *v.t*, mūto (1)
transgress *v.t*, vĭŏlo (1); *v.i*, pecco (1)
transgression (fault) dēlictum, *n*
transit transĭtus, *m*
transitory cădūcus
translate *v.t*, verto (3)
translation (a work) ŏpus translātum, *n*; **(act)**, translātĭo, *f*
translator interpres, *c*
transmigrate *v.i*, transmĭgro (1)
transmit *v.t*, transmitto (3)
transparent perlūcĭdus

transpire *v.i*. **(get about)**, vulgor (1 *pass*)
transplant *v.t*, transfĕro (*irreg*)
transport *nn*, *use vb. below*; **(joy)**, laetĭtĭa, *f*, exsultātĭo, *f*
transport *v.t*, transporto (1), trāĭcĭo (3)
trap *nn*, insĭdĭae, *f. pl*; **(for animals)**, lăquĕus, *m*
trap *v.t*, *use phr*, illĭcĭo (3) in insĭdĭas **(entice into a trap)**
trappings insignĭa, *n.pl*
trash scrūta, *n.pl*, nūgae, *f. pl*
travel *nn*, ĭter, *n*
travel *v.i*, ĭter făcĭo (3)
traveller vĭātor, *m*
traverse *v.t*, ŏbĕo (4)
travesty (mockery) lūdĭbrĭum, *n*
tray fercŭlum, *n*
treacherous perfĭdus
treachery perfĭdĭa, *f*, fraus, *f*
tread *nn*, grădus, *m*
tread *v.i*, ingrĕdĭor (3 *dep*); *v.t*, **(— on)**, calco (1)
treason māiestas, *f*
treasure ŏpes *f. pl*; **(hoard, treasure-house)**, thēsaurus, *m*
treasure *v.t*, **(regard highly)**, magni aestĭmo (1); **(store up)**, rĕcondo (3)
treasurer praefectus (*m*) aerārĭi **(director of the treasury)**
treasury aerārĭum, *n*
treat *nn*, dēlectātĭo, *f*
treat *v.t*, **(deal with, behave towards)**, hăbĕo (2); **(medically)**, cūro (1); **(discuss)**, ăgo (3)
treatise lĭber, *m*
treatment tractātĭo, *f*; **(cure)**, cūrātĭo, *f*
treaty foedus, *n*
treble *adj*, trĭplex
treble *v.t*, trĭplĭco (1)
tree arbor, *f*
trellis cancelli, *m. pl*
tremble *v.i*, trĕmo (3)
trembling *nn*, trĕmor, *m*
tremendous ingens
tremulous trĕmŭlus
trench fossa, *f*
trepidation trĕpĭdātĭo, *f*
trespass (crime) dēlictum, *n*

trespass *v.i, use phr. with* ingrĕdi **(to enter),** *and* tē (mē, *etc.*), invīto **(without your (my) permission)**

tress (hair) grădus, *m*

trial (legal) iūdĭcĭum, *n*; **(experiment),** expĕrĭentĭa, *f*

triangle trĭangŭlum, *n*

triangular trĭangŭlus

tribe (Roman) trĭbus, *f*; **(other),** pŏpŭlus, *m*

tribunal iūdĭcĭum, *n*

tribune trĭbūnus, *m*

tributary *adj,* **(paying tribute),** vectīgālis

tributary *nn,* **(river),** *use phr,* qui in flūmen influĭt **(which flows into a river)**

tribute trĭbūtum, *n,* vectīgal, *n*

trick *nn,* dŏlus, *m,* fraus, *f*

trick *v.t,* dēcĭpĭo (3)

trickery dŏlus, *m*

trickle *v.i,* māno (1)

trickster hŏmo dŏlōsus, fallax

tricky (dangerous) pĕrīcŭlōsus

trident trĭdens, *m*

tried (well —) prŏbātus

trifle *nn,* rēs parva, *f,* nūgae, *f. pl*

trifle *v.i.* lūdo (3)

trifling *adj,* lĕvus

trim *adj,* nĭtĭdus

trim *v.t.* pŭto (1)

trinkets mundus, *m*

trip *nn,* **(journey),** ĭter, *n*

trip *v.t.* supplanto (1); *v.i.* **(stumble),** offendo (3), lābor (3 dep)

tripe ŏmāsum, *n*

triple trĭplex

tripod trĭpus, *m*

trite trītus

triumph (Roman celebration of victory) trĭumphus, *m*; **(victory),** victōrĭa, *f*

triumph *v.i, and v.t,* trĭumpho (1)

triumphant victor

triumvirate trĭumvĭrātus, *m*

trivial lĕvis, vīlis

troop (band) mănus, *f*; **(— of cavalry),** turma, *f*; **(—s),** cōpĭae, *f, pl*

troop *v.i,* conflŭo (3)

trooper ĕquĕs, *m*

trophy trŏpaeum, *n*

trot *nn,* lentus cursus, *m*

trot *v.i,* lento cursu ĕo (4); **(proceed on a slow course)**

trouble *nn,* **(disadvantage),** incommŏdum, *n*; **(exertion),** ŏpĕra, *f*; **(commotion),** tŭmultus, *m*; **(annoyance),** mŏlestĭa, *f*

trouble *v.t,* **(disturb),** sollĭcĭto (1); **(harass),** vexo (1); **(— oneself about),** cŭro (1)

troublesome mŏlestus

trough alvĕus, *m*

trousers brăcae, *f. pl*

trowel trulla, *f*

truant *nn, use phr,* qui consultō ăbest **(who is absent deliberately)**

truce indūtĭae, *f. pl*

truck plaustrum, *n*

truculent (grim) trux

trudge *v.i, use phr,* aegrē ambŭlo (1) **(walk with difficulty)**

true vērus; **(faithful),** fīdus

truffle tūber, *n*

truly *adv,* vērē, prŏfectō

trumpery scrūta, *n.pl*

trumpet *nn,* tŭba, *f,* būcĭna, *f*

trumpeter tŭbĭcen, *m*

truncheon fustis, *m*

trundle *v.t,* volvo (3)

trunk truncus, *m*; **(of elephant)** prŏboscis, *f*; **(box),** arca, *f*

truss fascĭa, *f*

trust *nn,* fīdes, *f*

trust *v.t,* confīdo (3 *semi-dep*) (*with dat. of person*), crēdo (3); commit to), commĭtto (3)

trustworthy, trusty certus, fīdus

truth vērĭtas, *f*; **(true things),** vēra, *n.pl*; **(in —),** *adv,* vēro

truthful vērax

truthfulness vērĭtas, *f*

try *v.i,* **(attempt),** cōnor (1 *dep*); *v.t,* **(put to the test),** tento (1); **(— in court),** iūdĭco (1)

trying *adj,* mŏlestus

tub lābrum, *n*

tube tŭbŭlus, *m*

tuber tūber, *n*

tubular tŭbŭlātus

tuck up *v.t,* succingo (3)

tuft crīnis, *m*

tug *v.t,* trăho (3)

tuition   instǐtuutǐo, *f*
tumble   *nn*, cāsus, *m*
tumbler (beaker)   pōcūlum, *n*
tumour   tŭmor, *m*
tumult   tŭmultus, *m*
tumultuous   tŭmultŭōsus
tun (cask)   dōlǐum, *n*
tune (melody)   cantus, *m*; **(out of —)**, *adj*, absŏnus
tune   *v.t*, **(stringed instrument)**, tendo (3)
tuneful   cănōrus
tunic   tŭnǐca, *f*
tunnel   cănālis, *m*, cŭnīcŭlus, *m*
tunny fish   thunnus, *m*
turban   mǐtra, *f*
turbid   turbǐdus
turbot   rhombus, *m*
turbulence   tŭmultus, *m*
turbulent   turbŭlentus
turf   caespes, *m*
turgid   turgǐdus
turmoil   turba, *f*, tŭmultus, *m*
turn (movement)   conversǐo, *f*; **(bending)**; flexus, *m*; **(change)**, commūtātǐo, *f*; **(by — s, in —)**, *adv*, invǐcem, per vǐces; **(a good —)**, offǐcǐum, *n*
turn   *v.t*, verto (3); **(bend)**, flecto (3); **(— aside)**, dēflecto (3); *v.i*, sē dēclīnāre (1 *reflex*); **(— away)**, āverto (3); **(— the back)**, *v.i*, tergum verto (3); **(change)**, *v.i*, mūtor (1 *pass*); **(— back)**, *v.i*, rĕvertor (3 *pass*); **(— out)**, *v.t* ēǐcǐo (3); *v.i*, ēvēnǐo (4); **(— round)**, *v.t*, circumăgo (3); *v.i*, circumăgor (3 *pass*)
turning   *nn*, flexus, *m*
turnip   rāpum, *n*
turpitude   turpǐtūdo, *f*
turret   turris, *f*
turtledove   turtur, *m*
tusk   dens, *m*
tutelage   tūtēla, *f*
tutor   māgister, *m*
twang   *nn*, sŏnǐtus, *m*
twang   *v.i*, sŏno (1)
tweak   *v.t*, vellǐco (1)
tweezers   volsella, *f*
twelfth   dŭŏdĕcǐmus
twelve   dŭŏdĕcim; **(— each)**, duodēni

twentieth   vīcēsǐmus
twenty   vīginti
twice   *adj*, bis
twig   rāmŭlus, *m*
twilight   crĕpuscŭlum, *n*
twin   *nn and adj*, gĕmǐnus
twine   *nn*, līnum, *n*
twine   *v.t*, circumplǐco (1); *v.i*, circumplector (3 *dep*)
twinge   *nn*, dŏlor, *m*
twinkle   *v.i*, mǐco (1)
twirl   *v.t* verso (1)
twist   *v.t*, torquĕo (2); *v.i*, sē torquēre (2 *reflex*)
twit   *v.t*, ōbǐcǐo (3) (*acc. of thing and dat, of person*)
twitch   *v.t*, vellǐco (1)
twitter   *v.i*, **(chirp)**, pīpǐlo (1)
two   dŭŏ; **(— each)**, bīni
two-fold   dŭplex
two-footed   bǐpes
two hundred   dŭcenti
type (class, sort)   gĕnus, *n*; **(example)**, exemplar, *n*
typical   *use adj*, ūsǐtātus **(familiar)**
tyrannical   tўrannǐcus, sŭperbus
tyrannize   *v.i*, dŏmǐnor (1 *dep*)
tyranny   dŏmǐnātǐo, *f*
tyrant   tўrannus, *m*

U

ubiquitous   praesens **(present)**
udder   ūber, *n*
ugliness   dēformǐtas, *f*
ugly   dēformis
ulcer   vŏmǐca, *f*
ulcerate   *v.i*, suppūro (1)
ulceration   ulcĕrātǐo, *f*
ulcerous   ulcĕrōsus
ulterior   ultĕrǐor
ultimate   ultǐmus
ultimatum (to present —)   ultǐmam condǐcǐōnem ferre (*irreg*)
umbrage (to take — at)   *v.t*, aegrē fĕro (*irreg*)
umbrella   umbella, *f*
umpire   arbǐter, *m*
un-   *prefix, often* nōn, haud, *can be used*
unabashed   intrĕpǐdus; **(brazen)**, impŭdens
unabated   immǐnūtus

unable *use vb. phr. with* non posse **(to be unable)**
unacceptable ingrātus
unaccompanied incŏmĭtātus
unaccomplished infectus
unaccountable inexplĭcābĭlis
unaccustomed insŏlĭtus
unacquainted ignārus
unadorned ĭnornātus
unadulterated sincērus
unadvisable (foolhardy) audax
unadvised inconsĭdĕrātus
unaffected (natural) simplex; **(untouched)**, intĕger
unaided *use adv. phr*, sĭne auxĭlĭo **(without help)**
unalloyed pūrus
unalterable immūtābĭlis
unambitious hŭmĭlis
unanimity ūnănĭmĭtas, *f*
unanimous ūnĭversus **(all together)**
unanimously *adv*, ūnā vōce
unanswerable non rĕvincendus
unanswered *use vb*. rēspondĕo (2) **(to answer)**
unappeased implācātus
unapproachable nōn ădĕundus
unarmed ĭnermis
unassailable ĭnexpugnābĭlis
unassailed intactus
unassuming mŏdestus
unattainable *use phr. with vb*. attingo (3) **(to reach)**
unattempted ĭnexpertus
unauthorized illĭcĭtus
unavailing fūtĭlis
unavoidable ĭnēvītābĭlis
unaware inscĭus
unawares *adv*, dē imprōvīso
unbar *v.t*, rĕsĕro (1)
unbearable intŏlĕrābĭlis
unbecoming indĕcōrus
unbelieving incrēdŭlus
unbend *v.t*, rĕmitto (3)
unbending rĭgĭdus
unbiassed intĕger
unbidden iniussus
unbind *v.t*, solvo (3)
unblemished pūrus
unbound sŏlūtus
unbounded infīnītus
unbreakable *use phr*, quod frangi

non pŏtest **(that cannot be broken)**
unbridled effrēnātus
unbroken intĕger, perpĕtŭus
unbuckle *v.t*, diffĭbŭlo (1)
unburden *v.t*, exŏnĕro (1)
unburied ĭnhŭmātus
uncared for neglectus
unceasing perpĕtŭus
uncertain incertus, dŭbĭus; **(to be —)**, *v.i*, dŭbĭto (1)
uncertainty dŭbĭtātĭo, *f*
unchangeable immūtābĭlis
unchanged constans; **(to remain —)**, *v.i*, permānĕo (2)
uncharitable inhūmānus
uncivil ĭnurbānus
uncivilized incultus
uncle (father's side) pătrŭus, *m*; **(mother's side)**, ăvuncŭlus, *m*
unclean inquĭnātus
unclouded sĕrēnus
uncoil *v.t*, ēvolvo (3); *v.i*, se ēvolvĕre (3 *reflex*)
uncombed incomptus
uncomfortable mŏlestus
uncommon rārus, insŏlĭtus
uncompleted imperfectus
unconcerned sēcūrus
unconditional simplex; **(to surrender —ly)**, mănus do (1)
uncongenial ingrātus
unconnected disiunctus
unconquerable invictus
unconquered invictus
unconscious (unaware) inscĭus; **(insensible)**; *use phr*, sensu ablāto **(with feeling withdrawn)**
unconstitutional non lēgĭtĭmus
uncontaminated incontāmĭnātus
uncontested *use phr*, quod in contentĭōnem non vēnit **(that has not come into dispute)**
uncontrollable impŏtens
uncontrolled lĭber
uncooked incoctus
uncouth incultus
uncover *v.t*, dētĕgo (3)
unction unctĭo, *f*
uncultivated incultus; **(person)**, ăgrestis
uncut (hair) intonsus, prōmissus
undamaged intĕger

undaunted fortis
undeceive *v.t*, errōrem ērĭpĭo (3)
undecided incertus; **(of a battle)**, anceps
undefended nūdus, indēfensus
undeniable certus
under *prep*, sub (*with abl. to denote rest, and acc. to denote motion*); infra (*with acc*); **(— the leadership of)**, *use abl. phr*, e.g. tē dŭce **(— your leadership)**
underclothes sŭbūcŭla, *f*
undercurrent flŭentum subterlăbens, *n*
underestimate *v.t*, mĭnōris aestĭmo (1)
undergo *v.t*, sŭbĕo (3), fĕro (*irreg*)
underground *adj*, subterrānĕus
undergrowth virgulta, *n.pl*
underhand *adj*, clandestīnus
underlying (lying hidden) lătens
undermine *v.t*, subrŭo (3)
undermost *adj*, infĭmus
underneath *adv*, infrā
underrate *v.t*, mĭnōris aestĭmo (1)
understand *v.t*, intellĕgo (3), comprĕhendo (3)
understanding *nn*, mens, *f*; **(agreement)**, conventum, *n*
undertake *v.t*, suscĭpĭo (3); **(put in hand)**, incĭpĭo (3)
undertaker vespillo, *m*
undertaking, *nn*, inceptum, *n*
undervalue *v.t*, mĭnōris aestĭmo (1)
undeserved immĕrĭtus
undeserving indignus
undesirable *use phr. with* nōn *and* cŭpĭo (3) *or* expĕto (3) **(to desire)**
undetected tectus
undeveloped immātūrus
undigested crūdus
undiminished immĭnūtus
undisciplined ĭnexercĭtātus
undisguised non dissĭmŭlātus
undistinguished ignōbĭlis
undisturbed stăbĭlis, immōtus
undo *v.t*, solvo (3); **(render ineffectual)**, irrĭtum făcĭo (3)
undone infectus
undoubted certus

undoubtedly *adv*, sĭne dŭbĭo
undress *v.t*, vestem dētrăho (3) (*with dat. of person*)
undressed *adj*, nūdus
undue nĭmĭus
undulate *v.i*, fluctŭo (1)
unduly *adv*, **(excessively)**, nĭmĭum
undying immortālis
unearth *v.t*, dētĕgo (3)
unearthly *adv, use* terrĭbĭlis **(frightful)**
uneasiness anxĭĕtas, *f*
uneasy anxĭus
uneducated indoctus
unemployed ōtĭōsus
unending aeternus, infinītus
unenterprising ĭners, ĭnaudax
unequal impar, ĭnīquus
unequalled singŭlāris
unequivocal non dŭbĭus
unerring certus
uneven ĭnaequālis; **(of ground)**, ĭnīquus
unevenness ĭnīquĭtas, *f*
unexampled ĭnaudītus, ūnĭcus
unexpected ĭnŏpīnātus
unexpectedly *adv*, ex (*or* dē) imprōvīso
unexplored ĭnexplōrātus
unfailing pĕrennis
unfair ĭnīquus, iniustus
unfairness ĭnīquĭtas, *f*
unfaithful infĭdēlis, perfĭdus
unfaithfulness infĭdēlĭtas
unfamiliar insŭētus
unfashionable *use phr. with* extrā consŭētūdĭnem **(outside of custom)**
unfasten *v.t*, solvo (3), rĕfĭgo (3)
unfathomable infinītus
unfavourable ĭnīquus; **(omen)**, sĭnister, infēlix
unfeeling dūrus
unfeigned sincērus, simplex
unfinished imperfectus; **(task)** infectus
unfit incommŏdus
unfitness ĭnūtĭlĭtas, *f*
unfitting indĕcōrus
unfix *v.t*, rĕfĭgo (3)
unfold *v.t*, explĭco (1)
unforeseen imprōvīsus

unforgiving implācābĭlis
unforgotten *use phr. with*
mĕmor, *adj*, **(remembering)**
unfortified immūnītus
unfortunate infēlix
unfounded (groundless) vānus
unfriendliness ĭnĭmīcītĭa
unfriendly ĭnĭmīcus
unfulfilled irrītus, ĭnānis
unfurl *v.t*, pando (3)
unfurnished nūdus
ungainly rŭdis
ungentlemanly illībĕrālis
ungodly incestus
ungovernable impŏtens,
indŏmĭtus
ungraceful ĭnēlĕgans
ungrateful ingrātus
unguarded incustōdītus; **(speech
or action)**, incautus
unhappiness mĭsĕrĭa, *f*
unhappy mĭser, infēlix
unharmed incŏlŭmis
unhealthiness vălētūdo, *f*; **(of
place, etc.)**, grăvĭtas, *f*
unheard (of) ĭnaudītus
unheeded neglectus
unhesitating cofidens
unhindered expĕdītus
unhoped for inspērātus
unhorse *v.t*, ĕquo dēĭcĭo (3)
(throw down from a horse)
unicorn mŏnŏcĕros, *m*
uniform *nn*, **(military —)**, hăbĭtus
mīlītāris, *m*
uniform *adj*, aequābĭlis
unimaginable *use phr*, quod
mente concĭpi non pŏtest **(that
cannot be conceived in the mind)**
unimpaired intĕger
unimportant lĕvis
uninhabitable ĭnhăbĭtābĭlis
uninhabited dēsertus
uninitiated prŏfānus
uninjured incŏlŭmis
unintelligible obscūrus
unintentional non praemĕdĭtātus
uninteresting (flat, insipid) frīgĭdus
uninterruped contĭnŭus
uninvited invŏcātus
union (act of joining) iunctĭo, *f*;
(— of states), cīvītātes foedĕrātae,
f.pl; **(agreement)**, consensus, *m*

unique ūnĭcus
unit (one) ūnus
unite *v.t*, coniungo (3), consŏcĭo
(1); *v.i*, sē consŏcĭāre (1 *reflex*), sē
coniungĕre (3 *reflex*)
united consŏcĭātus
unity (one) ūnus; **(agreement)**,
concordĭa, *f*
universal ūnĭversus
universe mundus, *m*
university ăcădēmĭa, *f*
unjust ĭniustus
unjustifiable *use phr*, quod
excūsări non pōtest **(that cannot
be excused)**
unkind ĭnhūmānus
unkindness ĭnhūmānĭtas, *f*
unknowingly *adj*. imprūdens
unknown ignōtus, incognĭtus
unlawful (forbidden) vĕtĭtus
unlearned indoctus
unless *conj*, nĭsi
unletered indoctus, illittĕrātus
unlike dissĭmĭlis (*foll. by dat. or
genit*)
unlikely non vēri sĭmĭlis **(not like
the truth)**
unlimited infīnītus
unload *v.t*, exōnĕro (1); **(goods,
etc.)**, expōno (3)
unlock *v.t*, rĕsĕro (1)
unlooked for ĭnexpectātus
unloose *v.t*, solvo (3)
unlucky infēlix
unmanageable impŏtens;
(things), ĭnhābĭlis
unmanly mollis
unmarried caelebs
unmask *v.t*, **(plans, etc.)**, ăpĕrĭo
(4)
unmerciful immĭsĕrĭcors
ummindful immĕmor
unmistakable certus
umitigated mĕrus
unmolested intĕger
unmoved immōtus
unnatural monstrŭōsus;
(far-fetched), arcessītus
unnavigable innăvĭgābĭlis
unnecessary non nĕcessărĭus,
sŭpervăcānĕus
unnoticed *use vb*, lătĕo (2) **(to lie
hidden)**

unnumbered innŭmĕrābĭlis
unoccupied (at leisure) ōtĭōsus; (of land), ăpertus
unoffending innŏcens
unopposed (militarily) *use phr*, nullo hoste prŏhĭbente **(with no enemy impending)**
unpack *v.t*, exŏnĕro (1)
unpaid *use* rĕlĭquus **(remaining)**
unparalleled ūnĭcus
unpitied immĭsĕrābĭlis
unpleasant iniūcundus
unpleasantness (trouble) mŏlestĭa, *f*
unpolished impŏlītus
unpolluted intactus
unpopular invĭdĭōsus
unpopularity invĭdĭa, *f*
unprecedented nŏvus
unprejudiced intĕger
unpremeditated sŭbĭtus
unprepared impărātus
unpretentious hŭmĭlis
unprincipled (good for nothing) nēquam (*indeclinable*)
unproductive infēcundus
unprofitable non quaestŭōsus
unprotected indēfensus
unprovoked illăcessītus
unpunished impūnītus
unqualified nōn aptus; **(unlimited)**, infinītus
unquestionable certus
unravel *v.t*, rĕtexo (3); **(a problem, etc.)**, explĭco (1)
unreasonable inīquus
unrelenting ĭnexōrābĭlis
unremitting assĭdŭus
unreserved līber
unrestrained effrēnātus
unrewarded ĭnhŏnōrātus
unrighteous iniustus
unripe immātūrus
unrivalled praestantissĭmus
unroll *v.t*, ēvolvo (3)
unruffled immōtus
unruly effrēnātus, impŏtens
unsafe intūtus
unsatisfactory nōn aptus
unscrupulous (wicked) mălus
unseal *v.t*, rĕsigno (1)
unseasonable intempestīvus
unseemly indĕcōrus

unseen invīsus
unselfish (persons) innŏcens; **(actions)**, grātŭītus
unselfishness innŏcentĭa, *f*
unserviceable ĭnūtĭlis
unsettle *v.t*, turbo (1)
unsettled incertus, dŭbĭus
unshaken immōtus
unshaved intonsus
unsheath *v.t*, stringo (3)
unship *v.t*, expōno (3)
unsightly foedus
unskilful impĕrītus
unskilfulness impĕrītĭa, *f*
unslaked (thirst) nōn explētus
unsociable diffĭcĭlis
unsophisticated simplex
unsound (of health or opinions) infirmus; **(of mind)**, insānus
unsoundness infirmĭtas, *f*, insānĭtas, *f*
unsparing (severe) sĕvērus; **(lavish)**, prōdĭgus; **(effort, etc.)**, non rĕmissus
unspeakable infandus
unspoiled intĕger
unstained pūrus
unsteadiness mōbĭlĭtas, *f*
unsteady instābĭlis, vărĭus
unstring rĕtendo (3)
unsuccessful irrĭtus; **(person)**, infaustus
unsuitable incommŏdus
unsuitableness incommŏdĭtas, *f*
unsuspected non suspectus
unsuspecting incautus
untameable impŏtens
untamed indŏmĭtus
untaught indoctus
unteachable indŏcĭlis
untenable (position) *use phr*, quod tĕnēri non pŏtest **(that cannot be held)**
unthankful ingrātus
unthinking (inconsiderate) inconsīdĕrātus
untie *v.t*, solvo (3)
until *conj*, dum, dōnec
until *prep*, ad, (*with acc*)
untilled incultus
untimely *adj*, immātūrus
untiring assĭdŭus
untold (numbers) innŭmĕrābĭlis

untouched intĕger
untried ĭnexpertus
untroubled sēcūrus
untrue falsus
untruth mendācĭum, *n*
unused (of persons) insŏlĭtus; (things) intĕger
unusual insŏlĭtus, ĭnūsĭtātus
unutterable infandus
unveil *v.t*, dētĕgo (3)
unwarily *adv*, incautē
unwarlike imbellis
unwarrantable ĭnīquus
unwary incautus
unwavering constans
unwearied indēfessus
unwelcome ingrātus
unwell aeger
unwholesome grăvis
unwieldy ĭnhăbĭlis
unwilling invītus; (to be —), *v.i*, nolle (*irreg*)
unwillingly, unwillingness use adj, invītus (unwilling)
unwind *v.t*, rĕtexo (3), rĕvolvo (3)
unwise stultus, imprūdens
unworthiness indignĭtas, *f*
unworthy indignus, immĕrĭtus
unwrap *v.t*, explĭco (1)
unyielding firmus, inflexĭbĭlis
unyoke *v.t*, disiungo (3)
up *prep*, (— stream or hill), adversus (*in agreement with noun*); (— to), tĕnus (*with abl*)
up *adv*, sursum; (— and down), sursum dĕorsum
upbraid *v.t*, obiugo (1)
upbraiding *nn*, exprŏbrātĭo, *f*
uphill *adv. phr*, adverso colle
uphold *v.t*, sustĭnĕo (2)
uplift *v.t*, tollo (3)
upon *prep*, sŭper (*with acc*); (on), in (*with abl*)
upper *adj*, sŭpĕrĭor; (to get the — hand), sŭpĕrĭor esse (*irreg*)
uppermost *adj*, summus
upright rectus; (of morals), prŏbus
uprightness prŏbĭtas, *f*
uproar clāmor, *m*
uproarious tŭmultŭōsus
uproot ēvello (3)

upset *v.t*, ēverto (3)
upset *adj*, mōtus; (troubled), anxĭus
upshot exĭtus, *m*
upside down, (to turn —) *use vb*. verto (3) (to overturn) *or* miscĕo (2) (throw into confusion)
upstart nŏvus hŏmo
upwards *adv*, sursum; (of number, — of), amplĭus quam
urbane urbānus
urbanity urbānĭtas, *f*
urchin pūsĭo, *m*
urge *v.t*, urgĕo (2); (persuade), suādĕo (2) (*with dat. of person*)
urgency grăvĭtas, *f*
urgent grăvis
urine ūrīna, *f*
urn urna, *f*
us *obj. pron*, nos
usage mos, *m*
use ūsus, m; (advantage), commŏdum, *n*
use *v.t*, ūtor (3 *dep. with abl*)
useful ūtĭlis
usefulness ūtĭlĭtas, *f*
useless ĭnūtĭlis
uselessness ĭnūtĭlĭtas, *f*
usher in *v.t*, intrōdūco (3)
usual ūsĭtātus, sŏlĭtus
usually *adv*, plērumque, fĕrē
usurer fēnĕrātor, *m*
usurious fēnĕrātŏrĭus
usurp *v.t*, occŭpo (1); (seize), răpĭo (3)
usury fēnĕrātĭo, *f*, ūsūra, *f*
utensils vāsa, *n.pl*
utility ūtĭlĭtas, *f*
utilize *v.t*, ūtor (3 *dep. with abl*)
utmost extrēmus, summus
utter *adj*, tōtus
utter *v.t*, dīco (3)
utterance dictum, *n*
utterly *adv*, omnīno

V

vacancy (empty post) lŏcus văcŭus, *m*
vacant *adj*, văcŭus, ĭnānis
vacate *v.t*, rĕlinquo (3) (a post), ējūro (1)
vacation fērĭae, *f.pl*

vacillate *v.i*, văcillo (1)
vacillation văcillātĭo, *f*
vacuum ĭnāne, *n*
vagabond erro, *m*
vagabond *adj*, văgus
vagary lĭbīdo, *f*
vagrant *adj*, văgus
vague incertus
vagueness obscūrĭtas, *f*
vain vānus; **(boastful, etc.)**,
  glŏrĭōsus; **(in —)**, *adv*, frustrā
vainglorious glŏrĭōsus
vainglory glōrĭa, *f*
vale valles, *f*
valet cŭbĭcŭlārĭus, *m*
valetudinarian vălētūdĭnārĭus, *m*
valiant fortis
valid firmus, vălĭdus
validity grăvĭtas, *f*
valise capsa, *f*
valley valles, *f*
valorous fortis
valour virtus, *f*
valuable prĕtĭōsus
valuation aestĭmātĭo, *f*
value *nn*, prĕtĭum, *n*
value *v.t*, aestĭmo (1); **(— highly)**,
  magni dūco (3) **(— little)**, parvi
  dūco
valueless vīlis
valve ĕpistŏmĭum, *n*
van (vanguard) prīmum agmen, *n*
vanish *v.i*, vānesco (3), dīlābor (3
  dep)
vanity vānĭtas, *f*, iactātĭo, *f*
vanquish *v.t*, vinco (3)
vanquisher victor, *m*
vantage-point lŏcus sŭpĕrĭor, *m*
vapid văpĭdus
vapour văpor, *m*
variability mūtābĭlĭtas, *f*
variable vărĭus, mūtābĭlis
variance dissensĭo, *f*; **(to be at —**
  with), dissĭdĕo (2) ab (*with abl*)
variation vărĭĕtas, *f*
varicose vărĭcōsus; **(a — vein)**,
  vărix, *c*
variegated vărĭus
variety vărĭĕtas, *f*, dīversĭtas, *f*
various vărĭus, dīversus
varnish *nn*, ātrāmentum, *n*
vary *v.i and v.t*, vărĭo (1)
vase vās, *n*

vassal clĭens, *m, f*
vast vastus, ingens
vastness immensĭtas, *f*
vat cūpa, *f*
vault fornix, *m*
vault *v.i*, sălĭo (4)
vaunt *v.t*, iacto (1); *v.i*, glŏrĭor (1
  dep)
vaunting *nn*, iactātĭo, *f*
veal vĭtŭlīna căro, *f*, **(calf's flesh)**
veer *v.i*, sē vertĕre (3 *reflex*)
vegetable hŏlus, *n*
vehemence vīs, *f*
vehement vĕhĕmens, ācer
vehicle vēhĭcŭlum, *n*
veil *v.t*, vēlo (1), tĕgo (3)
veil *nn*, rīca, *f*; **(bridal —)**,
  flammĕum, *n*; **(disguise)**,
  intĕgŭmentum, *n*
vein vēna, *f*
velocity vēlōcĭtas, *f*
venal vēnālis
venality vēnālĭtas, *f*
vendor vendĭtor, *m*
veneer *nn, use* cortex, *m*, **(bark,**
  shell)
venerable vĕnĕrābĭlis
venerate *v.t*, cŏlo (3), vĕnĕror (1
  dep)
veneration cultus, *m*
venereal vĕnĕrĕus
vengeance ultĭo, *f*; **(to take —)**,
  ulciscor (3 *dep*)
venial *use phr*, cui ignosci pŏtest
  (that can be pardoned)
venison fĕrīna căro, *f*
venom vēnēnum, *n*
venomous vĕnēnātus
vent *nn*, spīrāmentum, *n*
vent *v.t*, **(pour out)**, effundo (3)
ventilate *v.t*, ventĭlo (1); **(discuss,**
  etc.), *use vb*, prōfĕro (*irreg*) **(to**
  bring out)
ventilator spīrāmentum, *n*
ventricle ventrĭcŭlus, *m*
venture *nn*, **(undertaking)**, rĕs, *f*,
  inceptum, *n*
venture *v.t*, pĕrīclĭtor (1 *dep*)
venturous audax
veracious vērus
veracity vērĭtas, *f*
veranda pŏdĭum, *n*
verb verbum, *n*

verbal   *nn, see adv,* **verbally**
verbally   per verba **(by means of words)**
verbatim   *adv,* tŏtĭdem verbis **(with the same number of words)**
verbose   verbōsus
verdant   vĭrĭdis
verdict (of a person or jury) sentẽntĭa, *f;* **(of a court),** iūdĭcĭum, *n*
verdigris   aerūgo, *f*
verge   *nn,* ōra, *f,* margo, *c;* **(on the — of)** *use phr.* minimum abest quin ... **(it is very little wanting that ...)**
verge   *v.i,* vergo (3)
verger   appārĭtor, *m*
verification   prŏbātĭo, *f*
verify   *v.t,* prŏbo (1)
veritable   vērus
vermilion   mĭnĭum, *n*
versatile   vărĭus
versatility   ăgĭlĭtas, *f*
verse   versus, *m*
versed in   *adj,* exercĭtātus
versify   *v.i,* versus făcĭo (3)
version   *use vb,* converto (3) **(turn)**
vertebra   vertĕbra, *f*
vertical   rectus
vertigo   vertīgo, *f*
very   *adj, use emphatic pron,* ipse
very   *adv, use superlative of adj. or adv, e.g.* — **beautiful,** pulcherrĭmus; — **quickly,** cĕlerrĭme; *otherwise* maxĭmē, valdē, admŏdum
vessel (receptable) vās, *n;* **(ship),** nāvis, *f*
vest   *nn,* tūnĭca, *f*
vest   *v.t,* **(invest, impart),** do (1)
vestal virgin   vestālis virgo, *f*
vestibule   vestĭbŭlum, *n*
vestige   vestīgĭum, *n;* **(mark),** nŏta, *f,* indĭcĭum, *n*
vestry   aedĭcŭla, *f*
veteran   *adj,* vĕtĕrānus; **(— soldier),** vĕtĕrānus mīles, *m*
veterinary   vĕtĕrīnārĭus
veto   *nn,* intercessĭo, *f*
veto   *v.i,* intercēdo (3) *(with dat)*
vex   *v.t,* vexo (1), sollĭcĭto (1)
vexation   indignātĭo, *f,* dŏlor, *m*
vexatious   mŏlestus

vial   lăgēna, *f*
viands   cĭbus, *m*
viaticum   vĭātĭcum, *n*
vibrate   *v.i. and v.t,* vĭbro (1)
vibration   ăgĭtātĭo, *f*
vicarious   vĭcārĭus
vice   turpĭtŭdo, *f*
viceroy   lēgātos, *m*
vicinity   vīcīnĭtas, *f*
vicious   vĭtĭōsus; **(fierce),** fĕrus
vicissitude   vĭces, *f.pl,* vĭcissĭtūdo, *f*
victim   hostĭa, *f,* victĭma, *f*
victor   victor, *m,* victrix, *f*
victorious   victor
victory   victōrĭa, *f*
victual   *v.t, use phr,* rem frūmentārĭam prōvĭdĕo (2) **(to look after the supply of provisions)**
victuals   cĭbus, *m*
vie with   *v.i,* certo (1) cum *(with abl)*
view   *nn,* aspectus, *m,* conspectus, *m;* **(opinion),** sentẽntĭa, *f*
view   *v.t,* conspĭcĭo (3); **(consider),** *use* sentĭo (4) **(to feel)**
vigil   pervĭgĭlātĭo, *f*
vigilance   vĭgĭlantĭa, *f*
vigilant   vĭgĭlans
vigorous   impĭger
vigour   vīs, *f,* vĭgor, *m*
vile   turpis
vileness   turpĭtŭdo, *f*
vilify   *v.t,* infāmo (1), dētrāho (3)
villa   villa, *f*
village   pāgus, *m*
villager   pāgānus, *m*
villain   hŏmo scĕlĕrātus
villainy   prāvĭtas, *f,* scĕlus, *n*
vindicate   *v.t,* vindĭco (1); **(justify),** purgo (1)
vindication   purgātĭo, *f*
vindictive   *use phr,* ăvĭdus iniūrĭae ulciscendae **(eager to avenge a wrong)**
vinegrower   cultor, *(m)* vītis
vine   vītis, *f*
vinegar   ăcētum, *n*
vineyard   vīnĕa, *f*
vintage   *nn,* vindēmĭa, *f*
vintner   vīnārĭus, *m*
violate   *v.t,* vĭŏlo (1)

violation vĭŏlātĭo, *f*
violator vĭŏlātor, *m*
violence vīs, *f* vĭŏlentĭa, *f*,
impĕtus, *m*
violent vĭŏlentus, impŏtens
violet *nn*, vĭŏla, *f*
violet *adj* (— colour), ĭanthĭnus
viper vīpĕra, *f*; *adj*, vīpĕrīnus
virago vĭrāgo, *f*
virgin *nn*, virgo, *f*
virgin *adj*, virgĭnālis
virginity virgĭnĭtas, *f*
virile vĭrīlis
virtually *adv* re ipsā
virtue virtus, *f*, hŏnestas, *f*; (by —
of), *use abl. case of noun alone,
or use per* (*with acc*)
virtuous hŏnestus
virulent ācerbus
viscous lentus
visible (noticeable) mănifestus; *or
use nn.* conspectus, *m* (view)
vision visus, *m*; (phantom,
apparition), īmāgo, *f*, spĕcĭes, *f*
visionary vānus
visit *nn*, (call), sălūtātĭo, *f*; (stay),
commŏrātĭo, *f*
visit *v.t* vīso (3)
visitor sălūtātor, *m*, hospes, *m*
visor buccŭla, *f*
vista prospectus, *m*
visual *use phr. with* ŏcŭlus, *m*,
(eye)
vital vītālis; (important), grăvis
vitality vīs, *f*, vīvācĭtas, *f*
vitiate *v.t*, vĭtĭo (1), corrumpo (3)
vitreous vĭtrĕus
vituperation vĭtŭpĕrātĭo, *f*
vituperate *v.t*, vĭtŭpĕro (1)
vivacious ălăcer
vivacity ălăcrĭtas, *f*
vivid vīvus
vivify *v.t*, ănĭmo (1)
vixen vulpes, *f*
vocabulary verba, *n.pl*
vocal vōcālis
vocation offĭcĭum, *n*
vociferate *v.i*, clāmo (1)
vociferous clāmōsus
vociferously *adv*, magno clāmōre
vogue mos, *m*, (custom)
voice *nn*, vox, *f*
voice *v.t*, dīco (3)

void *nn*, ĭnāne, *n*
void *adj*, ĭnānis; (— of), văcŭus
(*with abl*)
volatile lĕvis
volcano mons qui ēructat flammas
(a mountain which emits flames)
volition vŏluntas, *f*; (of his own —),
sŭa sponte
volley (of javelins) tēla missa, *n.pl*
volubility vŏlūbĭlĭtas, *f*
voluble vŏlūbĭlis
volume (book) lĭber, *m*; (of noise),
magnĭtūdo, *f*
voluminous cōpĭōsus
voluntarily *adv*, sponte (of one's
own accord) *with appropriate
pron*, mĕā, tŭā, sŭā
voluntary vŏluntārĭus
volunteer *nn*, mīles vŏluntārĭus,
m
volunteer *v.i*, (of soldiers), *use
phr*, ultro nōmen dăre (enlist
voluntarily)
voluptuous vŏluptārĭus
voluptuousness luxŭrĭa, *f*
vomit *nn*, vŏmĭtĭo, *f*
vomit *v.i. and v.t*, vŏmo (3)
voracious ĕdax, vŏrax
voracity ĕdācĭtas, *f*
vortex vertex, *m*
vote *nn*, suffrāgĭum, *n*, sententĭa, *f*
vote *v.i*, suffrāgĭum fĕro (*irreg*);
(to — in favour of), in sententĭam
īre (*irreg*) (*with genit*)
voter suffrāgātor, *m*
voting-tablet (ballot paper) tăbella, *f*
vouch for *v.t*, praesto (1), testor
(1 *dep*), testĭfĭcor (1 *dep*)
voucher (authority) auctōrĭtas, *f*
vow vōtum, *n*; (promise), fĭdes, *f*
vow *v.t*, prōmitto (3), vŏvĕo (2)
vowel vōcālis littĕra, *f*
voyage *nn*, nāvĭgātĭo, *f*
voyage *v.i*, nāvĭgo (1)
voyager pĕrĕgrīnātor, *m*
vulgar vulgāris, plēbĕius,
sordĭdus
vulgarity (of manner, etc.) *use
phr*, mōres sordĭdi, *m.pl*
vulgarize *v.t*, pervulgo (1)
vulnerable ăpertus
vulture vultur, *m*

W

wadding   *use* lānūgo, *f*, **(woolly down)**

wade   *v.i, use phr*, per văda īre (*irreg*) **(to go through the shallows)**

wafer   crustŭlum **(pastry)**

waft   *v.t*, fĕro (*irreg*)

wag   *nn*, **(jester)**, iŏcŭlātor, *m*

wag   *v.t*, quasso (1)

wage (war)   *v.t*, gĕro (3) (bellum)

wager   *nn*, sponsĭo, *f*

wager   *v.i*, sponsĭōnem făcĭo (3)

wages   merces, *f*

waggish   făcētus

waggon   plaustrum, *n*

wagtail   mōtăcilla, *f*

wail, wailing   *nn*, plōrātus, *m*, flētus, *m*

wail   *v.i*, plōro (1) flĕo (2)

waist   mĕdĭum corpus, *n*

waistcoat   sŭbūcŭla, *f*, **(undergarment)**

wait   *v.i*, mănĕo (2); *v.t*, **(to — for)**, exspecto (1); **(serve)**, fămŭlor (1 *dep.*); **(— in ambush)**, insĭdĭas făcĭo (3) (*with dat*)

wait   *nn*, mŏra, *f*

waiter   fămŭlus, *m*

waiting   exspectātĭo, *f*, mansĭo, *f*

waive   *v.t*, rĕmitto (3)

wake   *v.t*, excĭto (1); *v.i*, expergiscor (3 *dep.*)

wakeful   vĭgĭl

wakefulness   vĭgĭlantĭa, *f*, insomnĭa, *f*

walk   *nn*, ambŭlātĭo, *f*; **(gait)**, incessus, *m*; **(— of life, occupation)**, quaestus, *m*

walk   *v.i*, ambŭlo (1), grădĭor (3 *dep.*), incēdo (3)

walker   pĕdes, *m*

walking   *nn*, ambŭlātĭo, *f*

wall   mūrus, *m*; **(ramparts)**, moenĭa, *n.pl*; **(inner —)**, părĭes, *m*

wall   *v.t*, mūnĭo (4) **(fortify)**

wallet   saccŭlus, *m*

wallow   *v.i*, vŏlūtor (1 *pass*)

walnut (tree and nut)   iŭglans, *f*

wan   *adj*, pallĭdus

wand   virga, *f*, cădūcĕus, *m*

wander   *v.i*, erro (1), văgor (1 *dep.*)

wanderer   erro, *m*

wandering   *nn*, error, *m*

wane   *v.i*, dēcresco (3)

want   *nn*, **(lack)**, ĭnŏpĭa, *f*, pēnūrĭa, *f*; **(longing for)**, dēsīdĕrĭum, *n*; **(failing)**, dēfectĭo, *f*; **(in —)**, *adj*, ĭnops

want   *v.i*, **(wish)**, vŏlo (*irreg*); *v.t*, **(to lack)**, cărĕo (2), ĕgĕo (2) (*with abl*); **(long for)**, dēsīdĕro (1); **(desire)**, cŭpĭo (3)

wanting (to be —, to fail)   *v.i*, dēsum (*irreg*)

wanton   *adj*, lascīvus, lĭbīdĭnōsus

wantoness   lascīvĭa, *f*

war   bellum, *n*; **(civil —)**, bellum cīvĭle, *n*; **(in —)**, *adv*, bello; **(to make — on)**, bellum infĕro (*irreg, with dat*); **(to declare — on)**, bellum indīco (3) (*with dat*); **(to wage —)**, bellum gĕro (3)

warble   *v.i*, căno (3)

warcry   clāmor, *m*

ward   pūpillus, *m*, pūpilla, *f*; **(district)**, rĕgĭo, *f*

ward off   *v.t*, arcĕo (2)

warden   cūrātor, *m*

warder   custos, *c*

wardrobe   vestĭārĭum, *n*

warehouse   horrĕum, *n*

wares   merx, *f*

warfare   mīlĭtĭa, *f*

warily   *adv*, cautē

wariness   cautĭo, *f*

warlike   *adj*, bellĭcōsus, mīlĭtāris

warm   călĭdus; **(to be —)**, *v.i*, călĕo (2)

warm   *v.t*, călĕfăcĭo (3)

warmly (eagerly)   *adv*, vĕhementer

warmth   călor, *m*

warn   *v.t*, mŏnĕo (2)

warning   *nn*, **(act of —)**, mŏnĭtĭo, *f*; **(the warning itself)**, mŏnĭtum, *n*

warp   *nn*, stāmen, *n*

warp   *v.t*, **(distort of mind, etc.)**, dēprāvo (1)

warrant   *nn*, mandātum, *n*; **(authority)**, auctŏrĭtas, *f*

warrant   *v.t*, **(guarantee)**, firmo (1), praesto (1)

warranty   sătisdătĭo, *f*

warren   lĕpŏrārĭum, *n*

warrior mīles, *c*, bellātor, *m*
wart verrūca, *f*
wary prōvĭdus, prūdens
wash *v.t*, lăvo (1); *v.i*, lăvor (1 *pass*)
wash, washing *nn*, lăvātĭo, *f*
washbasin ăquālis, *c*
wasp vespa, *f*
waspish ăcerbus
waste *nn*, damnum, *n*; (careless throwing away), effūsĭo, *f*; (— land), vastĭtas, *f*
waste *adj*, vastus, dēsertus
waste *v.t*, consūmo (3), perdo (3); (— time), tempus tĕro (3); *v.i*, (— away), tābesco (3)
wasteful prŏfūsus
wastefulness prŏfūsĭo, *f*
watch (a — of the night) vĭgĭlĭa, *f*; (watching on guard), excŭbĭae, *f.pl*
watch *v.t*, (observe), specto (1); (guard), custōdĭo (4); *v.i*, (not to sleep), excŭbo (1)
watchful vĭgĭlans
watchfulness vĭgĭlantĭa, *f*
watchman custos, *m*
watchword tessĕra, *f*
water ăqua, *f*; (fresh —), ăqua dulcis, *f*; (salt —), ăqua salsa, *f*
water *v.t*, rĭgo (1), irrĭgo (1)
water-carrier ăquārĭus, *m*
water closet lātrīna, *f*
water snake hydrus, *m*
waterfall ăqua dēsĭlĭens, *f*, (water leaping down)
watering place ăquātĭo, *f*; (resort), ăquae, *f.pl*
waterworks ăquaeductus, *m*
watery ăquātĭcus
wattle crātis, *f*
wave *nn*, unda, *f*, fluctus, *m*
wave *v.i*, undo (1), fluctŭo (1); *v.t*, ăgĭto (1)
waver *v.i*, fluctŭo (1) dŭbĭto (1)
wavering *adj*, dŭbĭus
wavering *nn*, dŭbĭtātĭo, *f*
wavy (of hair) crispus
wax *nn*, cēra, *f*; *adj*, cērĕus
wax *v.i*, cresco (3)
way vĭa, *f*; (journey), ĭter, *n*; (pathway), sēmĭta, *f*; (course), cursus, *m*; (manner), mŏdus, *m*;

(habit), mos, *m*; (system), rătĭo, *f*; (in the —), *adj*, obvĭus; (in this —), *adv*, ĭta, sīc; (out of the —) *adj*, āvĭus; (to give or to make —), *v.i*, cēdo (3); (to get one's own —), vinco (3)
wayfarer vĭātor, *m*
waylay *v.t*, insĭdĭor (1 *dep.*) (*with dat*)
wayward pertĭnax
we *pron*, nos; *often expressed by 1st person plural of vb, e.g* we are, sumus
weak infirmus, dēbĭlis; (overcome), confectus; (of arguments, etc.), lĕvis
weaken *v.t*, infirmo (1), dēbĭlĭto (1); *v.i*, languesco (3), dēfĭcĭo (3)
weak-hearted pŭsilli ănĭmi (of weak heart)
weakness infirmĭtas, *f*, dēbĭlĭtas, *f*, lēvĭtas, *f*
weal (the common) bŏnum pūblĭcum, *n*; (on skin), vībex, *f*
wealth dīvĭtĭae, *f.pl*, ŏpes, *f.pl*; (large supply), cōpĭa, *f*
wealthy dīves, lŏcŭples
wean *v.t*, lacte dēpello (3) (remove from the milk)
weapon tēlum, *n*; (*pl*) arma, *n.pl*
wear *v.t*, (rub), tĕro (3); (— out), contĕro (3); (— a garment), gĕro (3); *v.i*, (last), dūro (1)
weariness lassĭtūdo, *f*
wearisome lăbŏrĭōsus
weary *adj*, fessus, fătīgātus
weary *v.t*, fătīgo (1); *v.i*, (grow —), dēfătīgor (1 *pass*)
weasel mustēla, *f*
weather *nn*, tempestas, *f*
weather *v.t*, (endure, bear), perfĕro (*irreg*)
weave *v.t*, texo (3)
weaver textor, *m*
web tēla, *f*
wed *v.t*, (of the husband), dūco (3); (of the wife), nūbo (3) (*with dat*)
wedding *nn*, nuptĭae, *f.pl*; (— day), dĭes (*m*) nuptĭārum
wedge *nn*, cŭnĕus, *m*
wedlock mātrĭmōnĭum, *n*
weed *nn*, herba ĭnūtĭlis, *f* (harmful plant)

weed

weed *v.t*, runco (1)
week *use phr*, spătĭum septem
dĭērum **(a space of seven days)**
weep *v.i*, lăcrĭmo (1)
weeping *nn*, flētus, *m*
weeping willow sălix, *f*
weevil curcŭlĭo, *m*
weigh *v.t*, pendo (3), penso (1),
(consider), pondĕro (1);
(— down), grăvo (1)
weight pondus, *n*; **(a —)**,
lībrămentum, *n*; **(influence, etc.)**,
use adj. grăvis **(important)**
weightiness grăvĭtas, *f*
weighty grăvis
weir **(dam)** mōles, *f*
welcome *adj*, grātus, acceptus
welcome *nn*, sălūtātĭo, *f*
welcome! salve! **(***pl*. salvēte!**)**
welcome *v.t*, excĭpĭo (3)
weld *v.t*, ferrūmĭno (1)
welfare bŏnum, *n*, sălus, *f*
well *adv*, bĕnĕ; **(very —)**, optĭmē
well *nn*, pŭtĕus, *m*
well *adj*, **(safe)**, salvus; **(healthy)**,
sānus, vălens; **(to be —)**, *v.i*, vălĕo
(2)
wellbeing *nn* sălus, *f*
well-born nōbĭlis
well-disposed bĕnĕvŏlus
well-favoured pulcher
well-known nōtus
well-wisher *use adj*, bĕnĕvŏlus
(well-disposed)
welter *v.i*, vŏlūtor (1 *pass*)
wench pŭella, *f*
west *nn*, occĭdens, *m*
west *adj*, occĭdentālis
westward *adv*, ad occĭdentem
(sōlem)
wet *adj*, hūmĭdus, mădĭdus
wet *v.t*, mădĕfăcĭo (3)
wether vervex, *m*
wet nurse nūtrix, *f*
whale bālaena, *f*
wharf nāvāle, *n*
what *interrog. pron*, quid?
interrog. adj, qui, quae, quod;
relative pron, quod, *pl*, quae;
(— for, wherefore, why), quārē;
(— sort), quālis?
whatever *pron*, quodcumque;
adj, quīcumque

wheat trītĭcum, *n*
wheel *nn*, rŏta, *f*
wheel *v.t*, circŭmăgo (3)
wheelbarrow păbo, *m*
wheeling *adj*, circumflectens
whelp *nn*, cătŭlus, *m*
when? *interrog*, quando?
(temporal), cum *(with vb, in
indicative or subjunctive mood)*,
ŭbĭ *(vb. in indicative)*
whence *adv*, undē
whenever *adv*, quandōcumque
where? *interrog*, ŭbĭ?; *(relative)*,
quā; **(— from)**, undē; **(— to)**, quō;
(anywhere, everywhere), *adv*,
ŭbīque
whereas *adv*, quŏnĭam
wherever quācumque
wherefore *adv*, quārē
whereupon *use phr*, quo facto
(with which having been done)
whet *v.t* **(sharpen)**, ăcŭo (3)
whether *conj*. *(in a single
question)*, num, nĕ; *(in a double
question*, whether ... or**)**, ŭtrum
... an; *(in a conditional sentence)*,
sīve ... sīve
whetstone cōs, *f*
whey sĕrum, *n*
which *interrog*, quis, quid;
(relative), qui, quae, quod; **(which
of two)**, ŭter
while *conj*, dum *(often foll. by
vb. in present tense indicative)*
while *nn*, tempus, *n*, spătĭum, *n*;
(for a little —), *adv*, părumper; **(in
a little —)**, brĕvi (tempŏre)
while away *v.t*, fallo (3), tĕro (3)
whim lĭbīdo, *f*
whimper *v.i*, vāgĭo (4)
whimsical rĭdĭcŭlus
whine *v.i*, vāgĭo (4)
whinny *v.i*, hinnĭo (4)
whip *nn*, flăgellum, *n*
whip *v.t*, verbĕro (1), flăgello (1)
whirl *v.t*, torquĕo (2); *v.i*,
torquĕor (2 *pass*)
whirlpool *m*, gurges, *m*
whirlwind turbo, *m*
whirr *nn*, strīdor, *m*
whirr *v.i*, strīdĕo (2)
whiskers *use* barba, *f*, **(beard)**
whisper *nn*, sŭsurrus, *m*

whisper　*v.i*, sŭsurro (1)
whispering　*adj*, sŭsurrus
whistle, whistling　*nn*, sībĭlus, *m*
whistle　*v.i*, sībĭlo (1)
white　*adj*, albus; **(shining —)**, candĭdus
white　*nn*, album, *n*
whiten　*v.t*, dĕalbo (1); *v.i*; albesco (3)
whiteness　candor, *m*
whitewash　*nn*, albārĭum, *n*; v.t, dĕalbo (1)
whither　*(interrog. and relative)*, quo
whiz　*v.i*, strīdĕo (2)
whiz, whizzing　*nn*, strīdor, *m*
who　*interrog*, quis? *(relative)*, qui, quae
whoever　*pron*, quīncunque
whole　*adj*, tōtus; **(untouched)**, intĕger
whole　*nn*, tōtum, *n*, ūnīversĭtas, *f*, or use adj, tōtus, *e.g.* **the — of the army**, tōtus exercĭtus, *m*
wholesale trader　mercātor, *m*
wholesale trading　mercātūra, *f*
wholesome　sălūbris
wholly　*adv*, omnīno
whoop　*nn*, ŭlŭlātus, *m*
whom　*acc. case of rel. pron*, quem, quam; *pl*, quos, quas
whore　mĕrĕtrix, *f*
whose　*genit. case of rel. pron*, cūius; *pl*, quōrum, quārum
why　*adv*, cur, quārē
wick　ellychnĭum, *n*
wicked　scĕlestus, mălus, imprŏbus
wickedness　scĕlus, *n*, inprŏbĭtas, *f*
wicker　vīmĭnĕus
wide　lātus; **(— open)**, pătens
widen　*v.t*, dīlāto (1); *v.i*, sē dīlātāre (1 *reflex*)
widow　vĭdŭa, *f*
widower　vĭdŭus vir, *m*
widowhood　vĭdŭĭtas, *f*
width　lātĭtūdo, *f*
wield　*v.t*, tracto (1)
wife　uxor, *f*
wig　cāpillāmentum, *n*
wild　indŏmĭtus, fĕrus; **(uncultivated)**, incultus; **(mad)**, āmens

wilderness　dēserta lŏca, *n.pl*
wildness　fĕrĭtas, *f*
wile　dŏlus, *m*
wilful　pervĭcax
wilfully　*adv*, pervĭcācĭter; **(deliberately)**, consultō
wilfulness　pervĭcācĭa, *f*
wiliness　callĭdĭtas, *f*
will (desire)　vŏluntas, *f*; **(purpose)**, consĭlĭum, *n*; **(pleasure)**, lĭbīdo, *f*; **(decision, authority)**, arbĭtrĭum, *n*; **(legal)**, testāmentum, *n*
will　*v.t*, **(bequeath)**, lēgo (1)
willing　*adj*, lĭbens
willingly　*adv*, lĭbenter
willingness　vŏluntas, *f*
willow　sălix, *f*
wily　callĭdus, văfer
win　*v.i*, vinco (3); *v.t*, consĕquor (3 *dep*), ădĭpiscor (3 *dep*)
wind　ventus, *m*; **(breeze)**, aura, *f*
wind　*v.t*, volvo (3)
winding　*nn*, flexus, *m*
winding　*adj*, flexŭōsus
windlass　sŭcŭla, *f*
window　fĕnestra, *f*
windward　*use phr*, conversus ad ventum **(turned towards the wind)**
windy　ventōsus
wine　vīnum, *n*
wine cask　dōlĭum, *n*
wine cellar　ăpŏthēca, *f*
wine cup　pōcŭlum, *n*
wine merchant　vīnārĭus, *m*
wing　āla, *f*; **(of army, etc.)**, cornu, *n*
winged　pennĭger
wink　*nn*, nictātĭo, *f*
wink　*v.i*, nicto (1); **(overlook)**, cōnīvĕo (2)
winner　victor, *m*
winning　*adj*, **(of manner)**, blandus
winnow　*v.t*, ventĭlo (1)
winter　*nn*, hĭems, *f*
winter　*adj*, hĭĕmālis
winter　*v.i*, hĭĕmo (1)
wintry　hĭĕmālis
wipe　*v.t*, tergĕo (2)
wire　fĭlum, *n*, **(thread)**
wisdom　săpĭentĭa, *f*, prūdentĭa, *f*
wise　*adj*, săpĭens, prūdens
wisely　*adv*, săpĭenter, prūdenter

wish *nn*, (desire), vŏluntas, *f*; (the wish itself), optātum, *n*; (longing), dēsīdĕrĭum, *n*

wish *v.t*, vŏlo (*irreg*), cŭpĭo (3), opto (1); (long for), dēsīdĕro (1)

wishing *nn*, optātĭo, *f*

wisp mănĭpŭlus, *m*

wistful cŭpĭdus (longing for); (dejected), tristis

wit ingĕnĭum, *n*; (humour), făcētĭae, *f.pl*; (out of one's —s), *adj*, āmens

witch sāga, *f*

witchcraft ars măgĭca, *f*

with *prep*, cum (*with abl, but when denoting the instrument, use abl. case, alone*; (among, at the house of), ăpud (*with acc*)

withdraw *v.i*, cēdo (3), sē rĕcĭpĕre (3 *reflex*); *v.t*, dēdūco (3), rĕmŏvĕo (2)

withdrawal regressus, *m*

wither *v.i*, languesco (3); *v.t*, (parch), torrĕo (2)

withered flaccĭdus

withhold *v.t*, rĕtĭnĕo (2)

within *adv*, intus

within *prep*, (time and space), intrā (*with acc*); (time), *use abl. case alone, e.g.* within three days, trĭbus dĭēbus

without *prep*, sĭne (*with abl*); (outside of), extrā (*with acc*); *when* without *is followed by a gerund* (*e.g* I returned without seeing him) *use a clause introduced by* nĕque, quĭn, ĭta ... ut: *e.g.* rĕgressus sum, nĕque ĕum vīdi

without *adv*, extrā

withstand *v.t*, rĕsisto (3) (*with dat*)

witness *nn*, (person), testis, *c*; (testimony), testĭmōnĭum, *n*

witness *v.t*, testor (1 *dep*), testĭfĭcor (1 *dep*); (to see), vĭdĕo (2)

witticism făcētĭe, *f.pl*

witty făcētus; (sharp), salsus

wizard māgus, *m*

woad vĭtrum, *n*

woe dŏlor, *m*, luctus, *m*

woeful tristis

wolf lŭpus, *m*

wolfish (greedy, rapacious) răpax

woman fēmĭna, *f*, mŭlĭer, *f*; (young —), pŭella, *f*; (old —), ănus, *f*

womanish, womanly mŭlĭĕbris

womb ŭtĕrus, *m*

wonder mīrātĭo, *f*; (a marvel) mīrācŭlum, *n*

wonder *v.i.* and v.t, mīror (1 *dep*)

wonderful mīrus, mīrābĭlis

wont, wonted *adj*, sŭētus

wont *nn*, mos, *m*

woo *v.t*, pĕto (3), ămo (1)

wood (material) mātĕrĭa, *f*; (forest), silva, *f*

wood-collector lignātor, *m*

wooded silvestris

wooden lignĕus

woodland silvae, *f.pl*

woodpecker pīcus, *m*

wooer prŏcus, *m*

wool lāna, *f*

woollen lānĕus

word verbum, *n*; (promise), fĭdes, *f*; (information), nuntĭus, *m*; send word, *v.t*, nuntĭo (1)

wordy verbōsus

work *nn*, ŏpus, *n*; (labour), lăbor, *m*

work *v.i*, ŏpĕror (1 *dep*)

work *v.t*, exercĕo (2); (handle, manipulate), tracto (1); (bring about), effĭcĭo (3)

worker ŏpĭfex, *c*, ŏpĕrārĭus, *m*

workman ŏpĭfex, *c*, ŏpĕrārĭus, *m*

workmanship ars, *f*

workshop offĭcīna, *f*

world mundus, *m*, orbis (*m*) terrārum; (people), hŏmĭnes, *c. pl*

worldliness *use phr*, stŭdĭum rērum prŏfānārum (fondness for common matters)

worm vermis, *m*

worm-eaten vermĭnōsus

worm (one's way) *v.i*, sē insĭnŭāre (1 *reflex*)

wormwood absinthĭum, *n*

worn (— out) *adj*, trītus; (as clothes), gestus

worry *nn*, anxĭĕtas, *f*

worry *v.t*, vexo (1); *v.i*, cūrā affĭci (3 *pass*) (to be affected by worry)

worse *adj*, pēior
worse *adv*, pēius
worship *v.t*, vĕnĕror (1 *dep*), cŏlo (3)
worship *nn*, vĕnĕrātĭo, *f*, cultus, *m*
worshipper cultor, *m*
worst *adj*, pessīmus
worst *adv*, pessīmē
worst *v.t*, vinco (3)
worth *nn*, **(price)**, prĕtĭum, *n*; **(valuation)**, aestĭmātĭo, *f*; **(worthiness)**, virtus, *f*, dignĭtas, *f*; **(— nothing)**, nĭhĭli; **(to be — much)**, *v.i*, multum vălĕo (2); **(*adj*)** dignus
worthiness dignĭtas, *f*
worthless vīlis
worthy (*with noun*), dignus (*with abl*); (*with phr*) dignus qui (ut) (*with vb. in subjunctive*); **(man)**, prŏbus
wound *nn*, vulnus, *n*
wound *v.t*, vulnĕro (1), saucĭo (1)
wounded vulnĕrātus, saucĭus
wrangle *v.i*, rixor (1 *dep*)
wrangle, wrangling *nn*, rixa, *f*
wrap *v.t*, involvo (3)
wrapper invŏlūcrum, *n*
wrath īra, *f*
wrathful īrātus
wreak vengeance on *v.t*, ulciscor (3 *dep*)
wreath *nn*, serta, *n. pl*
wreathe *v.t*, torquĕo (2)
wreck *nn*, naufrăgĭum, *n*
wreck *v.t*, frango (3)
wrecked naufrăgus
wren rēgŭlus, *m*
wrench away, wrest *v.t*, extorquĕo (2)
wrestle *v.i*, luctor (1 *dep*)
wrestler luctātor, *m*
wrestling *nn*, luctātĭo, *f*
wretch perdĭtus, *m*
wretched mĭser
wretchedness mĭsĕrĭa, *f*
wriggle *v.i*, torquĕor (2 *pass*)
wring *v.t*, torquĕo (2)
wrinkle rūga, *f*
wrinkled rūgōsus
wrist *use* bracchĭum, *n*, **(forearm)**
writ (legal —) mandātum, *n*

write *v.t*, scrībo (3)
writer scriptor, *m*; **(author)**, auctor, *c*
writhe *v.i*, torquĕor (2 *pass*)
writing scriptĭo, *f*; **(something written)**, scriptum, *n*, ŏpus, *n*
wrong *adj*, falsus; **(improper, bad)**, prāvus; **(to be —)**, *v.i*, erro (1)
wrong *nn*, nĕfas, *n*, peccātum *n*; **(a —)**, iniūrĭa, *f*
wrongly *adv*, **(badly)**, măle; **(in error)**, falso
wrong *v.t*, fraudo (1), iniūrĭam infĕro (*irreg*) (*with dat*)
wrongful iniustus
wroth īrātus
wrought confectus
wry distortus

Y

yacht cĕlox, *f*
yard (measurement) *often* passus, *m*, **(5 ft/1.5 m approx.) (court —)**, ārĕa, *f*
yarn (thread) fīlum, *n*; **(story)**, fābŭla, *f*
yawn *nn*, oscĭtātĭo, *f*
yawn *v.i*, oscĭto (1)
year annus, *m*; **(a half —)**, sēmestre spătĭum, *n*; **(space of six months)**
yearly *adj*, **(throughout a year)**, annŭus; **(every year)**, *adv*, quŏtannis
yearn for *v.t*, dēsīdĕro (1)
yearning dēsīdĕrĭum, *n*
yeast fermentum, *n*
yell clāmor, *m*, ŭlŭlātus, *m*
yell *v.i*, magnā vōce clāmo (1)
yellow flāvus
yellowish subflāvus
yelp *v.i*, grannĭo (4)
yelping *nn*, gannītus, *m*
yeoman cŏlōnus, *m*
yes *adv*, ĭta
yesterday *adv*, hĕri; *nn*, hesternus dĭes, *m*
yet *adv*, **(nevertheless)**, tămen; (*with comparatives*) ĕtĭam, *e.g.* **yet bigger**, ĕtĭam māior; **(of time; still)**, ădhuc

yew   taxus, *f*
yield   *v.i*, cēdo (3) (*with dat*);
  (surrender), sē dēdĕre (3 *reflex*)
yielding   *nn*, concessĭo, *f*
yielding   *adj*, **(soft)**, mollis
yoke   *nn*, iŭgum, *n*
yoke   *v.t*, iungo (3)
yoked   iŭgālis; **(— pair)**, ĭugum, *n*
yolk   vĭtellus, *m*
yonder   *adv*, illic
yore   *adv*, ōlim **(once, in time
  past)**
you   *pron, often not expressed,
  e.g.* **you come**, vĕnis; *pl*, vĕnĭtis;
  otherwise use appropriate case of
  tu; *pl*, vos
young   *adj*, iŭvĕnis, parvus;
  (child), infans; **(— person)**,
  ădŏlescens
young   *nn*, **(offspring)**, partus, *m*
younger   iŭnĭor, mĭnor nātu **(less
  in age)**
young man   iŭvĕnis, *m*
youngster   iŭvĕnis, *c*
your, yours   *(singular)*, tŭus; **(***of
  more than one***)**, vester
yourself   *(emphatic)*, *use* ipse *in
  agreement with pron*; *(reflexive)*,
  te; *pl*, vos
youth (time of —)   iŭventus, *f*,
  ădŏlescentĭa, *f*; **(young man)**,
  ădŏlescens, iŭvĕnis, *c*; **(body of
  young persons)**, iŭventus, *f*
youthful   iŭvĕnīlis

Z

zeal   stŭdĭum, *n*
zealous   stŭdĭōsus
zenith   *use* summus, *adj*, **(top of)**
zephyr   Zĕphўrus, *m*, Făvŏnĭus, *m*
zero (nothing)   nĭhil
zest   ălăcrĭtas, *f*
zodiac   signĭfer orbis, *m*,
  (sign-bearing orb)
zone   lŏcus, *m*